TWILIGHT OF THE
PANTHER

TWILIGHT OF THE
PANTHER

Biology, Bureaucracy and Failure
in an Endangered Species Program

by Ken Alvarez

MYAKKA RIVER
PUBLISHING
Sarasota, Florida

Cover design and maps by Jono Miller

Grateful acknowledgment is made to the following for permission to reprint excerpts from previously published material:

Environmental Politics and Policy by Walter A. Rosenbaum. Copyright © 1985, Congressional Quarterly Inc. Reprinted by permission of the publisher.

"The Grizzly and the Juggernaut" by Alston Chase. Reprinted by permission from *Outside* Magazine Copyright ©1986, Mariah Publications Corporation.

Reprinted from *Thinking Like A Mountain: Aldo Leopold and the Evolution of an Ecological Attitude Toward Deer, Wolves and Forests* by Susan Flader, by permission of the University of Missouri Press. Copyright ©1974 by the Curators of the University of Missouri.

National Parks: The American Experience, by Alfred Runte. Reprinted by permission of the publisher. Copyright ©1979 and 1987, University of Nebraska Press.

Reprinted from *Memoirs of a Naturalist*, by Herbert L. Stoddard, Sr., by permission of the publisher. Copyright ©1969 by the University of Oklahoma Press.

Reprinted from *The United States Fish and Wildlife Service*, by Nathaniel Reed and Dennis Drabelle, Copyright ©1984, by permission of Westview Press, Boulder, Colorado.

First printing 1993

Library of Congress Catalog Card Number: 93-77355
ISBN 0-9635656-0-5

Printed in the United States of America
on recycled paper

To my colleagues on the
Florida Panther Recovery Team

Sonny Bass
Robert Baudy
John Eisenbrg
Mel Sunquist

Things and actions are what they are,
and the consequences of them will be what they will be:
why, then, should we desire to be deceived?

Bishop Joseph Butler
1692 - 1752

Far more crucial than what we know or do not know is what
we do not want to know. One often obtains a clue to a person's nature
by discovering the reasons for his or her imperviousness
to certain impressions.

Eric Hoffer
The Passionate State of Mind

ACKNOWLEDGMENTS

For permission to quote from her father's papers on the tick eradication program of the 1940s, thanks to Mrs. Nina Leopold Bradley.

I would like to proclaim gratitude to persons who made contributions. To those who reviewed chapters or provided information, thanks to Melvin Sunquist, Melody Roelke, Kenneth Dodd, Robert C. (Chris) Belden, Douglas Miller, David Maehr, Larry D. Harris, Walter McCown, John Lukas, Otie G. (Greg) Brock, William B. Robertson Jr., Fred Lohrer, David Gluckman, Archie (Chuck) Carr III, Oron P. (Sonny) Bass, Max Schroeder, James Schortemeyer, Jay Sheppard, Eugene Knoder, John (Jack) Pons and Jerry Cutlip. Special thanks to Richard (Dick) Fuhr who read the manuscript and commented as a layman on the clarity or obscurity of biological matters.

For information and reviews on the black-footed ferret chapter, thanks to Brian G. Miller of the National Zoological Park and Tim Clark, presently with the Northern Rockies Conservation Cooperative. For assistance with the dusky seaside sparrow, thanks to William J. Hardy and especially to Herbert Kale, who struggled many years to stem the ebbing fortunes of this tiny bird. For assistance with the California Condor Chapter, I am beholden to John Ogden, now working to save the Everglades, and to Noel Snyder.

Thanks to Jerry Gerde for "legal" assistance. My gratitude goes to Peter B. Gallagher for loaning me video tapes of the James Billie trial and of public meetings on the panther, and for the use of his collection of panther articles written for the *St. Petersburg Times*. Thanks also to Robert Dye who granted me three months leave to work on the book. My appreciation to Bill Partington, of the Florida Conservation Foundation, who mailed me his files on the Tosohatchee controversy, and on his history of trying to enlist a reluctant Florida Game and Fresh Water Fish Commission as an ally in promoting a statewide system of interconnected wildlife habitat.

I am grateful to John Eisenberg, James Layne, and Robert Dye for reviewing the entire manuscript. I should add that the body of opinions given in the pages that follow are my own. Not all of the reviewers would agree with all of them, and, of course, I bear responsibility for any errors. Particular thanks to Catherine (Penny) Spurr and to Fiona Sunquist for editorial guidance. However, since I did not always follow what I suspect to be perfectly sound advice, I claim sole responsibility for any editorial shortcomings. Special thanks to Linda Backer of the Ann Marbut Environmental Library of Sarasota, Florida, for her zeal in collecting many far-flung documents. I found that in writing a book there are few assets to compare with an enthusiastic librarian. Thanks also to Carol Sellars for proofreading the galley. And finally, special thanks to Belinda Perry for patience, many volunteered weekends and endless hours at the computer.

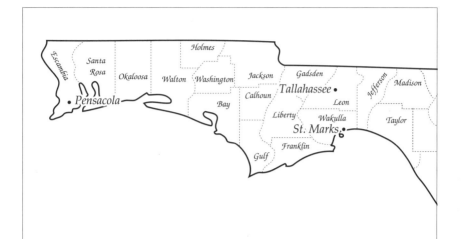

Map of Florida

*showing the names of the
counties and selected places
mentioned in the text*

Nassau

Jacksonville

Jefferson Madison Hamilton

Columbia

Duval

Taylor Suwannee Baker

St. Augustine

Layfayette Union Brad-ford Clay St. Johns

Dixie Gil-christ Alachua Putnam

Gainesville

Flagler

Marion

Levy Volusia

Lake

Inverness Leesburg

Citrus Seminole

Sumter Orlando

Hernando Orange

Pasco Osceola

Hillsborough Polk

Tampa Brevard

Sebastian

Indian River

Manatee Hardee Okeechobee

De Soto Highlands St. Lucie

Sarasota Ft. Ogden Hobe Sound

Martin

Punta Gorda

Charlotte West Palm Beach

Gasparilla Island Moore Haven Palm Beach

Ft. Myers Lee Hendry Lantana

Estero

Bonita Springs Immokalee

Naples Collier Broward

Ft. Lauderdale

Marco Island Dade

Everglades City Miami

Monroe

Homestead

Cape Sable

Florida Bay

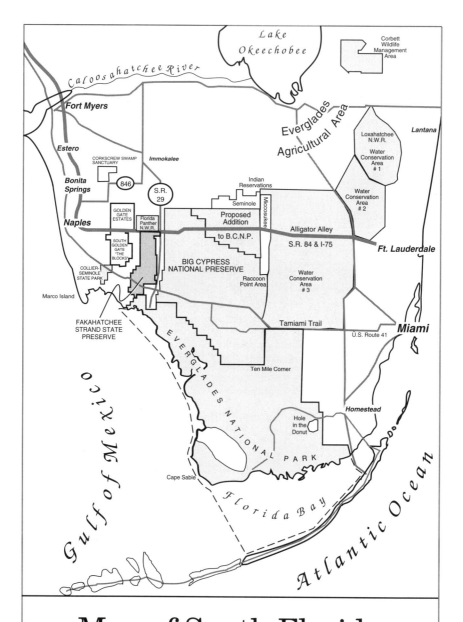

Map of South Florida

Emphasizing (in grey) the major areas of public ownership in 1987.

TABLE OF CONTENTS

INTRODUCTION

The pages to come will trace the fate of a large, endangered predator upon its consignment to the solicitude of four government agencies and the committees that serve as appendages to them. Because the nomenclature of bureaucracy can be a confusing field for laymen, I offer here some explanatory remarks and a diagram to help the reader through the morass. Of the four agencies, two are federal instruments while two operate within the state of Florida. A sketch of the federal agencies first.

The National Park Service name is linked to images of the grand features of the North American landscape. It is one of the best known arms of the American government and is perhaps the most popular. The U.S. Fish and Wildlife Service oversees the country's fish and wildlife resources, in part through a system of refuges. It has in addition numerous administrative branches to regulate activities potentially injurious to fish and wildlife and for liaison with other federal and state instrumentalities. When discussing the U.S. Fish and Wildlife Service in the narrative, the initials "U.S." have been omitted in the interest of brevity.

Now for the state agencies.

First is the Florida Department of Natural Resources (hereinafter shortened to Florida DNR). Its role in this affair, as we will see in the unfolding narrative, is important but less preponderant than the others. The Florida DNR is a sprawling mechanism of many parts; foremost among these for the purpose of the panther story is the Florida Park Service, which controls a parcel of land where panthers live.

Departments to safeguard species of fish and game began appearing in the late 1800s, sprouting in state after state. The process was completed during the first half of the twentieth century. The Departments of Fish and Game are unusual among American land-management institutions in having attained a degree of independence from the executive branch of government. They came, one by one, under the direction of commissions of highly qualified citizens, the date being determined by a sequential upwelling of citizen support. Details of this evolution will be supplied later.

In most states, the title "Game and Fish Commission," applies solely to the commissioners, not to the department they superintend which is properly referred to by its own separate title. However, in Florida, both the appointed commissioners, and the body of career professionals that executes the commission's policies, are collectively called the Florida Game and Fresh Water Fish Commission. This has been shortened in the text to "Game Commission." All state game agencies bear a family likeness, not only in structure but also in bureaucratic behavior. Since this point is important in following the analysis to come, I have, when writing about the game and fish departments in California and Wyoming, used the term "commission" to encompass the institution collectively.

Now for the extra-agency arrangements.

In 1976 the Fish and Wildlife Service formed a *Florida Panther Recovery Team*, composed of citizen experts and government biologists. Its purpose was to write a plan aimed at saving the panther from extinction. When the plan was finished in 1981 the team was disbanded.

In l983 the Florida legislature created a *Florida Panther Technical Advisory Council* to advise the Florida Game Commission in its endeavor to coax the animal back from the brink of extinction. I have shortened the name of this group to "Panther Advisory Council." It still functions today.

In 1986 the two federal and two state agencies named above, banded together around the panther program, calling themselves the *Florida Panther Interagency Committee*. In the book I distinguish this entity by its acronym — FPIC — to avoid confusion with the Panther Advisory Council. The former (the Committee, or FPIC) is an ad hoc organization, the latter (the Council) is mandated by statute.

Now to explain one last complexity: the *Technical Subcommittee* (TS), a body formed by the FPIC, ostensibly to advise it on the technical aspects of saving panthers (this in addition to the Panther Advisory Council which advises only the Game Commission). But as we shall see this purpose has been a fiction, pure and simple. The Technical Subcommittee is composed of representatives of each of the four agencies; its complexion therefore has been more parochial than technical.

The following table of organization illustrates the agencies in relation to each other and to their adjunct advisory arms.

TABLE OF ORGANIZATION:
FLORIDA PANTHER RECOVERY PROGRAM

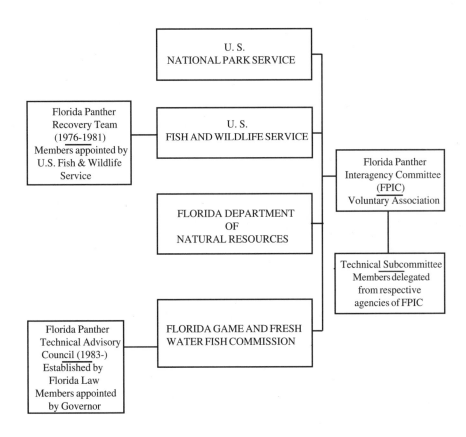

PART ONE: THE SITUATION

Chapter 1

FELIS CONCOLOR:
THE GREAT AMERICAN UNSPOTTED CAT

Yes — and painters, prowlin' 'bout,
Allus darkest nights. Lay out
Clost yer cattle. — Great, big red
Eyes a-blazin' in their head,
Glitter'n 'long the timber-line —
Shine out some, and then unshine,
And then shine back — Then steady! Whizz!
'N'there yer Mr. Painter is
With a hole bored spang between
Them-air eyes! . . .

James Whitcomb Riley

In November pleasant weather arrives in southern Florida. The monsoon summer has faded; the daily downpours end; humidity subsides to comfort, and a cumulonimbus sky gives way to one of daylong blue. On a bright November morning in 1983, three helicopters lifted off from Everglades City, a fishing village nestled in a mangrove forest at the tropical tip of Florida. They carried five persons newly appointed by the governor to advise the state game agency in its endeavors to save the Florida panther from extinction. I had been elected to chair this body and immediately organized a field trip to panther country so that members could see its salient features. The first leg of the flight took us over the Fakahatchee Strand, a swamp known for its rare tropical plants, where royal palms towered above a lush, green canopy that reached north beyond the limits of vision. Over the intercom, the pilot, above the Fakahatchee for the first time, said it looked like Vietnam, but without tracer bullets coming up to greet us. Soon we crossed Alligator Alley, an asphalt ribbon stretched tight across the soggy wilderness to speed motorists between its Atlantic terminus at Fort Lauderdale and Naples on the Gulf, and swung eastward toward Bear Island—as the northernmost extension of the Big Cypress National Preserve is known. The vista below centered on a broad marsh, bordered by hammocks of oak and cabbage palms. Beyond the hammocks, scattered pines stretched away to the horizon. Far to the east we flew, helicopter shadows moving swiftly over the grounds of an Indian reservation, before turning southwards toward the heart of the Big Cypress Swamp where a sweeping, cypress-

introduced to Europeans as a "lion" because of its obvious resemblance to the Old World cat of that name. Credit for the introduction goes to Christopher Columbus who observed the animal while exploring the coast of Honduras and Nicaragua during his fourth voyage in 1502.[2]

Though presently called by several common names such as cougar, mountain lion, panther and el leon (in Latin America), it has 83 denominations of record in English, Spanish and native American dialects.[3] "Puma" is said to be one of the few Inca words to have entered the English language[4] and is thought to have first appeared in print in 1783,[5] probably as a phonetic rendering in Spanish of a native American pronunciation. Some early Spanish writers also referred to the cat as a "red tiger."[6] Also, in the New Netherlands of colonial North America—present New York State—the term "tiger" was applied,[7] and in Florida it was called a tiger well into the nineteenth century. "Cougar" is reputedly derived from a misspelling in eighteenth-century France.[8] In the United States, "mountain lion" has served in the Rocky Mountains, while "cougar" has been heard more often in the Pacific Northwest.[9] "Catamount" and "panther" were used east of the Mississippi River. It has been written that the animal was called a "panther" in northwestern Iowa in the late 1800s.[10] In rural dialects "panther" was sometimes corrupted into "painter." Thoreau, writing in New England in 1856 of the nobler animals exterminated from that region, used the word panther as well as cougar.[11] The first Latin inscription dates from the eighteenth century, when the binomial *Tigris fulvus* was given to the form known as the "tigre rouge" in Cayenne. Carl Linneaus, who devised our system of classifying organisms, christened it *Felis concolor* in 1771; the Latin can be rendered in English as cat-of-one-color or one-colored cat. In this narrative the name panther, or Florida panther, will refer to the form of the southeastern United States. Where the cat is mentioned in other regions the term puma will be used whenever possible.

Breeding populations of the puma have been virtually eliminated from eastern North America except in southern Florida. Specimens have been confirmed for Louisiana in 1965, Pennsylvania in 1967, Oklahoma in 1968, Arkansas in 1969, Tennessee in 1971 and a second one from Oklahoma in 1975, but there is no recurring proof as would be expected if cats were established in these regions.[12]

Physical and Social Characteristics

An adult puma may be nine feet long from nose to tail. Males may attain a weight of 150 pounds or more. Females are smaller at 80 to 100 pounds. These figures will vary somewhat, and there are on record a few unusually large males that surpassed 200 pounds.

With the exception of African lions, which typically live in groups, most of the world's big cats are characterized as solitary. The description is apt since they spend much time alone and usually seem intolerant of one another's presence— except when male and female meet for mating encounters and when females are caring for young. During breeding, male and female pumas have been known to remain together for as long as 16 days.[13] But use of the term "solitary" may veil the fact that this big cat does have a social system which apportions its environment into separate units of occupation by individuals and yet allows its members to stay in contact with one another. This arrangement has come to be called a land-tenure system because, once in possession a unit of ground, an adult usually holds its tenantry until death.

The home range of a puma is relatively large, and the inhabitant continually advertises the occupancy of a locale by leaving signs that can be seen and smelled by others of its kind. In addition to depositing feces in traveling about its domain, the cat also frequently marks the ground with the rear feet by raking leaves and debris into a small pile upon which it urinates. These scented scrapes reveal to others of the species the recent passage of the occupant and its direction of travel. The odor may also advertise the female's receptivity to breeding. Male pumas make scrape marks more frequently than females. Another rare sign of a puma's presence, called a mound, is made of leaves, pine needles or other material raked into a shape, four or five feet in diameter. The reason for mounds is not known; it is suggested that they are made by females and are related to birth or to the presence of young litters. A researcher in Arizona reported seeing only two mounds in eight years of field work.[14] Only three mounds have been observed in panther habitat in southern Florida during 13 years of study.[15]

The contiguous home ranges of several females are frequently within the much larger range of a male with whom they periodically mate. So although individual pumas spend much of their time alone, each is aware of the presence of its neighbors and of the way their movements relate to its own. There are usually no rigid demarcations between home ranges of adjacent cats. Incursions by pumas into the environs of a neighbor are common and ordinarily tolerated, except that strife may ensue among males over the right of access to females. There are no well-defined boundaries to be defended as with the territories of some other wildlife species, and so the boundary between the tenured ground of individual cats may be visualized as being in a state of flux or as overlapping the one next to it.

When a puma home range is vacated, which usually comes about only upon the death of its occupant, it may be taken by a transient puma—usually a younger one searching for an accommodating plot of ground where it can join an interacting group. Alternatively, when a home range becomes vacant, adjacent pumas may begin utilizing the newly available space; or some combination of these two events may cause a good deal of territorial shifting, leading to fighting, and perhaps deaths among the cats, until a mutually acceptable spatial arrangement is restored. When young pumas become old enough to leave the mother, they disperse to wander in search of a place of their own. The ranges of large felines are capacious because large prey are needed if the predators are to satisfy their demands for energy. Consider for example that a puma may kill thirty or more deer during a year. It can be seen that a very large hunting ground is necessary, particularly since large prey also usually need foraging space in proportion to their size. The puma's wide spacing is an adaptation to the scale of its food requirements.

Breeding

Female pumas usually reach sexual maturity between two and three years of age, and males after three years, although in Florida one-and-a-half to two years has been documented.[16] Both sexes tend to defer breeding until a territory can be claimed. However, Game Commission biologists in Florida recently documented, for the first time, the first reproduction of a female of known age. She conceived before 20 months and gave birth before age two. She also established residency in the home range of her mother who tolerated her presence, it is thought, because prey were plentiful in that vicinity.[17]

Females ordinarily breed every other year, since their kittens typically take a year-and-a-half or more to become independent. If females lose their young, which happens at times, they can conceive again shortly thereafter. Thus pumas may breed in any month of the year; ordinarily though, there is a peak period or "season" during the year. Pumas are believed to live approximately ten to eleven years. In captivity they have survived for 16 to 18 years or more.

Prey Species

An inadequate food supply for panthers will affect the productivity of the population and its density. The measure of energy required by female panthers for body maintenance is roughly equivalent to that of humans: about 3,000 calories per day. Females must have additional calories to carry through a pregnancy, and after the young are born obtaining prey becomes critical in raising them to maturity. Very young kittens are vulnerable when left alone by a mother who must hunt. In time the kittens can travel with her, but she must kill often to feed the growing dependents. A female with a single offspring may use over 8,000 calories daily for the two of them as the young cat approaches the age of independence; a female with four growing kittens may eventually need 20,000 calories a day.[18] The number of young that can survive to adulthood will strongly correlate with the calories available. In conditions of severe scarcity, young cannot be produced at all.

Predators are not successful in every attempt upon prey. There are often misses, sometimes several in succession, before a hungry puma brings down a quarry. Natural selection has favored in the puma's preferred prey—deer— qualities of alertness, quickness, speed and stamina that often enable them to avoid becoming a meal. Deer may—by sight, sound or smell—sense the cat during its initial approach or during the stalk; or if the puma is compelled by circumstances to launch its rush under conditions marginal to success, a quick reaction by the intended target can enable an escape. Of 12 complete stalks of deer by tigers during a study in India, only one ended in a kill.[19] A puma study in Idaho estimated that a kill was usually made if the cat reached a position to launch an attack. However, conditions did not permit an assessment of success in the initial approach or during the stalk.[20] The opportunities for successful hunting in any habitat depend on the density of the prey. The odds for encounters increase when prey are more numerous.

Pumas will occasionally eat carrion and even other pumas. Males, given the opportunity, will sometimes eat young pumas.[21] Pumas will kill and eat almost any vertebrate, but if a population is to sustain itself it normally requires an adequate supply of big animals to provide the caloric requirements—much greater for the females, who must bear and raise the young. At the beginning of the historic period in the Americas, pumas appear to have been everywhere that suitable prey were present in densities adequate to sustain them.

At least 40 different prey species have been given for the puma in North America and seven species from South America.[22] Most food habit studies have been done in North America and prove that deer are the most important prey, comprising the largest volume of food consumed. This finding has showed some variation with recent studies of the Florida panther. Here, some individual cats live where feral hogs are plentiful. In such situations the hogs may comprise as much as 80 percent of the diet.[23] Florida panthers in some locations subsist on small animals such as raccoons and armadillos, but in these cases the female panthers are often in poor physical condition and have a low rate of productivity—or none at all.[24] If a predator population's food supply is diminished, it will initially be reflected by an altered age structure, with younger animals becoming a smaller percentage of the total. If the trend holds, the population will sink toward extinction unless corrective measures can be put in place. Thus it would be possible to exterminate a predator population simply by reducing its prey.

What effect does puma predation have on a deer herd? Two extremes have been demonstrated by research. A five-year study in Idaho on mule deer and elk, in a region where they are relatively abundant, showed that pumas did not limit the ungulates.[25] However, predation on deer which are present at a low density may prevent them from increasing, as was observed in California where a herd estimated at 17,000 in 1950 declined to 2,600 in 1984. It was presumed that livestock grazing and forestry practices had combined to impair the carrying capacity of the range, and a ten-year program of habitat improvement was started in 1970. But the deer herd failed to grow. Research showed fawn production to be high, but recruitment (the number of young animals entering the herd as breeding adults) was low. The herd kept shrinking. When fawns were radio-collared it was learned that 64 percent were killed by several species of predators. Computer modeling indicated that fawns lost to just one species of predator, the puma, were being killed at a rate sufficient to bar the herd from rebounding.[26] So although births were high, they could not overcome total losses, a significant portion of which were due to predation.

In Florida feral hogs are also an important prey species. Hogs came to Florida with Hernando DeSoto who passed through at the beginning of an epic 3,000-mile journey in 1539. His original 13 animals, we are told, increased to 300. Some of this stock must have escaped and thrived, because when the French briefly settled near present-day Jacksonville in 1560, Indians supplied them with pork.[27] Hogs spread through the lower plain of the Atlantic and Gulf Coasts.[28] In Florida they are found in 66 of 67 counties.[29]

The Setting for the Story

Impoverished soils and a seasonally flooded landscape left the lower Florida peninsula little altered during the period when the fertile, forested lands of eastern North America were being reshaped by settlement. Some wildlife species that faded from these more intensively peopled regions survived in Florida on land not coveted by humans. The flat topographic region of Florida which extends inland from the coast, gradually attaining an elevation of 100 feet, is known as the coastal lowlands. It varies in width in the northern portion of the state, but in the south extends from coast to coast. The soils of this lowland zone are recently emerged marine sediments; they are sandy, usually acidic, and seasonally wet. On this siliceous base grows a vegetative community called pine flatwoods, which is dominated by pine trees, wire grass and a shrubby palm known as saw palmetto. Before the advent of chemical fertilizers, flatwoods soils were poorly suited to the cultivation of crops. Cattle ranching was the principal land-use activity in much of peninsular Florida throughout the frontier period and is still common. The conversion of native range to improved pasture did not begin until the 1920s, and then only in a tentative way. In all the vastness of the Eastern continent, it was in this forbidding and little disturbed terrain that the panther was able to linger on to the present time.

Southern Florida is flat and wet; its dominant feature is Lake Okeechobee. Historically the lake overflowed in the season of rains, sending its summer surfeit of water south through a broad, shallow depression to Florida Bay. The visual impress of this wide, flat reach of grassy water, spreading to a distant skyline, has inspired euphonious sobriquets: the River of Grass, the Everglades, and in the lyrical rendering of an Indian tongue, the Pa-hay-o-kee. The term "Everglades" is not always used with a precise application, partly because the original River of Grass has been altered by human impact. Immediately south of the lake, much of it has now been drained to become the Everglades Agricultural Area. The next segment to the south was enclosed by dikes in conformance with a gigantic water management scheme to store water for the coastal cities. Only at the extremity of the long peninsula was the river left undisturbed. Here, in Everglades National Park, the colloquial name, "Shark River Slough," identifies the sole fragment of the original flow whose waters once coursed unvexed from Okeechobee to the sea.

The Big Cypress Swamp lies to the northwest of Everglades National Park. It is a flat, limestone plain, emerged from the sea in recent geologic times. The vegetation mosaic is sharply contrasted: scattered clusters of pine and cypress trees alternate with spreading prairies and narrow, linear swamps called strands, the latter rooted in a depth of organic detritus accumulated over centuries in elongated fissures in the limestone. The largest of the strands—the Fakahatchee Strand—is, in most of its southern length, a state preserve; the northern extremity has recently become the Florida Panther National Wildlife Refuge, under the administration of the Fish and Wildlife Service. While the whole of the swamp is "big," most of the individual cypress trees are not, excepting those that rise out of the rich peat of the strands to attain an impressive size. The adjective "big" refers to the proportions of the swamp, not to the height of its trees. Beyond the pockets of organic soil the smaller cypresses are rooted in nutrient-poor marl. A portion of the Big Cypress Swamp is administered by the National Park Service in a preserve of that name. It has a second landlord to oversee hunting: the state game agency. For that activity, the Preserve has been administratively divided into units. "Raccoon Point" is a colloquial term of obscure origin that names, not a specific geographical feature, but the eastern portion of the Monument Unit. Raccoon Point will appear frequently in the following chapters.

Civilization made a tardy arrival in this inhospitable sub-tropical finger-tip of North America, but a nation growing in wealth wanted resorts, so railroads were pushed south to the frost-free Atlantic beaches near the end of the past century. In the 1920s, a highway, the Tamiami Trail, crossed the Everglades to link Tampa with Miami; it is officially known as U.S. 41. In Collier County, another highway of the 1920s, now State Road 29, reached southward from the farming community of Immokalee to connect with coastal Everglades City. In the 1960s Alligator Alley was built to link the lower peninsula from the Atlantic to the Gulf of Mexico.

Also in the 1960s, in the cypress country east of Naples, 173 square miles of swamp, purchased cheaply, was laced with a grid of canals and roads and

through succeeding generations. Therefore, an important management goal for a small population is to expand it as quickly as possible.

A rule-of-thumb figure of 50 breeding adults has been proposed to defend against inbreeding.[32] It is derived from what has been learned from breeding domestic and zoo animals, reinforced by theoretical genetics. However, for 50 breeding adults to avert a loss of genetic variation, pairs would have to mate completely at random through successive encounters to insure a continual mixing of all possible genetic combinations. Since this would not always happen in nature, 50 is an ideal figure. In the wild, the actual number needed to insure the scope of random mating for complete mixing of genes (called panmixis) would have to be larger. This "real" or actual number of breeders has been designated the *effective population number* (or size). The effective population number will vary with the species, the harshness of its habitat and other factors, but the number may be in the low hundreds in some situations.

Several management imperatives follow from the need to establish an effective population number. Time, as previously mentioned, is one of the most important. Those who assume responsibility for the endangered population cannot dawdle. The margin of safety can never be calculated with precision. The small, endangered wildlife population is not unlike an injured patient brought to a hospital emergency room. The nature of the injuries must be swiftly assessed by following a prepared doctrine for emergencies. Unfortunately, many key decision makers in our land-management agencies will not concede a need for haste, and no exigent procedures have ever been thought out by the responsible institutions. When confronting a crisis, the agencies have sometimes behaved as if the patient were in no extreme difficulty and had by its unexpected arrival caused an annoyance to the tranquil routine of the undisturbed emergency room.

Next, after an effective population size has been calculated, a habitat must be identified that might serve as a refuge. It may not be possible to quantify these objectives with precision at the outset, given the initial state of knowledge, but crude calculations can be made, as a basis for planning and primary action, while research is put to work supplying more refined data. Every available theory and technique must be weighed for use in the extremity. A captive population, to serve as insurance against disaster befalling the wild one, can be vital and should be encouraged early in the program. The black-footed ferret, which almost disappeared as it was being studied, stands as a grave illustration of the vulnerability of small, isolated populations to random events, regardless of the intensity of field conservation efforts.[33] The same is true for the dusky seaside sparrow which plummeted to extinction as a refuge was being acquired for it. Captive animals can also serve as a "bank" for genetic material which might be lost through attrition in the wild. To continue with the bank analogy, in extreme cases of peril it may be prudent to "bank" all the animals as capital from which the "interest" can be used to restore them to the wild.

Outbreeding is a management option related to captive breeding. If inbreeding has impaired the evolutionary potential of an isolated population, it may be desirable to outbreed with more genetically fit animals from another region, assuming of course that suitable stock is available. Outbreeding will be examined in Chapter 6.

Obviously it will often be inadequate just to protect a remnant population within the confines of a nature preserve or a national park. Animals in dire straits cannot simply be left alone if they are to survive. Humans will have to take a hand, to an extent previously looked upon as undesirable in our National Parks. The term *intervention* has been coined to identify measures called for by the crisis. The term can mean genetic intervention to insure a mixing of genes that could not be otherwise anticipated; it can also mean employing conventional wildlife management techniques to spur the growth of a population, or to otherwise provide security. In some situations both kinds of intervention might have to be employed. The initial phase of management should aim at keeping the death rate to a minimum while promoting births to the maximum.

One more solemn matter should be mentioned; the figures given thus far for an effective panther population size might not be adequate over the very long term. Even more breeding adults, up to 500, have been hypothesized as the minimum that would safeguard evolution against the prolonged rigors of environmental trauma.[34] A lesser number might be adequate to stave off decline through inbreeding but would not necessarily be large enough to adapt to future environmental changes.

A fact about wildlife in our time, perhaps not widely recognized, is that for many isolated populations, evolution by natural selection—the process that created the living world as we know it—has ceased. Most of the planetary reserves and parks are not large enough for all the species within them to continue evolving by natural selection.[35] The "saved" populations are too small; the gene pools lack the variance that would grant them the widest adaptive margin. So long as the environments of these animals remain stable, they may be secure, but a shift in some variable could bring a swift end—climatic change a century from now, for instance, or a new virus next year, virulent enough to kill all or most of the individuals, or bring them below that critical point where one, or a combination of impacts, could send the rest spiraling into extinction. Against these dismal possibilities, management strategies have been proposed that would simply aim at keeping populations alive to preserve management options for the next generation. Captive breeding would often be essential to the strategy. The genetics of the captive aggregation could be managed through planned breeding; the hope would be that at some future date, improved circumstances would permit a return to the wild, for at least some species, to conditions as close as possible to those under which they evolved.[36] Given this assessment we should conclude that the long-term survival of the Florida panther is by no means assured, and certainly not in Florida. The population has been at a small, but undetermined size, for an unknown length of time. There is evidence of inbreeding as we will see later on. Inbreeding is only one hazard for the Florida panther, but it is one that could most easily be deflected—at least in theory.

Field research since 1976 suggests that established social groups of panthers are probably confined to a zone extending from Lake Okeechobee southwards, although another opinion holds that research has been inadequate to define their northern limits, and that intensive field work could shift this arbitrary boundary northward. Individual cats have been captured as far north as Highlands County, but they were young and could have been transients dispersing from the region of known habitation farther south. Panthers sign has been documented in northeastern Florida, in Flagler County, but field searches have failed to confirm a settled population there.

Chapter 2

FELIS CONCOLOR CORYI:
THE FLORIDA PANTHER

They call him "puma" in the zoo;
Down South he's known as "panther" too;
In many places way out West
Folks think that "cougar" suits him best.

So you can give him any name
And still he'll look and act the same.
He's just a great big yellow thief
That likes to steal the rancher's beef.

David Newell
Verse written for children, 1935.

The panther by some lost name was featured in the art and religion of the pre-Columbian inhabitants of Florida. A well-preserved wooden carving of a stylized panther, dating from the fifteenth century, was unearthed during archaeological investigations on Marco Island. It was written of this find that "nothing thus far found in America so vividly calls to mind the best art of the ancient Egyptians or Assyrians, as does this little statuette of the Lion-God, in which it was evidently intended to represent a manlike being in the guise of a panther."[1]

We cannot know how many panthers once lived within the present-day boundaries of Florida, but a theoretical estimate of approximately 1,360 has been suggested. The total was derived by appraising what is presently known about the carrying capacity of the present-day habitats of large prey, principally white-tailed deer. This theoretical food supply was assessed for cropping by all predators—including aboriginal humans—to calculate the abundance of panthers it might have sustained.[2]

The presence of panthers became a matter of record soon after the European discovery of Florida. Hernando deSoto landed in 1539 at what is now Tampa Bay. He carried a contract from the Spanish crown to conquer, pacify, and settle the interior of *La Florida*. A narrative of his expedition told of "many lions and bears in Florida, wolves, deer. . . ."[3] Indians were described placing bodies of the dead in chests above ground at a place some distance from their village and at times being angered when "lions" carried the deceased away.[4] France ferried explorers to Florida's Atlantic shore in the 1560s. They encountered an "animal which differs very little from the lion of Africa."[5] The French fortified a site near present-day Jacksonville, but the garrison was short-lived. It was ruthlessly extinguished by Spaniards, alarmed at the prospect of a French base on a coast which would have to be passed by their treasure fleet on its annual voyage to Spain. To frustrate further encroachments by its European rivals, Spain planted its own base at St. Augustine in 1565.

Florida was an outpost of the Spanish empire for the next two-and-a-half centuries except for a brief interlude under the British (1763-1783). During the British colonial period the Philadelphia naturalist, William Bartram, made his visit which, to the enlightenment of posterity, he recorded in detail. While traveling through Georgia he observed that "bears, tygers [panthers], wolves and wild cats (*Felis cauda truncata*) are numerous enough."[6] If the centuries of Spanish occupation had any effect on panthers, it would probably have been in a favorable way. The Spanish presence rested lightly on the land. There were small settlements at Pensacola, St. Augustine and St. Marks, but little activity in the interior aside from some cattle ranches in the vicinity of present-day Duval and Alachua Counties (la Chua was the name of a large Spanish cattle ranch),[7] and a smattering of missions in the northern parts. In fact much of the land was virtually depopulated as the original Indian inhabitants were devastated by European diseases. The survivors were gathered into the mission settlements which were themselves destroyed in the colonial fighting spawned by several European wars. Not only would competitive predation by humans for deer have been lessened, but an additional important prey animal, the feral hog, was introduced. In the latter part of the eighteenth century, some 200 years after the arrival of the Spanish, Indian immigrants from several Creek tribes—who would come to be known collectively as Seminoles—began to enter Florida.

Official persecution of the panther came to Florida when it was joined to the United States. The cats were apparently common in the new territory and regarded as a menace. The territorial legislature enacted a law in 1832 to reward persons for killing them. The amount of the bounty was to be set by the counties. In 1837 John Lee Williams, an assistant to John James Audubon during a visit to Florida, wrote that panthers were numerous in some parts and were particularly destructive to calves. In 1887 another bounty law was passed, this time authorizing a statewide $5.00 payment for panther scalps.[8]

While extermination was the fashion, science began to take an interest. In the late nineteenth century there took form in the United States what might be called a scientific establishment, with practitioners taking to the field to collect objects of natural history for museums. The scientist, Charles B. Cory, journeyed to Florida in the 1890s, combining sport hunting with a scientific endeavor. Cory was the first to offer a detailed description of the panther and to distinguish it from specimens collected from other regions. An ornithologist, and a member of several scientific societies, he was also an avid hunter and fisherman who made several excursions into the Everglades. In 1895 he set out from the lower east coast with an expert guide and six hunting dogs. His intent was to collect a panther.

The prey proved elusive; although tracks were seen several times, conditions were never suitable for the dogs to stay on a trail. After two months of hunting, he finally killed a female about 35 miles south of Lantana. She measured seven feet from nose to tail-tip. Cory declared the Florida panther separable from those in the north by a more reddish brown color, with longer legs and smaller feet. He designated it a subspecies, calling it *Felis concolor floridana*.[9] The name was to survive only three years. It was changed by another scientist, Outram Bangs, who pointed out that the name *Felis floridana* had previously been used for a bobcat and so another would have to be found. He honored Charles Cory by proposing, *Felis coryi*, thereby elevating it to the rank of species.[10]

Bangs, in a paper published in the proceedings of the Biological Society of Washington in 1899, wrote of his collection that it "now contains six specimens of *F. coryi* (skins and skulls complete), all taken by F. R. Hunter in the same general region of Florida, namely, the great wilderness back of Sebastian in Brevard and Osceola counties. . . ." From his specimens Bangs provided numerous measurements of the dimensions of skulls and skins and of the skin color and characteristics. Designating the skin of an old female as the "type specimen," he observed "little bunches of white hair scattered here and there" on the upper surface of the neck and back. . . . Its long limbs, small feet and rich ferruginous color are the best characters by which to distinguish it from other North American pumas. It needs no comparison with the small pumas of northern South America or Central America."[11]

Bangs followed a school then current holding that pumas from different geographical regions, which could be told from those of other regions by distinct and non-overlapping physical characters, were separate species. The question of how to distinguish species from subspecies has been an interesting one in the history of biological science and will be presented in a later chapter. Bangs thought the Florida panther to be geographically isolated from pumas in other regions. That apparently was sufficient grounds to declare it a species, since he believed it could no longer interbreed with others of its kind and perhaps never had.[12] Nearly a half-century later when two scientists, Stanley Young and Edward Goldman, made a search of puma reports, they found references to the cat's presence in the Carolinas,

Tennessee, Georgia, Alabama, Louisiana, Mississippi, Missouri, and the Midwest.[13] It seems inconceivable that those in the Florida peninsula would not have intergraded with other forms.

During the nineteenth century the practice of referring to the puma in Florida as a tiger yielded to "panther" as the exclusive term. William Bartram had written in the late 1700s that "this creature is called in Pennsylvania and the northern states 'panther' but in Carolina and the southern states, is called 'Tyger'; it is very strong, much larger than any dog, of a yellowish brown, or clay colour, having a very long tail; it is a mischievous animal, and preys on calves, young colts, etc."[14] The term "tiger" is enshrined in numerous Florida place names. There are Tiger Creeks, Tiger Islands, Tiger Hammocks and Tiger Branches (in Florida a hardwood forest, or any closed-canopy forest, is called a hammock, and a small creek is sometimes called a branch). A well-known Indian chief (a Tallahassee) of the Second Seminole War (1835-42) had been dubbed "Tigertail" by American contemporaries. The nickname originated at an Indian ball game where he was observed wearing a strip of panther skin dangling at his belt.[15] His real name, rendered phonetically as Thlocklo Tustenuggee, was not one that would have rolled easily off the Anglo tongue. It may have prompted the improvisation of a manageable substitute with some audible similarities. Tigertail Island, in the Homosassa River, is a reminder of this historical footnote.

Toward the end of the past century, hunting panthers for sport became popular among men of means from the Northeast. Several accounts of hunting expeditions are preserved in contemporary books and sportsmen's magazines. A narrative of a panther killing along Sebastian Creek near Hobe Sound, by F. A. Ober in 1874, mentions the names panther, tiger and catamount. "This animal," declared Ober, "is more generally known by the name tiger than any other, and as such is spoken of with dread by the 'crackers.'"[16] The ornithologist Charles Maynard (who discovered the dusky seaside sparrow, written about later in this book) made notes on mammals as well as birds during eight winter visits to Florida between 1868 and 1882. Writing in 1883 he confirmed that residents spoke of tigers and elaborated on their dread of the cat: ". . . old hunters warned me against passing through the thick woods in the early morning or late in the evening as they said the Tigers were usually on the alert at such times and might be tempted to spring upon one if he were alone."[17] However, the name "panther" seems to have been settled upon by the 1890s—at least by the literate. Charles Cory used the term exclusively in his 1896 book. Jim Bob Tinsley, who published an informative little book on the Florida panther in 1970, included some news clippings from the *Jacksonville Times-Union* in 1895 that reported local episodes involving "panthers."[18]

The Decline of Panthers

How, when, and at what rate panthers began to decline in Florida can only be speculated. Settlement began in the panhandle and in the northern peninsula where soils were more suited to growing cash crops. There were cotton and tobacco plantations and small towns in this region before the Civil War. Even so, the state was lightly populated at mid-century. A settler named Abel Miranda settled on the wild Pinellas Peninsula about the time of the Civil War. He reportedly killed 11 bears and a panther the first year he was there.[19]

Conventional wisdom has it that pumas were lost to persecution in the East.[20] But although it is well-known that they were enthusiastically destroyed, the opinion may be questioned. Pumas persevered through decades of well-financed government programs to eradicate them in the West where states offered bounties as recently as the 1960s. Arizona paid until 1971.[21] Although wolves and grizzly bears were systematically eradicated by government programs, the big cats proved resilient beyond all expectations.[22] Like wolves and bears, pumas are large predators that live at a low density—meaning that there are relatively few individuals per unit area of land. However, it was the misfortune of wolves and bears to be readily lured to poison baits—which made for relative ease of extermination. Authorities in Arizona believed that pumas were ineradicable because, in addition to the difficulty of poisoning, there would be an influx of animals from "remote strongholds" when numbers were reduced locally.[23] In these wild and rugged sanctuaries sustained eradication efforts were not practical. However, these conditions described for the Southwest would apply to Florida well into the twentieth century. The interior of lower Florida was virtually unpopulated throughout the 1800s, and the waterlogged southern extremity was avoided well into the present century.

Contrary to what laymen sometimes suppose, killing wild animals does not necessarily reduce their numbers. That result cannot be obtained by this practice unless, for an extended period of time, deaths exceed the number being born and recruited as breeding adults. Also, if the population drops below the capacity of the habitat, it tends to respond with a higher rate of production and recruitment because, with fewer individuals competing for resources, there is a relative abundance available to each individual. Since a female puma can raise up to four or more kittens every other year, a generous supply of prey can fuel a remarkable rate of fecundity—which means that high losses can be compensated for. In California 12,000 bounties were paid on pumas between 1908 and 1963. The cats persisted though they may have been reduced during this time. The number taken during the first eight years averaged 290 per annum. During the final eight years of the bounty period the average annual kill figure had dropped to about 135.[24]

In Colorado the *Denver Post* newspaper paid a total of 890 bounties between 1920 and 1939. The state of Colorado followed suit in 1929, paying 1,457 bounties until 1965. Puma numbers in Colorado have been estimated at between 165 to 350. At the lower figure biologists estimate that the population could sustain a kill of 50 a year without declining.[25] In Utah the average minimum (not all pumas taken were reported) number of pumas taken between 1977 and 1984 by hunters and professional trappers was 211 per year.[26] These figures give an idea of the resilience of pumas in the face of persecution. So long as there is adequate food (and assuming no other limiting factors), an annual increment of young will reach maturity and disperse, each to search for a place of its own. The most likely explanation for the disappearance of pumas from the East is the unregulated exploitation of the deer herd—with persecution as an added factor. Rainer Brocke, who investigated the decline of pumas and deer in the East through historical records, suggested persecution as the probable cause of puma extirpation. The material available to him gave evidence that the demise of the puma preceded that of white-tailed deer by several years.[27] However, in Florida documents tell a different story.

It is well known that white-tailed deer were virtually obliterated from eastern North America in the nineteenth century.[28] In many areas where they survived, deer were held at a low density by unrelieved hunting pressure. It was primarily the vigorous and persistent political efforts of organized sportsmen that enabled deer to persist and eventually recover—after the passing of the puma. As will be explained later, the question of an adequate provision of deer for the panther in southern Florida may be an important one if plans are to be made that will enable it to persist.

McCauley's Thesis

To determine why panthers held out in southern Florida, it is useful to investigate what is known about the cat, and its prey, in the state during the past. A search for panther records was undertaken by Melinda McCauley, a graduate student, in 1977.[29] She found 150 published accounts, with locality data, spanning the decades from 1871 to 1976. She also analyzed 391 unpublished records for the span, 1934 to 1976. Some were of specimens, so it is possible to pinpoint with confidence sites where some panthers were killed at various periods. She arranged her findings into segments of time: pre-1900, 1901-1940, 1941-1950, 1951-1960, 1961-1970 and 1971-1976.

Sporadic accounts from the colonial and territorial periods (until 1845) indicate that panthers were common. McCauley believed that "no doubt panthers have steadily declined since the white man's arrival."[30] This assertion has been echoed by subsequent writers but cannot be supported by the history of human demographic trends. Aboriginals virtually disappeared under Spanish rule, leaving Florida largely vacant of people for two-and-a-half centuries. A few Seminole Indians took up residency in northern Florida during the late 1700s, and American immigrants began filtering into Spanish Florida during the early 1800s.

From 1876 to 1900, discussed previously relative to the activities of Charles Cory and other sportsmen-scientists, McCauley found records of specimens collected in Volusia (1), Brevard (1), Indian River (2), Martin (2), and Palm Beach (1) counties. Two anecdotes from northern Florida during this span of years, not included by McCauley, are worth retelling. The first is from a chronicler visiting the state with General Grant in 1880, who said that "the haunts of bears and panthers are mostly on the islands and in the southern counties; but they are scared up in all parts of the state, usually right where and when least expected, of course."[31] The second account is from 1890 when a cattleman named Bronson Lewis, of Alachua and Levy counties, heard a disturbance in his cow pen. He went out for a look and found a panther crouched over a dead calf. The cat suddenly jumped on him and they both fell to the ground. The cattleman somehow got a rope around the cat's neck and tied it to a stump. He then beat it to death with a fence rail. Lewis, according to the account, was literally "torn to pieces" in the fight. It was months before he could stand on his feet, and he remained partially crippled the rest of his life.[32]

From 1901 to 1940 the lower west coast of Florida was yielding to settlement. Rail and auto roads were being pushed southward to Naples by the 1920s. Several panther specimens were reported from this region by McCauley. Two came from Collier County and four from Lee. A specimen was taken in Dade County in what is today the Long Pine Key area of Everglades National Park where panthers still roam. Four more were collected on Cape Sable, also now in Everglades National Park, but a place where recent investigations have not turned up evidence of the cats. Well to the north of this cluster of records, two specimens were taken along the St. Johns River in Lake County. There were in addition two sighting records from the Florida Keys on Key Vaca and on Lower Matecumbe Key. There are several other accounts from the Keys from other periods.[33] If reports from the upper Keys are valid, the occurrence of cats there would have surely been accidental. These islands are small and narrow, and too depauperate in prey to feed even a single panther. There is a deer herd in the lower Keys, but panthers would have had to swim from island to island, some of them separated by miles of water, to get there.

An event of the 1930s is not mentioned in McCauley's thesis. In the summer of 1935, an article in *Saturday Evening Post* magazine told of a panther hunt during January of the same year in the Big Cypress Swamp of Collier County.

The author was David Newell, a Floridian (from Leesburg) who expressed a common belief of the day. "In so far as I know, the Florida Everglades and Big Cypress Swamp are the last strongholds of the panther in the eastern United States." Newell mentioned, however, that "I have known of four being killed in Central Florida during the last eight years."[34] Two years earlier, Newell had tried hunting panthers in the Big Cypress with his own pack of dogs, but had taken only one. He attributed this paltry luck to inexperienced dogs which had been trained for bears. Given that panthers are exceedingly reclusive and difficult to kill without specially trained dogs—even in an environment where they were known to be present—the evidence of four panthers killed in Central Florida (if true) might indicate that they could have been more common than supposed. In fact, Newell commented about the panthers in southern Florida that "even some of the settlers who live on the edge of the `glades country' are unaware of his [the panther's] existence in any appreciable quantity."[35]

For the 1935 hunt Newell had arranged to bring experienced puma hunters and their pack of hounds from Arizona. The excursion lasted six weeks, interrupted by brief visits to civilization. The first morning out, the party took a panther found at its kill: a 200-pound wild boar. The next day two more panthers were shot; they were both old females. During the remaining six weeks of the hunt, five more panthers were taken, for a total of eight. The skins were prepared for shipment to the Academy of Natural Sciences in Philadelphia. Newell stated that the stomachs of six of the eight "were full of fresh venison, one had deer bones and hair in the intestines and one was empty."[36]

In the 1941-1950 decade, according to McCauley, specimens were taken near the adjoining boundaries of Lee, Hendry and Collier counties, where panthers are still active today. There were two from Hendry, two from Collier and one from Lee; two more were collected in Highlands County, not far removed to the north. McCauley's map shows two clusters of sighting reports during the 1940s, one in the Gulf Hammock region (Citrus and Levy counties) and another near present-day Myakka River State Park (Sarasota and Manatee counties).[37]

Early Protection

In the decade 1951-1960, a low point in panther numbers has been presumed, and that is probably correct.[38] There are few reliable records. Another ironic indication is that 1950 is the year the Game Commission extended the first tentative protection to the big cat by making it a game animal, thus limiting by season and number the allowable kill. The commissioners were careful to make provisions that any panther destroying livestock could be taken by permit. Remember that in the West, in 1950, puma eradication programs were still following their ineffectual course. Florida cattlemen were still politically strong enough in that year to have blocked protection had they been opposed. The fact that they did not would seem to indicate that they no longer thought it a threat to stock. Furthermore, it is reported that a well-known Collier County panther hunter named Steve Hunter was no longer taking panthers in 1952 because he could no longer find them.[39]

I am not aware of any records, either of depredation permits being issued, or of panthers taken by hunters after 1950. Eight years after its initial protective measure the Game Commission felt confident enough to take the next step. The panther was taken off the game list and given complete protection.[40] Earl Frye of the Game Commission led the way in this crusade. It is interesting to read, in an article written by him in *Florida Wildlife* magazine to promote his case, that he cast his arguments to appeal to hunters, nature lovers, timber growers, and to cattlemen.

> Back in the old days when farms were widely scattered and stock was mostly free ranging, the panther represented only a menace to the livelihood of the settler. Today, with more intensive agricultural and stockraising practices, the movement of the small farmer from the large cattle ranches and timber holdings, and the relegation of the panther to the more remote woodland areas of the state, this aspect of the habits of the panther is of less importance. The panther is still capable of destroying livestock but its opportunities for doing so are now more limited.

> No one questions the ability and the occasional tendency of the panther to kill cattle or horses, but by far its greatest potential damage to livestock in Florida lies in the destruction of free-ranging hogs. The question immediately arises: does the pleasure the hunter or nature lover receives from hunting or merely seeing this animal outweigh the loss of a few razor-back hogs. This question is of particular significance when one considers the fact that the free-ranging hog is deemed more of a nuisance than a benefit by most cattlemen and timber growers due to its rooting pastures, its reputation as a carrier of screw worm, and its destruction of young pine trees. In addition, the semi-wild hog is recognized by most wildlife authorities and sportsmen as one of the greatest competitors of deer, turkey, and other forms of wildlife for natural foods such as acorns. It is entirely possible that in most of Florida, a taste for pork is more in favor of these big cats than against them.[41]

It is reasonable to wonder if there were any panthers left by the 1950s. McCauley found 54 records from the years 1951-1960, but most are of questionable reliability. Only one is a published record of a specimen (from Broward County), as opposed to six from the previous decade. Panthers, and possibly pumas from elsewhere, were being held in captivity in Florida in the 1950s. It could be speculated that panthers in the wild disappeared during this period and were replaced by released captives of uncertain pedigree, or alternatively that released animals interbred with the few remaining cats in the wild. However, in the 1970s and 1980s when cats from the wild again became available for examination by investigators, their skins and skulls closely resembled the ones collected years earlier. Biologists who had an opportunity to compare these characters have no doubt the animal persisted.[42]

McCauley ventured that from 1900 to the mid-1950s the panther population trended downward—an opinion buttressed by documents as well as anecdotes, although the evidence available to her was too vague to speculate on the rate of decline. She followed the conventional belief of an earlier commentator—John Davis in 1943—who blamed indiscriminate killing.[43] Much North American wildlife was depleted by unrestrained killing; it is reasonable to presume the same about panthers, but again, the story from the West suggests that pumas in a sparsely settled land, well supplied with prey, cannot be eliminated even when assailed by governments. So the panther's fortunes were likely linked to its prey resources, principally white-tailed deer and feral hogs.

The Decline of Deer

As mentioned above, Seminole Indians trickled into northern Florida in the late 1700s. William Bartram's journal hints that Seminole society might have begun making inroads into the deer herds, at least in certain locales. Although the Indians were "weak with respect to number," as Bartram phrased it, their economy gained from "the hides of deer, bears, tigers and wolves, together with honey, wax and other productions of the country [which were used to] purchase their cloathing [sic], equipage, and domestic utensils from the whites." The intensity of the trade was lamented by Bartram: "They wage eternal war against deer and bear, to procure food and cloathing [sic], and other necessaries and conveniences; which is indeed carried to an unreasonable and perhaps criminal excess, since the white people have dazzled their senses with foreign superfluities."[44]

Richard F. Harlow and F. K. Jones, in their volume on *The White-tailed Deer in Florida*, speculate on the probable impact of the English colonial fur trade on deer.

Frontier trade was a rigorous business for both the traders and their clientele. The distances between trading posts and the main trading centers of St. Augustine, Pensacola, Mobile, and Charles Town were great. The principal item of trade was deer hides for use as leather as opposed to fur and as late as the 1750's deer hides brought greater returns than all other commodities combined. The volume of trade fluctuated greatly with the luck of the hunters, numbers of traders, and intertribal and international warfare. The trade was lighter from St. Augustine where in 1771 only four thousand pounds of hides were traded than from Pensacola where during the same year the combined export from Pensacola and Mobile was 250,000 pounds of hide. The annual export from Charles Town between 1739 and 1762 was from 131,000 pounds to 355,000 pounds and from Georgia between 1765 and 1773 was more than 200,000 pounds. This represents quite an impressive volume of trade as the average hide weighs one and one-half pounds. It is hard to judge the effect that this hunting had on the deer population but locally it must have represented a heavy pressure and diminished herds. An early writer (1682) said. . . . These exports represent a great slaughter and the "infinite herds" of the late seventeenth century must have been seriously diminished particularly in parts of the Carolinas, Georgia, Alabama and North Florida. The trade, because of transportation problems, probably did not affect peninsula Florida to a great extent. . . .[45]

American migration into northern Florida surged in the early nineteenth century, and by the end of the second decade we can see evidence that the newcomers were depleting deer. Spain had ceded Florida to the United States by treaty in 1821. In 1828 the territorial legislature enacted a prohibition against fire-hunting west of the Suwannee River; later that year the act was extended to the entire territory. In 1851 the state legislature moved to regulate camp hunting in Escambia and Santa Rosa counties and, in 1859, banned hunting on Sunday.[46] The latter act though, may have been intended to aid in the saving of souls as much as deer.

Anecdotal data from the late nineteenth century relates that deer were then vanishing from the more populated northern parts of the state. In 1874 an English Guards officer, F. Trench Townshend, hunted and explored in Florida leaving an informative and entertaining account of his adventures.[47] Townshend gave the population of Florida as 187,000, presumably quoting the census of 1870. Jacksonville, where he outfitted and inquired about places to hunt, was Florida's largest city with 10,000 citizens. Captain Townshend was told that big game was harder to find every year. He resolved to make for the southwestern part of the state which was barely inhabited. From a village on the Manatee River he scouted the countryside, but "got little shooting at Manatee, the reason being that the country around had been hunted out."[48] However, deer and other game were found a few days travel from civilization. The officer camped at what is now Myakka River State Park. Near a spring (Little Salt Springs in present-day Sarasota County) he found small herds of six or seven deer "with some fine heads among the stags and all tame enough to get within easy shot."[49] At this place a panther was killed when the unsuspecting cat came leisurely trotting toward the hunting party.

Townshend traveled to Cuba, then returned to make his way up the east coast of Florida to St. Lucie, which he described as a "few wooden houses straggling along the bank of the Sound . . . a couple of stores and a post-office. St. Lucie was reached by hiring a small cutter or schooner for three dollars a day, but only a few hunters or tourists penetrate so far south." Along the so-called Indian River, the narrow coastal waterway separating the mainland from the offshore barrier islands that parallel it, game populations were scarce, but "a little way up some of the inflowing creeks tolerable sport may be had."[50] A few miles up the St. Lucie River he found deer and turkey common. Townshend made several references to ocelots in Florida, which is puzzling since the animal is not known to have ever existed here, and the author leaves an impression of being a careful and reliable observer. His story intimates that the unregulated hunting practices of the day were removing deer from the vicinity of the advancing settlements.

There is an item of particular interest in the author's commentary on hunting near St. Lucie on the east coast and Manatee on the west coast. Townshend says that there were no suitable dogs available in either place to hunt panthers— a fact that would have made purging them from the hinterland problematical.[51] When Charles Cory came to the east coast of Florida to collect a specimen, 22 years after Townshend's visit, it took two months of effort to get one. But the time required seems less a reflection on the scarcity of panthers than on the lack of trained dogs. The dogs of his guide often trailed deer; moreover, the warm temperature often limited hunting to the cool hours of morning and evening. During his 1935 hunt, Dave Newell had to send to Arizona for properly trained dogs before he could achieve more than mediocre success. Admittedly the clues are sparse, but the impression from this brief review is that the persecution of panthers in Florida may not have been conducted with the efficiency of later predator control programs for pumas in the West.

The wars against the Seminole Indians by the U.S. Government had the object of transferring them to the West. Many were removed, but final obstacles were insurmountable. The Indians dispersed in small groups that fought guerilla style while living off the land, and the Florida environment in those days was a crippling one for military campaigns; it killed and disabled soldiers far more effectively than the Indians. At the close of the Third Seminole War (1855-58) less than 300 Indians remained in southern Florida.[52] They were scattered through the interior living in small encampments. Beginning in the 1870s the Indians periodically entered the small coastal settlements at Miami, Fort Lauderdale and Fort Myers to trade pelts, hides and bird plumes for commodities such as ammunition, salt, cloth and decorative items. In the 1870s dressed deer skins brought 40-50 cents a pound, and skins died with red mangrove bark, a dollar per pound.[53] When the Indians were in the vicinity of white settlements they also found a ready market for venison.[54]

There is little indication (from what was an admittedly cursory survey) that the Seminole trade in the late 1800s would have had a great impact on deer. The Bureau of Ethnology estimated in a report in 1883-84 that the Seminoles were killing 2500 deer a year.[55] The Seminoles of this period were few in number and traded animal products when they had a need for commodities, as opposed to being motivated by a desire for profit, as was the case with whites. Harry Kersey, who researched the Seminole trade, comments: "For the first twenty years of the heavy trading period, the Indians were the dominant factor, but by the 1890s increasing numbers of professional white hunters had arrived in the region. They were generally better armed, well organized (especially the plume hunters, who could systematically exterminate a rookery in a day or two), and, as a group, quite ruthless in their wanton destruction of game."[56]

In the early 1880s, James A. Henshall, a medical doctor of Cynthiana, Kentucky traveled the peninsular coast on a hunting and fishing expedition. His route and routine resembled that of Captain F. Trench Townshend, with the exception of proceeding in the reverse direction, southward along the Atlantic Coast, with the return being made up the west side of the state. His travelogue suggests that deer abundance was unaltered since Townshend's visit nearly a decade earlier. Deer were still common near St. Lucie and venison could "be had for the taking."[57] In one interesting incident, Henshall spent the night in an Indian village where he had paddled his canoe. The village chief was the son of Tigertail, mentioned earlier in the chapter. The old chief had been killed by lightning, two years previously, having endured two wars with the U.S. Government and evading deportation to the West.[58] In another incident, Henshall, hoping to get a turkey, concealed himself in heavy brush where he had found sign of the birds' activities. He tried calling them to his blind, but was not rewarded. He emerged from concealment to find the tracks of a panther which had approached within six feet of his position, apparently attracted by his turkey calls.[59]

Farther south in his voyage, Henshall observed on the savannah bordering the Everglades that "deer are quite plentiful."[60] Along the western coast, he found deer and turkeys common near the Caloosahatchee River. Deer were seen on Big Gasparilla and Little Gasparilla Island (where they do not occur today). Along the Myakka River and Pease Creek (the present Peace River), deer and turkeys could be found in numbers "to satisfy the greediest hunter."[61] Years later a resident of southwest Florida, reminiscing about this region, remembered that "you could go out east of Fort Ogden when I first went there in 1883 and see 50 deer in a herd feeding in the prairie and could go south from Cleveland and Punta Gorda in the hammock ponds and see 25 or 30 deer feeding in the woods but there is none there now. Down southeast of Fort Ogden on the edge of the prairie at the head of Lee's Branch was Stink Pen Hammock where the cattlemen used to poison beef and leave it to kill wolves. There was some of them there."[62]

Like Townshend, Henshall found game wanting around the larger settlements, like Tampa. He did find "deer and other game" on some of the keys near Point Pinellas. He bagged a deer farther north along the Homosassa River, and his descriptions of wild Hernando County indicate that it was a sportsman's paradise. ". . . in the swamps and low hamaks [sic] can be found panthers, bears, wild cattle and hogs. . . ."[63] Charles Maynard wrote of this area in 1883, at about the time Henshall was hunting there: "I learned last winter that not more than three [panthers] had been shot in the Gulf Hummocks [sic] in western Florida during five years."[64] However, the wilderness of the northern peninsular Gulf Coast may not have remained a prolific hunting ground long after Henshall's visit. In the 1880s, in Gulf Hammock, two market hunters are alleged to have killed 1100 deer in just nine months.[65]

T. Gilbert Pearson, a prominent early twentieth-century conservationist, spent his boyhood in Alachua County in the 1880s. His autobiography offers insights into the rapid disappearance of wildlife near settlements.

> There was a great deal of hunting. Nearly every man carried a gun when he came to town or traveled about the country. We would sometimes see six or more pale, lanky white men with wide-brimmed slouch hats riding together along the road, each with a gun across the front of his saddle. Often on Saturday nights there was much shooting, frequently mingled with the sound of running horses, hilarious hunting calls and rebel yells as some of the crackers made their way home after an evening in the saloons. Boys had guns before they were strong enough to hold them out and aim. People killed any wild bird or animal on which they were willing to waste a bullet.[66]

The head of Florida's first game agency, E. Z. Jones, in 1914, lamented the wastage of Florida's birds and game.[67] There is evidence that deer in the peninsula suffered another heavy blow in the first decade of the new century. The state was widely if thinly settled by that time, and there was no enforcement of game laws worthy of the name. In the eastern United States, large-scale hunting for city markets had emptied the forests of deer and other species as well. Interstate commerce in game animals had been outlawed by the federal government in 1900, but hunting for local markets was still practiced in Florida. The going price for a deer was 50 dollars in 1915.[68] That would have been a fat sum for the cash-poor crackers who lived from the offerings of this southern frontier.

In 1915 E. Z. Jones attempted Florida's first deer "census." In that year he presented his findings to the governor, affirming that "the information shown as to the number of each of some of the different kinds of animals and birds of this state was arrived at by securing from each county estimates of different persons and making such allowances as would seem proper and while it's more or less guess work a certain degree of accuracy may be placed upon it."[69] This statement is probably true enough in the case of deer. His figure was 13,460.[70] Nearly a quarter of a century later the Game Commission's statewide estimate would be roughly the same.[71] So it appears that deer in the peninsula diminished during the first decade of the twentieth century. As late as 1893 a new arrival in Fort Lauderdale had written that there were ". . . wild cats, otter, deer, alligators all the game anyone wants. . . ."[72] Three years later the locomotives of Henry Flager's Florida East Coast Railroad steamed into Miami bringing with them a flush of communities along the lower east coast. In 1915 E.Z. Jones "guessed" the deer population of Dade County at 25 animals. That was perhaps an underestimate, considering the tribulations of pursuing deer into the Everglades marsh, but surely an indication that deer could not be found near the coast.

On Florida's west coast the rails had pushed south to Punta Gorda in 1886 and to Fort Myers in 1904. E. Z. Jones put the deer population of Lee County (which then included present-day Collier County) at 1,000 (the largest estimate, by far, for any county). In the year of Jones' census in Lee County the *Fort Myers Press* announced that C. B. Douglas, a cattle rancher from Immokalee was organizing a party to help him "in destroying some of the bears and panthers of the Big Cypress that had lately been doing considerable damage to his young stock."[73] To Immokalee went the locomotives in 1921, and to Naples in 1926, only two years ahead of the Tampa to Miami highway (the Tamiami Trail).[74] However, the arrival of these transportation arteries did not immediately foster the boom that had spread over Florida's lower Atlantic Coast. Development was slowed by a national economic depression beginning in 1929. The domestic calamity was followed by a world war. It seems probable that the bustling towns spawned by the advancing railroads led to the final reduction of the peninsular deer herd by about 1910. Deer were never completely eradicated, because much of this region is swamp or marsh. Access was formidable, granting a tenuous sanctuary due to the barriers posed by terrain. But for the first half of this century, deer would have been too few and widely scattered to have sustained many panthers.

It would not be until after midcentury that Florida was able to restore its deer herd, although there were a few local successes in protected preserves. The first attempt to found a state game agency lasted through one interregnum of the biennial legislature. The Department of Game and Fish was abolished in 1915 and was not to reappear until 1925, and even when resurrected the agency was poorly funded until after World War II; law enforcement prior to that time was ineffective in restoring deer numbers—in contrast to most other states. In 1938 the Game Commission estimated that the deer range in Florida could support 2,000,000 animals (undoubtedly a high estimate), but actual numbers were put at just under 17,000.[75] The recorded legal harvest of deer for the 1938-39 biennium was 1,539.[76] Deer recovery was further hindered by the arrival of the screw-worm fly in the Southeast in the 1930s, a pest that would not be eradicated until 1958.[77] In 1944 Game Commission statistics showed 1,293 deer harvested the previous hunting season, a year when the agency estimated that there were 25,000 deer in Florida.[78]

The Tick Eradication Program

McCauley suggested that "another factor that may have contributed to [panther] population reduction in the late 1930s was the deer eradication program instigated by Florida's cattlemen to control the Texas cattle fever ticks . . . which were known to occur occasionally on deer. This program which was carried on from 1937 to 1939 was responsible for drastic reductions of deer herds in Orange, Osceola, Highlands, Glades, Polk, Okeechobee, Charlotte, Hernando, Collier and Hendry counties (Marshall et al., 1963)."[79] Since the data I discovered indicated that there were relatively few deer to be reduced, I researched the tick affair.

In the early 1900s southern cattlemen tried to breed a more competitive grade of beef. The endeavor was frustrated by a variety of tick which propagated itself only on cattle, infecting them with a blood disease. The longhorns in Texas and the scrub cattle in Florida may have been resistant, but imported breeds sickened or died. The states harboring these ticks collaborated with the federal government to get rid of them. Research proved that dipping all the cattle in a given region in an arsenic dip once every 14 days, for a period of 14 months, eradicated the ticks. Dipping began at the northern edge of the tick's geographical range, progressing southward through designated treatment zones. Cattle in the untreated zones were quarantined from the tick-free area. The program reached Florida in 1923. When it had advanced to Orange County in 1931 an obstacle appeared. Orange County had been scheduled for release from quarantine in 1932, but the cattle still had ticks. A second round of dipping was initiated; it too, proved unsuccessful.

Specimens of ticks were then sent to scientists in Washington, D.C., who discovered them to be a tropical variety not previously known in the United States. Additional field studies found that deer, and only deer, were an alternate host for the tropical tick, which had a limited distribution in several counties in southern Florida. An intensified effort was made to rid Orange County of ticks; it failed. In 1937 the State Livestock Sanitary Board—the responsible agency—concluded that two options remained: either eradicate the ticks by killing deer prior to cattle dipping, or try to hold the quarantine line where it stood to prevent a general reinfestation.[80] The cattlemen had no sympathy for option two, and they were a powerful political force in the 1930s. Local legislators introduced bills in the 1937 session to destroy deer in the infested areas. In so doing they brought themselves head-on into conflict with sportsmen's groups and other conservationists. The bills passed and controversy flamed. The Florida Deer Protective Association got an injunction from the state supreme court to block the killing, but it was soon overturned.

Subsequent events can be followed through newspaper accounts. Licensed hunters were given first crack at the deer. A season was opened from July 1 to October 31, 1939, the hunt to center on a game refuge near Naples. An early strategy of what was called the game protective movement had featured protected refuges for game where no hunting was permitted. One of these sanctuaries sprawled over 390,000 acres in Collier County, and it unquestionably held the only deer population of any size in Florida.[81] In 1939 it had been guarded for 12 years. It was here that news reporters and photographers gathered. The Game Commission detailed men to record the number and sex of deer killed. At the close of the season, professional hunters were hired at $80 a month to finish the work.

The deer kill was a heated issue and some newspapers openly took sides. The outdoor writer from the *Miami Herald*, Erl Roman, waxed apoplectic.

> . . . All our deer have been ruthlessly slaughtered by hired deer butchers through legislative decree. . . . Taking it all in all, we do not believe even Hitlerite Germany can match it. . . . Sportsmen of the state and notably the Florida Deer Protective Association . . . collected a fund to prevent the slaughter . . . they obtained from the Florida Supreme Court an injunction stopping the livestock board from carrying out the provisions of the nefarious law.
>
> They pointed out that the killing of deer would no more eliminate the ticks than would the killing of a 1,000 cats and dogs eliminate

fleas. Now as everyone who knows wild deer is aware, these creatures are the dearest of God's creatures. They are so constructed that they can pick ticks from any part of their limbs or bodies—even out of their ears.[82]

Roman suspected dirty politics. He saw the whole affair as a political deal, "where by the livestock board had invented the mysterious tick . . . in order to furnish jobs to the political faithful." He renewed the attack, following the special hunting season:

> ". . . 80 paid slaughterers will be sent into the region to "clear up" the work of exterminating the deer. . . . As for the deer, the most innocent, timid and loveable creature of nature, they have been slaughtered and pursued until they are frantic with fright. Out there in the wilderness of hammocks and sawgrass, lie the bleeding carcasses of the noble bucks, does and fawns rotting and stinking to high heaven of the outrages foisted upon them by man. Those yet alive do not know which way to turn for everywhere they go they face an enemy—a paid killer, paid for by you and me.[83]

The *Orlando Sentinel,* in the heart of cattle country, took a different view: "Shall a giant industry be destroyed to please hunters a few weeks each year?"[84]

The war on deer encountered resistance when it came to the Indian reservation adjacent to the Collier County preserve. The Indians needed the deer for food. The Secretary of the Interior, Harold Ickes, refused to allow the killing. The Florida congressional delegation, apparently with support from other southern states, put the pressure on, but newspaper accounts reveal that Ickes was no pushover. He dug in and fought back, garnering support from national conservation leaders. It so happened that both Ickes and his wife had a knowledgeable interest in, and sympathy for, the American Indian. His wife had written a book on the Pueblo and Navajo Indians, and Ickes had appointed a friend, John Collier, as the head of the Bureau of Indian Affairs. Ickes was also an old-time righteous crusader for noble causes. He thrived on attention from the press, and had a combative personality and a volcanic temper which at times reduced him to incoherence. His boss, Franklin D. Roosevelt, called him Donald Duck behind his back.[85] The conflict at the Indian reservation was a fight made to order for Ickes.

The National Audubon Society, directed by John Baker, joined in to protect the deer. Baker enlisted Aldo Leopold, then at the University of Wisconsin, who was regarded as the foremost wildlife expert in the country. Leopold backed the Audubon Society. Baker also contacted Herbert L. Stoddard, another wildlife expert who was working in southern Georgia, and asked him to investigate. Stoddard traveled south to Collier County in the summer of 1941, taking with him two young biologists, Roy and Ed Komarek. Ickes had denied the State of Florida permission to kill deer on the Indian reservation on the grounds that there were insufficient data to show that reservation deer were actually carrying the fever ticks. Following Stoddard's reconnaissance, he arranged that Roy Komarek would work under contract to National Audubon to determine if the reservation deer harbored the ticks.[86]

There are records of several panthers being taken at the time deer were being killed. The mammalogist, W. J. Hamilton, visited Fort Myers in the spring of 1939 and again in 1940. He reported a 145-pound panther killed a mile from Bonita Springs on October 10, 1939 and an even larger cat shot near Estero on November 20. In 1941 a cowhand was reported by Hamilton to have shot a large female near Immokalee. The cat was exhibited with its two live kittens in Fort Myers on the same day.[87] There is reason to believe that with the sudden, heavy loss of deer in Collier County, the panthers turned to preying on cattle, which in turn spurred local ranchers to persecute panthers. The day after Christmas in 1939, an individual named Ransom Page from Bergen, New York, wrote a letter to the chief of the Regional Biological Division of the Soil Conservation Service in Upper Darby, Pennsylvania.

Dear Ed:

I am enclosing a photo of a puma shot in lower Florida. I spent part of November and December this fall in the same locality—near Naples, Collier County, and while there two pumas were shot in that vicinity. It seems they have been especially destructive of cattle since the State of Florida started a deer extermination campaign in this county to clear out the fever tick and improve the "cattle range", and consequently more are being hunted and shot.

Seventy-five hunters have been afield in Collier County since last spring, hunting largely at night, shooting from horseback with jacklight, collecting a bonus on each deer hide in addition to monthly pay.

Both panthers, as they are locally called, that I saw after being shot, were credited with killed [sic] 20-30 head of cattle and the cattlemen are still having trouble.

It is planned to put paid hunters in Hendry and other lower Florida "cattle counties" soon to continue the deer extermination.

Looks as though the wiping out of the deer may mean the end of this last frontier for the puma in eastern United States.

Thought you might be interested in this little angle.

As ever,
/s/ Ransom Page[88]

The recipient of this letter, sent it on to his superior in Washington, D.C. and copied Aldo Leopold.[89] Leopold sent copies to John Baker; to Ira Gabrielson, Chief of the U.S. Biological Survey; to the president of the American Society of Mammalogists and to the head of the Rare Species Committee of the American Ornithologists' Union.[90] He then wrote to Harold Ickes. Leopold had a poor opinion of Ickes who was a covetous, bureaucratic empire-builder. Ickes tried to gain control of every government program and agency in sight, and sometimes succeeded. He wrested the Bureau of Fisheries from the Commerce Department, and the Bureau of Biological Survey from the Department of Agriculture. The two bureaus were reorganized into the agency known today as the Fish and Wildlife Service. But Icke's appetite was insatiable. He kept trying for the U.S. Forest Service, an agency where Leopold had once worked. Though failing to capture this prize, his intrigues never slackened. He plotted tirelessly to get the nation's forests into his department during his entire 13-year tenure at Interior.[91]

Leopold had, on other issues, criticized Ickes publicly; privately he likened the man's unrestrained bureaucratic predation to that of Adolf Hitler on the international scene, differing principally in that "Mr. Ickes doesn't have an army—yet."[92] However, in assessing tick eradication, Leopold found himself in a situation calling for conciliation—and support for Ickes.

Dear Mr. Secretary:

I have, on occasion, been critical of your conservation policies. It now gives me satisfaction to uphold and endorse your refusal to permit the attempt to exterminate deer on the Seminole Reservation in the interest of cattle fever tick control.

I am interested not only in deer, but in the last easterly remnant of cougar which will certainly pass out when the deer do. Florida

The 1928 statistics of the Florida Game Commission also give the returns from the state's hunters. The tallies clearly show that panthers were not surviving on deer. Of 50,000 licensed hunters, 10,000 reported a harvest of 577 deer.[104] To put these figures in perspective, during the early 1970s hunters in Florida were taking 50,000 to 60,000 deer annually.[105] A local disparity between deer and panther numbers is suggested by statistics from Palm Beach County where three panthers were taken by trappers while hunters reported killing only six deer. The highest harvest figure of deer from a single county was 76. Such an informative county-by-county breakdown of figures was never repeated by the Game Commission (or at least not given in the annual and biennial reports).

If panthers require a supply of large prey animals, and there were panthers in Florida but few deer, the population of feral hogs may have made the difference. The World Almanac for 1927 (the year that 577 deer were reported killed by hunters) reveals that there were more than 500,000 hogs in Florida.[106] The census figures are listed under "livestock on farms," but the common practice in Florida was for hogs to range freely in the woods, foraging on their own. They were periodically baited to traps to be harvested, or else captured with specially bred and trained dogs which caught the animals by the ears and held them until the owners could arrive. The U.S. Department of Agriculture's statistics on hogs in Florida date back to 1924. In that year 640,000 hogs were reported from the state. Outbreaks of hog cholera occurred periodically, but the statistics do not indicate any drastic declines in overall numbers, which in most years fluctuated rather erratically between 400,000 and 600,000 until 1962 when the figures drop permanently below 400,000.[107] Feral hogs are widespread in Florida, occurring in 66 of the state's 67 counties.[108] The distribution is not uniform; the animals are absent from much of the state's upland areas except where the uplands are penetrated by the swamps of river floodplains. Hog populations of high and medium density are concentrated in Florida's coastal lowlands topographic region. So, even though Florida's deer were few and fugitive after the turn of the century, feral hogs remained abundant and widespread and may account for the survival of the panther after 1910. Harvest statistics suggest that panthers remained widely distributed in Florida at least into the 1930s—a good 20 years after the deer faded, and during the period when public sentiment favored exterminating panthers. Why then did panthers ultimately decline? If attributed to persecution, why did panthers not rebound after 1950 when they became protected? There was an abundant supply of feral hogs, and after midcentury the deer herd began a rapid expansion.

Adequate habitat for panthers was available in Florida during the 1950s. In fact the situation then may have been more favorable than at any time since the reduction of deer at the beginning of the century, because large numbers of squatters and smaller landowners began leaving the hinterland during the 1940s and 1950s. During the depression years of the 1930s, many large tracts owned by timber companies became tax-delinquent. These properties were claimed by Florida under the Murphy Act of 1937 and offered at public auction. Cattlemen acquired them at little cost since most could be had for the price of delinquent taxes. Many homesteaders (or squatters) living on these lands were forced to sell their holdings for little or nothing.[109] Between 1930 and 1944, the average number of acres owned by individual Florida cattlemen increased from 88 to 870.[110]

The post-World War II prosperity enabled wealthier ranchers to buy even more land, reducing the amount available to poorer cattlemen. The practice of open range continued in Florida until collisions between cattle and the proliferating automobile became scandalous. In 1949 the state legislature finally required all stock owners to fence in their cattle.[111] The end of open range also terminated marginal cattle operations whose owners could not afford fencing. All these events consolidated Florida's rural lands in the hands of fewer owners, while smaller landholders and squatters were gradually forced off. This had the practical effect of protecting deer, since many of the departed were not scrupulous abiders of game laws. The Game Commission's biennial report of 1950 was finally able to report that "the deer population in Florida has shown a definite increase in the past few years due to three major factors: (1) better enforcement of game laws; (2) the posting of large tracts of land by cattlemen and other private interests; (3) the general movement of homesteaders from rural areas, particularly in the ranching areas of southern Florida."[112]

The "definite increase" of deer, evident in 1950, was the beginning of a spectacular expansion. In 1944 Florida hunters had reported taking 1,293 deer from a population estimated at approximately 25,000. Six years later, in the 1950 season, the harvest tally was 6,100 deer. During the winter of 1963-64 it climbed to 16,800, and the deer herd was estimated to stand at 168,000. The continuing ascent in annual harvest statistics tells the story of a herd growing like Topsy, with the increase in total numbers racing ahead of the sharply rising harvest figures. In 1966-67 the legal kill was 33,800; one year later 43,900 were taken, and in 1972-73 the number of reported legally killed deer topped 58,000.

The sharp rate of growth was probably assisted by the eradication of the screw worm fly in 1958.[113] So we can see that the deer numbers rose dramatically during the 1950s, a situation that should have been favorable to panthers, but judging by all that has been learned from panther studies in recent years, the revival of deer was not accompanied by a proportionate recovery of the panther, and bear in mind that an alternate prey source, feral hogs, had remained abundant all along.

TABLE 1. WHITE-TAILED DEER IN FLORIDA:
ESTIMATES OF TOTAL NUMBERS
AND REPORTED NUMBERS HARVESTED
FOR SELECTED YEARS

YEAR	ESTIMATED TOTAL	LICENSED HUNTERS	HARVESTED
1513[A]	400,000	-	80,000
1915[B]	13,460	21,371	-
1928[C]	-	52,281	577
1936[D]	-	42,288	1,761
1938[E]	16,908	55,693	2,083
1940[F]	16,169	57,927	1,974
1944[G]	25,202	51,123	1,293
1951[H]	61,000	27,000	6,100
1964[H]	168,000	76,000	16,800
1968[I]	-	-	43,900
1971[I]	-	-	48,000
1973[I]	-	-	58,500

A. Cristoffer and Eisenberg, "Report No. 2, 1985 (see note no. 2)

B. Jones, *Second Annual Report,* 1915 (see note no. 74)

C. Royall, Report, *Biennium 1928* (see note no. 88)

D. *Biennial Report: Florida Commission of Game and Fresh Water Fish, Biennium Ending December 31, 1936* (Tallahassee: Florida State Library).

E. *Florida Commission of Game and Fresh Water Fish Biennial Report for Period Ending December 31, 1938* (Tallahassee: Florida State Library).

F. *Biennial Report 1940* (see note no. 81) The report noted that "...gains in Walton, Santa Rosa and Okaloosa counties, where deer have been given additional protection on the Eglin Field Military Reservation and the Blackwater River State Forest; and gains in several other areas are due to added protection; have partially offset the heavy reduction in Collier County [from the tick eradication program]..."

G. *Biennial Report 1944* (see note no. 83)

H. Harlow and Jones, *The White-tailed Deer in Florida,* (see note no. 49)

I. William B. Frankenberger and Robert C. Belden, "Distribution, etc." (see note no. 89)

When the Florida panther recovery program was initiated in 1976 it was soon discovered that panthers survived at the southern extremity of Florida. A question occurring to several of us was: why does this small population remain restricted to a region that is so poor in prey? Why after 25 years of protection, which saw a dramatic increase in deer, is there no evidence of panthers farther north in the state? An unofficial but popular hypothesis held that a heavy mortality rate among the remnant panthers had held them down. Since monitoring began in 1976 the documented rate of deaths has been high enough to lend some credence to this idea, but most of the known mortalities were caused by automobiles, whereas when the deer herd was expanding after 1950 the volume of traffic in panther country would have been minuscule compared to the post-1976 period. Also, most of the known highway deaths took place on Alligator Alley, which was not completed until the late1960s. Prior to its completion, much of today's occupied panther habitat was remote to hunters who were significantly fewer then than today. McCauley's thesis states that "panthers were not fully protected in Florida until 1958 and it seems safe to assume that the population continued to decline through legal hunting until that time."[114] However, I do not believe it safe to assume that the legal harvest of panthers, within the newly imposed constraints of a season (November 7 to January 7)[115] and a bag limit (one panther), would result in a "continuing" decline. Furthermore, there are no records known to me of panthers being taken between 1950-1958.

Another hypothesis to explain why panthers have not reestablished farther north is based on a suspicion that the species does not often colonize a new area.[116] This belief is based on the behavioral trait of "transients" or "floaters"— young cats which, upon becoming independent of the mother, disperse in a search for a "vacancy" in an area occupied by an established "community" of adults. It is thought that if no community is found, the young animal will simply wander on. In the West, marked pumas have been found more than 100 miles from their site of birth,[117] an indication that individuals may drift for great distances.

Another interesting hypothesis has recently been offered (informally) by Melody Roelke, a veterinarian employed by the Game Commission to work in the panther recovery program. The hypothesis has to do with the feral hog, which, as stated, may account for panther survival to the present time and yet may also pose an indirect threat. Roelke has investigated diseases, not only of the panther, but of its prey as well. Pseudorabies is a particularly virulent pathogen which she observed in feral hogs. Exposure by hogs to the virus is apparently fatal. Blood analyses have revealed no antibodies—a sign that hogs had withstood the disease. The virus is density-dependent. When individuals are scattered, relatively few animals are affected, but a dense population tends to suffer heavy losses during an outbreak. Where hogs occur at high densities in southern Florida, investigations have commonly shown infection rates higher than 50 percent; whereas samples of populations more dispersed, as in Collier County, have revealed lower rates of about 20 percent.[118] The disease is deadly to house cats which usually die before any immune response can be detected. If house cats are vulnerable to pseudorabies, panthers might also be. The disease progresses rapidly in house cats (24-36 hours) and might be hard to detect in a panther population.

Where hogs are abundant in southern Florida they are commonly taken by panthers. The three counties in southern Florida, which account for the only known established panther population (Collier, Hendry and Dade), have a low density of feral hogs. Hog populations of high density occur in two nearby areas—Fisheating Creek and Myakka River State Park. Though both of these areas appear favorable to panthers, the cats are either absent or uncommon there. Roelke, in a recent report wrote: "although the impact of PRV (pseudorabies) on the panther is largely conjecture at this time, there is circumstantial evidence that suggests that hogs carrying pseudorabies could be acting to limit and delineate the distribution of panthers in southern Florida."[119]

I would emphasize that this is only a tentative hypothesis, but one that should be explored since it has obvious implications for panther survival in southern Florida. Antibodies of feline panleukopenia (feline distemper) have also been detected in panthers. The disease can be devasting to domestic and captive felines.[120] An outbreak of panleukopenia at Archbold Biological Station, near Lake Placid, Florida in the winter of 1979 and 1980, killed 9 0f 18 radio-collared bobcats.[121] Yet another hypothesis to explain the failure of the panthers in southern Florida to expand beyond the confines of their presently known range has to do with the possible reduced fitness of individuals by reason of inbreeding. A recent panther death is believed to have been caused by a congential heart defect; pernicious anomalies of this kind would not be unexpected in an inbred population.

Attempts to reintroduce panthers farther north in the peninsula will confront another threat: the annually increasing volume of traffic on the state's crowded highways. Cats have demonstrated a remarkable propensity for getting run over by automobiles. A program to reintroduce Canadian lynx to the Adirondack Mountains in New York has suffered from highway mortalities. Of 18 lynx brought to the state in November 1988, four of them had died crossing highways by July 1989.[122]

Chapter 3

IN THE BEGINNING

At the present time, it is not known whether or where a viable population of <u>Felis</u> <u>concolor</u> occurs in Florida.

Robert C. Belden
December 1976

If a place and date can be said to mark the beginning of the Florida panther recovery program, it was the First Unitarian Church on Robinson Street, in Orlando, Florida, on March 17 and 18, 1976. There a conference was convened by Peter C. H. Pritchard of the Florida Audubon Society. Pritchard invited participants whom he generously alluded to as "experts" to tell what they knew, or thought they knew, about the Florida panther. The high estimate ran to 100 or more, a speculation that drew from sighting reports. But some who came doubted the animal's existence. The null hypothesis attributed the few confirmed records of recent years to released captives that were known to have come to grief in encounters with humans. The incidents were as follows: in the spring of 1967 the remains of a 70-pound male were found in the Ocala National Forest.[1] In March 1969 a photograph in the *Citrus County Chronicle* showed a male panther killed near Inverness by a deputy sheriff; it weighed over 100 pounds.[2] In February 1972, south of Moore Haven on State Road 25, a large male was injured by an automobile and later shot by a highway patrolman. In February 1973 a very old female was treed near Fisheating Creek by the dogs of a puma hunter, Roy McBride, who, in company with Ronald Nowak, had been hired by the World Wildlife Fund to search for Florida panthers.[3]

A Fish and Wildlife Service official had come to the meeting, hoping to assemble a recovery team from among the participants. He unfolded the monumental chore assigned to his agency by the Endangered Species Act of 1973. It had first to identify all the nation's endangered organisms, then to work out a means of rescuing them. The recovery team was an imaginative device for coordinating this labor. The idea was to select participants thought to be most knowledgeable about the species in hazard. The team would write a plan whose objective would be to "create a situation in which the animal (or plant) is no longer endangered or threatened by man and can assume a natural role in its ecosystem with assurance that measures will continue to prevent it from reverting to endangered or threatened status."[4] The goal was termed "recovery." The Fish and Wildlife Service was to be the administrative overseer and a source of funds. The planning framework left little to chance. It called for a blueprint that would, step by step, surmount each obstruction to recovery through a specific task. All would be placed in a sequence of priorities and parceled out to a combination of government agencies and perhaps to other organizations as well. An "implementation schedule" would identify a date for the completion of each task.

The recovery plan concept is impressive. It begins with a group of "experts," thinking the problem through. The weight of professional consensus ought, in theory, to keep the enterprise on a sure footing. As an additional safeguard the Fish and Wildlife Service would subject the draft to scrutiny by its own personnel and by other knowledgeable persons around the country. As a final check it controlled the purse strings. Other participating entities, if they balked at sensible measures, could (in theory) be denied funding. Of course in the real world bureaucracies do not submit to an idealistic planning design. Joint planning is often approached with caution by hesitant government agencies, fearing to be led down a path they do not wish to travel. The Fish and Wildlife Service was under no illusions here and, perhaps to allay anticipated fears, took pains to lure the participants into cooperating; it actually promised to not "require each cooperating agency to sign plans."[5] The federal officials were simply trying to accommodate a hard bureaucratic reality.

The Florida Panther Recovery Team came into being soon after the conference. The Game Commission was designated the lead agency. One of its biologists, Robert C. (Chris) Belden, became the team leader. Belden's specialty was large mammals including panthers, deer, and feral hogs. Peter Pritchard was put on the team. His expertise was in turtles, but he had assisted elsewhere with large projects on behalf of endangered species and had edited general publications on the theme.[6] James N. Layne was also picked. He was a mammalogist and director of the Archbold Biological Station, a field station of the American Museum of Natural History, sited in the south-central part of the state where panthers were frequently rumored. Another appointee was James Kushlan, a research scientist from Everglades National Park. The U.S. Forest Service sent Brian Knowles, a wildlife biologist assigned to the Ocala National Forest. I was asked to the team as a biologist from the Florida Park Service. The Fakahatchee Strand State Preserve was one of several parks for which I was responsible, and I had come to the meeting bearing tangible evidence of a panther: two plaster-of-Paris casts of tracks from the Preserve. Robert Baudy, a professional breeder and trainer of wild animals with an impressive record of success in breeding big cats, completed the slate.

We faced our job with some among us unsure if there were panthers in Florida. If they could be found, the next question would be whether they were a remnant of the original wild stock, or captive pumas that had been released, or perhaps a mixture. These uncertainties influenced the course of early investigations by the Game Commission. Two initial tasks were to delineate any existing populations and to determine the distinguishing characteristics of the Florida panther. The latter subject will be covered in a chapter to come.

The Clearinghouse

To begin, the Game Commission set up a clearinghouse that would evaluate reports and assign them to one of five categories. The first two were for confirmed panther records; the first was for specimens that could be examined, either by capture, or the remains of a dead one; the second category was for positive evidence, short of a specimen in hand—plaster casts of tracks, photographs or other unquestionable documentation would suffice. Two categories were needed for the confirmed status, because in the second case the evidence might be from a former captive which had escaped or had been released.

Categories three through five, were for unconfirmed claims—observations of the animal or its sign, not documented by physical evidence. Category three was for an account by someone presumed to be reliable, such as a wildlife biologist or a forest ranger. Category four was reserved for a sighting from anyone else. A fifth category was added for reports that were plainly erroneous, for instance where tracks had been investigated and found not to be those of a panther, or a report from mid-city or some other unlikely place.[7] By the end of June 1978, the clearinghouse had received 752 reports. Forty-one were investigated. Only one gave conclusive evidence of a panther. Of the rest, 35 percent were attributed to dogs, and 20 percent to bobcats. In 37 percent of the reports no sign of the animal could be found. Otters, bears, and raccoons were among the creatures mistaken for panthers.

Field Searches

Field searches were made at promising sites, most of them carried out by Chris Belden, with others on the recovery team assisting locally when circumstances permitted. Belden went first to West Texas to be tutored in reading sign by Roy McBride, who three years earlier had been sent by the World Wildlife Fund to look for panthers in Florida. McBride had tracking skills that few people today have an opportunity to cultivate. Back in Florida Belden traveled widely. Sign was found in the Fakahatchee Strand, and park biologists in Everglades National Park discovered tracks there. A few of the big cats still roamed the swampy lands of southern Florida.

Early in 1978 a wildlife officer received a tip that a panther was hanging in an ice plant in Homestead. He went there with a search warrant, found the evidence and arrested the plant manager, who claimed his son had killed the cat in mid-air as it was in the act of springing on the son's girlfriend. This drama was said to have been enacted in the eastern part of the Big Cypress National Preserve. The ice plant manager said the panther had been refrigerated in anticipation of making a rug of it.[8] The carcass was necropsied in Miami by the Dade County medical examiner and found to have been hit at long range by shotgun pellets as it was quartering away from the direction of the shot. The accused was given a maximum sentence of 30 days in the Dade County jail, plus a $500 fine; under state law, killing a panther was only a misdemeanor. The publicity that attended the crime promoted the penalty to a felony during the next session of the State Legislature.

In 1978 the Game Commission hired a biologist, Kent Reeves, to roam the Big Cypress National Preserve in search of panther tracks. Reeves had experience with pumas in California where he had studied under Carl Koford, a wildlife scientist at Berkeley. Koford had recently undertaken a survey of California's pumas working primarily with track data. Reeves spent 30 days in the Preserve with two objectives: The first was to discover if the general area of the recently killed panther supported a reproducing population; secondly, he was to look at parts of the Big Cypress that had not yet been checked. Reeves covered 233 miles on foot and by swamp buggy, exploring Raccoon Point, the Stairsteps, the Deep Lake unit, the Bear Island unit and the Seminole Indian Reservation. He estimated that five panthers were in the Raccoon Point area—the only place sign could be found, aside from a single scrape on the Indian reservation. Tracks of varying size seemed to have been made by five individuals: two adult males, two adult females and a juvenile.[9]

Drafting the Recovery Plan

In the late months of 1978 the recovery team mailed a draft plan to the Fish and Wildlife Service. Writing it had taken two years. This was perhaps not a bad record given the size of the committee and the paucity of information at the outset about the subject. Even so, we were relieved to see the document off. No one had any inkling that it would take the federal bureaucracy two-and-a-half years to complete its review and get it published. While the draft plan was incubating in Washington, D.C., the recovery team busied itself with other chores. Robert Baudy, who as a private businessman had little patience with the tempo of government bureaucracy, started his own captive breeding project about which more will be said later. The question of public hunting in the Fakahatchee Strand State Preserve also attracted our deliberations since panther activity was so obvious there. The Preserve was inadequately protected, only a fraction of it having been acquired. Thousands of private owners held title to small lots, purchased during the 1960s in a massive land-sales scheme. Hunting camps, built by squatters, had sprouted throughout the swamp and were not easily policed. To safeguard panthers, Game Commission biologists urged a closure-to-hunting rule by the Commissioners, but it would be years before anything came of this.

Exploring Research Techniques

As the decade of the 1970s was winding down, consistently documented evidence of panthers came only from Everglades National Park, the Big Cypress National Preserve and the Fakahatchee Strand. The panther's status was still too poorly understood to predict survival. More information was needed.

The miniaturization of electronic components, that allowed radio-transmitters to be lofted into the heavens in satellites in the late 1950s, led to a new means of studying the more elusive animals. It wasn't long before someone got the idea of attaching a tiny transmitter to a collar, which could be fastened to an animal's neck. Its whereabouts could then be plotted by the operator of a portable receiver. In the years since, radios have been used to investigate fauna, from manatees and alligators, to rattlesnakes and the California condor. The shadowy behavior of certain creatures was well illustrated by the big cats, particularly the puma, whose wraithful and furtive meanderings so rarely reward the eye. When our culture came belatedly to place a value on understanding pumas, they had been purged from wide stretches of the continent.

During the 1960s, in the western United States, Maurice Hornocker, at the University of Idaho, embarked on the first systematic field study of the puma in a remote mountain range where the cat and its prey were abundant. Although he used a familiar method known as mark and recapture, his elusive subject called for new technologies. Pumas were first treed by dogs and then made amenable to handling by being calmed with injections of a drug from a specially designed gun. Transmitters were not used in the early studies, but several devices served as markers, including color-coded collars on all adults; this permitted identification of individual cats when they were treed. Work was intensified in winter when snow facilitated tracking. By these means the adult puma population in a 200 square-mile region was monitored for five years, along with its principal prey—elk and mule deer.[10] In 1970 a researcher named John Seidensticker carried the project a step further. He fastened the first radio-collars to pumas and followed their movements for the next two-and-a-half years.[11] Within a decade the shroud around the "mysterious American cat," as it had once been called, was pulled away, revealing in the reclusive cat's behavioral traits an intricate design for survival.

The relative quickness with which radio-telemetry could furnish data on secretive animals was not a lesson to be ignored when evaluating methods to acquire information on endangered wildlife. Capturing animals with drugs afforded opportunities to assess the population's age structure, physical health and, by the collection of tissue samples, its genetic condition. However, these tools were not always accepted readily by the public. Capturing a wild animal with or without drugs cannot be done without risk. The same proprietary citizen support that produced legislation and funding to prevent the loss of endangered animals was trigger-quick to anger when one of them died at the hands of biologists. It would not be long before the Florida panther recovery program would be running a gauntlet of outrage over the death of a cat. And the experience would be repeated with the California condor.

In preparing for the research, Chris Belden undertook a review of all the scientific literature then extant on puma captures, summarizing his findings early in 1981. Over 230 pumas had by that date been captured in the field in excess of 460 times. At least 54 of the cats had been fitted with radio-collars, and all had been treed by dogs and tranquilized with drugs. Fifteen had died; six (40 percent) were kittens that were caught on the ground by dogs; five (33 percent) were fatally injured by falling from high trees after being completely immobilized with Succinylcchloline chloride. These two kinds of accidents had caused the majority of deaths. Of the remainder, one kitten had died when a syringe punctured its lung; one female had broken off her canine teeth in a holding cage; two reportedly had died from heat exhaustion. Belden planned to lower mortality risks by working in winter (to avoid overheating), by using drugs that would tranquilize rather than completely immobilize and by being selective at the capture site (not darting cats too high in trees). He estimated a 97-98 percent chance that "nothing would go wrong" and believed the information gained was well worth the risk.[12] In this opinion he was backed by the recovery team—with the exception of Robert Baudy.

Controversy

Robert Baudy was an accomplished breeder of rare felines. He was the first to breed clouded leopards—a small, tree-dwelling species that lives in the upper levels of tropical forests in Southeast Asia. Female clouded leopards reportedly appropriate the nests of eagles to raise their young. These cats can leap astonishing distances from one branch to another; their antics, so fascinating to watch in captivity, are more remindful of squirrels than cats.

Baudy, naturally, was intent on breeding Florida panthers and prematurely set off on his own. He was also an indefatigable correspondent and kept up a lively epistolary duel with Chris Belden, with whom he was frequently at odds. The theme of his letters centered on his interest in captive breeding and on his reservations about the impending radio-telemetry research. Baudy acquired on loan what he, and others, believed to be Florida panthers from Everglades Wonder Gardens, a roadside tourist attraction in Bonita Springs. He also advocated "borrowing" at least one adult male from the wild to "insure the necessary injection of fresh new blood."[13]

The main catch in Baudy's advocacy resided in doubts that had been cast on the pedigree of the cats he had borrowed. It was rumored that a South American puma was ancestral to this stock. Federal support, including money, was legally constrained at the time (and perhaps now) by a departmental ruling that placed great store by the integrity of a subspecies. The Florida panther is the only subspecies of *Felis concolor* extant that is officially endangered. Work was then underway to resolve what a Florida panther was supposed to look like. Under these circumstances the other team members could see no obvious advantages in extracting even a single wild animal from what seemed a precarious few. There were no risk-free options, but most of the recovery team favored the conservative path of learning more about the wild stock prior to making a judgement on captive breeding. Radio-telemetry became the only issue on which the recovery team ever took a formal vote. Baudy voted against; three members voted for; Peter Pritchard abstained, although later when a panther died during a capture he stood by the collaring.[14] On that occasion he was instrumental in getting a resolution of support for radio-telemetry from the Florida Audubon Society's Board of Directors.[15]

The First Capture

Preparations for the capturing and collaring of panthers moved forward. The plan was to begin in the Fakahatchee Strand State Preserve. Roy McBride, the professional puma hunter, drove in from the West with his dogs and bedroll in a pickup truck. He would be the "houndsman" of the project for years to come. He had six dogs, the minimum he preferred in a pack; two were proven veterans, but getting on in years; two were in their prime, and two were youngsters learning the work of trailing cats.

The big day came on February 10, 1981. McBride went ahead into the swamp, splashing on foot, carrying a walkie-talkie. He usually hunted alone with his dogs in remote areas of the Southwest and in Mexico, and they were not accustomed to seeing anyone but their master. The presence of other people was sometimes so disconcerting that the pack would quit hunting and just join the group and become "sociable." The others of the party, each holding a radio, were strategically spaced several miles apart and parallel to the swamp, along roads, so that at least one of them would be near enough to hear a radio message when a cat was treed. At 8:25 a.m. McBride radioed. His dogs were in full and joyous clamor on a warm trail. The team members fidgeted and waited. At 8:45 a.m. there was another message that the chase was moving northeast through the swamp and for everyone to stay put. At 9:00 a.m. word came that the panther was in a tree. A general location was given.

The team assembled with adrenalin pumping, hoisted on its equipment, and set off in a file down into the swamp on an old logging road which led toward their quarry. Although the roadway was overgrown with vegetation, it was elevated above the swamp, thereby facilitating movement somewhat. Extra radio-collars had been placed on McBride's dogs. Chris Belden carried the receiver and antenna listening to the beeping signal growing stronger in his earphones. When he judged the moment right he led the team down off the road and in among the cypress knees and into a rank growth of ferns. They went sloshing through the dense, tropical undergrowth, sweating heavily in the humid air. Spurred on by excitement, they reached McBride and the dogs by 10:30 a.m.

Peering down from the limb of an oak tree, 15 feet above the ground, was the first wild panther any of them (with the exception of McBride) had ever seen alive. Heads titled back, they looked with wide-eyed fixation, aware that the cornered cat represented the first step in a journey of understanding that all hoped might insure the presence of panthers in Florida. A supreme challenge and dream of wildlife professionals—the coaxing of an endangered creature back from the abyss of extinction—was embodied in the frightened animal clinging to a limb above their heads.

The necessity of getting on with the capture brought the momentary contemplation to an end. The weight of the panther was estimated by McBride, and a dart was loaded with an appropriate amount of tranquilizing drug (a mixture of ketamine and acepromazene). McBride shot the dart into the cat's rump. Within seven minutes it was visibly beginning to relax. Belden took a rope and started climbing with the intent of lowering it from the tree. His scheme went awry when the cat fell and both of them came crashing to the ground together. The panther ran weakly for a few hundred feet before McBride caught it by the tail. Another small dose of the drug was administered. The biologists hurried to finish, knowing the drug would soon lose effect. The collar was adjusted; it had to be tight enough to stay on, but not so tight as to impede swallowing; it was fastened with screws. Next the specimen was weighed by being hoisted in a sling attached to a scale, suspended from a portable tripod. It was a 120-pound male. Fecal and blood samples were taken and the pelage was inspected for ticks, which might yield information on disease. The job was done in less than half-an-hour, by which time the animal was showing signs of recuperating. When it could move about steadily the group headed out of the swamp wet, muddy, scratched by thorns, but with an immense feeling of relief and accomplishment. The capture was the first of many to come.[16]

Ten days later in the Fakahatchee Strand State Preserve, a second cat was collared. Monitoring its movements began at once; locations were checked twice daily and plotted on a map. A curious thing about the two cats was that, like the one McBride had captured seven years before, both were old and impoverished, their teeth worn nearly to the gums. The second male had weighed only 108 pounds. McBride guessed the ages at approximately 10 and 12 years respectively.[17] In late May the ground being traversed by each of the panthers was delineated by drawing on a map a line connecting the outer points of the radio-location plots. The activity of one cat covered 45 square-miles; the home range of the other one sprawled over an area nearly twice that size.

In January 1982, the Florida panther recovery team gathered in Gainesville for what would be its final meeting; the recovery plan was at last ready for approval. Chris Belden summarized the preliminary yield from the research. The two collared panthers had been checked closely during the 1981-1982 hunting season for signs of behavioral changes in response to hunting activity. None were evident. Robert Baudy again made a pitch to start a captive breeding project, stressing that the removal of a wild specimen would not have to be permanent. Belden answered that captive breeding was still an option, but that the status of the wild population was too poorly known to justify withdrawing any animals.[18]

The same month saw an expansion of the radio-telemetry research. The plan for 1982 called for collaring up to ten cats, but as it turned out only five more were collared: three males and two females. One of the previously collared males was caught and checked. The searchers traveled to Raccoon Point in the Big Cypress National Preserve, bagging two more, raising to seven the radio signals now streaming in from two widely separated regions, and greatly improving prospects for an expanded picture of panther activity.

On March 9, 1982 Governor Bob Graham signed a bill designating the Florida panther the state animal. It had been chosen by students in a poll during the previous year, beating other contenders such as the manatee and the alligator. The choice signaled a strong undercurrent of sympathy in the state toward the panther.

In September of 1982 the estimate for panthers in southern Florida was put at 20. The sex ratio was thought to be between 50:50 and 60:40, slightly favoring males. Six mortalities were known thus far: four roadkills and one by gunshot. The cause of another death was given as unknown blunt trauma; it was suspected that the end had come in a fight with another of its kind. One female had been seen with kittens. A female killed on the highway had been carrying four fetuses. The known rate of deaths was averaging about one a year—about five percent of the known population. By what he could see, Chris Belden thought the population was stable, but warned of an accelerating loss of habitat. Eighty to 90 percent of the cats were from six to 12 years old.[19] It seemed an aging population.

Monitoring went on through 1982. The following January, at the end of 1982-83 hunting season, the capture team headed back into the field hoping to find panthers yet uncollared, and to recapture those carrying transmitters in order to check the radios and the animals wearing them. On January 17, after a capture—an activity that had by now become routine—the team members were stunned when the panther they had just darted and taken down from a tree, suddenly died.

Controversy and Independent Advisors

Word got to Game Commission headquarters in Tallahassee as soon as a telephone could be reached. The message caused the greatest consternation. Anger at collaring panthers had been aired in newspapers and magazines around the state, and some prominent persons had spoken against it. Now the worst had happened, and it was sure to raise a storm of criticism. Like any land-management agency, the Game Commission is acutely attuned to the potential entanglements brought on by public wrath. The death of a California condor chick, during a capture in 1980, had raised a spectacular furor in that state.

The agency's reaction was as immediate and decisive as a reflex. After a hurried conference, letters were sent from the executive director's office that day "appointing" people with "technical knowledge and expertise in wildlife conservation and management" to a committee that would, "serve in an advisory capacity to the Game Commission."[20] In fact, Peter Pritchard had been advocating such an advisory body since the termination of the Florida panther recovery team a year-and-a-half before. Officials had now wakened with a start to the usefulness of such a body. Government agencies know that advisors may turn out to have minds of their own and may not always give wanted advice. For an agency to call up its own independent advisors (particularly without limiting their tenure) is an extraordinary event. Needing support, the Game Commission took the plunge, picking persons like me who were known to believe in radio-telemetry.

It would probably have been hard to find a biologist who would not have backed the research. More had been learned about the Florida panther in two years using radio-collars than in the previous 50. Highway deaths were mounting. Radio-locations showed that panthers often crossed Alligator Alley at specific points. This information would be used later to elevate the road over a series of engineered "wildlife crossings" when it was converted to an interstate highway. Other behavioral traits had come to light; some promised to aid management decisions. During summer panthers moved only at night, resting in the heat of the day. But in winter they were active during the day as well. They sometimes traveled 20 miles in a night, but at other times movement would subside for a week or more. They frequently crossed highways and swam canals. In the Everglades marsh (the Water Conservation Areas) panthers waded or swam from one tree island to another.

When approached by humans, they would either be still or try to circle behind the interlopers. The cats became accustomed to man-made noises such as rock-quarrying, highway traffic or an aircraft and, once used to the sounds, became unwary of them. Radio signals showed the affinity of panthers for the dense cover afforded by cypress strands and by forest vegetation in general.[21] They were attracted to woodland fires and often stayed near recent burn sites for days—an interesting observation; deer are drawn to burned sites where they feed on the shoots of resprouting vegetation.

The panther's death became a featured news item, fanning the hostile opinion that had been feared. Attacks on radio-telemetry would go on for years, but the Game Commission received strong support. The Florida Audubon Society sent a resolution from its board of directors.[22] The agency was able to ride out the storm, and the capture team was back in the field within ten days. Reactions to the panther's death were typified by the excerpt from the following letter sent to the governor:

Dear Governor Graham:

We, concerned citizens for the preservation of the Florida panther, implore you, governor of the state, to use your POWER and AUTHORITY to STOP THE HARASSMENT OF THE PANTHERS! by the Florida Game and Fresh Water [Fish] Commission who plan to equip six to eight panthers with telemetry radio systems. . . .[23]

There were many letters to newspaper editors in the tone of this excerpt from one to the *Miami Herald*:

Sir:

. . .These well-meaning and scientifically trained biologists want to know every fact obtainable about the species including where it feeds and breeds so they can report it in a scientific journal. . . . What could be more terrifying to a wild panther than barking dogs and men with guns, associated in the minds of animals with death? Whether the guns are loaded with bullets or tranquilizers, the terror is the same.[24]

And the *Miami Herald* editorialized as follows:

. . .This is an outrage. The panthers should be left alone indefinitely. Let them breed and perhaps replenish their numbers, or let them live out their lives free, and wild, and in peace. Now is not the time to wire them up. Gov. Bob Graham ought to urge the game commission to do that, before it's too late.[25]

The hostility lingered. Three years later, the following snippet appeared in the *Fort Myers News-Press*:

PANTHER RX: HANDS OFF

. . . How can it help the few panthers remaining in the Everglades to be constantly tracked and trailed - on the ground and from the air - by wildlife officers trying to spot them, catch them and tag them with radio-signalling collars so they can be spied on the rest of their lives. . . . What the panthers need most is be left alone.[26]

The Game Commission's new advisory body met within a month. Stephen R. Humphrey, a mammalogist from the Florida State Museum, had been asked to the Chair. The advisory body didn't take long to do its work. We supported the radio-telemetry, urging a close watch on females to learn more about reproduction. Some members were bothered by the scarcity of young and the apparent small population size—which raised questions about inbreeding. We advised taking blood samples for genetic analysis. Questions about recreational hunting came up for an airing. Several days after the meeting Colonel Brantly sent a letter of thanks to each advisor. "The recommendations," it said, "reflect the type of technical review of our program I had hoped would emanate from the committee."[27] The meeting of this appointed body, as it turned out, was the only one ever held.

In July 1983 a memo arrived from Steve Humphrey with news that the Game Commission-appointed advisory body was to be replaced by a legislatively mandated Panther Advisory Council, its members to be named by the governor. The Act provided for five positions representing government agencies, universities or associated institutions and the general public.[28] With the memo was a copy of a Florida Panther Recovery Status Report that Colonel Brantly had just sent to the Governor and Cabinet. It opened encouragingly, ". . . [the Game Commission] is optimistic that the Florida panther will be recovered from extinction to remain a viable member of the diverse wildlife community that is unique to our state." This was surprising; there were no grounds for making such an optimistic prediction the foundation of a status report; it was also in striking contrast to a letter the executive director had sent to the governor only nine months earlier. The previous letter had argued against allowing an access road into the Big Cypress National Preserve, warning that "Perhaps fewer than 20 total panthers remain, making the species [sic] one of the most endangered in the world. Our margin for exploiting its habitat is obviously extremely narrow." The later, optimistic report also grew defensive: "Certain interested groups have expressed the opinion that hunting is not an appropriate form of public use of the Preserve and that hunting is not compatible with the safety of the panther. To the contrary, public hunting has coexisted for years with Florida panthers, white-tailed deer, and other species of wildlife, and the Commission has not observed evidence at this time that those activities have impacted panthers or other wildlife in the area. . . ."[29]

I knew from previous conversations with certain agency biologists that they would not have supported this statement by their executive director. However, the assertion that "hunting has coexisted for years with Florida panthers" would become a Game Commission catchphrase, this despite the next paragraph in Brantly's report warning of "new types of off-road vehicles being used in the Preserve . . . that are more versatile and affordable than the traditional 'swamp buggy.'" In addition, there was a ". . . rapid increase in the number of people now using the area for recreational purposes." He predicted that " . . . if pressures of public use are allowed to continue accelerating the Florida panther will likely be impacted as will the quality of deer hunting . . . ."[30] It was no secret that human activity in the Big Cypress had been rising sharply. The question was whether the level might already be undesirable. With less than 20 panthers accounted for, it was not a situation that justified optimism or complacency.

Shortly thereafter the governor's office made its appointments to the new Panther Advisory Council. Robert Baudy filled the general public slot. Baudy and I were carryovers from the recovery team. I represented a government agency, as did Oron (Sonny) Bass, a research biologist from Everglades National Park. John Eisenberg and Melvin Sunquist, both from the University of Florida, were from academia. Sunquist had published papers on tigers, leopards and ocelots. Eisenberg was widely known as a mammalogist. Leopards and deer were among several species he had studied in Sri Lanka. These two men would bring both a broad perspective and a specialized knowledge which was not available in the government sector.

In September 1983 there was a brief transitional meeting at the Florida State Museum in Gainesville between the outgoing Game Commission advisory body and the newly appointed Panther Advisory Council. Tom Logan, who directed the agency's Bureau of Wildlife Research, outlined plans for the coming year. The recovery program, which had started eight years before on a shoestring budget, would receive $250,000 in 1984. Veterinarians would go along with the 1984 capture team to help ensure the safety of panthers, and to boost the collection of biomedical data.[31] I was elected to the Chair, and so, with arrangements thus settled, we made a field trip to southern Florida to look over panther habitat.

The Council Meeting

Following our field trip and a helicopter tour described in the opening of this book, we gathered for the first meeting. The Game Commission staff was well represented and there was a palpable wariness on the part of some of them towards advisors of unknown quantity, imposed by legislative mandate. Chris Belden presented maps of panther movements, and oil drilling was brought up. The main worry about this activity was from new roads that would lead to drilling platforms, thereby facilitating access into a region hitherto difficult to reach.

Fred Fagergren, superintendent of the Big Cypress National Preserve, briefed the Council on hunting. The peak period of use came during the first nine days. The Game Commission had recently set a hunting quota during this period of 4,200 permits. There was no quota after the first nine days. The general gun season lasted for 60 days, and there were other designated hunting seasons during the year, including archery, primitive weapons, raccoon, small game, and spring gobbler (for wild turkey); it was during spring gobbler season in 1978 that a panther had been shot. A yearly total of 222 days of hunting was authorized. Hunting camps dotted the Preserve. Six thousand off-road vehicles were registered for use there, representing a 41 percent jump in two years. The swamp buggy, the vehicle of tradition in cypress country, was usually a home-made rig with high clearance, riding on tractor or airplane tires. Many of the new permits were for all-terrain vehicles (ATV's) which had arrived on the market in the 1970s and could be bought for as little as $600. The ATV's were small, three or four-wheeled, balloon-tired machines. They would go anywhere and could be transported in a pick-up truck. The use of ATV's had soared with no sign of approaching a peak.[32]

We were troubled by this growing mechanization in a sanctuary of a size that might have held more panthers than had been found. The ones captured were old and undernourished. Hunters and panthers were competing for the same prey— deer and hogs, of which few were being harvested (according to a spotty checking system), even though both species were hunted with dogs, thereby giving the hunter an edge. When we questioned the impact of all this, the Game Commission men replied with the stock answer: hunting had co-existed for years with panthers, and there was no evidence that it was having any impact on them.[33] There were few data on deer.

In making our first recommendations, we skirted hunting, hoping a deer study slated for the year ahead might produce more information. We did recommend that the Game Commission urge the adjacent Everglades National Park to study its deer; they had been protected since 1947. No one suspected at the time the kind of stubborn resistance to this proposal that would be met with from the superintendent of Everglades National Park. For the Big Cypress National Preserve, we suggested an experimental design that would eliminate vehicles from a control area so as to measure any bearing that ORV's might have on both deer and panther movements (this was never attempted). We pointed out the need to safeguard more habitat (land purchases have continued to this day, although that alone will not insure the survival of panthers in southern Florida. The land must be properly managed, as will be explained later). We encouraged the Game Commission in its striving to have wildlife crossings incorporated into the Interstate-75 design (the initiative was not being well-received by the Federal Highway Administration).[34] We also called attention to an infestation of melaleuca trees which had overrun the countryside.

Robert Baudy made another pitch for captive breeding, iterating his motif that with the panther's status so pinched, common sense demanded a captive stock to guard against extinction.[35] His collective arguments made a strong case, but the others on the Council were reluctant to see cats removed because of an imponderable risk to the indeterminate few left behind. Baudy proposed to allay this concern by capturing kittens. This tactic had been suggested originally by Jim Layne and, in fact, the Council would endorse it later, but our mood at this early stage was conservative. The recommendations were signed by each Council member and sent off in a letter to the Game Commission headquarters. In contrast to letters of the previous February from advisors the agency had appointed, and to the communication sent from the joint Committee/Council transitional meeting in September, there was no answer. Nor was there an acknowledgement that our letter had been received.

Chris Belden's presentation at the meeting on panther activity in southern Florida was his last on that particular subject. The Game Commission had taken its only biologist with field experience of panthers out of the field and reassigned him. Chris's opinions of panther recovery had always been guided entirely by the emerging results of the research, and he had always been clear and forthright in stating his opinions. Chris once told me that his lead position in the recovery program made him feel that the whole weight of success or failure rested on his shoulders—a feeling I would come to know well. If he saw a problem that required action, he felt a responsibility to push for it. He couldn't back off because the opinions weren't welcome. If he didn't press who would? He had raised questions about hunting, and persisted in them. In my experience most agency biologists will not go on pushing their views when warning lights come on from above. There are no rewards and it can sometimes be professionally hazardous. There are many who resign themselves to management decisions that are biologically unsound (or foolish), or even arguably unethical, and it is an easy matter to rationalize when no apparent disastrous consequences are likely to result. But a failed effort to save an endangered organism ends an evolutionary process that spans a time the mind cannot grasp, and it cancels a potential benefit to all which extends further into the future than anyone can see. This awareness can become a ruthless and reckless stimulus to some who find themselves carrying the responsibility.

More Captures

The capture team went back to the swamps early the following year under the leadership of John Robosky, who had replaced Chris Belden. A total of eight cats were now wearing collars; three had died, including the one killed during the capture the year before; another was lost to a car and two had perished from unknown causes. The radio on another cat had stopped transmitting. The team goal for 1984 was ten panthers but it was not to be. There were mechanical breakdowns; new custom-built swamp buggies were on order, but the equipment then in use was old and unreliable. More significant was the difficulty of finding panthers on public lands.

A collared panther was immobilized in the Fakahatchee Strand and fitted with a new transmitter, powered by two-year batteries designed to reduce the frequency of recapture. A second collared male, very old, was treed but was so emaciated the team was unwilling to chance drugging him. The revised capture procedures posited three "capture vetoes" within the team: the team leader, Robosky, the veterinarians and Roy McBride whose wealth of experience made his judgement essential. Several factors entered the decision. A visual evaluation of the panther's health was one. Another was the temperature; no chance was taken if the cat was over-heated. The precautions against accidental death were extraordinary. Sixty pounds of medical equipment were back-packed into the capture site— a virtual field hospital. A crash bag was invented by John Robosky and fellow biologist, Walt McCown, to be placed on the ground beneath a treed cat in case the animal fell when tranquilized.

For the capture team the 1984 search became a numbing routine of weeks that began each day at 3:00 a.m. with breakfast and coffee, with cobwebbed heads, and with bodies that moved by habit through the dark, driving to the off-pavement starting points. The buggies were backed down the ramps of their trailers and driven sloshing across the prairies while the occupants sat quietly, bundled against the pre-dawn chill. The routine was leavened by the spell of magic in the transformation of each starry blackness into a sub-tropical dawn. The slow-moving vehicles slipped past the silent cypress trees, their bromeliad-festooned branches illuminated in finer detail as the day advanced and the expedition crept mile after mile into the swamp.

After searching the Fakahatchee Strand, the team moved on to Raccoon Point. There they hunted—or more accurately, they waited, expectantly in their swamp buggies, while McBride hunted with his dogs—for six boring weeks, fidgeting time away as the warming winter sun climbed to a low apogee in the southern sky, taking with it on its downward arc another day's hope for action. Bouts of conversation alternated with long silences. They read, dozed and scribbled notes in journals or identified birds that flitted by.

After what seemed an eternity, it happened. McBride's voice crackled terse instructions out of the portable radio. "Don't lose track of the dogs. Stay within a quarter mile of me. No closer." The slumped forms on the swamp buggies jerked upright. One stood up with the telemetry antenna held high, rotating it slowly to get a fix on the radios carried by the dogs. The engines came to life, and the vehicles threaded their way among clumps of trees, guided by the hand-held radio receiver and antenna now functioning as the expedition's radio compass.

The panther went up a tree. The party drove as close to the site as possible and dismounted, to eagerly pull on packs that held the capture tent, climbing gear, scales and tripod, oxygen tanks and other medical paraphernalia, and filed vigorously off into the trees behind John Robosky who, with antenna held aloft, looked like nothing so much as a khaki-shirted Statue of Liberty leading a mad parade of backpackers through a swamp. At the base of the tree, six yelping hounds sprang frantically up, again and again, at the trunk they could not climb. Outside the noisy ring of bouncing dogs, McBride slowly circled with a grim look on his upturned face. Breathing heavily, the arriving team members slipped off their packs as they came up one by one to the tree with the frantic bouncing dogs and the motionless panther draped over a branch 30 feet up. The cat, a female, looked abysmal. Bones protruded, and her skin hung in slack folds at her chest. Within leaping distance was another taller tree to which she could, if so inclined, climb higher—not an uncommon reaction by panthers when hit by the tranquilizer dart. The day was warming, and if she elected to ascend it could take a long time for a climber to get her down from the higher tree.

The old cat stared intently down at the solemn visages that looked alternately up and at one another, their murmuring voices floating up from below. Then there was quiet while the group looked up. Then the voices started again, and the figures paced around the tree looking up. And again they were still, and there was a long silence. And once more a brief chatter. At last the voices stopped. The figures below moved to their bundles on the ground. Everyone was quiet. Heavy packs were hefted onto sweat-soaked backs, and they went one-by-one out of the trees and across the prairie behind their leader in a well-spaced file, eyes on the ground before them. From her perch in the tree, the old she-cat heard only the fading, ragged cadence of wheezing, water-logged shoes. She gazed intently, yellow eyes fixed on a distant wall of cypress trees which absorbed the bobbing walkers, one by one, until she was alone again in the wilderness.[36]

Another female was captured two weeks later. A total of four panthers were treed in the 1984 season, all about ten years old and believed nearing the end of their lives. Two had been emaciated, with bones protruding from their sagging, lusterless hides. The veterinary report for the season made somber reading. After four years, no captured panther was believed to have been under four years of age. One radio-collared female had given birth to two kittens, an opinion reached by searching in the vicinity of her radio-signals and spotting the tracks of the young. The tracks of the mother, with those of the kittens, had been glimpsed repeatedly over a span of 16 months—at which time the young commonly go off on their own. It was presumed that they had attained maturity—and independence. A few young adults of uncertain origin, but obviously from outside the study area, had been killed, either illegally or by highway traffic, but the data did not present a picture of flourishing cats. The symptoms were of a small, sparse, aging population with few young entering the ranks.

The veterinarians also documented feline distemper and hookworms. All forms of wildlife are subject to diseases and parasitism. It is commonly presumed that individual animals in good health are resistant to parasites and pathogens native to their environment, but if the population is physiologically stressed, because of nutritional deficiencies for instance, its immunity to these harmful agents is lowered. The young are most susceptible and usually die first. Feline distemper had been documented in bobcats, and elsewhere in pumas, but nothing was known of its historical prevalence among Florida panthers. The same could be said of a species of hookworm; it had been found in Central and South American cats, but nothing could be said for certain about its life cycle or how it might affect a host, either acting independently or in combination with other stresses. It was known however that other hookworm species were deadly to domestic kittens and puppies.[37]

Hunting Reconsidered

When the Panther Advisory Council met again in the spring of 1984 the hunting issue could not be ignored. Our recommendations opened with a statement indicating our feeling that hunting, as it was practiced in the Big Cypress, had reduced the deer population well below the capacity of the Preserve. The available data were not adequate to support this opinion—a point that was made in the narrative that followed. But the evidence painted a perilous picture—a swelling volume of hunters and very few deer. We decided that if we erred, it would be on the side of the panther, not in favor of the status quo. Presuming that the herd was below carrying capacity, we proposed a strategy that would strive to improve deer numbers in the Big Cypress (we did not address hunting in the Fakahatchee Strand State Preserve at this time), while stepping up research north and south of the public hunting areas. To the south was Everglades National Park, where game had been protected since 1947. To the north, the land was mainly used for cattle ranching with some light hunting.

We encouraged the Game Commission to meet with the National Park Service to evaluate nine options: (1) limits on the number of hunters and ORV's [quota system]; (2) elimination of dogs; (3) reducing the length of the season; (4) mandatory check stations; (5) institute a tagging system for deer in which a hunter is given a number of tags equal to the number of deer he is permitted to kill during the season—two in this instance. When he kills a deer the tag is attached to it. This, in theory, limits the number of deer he can take; an untagged deer in possession of a hunter is illegal; (6) establishing a checkerboard pattern of use, whereby areas could be alternatively opened and closed to give local deer populations an opportunity to recover; (7) making certain areas off-limits to ORV traffic; (8) suspending hunting temporarily to give the deer herd an opportunity to recover; (9) accelerating the removal of hunting camps.

We also urged a moratorium on hunting in Bear Island, where recent data suggested a deer herd below capacity. A suspension, we reasoned, might show whether hunting was suppressing deer. Bear Island was more conducive to this kind of investigation than any other management unit, being the smallest, with the best road net, and with controllable access points. In retrospect, the moratorium idea was probably unsound. The experiment, whatever its findings, would have had questionable relevance elsewhere in the Big Cypress National Preserve, where the habitat differed markedly. Although deer densities on Bear Island deer seemed low, they were still the highest in the Preserve and adequate to sustain a resident female panther who regularly raised young. Any closure-to-hunting suggestion, even temporary (the recommendations included reopening the unit after several years to assess a renewed harvest), roused suspicions in the Game Commission and inspired a tenacious resistance. The Panther Advisory Council would expend considerable energy belaboring the Bear Island issue, with no result except to fuel the anti-hunting paranoia of game officials.

Other Recommendations

We also pointed out a fundamental problem. The contiguous public lands that were guaranteed as a future habitat were being managed in accord with different agency philosophies. The merit of treating them as a single management unit for panthers is too plain to call for elaboration, but our counsel on this issue would accumulate a history of the most stolid and unanimous rejection of any we put forth. We also advised preliminary steps toward a captive propagation center with the goal of reintroducing panthers to northern Florida. There were other lesser recommendations; all were circulated to Council members for a signature and then sent off by mail.[38] Again, the weeks went by and there was no reply—not even the acknowledgement of receipt required by professional courtesy. I believe any objective evaluation of these early proposals for hunting would find them moderate. In the years to follow, the Game Commission, on its own, would gradually add more restrictions than those advocated by the Panther Advisory Council in 1984. But at the time they were greeted with a cold bureaucratic shoulder. It seemed to me that we were going to be ignored. I called a long-time acquaintance and environmental activist, Bill Partington, to talk about the blockage.

Partington is a one-man environmental army. In 1971 he became the first president of a crusading group called Florida Defenders of the Environment (FDE), which had been hammered into form by the energies of an able citizen named Marjorie Carr. The state's conservationists of that day had sunk into the state of vitiation that periodically enfeebles institutions. They were demoralized by the specter of the impending cross-Florida barge canal (among other things), a pork-barrel scheme of calamitous proportions, and were fatalistic about stopping it. In the teeth of great odds FDE shut the canal down in mid-construction after millions of dollars had been poured in. Following the demise of the barge canal, Partington created his own organization, the Florida Conservation Foundation, using a grant from the Ford Foundation. It continues to this day, often limping along on a shoestring budget, providing useful environmental services. Several times each year Partington sends out a publication (*ENFO*), usually a monograph on some timely topic; it is widely read in Florida. I suggested that an *ENFO* on the panther logjams might alert the Game Commission to the existence of its Panther Advisory Council.

Gerald Grow, a volunteer environmental writer, took the assignment and, "New Threats to the Florida Panther," appeared in October, 1984. Grow's article came to the following summary:

> To the Florida Panther Technical Advisory Council, there is no proof that hunting is not hurting the panther, and many signs to suggest that it is.

> To the Game and Fish Commission, there is no proof that hunting is hurting the panther, although they cannot prove that it is not.

> In the absence of "unassailable data," the Advisory Council advises the Commission to act with extreme caution, take no chances, and take every imaginable step that might aid the survival of the state animal.

> In the absence of "unassailable data," the Game and Fish Commission chooses to keep things as they are, study the

situation, and maintain present levels of hunting until there are solid data to support changing things.

The Advisory Council speaks of the panther as an animal in extreme danger of extinction, under great stress, threatened by an epidemic of a fatal disease, and in need of immediate, urgent, intensive, coordinated action if it is to survive.

Although last year the Game and Fish Commission stated that the panther was severely endangered, it is now "optimistic" about the Florida panther, and speaks of the panther as an animal that has cohabited with hunting for centuries, is showing up in greater numbers than we first believed, and is the topic of an enormous advance in knowledge in a very short period—knowledge which will lead us to the proper management actions to preserve it forever. . . . in discussions and interviews, a variety of different people expressed concern to me that the Florida Game and Fresh Water Fish Commission, due to its dedication to hunting, might have difficulty administering the endangered species program and the new non-game wildlife program. This concern was expressed to me not just by environmentalists, but also by an official in the Department of Natural Resources, an aide in the Governor's Office, the aide in a major Senate committee, an administrator in the Department of Environmental Regulation, two researchers in private scientific organizations, and several university scientists. . . .[39]

Soon after this, I was surprised by two phone calls. One was from Estus Whitfield, an aide in the governor's office, who said the governor wanted to meet personally with the Panther Advisory Council. The other call was from the executive director of the Game Commission who said he also wanted to address the Council to explain his ideas on curtailing the deer harvest in the Big Cypress. The *ENFO* story had attracted some high-level attention. The Council and the Colonel came together with Governor Graham in Tallahassee, in November 1984. The governor firmly made the point that he wanted his appointed advisors listened to. Two months later came the meeting with Colonel Brantly and his staff. There, we made one brief recommendation of preeminent importance: an investigation into planning the linkage of existing public lands across the state so that they would form a continuous refuge. John Eisenberg had recently sent me a paper coauthored by Larry Harris, a professor of wildlife ecology at the University of Florida, and one of his students, Reed Noss. It pointed to a worldwide trend in forest destruction which was leaving protected forests isolated as islands of habitat—precisely the case in Florida. One consequence would be the eventual loss of many wide-ranging species—like bears and panthers. Avoiding these misfortunes would require a comprehensive approach to landscape planning, one aspect of which would feature an interconnected network of nature preserves. Something of the sort would have to be fashioned in Florida if there were to be any prospects for the state animal. The fate of this idea will be recounted in Chapter 17.

The Game Commission had selected two of our several recommendations of the previous year: a ban on dogs for hunting deer and hogs, and a ban on off-road vehicles—except for the traditional swamp buggy. The prohibited vehicles would include all-terrain vehicles, tracked vehicles and trail bikes. It sounded like a big step. Fewer recreational vehicles and less efficiency in hunting might significantly ease pressure on the deer herd. We were gratified; but when the new policy was implemented it was less restrictive than we had been led to expect. It must be understood that the executive director does not change rules by fiat. He submits them to the five citizens who comprise the Game Commission. Prior to approval, the proposals must be aired in public forums for the scrutiny of those who will be affected by them. Brantly's parting words to the Council stuck in my mind. "I wish," he said, "that you would come to these meetings and see what we're going to have to go through."

The hunters hit back in force. The commissioners and staff were deluged with almost 1,000 letters of opposition (approximately 500 in favor came in). A meeting held by the Game Commission in south Florida was packed with hundreds of angry hunters who registered a thunderous antagonism to the rule changes. The day before the commissioners were to gather for a decision, an agency staffer called to tell me that they had caved in under the pressure and were not going to enact the regulations. However, Governor Graham got wind of this irresolution, and by the next day the commissioners had reconsidered—somewhat. The regulations were weakened, but survived. They prohibited the use of dogs—except during the first nine days of the season. This, of course, was the period of intensive hunting when most deer and hogs were taken. All-terrain vehicles were not banned, although it was prohibited to hunt from the machines or transport firearms on them.

The outcome made it clear that every forward step would confront the most stubborn opposition. If not for the intervention of Governor Graham, there would have been no progress at all. I did not realize at the time how many feasible measures to benefit the panther were going to prove impossible, and in the end the Game Commission would demonstrate more flexibility than some of the other agencies. As for the new hunting regulations, though falling short of what had been promised they did trim the deer harvest and cut ATV use.

Big Guy

Early in the morning of November 11, 1984, Ronald Townsend, a Naples restauranteur, was driving a produce truck across the Tamiami Trail from Miami to Naples. Crossing a bridge he saw a panther along the side of the road. Stopping, he could see that it was badly injured. He sped up the highway to the nearest highway patrol station and set in motion a remarkable rescue operation. The patrol station called John Robosky at his home in Naples. Robosky and Walt McCown headed to the site.

The College of Veterinary Medicine at the University of Florida had planned for such a contingency. Ned Johnson, a Naples veterinarian, was helicoptered to the scene. The cat had two mangled rear legs, one a compound fracture. It was treated for shock and flown to the St. Francis Animal Clinic in Naples. Two veterinarians, George Kallias and Melody Roelke, arrived that afternoon. They loaded the panther, now being solicitously addressed as "Big Guy," into a chartered plane and flew with him to Gainesville. There he endured five hours of surgery by a team of eight veterinarians, lasting until 1:30 a. m. Three days later there was another orthopedic operation. Steel plates were put in the cat's legs.[40] Melody Roelke, the Game Commission veterinarian, lived with Big Guy for the next six weeks. He was a moody, difficult patient. He would not rest and launched savage attacks on the walls of his chain-link ward, breaking his canine teeth (dental surgery gave him replacements). Big Guy's medical bill had mounted to $7,000 early in 1985.[41] The administrative outcome of this cat-in-hand was that the subject of captive breeding, long on the back burner at Game Commission headquarters, moved to the fore.

The Panther Advisory Council assembled in May on the topic of captive breeding. A year-and-a-half before, we had affirmed that priority should go to strengthening the wild population before taking any animals from it.[42] However, an alarming trend in panther deaths had made worries about the small number of cats in the wild irrelevant. Nine were known to have been killed since our previous deliberations on captive breeding in November of 1983: three by firearms, one apparently in a fight with another of its kind, one from an unknown cause and four on the highway. The prudence of tucking animals into safekeeping could no longer be ignored and we advised accordingly—to no avail. This repudiation of common sense will unfold in Chapters 7 and 19.

1985

1985 was the year in which the salient essentials of a panther strategy in southern Florida came into sharp relief. It was also in this year that another obstacle loomed. Recommendations to study deer and panthers in Everglades National Park were not being well-received at park headquarters. This was baffling. The panther's hopes were looking grimmer all the time. Attention had settled on poorly regulated hunting and its uncertain pressures on the panther's food supply. The national parks are strongly biased against the harvest of game and a study of deer-panther relationships in Everglades National Park might have been expected to shed light on a possible hunting problem next door in the Big Cypress National Preserve. In February 1983, recommendations for a deer study had been made by the Game Commission's agency-appointed advisory body, and the Panther Advisory Council had made them again later that year. It takes at least a year to get results from work of this kind, and three years of data is a desirable minimum. The panthers were clearly in trouble and time was slipping away. One of the basic determinants of health in a wildlife population is its food supply, thus the need to look at deer. In the absence of sound data on the deer herd, everyone was making guesses—according to his favorite bias.

Officials in land-management agencies often cultivate a wariness about any issue that is potentially flammable. It required no subtlety to spot the tumult lying dormant in an undertaking to catch panthers in the National Park. Reverberations from the Game Commission's mishap were still being read in the letter columns of local newspapers. That, the Panther Advisory Council speculated in private, might account for the park superintendent's aversion. Whatever the reason, the recovery program wanted a more thorough data base to proceed with confidence. We tried again at our May 1985 meeting by asking the Game Commission to formally urge the National Park Service to initiate radio-telemetry studies of deer and panthers in Everglades National Park.[43]

Soon thereafter, Colonel Brantly penned an official request to the park superintendent.[44] The return letter was a bureaucratic special. The author, it seemed to me, was uninformed about the role of research in wildlife conservation. He emphatically and repeatedly agreed that the subject research would have to be done; but there were preconditions: "There is a huge amount of research that still remains to be performed in. . . . (there followed a listing of all possible sites outside the park)." His opinion was that the "unique significance of the animals living within the park is that they are probably the least disturbed [by man] of all the remaining population. I feel strongly that it is important to protect this undisturbed aspect as much as possible." Doing the research somewhere else would, he implied, lead to better techniques. "The longer we wait to begin on the undisturbed animals, the safer, more complete and more meaningful the research will be."[45]

I would point out here that the panthers living in Everglades National Park were then estimated at five or six, based on a recent track survey by Roy McBride (this represented about 25 percent of the total estimated for Florida). The letter went on. "As I have expressed on numerous occasions, I do not agree with their [the

Panther Advisory Council's] urgency to radio-collar panthers at this time." The communication ended with a vague reference to the founding of an "inter-agency advisory group" which, he said, "would be the perfect forum for topics such as this."[46]

The arguments made no sense to me. After reading this discouraging reply, I could not sit still and sent off a letter of my own to William Penn Mott.[47] Mott, the former director of California's state parks, had recently been picked by President Reagan to oversee the National Park Service. I had read statements of his proclaiming a commitment to the preservation of endangered species, and thought that if Mr. Mott were told one of his superintendents had been given an opportunity to cooperate in saving an endangered mammal, and was behaving in a disappointing way, that Mr. Mott would put an end to the resistance. I still had a few things to learn about bureaucracy.

I routinely forwarded a copy of my letter to central office and was soon listening to a chastening phone call. My superiors were horrified at this breach of etiquette. Low-level agency employees do not write letters to the heads of other agencies, particularly to criticize the other's subordinates. I didn't have to be told this, but judged that having been put by the governor in a position that functioned outside my agency, I shouldn't sit idle when something needed doing. "How do you know," said the voice on the telephone, "that the park superintendent doesn't have some policy that would prevent him from collaring panthers?" I couldn't imagine why anyone would presume such a thing, but decided not to argue. "What do you meeean, "said the voice in a rising inflection, "using words like DILATORY?" No answer came from me. I hadn't thought dilatory such a venomous adjective, but could see that it had a jarring impact in Tallahassee. The voice gradually settled down to a normal pitch and we moved the conversation to a close. I promised to try and do better in the future. In this I would fail.

The return letter from Mott came in two months. It was a soothing epistle backing the park superintendent. "I hasten to assure you," it said, "that this position is not based on resistance, lack of urgency or lack of concern. The position is based upon a deep concern that we take full advantage of the one significant remaining untapped research opportunity available to us to help insure the continued survival of the panther." It went on in this vein and concluded by seconding the superintendent's earlier call for another administrative mechanism to deal with the panther recovery program.

> The National Park Service strongly supports a proposal, evolved
> from Superintendent Morehead's earlier call for an Interagency
> Panther Advisory Council, for instituting a Federal-State-private
> Interagency Florida Panther Committee to be modeled after the

highly successful Interagency Grizzly Bear Committee (see enclosed copy of the Memorandum of Agreement). As in the case of the grizzly bear, we are convinced that interagency discussion consensus, and cooperative agreement on joint research and management actions are far preferable to individual agency action and, in the long run, offer the only true hope for the survival of the Florida panther. Such a goal-oriented and action-oriented committee not only can catalyze the type of research cooperation you are seeking, it also can provide the cooperative strength needed to initiate some of the obvious, necessary, and immediate but difficult management actions that must be taken now if the Florida panther is to survive.

I look forward to your actively joining the National Park Service as a partner in the formation of this interagency committee.[48]

Keep the penultimate paragraph in mind, dear reader; we will have opportunities to examine the "accomplishments" of this "goal-oriented and action-oriented committee." Well there it was. Instead of moving forward with the research he had been stalling, the superintendent was going to create a take-action-now super-committee which could do it even better. It would take another seven months to get this bureaucratic monstrosity in motion.

Also in 1985, in May, just before the Panther Advisory Council meeting that would take up the topic of Big Guy, I received a call from Tom Logan at the Game Commission, expressing an official interest in our January recommendation for a state-wide habitat network. I was delighted and we talked for a few minutes. The recommendation had simply introduced a theoretical scheme and extolled its virtues, while admitting that we were "proposing a novel concept without any practical suggestions for converting it to a workable program."[49] Now came the challenge of what to do next. I couldn't think of anything at the moment. Neither could Logan. His comment as I recall was "this is just bigger than everything." I promised to bring some ideas to the meeting.

In thinking it over, I figured there would have to be a workshop of some kind to bring the pertinent parties together: environmentalists, agency representatives, academics and, with luck, a few key legislators and, of course, the press. With that kind of a kick-off, a working group might follow to draft a bill for the next legislative session. With the Game Commission's backing, we might put it over. But on the meeting day no one would take responsibility for setting up a workshop. The excuses were that no one had time to work on it. I tried to be tactful but wondered how the staff imagined that the idea could become a reality. A program like this wouldn't create itself. Someone had to take charge and shepherd it along.

Back at the office I again turned to Bill Partington, knowing that he was experienced in organizing conferences. As always, Bill was enthusiastic about any good idea and willing to tackle it at the drop of a hat. I then called Larry Harris at the University of Florida, and the three of us planned the workshop by telephone. It was a huge success, attended by over 200 people, including key environmental leaders, legislators, representatives from the governor's office—a gubernatorial candidate and sundry newspaper reporters. It appeared to be an idea whose time had come, but years would pass before anything was done. We shall pick up this thread of the story later.

More Research

Two interesting reports were completed by the National Park Service in mid-1985. The previous year, the agency had contracted with Roy McBride to survey panthers in Everglades National Park by searching for tracks and other evidence. A secondary objective was to estimate prey abundance wherever panther sign was found.[50] In his report McBride reckoned that "fifty-five percent or more of the known population is on privately-owned lands and. . . development threatened to remove these private lands from the overall habitat available to the Florida panther. Therefore, the future of the Florida panther could rest entirely on its ability to survive on the federally-owned lands in southern Florida."[51] At this time McBride was undoubtedly the most qualified person to attempt a broad assessment. For 28 years he had tracked cats in the American West, Mexico and South America and had been part of the field research since its inception, longer than anyone. He gave the clearest picture to date of the extent and abundance of panthers. It was served up with opinions on prey availability.

By this stage the known distribution of the cats could be clumped in three distinct areas. The central portion of the range—the Fakahatchee Strand and the Big Cypress National Preserve—was best understood, since it was the only place where radio-collars had been used and panthers physically examined. The plight of these animals was not encouraging. Since 1981 there had been no sign that any female had raised young to maturity in the two preserves where they had been studied; there the population seemed to be aging and perhaps shrinking. To the south lay Everglades National Park. McBride doubted that more than six adults lived there. There were large cattle ranches to the north. McBride believed that those lands from Alligator Alley north to Highway 846 had the highest panther densities of any he had surveyed, including the 38,000-acre Bear Island unit of the Big Cypress National Preserve. He wrote: "While searching for panther sign during good tracking conditions, as many as thirty-five different urine markers (scrapes) were found in one day, along with sign of four different tracks and a half-dozen droppings. It is obvious that this population is dynamic and part of the increment is represented in the increased road kills on Highways 29 and 84. How far north of 846 the panther range continues is not known at this time but it is known that this area is changing in land use patterns."[52]

McBride could see alterations underway: "An increased demand for larger schools to serve the growing communities, plus other public services, is increasing the pressure for higher taxes on all the agricultural land. Cattle raising is the poorest form of economic return from the raw land; therefore it is giving way to improved pastures, citrus and development."[53] He finished with some general and practical thoughts. ". . . If the panther can be saved anywhere in the eastern United States, south Florida holds the best opportunity. Nowhere else east of the Mississippi exists an undeveloped area of such size. . . . The evidence that panthers can exist in south Florida is unassailable. The extent to which the public is willing to sacrifice the growth and utilization of the remaining habitat will determine the ultimate outcome. . . ."[54] McBride was also pushing the opinion that preserved land should be managed to produce more deer. Two areas he named were the Fakahatchee Strand State Preserve and Hole-in-the-Donut in Everglades National Park.[55]

Another useful document in 1985 was authored by William B. Robertson Jr., a research scientist at Everglades National Park, who was perhaps best known for ornithological studies. His treatise, which relied heavily on data gathered by Sonny Bass and Roy McBride, was a masterfully concise 11-page summation of everything that had been learned about the Florida panther to date. It observed that there were still significant informational gaps which should be filled. Robertson concluded that, after four years of field research, the "core area of panther survival" could be defined as the contiguous public lands and those lands immediately west and north of the Fakahatchee-Big Cypress. That was where panthers had been documented. "The few undoubted records in the 1980s outside this area," he wrote, "most likely were wandering individuals."[56]

> . . . Thus, over a vast extent of protected public lands constituting the heart of its remaining range the Florida panther appears to be declining toward extinction. Conversely, in two much smaller peripheral areas, one of which is unprotected private land, panthers appear to be reproducing normally, but relatively little is known about these more successful population segments. Ten animals, half the presently known population, are on private lands in an area where clearing for citrus groves and other large-scale development has already begun. . . . In a biological sense, the Fakahatchee/Big Cypress population could be considered already extinct because there has been no definite evidence of local recruitment for many years.

The situation outlined above would seem to need rather urgent consideration and investigation of the reasons for the sharp dichotomy between the successful and failing population segments would seem to be a useful first step.[57]

He concluded with an elaboration of "unanswered questions" and suggested a research direction to answer them.

The Summary For 1985

Florida's fiscal year terminates at the end of June. Game Commission biologists then begin writing up their previous year's research. These "annual performance reports" are completed in August or September. The Panther Advisory Council fell into the habit of a two-day meeting each fall, after we had perused the reports. In late 1985 we assembled with the Game Commission staff. On the first day the biologists presented the past year's discoveries. Melody Roelke, who would become the veterinary fixture of the recovery program, led off with a biomedical presentation. Roelke, whose competence is enhanced by extraordinary energy, presented graphs and tables on everything imaginable, from hematology to parasites—which would be expected from a veterinarian, and moreover she had also swept up all the idle raw data in sight; from this she displayed graphics on the population, its age structure and sex ratio, and a thorough analysis of mortality patterns—to name a few. Her briefs were well received by the Panther Advisory Council members, who had been thirsting for data.

Roelke provided graphics and commentary on some of the information that had been offered in narrative form earlier in the year by McBride and Robertson. When age data from 1981-1985 were compared to those available from the western pumas, it was seen that juvenile panthers comprised only an estimated eight percent of the population, whereas juveniles from five populations studied in Colorado, New Mexico, Idaho and Nevada (two from Nevada) accounted for 37 to 57 percent of the total. If the date of accounting the age structure for the Florida population was pushed back to 1978, so that it included several young panthers killed in those years, the juvenile percentage of the population showed an apparent increase to 22 percent—still well below the profiles from the West. In private debates it was contended that the larger proportions of young in the West was because pumas there were hunted. The regular cropping of adults, it would said, would tend to expand the younger end of the spectrum. This opinion was countered by arguing that although panthers in Florida were not hunted, the number of adults known to be killed illegally and on highways should mimic its effects, yet the juvenile class was still comparatively small compared to that for adults.[58]

There were striking contrasts in the health of panthers from different locales. North of Alligator Alley they were considerably heavier and healthier looking than those to the south. Female panthers in the State Preserve were below their potential weight. The poor physical condition of panthers in the Fakahatchee Strand State Preserve, and in the Big Cypress National Preserve, raised questions in the mind of the veterinarians as to whether females in these refuges could have proper reproductive cycles, conceive, and carry a full-term pregnancy, or could even raise offspring if they did.[59] The females examined in these prey-poor environments were under greater physiological stress than the males, probably due to the greater nutritional demands of pregnancy and caring for young. All the data thus far argued that the panther's plight was desperate.

Chapter 4

THE FLORIDA PANTHER INTERAGENCY COMMITTEE

They were indeed a queer-looking party that assembled on the bank . . . all dripping wet . . . . The first question of course was how to get dry again . . . said the dodo solemnly rising to its feet, "the thing to get us dry will be a caucus race." "What is a caucus race," said Alice . . . . Why," said the dodo, "the best way to explain it is to do it." First it marked out a race course in a sort of circle. "The exact shape doesn't matter," it said. And then all the party were placed along the course. There was no one, two, three and away, but they began running when they liked and left off when they liked, so that it wasn't easy to know when the race was over. However, when they had been running half an hour or so and were quite dry again, the dodo suddenly called out, "the race is over!" And they all crowded round him panting and asking, "but who has won?" This question the dodo couldn't answer without a great deal of thought and it sat for a long time with one finger pressed upon its forehead while the rest waited in silence. At last the dodo said, "everybody has won and all must have prizes!"

Lewis Carroll
Alice in Wonderland

In December 1986 a grizzly bear stared out at me from the cover of *Outside* magazine. "Say Goodby to the Grizzly," said the caption above the bear. The subtitle posed a question: "Last Stand in Yellowstone?" I turned to the article. Like many others, I had for years been vaguely aware of grizzly bear research in Yellowstone National Park. It had been much written about and portrayed in television documentaries, and I recalled that the researchers, the Craighead brothers, had gotten into a dustup with the National Park Service and were sent packing. The magazine article, by Alston Chase, was entitled, "The Grizzly and the Juggernaut." The bears in Yellowstone were dying out, the article claimed, despite an elaborate program to save them. The federal government had spent nearly $3,000,000, a group of scientists closely monitored the grizzly activities, the leading environmental organizations in the nation had taken an active interest, and the bears appealed easily and often to the news media. But according to Alston Chase their prospects had not brightened. Why, I wondered, with the enthusiasm and resources of the world's wealthiest nation committed to the rescue, was the outlook so gloomy?

In Chase's opinion "this tragic course of events could, very possibly, be reversed tomorrow, if there were the bureaucratic will to do so. But if history is any guide, that almost certainly will not happen." The National Park Service program, he claimed, had solid bureaucratic support and was backed by many environmental organizations as well. "The grizzly," he said, "is serving a variety of hidden political agendas."[1] (An "agenda," simply put, is what someone or some group would like to accomplish.)

According to the author, scientific research on the grizzly bear had been curtailed during the past 17 years; careers had been derailed; information had been manipulated and withheld, and 325 bears had been killed since the program began. The real culprit, Chase alleged, was the National Park Service's management policy, called ecosystems management. He quoted the agency's deputy chief scientist on ecosystems management, ". . . to maintain or re-create when necessary . . . those ecological conditions that would currently prevail were it not for the advent of post-Columbian man and his cultural impact." This policy, the author explained, featured "the attractive goal of restoring Yellowstone to the conditions it enjoyed before the first white man set foot there."[2]

I could easily relate to Chase's interpretation since my agency, the Florida Park Service, had in the early 1970s adopted the same ambitious philosophy of land stewardship. Ecosystems management is based in part on an awareness of ecological principles that began spreading beyond the walls of academia in the 1960s, and it is partly a philosophical and aesthetic ideal rooted in the American historical experience. In our time it has acquired an immense prestige. As a science of management it has definite limitations not always recognized by its practitioners—a subject to be developed later.

The Grizzly Saga

A good time to begin the Yellowstone grizzly story, as related by Chase, is in 1959 with the Craighead brothers, John and Frank. They were contracted by the National Park Service to study the big bears. Their research entailed the census of bears at park garbage dumps where they could easily be counted and individuals identified. The Craigheads also sedated bears and marked them with colored tags to identify them and plot their movements. During the course of this research the new technique of radio-telemetry came to hand, and the Craigheads were the first to employ it. While the two brothers were happily uncovering the mysteries of grizzly bear biology, another actor in the impending drama was making his collective way onto the stage: the park visitor.

With the spreading affluence and leisure time that followed World War II, visitation rose steadily in the national parks, swelling to proportions undreamed of in the past. Backcountry use grew in popularity, and visitors spilled out of the park centers onto hiking trails that led to the quiet and solace of the wilderness. All big, strong animals are potentially dangerous, although most wild creatures today fear and avoid humans, but at some point of human saturation in the realm of a potentially dangerous beast an injurious or lethal encounter is inevitable. In the National Parks the fatal convergence of humans and grizzly bears came in 1967. On a night in the summer of that year, among the sharply sculptured peaks of Glacier National Park, in incidents miles apart, two teen-age girls were killed in their sleeping bags.

The tragedy prompted a rigorous review by the National Park Service of its wildlife policy. Contact between visitors and grizzlies had always been treated casually. The feeding of roadside bears by visitors from automobiles was a common sight. At one time bleachers had been built at a garbage dump so visitors could enjoy the spectacle of bears rummaging for food. Now, to scale down encounters, a strict policy was adopted to keep the park's bears away from sites where humans gathered. Rules against feeding bears were strictly enforced; a visitor who left food unattended might be fined. I spent ten days in Yellowstone in 1977 and remember the extreme precautions taken against bear incidents. Rangers patrolled the campgrounds in the evening to ensure that no food was left out overnight; there was a thorough campaign to educate visitors; pamphlets were given out at the park entrance; information was prominently posted in the campgrounds, and every evening's campfire talk was preceded by a brief message on the bruins. Those that showed up in a use area, visitors were told, were immediately trapped and removed to the backcountry. If one should return it was trapped again. On the third occasion (if my memory is correct) it was killed. The park garbage dumps also came under scrutiny. The new policy of ecosystems management had been formally approved in the 1960s. It melded perfectly with the aspiration to keep bears away from people. The garbage dumps, it was decided, must go; and there was planted the seed of conflict.

Grizzlies had charmed visitors at Yellowstone since it became the world's first national park in 1872. When lodges were built in the late 1800s to accommodate tourists, garbage dumps, a necessary accompaniment, became a supplementary food source for the bears, some of whom spent part of each year foraging in them. As visitation swelled with the decades the dumps grew apace and presumably so did the bear population. By the 1970s bear numbers within the park were greater than they would have been in the absence of the additional food. But by this time bear habitat beyond the park boundaries had become inhospitable. The twentieth century had brought settlement and livestock, and human incompatibility with giant bears. When Yellowstone was made a park, a century before the dump closure, grizzlies had prowled from the Rocky Mountains to the Pacific, southward into Mexico and north into Canada, but in the 1970s they were gone from the United States except for small, remnant pockets in the northern Rocky Mountains.

These unextinguished residuals of a formerly widespread multitude, owed their existence to islands of reserved land administered by the National Park Service and the U. S. Forest Service. The largest of the vestigial populations was centered on Yellowstone. The grizzly strongholds of the 1970s had so shrunk that, if the bears were to have any hope of persisting, it might now be essential to hold them at an "artificially" high number in the few refuges left to accommodate them. Unfortunately this concept of wildlife preservation collided with the aforementioned park policy which aimed at returning wildlife populations to "natural" densities—those believed to have prevailed before the arrival of modern man. This dilemma of wildlife in shrinking refuges, encapsulated by the grizzly drama in an American National Park, is now drawing attention worldwide as habitat around nature preserves deteriorates.

The Craigheads argued against abruptly shutting down the dumps. The brothers contended that the problem of contacts between bears and humans, which dump closure was meant to curtail, might worsen as hungry bears wandered to areas of human activity in search of food. They also warned that it might bring a crisis down on the Yellowstone grizzly. If its numbers had been inflated by the dumps, and the dumps were closed, then the bear population, deprived of much of its food, might come spiraling down—with terminal consequences. The Craigheads suggested a gradual phase-out of the refuse sites while keeping the bears under surveillance. They reasoned that if, during the transition, the census data showed a downward slope, the Park Service would want to modify its new policy by continuing supplemental feeding in some way. They saw an imaginative alternative for such a contingency in the park elk herd, whose tendency to expand beyond the capacity of its range had been recognized (at least by some) as a problem in Yellowstone for nearly a century. The Craigheads advised that elk might be culled to supply carrion to grizzlies. This innovation would restore a food source to bears which had been chronicled by Lewis and Clark. That expedition had observed grizzlies feeding on the carcasses of bison killed by Indians who had driven them off cliffs. The burgeoning elk herd was also suspected of having supplanted other animals such as mule deer, white-tail deer and beavers.

Culling elk was a creative suggestion to keep survival odds in favor of the bears. But the Craighead's ideas were not welcome; the official mood did not dispose it to heed the most informed scientific guidance available. The opinions of the two brothers held no sway in the policy decision. They had postulated that a quick end to the dumps might menace humans by fostering more contacts with bears. Killing the offending bears, they also pointed out, would be illegal because in 1967 grizzlies had been placed on the first endangered species list. The National Park Service handily swept this obstacle away. Early in 1969 the bear was taken off the endangered species list. It is probably not possible to identify a more crass act by a government agency responsible for the management of an imperiled species. It is interesting to speculate what sort of outcry might have been raised by environmentalists if some commercial enterprise, say for oil exploration, had tried to remove the grizzly from the endangered list to further its ends.

The Craigheads would not be silent about what they regarded as a rash and exigent policy that might leave Yellowstone bereft of its famous bears. In speaking out they brought a reprisal. When their research permit came up for renewal in 1971 the park authorities said no, unless the brothers promised not to speak to the public or publish without first obtaining the agency's permission. The Craigheads saw this as an infringement of academic freedom and refused.[3] They were out of the park. A 12-year study, one of the few long-term studies of a North American wildlife species, was terminated. The following year the National Park Service began catching collared bears—to remove the collars. The radio signals, which for years had streamed data on the movements and interactions of grizzly bears to portable receivers were silenced. Whatever impact the new policy might have on bears the National Park Service was not going to know about it.[4] At this point in the narrative I could not help wondering if the park superintendent at Everglades National Park, who had for so long blocked the use of radio-collars, hadn't seen the long shadow of the Yellowstone grizzly fracas falling across his park.

All the park dumps were closed by the end of 1971. The first grizzly-caused human fatality in the park in 30 years followed in 1972. Encounters between grizzlies and humans went up sharply, and officials began killing bears—189 of them between 1968 and 1973. The Craigheads watched the ebbing statistics with alarm. In 1972 they warned that deaths had risen to more than double the birth rate —a trend that if carried on must finish off the bears. Their outspokenness, by 1973, was beginning to cause rumblings, and officials took steps to quell the incipient tempest. It restored the research program, but this time under the control of government scientists.

Land-management agencies ordinarily prefer to conduct their affairs without guidance from outsiders, but if the going gets sticky will sometimes entertain advisement from "experts" with the hope that it will be supportive. The appointment by the Florida Game Commission of its own independent advisory committee upon the death of a panther in 1983 was an example of this reflex. So now the National Park Service, sensing a rising storm, reacted by inviting other state and federal agencies to a cooperative study of grizzly bears in Yellowstone. The Interagency Grizzly Bear Study Team (IGBST) would be directed by a Park Service employee. The study team would in turn be supervised from Washington by another ad hoc aggregation known as the Interagency Grizzly Bear Steering Committee.

However, apart from these maneuvers a genuinely promising step was taken. The Interior Secretary, Roger C. B. Morton, asked the National Academy of Sciences to investigate. The Academy made its report in 1974; it was, according to Chase, virtually a complete confirmation of the Craigheads' conclusions. It observed that by 1974 bear fatalities were averaging more than 30 a year, and that the population could not, over the long run, endure a man-caused mortality rate greater than ten. Among its corrective proposals the Academy urged a coordinating body that would be free of control by the agencies. The National Park Service lost no time squashing that recommendation. A Department of Interior solicitor's opinion claimed that such a body "would be an improper and unauthorized delegation of authority."[5] Rather than independent research chaired by a neutral person, the work would be carried out by the new research team, which was firmly under department control.[6]

Meanwhile, some wildlife organizations lobbied Congress to force the Department of Interior to restore the Yellowstone grizzly to the endangered species list.[7] The 1966 law had been strengthened by a subsequent measure in 1969. In 1973 yet another act was passed to shore up lingering weaknesses; one shortcoming had been that only species in extreme peril could be listed, thus granting statutory beneficence rather late. The Act of 1973 attempted a remedy by creating a "threatened" category for species judged likely to become endangered within the foreseeable future.[8] The new legislation cleared the way for a semantic compromise on listing the Yellowstone grizzly; in 1975 it was consigned to the threatened category. Thus the creature that had been declared endangered in 1967, and then removed from the list, was demoted to threatened in 1975, although by that time it appeared greatly diminished by the press of park service policy since 1967. The threatened species provision in the federal act had obviously been intended to allow preventive action before the organism reached a state of crises, not to be a contrivance whereby government agencies could evade legally mandated responsibilities that collided with a favored doctrine.

The research team set to work with a will, but had poor luck in finding bears. After five years of searching, it had recorded only 46. Under government control or not, the researchers could only state what the data revealed, and the estimates they arrived at were not in line with the recent optimistic pronouncements of officials. In 1975 the superintendent of Yellowstone National Park had declared, "none of us believes that there is scientific evidence or facts indicating the grizzly is threatened with extinction. . . . Plainly it does not need help in the Yellowstone area." The agency had stood for a decade on the figure of 350 bears in Yellowstone. But the researchers, even by the most optimistic amplification of the data, could only postulate a maximum of 200. More importantly, numbers appeared to be still falling. The team leaders concluded that the downslide was eliminating bears at a rate of about two percent a year. They sent their conclusions to the steering committee head in Washington, who dutifully informed his colleagues by memorandum that "the survival of grizzly bears within the greater Yellowstone ecosystem . . . is dependent upon reversing the current population decline." The memo quickly leaked to the press causing another flurry of embarrassing publicity. There were articles in *The New York Times* and a news special by CBS. In response to the outcry there was again a display of bureaucratic busyness. Yet another committee was formed, this one to be called the Interagency Grizzly Bear Committee (IGBC).[9]

At this point in the narrative I sat up and took notice. This was precisely the bureaucratic device that the National Park Service was now promoting to take charge of the Florida panther. The proposed Florida Panther Interagency Committee being aired by William Penn Mott was to be explicitly modeled on the Interagency Grizzly Bear Committee.[10]

In Yellowstone the Craighead brothers had gone on futilely pleading from the sidelines for the National Park Service to quit horsing around and to get to the root of the problem. If the bear mortality was due to inadequate food, the solution was to provide the bears with more. If the refuge was too compressed to furnish food enough for a population of sustainable size, then numbers would have to be augmented by bolstering the provision from nature. The alternative was to sit and watch the census graph slide downward, hoping without any good reason to do so that the descending line would bottom out before the threshold of extirpation was crossed. In the ensuing bustle John Craighead was recalled to service. Early in 1983 yet another committee was formed, this one was at last to tackle the substantive issue of supplemental feeding. The Craigheads had kept promoting the scheme to feed grizzlies from the elk herd. Surplus elk could be put out for the grizzlies at remote places in the park. The report from this committee confirmed that the bear decline was related to the dump closure, and that enticing the bears to the backcountry with carrion would not only elevate their nutritional plane, but dampen the impulse to wander so widely and into places where they would have to be destroyed.

But then the supplemental feeding committee refused to endorse supplemental feeding. It had been given a majority known to oppose the innovation. Bureaucrats know that controversies of this kind have a brief life span. If an issue doesn't have a direct impact on the public it is soon displaced by others. A flurry of apparent remedial actions, a committee set up to look into the matter (which in fact may be thoroughly understood by the reviewers, having been hashed over by them for years) and interest wanes. The agency can then return to the course from which it never had any intention of deviating. The committee rejected the proposal to feed surplus elk to the grizzlies, because if some elk were killed the others might become "more secretive than at present, seriously damaging their value to park visitors."[11] Surplus elk by this line of reasoning could not be utilized to aid grizzlies because a park visitor might then find it harder to see one. This was a visual, not a biological consideration. It bypassed the question of what to do about too many elk and too few grizzly bears, but in the collective mind of the National Park Service the scenery and biology of a park can become hopelessly confused. The reader should mark this incident. Time and again in the course of this book we will see recommendations made to aid endangered wildlife, rejected by land-management agencies (not just the National Park Service) on grounds having nothing to do with biology.

The Parallel in Florida

The state of things in Yellowstone was remarkably like that in Florida. Both situations featured refuges that seem enormous in size by conventional American park standards, and both involved species of large, wide-ranging animals, but the survival requirements of the respective species dwarfed the capabilities of the refuges to sustain them—under "natural" conditions. Management would have to intervene in some way to make up the deficiency or at least investigate the possibility of doing so. Given adequate food the refuge might be more favorable. Intervening in southern Florida would mean that additional deer would have to be produced. Intervening in Yellowstone would mean that the elk herd, which had expanded at the expense of other wildlife species, would have to be culled.

In both cases the National Park Service held a key, and in both cases its policy was as immovable as the Rocky Mountains. It would hear no argument that seemed inimical to its management ideal. In Yellowstone, three feeding centers for grizzlies had been urged. On the public lands in southern Florida, it had been recommended that Hole-in-the-Donut in Everglades National Park be used to boost deer numbers, and that two other areas, the Big Cypress National Preserve and the Fakahatchee Strand State Preserve (managed by the Florida Park Service), also try to raise the deer population above the capacity of its natural habitat. And the most striking parallel of all was that the National Park Service was now going to saddle the Florida panther recovery program with an interagency committee modeled after the one that was sitting ponderously astride grizzly bear policy in Yellowstone National Park. History was about to repeat itself. I knew the depth of departmental feeling about its sense of mission and its keen attunement to any imagined threat. I also knew the vigorous counterstrokes that could be mounted when a threat took form. Alston Chase had done a great service. He had held up a crystal ball that afforded a tantalizing glimpse into the future.

There could be no doubt about the character of the looming Florida Panther Interagency Committee. The appearance of a "team" of cooperating agencies, pooling resources in an all-out campaign to save the panther, would be an image, nothing more. Behind this masque the National Park Service would assiduously dodge initiatives that seemed incompatible with its doctrine. The circumventions could be easily handled in the group dynamics of committee meetings. Agencies are loath to squabble openly and would be unlikely to do so, even if the other delegates were astute enough to see the game.

Enlisting the Environmental Organizations

But, I thought, in Florida the blockage could be overcome. Saving the panther has a wide appeal in the state. If the environmental organizations were briefed about the obstructions facing recovery and the reluctance of the agencies to bring their weight against them, the organizations would be quick to act. They had moved with alacrity to pressure the Game Commission when it balked at tightening hunting regulations, and they would be equally quick to push a foot-dragging National Park Service—or so I thought.

The most important tasks at the beginning of 1986 were to ease hunting pressure on the Big Cypress deer herd and to get panther research underway in Everglades National Park. The intransigence of the National Park Service had become a source of frustration to every biologist in the program. Early in the year I made the rounds: a Florida Sierra Club gathering in Sarasota, a Florida Audubon Society board meeting in Orlando, and Florida Defenders of the Environment in Gainesville. In Gainesville I proposed a panther conference. The suggestion was adopted instantly. The new executive director, William (Bill) Branan, was instructed forthwith to organize a conference for April (just over two months away). Branan had taken a doctorate in deer management at the University of Georgia. He could not have fitted in more perfectly.

In January I briefed a working group of the Everglades Coalition, an assembly of state and national environmental organizations that had coalesced to back Governor Graham's "Save the Everglades" campaign. The delegates gather each year in southern Florida to survey the many ailments of the Everglades. Among other subjects, I talked about the Game Commission's aversion to hunting modifications and told them also that the superintendent of Everglades National Park was holding up research. The Coalition answered with an endorsement of these measures that could not easily be ignored, and further, it backed a recent Panther Advisory Council recommendation to close the Fakahatchee Strand State

Preserve to hunting—which had been advanced by Game Commission biologists eight years before. All this bracing would bear fruit. The Coalition's brief was delivered to Governor Graham.[12]

Creation of the Interagency Committee

In February Everglades National Park became the setting for a personal project of the park superintendent, who wanted to make his pitch for an interagency committee like the one that was oppressing grizzly bears in Wyoming. All government agencies affiliated with the recovery program were to attend. Just prior to this event, the Panther Advisory Council met with the Game Commission staff to frame a strong statement about the importance of getting research started in Everglades National Park. There was now a rumor that the park superintendent had softened his position somewhat (perhaps not surprising since a groundswell of criticism from environmentalists was palpable). He was now saying that he had never been presented with a plan of research. Well, that was easy enough. I asked John Eisenberg to rough out a plan; he quickly mailed a draft; I worked it over by telephone with Mel Sunquist, and there it was. Now admittedly, it skimped a bit on detail, but if anyone was interested to begin research, the whys and wherefores and methodology were adequately outlined.

The Everglades assembly consumed two days. All of the agency administrators overseeing panther management were present to interact for the first time. It turned out that each one had brought a private agenda, intending to use the gathering as a platform to promote his own aims. The regional director of the National Park Service was there. The superintendents of both Everglades National Park and the Big Cypress National Preserve were present with several of their staff. The regional director of the Fish and Wildlife Service chaired the meeting. He had brought staff from Atlanta as well as from his agency's Florida endangered species office in Jacksonville. The executive director of the Florida Department of Natural Resources had arrived with a retinue from the Florida Park Service. The executive director of the Game Commission brought a bevy of biologists. The only representative of an environmental organization to attend was Bill Branan, the executive director of FDE.

Fish and Wildlife Service officials wanted to update the five-year old recovery plan to accommodate current knowledge. They aired a list of 27 issues which would become the working basis for a first draft of the new recovery plan. It was during the drawn-out deliberation on these topics that the parochial themes which had been brought to the assembly made their debut. The goal of the superintendent of Everglades National Park, as mentioned before, was to sell the idea of a Florida Panther Interagency Committee. This was agreed to after much palaver. A convening of the agency heads was scheduled for May to formally inaugurate the FPIC (the acronym will be used hereafter in the narrative for simplicity, and in the hope that it will avoid confusion with the Panther Advisory Council). Although the park superintendent was successful in launching his project, he was embarrassed in verbal exchanges wherein it was implied that he had been obstructing research.

I brought up the need for the National Park Service to manage for a greater abundance of deer, singling out the Hole-in-the-Donut as suitable for experimentation. The park superintendent was quick to answer that in 1982 Congress had forbidden the National Park Service to use exotic plants in the parks or to practice single-species management. This was an odd claim which I have since been unable to substantiate, but the park superintendent made it plain that under no circumstances would he entertain the idea of an "unnatural" number of deer. That doctrinaire assertion has been reinforced many times since. The National Park Service is uncompromisingly opposed to altering its management thinking—even for a large, endangered predator.

The Game Commission scheme was soon in the open. It aimed at putting an end to the tiresome attacks on hunting. A proper understanding of this gambit will require backtracking a few months. In the summer of 1985 the National Park Service commissioned four nationally known authorities on the white-tailed deer to look at the impact of hunting on deer in the Big Cypress National Preserve. There was anecdotal evidence to suggest that deer numbers were higher on private lands immediately to the north where no public hunting was permitted. Private opinion in the National Park Service held that hunting had lowered the Preserve deer herd. There can be little doubt that the Park Service believed that the deer review panel would reach the same conclusion.

But the panel's draft report, in December 1985, must have been a disappointment. It ventured that the bucks-only hunting regulations that had been put in force by that time—provided they were adhered to by the hunters—should not hinder the productivity of the deer herd.[13] Consequently, the Park Service simply sat on its discouraging document. Whereas the report brought gloom in the Park Service, it unquestionably delighted the rival camp. The Game Commission and the Park Service wrangled ceaselessly over hunting regulations, with the Park Service urging more restrictions and the Game Commission resisting unless, in its view, there was a clear indication that hunters were damaging the resource. The best tactical move for the Park Service would have been to get the paper out and deal with it. Since the Game Commission had the report, it could be assumed that it had been passed on to hunting organizations. It could have further been assumed that the rival agency would utilize the report for maximum advantage at a time of its choosing (which, as it turned out, was the February meeting at Everglades National Park). In fact, the investigation had acknowledged that there were several unknowns in the equation if the goal was to manage the deer herd to the advantage of panthers: the illegal kill was incalculable, and the take by panthers was unknown. It suggested further restricting the harvest and expanding data collections in order to peer with more precision into the hazy statistics of deer mortality.

But the Game Commission now intended once and for all to end debate on hunting in the Big Cypress. A representative of the agency took the floor and delivered a forceful oration on the need to put such divisive discussions aside and get on with the business of saving panthers. His arguments leaned heavily on a point made in the draft report of the deer management review panel that bucks-only hunting rarely removes more than ten percent of the deer.

Bill Branan was virtually unknown to the assembly at the time. However, he had recently reviewed the draft report. It also happened that he was well-acquainted with two of the authors and had talked at length with one of them by phone. Branan interrupted the peroration to inquire if anyone present was aware of any research measuring the combined effects of hunting and natural predation on a deer herd (there were no completed studies at that time). The speaker on the floor might have anticipated this riposte in preparing for the debate, since the problem had been alluded to in the paper, but he was at a loss to counter it. Consequently, attention shifted to Branan who began entertaining questions from around the room, while the Game Commission speaker stood idle in the middle of the floor. His offensive lost its momentum and never did revive.

Branan's involvement did not end here. He lobbied some of the authors to insert the volatile closure-of-Bear-Island-to-hunting recommendation as one of its proposals. The deer management panel modified its final product in March, 1986 to suggest closing half of Bear Island. The upshot of all this was that the report, which in draft form had been awkward for the Park Service and a useful lever for the Game Commission, now became awkward for the latter agency. Deprived of all its political leverage, the blue ribbon report soon faded from sight.[14] Branan's stock soared in the National Park Service, but he was not popular at Game Commission headquarters.

The FDE Panther Conference

In the cities of the Roman Empire, judicial and public business was conducted in the open city square, then called the forum. The word has survived the centuries as an English noun meaning a public meeting. The statute creating the Panther Advisory Council stipulated that one of its purposes was to "provide a forum for technical review and discussion of the status and development of the Florida Panther Recovery Program." In April of 1986 a forum was supplied in grand style, with the generous assistance of Florida Defenders of the Environment.

The broad design for the FDE conference was simply to expose the surfacing issues of panther recovery to scrutiny and debate, thereby overriding the bureaucratic propensity for secluding them. A paramount topic was the inadequacy of the present refuge in southern Florida and the impossibly few panthers living there. We thought that if the deficiency was vividly presented, inescapable conclusions would have to be drawn: if properly managed, panthers on public lands might be increased; also, the privately owned lands in the region, which held half or more of the known population, were vital to a recovery strategy. We wanted to call attention to the precarious status of this depleting asset, hoping to stimulate creative ideas for securing some portion of it.

We specifically targeted the management philosophy of the National Park Service for attention. Representatives of that agency were requested to explain themselves on the subject. Beyond this set of pressing issues, the more obtuse matter of genetics demanded attention. The potentially harmful effects of inbreeding can be fatal, but may also be remedied—by outbreeding. That is to say that pumas from elsewhere might be bred to Florida panthers to neutralize the stealthy impact of consanguinity. This subject has been little remarked in the narrative thus far and will be relegated to a chapter of its own, where the complexities can be treated separately and in detail.

As a palliative to the alarmed agencies, a segment of the conference was allocated to them so they could expound on their recent accomplishments. Agencies can always produce such a list, and there were in fact some solid gains to boast of. Of course the point that counts about accomplishments in an endangered species program is that in sum (and in time) they must suffice to save the species from extinction.

Great expectations ascended the podium with the National Park Service spokesmen. First at the lectern was Robert (Bob) Baker, the regional director of National Parks in the Southeast. His acquaintance with the issues surrounding the panther's survival had been fairly recent, the audience was told. However, he had worked hard to understand them. "I am not satisfied with where we are," he asserted. "We in the National Park Service may not have been as actively involved as we should have been." Since the February meeting in Everglades National Park, he had asked for and received $180,000 to fund research in the coming year, and he had selected a new superintendent for that Park, based on the man's strong natural resource background (this all sounded very positive). "We are forming an Interagency Council [The term was incorrect. He was mixing the title of the new FPIC with that of the Florida Panther Advisory Council.] on behalf of the panthers. . . . Better coordination is needed. I feel that this Council [sic] will be effective and not an obstacle to the work that is needed." Baker then listed several preliminary chores the FPIC had assigned itself, one being to "establish a technical advisory group to assist us" (The FPIC's arrangements for technical advisors will be presented in the next chapter). Baker finished with optimism. "I am very excited that an extremely tough, difficult issue—the survival of the Florida panther—is bringing us together."[15] The man seemed to radiate a genuine resolve.

The next speaker was Jay Gogue, the chief scientist of the National Park Service's southeast region. Gogue's talk seemed a breath of fresh air from the Park Service bureaucracy. It began with a frank, no-nonsense, thumb-nail history of resource management in the National Park Service, its history, its failings, its biases, and its current flexibility and willingness to face the new challenge. The assembly was told that, in its early decades, the agency had embraced the bias of the time toward "good" and "bad" animals. Predators had been purposefully destroyed. "The loss of predators is the key reason why we now face the recurring need to artificially manage the elk herd at Yellowstone National Park." (Alston Chase, I recalled, had criticized the Park Service for leaving the elk herd to manage itself.) "I should point out that we in the National Park Service did not recognize the need to change; it was, in essence, forced on us by very knowledgeable conservation groups and key academicians."[16]

This was an admission of unexpected frankness, and it fitted a growing awareness in the back of my own mind. A land-management agency comes into being to serve a social need, infuses its mission with the highest ideals, and soon settles into a normative mode of thought and routine which becomes imbedded in doctrinal concrete. A tribal mentality takes hold; threats to the doctrine are forever coming forth from segments of society that do not share the agency ideals and may even be hostile to them. Other agencies may at times become rivals for the control of some piece of turf. This competition hones the protective instincts to a razor edge. The institutional environment may change over time, imposing a corresponding responsibility for mental adjustments, but rarely will the cadre of true believers directing affairs have the flexibility to reorient themselves.

Gogue explained that "in the early 1960s, as we were increasingly unable to respond to the strong criticism of how we managed our resources, the Congress called for several external reviews of our resource management. These committees, under the guidance of Dr. Starker Leopold, recommended a major change in the way we viewed our resources. They suggested that we embark on a policy of 're-creating' the scenes and resources in parks as they were first seen by the white man. This effort of re-creating pre-Columbian conditions moved the Service closer to integrated management of park resources. However, it did not fully appreciate the impacts of global changes and subsequent resource changes that had and are still occurring. . . ."[17] Here was another refreshingly frank admission. The policies introduced by the Leopold committee had become the current gospel.

Gouge deferred to the Endangered Species Act in any policy conflict. He cited examples: The Park Service was trying to increase the nesting of Atlantic Ridley turtles at Padre Island National Seashore—disregarding a low historic nesting density; in some parks artificial nests were aiding bald eagles; owls were being thinned out to ease predation in falcon nesting areas; an artificial habitat—a pond—had been constructed in Big Bend National Park for the Big Bend Gambusia, a small fish; in other parks fences had been strung to contain elk and bison. Gogue implied that his agency could supplement food for panthers, but preferably by planting native rather than non-native forage for deer. "Artificial supplemental feeding is something we try to avoid. It is a last resort technique and then viewed as a short-term, sporadic management tool."[18] These words were disturbing and did not seem consistent with other foregoing assertions. Intervention might have to be permanent. Was the artificial pond at Big Bend National Park only for the short term, and what about the other cases? And, if the Park Service was amenable to supplemental feeding, why the dogged refusal to try anything new with grizzly bears in Yellowstone?

This rigidity has confounded many persons who have struggled against its contradictions, believing that sooner or later the Park Service would have to see through its own tangle of illogic. Critics have charged (among other things) that it is has more of an incentive to protect its public image than to protect the environment.[19] But this is a shallow probe. It might be that in an age when positivist reason, reinforced by scientific achievement, rules our system of belief, spiritual dynamics are often inflected to a more consuming emersion in (and service to) nature and social causes—and to the institutions that are conduits for their energies. Here, the mission of the National Park Service shines forth like a beacon. Resource management in the National Park Service is based on an ideal: the recreation of the splendor of the original American landscape. Seen from the vantage point of a park service professional, it is an ideal that swells the institutional heart with pride and infuses its labors with a piercing purpose. The steep and arduous slope to such a goal only enhances its appeal; its attainment would be a gift to the ages. Participation in the task promises to invest a career with a transcendent meaning. Such a cause takes on the attributes of a secular faith, arousing powerful emotions. The defenders of this faith develop keen receptors that can detect threats, real or imaginary, far off on the horizon. The imaginative bureaucratic diversions that have been thrust forward one after another to oppose something so simple as trying to arrest the decline of grizzly bears in Yellowstone National Park tell us of the strength of these emotions. There is far more at work here than bureaucratic sluggishness or heavy-footed resistance to change.

At the end of his talk, however, Gogue concluded with a cautious but encouraging two-point summary.

1. It is accepted in the National Park Service to adjust or modify natural processes so long as the adjustments do not jeopardize other species or community types.

2. We can manipulate an array of factors which will benefit the endangered species, but these adjustments must be based on sound research and be in compliance with administrative procedures and appropriate statutes.[20]

The first point made is the key to a rational modification of the cherished policy. But in the end these fine words would come to nothing. It was the final phrase in Gogue's second point which the National Park Service would use to deflect change. As we shall see, the agency and its public support group, the National Parks and Conservation Association, would claim that the "appropriate statutes" prohibited any action to benefit a "single species." And Jay Gouge soon departed the Park Service. But these disappointments waited in a future which at the moment seemed to have brightened. The land-management agencies were in the spotlight, putting on their best performance. For their next act they would join forces as the FPIC and stride boldly forth together.

Chapter 5

THE FPIC IN ACTION

And what of that other mode of life in which man makes believe,
pretends — is it any less interesting? What is this strange,
ungenuine doing to which man sometimes devotes himself pre-
cisely for the purpose of really not doing what he is doing.

José Ortega y Gasset
Man and People

On a morning in May 1986, the heads of four government agencies, two state and two federal, met in southern Florida to sign a document creating an ad hoc organization to take charge of the Florida panther. I was directed by the head of the Florida Department of Natural Resources to attend, as the department expert on the panther. The gathering served up a fine opportunity to study the psychology of executives. Working at the bottom rung of an agency affords few opportunities to witness decision-making at the top and to watch leaders in action (or inaction as the case might be). I made notes and, as was often my habit during these years, compiled a detailed narrative the next day.

One agenda item aired the question of who should be allowed at the FPIC meetings. A Game Commission representative was not keen on having the public or press attend. A Fish and Wildlife Service man declared that they could not be excluded. Thus sapped of its vital juices the topic faltered and soon expired, but it had unveiled an attitude pronounced among the Game Commission staff, holding that matters of this kind are best conducted out of sight. Government agencies that ride out occasional storms of public wrath learn to "tip-toe" with certain issues. State game agencies, perhaps since they must perpetually reckon with volatile constituents, have enlarged wariness into paranoia and tip-toeing into a modus operandi—a subject for a coming chapter. As with most fears of this kind the nervousness would prove unfounded since it was unusual for anyone outside the official circle to show up at FPIC meetings.

Another agenda item was labeled "Public Information Needs."[1] It had to do with what people should be told and how the information should be disseminated. A newsletter was nominated to publicize the doings of the FPIC. A copy of a Grizzly Bear Interagency Committee Newsletter was passed around as a model.

Here the Game Commission was quick off the mark, volunteering to be the publisher. The Game Commission has often been slow to grasp the fundamentals of saving panthers, but in the realm of public relations its skills are finely honed. It did not fail to appreciate the value of having control of the Committee's medium of information. This subject of inordinate concern was a prolonged one. Unfortunately, the weight of commentary did not forecast a strategy devoted to educating citizens about the intricacies of saving panthers, but one preoccupied with showing officialdom in a favorable light.

Another agenda item was entitled "Designation of a Technical Subcommittee to FPIC." This topic brought out official sentiment on the formation of an independent body of experts to advise the FPIC, in the way that the Panther Advisory Council offered prescriptions to the Game Commission. Here Game Commission officials were emphatic and firm; they did not want to be further oppressed by unsolicited advice. The National Park Service seemed to concur. The state agency strongly resented its legislatively imposed consultants, who seemed full of disagreeable ideas. The upshot was that the so-called Technical Subcommittee of the FPIC would be made up of delegates from each of the four agencies, who would come to future meetings armed with their divergent biases. In the months that followed, the separate delegations would prove more keen to assuage parochial anxieties than in taking concerted steps to reverse the decline of an imperiled cat. The so-called Technical Subcommittee has functioned as a secretariat to the FPIC, brokering tribal concerns into a mutually acceptable position.

Next, attention settled on the job that would consume most of the day: a walk-through of the first draft of the revised Florida Panther Recovery Plan. It will be remembered that three months earlier at the meeting in Everglades National Park, Fish and Wildlife Service biologists had sponsored a broad review of 27 issues. Their notes had been taken back to the endangered species office in Jacksonville and there used to compile a draft of the new recovery plan. It was to this revision that the editors now turned.

I was prepared to be bored as we plodded through pages of minutia, but was soon aroused by the attention shown by some administrators in the document's every statement, and nuance of expression. Some of them objected to remarks, sentences and in some instances even entire sections in the plan. They wanted words changed and phrases recast; they went after the draft like academicians dissecting a student's thesis. But the aim was not to strengthen the biological foundation of the plan. The alterations and deletions being insisted upon had nothing to do with supplying the irreducible minima of preserving panthers. The reviewers (primarily laymen) had their conventional blinders on. They were worried that proposals might encroach on cherished ideas about management, or stir a controversy. The term "red flag" kept being used, as in "now this is going to wave a red flag" at such-

and-such a segment of the public. One agency administrator seemed to see his institutional environment filled with figurative angry bulls that would come charging in if any red flags went up. Changes were made helter-skelter, without questioning (and apparently without being aware of any need to question) how the final product would be tailored to the needs of panther recovery. It was a striking revelation of the variance between bureaucratic interests and the uncompromising demands of managing endangered wildlife.

The National Park Service delegation wanted a reference to radio-collaring panthers in Everglades National Park deleted. My heart sunk at the thought of fighting that battle again, after believing it had finally been won. In retrospect it seems that the agency was in fact at last committed to radio-telemetry but still chary of saying so. But the research couldn't be hidden, and what would happen if a cat died? The way to proceed with volatile issues is to build a case for the policy and use the agency's educational arm to cultivate a supportive opinion or, to at least strive for acceptance. It can prove disastrous to launch a potentially controversial policy in secret, and of course the management problem cannot be solved by avoiding it. Unfortunately, government agencies have a tendency to drift toward one or the other of these alternatives when they sense that a new challenge might cause an uproar. When lacking the self-confidence to deal openly with it, the tendency is to fall into the tactics of secrecy or deception —if they value the policy, or to sidestep the problem—if they do not.

When the question of outbreeding came up, the Game Commission spoke strongly against "wiping out *coryi*." An interesting story was related in which the executive director of the Game Commission, while briefing the Governor and Cabinet on the panther, was asked why he didn't simply bring in cats from out West rather than spending money on the remnant of panthers in Florida. The official's question necessitated a lengthy explanation of why it was thought important to preserve the physical traits seen in *Felis concolor coryi*. As explained earlier, the Florida panther had initially been defined on the basis of a crook in the tail, a "cowlick" and white spots on the head and neck. With the knowledge available to the executive director at the time of his appearance before the Governor and Cabinet, the defense had been correct, but the story was narrated to imply that having defended the uniqueness of the Florida panther in such a high council raised an intimidating (or perhaps insurmountable) barrier to any consideration of outbreeding.

However, subsequent biological questions had been raised about the wisdom of hewing to the three-character definition of a subspecies; the most important inquired about the effects of inbreeding—a problem given little thought in the early days of the recovery program, but at the time of this formative meeting of the FPIC, inbreeding was commanding attention (in the minds of a few), and the legitimacy of the three identifying characters was being challenged. This will be gone over in the next chapter, in which we will see an entrenched Game Commission's disinclination to weigh outbreeding and its dogged resistance to abandoning the three identifying characters. It is reasonable to wonder if this inflexibility doesn't have its origins in the give and take of the above-mentioned Cabinet meeting in Tallahassee. If so, it is one more case of an influence on the management of endangered species that has nothing to do with biology.

The bitterest disappointment for me came when the review of the draft recovery plan reached the topic of managing public lands for a greater number of deer. The National Park Service contingent came to life. They were outspokenly and vehemently adverse to any wording in this vein. They were adamant that language referring to "food plots," or even to the need to raise deer numbers above what was "natural" (natural was a word with strong emotional connotations), could not implicate the National Park Service. This rigidity in the privacy of a meeting room was in striking contrast to the impression of flexibility conveyed by the same officials in public only a month before at the FDE panther conference—where they had effused a willingness to entertain any and all measures. Now they stated emphatically that any proposal deviating from "natural systems management" would not be tolerated—even for the Hole-in-the-Donut in Everglades National Park, thousands of acres of former farmland now overgrown with non-native vegetation.

The Game Commission delegation showed alarm over an assignment calling for it and the Fish and Wildlife Service to jointly develop a plan for managing panthers on private lands north of the Big Cypress National Preserve. Another "red flag" issue; this one would wave at private landowners. This was not a promising start on preserving the private lands north of the Fakahatchee Strand and the Big Cypress Swamp. Admittedly, devising such a plan would be an uphill chore, carried out in uncertainty, and so would demand an effort of appropriate strength and resourcefulness, one worthy of a specially created government task force with a variety of talents and resources, that could pool its strengths, appeal to the environmental organizations and build on the broad public enthusiasm about the future of Florida's state animal. It would require an innovative body, say, like the FPIC, with all its imposing assets. But the FPIC has shown no awareness of the potential strength inherent in its unity, or of its tantalizing possibilities for ground-breaking achievements. Unfortunately the FPIC is not the sum of its parts; it is a confederation of entities, each guarding its favored modes and traditions, viewing its unity in terms of mutual safety and benefits. It is blind to the coherent strength that might attempt bold new feats of conservation. The unprecedented potential of this coalition for new moves in the field of natural resource management has never dawned on its ruling circle. The types who dominate it have shown a shrewd enough eye for opportunity—but primarily in a tribal context.

The Road Ahead

The meeting adjourned leaving me with a refined set of imprints about agency leadership, and also with some thinking to do about how reason might be made to prevail in the bureaucratic circus that was about to envelop the recovery program. I had not been unfamiliar with agency attitudes and the general way they might prove obstructive, but the details were now sharply in view. It was clear that the two most influential players were the Game Commission and the National Park Service. Administratively, the Game Commission oversees the recovery program in Florida and it, in theory, is responsible for managing wildlife in the Big Cypress National Preserve. The National Park Service administers the bulk of public land presently available for panther management in southern Florida. However, the weight of the two agencies does not derive from administrative responsibility or geographic accident; both have fervent and determined minds about the proper way to care for natural resources; these, at bottom, are incompatible. Both agencies also have strong, politically active constituents who toil on behalf of the institutional exemplars of their aspirations for the use of public land.

My growing suspicions of weakness in the Fish and Wildlife Service were confirmed. In the emending of the recovery plan, John Christian, of that agency, tried to defend the wording that his staff had written into it, but he was largely ignored. The other Fish and Wildlife Service representative, it seemed to me, had few opinions and just went along with what anyone else wanted. It was obvious that this federal agency was not going to put its foot down on anything. The great irony of the endangered species process in America is that the federal instrument which ostensibly drives the machine—by its responsibility under the Endangered Species Act, and by its control, in theory, of the purse strings—is politically the weakest among those it is supposed to guide. The others have constituencies that form influential links between the agencies and the legislative bodies. The endangered species branch of the Fish and Wildlife Service lacks such a power base. It is a political weakling which can be elbowed aside at any time.

The recovery plan exercise allowed each faction to eliminate or reword anything it found disagreeable—prior to having the draft go out for public review. It could be argued that legitimate editorial functions were involved, but the administrators had not made a disciplined analysis of panther survival. They were each trying to fit the design to long-standing notions of agency self-interest. Five years after this beginning, the effort to recover the panther in southern Florida would still be in motion, churning out optimistic statements and spending huge sums of money, with no idea of where it was going. And, as we shall see, the Fish and Wildlife Service would finally resort to contracting with a group of independent technical experts from around the country to try and impose sanity on the course of affairs.

But hope springs eternal, and I believed then that a meaningful direction could be mandated. The recovery plan, the administrative foundation of the effort, was the key. It was essential that the plan clearly identify the elements of the problem. If that were done then the solution would become visible and could be broken into its constituent parts for detailed evaluation and planning. That is not to say that the great labor ahead could be started with confidence or with precision; research would have to be structured to illuminate several dimly perceived corners, but certainly there was scope, within some field of magnitude, to set a sensible campaign in motion. It could be seen for instance that by projecting the trend of disappearing habitat in southern Florida into the future, a time would arrive when the remainder would be insufficient for a panther population. Five years of radio-telemetry data had given a picture of panther numbers, distribution, age-structure and productivity. It was clear enough that the status of the animals inhabiting the present refuge—the conglomeration of lands administered by several state and federal agencies—was without a hope unless management policies were modified in unison. The case seemed sufficiently precarious (I thought) to warrant a captive population, as insurance against any disaster that might overtake the wild one. The emerging evidence of inbreeding—whose insidious impact might not be visible until it was too late—meant (I thought) that prudence required at least making the administrative preparations for outbreeding, The essential matters, in addition to managing genes and accommodating the unforgiving dimension of time, were numbers and space. A number of panthers would have to be postulated as a management goal, and a space marked out to accommodate them. Management would have to adjust numbers to available space. The estimates thus derived would have to be conceptually fitted like an overlay to the map of Florida in order to inventory the asset of salvageable land; and so on, and so on, in such a sequence the thinking would have to go.

The bureaucrats wanted to fashion a plan on lines that would not give any of them heartburn. But they could be made to do the right thing, I thought, if the citizen activists who were showing such great interest were kept apprised of the wide gap between what would have to be done and what was actually being achieved. The obstacles that lay ahead were mountainous, but the energies of environmentalists had prevailed against previous blockages. I had listed them in the summary of my notes following the FDE panther conference: the initial refusal of the Game Commission to even acknowledge receipt of the Panther Advisory Council's correspondence; its disregard of recommended restrictions on hunting in the Big Cypress National Reserve; its indifference to suggestions that the Fakahatchee Strand State Preserve be closed to hunting; its unwillingness to change the legal limit on spike bucks from one inch to five inches; the resistance of the National Park Service to radio-telemetry research in Everglades National Park and its disdain to even hear of managing for an "unnatural" number of deer (unfortunately its concessions on this issue at the FDE panther conference later proved a decoy—as explained). All these obstacles (except the last) had been overcome. There was no reason to think that further gains could not be made.

However, my later attempts to mobilize environmental forces would fail. Although I made strenuous efforts to keep the leaders informed, there was no effective response. In the course of this long exertion I noticed a bias among these organizations. Whenever the Game Commission balked, the activists usually responded with alacrity, particularly when hunting was at issue, but when the National Park Service stonewalled, they could be extraordinarily difficult to rouse. Of course what I refer to as the "environmental organizations" are by no means homogeneous in outlook, but some of them set great store by the doctrines of the National Park Service which are thought to be highly advanced. Entrenched attitudes are not exclusive to the land-management bureaucracy. I must also say that some of the organizations that could have done far more for the Florida panther still make use of the animal when appealing for donations.

But the disappointing outcome of the revised recovery plan was a year ahead in May 1986. I departed the meeting with a copy of the draft plan. (It had been requested that all of them be turned in at the close of the meeting; I caused some annoyance by refusing to give mine back.) I planned to go through each successive draft and, from my base as chairman of the Panther Advisory Council, make as much noise as possible about its failings.

The Technical Subcommittee in Action

In June the FPIC's Technical Subcommittee began its labors. It would be absorbed during the first year in redesigning the 1981 recovery plan. I was not designated to attend, but was able to follow the proceedings through the minutes and other documents that were routinely mailed to interested parties. This mass of paper would have bored anyone not attuned to the unequal contest between the Fish and Wildlife Service, which was trying to design something that would work, and the other parties which were resolved that if the plan did not work to their special advantage, it would at least not work against them. To anyone who knew the game and the personalities, the stapled photocopies of letters, memos and minutes told a tale. The next few pages will trace some of the highlights of this lengthy exercise.

The initial meeting of June 1986, first took up the housekeeping questions: organizational arrangements, communications and so forth. It then moved on to the long delayed radio-telemetry project in Everglades National Park which at last was drawing near. Another priority agenda item was "to develop a public information strategy." A Game Commission representative "volunteered . . . to prepare a periodic newsletter which would detail the FPIC activities and summarize . . .

information on Florida panther recovery efforts."[2] We will dwell on this informational *tour de force* in Chapter 13.

On page three of the minutes, the Technical Subcommittee got down to editing the draft recovery plan. "The first item discussed was the recovery objective. It was felt important to understand where we are going with regard to panther recovery to properly evaluate research needs and management actions." True enough! The recovery objective given in the draft plan of May 1986, was "maintaining the presently known population in south Florida at its minimum viable population level (MVP), and establishing and maintaining at least two other MVP's within other areas of the former range of the panther." The next step of course was to aim for a number.

> From presently available data, it is not possible to provide a reliable MVP figure for the Florida panther. However, extrapolating from data for another large North American carnivore, the grizzly bear, it seems likely that to insure the survival of the Florida panther it will be necessary to substantially increase its present numbers. A MVP level for the grizzly bear has been estimated at between 40-125 animals, depending on the mortality rate within the population (Suchy, et al., 1985). Based on these estimates for the grizzly bear, the Service believes that for the Florida panther, which seems to have a high mortality rate, a MVP level of about 100 animals per population may be realistic.[3]

By choosing a number, it follows that serious thinking then becomes mandatory about such things as a refuge large enough to hold all the animals, and working out how it is to be managed—the fundamentals of a recovery plan. However, the minutes tell that "several of the subcommittee members took issue with setting a numerical recovery objective before we have identified a minimum viable population estimate."[4] The statement is unclear. As explained in the above offset quotes, the draft recovery plan postulated an MVP estimate. What the author wanted to convey (I presume) is that there was a desire by some, not to extrapolate a panther MVP from a grizzly bear MVP, but rather to apply panther data to a population model which would yield an estimate specifically for panthers. This might have the merit of greater precision and confidence, remembering, of course that an MVP model, while better than a guess, is still a theory to be tested by experience.

However, in the interim some number within the general minimum range of conventional theory could have usefully served as a guide to thinking about, and planning, the real-world solution to keeping panthers alive. For that the figure of 100 would have served; if that figure made someone nervous, then it might have been halved, but with more than 325,000 people a year pouring into Florida, and the land heavily threatened, there was a crying need to quit dithering and to bring the theory down to earth (literally) where it could identify a prospective refuge, or alternately, to make the assessment that panther recovery in southern Florida was unrealistic and to act accordingly. But the minutes inform that "it was agreed by the subcommittee members that the numerical objective would be removed from the recovery plan, and that a new 'research action' would be added to develop a population model and to apply such a model to develop a minimum viable population estimate."[5] (Yet when the recovery plan was completed a year later, there was no MVP estimate. Obviously someone did not want to endure the strain of such a troubling chore.)

Following each meeting, the Fish and Wildlife Service mail-outs, which reported the deliberations, arrived in the mail. They were sequentially numbered beginning with PANTHER INFO-1. PANTHER INFO-2 was a hopeful one. It included a half-inch thick stack of material on deer management techniques. Throughout the PANTHER INFO series it is possible to read the quiet and persistent efforts of the self-effacing types in the Fish and Wildlife Service to promote decisive planning. Time and again the minuted evidence appears; the controversial subjects are broached; the unwelcome questions raised. Time and again these cautious advances come to nothing. The Fish and Wildlife Service does not push; it will not insist. The hints about deer management in PANTHER INFO-2 would be ignored.

One environmental organization that did make some effort to steer the recovery plan in a sensible direction (without success) was Florida Defenders of the Environment. In July Bill Branan wrote John Christian, who was chairing the Technical Subcommittee, complaining that in the June 5 draft the National Park Service had not "stated how it will consider habitat reclamation on the abandoned farm land in the Hole-in-Donut area of ENP." He cited Bob Baker's declaration at the recent panther conference: ". . . policy in the NPS is very flexible . . . the NPS does not close the door on any management option. . . ."[6] In a meeting at the end of July, Branan's letter was taken up and disposed of rather breezily in the minutes, which encapsulate the discussion in a sentence and move on. "The committee discussed Dr. Branan's comment letter on the recovery plan. With reference to item 1 in his letter, the committee believed tasks 1312 and 13121 in the Step Down Outline addressed this point."[7]

That is so; the tasks addressed the point, but the committee evaded the issue. Branan had complained that the subtle shifts of wording in the June draft absolved the National Park Service of its charge to "consider implementing different habitat management techniques," which previously had been written into the May draft.[8] It was altered to read: "NPS will evaluate habitat protection and management actions in south Florida NPS units." In the narrative section that followed and elaborated upon the outline statements, the May draft had read: "to increase the density of deer, it may be necessary to manipulate the habitat to set back succession, using such techniques as selective thinning, clear cutting, burning, and food plots. To determine the effectiveness of each technique, it will be necessary to measure deer density, reproduction, mortality and habitat use, both before and after each technique has been applied." In the June draft the statement was altered as follows: "To perpetuate the natural distribution and abundance of the Florida panther and its primary prey, it will be necessary to evaluate current management, exotic species eradication programs, and habitat restoration programs. These management actions and programs will be adjusted as appropriate to improve panther habitat consistent with other natural resource management objectives."[9]

To the uninitiated these shifts in phrasing, and the fuss being made over them, may seem baffling. Like the subtleties of diplomatic phrasing they require a knowledge of underlying interests. The Technical Subcommittee was shading the wording of the recovery plan with the intensity of diplomats wording a joint communique. Land-management agencies are highly attuned to the kinds of actions that seem to threaten traditions, and of how words relate to those threats. And the sorts of things considered to be threats, though they might be incomprehensible to an outside observer, are clearly defined in the respective departmental catechisms. To the zealously protective personnel of the National Park Service, the shibboleth, "single-species management," and that of "ecosystems management," imply two mutually incompatible concepts; the former is seen as antagonistic to the latter. The logical defects of this ideology were touched on before and need not delay us here. The revised June draft sanctioned the status quo.

There are abandoned farm fields on National Park lands in southern Florida that are no longer in a natural condition. Hole-in-the-Donut in Everglades National Park is only the largest of these. Forage might be planted in them as an experiment to increase deer. However, the Park Service has so far refused to even evaluate the possibility. The old fields are infested with exotic plants that, under the Park Service's doctrine of ecosystems management, must be removed and the sites restored to a condition resembling the original. A costly restoration project was tried in the 1970s but failed, and the overgrown sites were ignored for years. However, "exotic species eradication programs" was nimbly spliced into the recovery plan as a measure "to perpetuate the natural distribution and abundance of the Florida panther and its primary prey."

Six months after the events chronicled above, on January 13 and 14, 1987, a two-day meeting of the Technical Subcommittee convened at Everglades National Park; it was followed on January 15 by a meeting of the four agency heads sitting as the FPIC. The minutes of the FPIC meeting are of interest because they show yet another try by the Fish and Wildlife Service to inject a measure of professionalism into the planning process, by making a presentation on "issue papers" and "peer review." It was proposed that papers should be written to summarize the important issues of panther recovery. The Technical Subcommittee would then make a recommendation on each issue, documenting the reason for doing so. Unfortunately, among the other parties there was a conspicuous lack of enthusiasm for issue papers. I believe only two were written.

The peer review proposal would have had qualified scientists examine the work of the FPIC and offer their comments. The peers would include persons not subject to the biases that blinker agency perspectives. The January minutes summarize the deliberations of the Technical Subcommittee on the subject:

> At the third FPIC Subcommittee meeting held on October 7-8, 1986, committee members discussed the establishment of a peer review group. The peer review group may be composed of both agency experts and those outside the agency. Outside agency review is encouraged. Peer review is important to insure all work, both management and research, is conducted in accordance with the best scientific knowledge currently available. As a result of the discussion, the decision was made not to develop a single peer review group but rather allow each agency to develop their [sic] own peer review process. This would save money and streamline the time allowed for review. The list of peer reviewers would be at each agencies' discretion, and the review would be completed prior to bringing the proposal to the FPIC. When a proposal is presented to the Technical Subcommittee, the agency responsible for the proposal would provide copies of comments from their reviewers. In this way agencies can modify proposals as necessary prior to presenting them to the FPIC.[10]

So there it is. Each agency was to arrange its own peer review—not a procedure likely to avoid biases, but it can be seen that the dedicated officials were constrained to weigh objectivity against the vital factors of time and money; planning should move with all expediency, and public dollars must be committed in the most efficient manner—about which more will be said later. Someone did think to add that the individual agencies should enter copies of the reviewer's comments into the record (I don't believe this was ever done).

The minutes of this meeting tell that panthers recently captured in Everglades National Park for the long-delayed radio-telemetry study were well-nourished and, surprisingly, they did not show the characters that had come to define the Florida panther. None had crooks in the tail, and only one had a cowlick. An implication was that panthers in the park were genetically distinct from all others previously captured; it followed that, by the Game Commission's working definition, these recently examined cats were not Florida panthers.

Now the subspecies conundrum had to be confronted. For two years the Panther Advisory Council had questioned the validity of these characters and the wisdom of adhering to them. The Fish and Wildlife Service duly brought the matter before the Technical Subcommittee in a paper which summarized the origins of the subspecific designation and recounted the adoption of the three characters: the crook in the tail, the cowlick and the white flecks—as the subspecific criterion. The Technical Subcommittee showed a practical bent in closing with this unexpected challenge. "Mr. Christian handed out a discussion paper on the taxonomic issue surrounding the Florida panther. It was agreed to edit the paper, and remove the third paragraph referencing the crook in the tail, the white spots and the cowlick as primary identifying characteristics. This was agreed to by the committee. The paper was redone, and will be sent out as PANTHER INFO-16."[11] Well that problem was out of the way. Or so it seemed at the time. We will revisit this topic in Chapter 7.

A report to the Technical Subcommittee from the Game Commission showed an intent to begin on one of the big challenges in southern Florida—that of the threatened habitat on the private lands north of the Big Cypress National Preserve which was facing conversion to citrus groves. Elsewhere in the minutes of this meeting the Technical Subcommittee was told that a single landowner had applied for a permit to convert 11,500 acres of land to citrus production.[12] The rescue of these lands could not begin too soon.

In 1985 the Panther Advisory Council had urged the Game Commission to draw up a map of critical private lands showing habitat types, ownership patterns and other useful data as a preparatory step in conservation planning. When a year passed without action, Larry Harris, who was trying to advance the cause of wildlife corridors in landscape planning, came to a Panther Advisory Council meeting in October 1986 with an offer to make the map, and seemingly made a favorable impression on Game Commission representatives. Now, in January 1987, the minutes of the Technical Subcommittee imply that the mapping scheme is moving forward: "Mr. Hines outlined several projects that were being discussed at the present time. One is working with Dr. Larry Harris on developing a land use map for Southwest Florida and projecting future development, and the second is working with the Florida Cooperative Research Unit in developing a population model for panthers. He said that a workshop was planned after this year's capture season with the Unit to discuss the modeling effort in more detail."[13] Yet in 1991, the map, which is essential to begin planning, had still not arrived.

In the FPIC meeting that followed that of the Technical Subcommittee, the agency heads heard what reviewers had said about the June draft of the recovery plan. One hundred and twenty copies had been sent out to designated reviewers; 24 of the recipients had responded. Their critiques had been categorized into topics, one being the still-undefined minimum viable population. The discussion was summarized as follows: "Some commentators believed it was essential to arrive at a number now and that such a number should appear in the recovery plan. The decision was made by the Directors to leave a number out of the plan until the panther population model is complete. It was the feeling of the FPIC that this would not detract from the urgency of developing an MVP."[14] The MVP will be taken up in Chapter 19. Suffice it to say, that the FPIC never bestirred itself to develop one.

The agency administrators next heard the reviewers' comments on the touchy subject of natural management versus artificial management: "Some commentors felt a more pro-active type of management needs to be developed for panther habitat on NPS lands. Because of the legislation establishing the Park Service property, the major emphasis will be on the eradication of exotics, encouraging natural succession and suppressing further invasion of exotic vegetation. The FPIC favored this approach as it will benefit the Florida panther and other native species."[15] In this cryptic statement can be read that the National Park Service objected to "artificial management" of National Park Service lands to benefit the panther—claiming that the law prohibited it—and the other FPIC members looked the other way. Those who acquiesced in this statement knew perfectly well that there would be no benefits to the panther.

On the topic of private lands, the FPIC seemed to take the bit in its teeth: "The importance of private lands was strongly emphasized by several commentors. The need for management strategies and habitat protection efforts was stressed. The importance of private lands to the panther is recognized by the FPIC and is evidenced by the fact that current data indicate that possibly up to one-half of the panthers occurring in south Florida presently occupy private lands. Because of this fact the FPIC places high priority on the protection and management of panther habitat occurring on private lands. Special emphasis will be placed on working with these landowners and closely coordinating all recovery efforts with them. A Comprehensive Land Management Plan will be developed for private lands. The cooperation and assistance of all landowners will be vital in the implementation of recovery efforts. All governmental agencies will be requested to utilize their full regulatory authorities and capabilities to ensure that maximum protection is afforded all panther habitat areas."[16] As of this writing, in 1991, there is no plan for private lands and, as repeatedly mentioned above, no map upon which a plan could be based. We will return to this topic in Chapter 17.

The FPIC now surveyed its handiwork and summarized: "It is the feeling of the FPIC that this plan has identified and addressed the issues relative to the panther known at this point in time and has developed practical, achievable recovery strategies based on available data, information, and knowledge."[17] Thus, the FPIC assured itself that it had done good. In March 1987, when the final draft of the recovery plan was again sent out for review, I began an exchange of lengthy letters with James Pulliam, the regional director of the Fish and Wildlife Service, sounding off about the fatal flaws in the recovery plan.[18,19,20] Of course this had no effect at all.

On June 22, 1986, the four leading bureaucrats of the FPIC met at White Oak Plantation and affixed signatures to their indecisive product. Four days later the momentous event was announced to the world in an FPIC news release.

INTERAGENCY COMMITTEE ADOPTS PLAN TO SAVE FLORIDA PANTHER

(YULEE, FLA.) —The Florida Panther Interagency Committee has approved a revised "Recovery Plan" that outlines what needs to be done to save Florida's state animal from extinction.

At a meeting here June 22, the committee also pledged full involvement and cooperation of two Florida State agencies, Florida Game and Fresh Water Fish Commission and Florida Department of Natural Resources, and two bureaus of the U. S. Department of the Interior, National Park Service and U. S. Fish and Wildlife Service, in the effort to save the panther.

Committee Chairman James W. Pulliam Jr., Southeast Regional Director of the U.S. Fish and Wildlife Service, said the Recovery Plan was revised to incorporate key comments received from the public and conservation organizations over the past seven months.

Pulliam said the plan "will serve as a blueprint for action by the four agencies and other groups and individuals to insure a future for the panther. . . ."

Robert Baker, Southeast Regional Director of the National Park Service, said, "The Florida panther serves as a symbol of the fragility of the ecosystems upon which people depend. Maintaining that natural system, restoring it, and the Florida panther which depends on it, will guarantee that the public will be able to enjoy the Florida panther and other wildlife-related uses associated with its habitat into the future.

The news release went on to tout a bold, new step by the FPIC: a resolution asking the State Legislature to change the name of Alligator Alley to Panther Parkway.[21]

Try, Try Again

The bureaucrats were ballyhooing an emasculated document which could not possibly lead to recovery—at least not in southern Florida, home of the only known panthers. But I was unwilling to give up. Hope dimmed with each passing day, but there were so many things that might be tried, at least tentatively, on an exploratory or experimental basis, if only a way could be found around the vast and imposing incapacities of the FPIC. I met with Bill Branan to plot where we might go next. We decided on a two-pronged tactic. The recovery plan had to be reviewed annually. My chore would be to stimulate letters to Florida's congressional delegation in the hope of pressuring the Fish and Wildlife Service to put some substance into the plan. We will see the outcome of this venture later. Branan for his part would initiate a legal review of the National Park Service's oft-repeated claim that the law forbad it practicing single-species management. He began by writing Bob Baker to draw out the official position. He asked for specific passages from the enabling legislation that prevented single species management for an endangered species.[22]

The answer came a month later:

Dear Bill:

In your recent letter you requested that I provide you with specific legislation that prevents single species management for endangered species and artificial planting.

The National Park Service is committed to ecosystem management. This mission is not unlike the emphasis provided in Section 2(b) of the Endangered Species Act which states: "The purposes of this Act are to provide a means whereby the ecosystems upon which endangered species and threatened species depend may be conserved, to provide a program for the conservation of such species. . . ."

The National Park Service Organic Act, 16 U.S.C. Sec. 1 et seq., remains after 70 years the definitive statement of the National

Park Service's mission, of the purposes of the parks, and is the core of its authority. That mission is "to conserve the scenery and the natural and historic objects and the wild life therein . . . in such a manner and by such means as will leave them unimpaired for the enjoyment of future generations." In 1970 Congress amended the Organic Act to affirm that unless Congress specified otherwise for a particular park unit, all park units were to be governed under the same mission. Moreover, the legislative history of the 1978 amendment to the Organic Act states: "The protection of the units of the [National Park] system is to be carried out in accordance with the maintenance of the integrity of the system, and management of these areas shall not compromise these resource values except as Congress may have specifically provided." (H. Rep. No. 95-581, p.21).

National Park Service management policies (Chapter IV-6) require that, "The Service will perpetuate the native animal life of the parks for their essential role in the natural ecosystems. Such management . . . will strive to maintain the natural abundance, behavior, diversity, and ecological integrity of native animals in natural portions of parks as part of the parks ecosystems."

The policy of the National Park Service was reaffirmed by Congress in the Act of December 2, 1980. The Senate report (96-416, page 171) accompanying Law 96-487 addressed this issue on a Servicewide basis as follows:

"The National Park System concept requires implementation of management policies which strive to maintain the natural abundance, behavior, diversity, and ecological integrity of native animals as part of their ecosystem, and the committee intends that concept is maintained."

Single species management that artificially alters the carrying capacity or results in game farming is generally inconsistent with the 1916 Organic Act. Special interest or protection of endangered species through closures and restrictive human access are generally appropriate to favor the recovery of an endangered species to its natural carrying capacity. Artificial plantings are in conflict with management policy to "maintain the natural abundance . . . and ecological integrity of native animals as part of their ecosystem. . . ."

Bill, I understand your concern but I feel that the interrelation-ships between the panther, the deer populations, and other resource management programs must be carefully evaluated and balanced in light of the overall ecological integrity, policy and compliance.

Sincerely,
[signed] C. W. Ogle
for Robert M. Baker[23]

Branan turned the letter over to Richard Hamann, an FDE legal expert. Hamann, who works at the Center for Governmental Responsibility at the University of Florida, assigned a student, John Tucker, to the project. Their study of 33 pages was finished in October 1987. It concluded as follows:

Legally, there are few impediments to imaginative habitat man-agement to restore the endangered Florida panther. The National Park Service has the power and the duty to act affirmatively under both its enabling legislation and the Endangered Species Act. The organic statutes of the NPS, ENP, and BCNP require the preservation of native flora and fauna. The ESA mandates that the NPS act affirmatively to conserve the endangered panther using any and all methods that will benefit the panther. The ESA takes precedence over the primary mission of any agency. These interpretations are supported by the courts.

The real issue is whether the NPS will adopt a more flexible affirmative role in effectuating the panther's recovery. The NPS is not being asked to abandon its management policy. Rather, it is being asked to recognize the limitations of that policy in a world of shrinking wildlife habitat and make appropriate adjustments. NPS management policies have taken this unfortunate environ-mental development into account in other places, for other species.

The law, public interest, and scientific study all support the conclusion that the NPS can and must act soon to save the panther. Habitat management of Brazilian pepper offers one expedient method of management since the land has already been significantly altered. However, other affirmative conservation actions must also be considered and implemented.[24]

124

Bill Branan posted this paper to the regional office of the National Park Service in Atlanta, under the cover of a tactfully worded letter: ". . . [Florida Defenders of the Environment] trust that this document will help the National Park Service manage more aggressively for deer and panther. . . ."[25] But the National Park Service was not helped at all by this scholarly instrument; it only wanted to manufacture a legal defense for its bias; it is as tenaciously adverse to change as ever.

It was around this time that I read, in thumbing through a copy of *National Parks* magazine, that a former superintendent of Everglades National Park had been named the winner of the prestigious Stephen P. Mather Award, given each year by the National Parks and Conservation Association. He had, the article said, "exhibited the combination of dedication and daring that was highly valued by the first director of the National Park Service, for which the award is named." The recipient of this bureaucratic medal-of-honor was the same individual who had delayed radio-telemetry research at Everglades National Park. The article said that the $1,000 cash prize was presented annually to an individual who had "demonstrated initiative and resourcefulness" and "taken direct action where others hesitated . . . possibly risking both job and career in the process." Listed among his several accomplishments was the formation of the Interagency Panther Advisory Council [sic] to help protect the endangered Florida panther.[26]

At the end of July 1986, a Game Commission news release opened as follows:

BATTLE TO SAVE PANTHERS RAGES ON TWO FRONTS

The Game and Fresh Water Fish Commission's wildlife biologists are battling on two fronts to save Florida panthers from the threat of extinction. Their foe is time. The battlefields are south Florida and White Oak Plantation, near Jacksonville [site of the so-called captive breeding project which will be discussed in Chapter 7.][27]

This has been the immutable pattern. The land-management agencies will not come to grips with the core issues and instead paste them over with inane news releases to assuage public opinion. Innovative and meaningful ideas are ignored, avoided or squelched. Those who maneuver to uphold the status quo are given awards. Words and forms triumph over substance. The Florida panther recovery program has been a masterpiece of bureaucratic art.

Chapter 6

INBREEDING, OUTBREEDING AND THE SUBSPECIES QUESTION

The practical aims of taxonomy demand that the subdivisions of the species, where such exist, be well-limited and well-defined units.The picture of the species, as presented by the taxonomist, is, however, not necessarily a very accurate rendering of the situation as it exists in nature.It is merely due to the need of the museum worker to identify every individual and to place it in a definite pigeonhole.

Ernst Mayr
Systematics and the Origin of Species

Why is so much time and money spent trying to nurse an apparently inbred remnant of a panther population to recovery, when cats of the same species could, within a matter of weeks, be trucked in from the West and released—quite economically. Are there compelling reasons to keep the Florida panther "pure," or should we compromise and "outbreed"—mix a little of some other subspecies to improve the inbred stock? This issue may be one of the most confusing to laymen. It may also be confusing to some officials who are supposed to have informed opinions. Ask representatives of different agencies about outbreeding, and a variety of opinions is guaranteed. Biases come into play, and there is a tricky legal question to be answered. All officials with a responsibility to think through the ramifications of the problem and formulate an opinion, or at least to define the terms for an informed debate, may not have done so. The pages that follow will try to make this question, which is perhaps a vital one, plain to the non-biologist.

Classification Explored

For background we must review some aspects of taxonomy and genetics, and the permutations that give rise to species and subspecies. Every large organization requires a filing system to arrange in an orderly fashion the information essential to its operations. Similarly, any system of thought, or any intellectual discipline, must systematically arrange its subject material before it can be used to expand knowledge. And so it was that the earth's vast array of organisms required a scheme of organization before an understanding of them could move forward.

Some organisms, while they are obviously different, can be grouped into a common category by similarities of form. A lion, a tiger and a lynx are plainly cats, each of a distinct type. Oaks are of different kinds, but all belong to a category of tree distinguished by the production of acorns. However, it was not always clear that the entire spectrum of living things could be understood by a single system. History records several attempts to solve the riddle before success came, in 1758, to a Swedish botanist named Carl Linnaeus. He found a solution by arranging all categories of living things in strata of descending order, beginning with the broadest and grouping each subsequent level according to traits in common. He assigned to this hierarchy, terms from the political organization of his day. All organisms belonged to one great empire. This empire of life comprised two kingdoms: one of plants, the other of animals. (Linnaeus also assigned the non-living substances of the world to a third kingdom—that of the minerals.)

The ranks were named. Phyla were at the top, divided into classes. A class was split into orders, orders into families and families into genera. Each genus was separated into the basic units of the system: species—the living, reproducing forms. To illustrate: several species of cats, including the lion, tiger and leopard, have been grouped into the genus *Panthera*, because of a likeness in body structure—even though the outward appearance of each one is strikingly distinctive. Linnaeus assigned the great American unspotted cat to the genus *Felis*, where it is in company with the bobcat, the lynx and several others, and named it *concolor*. All were placed in the family of cats. The name of an organism is given combined as the genus and the species, called the binomial. The binomial of the African lion for example is *Panthera leo*.

Elements of Linnaeus' system had been devised by others; it was his genius to synthesize them into a whole. The concept of the binomial had been previously advanced by Caspar Bauhin in 1623, as an improvement on the medieval practice of naming plants by linking together a series of descriptive Latin words.[1] This point is made to explain why, as discussed in an earlier chapter, *Felis concolor* had several binomials before Linnaeus' designation came into use. Linnaeus called each level of his system a taxon—taxa in the plural. Thus, the study of the classification of living things is known as taxonomy. The system of Linnaeus was sound and, with modifications, is still in use.

A century later Charles Darwin hit upon the general mode by which species have come to differ from one another. In 1831, Darwin, who at age 23 was blessed with good social connections, received an invitation to join a globe-circling scientific expedition aboard the brig, HMS Beagle. Early in the voyage a fertile seed-bed for novel ideas was readied in his mind when he began reading a currently popular book on geology. The author, Charles Lyell, advanced the then shocking theory that the earth's landforms had not been shaped by Noah's flood, as was

127

popularly supposed, but very gradually by the same natural forces presently at work: rain, wind, volcanoes, and so on. The alterations had gone unnoticed because the forces acted at so slow a rate that the effect was not apparent in the time-scale of human experience. In Argentina, Darwin discovered fossils of vertebrate animals from the remote past—the remains of species no longer extant, yet closely resembling living forms. It seemed to him from this evidence that organisms might change through the ages. However, the then popular belief about fossils was that they represented creatures that had unaccountably missed getting aboard Noah's ark and so had perished in the biblical flood.

In 1835 the Beagle arrived in the Galapagos Islands, a volcanic archipelago 500 miles off the western coast of South America. The islands would prove to be a workshop of evolutionary trends, illustrated by stark example. For instance, two kinds of large lizard were found; similarity of body structure indicated both were of the same genus, but they could not have been more different in habit. One lived on land; the other was a seagoing type which fed on submerged marine plants. The finches of the islands were even more striking. Darwin collected several. He saw the similitude of all forms, and yet observed that they could be classed into graduated types based on size and on the shape and size of beak. "Seeing this graduation and diversity of structure in one small, intimately related group of birds," he wrote, "one might really fancy that from an original paucity of birds in this archipelago, one species had been taken and modified for different ends."[2] Darwin learned from an official in the islands that the tortoises of the Galapagos, all of which were remarkable for great size, differed slightly in appearance from one island to another. He also noted that all the animals he observed resembled types found on the South American mainland.

Two additional ideas shaped Darwin's thinking. In 1838 he gained an insight into population growth when reading "An Essay on the Principle of Population" by Thomas Malthus. The author pointed out by historical illustration that the human population tended to expand at an ever-increasing rate and would overrun the earth if not held in check by war, famine and disease. It occurred to Darwin that the same principle of expansion applied, not just to humans but to all populations. But the multitudes were plainly held in check. Secondly, he was aware of the principle of selection in breeding domestic animals. The breeder selected generation by generation the characters he wanted in a new stock. The Galapagos fauna hinted that something of the sort must happen in nature. It appeared that the natural environment functioned as the selector of traits. Since the characteristics of all individuals vary somewhat, some will be favored over others in the intense competition to survive. Darwin called this winnowing, "natural selection." Nature continuously selected from among the many born only the fittest to survive. Over a great span of time, new species might originate through a sifting by nature for minor differences. Darwin could not divine the actual mechanics of variation; they

would not come to light until the turn of the century although, ironically, investigations were being conducted by a contemporary of Darwin's, an Austrian monk named Gregor Mendel.

Mendel observed variations of form in garden pea plants. Some plants were six feet tall; others rarely exceeded 18 inches. Some seeds were smooth and round; others were wrinkled. Some peas were yellow; while others were green. Mendel kept meticulous records on the kind and percentage of thousands of characters that appeared in succeeding generations of experimentally grown plants. When a plant with round seeds was cross-pollinated with one that produced wrinkled seeds, the plants of the second generation all had round seeds. However, when the plants of the second generation were self-pollinated, wrinkled seeds turned up in 25 percent of the third generation; the remaining 75 percent of the later seeds were again round and smooth. From hundreds of similar experiments Mendel observed that physical characters can be masked in one generation and reappear in the next.

Concluding that physical characters in individuals were controlled by factors that were either dominant or recessive, he proposed what would become known as the first law of inheritance: *characters are controlled by pairs of factors which do not blend during life and which pass into separate cells during reproductive processes prior to fertilization.* The pair of factors controlling each character may consist of two dominants or two recessives, or a mix—a dominant factor paired with a recessive one. The pairs split apart during the formation of sex cells, so each sex cell contains either one dominant or one recessive for each character. When the sex cells from two parents combine, the resulting embryo contains the randomly recombined dominants and recessives. If two recessive factors are joined together, the physical character expressed in the new plant will be the recessive one. A joining of two dominant factors gives rise to the dominant character. And the dominant character is also expressed by the union of a dominant with a recessive.

The advances of science in the first half of the twentieth century refined our understanding of a process that Mendel could only perceive indirectly. The "factors" of inheritable characteristics are called genes; they are arranged on elongate structures called chromosomes. When the sperm and egg—the sex cells of animals—are formed, each chromosome divides along its length and takes half the genes into the sex cell. Thus, each sperm or egg contains half the individual's complement of genes. When sperm and egg unite, chromosomes recombine, joining pairs of genes in various dominant-recessive combinations. In humans the gene for brown eyes is dominant; the gene for blue eyes is recessive. A brown-eyed couple, provided each one has the recessive, blue-eyed gene will tend to produce offspring at a ratio of three brown-eyed to one with blue.

Within-species Classification

Linnaeus followed the popular theological view of his day in believing that all the earth's species then extant had been distinct and unchanging since the creation. Darwin upset this theological convention when he showed in 1859 that one species can give rise to another. In doing so he caused a controversy which hasn't died away yet, but the offended view of creation was actually a late historical development among the thinkers of Christendom. Thomas Aquinus, the medieval theologian, had believed that new species were being created all the time —though not by evolution.[3]

Darwin's insights introduced to Linnaeus' scheme a complication. Species were no longer seen as fixed in time, but as forms that could be modified by a changed environment. Thus, individuals of a species of finch from the South American mainland, carried by rare accident on winds to the Galapagos Islands, a distance adequate to insure no further interbreeding with mainland birds, could, over many generations be modified by an unaccustomed environment into several new forms, similar in appearance yet recognizably different. Linnaeus knew that the individuals of a species sometimes varied in appearance. Later taxonomists could see that widespread species varied somewhat from region to region. As early as 1844 ornithologists devised the trinomial to denominate the geographical variations of form within bird species. Thus a third name w as added to the specific binomial; and in this manner subspecies came into being (in botany the term "variety" became the name used for variations within species). Darwin's subsequent demonstration that species can change through selection, by adapting to differing environments, gave rise to new ways of looking at geographical variation. It implied localized adaptations to different conditions, and also perhaps that the variants represented early stages in the evolution of new species.

As is often the case with innovations, the subspecies concept provoked immediate opposition when it was introduced in the 1840s.[4] However, by the late 1800s the idea had become accepted by enough scientists to give it an aura of legitimacy. The subsequent enthusiasm with which the search for subspecies was pursued carried it overboard, so that slight differences of form among a few specimens often led to the describing of a new subspecies. In retrospect it can be seen that many of these designations were often hasty.

Panther Taxonomy

The terms "splitters" and "lumpers" arose in the argot of taxonomy to distinguish professionals with a proneness to split species into many types based on slight variations, as against those with more conservative leanings. It was during

this phase of interest in finding subspecies that Charles Cory first described the Florida panther as such—based on observations of a few specimens from southern Florida. As related earlier, Cory dubbed the Florida panther *Felis concolor floridana* in 1896. Three years later the name was changed by Outram Bangs to *Felis coryi*, thereby elevating it to the rank of a species. A year following Cory's description the name *Felis hippolestes* was applied to a form in the western United States, and a western subspecies was designated as *Felis hippolestes olympus*.[5]

In 1901 C. Hart Merriam gathered all available specimens and made the first attempt to impose taxonomic order on puma classification. He distinguished six species of eleven "forms." The early disparity of views on how to categorize the puma is perhaps a reflection on the tenuous nature of taxonomic methods at the turn of the century. Merriam added a seventh species in 1903; yet another was described from Baja California in 1912, and a further one from Ecuador in 1913.[6]

In 1929 Merriam's classification was revised to accommodate the findings of the previous 28 years. The authors of the new revision, Edward Nelson and Edward Goldman, reduced Merriam's several species to one, within which they recognized 19 subspecies. Specimens continued to accumulate in museums, many of them from government predator control programs which had by now become pervasively institutionalized in the American West.

In 1946 this accumulated material prompted yet another revision by Goldman, now working with a colleague named Stanley Young. Their classification, the most recent, left us with a definition of the Florida panther which is still in use. Young and Goldman had examined a great many specimens; some were skulls without skins; others were skins without skulls.[7] The authors found that skull measurements provided more consistency of regional characters than skins, which varied widely. It was for this reason that the investigators relied primarily on skulls."[8] It cannot be known to what extent the subspecific boundaries drawn by Young and Goldman represent the actual variation in appearance of pumas at the time of uninterrupted distribution. The spotty arrangement and uneven abundance of specimens left much to be desired when designing a classification system for subspecies.

Implications of Genetic Diversity

There is no inherent sanctity in the division of subspecies that has come down to us. The important thing to understand is that many of the minor differences observed from region to region in a widespread species are an indication that the environment has been at work in each respective region, selecting characters that best adapt the individuals to a local setting. Observable differences therefore reflect

regional genetic variation that cannot be seen. Terms have been coined to distinguish between the visible characters and the purely genetic ones. The observable characters are collectively called the "phenotype," while the term "genotype" refers to the constituency of genes in an individual. Today several methods are available through biochemistry and statistical procedures that can be used to supplement observations of the phenotype as a means of gauging variation in organisms. Some of these methods offer glimpses into the genotype. None is unambiguous in describing genetic heterogeneity, but collectively they are far more sophisticated than the methods available to Young and Goldman.

It should be known that there are two fundamentally different contexts in which subspecies occur. In the best-defined cases, subspecies have become geographically isolated from one another, so that interbreeding between the isolates is no longer possible. Here it may be expected that eventually evolutionary divergence would render them incapable of interbreeding, at which time they would be rated as distinct species. More problematical are species distributed continuously across a broad land mass. These usually show localized differences that invite subspecific classification, and yet there may not be clearly defined boundaries between the differing types.

The term "cline" was proposed by Julian Huxley in 1938 to describe a gradation of characters in widespread species. Huxley had in mind a variety of clinal dimensions: geoclines, ecoclines, etc., but the term has settled on the geographic meaning and implies a uniform rather than an irregular change in characters.[9] However, it has been recognized today that, at least in some animals, there may be localized differences in behavior or ecology which do not coincide with differences in appearance, but which may also reflect a difference in genotype. Consequently, the study of non-morphological characters has become significant in the study of subspecies.

These multiplying complications in devising a within-species classification system have led to the suggestion that the primary use of subspecies today is as a sorting device in museum collections.[10] It can arrange observable physical distinctions as a starting point for the study of less obvious traits. A growing understanding of genetics has illustrated that not all variation within a species is readily seen. However, it has also brought an awareness that perceptible distinctions are related to genetic variation, and so the subspecific classifications of an earlier time may still have their uses in an endangered species strategy.

Inbreeding

Genetics can explain the danger of inbreeding. Some recessive genes can be harmful if expressed. A few rare genes are lethal in combination. Certain

aggregates of recessive genes can also be lethal, or at least damaging, subjecting the individuals who inherit them to a degree of risk. Hemophilia, congenital blindness and a suppressed immune system are only a few of the severe possibilities. The deleterious effects of other recessives may be more subtle.

A large population, in most instances, will contain an immense variety within its pool of genes. Individuals born into the population are allocated by chance a sample selection from the total pool. Those favored by combinations that fit them well for survival tend to pass the genes on to the next generation. Chance combinations not favorable, or less favorable, to survival tend more often to be lost when the unfortunate individuals who inherit them perish. When a population is greatly diminished, many genes from the total pool can be lost permanently, because there no longer will be enough remaining animals to harbor them all. This dwindling of genetic assets can put the population at risk for several reasons.

First is the question of what happens to the lethal genes which lurk in every population. Chance may dictate that they be expelled by the death of the individuals carrying them, but if they survive as recessives they will begin to reappear with increasing frequency. If they become "fixed" in a small population they can precipitate extinction. Deleterious recessive genes may also become fixed, and even if early extinction is avoided, the "fitness" of the population can be reduced; the degree will depend on the kinds and combinations of recessives that become fixed, and on the vagaries of a given environment. In a demanding environment, lowered fitness can precipitate a plunge to oblivion. In more stable surroundings the same population might persist longer—perhaps for centuries in the most favorable case. Population size, however, also becomes a key to survival when fitness is compromised; a very small inbred population like the Florida panther would be at greater risk than a large one—all other things being equal.

The loss of genetic diversity means that the environment has fewer combinations of genes from which to select when randomly determining who will survive. Drastic change in an environment, such as a severe climatic shift, can impose a fatal penalty on a population unsecured by an abundance of dissimilar genes that might cope with such emergencies. And there are other hazards. New strains of pathogenic viruses and bacteria can take a toll on a population that fails to offer adaptive combinations which could survive. Five of the world's 60 remaining Javan rhinoceroses suddenly perished from an unknown disease in 1982.[11]

The cheetah has demonstrated the effects of this weakness. A viral infection called feline infectious peritonitis has been devastating to captive cheetahs, although in colonies of domestic cats it seldom kills more than 10 percent. The cheetah's genetic condition has only recently been discovered. The difficulty

of breeding cheetahs in captivity has been a perplexing problem for centuries. The Philadelphia Zoo was the first to successfully produce a litter in 1956, but even following this feat, the subsequent successful reproduction by adults caught in the wild was only 10 to 15 percent. Mating attempts often failed, and even when they were consummated, conception rates were low with infant mortality high. In 1971 a cheetah-breeding facility was built in Pretoria, South Africa, and in ten years became the world's most successful; but even there, infant mortality was 37 percent.[12]

An intensive biomedical investigation of cheetahs was launched in the 1980s, finding 71 percent of the sperm to be abnormal. It is known that the average in domestic cats is 29 percent, and that in domestic bulls a 10 to 20 percent abnormality can cause infertility or sterility. Genetic sampling showed a startling fact: the cheetah had virtually no diversity. Nearly every gene pair was either dominant or recessive; there were few mixed combinations. Prior to the work on the cheetah, some 250 wildlife species had been searched for genetic diversity. Levels varied, but the genetic uniformity of the cheetah had previously been observed only in intensively inbred laboratory mice.[13]

A likely explanation for this condition is that, for reasons unknown, cheetahs were long ago reduced to a low number, perhaps more than once. Loss of genetic diversity is not only the outcome of an extreme reduction in numbers, but also of the length of time the population remains low, prolonging the effects of inbreeding. This low point of reduction, followed by expansion, is known as a genetic bottleneck. The subsequently enlarged population exhibits an altered gene pool with a reduced variation—perhaps extremely so as with the cheetah; it is unusually susceptible to some diseases and has difficulties with reproduction not ordinarily seen in other species.

The cheetah survives, however, in spite of its impairment. Survival may be favored by its relative abundance and wide distribution—which buffers the population against threats that might arise in a particular locale, and perhaps also because the cat inhabits a stable environment. Estimates of cheetah numbers vary widely from 2,000 to 25,000.[14] It is distributed across the length of Africa, one of the most naturally stable terrestrial environments on earth. The Continent's southerly latitude and high plateau spared it the ice age ravages of climatic extreme and submergence. Its spectacular wildlife represents the most impressive remnant of the earth's Pleistocene fauna.

Whereas the highly inbred cheetah showed 72 percent of sperm to be abnormal, the Florida panther has showed over 96 percent abnormalities. Several male panthers examined since 1984 have exhibited a deformity in which one testicle does not descend properly into the scrotum. The retained testicle generally

atrophies and is sterile. This condition, known as cryptorchidism, is controlled by a recessive gene. The malformed sperm are also probably genetically influenced. Both traits create suspicion of long inbreeding, as would be expected in such a shrunken population. There is as yet (in 1988) no solid evidence that inbreeding in the Florida panther has caused the kinds of problems seen in the cheetah. But fatal genetic impairments could be present; prolonged inbreeding in a small population should always warrant the greatest concern.

Preliminary tests have measured genetic diversity in the Florida panther. Cats from Florida were compared with populations from California, Oregon, Texas and with zoo animals. Of these, genetic variation was lowest in the Florida population, although it did not approach the extreme condition of the cheetah, and was highest in the zoo animals, as expected. In zoos, individuals from widely separated geographic regions are often bred indiscriminately. A single puma from Arizona was tested and showed less variation than the Florida panther. However, a sample of one is not a reliable indicator.

All these findings are tentative and await the outcome of work planned for the future.[15] But testing aside, common sense should caution that the panther may be breeding itself into extinction, and when genetic calamity comes there may be little time for preventive action. The total number of Florida panthers is not believed to exceed 30—a figure low enough to anticipate extinction through inbreeding. The panthers may have been in this diminished state for several decades. There is a clear responsibility to take preventive measures.

Outbreeding

An antidote to loss through inbreeding is by outbreeding. Outbreeding can increase genetic variation by breeding with another subspecies. The offspring may then be better prepared to deal with the slings and arrows of environmental fortune. Three concerns arise when considering outbreeding. The first involves a legal question and a precedent set by another endangered subspecies. The seaside sparrow inhabits coastal marshes of the Atlantic and Gulf coasts of the United States. One subspecies, the dark-hued "dusky," was confined to a single county in Florida. It once nested in the thousands but waned with its deteriorating habitat in the 1960s. In the 1970s the small bird became the intended beneficiary of one of the nation's first recovery programs, but the sparrow population plummeted, and by the late 1970s no females could be found. In 1980 the remaining five males were brought into captivity, and a last-ditch effort was proposed to save the bird by outbreeding with females from another subspecies. By subsequently backbreeding with the offspring much of the remaining genetic material could have been preserved in a reconstituted subspecies. However, solicitors in the U. S. Department of Interior in 1977 issued a legal opinion that "hybrids" are not condoned by the

provisions of the Endangered Species Act.[16] Thus loss of funding and moral support from the federal government reared up as an obstacle at a critical moment.[17] The dusky story will be detailed later. The legal opinion is merely a convention which in theory can be overcome, but then that can be said of most obstacles in the Florida panther recovery program, and in some others as well.

The second concern has to do with the phenomenon of outbreeding depression. As previously explained, inbreeding can cause a loss of vigor, fertility and disease resistance, with fatal consequences for a small population. These defects can be countered through outbreeding. However, there have been demonstrated instances of loss of fitness following outbreeding. It is known today that genotypes may differ enough between some distant subspecies to harm the offspring if the distant forms are mated. This is called outbreeding depression. A well-known case involved some ibex reintroduced to Czechoslovakia from Austria to replace a herd that had been hunted to extinction. The reintroduction seemed to work, until additional ibex from Turkey and Sinai were brought in. The mature offspring from crosses with the latter arrivals had an altered breeding time. They gave birth to young during the coldest month of the year. Soon all were gone.[18] Thus it is prudent to take precautions when outbreeding. But if a population has been reduced to a small size, the genotype may have been altered to a detrimental, perhaps fatal, degree. Under such circumstances outbreeding would be provident, if it can be done without creating the hazards alluded to above.

The third concern has to do with identifying the most suitable animals from which to select outbreeding stock. It is generally assumed that populations geographically closest to the one threatened are genetically closer than more distant ones, particularly if the animals live in the same latitude and in a similar habitat. But this is no more than a rule of thumb. The descriptions by Young and Goldman suggest *F. c. stanleyana* as the existing subspecies of closest resemblance. Therefore it becomes a candidate. There is an another possibility: the animals from the Piper collection which have been retained by Robert Baudy.

Defining the Florida Panther

As explained earlier, at the formative meeting on panther recovery in March 1976 there was a lively debate on how many panthers remained. Estimates ranged from a possible high of 300, based on sighting reports, to an opinion of none. The ensuing quest to learn if the rediscovered panthers were "real" Florida panthers was driven by the practical criterion of funding. A research and management program for an elusive, wide-ranging animal like the panther is expensive. In 1976 it ran on a shoestring budget of donated money. The most promising source of long-range support was the Fish and Wildlife Service. If that agency judged that a state's proposal for conserving endangered species met certain criteria under the Endan-

gered Species Act, it could make the state eligible for federal grants that might defray as much as three-fourths of the cost.[19]

So the question of the validity of the subspecies was one of great importance. Early on, Chris Belden sent a letter to the regional office of the Fish and Wildlife Service outlining the uncertainties and asking for guidance. From Atlanta the query was forwarded to the Washington Office for a decision. The answer was a refreshingly unbureaucratic directive to get on with the work: ". . . there is a continuous chain of specimen records and documented information from the nineteenth century to the present to demonstrate that the panther has existed all along in Florida. In such a situation there is no reasonable choice except to assume that we still have the original unmodified population."[20] Nevertheless, the question remained hanging in the air with all its vital implications intact. There was, I believe, a desire on the part of most of us present, even the doubters, to find verifiable Florida panthers; a devil's advocacy was not encouraged. So from the beginning there was an uncritical stimulus to define the features of a Florida panther.

Momentum gathered slowly, as narrated in an earlier chapter. The first priority was to find panthers. By 1978 tangible evidence of the cats was collected in the Fakahatchee Strand. Early in 1978 a specimen came to hand, when a tip-off led a wildlife officer to an illegal kill in a Homestead ice plant. Chris Belden noticed on this specimen, and later on others, the white flecking on the upper neck which had been noteworthy to Outram Bangs in the 1890s. Belden found two other characters not mentioned by Bangs: a crook in the end of the tail and a whorl of hair or "cowlick" on the back.

In fiscal year 1980-1981 the Game Commission contracted with Laurie Wilkins, a museum technician at the Florida State Museum in Gainesville, to investigate a large number of puma skins in museum collections in a search for comparative characteristics among the various subspecies. By this time, panther mortalities and the immobilizations for radio-telemetry research were making additional specimens available for examination. Wilkins and Belden prepared a paper on the investigation in 1982. It was based on an examination of 480 *Felis concolor* skins in museum collections, 24 of which were Florida panther specimens. The remaining 449 skins represented 19 of the 30 recognized subspecies from North, Central and South America. The study included seven panthers captured for radio-collaring. All were checked for white flecking, the cowlick and the crooked tail. The report found that:

> . . . *F.c.coryi*, however, has three distinctive characteristics that are being expressed in addition to the general appearance of the skull and pelage coloration (both of which are variable). These

are the white flecks on the shoulder, neck, and head region; a mid-dorsal whorl; and a crook in the end of the tail. Although these characteristics occur randomly in individuals of other subspecies, only in *F.c.coryi* do they occur in combination. This combination of traits make the Florida population distinctive and it is possible to make a conclusive identification based on a combination of skeletal and pelage characters or with assurance on the pelage alone. This can be especially important to researchers and law enforcement officials considering the large number of animals currently in captivity (which occasionally escape or are released). Only animals exhibiting these characteristics should be used in a captive breeding program for the subspecies should such a program be deemed necessary.

Data obtained in this study suggested that the flecks, whorl, and crooked tail are carried in the gene pool of the species at a low frequency but are expressed at a high frequency in the Florida population, probably due to isolation. The flecks and crooked tail appear to be fixed in the population whereas the whorl is not. The presence of the whorl in four infants while it was absent in the mother suggest that it is a dominant rather then a recessive trait however.

Although this study was intended to provide a more detailed description of the little-known subspecies, *F.c.coryi*, and not a taxonomic analysis or review, it does point out the need for a through taxonomic review of the species based on modern techniques and adequate sample sizes. . . . [21]

Thus, at the beginning of the 1980s, the white flecks on the hind neck and shoulders, the mid-dorsal whorl of hair (cowlick) and the crook in the end of the tail—came to officially describe a Florida panther.[22] A vital question had been laid to rest, or so it was thought. The definition would in fact prove to be too hasty and simple a solution.

Subspecies Criteria Questioned

At the first Panther Advisory Council meeting in September 1983, a member, John Eisenberg, brought a new perspective to the deliberations on the subspecies question. He immediately raised the threat posed by inbreeding and mentioned the legal barrier to outbreeding that could arise from a convention of legitimacy growing up around certain external characters—which he thought had a shaky taxonomic justification. This altered perspective and challenge of assump-

tions illustrates the value of expert, independent technical review. The recovery team had understood that visible characters could be the expressions of recessive genes. However, the motivation of the time left little room for skepticism. The need to define the subspecies was prompted by the suspicion that panthers in the Florida wilds might be escaped or released captive animals. By the early 1980s over 1,000 captive pumas were held in Florida, and the Southeast Coast was known to be a "hot spot" for dealers in exotic animals.[23] The desire to "prove" that panthers in the wild were indeed the native stock had dominated thinking on the subject. And even more fundamental matters pressed for attention at that period, such as proving the creatures actually existed, then getting radio-telemetry underway (including overcoming opposition to it) and nursing the program along on a trickle of funds. An awareness of inbreeding risks had not pervaded agency thinking to the extent that it since has (although it has yet to penetrate in some cases).

In the late 1970s and early 1980s the field of conservation biology was taking form. It came about through advances in the understanding of genetics, coupled with a growing anxiety in some scientific circles about the isolation of reduced wildlife populations. The new discipline was grappling with the question of how to preserve organisms under such duress. There was a lag between the emerging concepts and their dissemination to the field of management. John Eisenberg had served for a decade as assistant director of the National Zoo, where he was unavoidably attuned to inbreeding problems and in a position to follow developments in genetics. He had also contributed a chapter in the first volume to appear on the subject of conservation biology in 1980.[24] The view he brought to the recovery program from these experiences was a valuable one.

In 1986, as told in an earlier chapter, I worked with Bill Branan of Florida Defenders of the Environment to organize a conference on the Florida panther. One issue we wanted to cover was the newly raised one of taxonomic status and the legalities of outbreeding. Richard Hamann of the University of Florida Law School, and a Florida Defender's trustee, was asked to research the legal aspects. The question put to a panel at the conference was: is it possible or desirable to introduce genes into the Florida panther stock by translocating western cats?

Eisenberg, as a panel member, explained the taxonomic history. Prior to 1946 the subspecific definition had rested on a few specimens from the lower Florida peninsula. Young and Goldman had merged 15 specimens from Florida, which included ten skulls, with two skulls from Concordia Parish in Louisiana. The authors had noted that most of the skins had flecks of white on the shoulders. They did not allude to a crook in the tail which might not have been noticeable on tanned skins (They also did not describe the "whorl" of hair, however a crook in the tail can be seen today in a photograph of a panther killed in the 1930s),[25] but Eisenberg pressed the point that the 1946 definition, the most recent, had emphasized skull

dimensions, not skin characters. This was in contrast to the weight then being given to such traits—which might simply be due to inbreeding. The three observable characters could have as easily been regarded as a warning sign, as the mark of a subspecies. Eisenberg cautioned about boxing the recovery strategy into a legal trap which might preclude outbreeding, should it become necessary.

During the panel discussion, the following exchange was recorded between Eisenberg and Tom Logan, a panel member representing the Game Commission.

> Logan - John, do you feel that *F.c.coryi* is distinct, but we should not let that stand in the way to manipulating the gene pool to preserve it —or —do you feel that *F. c. coryi* is not distinct?

> Eisenberg - The south Florida population is clearly phenotypically distinct, but during the last revision by Goldman, 1946, he disregarded the phenotypic differences of the south Florida population and made a broader definition of *F. c. coryi* based on the similarities of the inflated nasal bone, thereby combining the Louisiana population and the Florida population into one subspecies. Today, because all we are left with is the Florida population, we've begun to think of *F. c. coryi* in the more restricted sense. Goldman saw *coryi* as a living subset of what he conceived of as a broader subspecific definition. Bangs had considered it to be a different species, but from a legal point, we have to go with the last accepted definition, which is Goldman, 1946. We now have a rather inbred subset of Goldman's conception of *F. c. coryi* in 1946.

> Logan - Regardless of whether animals in Louisiana were genotypically part of the same group, we now have a unique representation of what once occupied some range in the southeastern United States, and it's very important that this not be confused with any notion that the animal is not unique. We can't allow such a confusion to be perpetuated. There has been some suggestion that in lieu of spending great sums for protection and land acquisition, that we merely go out West, capture some cougars, bring them to Florida and turn them loose. It's important that we recognize that the Florida panther, as it occurs today, is very distinct.

> Eisenberg - It certainly is, as it exists today.[26]

Richard Hamann, in his presentation, ventured that there were provisions in the law that would allow outbreeding. "The Endangered Species Act doesn't just provide protection for the taxonomic classifications of subspecies. It also provides for the protection of species which are endangered over some significant portion of their range. If this was to be viewed simply as *F. concolor* which was limited to the Southeast, it is clearly still endangered. In order to retain the protection, it would be necessary to designate '*F.concolor* in Florida' as an endangered species. That's certainly a possibility."[27] (The definition in the Endangered Species Act reads as follows: "The term 'species' includes any subspecies of fish or wildlife or plants, and any distinct population segment of any species or vertebrate fish or wildlife which interbreeds when mature."[28]) Hamann continued: "There is also a possibility under the Endangered Species Act to list *F. concolor* for protection as a species which is similar in appearance to *F. c. coryi* in South Florida, to prevent disputes over alleged past introductions of other cats. Species similar in appearance can be listed for certain geographic areas to aid the enforcement program, and would also allow genetic introduction from other populations."[29]

In Hamann's interpretation of the law, it would be possible to introduce new genes without affecting the vital assistance offered by the Endangered Species Act for protection, research and acquisition of habitat. (This, of course, raises interesting questions about the legal opinion from the Department of Interior that terminated funding for the dusky seaside sparrow when outbreeding was proposed.) There was a necessary administrative procedure; it would consist of "relisting" the endangered animal as a population of *Felis concolor*, rather than as the endangered subspecies: *Felis concolor coryi*. The procedure could be initiated by anyone, by submitting a petition to the Secretary of the Interior. Representatives of the Fish and Wildlife Service appeared to be surprised by Hamann's interpretation. During the next break in the assembly, one of them telephoned the chief of the Office of Endangered Species in Washington to get a reaction.[30]

The final session of the conference was a panel of Bill Branan, Richard Hamann, Archie Carr and James Wolfe, a mammalogist from Archbold Biological Station. Carr ventured that officials ought to explore increasing genetic diversity in the Florida panther, but wanted to know if officialdom was going to be "irked" by the proposal and ". . . question our good sense. . . ."[31] A Fish and Wildlife Service man answered that he foresaw resistance: "We get various directions from the solicitors office of the Department of Interior and our agency, and they are slow to change. I think that our work is cut out for us to explain the situation and to come up with some clever ways to explain it, the situation where we are and how we anticipate that that's the change that we might want. But I would envision that there will be some resistance within the Department of Interior to that type of thing."[32] However, he promised to work on the issue at once: "I think that it's something we need to get on right away. Something that I'll start Monday, writing some stuff and

getting it along the way. . . . I think there is an out, but I think we've all got a lot of work ahead of us. I think it can be done."[33]

Six months after the conference, Bill Branan wrote to agency participants who had promised action. The Fish and Wildlife Service was queried as to what progress it had made on relisting the Florida panther. He was told that ". . . the remaining panthers . . . are in no immediate danger, and the state is actively working on . . . captive propagation. . . . I do not feel that we should take any action at this point. . . . If necessary we could . . . evoke our authority to undertake an emergency listing action. . . . Thank you for your continuing interest and involvement in the recovery of the Florida panther."[34] It would have been churlish for Branan to ask why the Fish and Wildlife Service would prefer to await an emergency before even beginning work on the administrative arrangements necessary to respond to it, so he did not inquire. The failure to relist was also excused on the grounds that captive propagation was impending, but there would still be no captive propagation project underway at the end of 1990. My guess is that officials ran into a wall—as they predicted at the panther conference. The incident shows once more the bureaucratic difficulties that obstruct the most elementary recovery measures.

Subspecies Criteria Undermined

During this period the white flecks had been losing credence. In her 1982 report, Laurie Wilkins had written that white flecks were present only on adults, but she did not think they were an age-related trait. However, several years later when more skins had accumulated, she and Melody Roelke went over all those from Florida, representing animals whose ages could be estimated; in this expanded analysis, the degree of white flecking did seem to correlate with the age of the cats. It was speculated that the white flecks might be caused by tick bites. Captured panthers regularly had ticks on the hind neck—a part of the body they could not reach to groom themselves. The white hairs seemed to grow out of scar tissue that remained when the ticks were gone. The amount of white flecking increased with age.

So by the mid-1980s, references to white flecking began to be omitted from Game Commission documents that referenced sub-specific characters—at least for a time. That left only the crook in the tail and the cowlick, neither of which had been in the early descriptions of the Florida panther.[35] But the challenges to the now-accepted criteria for defining the Florida panther did not sit well with everyone in the Game Commission. There, the definition was convenient and reassuring with regard both to the flow of federal funds and as an instrument of legal protection, to be used in prosecuting persons accused of killing panthers, and perhaps for other reasons. This adherence to the status quo withstood the tentative abandonment of the white flecking on the neck as one of the identifying characters.

Following adjournment of a Panther Advisory Council meeting in September 1986, Chris Belden engaged John Eisenberg in an impromptu debate on the subject, defending the existing definition. Up to this time every panther skin seen, excepting the remains of an illegally killed specimen from Palm Beach County in 1983, had shown the three characters. I don't remember all the details of the argument, but this was just prior to the long-delayed capture of panthers in Everglades National Park, and I remember Eisenberg asking, "and what are you going to do if the panthers captured in Everglades National Park don't have crooks in their tails? Will they qualify as Florida panthers or not?" I thought to myself that such a possibility was highly unlikely, but as it turned out, none of the panthers captured in the park had the deformity.

Six panthers were captured during the first season at Everglades National Park. Two were collared in December of 1986, one in January 1987 and three more in March. All had the white flecks on the back of the head and neck; one male had the cowlick; none had crooks in the tail.[36] It was now impossible not to rethink the issue. The mind turns to speculation here. Everglades National Park is the only documented reintroduction site. Several panthers were released into the park during the 1950s and 1960s. These cats were from the Piper collection and were supposedly from stock captured in southern Florida, although there are grounds to suspect that a puma from another geographic region had also been kept in the Piper compound. Are the characters seen in the park cats those bequeathed by the Piper animals? Why the consistent difference in appearance between panthers in the National Park and those seen in Collier and Hendry Counties? The Everglades marsh appears to be an obstacle to migration, but the documented use of Conservation Area 3A by panthers suggests that it is not an impassible one.[37]

When I called a Game Commission biologist to get his reactions to the findings in the national park, he ventured that maybe we should just deemphasize the subspecific characters and deal with the subject on a different basis. However, as explained before in this book, opinions in land-management agencies can change at the bottom of the organization long before they change at the top—where it matters.

Attempts at Relisting

On an evening in December 1983, a Seminole Indian named James Billie, chairman of his tribe, went deer hunting on reservation lands with a companion. Billie fired at a pair of green eyes reflected in the beam of his light and killed a panther. On the following day a wildlife officer, who obviously had been tipped off, seized the hide which Billie had dressed and draped over a cypress pole. Charges were brought but dismissed in 1985 by a circuit court judge in Hendry County. It is lawful for Indians to take wild game on the reservation at any time, if it is used

as food for themselves. But another state law prohibits the killing of endangered species, and in 1986 a state appeals court ordered Billy to stand trial. The case was brought to court in LaBelle, in October 1987. The state had the task of proving beyond a reasonable doubt two things: first, that James Billie did intentionally kill an animal and, second, that the animal killed was the endangered subspecies: *Felis concolor coryi*. The second task proved troublesome to the prosecution. The judge instructed the jury that any conviction of guilt in their minds which "wavered or vacillated" was a reasonable doubt, and "if you have a reasonable doubt you must find the defendant not guilty."[38]

The defense effectively used the disputed characters. Most of the defense attorney's closing argument bore down on the contradictions, making much of the cowlick, the crook in the tail and the white flecks. He pointed out to the jury that the cowlick and the crook in the tail had not been documented by Outram Bangs or by Young and Goldman, and further, that the white flecks had recently been discovered to be evidence of tick bites and discarded as an identifying character. The jurors were reminded that panthers recently captured in Everglades National Park lacked the cowlick and the crook in the tail. The question was put to the jurors as to whether these two characters might in the future also be discredited. The jury was told that the "experts" were confounded, that the verdict was obviously not in on what identified *Felis concolor coryi*, and therefore the verdict could not be in on whether James Billie had killed one.[39] Billie was acquitted.

The minutes of a 1986 Technical Subcommittee meeting reveal an apparent maneuver aimed at relisting the Florida panther. In December of that year, an issue paper went from the Fish and Wildlife Service's endangered species office in Jacksonville to the regional director in Atlanta. It summarized the taxonomic history of the panther through the 1946 work of Goldman, upon which the agency had in 1966 recognized the Florida panther as an endangered subspecies. A final paragraph noted the three characters identified by Wilkins and Belden.[40]

The topic was then placed on the agenda of an upcoming meeting of the FPIC's Technical Subcommittee, scheduled for January 1987. Following the meeting, Dennis Jordan, the Fish and Wildlife Service's newly appointed Florida Panther Coordinator, circulated a memo affirming that ". . . any panther found in Florida, which is not obviously escaped from captivity, must be regarded as a true Florida panther whether or not it displays any of the traits which recently have been said to be diagnostic for this species [sic].[41]

And so, the Fish and Wildlife Service's December issue paper on taxonomy, minus the last paragraph explaining the three characters named by Belden and Wilkins, became the new year's revised basis for defining the Florida

panther. The action was a practical one under the circumstances, agreed to by all four agencies of the FPIC. Or so it seemed at the time.

The apparent consensus by the FPIC to drop the skin characters, in combination with the James Billie prosecutorial fiasco, apparently encouraged an enterprising vigilant in the Fish and Wildlife Service to take the next step: relisting the Florida panther from an endangered subspecies to an endangered population. His proposal came down heavily on the demonstrated vexation of proving the subspecies in court and ventured that relisting would remove the legal obstacle by allowing protection to be extended to the Florida population. The proposal concluded with a cautionary paragraph: "We do not believe a change of this sort should require extensive paperwork. It is a technical and not a substantive change. We believe that a simple notice in the *Federal Register* should suffice to bring it into effect. Naturally, we would need to secure a Solicitor's opinion on the matter before proceeding."[42] The proposition was placed on the agenda of the December 1987 meeting of the FPIC's Technical Subcommittee. However, a mailout following that meeting hinted that it had not been well received in all quarters: "Action on the matter was delayed pending additional review and consideration."[43]

An event soon after, indicated that officials in the Game Commission were not entirely sold on the broader definition to which they had agreed the previous year. In March 1988 a panther was killed by a car near the community of Capps, in rural Jefferson County far to the north of any modern documented evidence of panthers. Game Commission spokesmen reported to the press that the animal had caused some confusion because it "did not have the characteristics of the Florida panther . . . typically having a crooked tail, white flecks, and a cowlick on the shoulder."[44] In the bizarre sequel to this story, it was disclosed that the dead cat, a male, had been released in company with a female from the Jefferson County plantation of Ted Turner, the television tycoon. However, the question is: why was there confusion over the absence of the three characters? (Note that the white flecks were resurrected.) Was there also still confusion over the panthers roaming in Everglades National Park? Were there any official thoughts on how clarity could be made to prevail?

In July 1988, the Game Commission, in a letter to the Fish and Wildlife Service, formally took a stand against relisting the Florida panther. Though admitting that federal law enforcement would be improved, the letter asserted that state law had recently extended protection to any wild panther. Then came the crux: "Reclassification may imply to some that *F. c. coryi* is not scientifically identifiable. This is not true and to contribute to any other opinion could be consequential to panther recovery."[45]

If there should be a genetic time-bomb in the remaining panthers, it is a far more vital issue for survival than the successful prosecution of panther slayers. Relisting would clear the way legally to deal with the biological problem. But attempts to get the animal relisted have never been able to get off the ground. The indications are that the Game Commission has been unwilling to concede the possibility of outbreeding. And so it goes with the Florida panther recovery program, where the most basic administrative precautions are forever bogging down in a bureaucratic mire.

Chapter 7

CAPTIVE BREEDING AND REINTRODUCTION

The wild or natural habitats of species are diminishing—not increasing. The character of the ecosystems will change through time, whereas our captive-bred animals or those in small wild reserves will not be subject to the same selective pressures. We must preserve as much genetic diversity as possible to provide the material for selection when animals are returned to these changed systems.

Strategy is a basic issue. I would seek a safe-to-fail strategy: a set of options for the maintenance of a species that will allow for a number of failures and catastrophes . . . .

Ulysses S. Seal
Animal Extinctions, 1986

Captive breeding has been an unsettled issue since the onset of the recovery program. It has been touched on in previous chapters; here it will be isolated for treatment. To begin we return to the formative meeting in Orlando in 1976. Peter Pritchard had invited Vernon Kisling of the Crandon Park Zoo, on Key Biscayne, and Robert Baudy, owner of the Rare Feline Breeding Compound in rural Sumter County. Both men made presentations. Baudy had successfully bred 14 species of cats. He had since 1960 raised 162 tigers, 324 leopards and 152 jaguars.[1] Baudy won a spot on the recovery team—as its captive breeding specialist.

Captive panthers had been on display for years in a roadside zoological attraction in Bonita Springs. This establishment, Everglades Wonder Gardens, was owned by the Piper brothers, Bill and Lester. The Pipers were represented at the 1976 meeting by Jim Vanas, an employee who recounted the history of the caged animals in Bonita Springs as it had been told to him by the Pipers:

> In 1941 a female panther was shot in an area known as Devil's Garden, northeast of Immokalee. Three kittens from this cat were found by the hunter's dogs and were taken to Everglades Wonder Gardens. They were raised tame and were the first Florida panthers the Pipers had. In about 1945 or 1946, two more

young cats (wildcat size) were brought to the Wonder Gardens from Felda—a town north of Immokalee. The later addition of a large male cat from the Sarasota area (about 1945) and a tamed female from the east coast of Florida (about 1958) accounted for the original breeding stock of Florida panthers at the Wonder Gardens. Presently, there are four male and four female cats at the Pipers'.

Past releases of captive raised panthers in Everglades National Park number either five or six. The Pipers' did not keep records of cats given to the Park and neither did Park officials. Writer-photographer Patricia Caufield took pictures of one of the releases for her book *The Everglades* (Sierra Club, 1970).[2]

These animals and their progeny, referred to as the "Piper stock," have popped up in captive breeding deliberations to the present time. Vanas was incorrect in assuming that park officials did not keep records. Information still in the park files tells of several releases. On October 31, 1957, two young males were turned out in the Park; one at Mahogany Hammock, the other at Bear Lake.[3] On September 29, 1965, two rangers from Everglades National Park picked up three nine-month-old panthers and freed them the same day.[4] Another two followed in 1968.[5]

1978

As the writing of a recovery plan dragged on through 1977, Robert Baudy grew discontented with the absence of a captive breeding project, which he expected to conduct. Baudy was a self-made businessman with no patience for the plodding pace of government operations. On June 1, 1978, his teammates received in the mail a one-page communique, under the letterhead of the Rare Feline Breeding Compound, which began: "To whom it may concern, this is to acknowledge that, on this day June 1, 1978, Mr. Robert E. Baudy, owner of the Rare Feline Breeding Compound and member of the Florida Panther Recovery Team, took delivery of one male and two female Florida Panther [sic] *Felis concolor coryi* from Everglades Wonder Gardens (owners Bill and Lester Piper)." The third paragraph announced that "all charges of boarding, maintaining and managing these three animals will temporarily be suffered by the Rare Feline Breeding Compound."[6] In Baudy's mind the logic of captive breeding was inescapable, so he promptly arranged his own project, anticipating reimbursement for expenses in due time. Anyone acquainted with the ways of bureaucracy would not have made such a miscalculation.

At this stage the recovery program was on a meager budget. The recovery team's attention was drawn to the demands of getting an administrative foundation

(the recovery plan) in place, and there were formidable questions to be answered about panthers in the wild. The only fresh evidence consisted of a few tracks and one specimen killed by a hunter in the spring of 1978. The biggest question was whether the cats could be confirmed, or disproved, as the true subspecies.

Baudy sent another letter a week later detailing the visit to Bonita Springs in which he had taken possession of the cats. He then gave a progress report on captive breeding. "The three animals are doing very well and on June 7, one of the females went in oestrus. Very obvious and surprising taxonomic differences between *F. C. Coryii* [sic] and other subspecies are quite evident now that these animals can be observed in large and sun exposed cages. These, of course, will be pointed out to the whole team during out forthcoming meeting at my place." The letter came directly to the delicate matter of money. "It is my hope that financial arrangement [sic] perhaps between the Game Commission, the U.S. Fresh [sic] & Wildlife Service and the Audubon, could be worked out as promptly as feasible to help us in the propagation of the panther. "He then broached suggestions for expanding the operation. "It is my recommendation that four additional animals of breeding potential, still located at the Pipers, should be relocated, as soon as possible next to these 3 panthers. Two older animals at the Pipers are obviously past breeding ability . . . . I would greatly appreciate your formal approval of this propagation blueprint if at all feasible, after, of course, due consultation with the team."[7]

The team gathering at the Rare Feline Breeding Compound was scheduled for September 27. A few days before that, captive breeding became an accomplished if officially unsanctioned fact, when copulation was observed by Baudy. He mailed a graphic minute of the event and predicted that Christmas, 1978 would be graced with ". . . the first captive-born Florida panthers earmarked for future reestablishment of the species [sic] in the Florida forests.[8] Four days later we toured Baudy's compound and thereafter drove to the nearby county seat in the rural community of Bushnell for the novel experience of meeting in the small brick courthouse. Bushnell is the site of an 1835 battle in which Seminole Indians won an overwhelming victory by inflicting casualties of 235 dead on the U.S. Army— for a loss of three killed on their side.

The majority sentiment of the 1978 recovery team about captive breeding is reflected in the record of deliberations on how the reintroduction of panthers would be treated in the recovery plan: "Belden noted that the teams [sic] consensus was that the first priority is to manage natural habitat, second to supplement populations with surplus animals, third to introduce captive-bred animals. He felt the plan adequately covered the options. . . ."[9] Baudy had written a lengthy report for the record emphasizing the importance of captive breeding. The week before, he had attended a meeting of the American Association of Zoological Parks and

Aquariums, where he chanced to have a lengthy conversation with Ulysses Seal, who was internationally known for his studies on the genetics of wild felids. Baudy's report drew heavily the opinions of Seal. Baudy raised ". . . a strong possibility that if the sub species [sic] is left alone it will soon become biologically terminated due to extreme inbreeding."[10]

Baudy pursued his project with a single-minded zeal that alienated some of his fellow team members who were inclined to advance more cautiously, and his later attacks on radio-telemetry did not win him any sympathy. And yet, with the advantage of hindsight, his arguments for gathering a captive stock seem sound. I believe he assessed the danger of inbreeding correctly, and he was right to press for urgent measures. If panthers had dwindled to 20 individuals, as it appeared, and if the deer in their habitat, which seemed at a low density, had been depressed, the situation was critical. There were grounds for removing wild panthers to a secure confinement at once. It may be that Baudy's opportunity to hear Ulysses Seal speak, and to talk with him, had given insights to Baudy that others of us on the recovery team did not have in those days. As we shall see, Seal would be brought in to advise on the Florida panther recovery program a decade later in 1989, and he would make recommendations similar to the ones made by Baudy in 1978—with like justification.

It was following the September meeting that Chris Belden mailed the fertile opinions of the recovery team off to Washington, D.C., in a draft recovery plan which would gestate for two-and-a-half years in the womb of the Fish and Wildlife Service.

1979

In January 1979, the recovery team assembled in Gainesville. This was during the months of waiting for the draft recovery plan to make its way through the labyrinth in Washington, D.C. The minutes tell that "Mr. Baudy stressed the need to remove a panther from the wild for captive breeding purposes. It was the opinion of the majority of members present that this might be a good idea. Jim Layne pointed out that if the panther's numbers in the wild are as low as thought by some this action would be necessary and if they are as high as thought by some the action would have no effect on the remaining population, particularly if subadults were removed. The team leader pointed out, however that the opposition the Team had for capturing animals for a telemetry study would be the same as for capturing the animals for captive reproduction. This opposition was centered around techniques for capturing and handling panthers without the use of dogs or drugs."[11]

The record shows that captive breeding was briefly pondered. No one was oblivious to the hazards that Baudy insisted were real. Jim Layne ventured that subadult panthers could be removed with minimal risk to the population. However, Belden was adverse. Unfortunately, the minutes do not give his argument clearly, and my memory of the exchange is vague. It may have been a riposte aimed at Baudy by Belden. Baudy had raised several objections to the radio-telemetry studies being planned at this time, among them the danger posed by dogs and drugs. Belden may have been making the ironic point that dogs and drugs would be as necessary to capture panthers for breeding as for radio-collaring. This is conjecture. In any case the recovery team's flirtation with the momentary allure of captive breeding passed without engagement.

1980-1982

Another year passed. In January 1980, Chris Belden sent word to the team that comments on the recovery plan would be forthcoming from Washington in May or June, and scheduled a meeting for the latter month. His memorandum also updated the team on the activities of Robert Baudy. ". . . on January 15, 1980, his last remaining Florida Panther female ("Sweet") gave birth to a single male kitten. He plans to hand raise this kitten as soon as it is weaned for use in future captive breeding efforts."[12] Baudy's exertions on behalf of captive breeding went on without cease. He kept up a barrage of correspondence putting his arguments before the recovery team.[13]

At the June meeting Chris Belden distributed his synopsis of past radio-telemetry studies on pumas in preparation for the impending research on the Florida Panther.[14] It was during and subsequent to this meeting that relations between Belden and Baudy began to heat up. Several long letters were exchanged between them during the summer of 1980, in which Baudy detailed his protests and Belden replied to the points he raised. This exchange was alluded to in Chapter 3 and will be passed over here—until we come to Belden's letter to Baudy, dated August 19, when having exhausted the debate on radio telemetry, the two correspondents moved into the subject of captive breeding and the pedigree of the Piper stock. Belden's views are summed up in a paragraph:

> . . . The captive-breeding program you continually refer to for the Florida panther that is being conducted at the Rare Feline Breeding Compound is being conducted with captive-born animals from the Piper's Everglades Wonder Gardens collection with no written records of their past history. You yourself mentioned several times at our meetings that at least one South American female was known to have been in the collection in the past. You knew this when you obtained the panthers from the

Piper's on breeding loan. Your reasoning being that they certainly were different from any other subspecies you had ever
looked at. . . .[15]

As explained in the previous chapter, the Game Commission's survey of
puma skins was completed in 1981, and the three characters: the crook in the tail,
the cowlick and the white flecks became the stamp of a Florida panther. The
recovery team minutes for the meeting of June 16, 1981, tersely note that "Mr.
Baudy brought the team up to date on the captive rearing project. The adult animals
will be returned to the Piper brothers. Mr. Baudy will keep the three offspring at
the rare feline breeding compound."[16]

The recovery team convened for the last time in January 1982. Baudy tried
again: "On the basis of the bleak outlook for the Florida panther, Bob Baudy,
advocated a captive breeding program. Chris Belden said that a captive breeding
program remained an option, but data was [sic] still not adequate to justify
withdrawing animals from the wild population at this time." Chris Belden
foreshadowed an impending episode by informing the team that he had written to
"the Superintendent of Everglades National Park in November requesting assistance in panther research, but had received no answer." In the final paragraph of
the minutes "captive breeding came up again. Bob Baudy said that the removal of
the specimen from the wild does not have to be permanent. Roy DeLotelle
[representing Environmental Science and Engineering, Inc.] suggested using
transient cats for captive breeding purposes since they appear to be lost from the
permanent population."[17]

1983

The curtain came down on the recovery team. A year later, in January
1983, a panther died during a capture, raising a furor over radio-telemetry. In the
spring of 1983 the Florida legislature wrote the Panther Advisory Council into law.
Robert Baudy and I were appointed—the only carryovers from the recovery team.
The first meeting of the new Council took place in September 1983. John Eisenberg,
who had recently arrived in Florida after ten years at the National Zoological Park,
had been asked by Tom Logan of the Game Commission to present his thoughts on
captive breeding. Eisenberg's remarks were brief and general, but they introduced
two perspectives which had as yet received little notice. The first was on the
enormous costs that would be incurred. His estimate for building a facility to hold
ten animals was $250,000. Annual operating expenses were put at $85,000 to
$120,000 a year; Eisenberg cautioned that the project would demand a long
commitment. It so happened in the next few years that millions of dollars would
be disbursed to save the panther, but that could not have been anticipated in 1983,
when expenditures since 1976 had averaged less than $40,000 per year.[18]

Eisenberg brought a second perspective—on genetics, raising the issue of a "founder stock." The ideal number to insure the maximum in genetic variation,100 of each sex, was an impossible attainment, "but," wrote Eisenberg, "the warning is there that a balanced captive population of males and females for propagation at the maximum tolerable by facilities and stock in the wild would be a desirable aim."[19] Eisenberg's appreciation, late in 1983, became the first document in this long-running enterprise to address genetic management in a small population. Baudy had first raised the specter of inbreeding in 1978, but the subject had stayed in the shadows. The thinking of most participants had been riveted to the recovery plan, which represented a somewhat provincial view rooted in the Florida panther paradigm of the late 1970s. Inbreeding was not mentioned in the first recovery plan.

At this formative gathering of the Panther Advisory Council, a November field trip to southern Florida was scheduled, in conjunction with a second meeting—an episode covered earlier. Members wanted to know how hunting might be affecting the panther's prey. The Game Commission representatives asserted that it was having no effect, but could produce no evidence to buttress the opinion. There was a feeling, I think, among the Council members at this period that if the apparent heavy pressure on the deer herd could be eased, the recovery problem might conceivably begin to correct itself.

Robert Baudy, whose ardor for his subject never cooled, put the case for captive breeding with his usual passion, but he stood alone. Our recommendations from this early gathering were somewhat unfocused and lacked a comprehensive grasp of the recovery problem. Baudy forwarded his own arguments to be appended to the recommendations. He repeated his opposition to radio-telemetry and urged taking young panthers to start a captive population: ". . . #1 Removed wild specimens used for captive breeding are not permanently removed from the wild. They will be released after a sound captive born generation is produced. They are only borrowed from the wild. #2 Removal of very young specimens from the wild will result in a prompt recycling and rebreeding, producing (subject to the mother not be disturbed by radio telemetry) in an INCREASED POPULATION. #3 Captive-breeding program should in a relatively short amount of time produce a large number of specimens, at no RISK to the survival of the subspecies   "[20]

1984

During 1984 captive breeding would lie dormant. But the Game Commission had taken a tentative step forward by asking John Eisenberg to submit research designs that would assess captive breeding and reintroduction. Eisenberg sent his proposals in December; they enumerated four tasks: one was a telephone survey to gauge Florida's receptivity to releasing panthers; the others dealt with the

mechanics of captive breeding and reintroduction. The studies were contracted for, and scheduled for completion during, the next two years.[21] As it happened the work would take longer, but an impression was created early in 1984 that decisions on captive breeding would be made upon its completion late in 1985. Eisenberg surveyed opinion in northern Florida, where attitudes more resemble those of the rural South in contrast to the more urbanized and cosmopolitan lower peninsula. His findings were of great interest. An overwhelming question was whether the rural populace would be willing to accept panthers. The question was of paramount interest to the Game Commission with its sensitivity to controversy. The polls proved to be a landslide in favor of reintroduction.[22]

The Panther Advisory Council came together again in the spring of 1984, producing recommendations aimed at relieving pressure on the panther's food supply in the Big Cypress National Preserve and urging research on the lands north and south of the Preserve. Captive breeding was mentioned briefly: "Preliminary investigations into the captive breeding and reintroduction of *F. c. coryi* into the wild have been undertaken by Dr. John Eisenberg. He has identified the general directions that such an effort should take, including the general locations of reintroduction sites."[23]

In November 1984 the Game Commission found itself unexpectedly in possession of a Florida panther. This was "Big Guy," the young male injured on the Tamiami Trail. By this time the apprehension of the Panther Advisory Council about what would happen to the remaining panthers, if a few were taken captive, was being overrun by events. Between the time of the November 1983 meeting and the injury of Big Guy, five panthers were known to have been killed. Big Guy was the sixth confirmed subtraction from the wild population, and there could have been others that had gone undetected. Panthers were being eliminated at a known rate of one every other month and the actual rate could have been higher. It was easily conceivable that mortalities were exceeding the rate of replacement.

Following Big Guy's arrival came another fortuitous circumstance. Captive breeding facilities were offered to the Game Commission—at no cost. John Eisenberg, in drafting a design for a captive breeding project, was aware of the financial burden it would bring. In discussing the dilemma with the director of the Florida State Museum, Wayne King, he learned of an excellent captive breeding complex near Jacksonville. White Oak Plantation is located on an 8,000-acre forested tract in rural Nassau County. Owned by the Gilman Paper Company, it is used as a zoological park for several endangered wildlife species. Wayne King was acquainted with the director, John Lukas; both men had formerly served with the New York Zoological Society. Eisenberg visited Lukas and was impressed with the spacious paddocks and holding pens, backed by substantial private capital, all situated near the Osceola National Forest, a potential reintroduction site in

northern Florida. Eisenberg urged Lukas to contact the Game Commission and offer his services. Lukas acted at once, and shortly thereafter signed a contract with the agency.

1985

In January 1985 the Panther Advisory Council traveled to Tallahassee for a short meeting with the executive director of the Game Commission and his staff to hear of the agency's impending hunting restrictions in the Big Cypress National Preserve. The issue, which was of intense interest, was the only topic on the agenda. At the end of the meeting I vaguely remember some comments being made about expediting the captive breeding project; they went past me at the time.

I was surprised on April 1, to be copied with a letter from the Game Commission to the superintendent of the Big Cypress National Preserve inquiring about the prospects of taking two female panthers for captive breeding.[24] Attached to the letter was a copy of an application to the Fish and Wildlife Service for the requisite federal permit. An accompanying statement of purpose weighed the pros and cons of withdrawals from the diminished remnant of panthers: "The implications of the removal of two females to the wild population of *Felis concolor coryi* are difficult to address. Certainly the wild population is low, but that fact argues for the removal as much as against it. Productivity of the wild population appears to be poor, but that may reflect inadequate data or a population at carrying capacity. The presence of feline distemper (panleukopenia) in the population may be a factor in the apparent poor productivity."[25] These dismal sentences found their inevitable way to an opinion that had now come to pervade the Panther Advisory Council and (obviously) had gained acceptance in the Game Commission: "The above information suggests to us that the prospects for panther survival in south Florida are tenuous in the short term. And those prospects can be enhanced by the artificial propagation of cats in captivity, regardless of subsequent reintroduction. A disease or other disaster could eradicate the remaining wild population very quickly."[26] Opinion from the Game Commission had now come about. It was echoing Robert Baudy.

The letter advocated going ahead to captive breeding without awaiting Eisenberg's studies, giving two reasons:"(1) It is the opinion of the Florida Panther Advisory Council, and shared by Commission staff, that valuable time and potential breeding stock may be lost unless the initial steps are immediately implemented; and (2) the necessity of immediate decision on disposition of the recuperating male now held at the Gainesville facility. If captive propagation is to be undertaken, it would be unwise to not make full use of an excellent specimen already in captivity. . . ."[27] I was aroused by these lines. Although the "opinion" referenced here was one that had been growing in all quarters, it had not come from

the Panther Advisory Council. From the outset I had adopted the practice of sending recommendations to the Game Commission in writing—after they had been signed by all Council members. In this way there could be no misunderstanding of our opinions, either outside the Council or within it (the practice was implemented to maintain harmony within the Council, since members did not always think alike on every issue).

I immediately sent off a letter objecting to a captive breeding project that excluded any input from the Panther Advisory Council.[28] A reply came (three weeks later) explaining to me how my inattentiveness had led to a misappraisal of the situation:

> As you well know, reintroduction of panthers has been an objective of the Florida Panther Recovery Plan as well as this agency's program for recovery of that species for several years. This is adequately stated in the attached documents which you have previously been provided. Furthermore, panther reintroduction and captive propagation had been discussed in some context at virtually every meeting of the Florida Panther Technical Advisory Council. The staff's recommendations for captive propagation of panthers as a means toward panther reintroduction were specifically discussed in detail at the January Council meeting receiving a verbal but clear statement of concurrence from you as chairman. These recommendations were then presented to our Commission on March 8, 1985, again receiving concurrence. You were informed of the Commission's response and notified that the staff is proceeding with all actions that are necessary to prepare for captive propagation. Final decisions regarding capture of wild stock, however, were to be discussed with the Council before any attempts are made for capture. This is still our intention.[29]

The letter prompted urgency, and suggested seizing the opportunity to minimize the cost to the taxpayer (always a guiding principle in Game Commission operations):

> I also assume you recognize that we are proceeding partly as a result of having the male specimen, with a decision required in the near future on whether he should be released or retained. We have a prime male already in captivity and, if an agreement can be reached, access to an outstanding breeding facility with an excellent staff to do the work at minimum cost to the taxpayer. Commission staff contend we should proceed as expeditiously as

possible with a captive breeding program as a means to panther reintroduction. We therefore see no point in delaying unless our cadre of experts can find flaws in the program. Certainly, we want to avoid, if we can, the situation that developed with dusky seaside sparrows.[30]

The matter clarified, a meeting date was set for the following month. By the time we convened in Tallahassee in May 1985, five additional panthers were known to have been killed since the injury of Big Guy, seven months earlier.

The Panther Advisory Council supported the captive breeding endeavor, explaining the shift in position.

> Exact data on the F. c. coryi population still leave much to be desired twelve months after our initial recommendations; however, the confluence of several developments have modified our original position: first, and most importantly, the appalling (known) number of mortalities and injuries which may be eroding the wild population at a rate we cannot determine; two, the providential appearance of a benefactor with an excellent captive breeding capability who is willing to underwrite the considerable cost of such an effort and; three, the appearance of "Big Guy" a potential breeding male specimen of F. c. coryi.[31]

We pointed out that it would first be necessary to determine if Big Guy could impregnate a female—something that could not be taken for granted (as it turned out, Big Guy was not talented as a breeder). We urged the Game Commission to first assure itself of a reintroduction site. We were mindful of projects like the red wolf and Mexican grey wolf, which had run out of momentum once the animals had been caught; twenty years later they were still in captivity. We made further recommendations.

> . . . Initial attempts to capture F. c. coryi captive breeding stock should target kittens, two to six months of age, rather than adult females so as to minimize risk to wild population.

> The Council's greatest concern - reducing the wild population (numbers unknown) to a further reduced unknown level - could be ameliorated by capturing kittens in the above-mentioned age bracket. The advantage is that the adult female would immediately recycle and breed again. The entire litter of kittens should be taken to ensure success. This might result in the availability of additional captive males as well as females. As Dr. Eisenberg

pointed out this approach would have the advantage of utilizing the interest of the wild population rather than digging into the capital. Also questions about the survivorship of young animals have been raised due to a high incidence of feline panleukopenia, raising the possibility that capture inoculations of young might be required as an extreme measure at some point in the future. The experience gained from capturing young for a captive breeding program would, therefore, cast some light on the feasibility of such a program.[32]

We recommended first releasing surrogate animals of another subspecies and watching the outcome, prior to freeing Florida panthers. We also felt a need to advise that the attention to panthers in southern Florida not be lessened "as the result of a captive breeding—reintroduction initiative for northern Florida."[33] There was a suspicion that if the northern initiative showed promise, the Game Commission would drift away from the daunting challenges in the south. We also proposed the making of arrangements to deal with any released panther that might become a nuisance. The Panther Advisory Council was still cautious. We were more inclined, based on the examples of captive wolves, to guard against bureaucratic irresolution that might stall the project once the animals had been captured, than we were to urge a no-holds-barred push to get the facilities and the breeding stock into being. But, regardless, we had given our support. The theme repeatedly hammered on by Robert Baudy, that prudence dictated a captive population against disaster striking the wild one, would now become a reality.

Or so it seemed at the time. In fact, years would pass without further progress (the first panthers would not be withdrawn for captive breeding until 1991, under circumstances that will come to light in Chapter 19). What happened? The 1985 reasoning of the Game Commission, quoted above, recalled the dusky seaside sparrow tragedy, where captive security had been neglected. The documents obviously mirrored thinking at the top: the need for urgency, the high vulnerability of low numbers, the appalling (known) mortality—and all that could be wished for in captive breeding pens and expert attention had been put at the service of the agency. The threats enumerated in 1985 have festered and swelled with the passing years. Why the change of mind? The agency would go on spurning opportunities— as we shall see. Several panthers would be temporarily brought into captivity for medical care and for other reasons, but they were always sent back to the wild. My continued pushing, as chairman of the Advisory Council, to promote a captive population for security would be answered with bland statements of optimism about the prospects of panther survival.

The Panther Advisory Council convened again in September 1985. As related in Chapter 3, it was at this time that the broad picture of the panther's plight

was taking form. No need was seen to make additional comments on captive breeding, since the project was presumed to be in the offing. This meeting was the occasion of "radical" recommendations for the National Park Service and the Florida Park Service to increase deer numbers, for the Game Commission to initiate a mapping project for private lands—which were becoming threatened as panther habitat, and for Everglades National Park to drop its resistance to panther-deer research, all of which we hoped would concert toward a dependable sanctuary for panthers in southern Florida.

In late October news carried nationwide that a calamity had overtaken the black-footed ferrets in Wyoming. The species had been thought extinct until a colony was miraculously found in 1981. The discovery had brought a stream of magazine and news articles to follow the fortunes of the ferrets. News of the population crash hit me with a jolt because of the similarities to the panther situation. It was a single, small population for which management responsibility had been given to the Wyoming Game Commission. Following the tragedy there were reports that independent advisors had repeatedly pressed officials to withdraw some ferrets to a captive facility. But the agency could not be moved to a sense of urgency, and suddenly it had been too late. I worried that perhaps the Panther Advisory Council had not underscored a need for expediency. Perhaps we had been too tentative in our recommendations. Now the perspective of captive breeding, previously colored by dead-end projects like the red wolf, had suddenly been altered by a catastrophe with the ferrets. Later in the day I called John Eisenberg. "Well," he said, "they've screwed around in Wyoming and lost the ferrets. When is our next meeting?" We talked briefly and agreed to try for another meeting to go over captive breeding, as soon as it could be arranged the following year. At least the project had been set in motion (we thought).

1986

The early months of 1986 were crowded. In January I briefed a working group of the Everglades Coalition on the Recovery Program. In February there was a Panther Advisory Council meeting in Gainesville. The sole purpose was to prepare a formal recommendation to the superintendent of Everglades National Park from the Game Commission to get research started there. This obstacle had commanded disproportionate attention. Later in the month came the two-day meeting in Everglades National Park to propose the FPIC (Chapter 4), and in April the FDE Panther Conference was held in Tallahassee. It wasn't until May that a Council meeting could be arranged.

We traveled to White Oak Plantation and toured the grounds. Its expansive pens held blackbucks, gaur, and barasinga from India. From Africa there were red lechwes, cheetahs, and roan antelope—to name a few. A large holding pen

for Big Guy had just been completed at a cost of $200,000. The captive breeding-reintroduction project seemed to be in motion, and we saw no need to push it. Chris Belden again had an active role in the recovery program; he had started work on a draft reintroduction plan which he presented. Our recommendations again stated a preference for capturing juvenile panthers. Game Commission representatives suggested the removal of an aged female from the Fakahatchee Strand State Preserve to see if she would breed. The animal appeared malnourished (as panthers in the Fakahatchee Strand State Preserve usually did). Radio telemetry data proved that she had consorted with males during the previous two years, but had not given birth; it was hoped that if put on a good diet, she might have a few productive years left and could be bred to Big Guy. The Panther Advisory Council endorsed this peripheral experiment.

Mindful of the ferret tragedy, we also advised the preparation of a contingency plan for removing all Florida panthers from the wild:

> This recommendation is prompted by recent events in the black-footed ferret situation in which a precipitous decline in the population brought that species to the brink of extinction. If an attempt had been made to foresee possible crises and plan for them, the crash of the ferret population might have been avoided or, at least ameliorated. The panther's predicament is certainly as precarious as that of the ferret. Bringing the remaining wild panthers into captivity would be an extreme, last-ditch measure to be undertaken at some point only if the remaining known number of panthers continue their apparent slow decline toward zero, or if the known numbers should begin a rapid decline. Both scenarios are realistic.[34]

This inspiration would accumulate an interesting history. Later in the month following this meeting, agency administrators gathered to sign the agreement creating the FPIC—and its Technical Subcommittee. The contingency plan idea soon went on the agenda of the Technical Subcommittee as a task to be identified in the revised recovery plan, and so it was when the plan was promulgated in June 1987; it was assigned to all four agencies. However, when I attended a Technical Subcommittee meeting in mid-1989, there was still no contingency plan. This thread of the story will be resumed in the last chapter.

The Game Commission response to our recommendations came in November. The commentary applicable to captive breeding was as follows:

> The Florida Game and Fresh Water Fish Commission shares the Council's concern for survival of the Florida panther. However,

we refuse to be stampeded into overreacting, particularly when our understanding of the dynamics of that population continues to improve as more data become available. For example, as recently as September 22, South Florida research personnel observed a heretofore unknown female panther and a spotted kitten in the "blocks." As such data become available, it is apparent that the danger you describe, while real, may be less eminent [sic] than you suggest. Certainly the long-term picture is very alarming due to shrinking habitat and possible disease and genetic problems, and these factors must not be taken lightly. We may not react as quickly and dramatically as you prefer, but I view our actions as a serious and realistic approach, which will best serve the needs of the panther in the long-run.

. . . A staff recommendation to remove the Fakahatchee Strand female from the wild under specified conditions has been prepared and will be submitted to the U. S. Fish and Wildlife Service for concurrence. The council will be kept informed as this recommendation develops. Under most circumstances, we agree with your position that juveniles are the best choice for removal to a captive-rearing program. Our rationale for removing the Fakahatchee female is based on her chronically poor health and productivity, and the premise that with improved health in captivity, she will benefit the subspecies as a captive breeder.

. . . We have discussed a contingency plan for removing all Florida panthers from the wild, and have concluded that development of such a plan is premature and an unnecessary use of manpower at this time. Furthermore, if such a need should arise, the level of investigation that is currently being devoted to the panther should reveal that need in ample time. I do think it should be pointed out that the parallel between the ferret and the panther is not entirely accurate. Panthers are not colonial and very probably are not as subject to catastrophic crashes due to disease as are ferrets. Also, we will soon have additional Florida panthers in captivity via our captive-rearing program. I will not rule out the potential for needing to prepare such a plan, but I do not feel it is an immediate priority.[35]

As mentioned before, there still would be no captive population at the end of 1990. The "Old Fakahatchee Female" was brought into captivity in 1987, where she died in 1988. She did not breed. The only male available for breeding her was Big Guy, who was refusing to have anything to do with females.

161

During this phase, when the recovery plan was undergoing revision by the FPIC, I repeatedly tried, by endlessly restating the warning about hazards to small populations, to dampen the new complacence that seemed to be infecting the Game Commission—such as that expressed in the above letter referencing the observation of a "heretofore unknown female panther and a spotted kitten."

Dear Sir:

Thank you for your letter of October 17. I think the Council's greatest concern with the Commission's approach to the Florida Panther Recovery Program is its continuing optimism which in the latest instance purports to be based on "recent documentation of panther reproduction." This will not stand up. There has always been reproduction, obviously. Continuing reproduction was demonstrated in the death-based life tables prepared by Melody Roelke in 1985. Intensified field work by the Commission during the past year has additionally permitted visual observations of young animals. This may be cause for relief, but no observations to date offer any reason for optimism about panther recovery in southern Florida.

The one young panther examined, was anemic and full of hookworms. His recruitment into the adult population was assisted by the veterinary ministrations he received. The fate of another young animal is unknown, following the recent death of his mother on Alligator Alley. This leaves the known surviving young at two in Bear Island and a possible two more in Everglades National Park. This reproduction must be seen against six known fatalities in 1985-86.

The balance-sheet aside, the reproduction rate as indicated by a considerable body of evidence appears to be very low relative to other documented situations, both with Felis concolor and other large felids. Also, Commission data call attention to an apparent problem between birthing and recruitment (Panther Health-Reproduction Annual Performance Report, 1984-85). Reproduction and recruitment problems could be partly genetic, but there is a considerable body of documented evidence that poor nutrition, resulting from inadequate supply of prey is implicated, regardless of genetics.

Stepping back to take a long view of the big picture in southern Florida, we see that panthers presently known to inhabit public lands with a secure future, number about a dozen. The remaining panthers are on private lands that might no longer function as habitat in the year 2000. Management measures that would permit an enlarged population of prey animals on the public lands have not been taken, and there is no conclusive evidence to date that the responsible government agencies are willing to take them.

For the reasons given above, any optimism about panther survival in southern Florida at the present time, must be considered a pipe dream.[36]

The young panther mentioned above could have been made captive; unfortunately he was not; soon after leaving his mother as a transient, he was killed by another male panther in January 1987.

My response to the comments about black-footed ferrets was as follows:

The lesson to be drawn from the black-footed ferret disaster is in observing, not that it is demographically dissimilar, but that it resulted from a flawed approach to an endangered species problem. Worst case assumptions and planning were not accommodated. The participants assumed a stable situation that would grant them time to work out a solution. We can now observe the consequences. The recovery program has moved into a last ditch phase with the handful of remaining ferrets in captivity, and survival odds further reduced. Stochastic events that cause fluctuations in large populations can be calamitous in small ones, whether they are concentrated (as with ferrets) or dispersed (as with panthers). We cannot predict the result of extreme events, as with a hurricane, or prolonged flooding, for example, on the remaining panthers and their prey.

The correct approach to endangered species recovery is to assume that the worst might happen. Time may be important. Urgency is justified. Every effort should be made to provide the remaining animals with the widest possible margin of safety; reasonable actions to this end should not await exhaustive data collections. Reasonable shortcuts should be sought after. The Council recognizes the genuine problem of manpower allocation. We can only hope that assumptions of ample time will not prove incorrect.[37]

In late October 1986 the Panther Advisory Council held its late-year meeting to review research from fiscal year 1985-86. Our report following this gathering highlighted several positive developments, among them were the steps taken toward captive breeding. "A second positive development is that the captive breeding facility at White Oak Plantation is finished and is gearing up for panther production. Considering the grave threats to the existing population, reintroduction in other locations will be essential for an added measure of security for panther recovery."[38]

But it happened that a mood of extreme caution was growing in the Game Commission toward releasing panthers into northern Florida. The attitude was understandable, but the Game Commission's extraordinary sense of caution becomes transformed into a snail-like mode of advance, stretching into years what might be accomplished in far less time. We attempted some encouraging remarks: "A third positive development is the apparent support of the general public in Florida for preventing the panther's extinction. There are two recent indications of this. The 1985 public opinion poll that was contracted by the Commission showed the public overwhelmingly in favor of saving the panther and of reintro-ducing it into northern Florida. Panhandle cattlemen who returned a mailed questionnaire approved of panther reintroduction provided they be compensated for stock killed by panthers. Recently the Palm Beach Post had asked citizens to vote on saving the panther—where it counts—with their pocketbooks. In a statewide environmental poll with a four percent sampling error, 57 percent agreed that public tax money should be spent to save the panther from extinction; 26 percent disagreed and 17 percent apparently don't care one way or another. . . ."[39]

It was during this period that I began to recognize one more centripetal tug making itself felt inside the recovery program. Well-funded research in the hands of competent biologists is an essential ingredient in recovering endangered species, but it also has the potential to become a vested interest, with the research faction fixating on the data-gathering activities. Soon after the October 1986 Panther Advisory Council meeting, I tried lobbying some of the field biologists to get support from the bottom in pushing for a captive population. I had a creeping suspicion that resistance from this quarter might be at least a part of the problem. It proved correct.

A female panther in the Bear Island unit of the Big Cypress National Preserve had regularly raised offspring and seen them off into the world. She was caring for two young kittens at this time. Over the phone I suggested to my auditors that the young be brought into captivity in accordance with recommendations long since made. I was taken aback by the abrupt reactions to this proposal, which in some cases bordered on hostility. I was even accused of wanting to "write off" the

panthers in South Florida. In one instance a biologist called back with a colleague on the line to counter-lobby the idea of establishing a captive population. The colleague made the astonishing statement that there might not be a captive-breeding project. Remember now, $200,000 had recently been spent on a facility at White Oak Plantation. (However, his prophesy proved correct—until a turn of events in 1991.) There was plainly apprehension among some field biologists that a captive breeding project might disturb their research.

1987

After testing the water on removing kittens from Bear Island, I chose for the moment not to wade in further, but another opportunity came in January 1987. In the northern part of the Fakahatchee Strand, the capture team found a pregnant female, wounded, having been hit in the foot with buckshot.[40] She was transported to Metrozoo in Miami for treatment. Trying to take advantage of a cat-in-hand (a pregnant one at that), I telephoned some of the field researchers again to poll them on the prospects for encouraging that the animal be used in the captive-breeding program. Again I ran into a wall of opposition. Those with whom I spoke wanted the panther and her prospective young returned to the wild where she could be studied.

Nonetheless, I telephoned the Panther Advisory Council members to ask for approval to send a letter to the Game Commission recommending that the panther be put into the lagging breeding project. The letter was sent, with the approval of four members of the Council, and against the opposition of one—who was involved in the field research:

> It has come to the attention of the Council that an injured, pregnant (with two to three fetuses) female panther has been captured and placed in the care of a zoo in Miami for rehabilitation. The Council would like to recommend that this adult female and her offspring be retained for the captive-breeding program.
> . . .
> The Council, as you know, has remained concerned about removing adults from the population for captive breeding purposes. However, bringing in an injured animal was obviously a responsible move and the removal is now a fait accompli. The panther's pregnancy could mean that, given a successful birth, a stock of potential breeders is now available on a no-risk basis. Such an opportunity is not likely to recur. . . .[41]

By this time the caution about using only young panthers was yielding to the desire to get a captive population by whatever means.

In January 1987, shortly after the injured female was taken to the zoo in Miami and after I had urged using it for captive breeding, the Technical Subcommittee of the FPIC met in Everglades National Park. The question of "the disposition of the injured female" was placed on the agenda. The Technical Subcommittee voted to return the female to the wild. The decision was considered important enough to warrant the preparation of an issue paper. The FPIC had scrupulously avoided the serious use of issue papers, but the research faction now used the medium to underpin its unwillingness to keep the injured cat in captivity. [42]

A month later came a reply from the Game Commission to the Panther Advisory Council recommendation to use the injured female for captive breeding.

Dear Mr. Alvarez:

Thank you for the recommendation of the Florida Panther Technical Advisory Council regarding disposition of the female panther that was evacuated from the Fakahatchee Strand State Preserve for medical treatment on January 9, 1987.

Following removal of that female from the wild, Commission staff considered the alternative of retaining her in captivity for captive breeding purposes. In addition, we took the matter to the Technical Subcommittee of the Florida Panther Interagency Committee for evaluation. In both cases, there was unanimous agreement that the female should be returned to her evacuated site as soon as medically feasible. She was, therefore, returned to the Fakahatchee Strand State Preserve in good health on February 12, 1987.

Her return to the wild was based on the following reasons:

1. The female is as demographically valuable as any single individual of the existing population. She is five plus years old, and is a proven breeder that has successfully raised at least one kitten and rebred in the Preserve during the past two years. There is no way that we could remove this female from the wild without impacting that population.

2. The female is instrumented and if we decide to remove her at a later date for captive breeding purposes, we still have that option.

3. As far as we know, she is the only productive female in the Fakahatchee Strand south of Alligator Alley. In light of planned efforts to improve the situation there for panthers, it seems to be a poor decision to remove the only reproductively viable female from that area at this point in time.

4. The male Florida panther we have in captivity has not yet successfully bred according to Dr. John Lukas. The male may require time to learn his breeding functions. This may be a minor problem that will work out in time. However, we do not have a proven male breeder to mate with any female at this time.

5. Even though we have made some progress in selecting potential release sites, that process is still not complete. Therefore, it seems unwise to prematurely commit such valuable genetic material to a breeding program which is not operational, and to a release program which has no introduction site.

Another major reason that we did not support keeping this female for the captive breeding program is that we also disagree with the Council's apparent view that the extinction of the Florida panther is imminent. There are simply no data to document such a conclusion. We have documented and continue to document reproduction as well as additional panthers as our knowledge and study areas expand. It is true there are some troubling spots such as in the Fakahatchee Strand and the long-term prospect for the subspecies is grim if habitat destruction, particularly in the private lands to the north of the Preserve, continues by current practices. However, those impacts will not manifest in total within the next two or three years and we certainly do not think the situation is so grave that it justifies the removal of this extremely valuable animal from the wild.

Thank you for your recommendations.[43]

It was (and still is) impossible to make any impression on the Game Commission that small populations have a tenuous hold on life. The tactfulness of my letters deteriorated as frustration grew.

Dear Sir:

Thank you for a prompt response to our February recommenda-

tion. I should attempt to clarify again that the Council is not committed to the proposition that the panther's extinction is imminent, but we are very much aware of the precariousness of any wildlife population that has been reduced to a very low number, and for which the conditions that would engender a reversal of the decline have not been created. We have previously referenced the black-footed ferret population. The precipitous decline of the dusky seaside sparrow is another case in point. The recent loss of twenty of the world's sixty Javan rhinoceroses to an unknown disease is yet another. The potential for increased susceptibility to disease in a small, inbred population is a factor that should be kept anxiously in mind. There are enough case histories to warrant a great concern for time, which is the unknown quantity in the recovery equation. An endangered species program should be managed always to maintain the balance of advantage in favor of the target species, to whatever extent possible.

As for the Commission aplomb over panther reproduction, I have been over that before, apparently to no avail.

The grim, long-term prospects referenced for panthers on private lands, leads directly to the conclusion that habitat on public land must be managed actively for more panthers if this animal is to have any long-term prospects for survival in southern Florida, and that this will require changes in the way the National Park Service manages its land—an ineludible fact that goes unremarked.

Regarding the five reasons for returning the female to the wild:

#1. The one kitten raised in this area—the only one since radio-telemetry studies began—was killed, apparently in intraspecific strife; so this female is not having any impact (to use your term) on the population in any case.

#2. This is true, if she isn't killed first.

#3. This argument might have merit if an improved situation was a fait accompli, or clearly impending. The coming efforts to improve habitat here are gratifying, but the initial work will be on a very modest scale and there is no reason to suppose it will benefit panthers any time soon.

#4. This is a sound argument and it identifies an obstacle to be overcome.

#5. If this genetic material is so valuable, why not try to conserve it rather than return it to a situation where there is a reasonable probability that it will be lost and little chance that it will be passed on? The habitat is clearly not conducive to recruitment, and known mortalities in this area have averaged two per annum since 1980.

Overall, this is a bad case, poorly argued.

As you suggest, it seems probable (but it is not certain) that panther numbers will not, within the coming two years, have started to decline as a result of habitat destruction on private lands. It is certain, however, that more of the habitat will have been destroyed; only the amount is in question. Time is not on the panther's side. We had hoped by our recommendation, to stimulate an enterprising action which would save some.[44]

At this time the Alice-in-Wonderland FPIC was rolling along to its rendezvous with destiny in the promulgation of a useless recovery plan. The FPIC was wont to pause in its labors on occasion, to reflect on its accomplishments. These were periodically minuted for the benefit of readers of the PANTHER INFO mail-outs. In April 1987 a mail-out ticked off a "Summary of Significant Accomplishments," one of which mentioned that "the panther 'Jim' [this was during a bizarre and futile attempt by the Game Commission to change Big Guy's name to Jim], injured on Alligator Alley [he was injured on the Tamiami Trail] was moved to White Oak Plantation, north of Jacksonville, for the purpose of captive breeding. Two female cougars from Texas were moved to the Plantation and 'Jim' and the older female have co-mingled—results unknown."[45]

The results might have been unknown, but they were strongly suspected. When the Texas female, in an appropriate state of passion, had been introduced to Big Guy, he had spat and swatted, driving her away. But no matter, the FPIC had to take accomplishments where it could find them. Also, on this remarkable list, the FPIC laid claim to fostering the FDE panther conference.[46] The FPIC's paramount achievement at this juncture was in transforming the captive breeding project into a meaningless exercise. Time was being wasted and money spent with nothing to show for it. In July, a PANTHER INFO reported on the successful capture of the "Old Fakahatchee Female"—the outcome of which has been revealed to the reader. The summary gave as a justification of the capture that it could

"possibly increase this panther's breeding potential." The justification also contained the howler that it would protect her "from almost certain premature death in the wild." It concluded with "the hope is that these efforts will lead to conception and birth of healthy Florida panther kittens, possibly as soon as the winter of 1987 or the spring of 1988."[47]

Now if we should be so brash as to take this message at face value, it might be concluded that the Game Commission wanted Florida panthers in captivity, perhaps to avoid the "situation that developed with the dusky seaside sparrows," as its assistant director had warned in 1985.[48] In applying for the capture permit, he had been emphatic ". . . that the prospects for panther survival are tenuous in the short term. And those prospects can be enhanced by the artificial propagation of cats in captivity, regardless of subsequent reintroduction. A disease or other disaster could eradicate the remaining wild population very quickly."[49] These 1985 arguments had buttressed a sound and unmistakable intent to add a layer of security against extirpation; that is what makes the subsequent behavior of this inconstant agency so incomprehensible. This was as close as the Game Commission would come in the 1980s to captive breeding. In 1987 it had a female too old to breed and a male that refused to. Seemingly, there was an absence of ideas about what, if anything, should be done next. The female died the following year. And so we can see bureaucrats haphazardly pursuing their aims by the most improbable method, while the simple solution is rejected.

During one week in March 1987, three young panthers were captured in Everglades National Park. They weighed 58, 37 and 38 pounds respectively. They might have been put into the captive breeding project, but were not. One of the young females (#23) exhibited what would come to be called an "orphaning problem," meaning that she tended to get separated from her mother before the age when it would be expected. She was appropriately dubbed "Annie" and was brought into captive safekeeping on two occasions. In May of 1987 a PANTHER INFO gave an update on Orphan Annie: "The ENP [Everglades National Park] kitten incident resulted when a female kitten estimated at between 5-6 months of age failed to reunite with her mother and sibling post-capture on March 18. Intervening action by the capture team was delayed until a point in time where it was decided that action would be necessary and appropriate to insure the kitten's health and survival. The kitten, mother and sibling, were all recaptured and placed in a temporary holding facility which had been constructed within the family's home range. After a short reuniting period they were released from the holding facility. To date the effort appears to have been a complete success. All movements and actions by the family group appear to have returned to normal.[50]

At a Technical Subcommittee meeting in June, it was noted that another large male panther [#20] had been injured by a pickup truck and was undergoing

treatment at Metro Zoo in Miami. This animal had a heart murmur and lacked a testicle.[51] After recuperating, it was returned to the wild—and found dead at Bear Island in August 1988. The minutes then move on to the next episode of Orphan Annie. A National Park Service spokesman said "the orphaning problem which resulted post capture with one of the young kittens (#23) back in the spring has recently reoccurred [sic]. The field crew is presently monitoring the situation and guidance from the FPIC may be needed before the conclusion of the meeting."[52] On page four, the minutes inform that ". . . (Roelke) presented a Bio-Medical update (Attachment 8). She indicated that she had just arrived from EVER [Everglades National Park] and that they had recaptured kitten (#23)[Orphan Annie] and would need guidance from the FPIC on how to proceed. . . ."[53]

On the second day of the meeting (page 6 of the minutes), Orphan Annie comes up again:

Everglades Kitten (#23) Issue: Brantly requested that the TS, with input from the various members of the field crews present, convene to explore the options available for addressing the subject situation and if possible recommend a course of action. After considerable discussion basically centering around whether to attempt another effort to reunite #23 with her mother and sibbling [sic] or to elect to keep her in captivity (either for later release back into the wild or for captive breeding), it was the collective decision of NPS (Baker and Findley [sic]) that the cat should be maintained in captivity, at least for the present time. This decision was largely based on the fact that earlier attempts to reunite the family had been unsuccessful over the long term and the increasing concern and fear that continued efforts could indeed result in compounding the situation and possibly compromising the health and safety of the other cats involved. It was abundantly clear that the kittens [sic] chances for survival in captivity were excellent, whereas, in the wild they were considered extremely questionable at best. The decision was that NPS (Finley) would coordinate a press release on the decision and would work out arrangements and details for long term maintenance of the animals by White Oak Plantation.[54]

So it seemed at last that another panther would be placed into the captive breeding program. But then late in the year the minutes of a Technical Subcommittee meeting in December inform that "#23 orphaned Everglades female kitten was moved to White Oak Plantation in August, is presently undergoing conditioning for release back into the wild."[55] And so it goes. In the minutes of the Technical Subcommittee meetings, the actors come and go; decisions are reversed, often

without explanation; no one is in charge; the different agencies and factions pursue their separate objectives; motives are sometimes discernible and sometimes not; the recovery program is a case of strategic aversion and operational chaos, organized only to the extent that it can avoid any action deemed undesirable by its component factions, as they project an image of industry and purpose while consuming a perennial flow of revenue.

In an October 1987 Technical Subcommittee meeting, a National Park Service spokesman warned that one of the collared sub-adults ". . . now frequently crosses U.S. 1 and the Card Sound Road. Based on the volume of traffic on these two roads he feels that it is just a matter of time until this cat will likely be another casualty unless something is done." This warning resulted in a "discussion" and then a "decision" that the National Park Service "would draft a recommended plan of action." This plan of action will then be sent to the Fish and Wildlife Service, which, in turn, would send it out to the Technical Subcommittee for review (the people who will do these various things are sitting together in the same room—this the FPIC's Technical Subcommittee). The exchange may have been more disputatious than the minutes imply. The final sentence states that "the plan should address the problem as supported by their telemetry data and make recommendations relative to whether an attempt should be made to relocate the animal or implement safety measures designed to provided [sic] for a safer territory."[56] And so the record deteriorates into an incomprehensible babble. The "plan" alluded to here does not reappear in future minutes of the Technical Subcommittee. Nothing was done, and in July 1988, the panther was struck by an automobile near the Card Sound Road.

The prolonged refusal to engage in captive breeding has denied the Florida panther a fundamental security precaution, permitting inbreeding to go on with its deadly work. It entails a rejection of the postulate that cataclysmic events can be fatal to small populations, and it rejects the lessons offered by the dusky seaside sparrow and the black-footed ferret.

Reintroduction

One objective of the first Florida panther recovery plan in 1981 was to "reestablish populations where feasible."[57] It was apportioned into tasks: obtaining breeding stock, developing a restocking plan, determining the best raising and breeding techniques to insure survival, and acclimation, of the released animals, and so forth. The tale of most of these has been told in foregoing chapters. In the 1987 recovery plan this objective was refined to read as follows: "The recovery objective for the Florida panther is to achieve three viable, self-sustaining populations within the historic range of the animal. First priority will be to secure a viable population in South Florida. Viable population level will be determined

when enough data are available to develop a panther population model [The latter essential was avoided—until imposed from without in 1989]. The other two populations to be established will require separate population goals. . . ."[58]

These vital projects have been in the hands of the Game Commission. Most of the field work has been under the supervision of Chris Belden. It began after his reassignment from southern Florida in 1983. The project has been divided into four phases: 1) evaluation of potential areas; 2) captive rearing and release of properly conditioned offspring of non-coryi as surrogates; 3) release of wild-caught translocated panthers of non-coryi as surrogates; and 4) release of Florida panthers.[59] Belden estimated that five resident panthers, two males and three females, would need an area of 200 square miles.[60] In 1985 Belden and Bill Frankenberger, another Game Commission biologist, began evaluating reintroduction sites, applying to them the criteria of size, prey availability and land use.[61] Using the five-panther minimum population unit for calculating food requirements, Belden and Frankenberger postulated 129-178 deer to satisfy bodily maintenance (without any reproduction), a density of one per 216-298 acres. More would be needed for the panthers to raise offspring.[62]

One criterion evaluated the density of human habitation and the frequency of paved highways. The fewer highways the better, since panthers are notorious for colliding with automobiles. But what about the compatibility of panthers with humans? The puma has come to be associated with the idea of wilderness, but as suggested in Chapter 2, the cat's disappearance in the eastern United States was more likely due to prey depletion than from settlement per se. Humans were intolerant of panthers and zealously destroyed them, but it is not proved that panthers cannot tolerate some degree of human settlement. Heavily populated California has pumas, and the monitoring of radio-collared panthers in southern Florida suggests that the animals will adapt to the proximity of humans. In Everglades National Park, panthers have selected daytime resting sites within a few feet of personnel residences and busy campgrounds. In a state park in southern Florida, panthers have regularly traveled along boardwalks at night and are believed to be attracted to the park dumpster to feed on raccoons that scavenge there.[63]

Belden and Frankenberger investigated land use and human attitudes. As explained before, opinion surveys in Florida show strong support for the return of panthers.[64,65] However, a minority has reacted with alarm. A large cattle ranch in southern Florida, owned by the Mormon Church, denied access to Game Commission biologists wanting to search for panthers.[66] Some owners of large properties fear that finding the animal on their property might lead to restrictions on land use. In rural Franklin County, in the Florida panhandle, deer hunters persuaded their county commissioners to notify the Game Commission that no panthers would be

welcome in their county. The hunters feared the reintroduction might restrict hunting privileges.[67]

The rate of human population growth around a potential reintroduction site was also a measure of habitat suitability. Belden and Frankenberger believed that "it would be best if this predicted growth does not exceed 10% between 1985 and 1995."[68] This succinct sentence exposes the great menace to all of Florida's dwindling wildlife habitat. The final land use criterion was ownership, on which the two biologists concluded: "it is generally accepted that public ownership of panther habitat gives greater protection against habitat loss. . . . This benefit depends on the goals and policies of the managing agency, however, and can be offset by inflexibility in management programs that do not feature the panther."[69] The concluding phrase is a veiled reference to the inflexibility of certain government agencies. In 1987, 11 candidate sites were appraised. The Apalachicola National Forest and the Osceola National Forest (and the nearby Okeefenokee Swamp National Wildlife Refuge) were rated tops. They best satisfied all the criteria and were not far from White Oak Plantation.[70]

In 1988 came the next step. From the outset there had been fears about reactions in the rural hinterland to releasing a large predator, particularly in the rural regions of northern Florida. Proposals to reintroduce wolves in the West have met a wrathful reception from the stock owning populace. These worries in Florida had been eased by the canvassing of rural opinion in 1984.[71] However, Chris Belden went a step further. In the 1980s the Fish and Wildlife Service had finally reintroduced the red wolf. Belden invited Warren Parker, the project leader, to brief Game Commission personnel on the challenges he had encountered. Based on Parker's experiences, Belden drew up a list of "key constituents"—persons near the proposed release site who might be influential in local opinion: elected officials, principal landholders, public agency heads, cattlemen, spokesmen for conservation and sportsmen's organizations. To head off emotional reactions to the news that panthers were about to be let loose on the countryside, these leaders were contacted in person a short time before a news conference was held in Jacksonville to announce the plans. Information packets were handed out at the news conference. Because there were several hunting clubs near the chosen site, a special meeting was scheduled to talk over plans with the hunters. Since the liberated cats might drift over the state line, the Georgia Department of Natural Resources was informed. That agency also distributed an information pamphlet to citizens in southern Georgia. To win over cattlemen, the Buckeye Cellulose Corporation agreed to indemnify owners against livestock losses up to $10,000.[72] In short, the Game Commission, represented by Chris Belden, conducted a model, local, short-term education program to prepare the public for panther reintroduction.

The reply from the key constituents was summarized as follows: "Of 46 key contacts made, 39 (85%) were supportive of the reintroduction project, 6 (13%) either did not care one way or the other or would not express an opinion, and 1 (2%) was opposed . . . The few concerns that were expressed were the ones that had been anticipated, e.g. concerns for livestock, land use restrictions, and potential effects on hunting. On the whole the response was positive, with the primary opposition coming from hunting clubs that lease land for deer hunting."[73]

For the surrogate phase of reintroduction, five pumas were flown to Florida from Texas in the spring of 1988. They were surgically sterilized, fitted with radio-collars and trucked through the pine flatwoods in portable pens to a remote site on the Gilman Paper Company land near the Osceola National Forest. The pen gates were opened and deer meat placed outside. The intent was to accomplish a gentle release and not alarm the pumas. At first the animals were reluctant to leave their accustomed confinement. After ten minutes one of the females moved out and started to eat. Gradually the other cats wandered off into the woods. A yearling female did not leave her cage until 2:00 a.m. the following morning.[74]

The narrative in the Game Commission's Annual Performance Report sketches the movements of the released pumas:

> The first two weeks of movements by the released mountain lions are as follows: #T13, an adult female, initially moved to the west, and she traveled all the way to I-75 west of Jasper, FL. She then came back east to the Suwannee River and went south until she came to I-10 just north of Lake City. She then went north between Hwy 41 and I-75 to Genoa, FL, then back south to White Springs and back north along the Suwannee River. The interstate highways appear to be a barrier to her movements.
>
> #T14, a yearling female, made small movements and tended to stay in the same location for several days at a time. She stayed in the vicinity of the release pens for several days and then moved north, then spent some time around a pine island in a clear-cut which had an active turkey-feeder. She may have been feeding on small mammals attracted to the feeder. She spent one night in Georgia.
>
> #T15, an adult female, after making a loop and coming back to the vicinity of the release pens on June 16, moved away in a northerly direction. She made a large north and west loop through Georgia north of Needmore and Pineland, started south around Statenville, GA and then turned east again around Jasper,

FL. She came east to the Suwannee River then turned south, went into the Osceola National Forest and spent several days around Deep creek on Drew Grade.

#T16, an adult male, left the release pen and went west to the Suwannee River, with subsequent movements being restricted to a 12-mile stretch up and down the river.

#T18, the other adult male, was the most mobile of the 5. He moved south, went to near White Springs, crossed both interstate highways at their intersection and moved west until he got to the Suwannee River at Dowling Park, FL. He spent several days around Dowling Park and then returned eastward, traveling a little north of his westerly travels. He crossed the interstate highways again at the intersection and was bumped by a car while crossing I-75. He continued northeasterly, apparently unhurt, into Impassable Bay in the Osceola National Forest and then went back to the vicinity of the release site where he spent several days.[75]

The general movement data showed a drift towards the west with pumas at first hesitant to cross interstate highways and rivers. Belden and Frankenberger speculated that the westing tendency might indicate a homing instinct in the cats.[76] Soon there were problems. One puma died of unknown causes, two were illegally shot and a third was injured during a recapture and had to be killed. Two additional pumas were set free in March 1989 to partly compensate for the four casualties. The following month a puma was brought back to captivity after it took to stalking exotic deer at a private hunting preserve. Another cat was retrieved when it wandered into the suburbs of Jacksonville. The researchers found it napping in a tree. The project was cut short in May 1989, when the two remaining pumas in the wild were ordered to be recaptured.[77]

Early in May, a memo referencing the recently terminated experiments went from the regional director of the Fish and Wildlife Service to administrators in the Game Commission, National Park Service and the Florida DNR. "By now we have all had an opportunity to reflect on the recent decision to remove from the wild all remaining animals serving as surrogates in the translocation experiment in North Florida. I suspect considerable thought has also been given to where we go from here." The communication affirmed that the data from the experiment would be analyzed and that the reintroduction project would go on.[78] It said also that there appeared to be "an excellent opportunity to launch a new thrust in our recovery program." The new thrust turned out to be a scheme to set the remaining neutered Texas female puma at large in the Big Cypress National Preserve—to see what

would happen.[79] A reasonable prediction would be (a) the cat would waste away to the deplorable state of health that had been observed in others before it, (b) the newcomer would clash with any resident panthers that might be present or (c) the cat would wander, possibly fighting with established panthers elsewhere in the region. It would be an experiment that might easily come to grief and from which no useful outcome could be predicted. Amateur hour was in full swing at the FPIC. A more promising experiment would be to try and increase deer numbers in the Big Cypress National Preserve to see if the panthers would benefit, but that was not a subject the agencies would talk about.

On May 24, 1989, the Panther Advisory Council came together in Gainesville. The members flatly refused to endorse the ill-considered proposal to release the Texas puma in southern Florida. A Game Commission official was asked to outline his agency's future plans, whereupon he informed the room that it was still committed to reintroduction. The first phase of the work had come to an end. It was now time to move on the next, which would be to condition kittens for release into the wild. I could not refrain from pointing out that phase two was impossible owing to the fact of no kittens being available for conditioning. This observation brought a long silence . . . "Yes," said the official at last, "that is a problem. We are behind schedule on that part of the project." Indeed!

PART TWO: THE PROBLEM

Chapter 8

THE FLORIDA GAME AND FRESH WATER FISH COMMISSION

There are two kinds of logic:
real logic and Game Commission logic.

Anonymous Game Commission biologist, 1986

"In the destruction of wild life I think the backwoods population of Florida is the most lawless and defiant in the United States. . . . From a zoological point of view, Florida is in bad shape. A great many of her people who shoot are desperately lawless and uncontrollable, and the state is not financially able to support a force of wardens sufficiently strong to enforce the laws, even as they are. It looks as if the slaughter would go on until nothing of the bird life remains. At present, I can see no hope whatever for saving even a good remnant of the wild life of the state."[1]

Thus declared William T. Hornaday in his crusading volume, *Our Vanishing Wildlife*, in 1913. Hornaday stumped the country early in this century promoting the cause of wildlife protection with the zealotry of an Old Testament prophet. He was a gifted speaker and a persuasive writer, a hunter by hobby and a taxidermist by profession, who in the 1880s came to be the chief taxidermist for the U. S. National Museum. Hornaday had collected and worked during the calamitous fall of American wildlife. He saw deer herds diminished in the East, and he watched bison vanish from the western plains. The animals were taken by the millions to be sold at market for meat and hides (and bones in the case of bison). The market hunter became the *bete noire* of the incipient wildlife protection movement.

Hornaday could see other species sliding toward the abyss. He preached salvation through a gospel of protection that prescribed strong laws, efficient enforcement and protected refuges. He was a single-minded, uncompromising, eloquent and choleric man who swung "a mighty sword with such vigor that he often laid open his allies along with his enemies."[2] He is largely forgotten now, but in his day he was the best-known advocate of wildlife protection in the country—with the possible exception of Theodore Roosevelt.

Hornaday was a driving force and despite the grating personality traits that accompany towering egos and fixed opinions his accomplishments were many and solid in the context of his times. In 1913 he judged the poor, rural state of Florida to be a hopeless case. But the winds of change, if not exactly blowing, were beginning to freshen. National attention was being called to Florida's laggard performance in protecting its wildlife. A few years earlier, when the Audubon Society had assigned a warden to guard bird rookeries in the Everglades, he had been murdered by plume hunters, creating a national sensation. When the Audubon Society hired a warden to protect federal bird reservations in Charlotte Harbor, he was found dead a few weeks later wedged under the seat of his patrol boat which had been holed and filled with sandbags to sink it.[3]

Neighboring Georgia and Alabama had their game departments in place by this time. The director of Alabama's wildlife agency had been inspired the year before to take Florida to task in *Forest and Stream*, a national hunting and fishing magazine. "Birds know no state lines, and while practically all the States lying to the north of Florida protect migratory birds and waterfowl, yet these are recklessly slaughtered in that state to such an extent as to be appalling to all sportsmen and bird lovers. So alarming has become the decrease of the birds and game of Florida that unless a halt is called on the campaign of reckless annihilation that has been ceaselessly waged in that state, the sport and recreation enjoyed by primeval nimrods will linger only in history and tradition . . . ."[4]

As early as 1828 Florida had put its first game law on the books when the territorial legislature prohibited fire-hunting west of the Suwannee River.[5] Other protective statutes had been enacted later, but with no agency of enforcement they were widely ignored. But the publicity of the early 1900s seems to have animated elected officials. In 1913 the Florida legislature established the post of State Game and Fish Commissioner to supervise a Department of Fish and Game. The enabling legislation of that year did not actually create a Game Commission in the modern sense; it simply decorated the head of the new Department with the title of commissioner.

But it was a beginning. The commissioner was to be appointed by the governor every two years and was to have an office and a clerk. The Department was to enforce the game laws and to issue hunting licenses and permits, which were required for the collecting of birds or their nests or eggs, and for the transport of "more than ten pairs of any one species of game, birds, or fish within or without this state."[6] Wardens were to be designated in each county, to be paid by one-fourth of the fines they collected. The commissioner was to be paid $2,500 a year. He was required to give bond of $5,000 to ensure he accounted for "all monies which may come into his hands in his official capacity."[7] It would appear that the integrity of public officials was not taken for granted in those days. The salary of the

commissioner, and the operations of his department, were to be paid from a Game and Fish Protection Fund to be raised from the sale of hunting licenses and from fines, penalties and forfeitures "arising from the Game Laws of this state."[8]

These funding provisions must have been inadequate. The new commissioner, E. Z. Jones, complained in his first annual report to the governor that "the Legislature unfortunately overlooked the necessity of providing means for the enforcement of laws they enacted to govern this department . . . . One can easily believe," he speculated, " that the laws were passed in their present form more for revenue to the state than for protecting the Game, Birds and Fish, which as a matter of course is not correct as the primary purpose of the laws is protection."[9] Jones also was not generous to the lawmakers who had just created his department: "Had the mental eyes of our Legislature of a few years ago only scanned the distance which now lies between our woods which were at that time teeming with such a sort of bird and wild game life and those same woods now practically denuded of the wealth they once possessed what a blessing to Florida it would have been."[10]

After drawing attention to the Legislature's lack of foresight in not creating his department sooner, Jones moved on to a rambling opinion of the motives of the legislators in acting when they did, and on their lack of acuity in general. "In the enactment of the laws creating this Department our legislators exhibited a great interest in the subject matter at their hands. Such interest which existed was not expected to accomplish as much good as was accomplished as most of them were dealing with a subject unfamiliar to them (as is often the case with legislators) and a subject to which they had not given the least thought and were therefore unable to see any distance beyond their own personal interest without very serious consideration."[11] Jones went on to catalogue deficiencies in the law, giving his thoughts on how they might be corrected. One recommendation was for a raise in his salary. He then made an acerbic forecast: "I have not the least idea that the larger percent of these recommendations will be provided. . . ."[12]

The Legislature answered these grievances at its next biennial session in 1915 by abolishing its fledgling Department of Fish and Game, thereby confirming William T. Hornaday's assessment of Florida. A later commentator remarked of E. Z. Jones that he was "earnest" but "not skilled in the game of politics as it was being played in Florida." Evidently not; the Legislature not only abolished Jones' position but apparently all the state's game laws as well.[13]

However, even if the state's first commissioner had been a diplomat, there are reasons to question whether Florida's nascent attempt to guard its fish and wildlife resources would have fared any better. New regulatory measures typically engender opposition. Those hindered by them may have been napping at the time of enactment, but they were soon aroused. Jones had reported in his second annual

report in 1915 that a large number of commercial fishermen had "organized in rebellion against enforcement of fish laws."[14] Their tactic was to agree among themselves to serve a jail sentence if apprehended, rather than pay a fine. Under the system of that day, the county and the warden were provided an incentive to arrest and convict, by being reimbursed a portion of the fine. There was no fishing license then. Jones advocated a license for each net; he did not, he wrote, believe there would be any strong opposition. The opinion gives pause since he also pointed out that the fishermen were in rebellion.[15] Jones also implied in his 1915 report that the performance of most of the state's county judges left something to be desired in the handling of cases brought before them. County judges of course were closely attuned to, and usually part of, local sentiment about game and fish laws.

Apparently economic trends did not favor game protection in Florida. In his 1915 report Jones explained that a "deficiency of receipts [from the sale of hunting licenses] of 1914-15 compared with receipts for 1913-14, should be attributed mainly to the financial conditions of the country, which has affected each and every commercial industry in the world"[16] (presumably a reference to the outbreak of World War I, in August 1914, which disrupted world commerce). While the economy was going into a slump and Jones was cracking down on the sale of game, demand and price were going up. Congress had banned the interstate sale of game in 1900 with passage of the first federal wildlife law, the Lacy Act, which was apparently ignored in Florida. "When this Department was created in Florida," wrote Jones, "quail was [sic] being shipped to various States and countries at not more than fifty cents each, and the price generally twenty-five cents each. By reason of the fact that I have refused for animals and birds to be shipped from this State for commercial purposes, prices have been steadily going up. There is a ready market for quails [sic] at thirty dollars per dozen; wild turkey hens, twenty dollars each, and gobblers, sixteen dollars each; wild otters, twenty-five dollars each; foxes, twenty dollars per pair; o'possums, twelve dollars per pair; coons, six dollars per pair; deer, fifty dollars each; skunk [sic], five dollars each. There is not a wild animal in the State but what has its own value for some purpose."[17]

There was an interesting postscript to the economic observation. The United States entered the war in 1917; the demand for food went sharply up, whereupon the archenemy of game protectionists, the market hunters, attempted a comeback—to contribute to the war effort of course. In several states, legislatures were lobbied to relax all hunting restrictions for the duration of hostilities. Conservationists fought back. Theodore Roosevelt thundered at the "profiteering proposal of the pseudo-patriots, the patriots for revenue only." Echoing Petain at Verdun he declared that the "united hosts of conservation reply: 'You shall not pass'."[18] Although the game laws came through the crisis, many fishing regulations were set aside, and state fish commissioners encouraged a greater use of fish to conserve meat. It is reported that Florida requested the Food Administration to

approve the killing of a million brown pelicans which were alleged to be eating $950,000 worth of food fish daily. This mad scheme was headed off by the Audubon Society,[19] but the fact that such a proposal could be made hints at the general mood in Florida. (When a reliable census of Florida's brown pelicans became possible in later decades, the total nesting population of the peninsula was estimated at about 13,000 adults.[20])

Florida's reaction to its first game agency was atypically harsh (although Missouri had an identical experience),[21] but the early game departments often navigated in hostile political currents. In a lecture at Yale University about this time, William T. Hornaday exhorted the citizen to support the commissions.

> No state game commission dares go to extremes in demanding more drastic protective laws, because to do so means incurring the open, active hostility of thousands of gunners who are ever ready to fight for their killing privileges, even unto the destruction of their own game commission. Any game commissioner who defies that body of men, in order to do his duty, takes his official life in his hands and must expect to meet his enemies in a death grapple before his legislature. . . . It is only the strongest of the state game commissions, those whose members are assured of strong outside support, who dare to advocate before their legislatures the drastic measure which alone will serve to save the present wildlife situation.[22]

The conservationists and sportsmen of Florida tried again. Another remarkable conservation leader, T. Gilbert Pearson, was thrown into the breach. Pearson was secretary of the National Association of Audubon Societies, a position he had held since 1905.[23] And during every legislative session since that year, he had been in Florida, lobbying for the creation of a game department. Success had crowned his years of labor in 1913 only to be blown away by the political winds of 1915. He journeyed once more to Tallahassee in 1917 to try and shepherd a game department bill through the legislature. Years later he reminisced about the confrontation: "In 1917, I was again working in Tallahassee, and again we got our bill through to establish a game department, but Florida had for Governor a Baptist preacher named Catts. As a bird lover, I naturally mistrusted any creature by that name, and my suspicions proved to be well-founded. He refused to sign the bill. Exhausted from pleading with him, I ran my handkerchief over my perspiring brow and departed for other fields."[24] It would take dejected sportsmen and conservationists nearly a decade to resurrect the machinery of game protection in Florida.

The Beginnings of Conservation

The American conservation movement took shape in the Northeast after the Civil War. It was a reaction to the destructive aspects of population growth and industrialization. At the outset of war in 1861, the East, though beginning to industrialize, was still agricultural while most of the West was an unexplored wilderness. But in the final years of the century the United States surpassed all nations in industrial and agricultural production. The country was rich in natural resources: vast coal fields and iron mines fed a new steel industry; oil, discovered in 1859 soon nourished a financial empire. Native manpower was inadequate to service this transforming scene, and the need was met by immigrants from Europe. The masses came and the cities to house them grew from the timber of forests that were recklessly felled with never a thought for the morrow. The booming populace needed protein, and the native fish and wildlife resources were shot, trapped and trawled to furnish it.

The industrialization that raised cities also created wealth, at first in the hands of a few, but the mass of well-to-do citizens grew steadily. Wealth gave them advantages of education and leisure. Among the activities at hand to fill the spare hours were field sports: the taking of fish and game primarily for enjoyment rather than of necessity. Thus a common pastime of wealthy classes in Europe found its way to adoption in America. However, the conflict that sprang from this confluence of forces still plagues us: the growth of human numbers, particularly when accompanied by wealth, is achieved by depleting the natural resources that wealth and leisure put us in a position to enjoy.

A conventional view has it that the conservation movement originated at the turn of the century under the driving personalities of Gifford Pinchot and Theodore Roosevelt, as evidenced by their enduring achievements in forest conservation, but although the two men popularized the term "conservation," the movement to conserve (via "protection") game animals for sport was in place well before 1900, and fish conservation began even earlier. These developments were researched by the historian, John Reiger. The movement to conserve fish was the first popular conservation crusade. In the 1860s several New England state legislatures were petitioned to stop the ravages of commercial netters. In Massachusetts alone petitions signed by almost 11,000 people were presented to the legislature in 1870.[25] Massachusetts founded a Commission of Fisheries and Game in 1865; it was probably the first state to do so.[26] Other states followed sporadically. As shown by the title of the agency in Massachusetts, wildlife was simply an adjunct responsibility handed to the early fish commissions in coastal New England. The first annual report of the New Hampshire Commission on Fisheries and Game devoted two paragraphs to wildlife and the rest to fish.[27] But wildlife worries were soon pressing.

The role of the states in marine fisheries was diluted in 1871 when the federal government set up the United States Fish Commission—the first federal agency formed to conserve a specific natural resource.[28] Federal responsibility was essential because the demands of protecting coastal fisheries reached beyond the boundaries of any single state. Wildlife, on the other hand, has remained prominent as a state responsibility even though a federal wildlife agency was eventually formed. And, as indicated in previous chapters of this book, when conflicts arise, the real authority of state wildlife agencies, vis-a-vis the fed, is usually greater than it appears to be on paper.

These early commissions, which became quasi-independent political institutions, were extraordinarily effective and efficient. They became "independent" in the sense that the authority for making and implementing game and fish policies was transferred (or more accurately, wrested) from the executive branch of government and entrusted to a board of appointed citizens. Such a shift in itself does nothing to promote an exceptional department of government. Its fineness of execution was owed to a design insuring that persons with the best professional qualifications were called to serve. Professional excellence, wedded to dedication of purpose, was institutionalized at the top.

The popular magazine was another novelty of this era. Several in the 1870s that were devoted to the interests of sportsmen supplied one of the indispensables for an effective system of wildlife protection: public education. To build a base of opinion that would bring the governmental correctives to fruition, the sportsmen's magazines preached the need to organize politically. In one year, during the winter of 1874-1875, nearly 100 local sportsmen's clubs sprang up around the country. Ten or twelve statewide associations were formed and one national association.[29] A new political force had arrived on the American scene; it remains to this day although other conservation branches with different orientations have since appeared.

Other states followed New England as the new breed of conservationists cast about for a mechanism to halt the destruction of wildlife. As more and more urban aficionados of field sports took to the field in pursuit of game, they found it disappearing before the ravages of commercial exploitation. The idea of the government setting aside land to protect and manage natural assets had not yet taken hold. Some of the sportsmen's clubs purchased or leased lands as private game preserves, but these holdings were too small to protect migratory or wide-ranging species. The great need of the day was simply protection from unregulated killing. Local game laws had been sporadically enacted since colonial times, but by the 1870s this legal patchwork was ineffectual. Ordinances regulating the taking of game were often left to municipalities or counties, so that they were not uniform

and were sometimes inadequate, or if local sentiment dictated, they didn't even exist.[30]

The sportsmen's clubs lobbied their legislatures to enact firmer laws. In 1879 the New York Association for the Protection of Game succeeded, after a hard fight, in pushing through a uniform state game code which removed the power to make game laws from the towns and counties and vested it at the state level. Enforcement though remained in local hands.[31] And the sportsmen would soon learn that the best laws are useless without a government mechanism to execute them effectively—a lesson still valid today.

Maine led the way in the 1870s with salaried game wardens.[32] In other states, sportsmen clamored for wardens. One by one, state legislatures began to authorize law-enforcement positions and a central administration to direct them. Unfortunately, the performance of these creations was frequently disappointing. In the days before civil service (or its equivalent at the state level), positions in the bureaucracy were filled by political patronage. The incumbent administration's selections were aimed at maintaining itself in power. The appointee's qualifications were usually an afterthought if they were thought about at all. If new laws conflicted with rustic traditions, they were seen in the countryside as something to ignore or circumvent; enforcement was trying and sometimes dangerous. In these circumstances, only men of the most willful and resolute character could make a name as wardens. The political spoils practice did not seek them out—a fact readily observed by the sportsmen who were sharply attentive to the game shortage and impatient for results.

Game protection was intolerant of laxity. Consider the white-tailed deer. If a herd has been reduced to a low density it can recover if given complete protection; but since, at the start of the rebuilding period, the number of deer is very low, only a few will reach maturity during each season. Some of this increment will be lost to predators and to other natural causes, so several years must pass before the herd reaches a threshold of substantial production. Even moderate killing by humans in the early phase can cancel the small annual increase. Years may pass without improvements in the shortage of deer.

The sportsmen's magazines next campaigned to free the departments from politics. Building an opinion stout enough to bring change in this field can be a drawn-out struggle, as it proved with the independent commissions. But the persevering sportsmen-editors knew what they wanted. One of the more influential, George Bird Grinnell of *Forest and Stream*, crusaded for 12 years to have the administration of New York's natural resources separated from politics; he endlessly repeated the point that efficient management of the state's natural assets would be obtained only in the hands of impartial experts.[33] Grinnell's exertions

were repaid in 1899 when his friend Theodore Roosevelt was elected Governor. Roosevelt first tried to restructure the state's Fisheries, Game and Forest Commission, but not even he could at first override the opposition to this idea. The commission was a source of patronage, and the state's politicians were unalterably against changing it.[34] Roosevelt did name men of exceptional ability to vacancies, but the "independent" commission was still in the future at this date.

In the mid-1880s an incipient interest in protecting non-game birds began to furnish allies to the game protectionists. George Bird Grinnell also helped to found in 1886 what would become the National Audubon Society, to stop the slaughter of wading birds which were being destroyed by the thousands to supply the millinery trade. Thus, the animus to conserve wildlife as a recreational resource was supplemented by the desire to conserve it for aesthetic reasons. The activists who sprang to these new principles came up hard against a prevailing view that saw wildlife as purely a commercial resource.

The movement to safeguard non-game wildlife was a different emphasis but not a divergent one—as it would sometimes tend to become later in the twentieth century. At the time, sport hunting was viewed as a masculine activity and the sportsmen's clubs were made up of men. The appreciation of birds with its emphasis on aesthetics was seen as something appropriate to women, although the practical needs of guardianship were energetically pursued by both sexes. Nonetheless, it was this novel endearment to birds that allowed the conservation movement to expand by incorporating a faction having no particular interest in the sporting aspect of wildlife preservation. The common stake in protection bonded the two forces.

It is interesting to note that the eradication of predators was also a common desire of the early conservationists. "There are several species of birds," wrote William T. Hornaday, "that may at once be put under sentence of death for their destructiveness of useful birds, without any extenuating circumstances worth mentioning. Four of these are *Cooper's Hawk*, the *Sharp-shinned Hawk*, *Pigeon Hawk* and *Duck Hawk*." He added that "fortunately these species are not so numerous that we need lose any sleep over them."[35] The attitudes of the early wildlife protectionists were still partly under the utilitarian influence, and they were proper Victorians as well who saw good and evil reflected back at them from the world of animals. Predators were powerful destroyers of the weak and innocent. The early wildlife protectionists had no grasp of the natural laws that governed the dynamics of wildlife interactions. Today we are prone to be amused (or dismayed) at such unsophistication, but although this particular black-and-white view of wild creatures is no longer with us, other mythical interpretations have taken its place.

In the days before the national income tax (which began in a modest way in 1913), there was no government bureaucracy to speak of, there being no way to pay for it. The few government institutions that could fund themselves out of their own receipts prospered, while others languished. For example, although the first National Park was created in 1872 out of land that did not require acquisition, it had to be staffed initially by the U. S. Army. As an institution the National Park Service was not possible until a dependable source of revenue could be tapped (the National Park Service was created in 1916—three years after the income tax arrived). By contrast, the vastly larger U.S. National Forest Service financed itself through the sale of its principal product, timber.[36] The state game agencies, in starting out, limped along on a trickle of disbursements from the state treasuries, until, in 1895, North Dakota introduced the hunting license. An idea whose time has come catches on quickly (provided that someone is bold enough to take the first step). By 1922 all but 14 states issued licenses.[37] However, many tip-toed into the business, at first stipulating that only out-of-state residents purchase them.[38]

Progress in Florida

Meanwhile, back in Florida the need for wildlife protection remained, and political support gained as the years passed. In 1925 the public will manifested itself in a legislative resurrection dubbed the Department of Game and Fresh Water Fish. The reborn agency came about under the stimulus of the Isaac Walton League. Florida became the forty-sixth state out of 48 to legislate a department "for the conservation of wild life."[39] The first biennial report of the new agency chronicled, among other things, the hunter casualties of the 1927-1928 hunting season. "E. E. Cone of Tampa was accidentally shot by a companion while hunting in Collier County. The two men were charged by a wild bull. Cone's hunting companion fired at the infuriated animal just as Cone ran between the gun and the bull. He was shot in the back. Death resulted." Another casualty: "An unknown man who was yelping like a turkey in woods near Callahan was mistaken for one by a nearby hunter who fired without assuring himself that the bird was there. The shot proved fatal."[40]

The new department, following a contemporary practice, set aside secure breeding sites for deer. A law of 1927 authorized the refuges, or breeding grounds, and by 1936 there were 65 of them in Florida.[41] Although most state game commissions were successful in rebuilding deer herds, Florida, as explained in Chapter 2, made little headway until after World War II. Deer prospered on a few refuges, but poaching was rampant and manpower short. In 1932 there were only 40 wardens to police 67 counties, although sportsmen's clubs helped to guard some of the breeding grounds.[42] A frustration for years in the state's rural counties was that the courts were sympathetic to poaching, an activity locally regarded as a traditional past-time and no business of the state government.

National concern for wildlife reached an unprecedented intensity in the mid-1930s. To the troubled American psyche, then trying to cope with the aftermath of a worldwide economic collapse, came the worst natural disaster in the country's history.[43] A prolonged drought of several years duration turned the topsoil of the western prairies into black powder which was picked up by the wind and carried all the way to the Atlantic coast. The skies over the Midwest were blacked out at mid-day. In Washington, D.C., at the time of an approaching continental dust storm, ". . . hearings were being held on the question of whether to give the Soil Erosion Service permanent official status." The storm closed in and darkened the committee room where testimony was being heard. "Congress quickly passed the bill that established a Soil Conservation Service. . . ."[44]

The dust bowl, as it came to be called, crushed wildlife as well as people. It virtually wiped out the waterfowl of central North America. Legislation erected administrative devices to mend the mayhem. In Florida the governor signed a bill in 1935 that amended an earlier act and created a State Commission of Game and Fresh Water Fish, to comprise five persons named by the governor, one from each congressional district.[45] Six years later the legislature went with the popular surge by adopting a constitutional amendment that shaped the agency in its present form, which the voters ratified in November.[46] The 1930s and 1940s were the popular high-water mark for these hard-won instruments of the American sportsmen. Under Florida's constitution the Game Commission was empowered to fix bag limits and seasons, and to regulate the manner of taking, transporting, using and storing wildlife, and to acquire property for its purposes. The legislature retained power to enact license laws and fix penalties.[47]

If the Game Commission was elated by its fortune in the 1940s it also had cause for alarm. The United States was at war again and fiscal prospects were bleak. Gasoline and ammunition were being rationed, and hunters were heading out to the distant theaters of combat. The agency's 1942 Biennial Report reads like a chamber of commerce brochure enticing the citizen to come hunt and fish:

> To those of us who remain to "keep the home fires burning" we wish to add this word of warning: if you have felt that you would put away your guns and fishing equipment we ask that you do not do so. Past experience has taught us that this annual harvesting of a portion of our game and crop is an essential part of our game management program. This fact together with the fact that the annual license fees paid by sportsmen for the privilege of hunting and fishing, without which the Commission cannot continue to function, prompt us to urge the continuance of these sports whenever possible. Our program of conservation must cease to

function when hunting and fishing ceases and the entire state will pay the penalty. Your trips for the purpose of hunting and fishing will of necessity be fewer, but make them when you can. Good, healthful recreation is as essential during these trying times as good food.[48]

The Audubon Societies fostered some of the early game departments. In one interesting instance, in North Carolina in 1903 —the first South Atlantic or Gulf State to provide for game wardens —the Audubon Society was made the executive agency.[49] In Florida, in 1913, E. Z. Jones had paid tribute: "The work of the Audubon Societies of the State should be appreciated very much, not only by the officers of this Department, but by every citizen of the State. By cooperating with them this Department can obtain valuable assistance and information pertaining to the nature, protection and value of wild life. . . ."[50]

T. Gilbert Pearson personified the bond between Audubon and the state game agencies by serving in turn during the 1930s as president of the National Audubon Society and president of the National Association of Game and Fish Commissioners.[51] In Florida, every year until 1940, the annual and biennial reports of the Game Commission paid tribute to the Florida Audubon Society, and later to the National Association. Wardens of the Audubon Society in Florida held honorary commissions as Conservation Officers of the Game Commission.[52] In later decades the Florida Audubon Society and the Game Commission would occasionally clash over issues. In the late 1930s, the Game Commission reports also began to pay tribute to the new Florida Wildlife Federation—an association of the statewide sportsmen's clubs.

The Coming of Wildlife Management

The sportsmen, after long travail, had forged an arm of government to safeguard their interest, and this great institution served the ends of wildlife protection well, restoring the country's depleted game animals and plume birds. The sportsmen-directed commissions were born of the evolving national quest for wildlife protection, an era whose dimensions were framed and filled by a 70-year crusade to install its design throughout the Union. But the currents of change are never stilled, and they were shifting again even as the movement was reaching fulfillment in the 1930s. In that decade the protection paradigm began the transition to the era of wildlife management. It had been discovered that some game animals went on declining despite protection and restocking. When the new era dawned, the protection system, now matured in its role, revealed a flaw. The organized hunters, always ready to fight at the drop of a hat, would not accept the prescriptions of the new breed of wildlife biologists. Resistance was most often triggered by deer policies, and the problem lingers to this day—as laments in the literature of deer

management will attest.[53] While the citizen commissioners had fortified the professionals of wildlife protection against indifferent or incompetent political appointees, they did not shield wildlife science from the political influence of uniformed hunters. Aldo Leopold was dismayed that the commissions failed to insulate the new profession from the force of this branch of opinion, so that it might take the long view of conservation rather than the short. His battles with emotional citizens, as a commissioner advocating the reduction of overly large deer herds, brought home to him the commission's vulnerability to uninformed sentiment.

Leopold's unshakable conviction of the need for herd reduction in Wisconsin raised public anger against him to a white heat. He doggedly pushed through a reduction policy—against frantic opposition—in 1943, but the remedy went awry. Unscrupulous hunters found a way to take "extra" deer by having their wives purchase a license. In one county, 500 women were issued licenses in contrast to 24 the previous year. Heavy snows forced hunters to concentrate in some areas with the result that deer herds in different regions were either decimated or scarcely affected. The hunt became known as the "Crime of '43," and Leopold became a target of wrath. Libelous articles were written about him. Undeterred, he pushed ahead, advocating further reductions; but the other commissioners capitulated. The fury had risen to such a pitch that some citizen groups wanted to abolish the Commission. Leopold's view of this crisis was that if the public would not tolerate intelligent deer management by its Commission, then it had no need of one. "The old system of political conservation football would do just as well."[54]

The Modern Era

Florida's Game Commission entered the modern era after World War II, hiring its first biologist, Earl Frye, in 1945. He later became the agency's executive director. A source of funding for wildlife research had been written into law in 1937. The Federal Aid to Wildlife Restoration Act (better known as the Pittman-Robertson Act) placed a federal excise tax on sporting arms and ammunition. The proceeds went to the states to be used for wildlife research and restoration. The 1947-1948 Biennial Report boasted that "two years ago the Game and Fresh Water Fish Commission had less than 200 employees, 170 of them wildlife officers. . . . for years, no technical or biological staff had ever been organized. Conservation education and public relations had not been developed to any extent. . . . Today the Commission has a total of 291 employees, 288 of whom are wildlife officers; 40 are biologists, technicians, or specialists in other fields and 23 are general administrative employees or laborers."[55] The post-war period was marked by game surveys and restoration projects, and extensive restocking of deer and turkeys. The Game Commission also acquired land for wildlife management areas and negotiated a number of hunting leases with owners of large tracts of private land.

With the coming of environmental awareness in the 1970s, the Game Commission added an environmental services section to monitor the impact of land-use practices, and another section to regulate the importation of exotic animals into the state. With change came ferment; the agency became mired in its first anti-hunting uproar in 1982, when animal rights activists blocked a hunt which had been scheduled to reduce a deer herd facing starvation in a flooded Water Conservation Area.[56] Officials had advocated shooting 2,200 deer in what it called a "mercy hunt." The activists wanted to capture the deer and remove them from danger, undaunted by fact that there was no unoccupied habitat that could have accommodated them. The affair turned into a media circus, and television news reporters had a field day. Would-be rescuers chased deer with air boats, catching 19 animals—13 of which died.[57] Deer are high-strung creatures subject to trauma and shock in this kind of capture, and they were weakened from hunger. Game Commission biologists foretold the outcome, but the rescuers were not prepared to be instructed. An avalanche of letters from around the country permanently stopped the hunt, and prolonged high water killed a good many deer (estimates are as high as 1,200).[58]

Following the uproar, Governor Graham appointed a multi-agency committee to submit a management policy for the deer herd in the Water Conservation Areas.[59] The recommendation was to keep deer "at a population level that closely approximates the number of animals that can reasonably exist in the area with water levels at the maximum regulation schedule, less 20 percent to account for times that the regulation schedule may be exceeded."[60] In plain words this meant that deer would be hunted heavily enough to hold them below carrying capacity, so that they would not become crowded during periods of flood. It was in effect a form of political wildlife management. Hunting pressure was applied and there was no more turmoil. After this event, not only would the Game Commission feel pressured to pander to the proclivities of hunters, but also to be wary of a hostile faction bent on bringing an end to hunting. These accumulating oppressions have not made for a forward-looking institution.

In the 1980s the agency took on the endangered species burden. Florida is a runaway growth state with an environment characterized by temperate and tropical biological components and also by an endemic biota. It harbors numerous endangered species. But fees from licenses and fines have been outpaced by growing responsibilities. In 1973 the Game Commission in Florida became the first in the Southeast to seek general revenues to supplement its internal sources. Two million dollars were received in that year and four million in 1976.[61] The current annual budget now exceeds $30 million; nearly half coming from the state's general revenue fund.[62]

The Game Commission Today

Today's executive director may have one of the more difficult jobs in state government; he must weigh the recommendations of his biological staff, filtering up from the field, and not just on their biological merits; he must intuitively gauge the temperament and leaning of his five bosses to assess how policy proposals might be greeted by them; he is ever conscious that each Commission meeting will be filled with representatives from hunting interests around the state, and that they will have a very definite and usually predictable, if not always well-informed, positions (supported by letter-writers back home) on policy. Representatives of hunting groups are not the only persons present at Commission meetings, but they predominate as can be seen in a review of the minutes of any meeting. Although today's Game Commission has been delegated to serve a broad range of environmental and wildlife interests, recreational hunters are still the most forceful presence in the agency's affairs. It is the only faction that, when satisfied, the Game Commission can always count as allies, and it is the only one perpetually ready to pounce when displeased. The hunters are vigilant and explosive constituents. In a political environment that has lately shown signs of hostility to hunting, and by extension to game commissions, support from hunters is not to be taken lightly. Their interests can never be ignored, and it should not be assumed that they can always be treated objectively by beleaguered commissioners, even when the interests of hunters come in conflict with a larger one. The agency's attentiveness to hunting also has an internal dynamic. It has traditionally drawn its personnel from those who enjoy hunting and fishing, although that has changed in recent years. Despite occasional conflicts over policy, there is a covenant between hunters and the agency, a bond perhaps heightened in recent times by the emergence of a mood which wants to eliminate sport hunting altogether.

Sport-hunting has a proud tradition, of which its responsible practitioners are fully aware. As described, it was one of the foundations of the American conservation movement. It embodied an unbending code of ethics that addressed personal conduct and responsibility toward wildlife as a component of responsible citizenship. The code was so rigid that it often impeded the advance of scientific game management, but it was, and still is, important to the way that responsible hunters view themselves and their place in society. This is unfathomable to opponents of the sport, but it has a powerful grip on hunters.

Of course, the commissioners do not owe their positions to the hunters. Gubernatorial appointments, in theory, insulate them from the anger of constituents displeased with unpopular decisions, but that is theory only. The hunting organizations are tireless and persistent in conveying their wants—and displeasures. The commissioners are not immune from the pressure—as has been

demonstrated. Thus it can happen that recommendations representing the best judgement from the field are not always adopted, and not in a timely manner if they are. In ordinary departmental decisions the result may only be poor management. With an endangered species it can prove fatal.

The Commission and the Panther

In 1976 the agency found itself abruptly in the lead role of a momentous enterprise to prevent the loss of a large predator. It was not prepared either in the way of staffing or of money. Several years would pass before finances were equal to the challenge. However, given the material constraints, it performed well at the outset. The inability of the Commission to act objectively was adumbrated in 1978 when its biologists advocated the precaution of closing the Fakahatchee Strand State Preserve to hunting.[63] But the appointed body took nine years to adopt the rules that would have been imposed at the first suggestion of its field staff, if institutional reasoning had been structured on the principle of minimizing risk to the endangered animal. By contrast, in another instance of an indirect threat to the panther, the Game Commission response was exemplary. In the early 1980s an oil company sought a permit to build a road into the Big Cypress Swamp from Alligator Alley. Environmentalists objected. In particular the hunters were adverse and made their displeasure known. The Game Commission was galvanized; its move against the oil drilling threat was a model of energy and administrative skill. With the solid backing not only of its traditional constituency, but of others as well, it could not have done more.

The executive director made a personal appeal to the governor, submitting his appreciation of the threat in writing:

> . . . Perhaps fewer than 20 total panthers remain, making the species [sic] one of the most endangered in the world. Our margin for error in exploiting its habitat is obviously extremely narrow. It is, therefore, incumbent upon the Commission, as the State agency responsible for managing Florida's terrestrial wildlife, to take all necessary measures to ensure the continued survival of that species [sic]. . . .

> The access road for which the Exxon Company has requested a permit to construct from Alligator Alley southward to the Eleven Mile Road is a dramatic example of the type of access that will adversely impact the Florida panther. . . .

> In 1976, when Eleven Mile Road was originally permitted, the Cabinet recognized the value of having a "master plan" for oil

production in the Big Cypress Preserve to use in evaluating future production plans and impacts to other natural values in the area (see attached copy of Cabinet minutes, July 20, 1976). Such a plan has not been prepared, and with the Florida panther having now become such an important environmental consideration, the need for such a "master plan," especially as it pertains to road construction, is even more important than it was six years ago.[64]

The upshot was the adoption of an access plan to regulate oil exploration.[65] It was the most that could be done. The Game Commission had been inspired, watching every move, acting decisively and fighting hard.

The above letter shows that it was keenly attuned to the shaky status of the panther as it was then known, and that it was quite capable of seeing the imperative for broad planning, and that the institutional memory was remarkable (it brought to the governor's attention the minutes of a cabinet meeting six years earlier, when the call for a master plan to guide the production of oil in the Big Cypress National Preserve had been made). How then in view of these demonstrated abilities can the agency's behavior during the revision of the Florida Panther Recovery Plan be excused? What justifications can there be for its persistent refusal to entertain any notion of a broad plan for managing panthers on the contiguous public lands of southern Florida—the only guaranteed future refuge for the animal?

It was about the time of this report to the governor that the Game Commission adopted for the panther an official management policy, ". . . committed to preserve Florida panthers where they now exist and to reestablish panther populations where it is socially and biologically feasible." The following points were stressed.

1. Research of panther life history and habitat requirements to provide information on which to base timely regulatory and management decisions of particular relevance to existing populations;

2. An information program to advise Floridians on the panther's status and requirements to gain public support of recovery efforts; and

3. Reintroduction of panthers into suitable areas of their former range to increase their numbers and to enhance their prospects for survival.

The Commission is firmly committed to taking all actions necessary and within its authority to assure recovery of the panther. These actions include regulation of public use; implementation of appropriate habitat improvement and population enhancement practices; and provision of sound information and recommendations to other agencies, groups and industry to encourage practices within their management programs that may further secure recovery of the Florida panther.

The Commission further maintains it is imperative that all decisions and actions affecting panther recovery, public use, and land management and preservation must be based on sound logic and scientific knowledge. Therefore, the Commission intends to support research in cooperation with other agencies to the extent necessary and feasible to provide this essential information for dissemination and timely application for recovery of the panther as a viable member of Florida's wildlife community.[66]

Bold words! And empty ones as it turned out.

It was also at this time that environmental organizations in Florida began to question the impact of hunters on panthers in the Big Cypress National Preserve. The Game Commission was regulating hunting there during the first nine days of a general gun season (that ran for 13 weeks) through a quota for each management unit. In reply to the disquiet, the agency proposed in the coming season to scale down the quotas. The Florida Audubon Society planned to appear before the Commission at the end of June 1983, to ask for a ban on hunting in the Preserve. It solicited support for its plan from Florida Defenders of the Environment, which assembled a technical group to evaluate the request. The FDE scientists did not embrace the closure proposition, feeling that so abrupt a move might alienate many potential allies of the panther. They did agree with the Florida Audubon Society that the situation seemed critical and agreed that an effective reduction of intrusions of all kinds, including hunting, was desirable. They complained that the announced quotas were inadequate to decrease hunting pressure in the management units having few deer. They also highlighted the importance of educating hunters in South Florida about the rationale for curtailing activities in the Big Cypress.[67]

Early in July, Colonel Brantly, the executive director, was summoned to brief the Governor and Cabinet on the status of the panther. His opening sentence (given in an earlier chapter) was one of optimism, " . . . that the Florida panther will be recovered from imminent extinction to remain a viable member of the diverse wildlife community that is unique to our state."[68] This gleaming assessment was made nine months after the warning that fewer than 20 of the cats remained,

that the panther was one of the most endangered animals in the world, that the margin for error in exploiting its habitat was extremely narrow and that it was incumbent upon his agency to take all necessary measures to ensure its survival. When the hunting issue raised its head, it seems to have caused a complete reappraisal about the panther's survival prospects. Since that July day in 1983 the optimistic statements issued by the Game Commission have seldom flagged. The report to the Governor and Cabinet continued:

> . . . Certain interested groups have expressed the opinion that hunting is not an appropriate form of public use of the Preserve and that hunting is not compatible with the safety of the panther. To the contrary, public hunting has coexisted for years with Florida panthers, white-tailed deer, and other species of wildlife, and the Commission has not observed evidence at this time that those activities have impacted panthers or wildlife in the area. Panthers have unfortunately been killed with firearms, but even these incidents have been outnumbered in recent years by those that have been killed by automobile collisions. . . .

> The Commission is firmly committed to taking all actions necessary and within its authority to assure recovery of the Florida panther. However, the success of these efforts and the continued existence of our state animal are contingent on effective resource management actions that can only be achieved with broad public support, active cooperation among all resource management agencies, and an appreciation that much greater emphasis must be given to the long-term irreversible processes associated with rapid human population growth that continue to impact south Florida and the state in general.[69]

Certainly no one could quarrel with the final paragraph. There is a need for effective resource management actions such as trying to raise more deer on certain public lands; and broad public support is important, of course, but it can't possibly be garnered if the Game Commission doesn't explain the predicament (the so-called public education program will be presented later). As for "active cooperation among all resource management agencies," an earlier chapter disclosed how enthusiastically the Game Commission cooperated with the Fish and Wildlife Service to write a meaningful recovery plan. And what about giving greater emphasis "to the long-term irreversible processes associated with rapid human population growth that continue to impact south Florida and the state in general"? The Panther Advisory Council did everything it could to spur officials to take on the private lands issue and to build a case for linking habitat statewide (this also will be reviewed later), but nothing productive ever seems to happen.

Today's Game Commission carries a heavy load of environmental and wildlife responsibilities, some with unprecedented technical requirements. But the mechanism is a relic of a bygone era, directed by five citizens chosen too often for political connections and ties to sport hunting, not by virtue of a professional understanding of today's pressing challenges. Threats to many of Florida's wildlife species are again reaching the alarming state that prompted the early wildlife protection movement, but converging pressures are placing the modern game commissions on longer and longer tightropes, constrained in movement, with balancing skills at a premium. The institution is not receptive to the novel requirements of endangered species management, with its unprecedented demands on professional operations.

This poor performance in Florida, in administering a complex endangered species program, is not singular; it is an institutional malaise. The universities may turn out trained wildlife biologists, but they cannot always perform as unfettered professionals in the political environment of wildlife management. An agency may be staffed with platoons of biologists, but their expertise often has a limited scope for expression and sometimes atrophies from lack of rigorous exercise. The folk wisdom in the state game agencies reflects the volatile environments to which they have had to adapt, and encourages submission to them. As cautious careerists ascend the ranks, they often arrive at the top knowing too much about politics and not enough about biology. The avoidance of controversy has come to be valued above management excellence. Questing for challenges is not encouraged, and when a new one arrives unexpectedly it is not welcome. Unprofessionalism has been institutionalized. The expedient of controversy-avoidance defines the line of march. This incompetence has gone unnoticed because it has not been as drastically dysfunctional as in the era of game protection, but it is coming into sharper relief.

Chapter 9

THE NATIONAL PARK SERVICE

"I pray you understand," quoth Sancho Panza,
"that those which appear there are no giants, but windmills."

Don Quixote de la Mancha
Miquel de Cervantes

A pleasuring ground for the nation. The idea originated in the United States; it has been called an American contribution to world civilization.[1] The origins and evolution of the national park concept have recently been traced by Alfred Runte.[2] This account of its unfolding is partly based on his history.

The national parks found their early expression in the scenic marvels of the American West, but the idea was conceived and advanced mainly by Eastern men of urban background. Among the early proponents were Horace Greely, owner and editor of the *New York Tribune*, Samuel Bowles, a popular travel writer, and Fredrick Law Olmsted who is perhaps best known for his role in creating Central Park in New York City. Olmsted was an early proponent of using magnificent natural spectacles as parks. John Muir, also a prominent formative force in the nation's parks, was an exception to the Eastern influence. Muir was a Scot immigrant who advanced landscape preservation in California; he is best known as founder of the Sierra Club.

In the early days of the frontier nation, educated men of what in a later day would be called "the establishment" were painfully awake to the disparity of cultural achievement between the United States and the nations of the Old World. The traveling elite of the early 1800s, in search of visual inspiration, toured the monuments, cathedrals and castles of Europe. The United States had nothing to compare. However, itinerant observers were awed by the surpassing visual qualities of the American wilderness. They extolled the "green old age" of the American earth, and its "earth monuments," standing supreme as spectacles of worth.[3] The inspiring native vistas glowed from the canvases of nineteenth century landscape paintings, the Hudson River School being the earliest.

Niagara Falls was the premiere spectacle of eastern North America and a must for the occasional European visitor. Unfortunately, the commercial instincts

of the new classless society had erected annoying impediments to the access and contemplation of the thing. The best overlooks were acquired and visitors charged for entry. Gatehouses and fences eventually "rimmed the falls from every angle."[4] Visitors were assailed by hackmen, curio hawkers and tour guides. More sensitive Americans were embarrassed by the acidulous commentaries of visiting Europeans. Two English visitors wrote that "one hardly has the patience to record these things; surely some universal voice ought to interfere and prevent the money seekers. Niagara does not belong to Canada or America. Such spots should be deemed the property of civilized mankind."[5] Alexis de Tocqueville made a prediction: "Already the forest around is being cleared. . . . I don't give the Americans ten years to establish a saw or flour mill at the base of the cataract."[6]

The influential citizens who later worked to save the awe-inspiring earth monuments of the West did so with a keen awareness, because of Niagara Falls, of what would happen if these treasures fell into private hands. John Muir said of scenic landscapes in America that "nothing dollarable is safe, however guarded."[7] When Americans reached the far West they found a topography that was overpowering. Unlike privately owned Niagara most of the monumental Western scenery was still in the public domain—states not yet having been formed to claim it.

Preserving the Spectacular

As is well-known, Yellowstone become the first national park in 1872. Runte offers an interesting perspective on how the first National Park came to be the largest. The pioneer sentiments about land were utilitarian—it was something to be "used," not "set aside." The attitude survived the frontier to be embodied as an official policy of conservation in the U.S. Forest Service, founded at the turn of the century. Public land, including its forests, water, minerals and wildlife was to be used not passively, but consumptively, according to a regulated program. Consequently, only sites of spectacular but unusable rock in the form of mountain peaks and canyons had any prospect of nomination as a national park, and then with boundaries compressed around features that were beautiful but "worthless." Hostility there was to shielding land having consumptive or extractive worth— often voiced by a vigilant and predatory U.S. Forest Service whose members pursued the utilitarian grail with the verve of crusaders. The Forest Service was then more politically powerful than the National Park Service, being better aligned with the prevailing sentiment about land use.

It was by accident that Yellowstone National Park came to enclose an expanse of "useable" land, because the Congress that made the park did not know the exact nature of the place; an expedition had to be dispatched to the wilderness to confirm fantastic rumors. The government explorers were awed, and their descriptions filled the press. Artists who accompanied the expedition displayed

their canvases. The wonders of Yellowstone became a revelation to the world; its superlatives a source of national pride—and its geographical obscurity precluded any claims by agents of commerce. Congress approved the chimerical park in a far-off land, with boundaries drawn suitably large to insure that everything noteworthy was included. After settlement of the region around Yellowstone, commercial interests would for years intrigue to get at the timber and minerals "unnecessarily" sequestered in the park. Subsequent national parks were better known when set aside, and the forces of utilization were stingy with peripheral configurations. The later boundaries were squeezed in by the widespread conviction that progress in the material sphere must never be impeded by a park.[8]

For decades the national parks were the step-child of American land management policy. Park supporters fought incessantly against profit-seeking encroachments. Conserving resources for sustained consumption was seen as an advance over the simple pioneer ethic of use, and this persuasion was legislated into the government's sprawling new forests. Yellowstone National Park antedated the national forests, but whereas an apparatus of administration came into being with the forests, it would be more than 40 years after Yellowstone before a National Park Service was approved in 1916. The Forest Service, guided by the able Gifford Pinchot, and nourished from the receipts of its own products, prospered and bustled about the business of "wise use" while the ideal of scenic preservation represented by the National Parks was thought extravagant. It had to be husbanded and guarded by a small but influential citizen elite. Geography played a part in this unequal contest. Until 1919, 90 percent of the population lived in the East while all parks of any size were in the West[9]—cheek by jowl with the national forests.

The damming of Hetch Hetchy Valley in Yosemite National Park was an early, oft-told battle pitting the forces of utility against those of scenic preservation. Utility won; the valley was dammed to store water for San Francisco. The loss of Hetch Hetchy pushed the defenders of scenic preservation toward a utilitarian strategy of sorts. The realization took root that parks would have to be exploited to some extent if they were to be preserved. Supporters began to promote them as an economic asset capable of generating dollars through tourism. The outcome of this shift in philosophy was an alliance with the railroads. Tracks were extended into the parks, and the railroads erected hotels, lodges, hostelries and Swiss-style chalets to house visitors. The goal of increased visitation would become a fixture of park service thinking until attendance climbed to a crushing volume in the 1960s.

The National Park Service was fortunate during its early decades in having leaders with both political and public relations skills. Stephen Mather and Horace Albright directed the institution from its beginning to 1933. At Mather's accession the patchwork system was only the geographical expression of a scenic and cultural idea, resting on an insubstantial legislative foundation. It was an

indifferent institution which roused the ire of visitors—like Mather—because of its incompetent caretakers. In 1916 the parks were given a firm legal sanction by the National Park Service Act. Mather and Albright provided an administrative structure and built a staff, instilling it with a sense of mission and an *esprit de corps*.

Preserving the Natural

In the twentieth century pressure grew for parks in the East. Here they would encounter novel obstacles, both financial and philosophical. The financial problem was that prospective sites would have to be purchased from private owners rather than simply being transferred from the public domain. Philosophical objections came from influential Park Service partisans who insisted on "scenic splendor" as the criterion for a national park. Scenic splendor had become firmly associated with the monumental topography of the West. Deviation from the conventional practice was viewed by some as debasing the standards upon which the parks were founded.

Acadia National Park was marked out on the coast of Maine in 1919; Shenandoah and Great Smoky Mountains followed in the 1930s. Purchasing difficulties for the last two named were overcome by generous donations from John D. Rockefeller. However, the suggestion for a park in the Everglades was thought unwarranted by some puritanical protectors.

> Few rumblings of dissent, however, were more disconcerting than the opposition of William T. Hornaday, long hailed as one of America's leading spokesmen for wildlife conservation. In the Everglades "I found mighty little that was of special interest, and absolutely nothing that was picturesque or beautiful," he asserted, recalling visits dating back to 1875; "both then and now, ... a swamp is a swamp." On a more charitable note, he conceded that "the saw-grass Everglades Swamp is not as ugly and repulsive as some other swamps that I have seen"; still he concluded:"it is yet a long ways from being fit to elevate into a national park, to put alongside the magnificent array of scenic wonderlands that the American people have elevated into that glorious class."[10]

In Hornaday we see the man who stayed too long. Grown powerful by the prestige of his early accomplishments, he continued to influence policy based on views no longer relevant. The National Parks Association (now the National Parks and Conservation Association), a citizens support group, was also hesitant about a national park in the Everglades. Its suspicions were aroused by the large acreage of private land within the boundaries of the proposed park; wily real estate

promoters were thought be at work. To this day the National Parks and Conservation Association remains as fiercely protective of the national parks, and as wary of altering course, as it was in the 1930s.

Runte marks Everglades National Park as a significant point of shift in the national park idea and in the philosophy of preservation. As a spectacle, the River of Grass flowed in flat and languid disaccordance with the great mountains, startling canyons and thundering waterfalls of the West. Its appeal to park partisans heralded a change in the sense of what should be saved. Henceforth the natural would vie with the grandiose vista in park selection; but the new emphasis could not be effectively promoted without broadening the accepted notion of what made worthwhile scenery. In 1932 the passage of 60 years since the naming of the first park had brought a new sentiment: that the natural was as unguarded before the power of the swelling populace to mar the land as the spectacular had been in an earlier day.

These pleasuring grounds for the nation grew out of a peculiarly American experience: the headlong and reckless alteration of a continent which had brimmed with a grand spectacle of nature's bounty. The transformation was so precipitous that those who witnessed it felt uneasy about the magnitude of change during their lives and often were oppressed by its aftermath. Recent historical research has shown that, contrary to what is commonly supposed, there were many from the beginning of the frontier era who recognized that something of value was being lost. Thoreau often serves as an example because of the enduring acclaim for his writings. His bent for solitude and independent stance on all matters may have bolstered the impression that his early lament of the passing wilderness was unusual, but the disquiet appears to have been widespread, not only for a diminished landscape, but also for the persecuted aboriginal cultures that adorned it.[11]

This mood that mourns the loss of the natural land—and the impulse to arrest its depletion—is still with us. It can be attested to by many residents of Florida (who have lived in the state more than two years). Americans so affected in the early days of nationhood could do little but record their feelings; a frontier society does not give rise to the means of preservation; the latter had to await urbanization and affluence, and a city-bound class of citizens with the motivation and time for political involvement. Today, the utilitarian sentiment still lives in the West and flourishes in Alaska. Preservation sentiment is strongest in the most urbanized parts of the country and grows steadily as a political force. As a foil to the perennial alterations of the land, the national parks were formed and have endured as an esteemed instrument of conservation—an institution embodying the best hope for holding fast to those dwindling stations at which we might receive primal messages from the earth.

The boundaries of the national forests were fixed nearly a century ago, but the national parks, which cannot be timbered or mined like the forests, have at intervals been enlarged, or authorized anew. They remain the hope of arresting the loss of a valued place, at a point in time, through the preservation of landscapes (and cultural sites as well). This helps to account for the perpetual growth and the immense popularity of the national parks. It imbues the Service with a rich sense of purpose and fuels an ardor to fend off any perceived threat. It is also an inoculate against criticism. The preoccupation with preserving the scenic quality of a site is a gleaming thread stitched through the history of the agency. Even though the original scenic wonders concept has been enlarged, requiring philosophical shifts to redefine national parks, the transcendent evocative power of the special view has remained paramount.

Re-creation; Ecology and Nostalgia

And so the extended idea of preserving natural landscapes first took form in the Everglades. In the 1960s the philosophy was further refined and articulated as an attempt to re-create the American past, gaining sanctity during that decade by being linked to ecological management. This expanded concept has come to underpin resource management policy in the National Park Service.

In the early 1960s a controversy detonated over an elk management policy in Yellowstone National Park. The burgeoning herd was thought to be damaging its range. In an attempted corrective the Park Service began shooting elk, thereby arousing the ire of animal rights partisans and local hunters. The strongest objections came from hunters who wanted to do the job by means of recreational hunting. When the pressure grew heavy the Park Service responded in the bureaucratic manner by appointing a committee, in this case of nationally known wildlife experts, chosen I suspect for known proclivities—of at least a majority—that could be predicted to yield a report favorable to the agency's management inclinations. This is conjecture, but it is often the course that beckons to officials when their departmental modus operandi is threatened.

At any rate the committee pressed for what the National Park Service wanted to hear: ". . . that every phase of management itself be under the full jurisdiction of biologically trained personnel of the Park Service. This applies . . . to all facets of regulating animal populations. . . . We cannot endorse the view that responsibility for removing excess game animals be shared with State fish and game departments whose primary interest would be to capitalize on the recreational value of the public hunting that could be supplied. . . ."[12] Though the verdict was anticipated by the Park Service, it likely mirrored opinion nationwide that hunting is not an appropriate activity in a National Park—a sentiment probably stronger today than in 1962.

But the importance of this product was not in its partisan findings. The committee was chaired by A. Starker Leopold, the eldest son of Aldo, who followed his father as a wildlife scientist and apparently in other ways as well. Aldo Leopold, one of the most remarkable figures in the history of land management, was the shaper of much of our present thinking on the subject. Trained as a forester, he is credited as the founder of wildlife management, the wilderness idea and the land ethic: the idea that land is a community to which we belong, not just a commodity. There were other capable thinkers and actors on the land-management stage with Leopold, but his renown is enhanced by the persisting appeal of his eloquent pen, which was canted always to a general audience. He believed that a scientist had a responsibility to share his knowledge and views with the laity, because "the real substance of conservation lies not in the physical projects of government but in the mental processes of citizens."[13] His conviction about the importance of having the specialist communicate with everyone is undoubtedly reflected in the 1962 Leopold Report written by the committee chaired by his son. It is a model of clear, non-technical prose.

The Leopold Committee had been charged with addressing wildlife management in National Parks, as a result of a controversy in one of them, but did not interpret its charge narrowly. Aldo Leopold had always tried to view specific wildlife management problems (in his case problems usually meant deer management) in a broad biological and social (and historical) context. He was also known to be unusually effective on committees.[14] Both these traits must have been passed on to Starker, who used the hunting issue as a platform. His document was a clear, simple, sweeping advocacy of new goals, policies and methods of resource management in the national parks: "As a primary goal [of wildlife management in the National Park Service], we would recommend that the biotic associations within each park be maintained, or where necessary recreated, as nearly as possible in the condition that prevailed when the area was first visited by the white man. A national park should represent a vignette of primitive America."[15]

Much of the subsequent wording spells out Starker Leopold's hopes that a new direction would redress the entrenched institutional thinking of the day, which had ruled from the outset and presumed a park to be "a place with no past and no future. It had not changed since the glaciers departed and was perfect as it stood."[16] An exception to this philosophy had eradicated predators—a practice that went on in some parks until the 1950s. Predators had been thought a decimating force, inimical to desirable animals—which, it should be noted, were prized as a feature of the park scenery. The Park Service was just awakening to the need for certain kinds of active management, the reduction of overlarge elk herds obviously being one. Everglades National Park had at this time been experimenting with fire as a management tool, but the practice had not gained a wide following. The

_____

managing principle rested firmly and with minimal imagination on the idea of protection.

The inspiration to recreate primitive America has its roots in the regrets of those who witnessed it vanish—as elaborated earlier. It was not a novel concept when advanced by Starker Leopold. It had been adopted in the late nineteenth century by sportsmen. They saw it not in terms of restoring the primitive scene but as resurrecting the role of the frontier hunter, who went forth in the wilderness to take his game by skill and stealth. The credo unfolded at a period when the setting for such vicarious reenactments was still within easy reach of the cities. Its most enduring embodiment was the Boone and Crockett Club founded by Theodore Roosevelt. The idea spread via the sportsmen's magazines and may have been absorbed either directly or indirectly by young Aldo Leopold who hunted with his sportsman father along the Mississippi River at the turn of the century.[17] Aldo Leopold later philosophized on the subject of atavistic values and practiced what he preached.[18] He early gave up his gun to hunt deer with bow and arrows, which he made himself. The ritual of recapturing bygone days by reenacting the frontiersman (or the Indian, in Leopold's case) concerted with the reigning utilitarian view of land. The later move to achieve the effect by restoring the natural landscape had to await a general unease about a deteriorating environment— which would coincide with the flowering of ecological science. Aldo Leopold's career encompassed both the utilitarian outlook and the maturing of ecological thought.

At the onset of his career, Aldo Leopold was fired by the utilitarian ideal, preached in the slogans of Gifford Pinchot, that conservation was "the use of the earth for the good of man"[19] and that forests should provide "the greatest good for the largest number for the longest time."[20] When the young forester arrived in the Southwest in 1909, the region had been sparsely settled and game animals not so badly depleted as in other parts of the country; their scarcity was just beginning to be noticed.[21] Leopold worked arduously at game conservation with the tools of the day: protected preserves, law enforcement, elimination of predators and a buck-only rule for the harvest of deer. These measures took hold sporadically throughout the country and eventually restored the deer herds.

The 1920s, 1930s and 1940s witnessed an overpopulation of deer— occasionally with striking die-offs, and with some deer ranges denuded of vegetation. There were a variety of causes, then poorly understood. It took time for the emerging discipline of wildlife management to decipher the dynamics of deer populations. Much of Aldo Leopold's later life was spent trying to learn the secret of getting deer in balance with a healthy land. He was tutored by the developing science of ecology. Two contrasting experiences in the mid-1930s profoundly influenced him. The first was a trip to Germany where he saw a highly manipulative

type of forest management that had banished natural deer foods, so that the herds had to be sustained by artificial feeding. The other experience was a wilderness vacation in northern Mexico.

> Protected from settlement and overgrazing, first by Apache Indians and then in succession by Pancho Villa's bandits, depression, and unstable land policies, the Sierra Madre in Chihuahua still retained the virgin stability of its soils and the integrity of its flora and fauna. "It is ironical," Leopold mused in a published account of his observatons [sic], "that Chihuahua, with a history and a terrain so strikingly similar to southern New Mexico and Arizona should present so lovely a picture of ecological health, whereas our own states, plastered as they are with National Forests, National Parks and all other trappings of conservation, are so badly damaged that only tourists and others ecologically color-blind, can look upon them without a feeling of sadness and regret."[22]

He tried in vain to stimulate an international research effort to compare the unspoiled Mexican site with its degraded counterpart across the American border, but the temper and the primitive finances of the day were not supportive. Years later, after his father's death, Starker Leopold finally mounted a research expedition.

> In summer 1948, a few months after his father's death, Starker Leopold returned to the Sierra Madre with a scientific team from the Museum of Vertebrate Zoology at Berkeley, intending finally to initiate the long-term study of deer and predators in virgin equilibrium that he and his father had envisioned on their bow-and-arrow expedition. What he encountered were graded logging roads, herds of cattle and sheep, and the Rio Gavilan flood-scoured and flowing sawdust. He understood then why his father had once written, "It is the part of wisdom never to revisit a wilderness," and he bade farewell in a moving essay, "Adios, Gavilan."[23]

These lessons made their mark on the younger Leopold, and when he found himself in the chair of a National Park committee, he seized the moment— as his father would have done. He saw that the National Parks could become a vehicle for restoring the land, at least portions of it, to the condition of health it once enjoyed or, it was hoped, to some approximation. As the many cautionary paragraphs of his 1962 report attest, he was under no illusions about the difficulty.

And thus it was that an ad hoc advisory group, convened as a political expedient, articulated what was to become a management gospel for the National Park Service. The advice was in harmony with the long standing institutional nous of landscape esthetics and the desire of sensitive citizens to preserve that archetypical animus evoked by the primal landscape. The recommendations also seemed consonant with the maturing science of ecology which had risen to prominence in biological circles and was about to burst onto the popular consciousness in the United States and elsewhere. It was a splendid convergence of a man, a moment and an idea. Unfortunately it now hinders the management of endangered species. It has moved beyond being a philosophical basis for scientific park management to become a stifling orthodoxy. In the Park Service it has come into the fervent, protective hands of lay park superintendents and partisan institutional supporters who defend it against any impending danger, although the defenders of this faith do not always judge well what is a threat and what is not. The refined philosophical guidance of the Leopold Committee has become a secular faith, infusing its adherents with the sense of possessing a superior management insight.

Aldo Leopold, through his early experiences in trying to make the land produce certain species of commercial or recreational value, had seen unantici-pated and sometimes unfortunate outcomes. The failings were due to misunder-standing the interdependence of the components of soils, water, plants and animals. As the evolving science of ecology began to reveal why the early efforts had gone awry, he labored unceasingly to mold a popular understanding of lessons he had learned the hard way. Leopold died in 1948. Then, in the 1960s, just as his thoughts and teachings were—through his son's involvement with the National Park Service—finally approaching institutional expression on a national scale, another scientific discipline with implications for land management was taking shape.

Parks as Islands

The Theory of Island Biogeography, by Robert H. MacArthur and Edward O. Wilson, was published shortly after the Leopold Report.[24] It announced a new discipline, island biogeography, to investigate the distribution of animal life on islands. The new school had a long incubation. The early classical work on island biogeography was authored in 1880, in London, by Alfred Russell Wallace, who had studied the apportionment of fauna across the island chain between Australia and the mainland of Asia. Thirty years later the American mammalogist, Joseph Grinnell, in surveying wildlife in the mountains of southern California, had noted a definite correlation between the number of species and the size of the life zones (the bands of distinctive habitat found at different altitudes) they inhabited on the higher elevations of mountain peaks.[25] Years passed before zoologists made quantitative investigations of how many species could be found relative to the size of the area they inhabited. Botanists, however, were soon making strides in this

field, plants being easier to census. While Grinnell speculated in California, Paul Jaccard, a Swiss botanist, counted the species in isolated plant communities high in the Alps, subjecting his figures to statistical analysis.[26] He was one of the first to study what would come to be known as the species-area relationship.[27] A decade later a Swedish botanist named Olaf Arrhenius censused plant species on several islands of different sizes near Stockholm. It was by then a "well-known and obvious fact," wrote Arrhenius, "that the larger the area. . . . the greater the number of species."[28] Investigations of this kind led in 1932 to the concept of the minimal area, defined as "the smallest area which can contain an adequate representation of an [plant] association."[29] A species-area curve took form when botanists plotted on a graph the number of species and the size of the area where they occurred.

In 1933 Aldo Leopold included in his book, *Game Management*, a section on "Minimum units of range and population" in which he noted both a minimum size in habitat and a minimum number of animals below which a game population could not survive.[30] These early investigations did not credit the role of genetics, which was an obscure laboratory science until the 1940s, when it would move ahead with the help of biochemical techniques. Leopold had simply speculated about the direct impact of cataclysmic natural events on small populations. However, it was during genetic research in the 1930s that the term "effective population number" entered the literature. It was further treated in publications of the 1950s and 1960s.[31] The term refers to the number of animals needed to buffer against the harmful effects of inbreeding. In 1957, Philip J. Darlington, in a volume on *Zoogeography*, devoted a chapter to "Island Patterns." It explored the statistical relationships of species to area on selected islands in the West Indies.[32]

When MacArthur and Wilson came to their task in the 1960s, they concluded that the number of species on an island was largely determined by its size and by its proximity to the mainland, or other islands, which might serve as a source of colonizing species. The authors announced that the principles of island biogeography would be increasingly applicable to the terrestrial landscape where once unbroken habitats were fragmenting under "the encroachment of civilization."[33] *Island Biogeography* appeared as an obscure scientific publication the same year that Starker Leopold joined the National Park Service, bringing his energy and skills to bear in fulfilling his father's dream, by turning the national parks into a model of ecological land management. Ironically, the great concern of the elder Leopold, that "natural land" (so called to distinguish it from the built environment) was not being managed properly, was now being overshadowed by the fact that much of it was vanishing altogether. Nature preserves were left isolated, a patchwork of natural remnants which, like islands, would be unable to sustain many of the species they were created to protect.

The year 1980 witnessed another arrival among the scientific disciplines addressing threats to the diversity of living things. Off the presses came *Conservation Biology: An Evolutionary-Ecological Perspective*. The volume represented the convergence of population biology, genetics and applied ecology.[34] Meanwhile, back at the National Park Service, the Leopold Report in 1962 appears not to have done anything except serve as a prestigious foil against pressure for recreational hunting in Yellowstone National Park. A self-satisfied bureaucracy does not amiably greet any proposed change of direction no matter how apropos. The Leopold Report may only have become the guiding management flame of the agency because Starker Leopold got himself hired as its chief scientist and fanned it into policy.

Ecosystem Management

In 1968, Leopold, as the new chief scientist, called together all National Park Service research scientists and management biologists at Grand Canyon National Park to discuss implementing his committee's report.[35] It was here that "ecosystem management" was first phrased.[36] The term "ecology" would come into common usage in the 1970s—often as an encomium, but it had a restricted currency in the previous decade and had been avoided in the Leopold Report. It was also at the Grand Canyon meeting that a momentous policy change was instituted for the management of grizzly bears in Yellowstone.[37] The consequences were told in a previous chapter. As the Craighead brothers predicted, bears suddenly deprived of a supplemental food source wandered to centers of human activity and had to be destroyed by the dozens and scores. In fairness, it should be added that in the early 1970s, there was not the widespread awareness among wildlife scientists of the genetic peril inherent in small populations that there would be a decade later. The Craighead brothers themselves may not have been conversant with the threat. In the early 1970s the salient awareness among scientists was of the pressing need for an ecological understanding in the management of land.

The boundaries of most national parks were drawn long ago and do not conform to anything that might reasonably be thought of as a self-regulating natural system (with the possible exceptions of some parks in Alaska). Enlarging a park to overcome a deficiency on that scale would be impossible in most cases. The National Park Service, for any practical consideration in the near future, will have to manage its natural resources within inherited boundaries. Adjustments and expansions will only occasionally be possible. The hang-up in the Park Service mind seems to be over any proposed management action that seems, however remotely, to imply a tampering, however slight, with the visual qualities of the landscape. The National Park Service has got the scenery confused with the ecosystem. A natural ecosystem is, in one sense, a product of the interactions of its biotic organisms with one another and with their abiotic (non-living) environment.

Managing for one species to prevent its loss may have an effect on other parts of the system, but allowing organisms to drop away will also. Whether the outcome will be positive, negative or neutral may be to some extent a value judgement. Each case has to be studied separately in deciding whether to intervene or to let the organism disappear. Ecosystems management, if it is to be worthy of the name, must at least think about conserving of the entire community of organisms, not just the scenic vistas. Resource management as conceived in the National Park Service owes more to esthetic and philosophical leanings than to any scientific discipline.

The insular fragments of nature that survive as parks will not be large enough to sustain all wildlife species within their boundaries. Many creatures will be lost, but others might be saved if certain actions are taken. First, the perimeters of the parks should be expanded where possible while it is still feasible to do so. Second, parks and nature reserves should be linked together where possible to form functionally larger units. However, many parks will inevitably be isolated, and managers should evaluate contingencies for species that might perish. This does not mean the plans have to be carried out, but there is a moral obligation to weigh them. "Intervention" is the term for such preservation measures. It has two aspects; the first is increasing the size of the population; the second is genetic intervention, or out-breeding. In some instances both together may be needed.

To date, Park Service responses to intervention proposals have fallen into three categories. The first has been the creative exercises in illusion that employ highly visible committees, research dollars and public relations techniques to convince that a vigorous no-nonsense, state-of-the-art rescue is underway. The second has been the repeated assertion that the idea is contrary to ecosystems management. The third has been to claim that the only permissible remedy is to expand the park to a size that will prevent the loss of its wildlife. This is a "magic wand" solution—a refusal to confront reality.

Perhaps the most lamentable aspect of this rigidity is that we are truly one world before the threat posed to biological diversity. The loss of a species is the cancellation of a universal inheritance; the prevention of such losses is the responsibility of all. The American National Parks could, without sacrifice, do much more than simply function as the planetary estates of a privileged class (those affluent enough to reach them). The institution is well-positioned to provide leadership in the world-wide protection of biological diversity. It is a transcontinental park system encompassing a wide representation of biological assemblages from the arctic to the tropics; it enjoys a broad enough base of public support to insulate it from the kinds of menace that stalks parks in some other countries; it is the product of a wealthy nation that has continually funded its expansion; it has access to a broad base of domestic scientific expertise to aid in research and management. The knowledge gained in recovering diminished wildlife popula-

tions might be usefully applied elsewhere in the world, but this potential contribution to a planetary cause is impossible given the pervading mentality.

We are trying now with increasing desperation to minister to the ills of an ailing planet. Many of the earth's life forms will come to an end during the next century. We can only hope, by great energy and by the disciplined application of science and reason, to limit the destruction. The greater part of this catastrophe will strike in planetary regions beyond the purview of the United States. Our capability to moderate the loss is constrained. We can contribute money and scientific expertise for research and management advice, and through financial institutions like the World Bank, creative use can be made of lending capital. But an important if indirect contribution would be to set an example within our own borders. The effort to prevent the loss of organisms in the United States presently has an unnecessarily limited scope partly because of the ingrown and defensive tribal attitudes of native land-management institutions. Some fresh thinking at home would go far in devising tactics to save life forms elsewhere. The National Park Service has much to offer the world, but it is giving little.

The Park Service and the Panther

Of all the agencies in the Florida panther recovery program, the National Park Service has been the most dogmatic and the most opposed to change. National Park Service biologists were urging the application of radio-telemetry to panthers as early as 1979, even before the Game Commission studies. It took increasing increments of pressure, and finally embarrassment of the agency, just to begin the research. In 1985 the Panther Advisory Council recommended that the Game Commission urge the National Park Service to manage the Hole-in-the-Donut area of Everglades National Park by replacing the exotic plant, Brazilian pepper, with species that would provide forage for deer. Since then the agency has shown signs of gearing up to take action in Hole-in-the-Donut, not to nourish deer but apparently to avoid having to do so.

After the signing of the revised *Florida Panther Recovery Plan* in June 1987, I made one final personal effort to have the document corrected. Several state environmental organizations I approached had declined to get involved, until Jerry Gerde, a Panama City attorney and a long-time environmental activist, got wind of the issue. He was decisive and energetic, instigating a letter-writing campaign by groups in his region to both of Florida's senators: Bob Graham and Lawton Chiles. The staffs in both senate offices were responsive and requested specifics on what emendations would be in order. I obliged by furnishing suggestions in two categories; the first was to require the National Park Service to experiment with forage for deer, a proposal that in Chapter 5 we saw excised from drafts of the recovery plan by the FPIC's Technical Subcommittee; the second suggestion was

for the agencies administering the conglomerate of lands at the southern tip of Florida to unite them through a common plan of management for panthers. Senator Chiles responded to these suggestions by mailing them to each of the four agency heads asking for comments.

The executive director of the Florida Department of Natural Resources answered favorably to having the National Park Service to increase its deer, but he was against a common plan on the grounds that "some of the agencies might have policies which would prevent them from doing it."[38] But why would anyone presume such a thing? And if it were presumed, why would it not be salutary to challenge such a shortcoming?

The Game Commission letter dodged the issues, and with a rambling commentary explained that the ". . . [Recovery] Plan does specify that each land management agency will prepare comprehensive land management plans for their respective properties. . . ." etc. It gave no information pertinent to the inquiry.[39]

The regional director of The Fish and Wildlife Service, in a letter to Jerry Gerde, agreed that proper management by the National Park Service of its habitat was important. "Your views concerning the importance of habitat management at Everglades National Park for the panther are equally shared by all of us on the FPIC. We are fully aware that Everglades NP along with the other areas in SW Florida under public control hold the key to the future for the Florida panther. . . ." However, the regional director said the specifics of what to do would be taken care of in the future—after further evaluation of the data."[40]

The regional director of the National Park Service, in his letter to Senator Chiles, opposed any mandate to manage for more deer. He resorted again to the now-discredited excuse that the National Park Service was prohibited by law from managing for a single species. He then pointed out that since the other three agencies had signed the recovery plan they must necessarily agree with his position.[41] This illustrates perfectly why the National Park Service drafts other agencies into collective arrangements like the FPIC. Things went awry somewhat in this instance in that Chiles' letter went to a new director of the Florida Department of Natural Resources, who had superseded the signer of the recovery plan, but that was a small matter. The National Park Service usually gets what it wants in the consensus decisions of these coalitions, and then insulates itself from criticism by claiming support from the others. In the Florida panther recovery program, state officials have watched the game through the filter of long-standing parochial interests, not from the vantage point of the animal they are supposed to be saving; and it must also be said here that state agencies can be country bumpkins when dealing with the politically sophisticated National Park Service. The Fish and Wildlife Service knows very well what is going on but won't say anything.

Senator Graham at first showed great interest in the letters which had been sent to him, but then, at the critical moment, did a curious thing. He asked the superintendent of Everglades National Park, Michael Finley, his opinion of the whole affair. Finley assured Graham that the national park position was supported by several scientists and environmental organizations.[42] The senator was satisfied with this explanation and the matter was dropped. Senator Chiles also lost interest. Graham, who as governor had moved with alacrity to press a balky Game Commission to modify hunting regulations in the Big Cypress National Preserve, and who had bypassed the resistance of the Federal Highway Administration to insure the construction of wildlife crossings under I-75, would not move against the National Park Service.

In fact, documentary evidence shows the only "position" articulated by the National Park Service is that: a) it will not manage its lands for the benefit of a single species because b) that would violate the principle of ecosystems management. The scientists and citizen alliances who support this position are not on record to my knowledge (with the predictable exception of the NPCA). In fact, although the environmentalists (as lamented in this book) have never gotten themselves together to pressure the National Park Service, they once passed resolutions expressing the opinion that officials there should overcome management inhibitions and produce more deer. On May 27, 1987, the Executive Committee of the Florida Wildlife Federation passed such a resolution.[43] Three days later, the Board of Trustees of the Florida Defenders of the Environment followed suit, and the National Wildlife Federation did the same.[44,45] Of course, none of these paper actions had any effect.

The genius of the National Park Service shines in defending the status quo of its management ideal, but not in managing the resources themselves. The record speaks loudly on this account. From the founding of Yellowstone, the parks have had to fight encroachments, attrition and abuse. Without skillful defenders there is no doubt that the nation's park resources today would be impoverished. Energetic and gifted partisans, both inside and outside the agency, who were sensitive to the esthetic values embodied in the parks, have always rallied to deflect threats. The legacy of this tradition is an institutional folk-wisdom, sophisticated in the methods and mechanisms of bureaucratic defense; but the Service has no comparable tradition of excellence in the scientific care of its natural assets. Resource management has traditionally been guided largely by intuition derived from philosophical precept. Historically, it has rarely been characterized by enlightenment or brilliance; the Park Service has been devoted to the status quo, perpetually behind the times, always being prodded into catching up, antagonistic to change and sluggish to respond when compelled. The responses even to orthodox management challenges are often inadequate and sometimes incompetent.

216

As an example of the inadequate, I offer the failure of the agency to eradicate melaleuca trees from the Big Cypress National Preserve, years after the park was established. Melaleucas are unquestionably the most serious menace to the biota of the public lands of southern Florida, and they should have been done away with long before now. This is not a matter of inadequate funding; it is an institutional incapacity to recognize a genuine threat and act. As an example of incompetence, I offer the botched and astronomically expensive failure to restore the Hole-in-the-Donut in the 1970s. The project is now being revived, certainly in part, because the Park Service regards suggestions for measures there to benefit the panther as more appalling than the Brazilian pepper infestation—which was left unattended for years. This going-into-lager around a Brazilian pepper patch cannot, by any stretch of the imagination, be construed as a defense against a threat to an ecosystem. It is a defense of the ideal of ecosystems management against the symbolic menace of single-species management. No matter that in the end the panther is lost, the ideal will have been saved. On the scale of values imprinted on the Park service cerebrum, it is the abstraction that is accorded primacy of place. The defenders of today's National Parks cannot distinguish giants from windmills.

The National Park Service is the most inflexible of all American land-management agencies, skilled in political maneuver and public relations, but disinclined to search out the inequities embedded in its dogma; it is blind to the contributions it could make to preserving biological diversity and oblivious to the harm it can do. Paradoxically, as in the days of predator control, it threatens to become—this time through its unwitting sins of omission—an agent of extermination of American wildlife. It could as easily become an innovative leader in pioneering the strategies and methodologies of preserving populations in isolated refuges.

Chapter 10

THE U.S. FISH AND WILDLIFE SERVICE

*In the eyes of many, the [Fish and Wildlife] Service
is not much more than an organizational nuisance.*

Jeanne Nienaber Clarke and Daniel McCool
*Staking Out the Terrain: PowerDifferentials among Natural
Resource Management Agencies*, 1985

The two political scientists who coauthored the book referenced above wrote also that ". . . the effectiveness of the act, as is the case with much of what the Service did and does, depended more on the voluntary compliance of others than it did on the actions of Fish and Wildlife [Service] coordinators."[1] The act referred to in this passage was the Fish and Wildlife Coordination Act of 1934, but the statement fits the Endangered Species Act of 1973. Anyone having the experience of working with the Fish and Wildlife Service in a multi-agency recovery program will soon see its inability to put pressure on another recalcitrant agency, even to implement the most essential measures.

The weakness of this branch of the federal bureaucracy, which has been put in charge of directing the national campaign to save imperiled organisms, is perhaps the single greatest impediment to fulfilling the intent of the Endangered Species Act. It offers the lesson that there are limits to what can be done by making laws and appropriating dollars. If the instrumentality is intimidated by those it is supposed to oversee, there is plainly a nullifying flaw in the mechanism. An effort to understand and repair this inadequate instrument would pay big dividends in the coming struggle to preserve biological diversity. The infirmities of the Fish and Wildlife Service have drawn the attention of political scientists;[2] the analysis given here will be a home-made one arising from my perceptions of its frailty in Florida, and in other programs examined in writing this book.

This unimposing arm is an administrative umbrella, spread wide to incorporate a variety of federal functions relating to fish and wildlife—a diffusion that sets it apart from its more specialized associates in the panther combination. In the century or so since the coming of the land-management agencies, their formative purposes have been modified or expanded, but they each have retained

a focus akin to the original one. Thus the energies of the U.S. Forest Service are still given to the provision of timber, the National Park Service to the iron custody of the nation's finest landscapes, and the state fish and game agencies are occupied with making fish and game resources available for recreational harvest.

The last three bodies named have bands of devoted adherents who form the sinews of institutional power. With the passing century there have been some adjustments in the relative strengths of these partisan backers. The non-consumptive land uses, such as passive outdoor recreation, have come to compete with the earlier utilitarian designs like the sustained-yield harvest of organic resources and the extraction of minerals. The animal rights movement has grown to challenge the taking of game (while usually being indifferent to fish). The shifting strengths of constituencies aside, they are all excitable and loud on behalf of agency champions. It should be expected that adjustments in this balance of interests will occur very gradually.

The Fish and Wildlife Service of today was not crafted by popular demand like the others mentioned. It grew by stages, accruing duties that relate in some way to fish or to wildlife. The fisheries side is descended from a commission formed by Congress to investigate a decline in food fishes in 1871. The wildlife branch traces its origins to 1885, when Congress decreed that the Department of Agriculture form within its Division of Entomology a branch of economic ornithology. There was in those days a growing awareness that birds could affect agriculture in a helpful or harmful way, and that these potentials might be investigated so that beneficial species could be protected and the bad ones checked. The United States was a rural nation then with agricultural interests strongly represented in the halls of political power. The newly authorized measure was intended by the congressmen to aid their agrarian constituents, and was officially installed the following year as the Office of Economic Ornithology and Mammalogy.

The Office was staffed by a naturalist and a clerk. The naturalist, C. Hart Merriam, had more interest in natural history than in practical research to aid farmers. Merriam seems also to have had an independent turn of mind. He angered congressmen by shunting the affairs of his office in the direction he believed they should take rather than where the august body had intended them to go. It is reported that the lawmakers once retaliated by shutting off appropriations to Merriam, which necessitated his rescue by President Theodore Roosevelt, a personal friend.[3] The Office placed its emphasis on studying the distribution of plants and animals, gradually adding biologists who carried out numerous surveys, particularly in the West. In 1896 Merriam's Office was renamed the Division of Biological Survey, thereby officially acknowledging his intentions for it. He stayed until 1910 having survived a fractious relationship with Congress.

In 1905 the Division of Biological Survey was upgraded to Bureau status. The Bureau's emphasis after Merriam, gravitated toward the utilitarian purpose intended for it: attending to wildlife species that hindered or succored economic activity. A new section was organized to study the relations of mammals to agriculture, which in 1915 became a going program to "control" animals judged to be injurious. After largely eradicating wolves and grizzly bears, it became controversial in scientific circles in the 1920s, and the ruckus has endured, reaching a peak in the 1970s and simmers still. However, in 1985 the Animal Damage Control Program, as it came to be known, was finally evicted from the Fish and Wildlife Service and sent to the Department of Agriculture.[4]

An important role of the Fish and Wildlife Service today is operating a nationwide system of wildlife refuges. At first refuges were brought into being by the stroke of a pen that extracted them from the public domain. The first, Pelican Island, a small patch of mangrove islands near Florida's east coast, was chosen by President Theodore Roosevelt in 1903. In 1929 the Migratory Bird Conservation Act authorized the purchase of private lands. Today refuge management has grown to be the largest single activity of the agency.[5] There are 89.9 million acres in the system—classified into 424 refuges, 149 waterfowl production areas and 58 wildlife management areas.

Ding Darling

One of the oddest episodes in the chronicles of this arm of government came to pass in 1934 when (still the U.S. Biological Survey) it fell into the hands of a political cartoonist. Jay Norwood Darling, known as "Ding" because he signed his cartoons "D'ing" (a contraction of his last name), was another mover and shaker in the American conservation movement who is almost forgotten now. But in his day, he was well-known because of his immensely popular cartoons. They appeared daily in the Des Moines *Register and Leader*, and were syndicated nationwide and eagerly anticipated by an army of fans. Darling twice won the Pulitzer Prize. A student of cartooning history has declared that as a cartoonist he was in a class by himself with no rivals, good imitators or successors.[6] Darling was gregarious and made friends easily, a facility enhanced by his nationwide renown. Since his political views found expression in his craft, his friendship would have been especially valuable to politicians, and he numbered prominent political figures among his friends. Among them were Herbert Hoover and Henry Wallace, Franklin D. Roosevelt's Secretary of Agriculture. Both men were fellow Iowans, as was Aldo Leopold, another friend.

But although Darling had built a prestigious Old Boy network, it alone did not account for a man in such an unlikely profession ascending to the head of a

wildlife bureaucracy—a position he neither sought nor took with any enthusiasm or material reward (among other things, he dropped from a six-figure income to a salary of $8,000 dollars a year).[7] Darling was an avid duck-hunter and a crusading conservationist, known throughout the country as such. He was a civic leader in Iowa, where his energy in public affairs was prodigious and fruitful.

By the 1930s the wildlife conservation movement had steadily gained strength, despite the pull of an economic depression on the nation's attention. However, as the sentiment to preserve wildlife had grown, waterfowl in North America had diminished. Franklin D. Roosevelt, upon entering his term of office, named a committee of three to investigate the trend and to prepare a strategy for the restoration and conservation of migratory waterfowl. The three were Ding Darling, Aldo Leopold and Tom Beck, an editor of *Collier's* magazine and chairman of the Connecticut State Board of Fisheries and Game. Beck was a friend of Roosevelt's and had proposed to him using federal relief funds for wildlife restoration. Beck's suggestion had led to the appointment of the committee.

The three men had iron personalities; Leopold and Beck held philosophically opposing views, and so the meetings were sometimes stormy. Beck represented a school of thought, now extinct, which held that the decline of game could be reversed almost solely by captive breeding projects; this strategy made no allowance for refuges, for regulating annual kill or for research into habitat requirements—which were insisted upon by Leopold. Beck also wanted his scheme administered by a new independent agency, presumably similar to the state game agencies. At this time the Bureau of Biological Survey had, in its habits of operation, fallen into a state of ineptness which periodically afflicts institutions. Leopold was aware of the decay, but he did not agree with dismantling the existing edifice and building anew in its place.[8]

Despite hard differences of opinion, the committee completed a "National Plan for Wildlife Restoration." It called for, among other things, federal purchase of some 12 million acres, at a cost of $25 million. Another $25 million would be allotted from the Public Works Administration and other New Deal relief measures for restoration and improvement of sanctuaries.[9] The recommendations led to the Duck Stamp Act of 1934 which financed National Wildlife Refuges. Beck's philosophy was not adopted, but it was obvious that new leadership, and an overhaul of the U.S. Biological Survey, was essential if it was to be fitted for fresh and obstinate challenges. Roosevelt appointed a surprised Darling, a solid conservative Republican, and an outspoken critic of the New Deal, to serve at an influential level in his administration.[10] Roosevelt, ever the skilled politician, had at once neutralized an influential critic and immensely pleased the country's conservationists by signing the man up on his team and inundating him with New Deal largesse—which absorbed Darling's energies in a useful task, dear to his heart.[11]

The reluctant new wildlife chief was a hard driving man of action who burned to see results. He was temperamentally unsuited to the tempo and hindrances of bureaucratic life, but agreed to take the job temporarily, provided that the wildlife refuge program would get immediate funding. Darling had no experience as an administrator, but knew what his agency was supposed to accomplish, and he had an eye for talent (and for deadwood). He overhauled the federal bureau in short order. His aggressiveness made him a successful bureaucratic brawler. He was soon battling Harry Hopkins for promised funds that had not been received. Hopkins, on Roosevelt's staff, could not grasp why, with so many people in dire straits, anyone would want to spend millions of dollars on birds.[12]

Darling clamped on the tightest restrictions in history on duck hunting and was soon assailed by congressmen whose constituents were angered by the new regulations. He met them head-on and refused to give an inch.[13] He got into a fight with Harold Ickes (a fight which Darling started), and the two men traded scurrilous insults through the newspapers. Ickes called Darling a vicious and conscious liar, willfully trying to destroy his (Ickes) effectiveness as a government agent. Ickes added for good measure that Darling "was a dirty little Republican anyway!"[14] (Ickes had been a Republican until appointed by Roosevelt; his selection came as a reward to midwestern independent Republicans who had rallied behind the New Deal.)[15] Darling and Ickes came around to a working relationship, but it can be seen that Darling created, and operated in, an atmosphere that crackled with tension.

In addition to shaking up the Bureau of Biological Survey and infusing it with new energy, Darling used his tenure in Washington for other notable and lasting accomplishments. He was a creative thinker in the realm of policy, and his calculations extended to the institutional structures needed to carry it out. He also had the rare talent to convert ideas into working arrangements. He used his position in a presidential administration, and his personal prestige as a nationally known figure, for leverage in bringing several organizational schemes to fruition.

In Iowa, while serving on the State Fish and Game Commission, Darling had been responsible for founding a cooperative wildlife research unit at Iowa State University. His goal was to supply the state agency with personnel trained for wildlife research. He crafted a three-way fiscal arrangement with the college and the Game Commission; each would pay for a third; Darling donated the rest.[16] He realized that innovative ideas have a better reception when money for them can be quickly found. The other ingredient is an uncommonly powerful driving force. He personally provided both.

In Washington, Darling went national with the wildlife cooperative research units. He put forth a proposal to install the units into nine land-grant

colleges. To bankroll this ambition, he called together a group of wealthy industrialists at the Waldorf-Astoria Hotel in New York City and made his pitch. The cooperative units are still at work. Darling also used the occasion as a platform to father a new conservation organization, later to be known as the National Wildlife Federation. His visionary plan was to unite the country's conservation groups into a powerful political force. He lamented that the conservationists of his day had never "influenced so much as the election of a dog catcher." His brain child emerged in 1936 (in the beginning it was called the General Wildlife Federation).[17] But Darling's dream of a single voting block of conservationists did not come to pass. Although the National Wildlife Federation has grown into the largest organization of its kind in the country, conservationists have remained impervious to unification.

Darling breathed renewed vigor and purpose into the U.S. Biological Survey, although he headed it less than two years. The obverse side of his hard-hitting, straight-ahead methods was that he came down hard on every toe in Washington. He saw that he was starting to cramp the style of many persons who could be helpful to the agency. That was among his reasons for stepping down.[18] Having put things on a firm footing he left the institution in the most capable hands he could find. His successor was Ira Gabrielson, a competent career employee who had caught Darling's eye. The newly energized Bureau of Biological Survey was transferred to the Department of Interior in 1939 (into the covetous hands of Harold Ickes). In 1940 it was merged with the Bureau of Fisheries, thereby assuming its modern form, which today is the U.S. Fish and Wildlife Service.

Ira Gabrielson headed the agency until 1946, when he left to head the Wildlife Management Institute and later the World Wildlife Fund.[19] The Bureau was apparently staffed at the upper levels with a number of capable wildlife scientists at this time, among them Durward Allen, a prominent wildlife scientist. Allen left the agency in dissatisfaction during the 1950s. In an interview years later he stated that the agency had been flooded with incompetents during the Eisenhower administration.[20] This vulnerability of the Fish and Wildlife Service to the upper level appointment of political hacks, or of those philosophically out of tune with its mission, is another key reason for its on again, off again performance. There is no guarantee that every non-professional appointee will be a Ding Darling. The appointments practice looms large in the record of this inconstant mechanism, which today has the same stale qualities shown by state game agencies in the time before the independent commissions.

The Endangered Species Act

The endangered species era was inaugurated in 1966, with the signing of an Endangered Species Preservation Act which blithely directed all heads of federal

agencies to protect native forms of wildlife that were threatened with extinction.[21] The first official listing of endangered species followed in 1967. The law further directed the Secretary of the Interior, after consultation with affected states and scientists having appropriate expertise, to "publish in the *Federal Register* the names of the species of native fish and wildlife found to be threatened with extinction. . . ."[22] Also in July 1966, the International Union for the Conservation of Nature published its *Redbook*, which identified rare and endangered species around the world.[23] The Fish and Wildlife Service set up an Endangered Species Office to administer the program. It consisted of one person.[24] The intent of the act was to protect about 35 species of mammals and 30-40 species of birds.[25] It was a primitive beginning.

A stronger law came three years later. The Endangered Species Conservation Act of 1969 furnished an enforcement authority lacking in the earlier act, and it upped the authorization of funds for buying habitat. Moreover, it banned the import or export of imperiled organisms while expanding the U.S. list of endangered species to global coverage. To regulate trade in wildlife products the statute further directed the Secretaries of Interior and State to convene an international ministerial meeting to make a treaty for the conservation of endangered species. The result was the Convention on International Trade in Endangered Species of Wild Fauna and Flora (CITES).

The 1970s ushered in a general fear about threats to the environment — which still holds sway because the threats have worsened. The decade had two important effects on the Fish and Wildlife Service. First, the agency came under the direction of an able environmentalist from Florida named Nathaniel Reed; and, secondly, new environmental programs and laws amplified the workload of the agency—without a commensurate increase in appropriations.[26] The new legislation was the Endangered Species Act of 1973. With subsequent modifications it became the legal foundation for the programs presently run by the Fish and Wildlife Service. A feature of the 1973 Act aimed at identifying a species for protective measures before it reached the precarious state of being "endangered." For this accommodation the category of "threatened" was authorized, a topic introduced in Chapter 4 relative to the Yellowstone grizzly controversy. There was also a provision for the listing of habitats critical to a species, with the intent to require all federal agencies to coordinate their activities within the area so designated; any proposed government action that menaced a species was to be prohibited.

The 1973 act soon ignited a controversy. The Tennessee Valley Authority, as is well known, has been erecting dams since the 1930s. We realize nowadays that dams, whatever their benefits—which frequently are grossly exaggerated—bring massive destruction to the environment mainly because they submerge great swaths of it. Environmentalists have more and more opposed dams and other federal water

projects by any means at hand. In 1973 the Endangered Species Act came to hand for a group opposed to the Tennessee Valley Authority's Tellico Dam, the construction of which was well under way. It happened that the dam would eliminate the habitat of a tiny fish called the Tellico snail darter.

The anti-dam crowd filed a lawsuit to bring the TVA in compliance with the Endangered Species Act. The case went to the U.S. Supreme Court which determined that the will of Congress required that the dam be stopped, whereupon Congress undertook a revision of its will, not having anticipated that it would be put to such unsettling uses. To make a long story short the dam was exempted from the act and went forward to completion. The act itself was not seriously impaired, but it has been under attack ever since. The national environmental organizations have battled tenaciously to keep the statute sound, deflecting several vitiating amendments, and nourishing it with a steady flow of appropriations. Among the ironies of the Tellico saga are, first, that the TVA, dismayed at the possibility of having its project terminated, bestirred itself and found a way to complete the structure while protecting the snail darter; and, second, other populations of snail darters were found which would not have been affected by the Tellico Dam.[27]

In 1978 Nathaniel Reed departed as Interior undersecretary in charge of the Fish and Wildlife Service, as did his boss, Russell Train, who as Secretary of the Interior had a strong commitment to environmental protection. Train's successor was Cecil Andrus. Then came James Watt.

The Watt Era

Watt attracted notice because of his tactlessness—and eventually was undone by it—but he was merely an executor of the presidential philosophy, as it expressed itself toward government land. Environmental problems are among several things modern presidents should know about which President Reagan did not. This blind spot in his weltanschauung formed one leg of his philosophy. Another was the notion that the unsatisfying performance of government can be improved by shifting its functions from the federal to the state level. But government (the bureaucratic part of it) can function incompetently at any level. This will not change unless more people try to understand what bureaucracy is, how it works (or fails to work) and what might be done to fix it. The Reagan idea of government reform was applied to the Fish and Wildlife Service by trying to make it produce more revenue and consume less of the budget. The idea is not in itself a bad one if the proper purpose of the agency rules the perspective.

Although Watt was the federal government's point man in looking out for the nation's wildlife, he was conspicuously unsuited to that responsibility and reportedly tried to dismantle the cooperative wildlife research units at universities

all over the country.[28] An impression emerges from Watt's actions and words that he felt the nation's chief wildlife agency ought to be more attuned to complementing the economy than with taking care of wildlife. He was against further purchases of land for National Wildlife Refuges (and National Parks) while wanting to bolster the revenues they generated. He announced, in a congressional appropriations hearing, that he intended to make "major—and I want to underline the word 'major'—there will be major changes in the management of the Fish and Wildlife Service." He added the revealing statement that, "it [the Service] need not stop economic activity, economic growth and job opportunities. In too many instances I believe that it has. . . ."[29]

Watt illustrates another debilitation that can render a land-management agency ineffective: the destruction of its morale. It's bad enough when a politically appointed executive is unfit by reason of incompetence. President Nixon once chose as director of the National Park Service an insurance salesman who had no experience with parks, or recreation, or preservation; the appointee eventually embroiled the agency in a financial scandal and had to be removed.[30] Watt's traits were worse; nothing will debase the spirit of an agency more completely than handing it to someone who is not in sympathy with its mission to society.

The mandate to prevent the loss of life forms is one for which Secretary Watt lacked even a trace of enthusiasm. The routine of adding new species to the endangered or threatened list is slow in the best of conditions. Under Watt, it virtually ground to a halt. The Reagan administration issued an executive order obliging every federal agency to examine its proposed rules and ponder whether they would have a significant economic effect —in effect, an economic impact statement created by executive fiat.[31] The Fish and Wildlife Service was told to analyze the economic ramifications for every species proposed for listing. The tactic brought a delay, on the average of a full year, in listing. Congress overcame this obstruction by overruling the executive order.[32] However, the event shows again how bureaucracy can be rendered useless by no fault of its career professionals who in fact become demoralized by their politically appointed chiefs. Environmental leaders rallied to defend the Endangered Species Act, and in the early 1980s we were treated to the unamusing spectacle of the nation's leading environmental organizations teaming up with the Congress to shield the endangered species program from the Department of Interior. The struggle went on for years.

The scale of this conflict is attested to in a recent book on the Fish and Wildlife Service by Nathaniel Reed and Dennis Drabelle:

> The Watt regime at Interior made no bones about its intention
> of managing the department through the budget process. In effect
> this meant repeated attempts to eliminate or at least paralyze

some programs by seeking zero or minuscule funding for them. . . . In the spring of 1983 conservationists organized themselves to meet the management - by - budget method head-on. Under the leadership of the National Wildlife Federation and the National Audubon Society, a kind of "shadow cabinet" of former executive branch officials in the natural resource agencies—Republicans and Democrats alike—appeared in tandem before the House Subcommittee on Interior and Related Agencies to present and advocate a comprehensive, alternative natural-resource budget for fiscal year 1984. The new tactic worked. The spending bill passed by Congress reflects the conservationist's priorities and figures, including those for the Fish and Wildlife Service far better than the administration's—the total amount appropriated was slightly over $8 billion, $1.3 billion more than the administration requested.[33]

The great pity here is that the environmental organizations, which should have been working in a partnership with wildlife officialdom, had to commit their resources to pushing money onto the Department of Interior that its leader didn't want, and then had to goad him into spending it.

The Malaise Today

The narrative now arrives at the present, leaving us to peer further into the 1990s where there will be much hard work ahead for the Fish and Wildlife Service. President Bush declared himself an environmentalist —in response to opinion polls suggesting that a prudent President should be one. But of four key environmental posts: the Environmental Protection Agency and the Departments of Interior, Energy and Transportation, he filled only one with an appointee who had demonstrated an understanding or a competence for dealing with environmental problems. That was William Reilly at the Environmental Protection Agency. Manuel Lujan didn't want the job at Interior, as he told reporters, but took it only because his friend the President asked him to. Lujan was rated by the League of Conservation Voters as having one of the poorest voting records in Congress on environmental issues.[34] In March, 1989, the *Los Angeles Times* reported that "Secretary of the Interior, Manuel Lujan Jr., displaying a lack of knowledge about matters central to his department, incorrectly insisted Wednesday that the government was being compensated with mineral royalties for the public lands it sells for just $2.50 an acre. . . . In a fireside session with reporters in his Cabinet office, Lujan also made clear that he did not understand regulations governing leasing for coal mining and other purposes."[35]

As the world drifted toward environmental crisis, the Bush administration gave oversight of America's natural resources to a placeholder who didn't have an environmental idea in his head. At a juncture in our history when the management of natural resources demands the most determined and enlightened leadership that can be found, the mechanism for selecting able administrators is bankrupt. In May 1990, in an interview with the *Denver Post*, Lujan vented his frustration with the Endangered Species Act which he saw interfering with economic development. He cited the Mount Graham red squirrel in Arizona, a subspecies standing in the way of a large telescope that the University of Arizona wanted to put there. Lujan wondered aloud if we needed to save every subspecies? He declared that no one had ever told him the difference between a red squirrel, a black one or a brown one.[36] If the Secretary had possessed views appropriate to the nation's top conservation official, he might have been moved to wonder how badly we needed another telescope. Why should the existence of an organism have to be justified against an apparatus that doesn't have to be built?

Only the blind can continue to see environmental threats as divorced from the economy, public health and other traditional measures of human well-being. A chronic and pervasive stress on the earth's life-support systems is ruthlessly fusing the issues. From this time forth we should strive for an environmentally compatible (or ecologically-oriented) economy. It must be made to function within the limits of the environment to sustain (among other things) the earth's remaining life forms. We will make little progress on this path so long as conservation oversight is given to those who cannot recognize that every additional loss is another spreading crack in the foundations of our future providence.

The Bush designee to head the Fish and Wildlife Service and the National Park Service was Constance Harriman, a nonentity whose experience of natural resource issues consisted of a two-year stint in the Department of Interior's Solicitor's Office from 1985 to 1987.[37] Unknown (and uninformed) appointees sometimes rise unexpectedly to the demands of an office, but such performances are atypical and fortuitous; they are not to be anticipated. It seems clear that these stewards at Interior were selected for malleability, not for demonstrated convictions, or even a suspicion, that they might have the discernment and drive needed to get a grip on environmental maladies that would be easier corrected now than later. The latest Director of the Fish and Wildlife Service, John Turner, is a Wyoming businessman and legislator, but one who does appear to have some knowledge of wildlife matters.[38]

In July 1989, soon after the *Exxon Valdez* disaster, the *Tampa Tribune* reported that the Department of Interior's Minerals Management Service, charged with overseeing offshore drilling operations, has not assessed a single penalty or

fine in more than six years—even though in the past four years alone, more than 16,000 violations of environmental and safety rules governing offshore drilling have been documented. The article charged that under the last three Secretaries of Interior—James Watt, William Clark and Donald Hodel—Interior was indifferent to offshore drilling regulations.[39]

In the failure of the federal bureaucracy to safeguard wildlife, one appalling case of incapacity follows hard on the heels of another. In July 1989, Robert Mosbacher, of the Department of Commerce, whose agency is the caretaker of marine turtles, caved in to shrimpers and announced that he was suspending enforcement of the rule that would have them install turtle excluder devices to prevent the drowning of turtles. The action was promptly challenged in court by the National Wildlife Federation as a violation of the Endangered Species Act.[40] But why should environmental organizations have to repeatedly sue federal agencies for refusing to carry out responsibilities prescribed to them by law? The breakdown begins in the political appointments practice in which presidential administrations have lately been compiling an irrefutable record of indifference; it does not seem to occur to recent chief executives that trustees of important environmental posts should have any particular qualifications or aptitude for the job. This is one place where reforms will have to be brought about if the bureaucratic rot is ever to be halted.

The important things to note from events to date are that the federal government has a woefully inadequate instrument with which to execute the Endangered Species Act, although the act is firmly in place despite repeated attempts to weaken it, and it is soundly if not lavishly financed. This is because most citizens want it to be. The public backing is there; the real weakness now in this vital crusade is not primarily in the law or the lack of capital; it is in the bureaucracy. A strong statute, well-funded, is still a weak instrument if the institutions responsible for its execution are incompetent or not enthused about using it. If the national environmental organizations have analyzed this flaw they have not devised an effective strategy to mend it.

The arm of government charged by federal law for overseeing the preparation and implementation of recovery plans is woefully ineffective. It has the legal authority, controls the purse strings and it is staffed with platoons of biologists eager to save the nation's endangered species. And in my experience, Fish and Wildlife Service biologists usually tend to be less hindered by dogma than those in some other land-management agencies. In theory, the agency has the outlook and the leverage to give balance to the programs, and the manpower to keep them moving toward well thought-out goals. That is theory only.

Employees of the Fish and Wildlife are not inclined to stick their necks out; they have seen enough heads roll to know better. One of the better-known victims was Kenneth Dodd, a herpetologist hired in 1976 to work in the agency's Endangered Species Office. In September 1979, Dodd saw in a local television report that Dominique's Restaurant in Washington, D.C. was touting rattlesnake on its menu. The snake in question was the timber rattlesnake from Pennsylvania. Dodd had recently read an article in the journal, *Biological Conservation*, that documented the worsening status of the species in Pennsylvania and suggested a plan for its protection. Though Pennsylvania had recently enacted a ban on commercial collecting, the reptile had not been federally listed—many deserving organisms had not been—but Dodd decided to take the restaurant to task anyway. He sent off a letter explaining the precarious status of the snake, ending his missive with the sentence: "I respectfully request that it be removed from your menu."[41] The return letter from the owner, Dominique D'Ermo, said he would comply immediately. D'Ermo requested Dodd's phone number so that he could check on any future item before placing it on the menu.[42] The exchange of letters led to a further telephone conversation, and the matter was satisfactorily ended—or so Dodd thought.

On September 20, the episode found its way to the gossip column of the *Washington Star*. Then the rumor mill at the Fish and Wildlife Service informed Dodd that Dominique's was a favorite restaurant of Cecil Andrus, the Secretary of Interior, who was a friend of the owner. Andrus, the rumor went, had been put out of humor by Dodd's letter and intended to fire him.[43] Dodd found the scuttlebutt incredible, but on October 10 he was stunned to receive a letter that began as follows:

Dear Dr. Dodd:

This is an advance notice of a proposal to remove you from your position of Zoologist, GS-12, and from the rolls of the U.S. Fish and Wildlife Service, no earlier than thirty (30) calendar days from the date on which you receive this letter for the following specific reasons: . . . .

Reason #1: Writing unauthorized correspondence which has jeopardized sensitive endangered species legislation which is essential to the continued operation of the U.S. Fish and Wildlife Service.

You recently directed a letter to Dominique's Restaurant regarding their serving of rattlesnake, stating that the Pennsylvania

population of the timber rattlesnake is approaching extinction and requesting that they remove it from their menu. The biological questions discussed in your letter are not at issue; however, you used Service letterhead and identified yourself by name, title, and office. The contents of such a letter could reasonably be construed by the general public and by the recipient as an official position by the Service and the Department of the Interior.

Your letter was alluded to in the "Ear Column" of the *Washington Star* on the evening of September 20, 1979 in a cavalier fashion during a time period in which members of the Department and the Service are conducting delicate negotiations with the Congress relative to pending endangered species legislation. It is Service posture and the position of the Department that the endangered species program remains vital to the national interest.

As a direct result of your letter, a serious matter was presented in the newspaper as trivial and frivolous to the public. Your action has jeopardized our efforts to maintain a viable, continuing endangered species program. . . .[44]

In this way Dodd learned that he had menaced the national interest, and that his correspondence, in the hands of a gossip columnist, might despoil the endangered species program. The letter went on to accuse him of "flagrant disregard for procedural directives."[45] The Environmental Defense Fund learned what was afoot and promptly provided Dodd with an attorney; the news media soon got wind of his impending dismissal, and it made the headlines. If the publicity generated by Dodd's actions had posed a threat to endangered species legislation, as alleged, it was spectacularly surpassed by the reaction of his superiors. When Andrus was queried by a reporter he said, "in four or five days it will all blow over."[46] But it didn't; conservationists rallied to the defense. One of Dodd's annual performance evaluations found its way to the *Washington Post*. It called Dodd "the most productive branch biologist" in the Office of Endangered Species (Dodd obviously wasn't sitting on his hands).[47] Dominique D'Ermo meanwhile had substituted western diamondback rattlesnakes from Texas—which he pronounced a tastier serpent.[48]

Andrus soon heard the snarls of congressmen, via letter and by the press. Sanguinary threats came from Representative John Dingell of Michigan, congressional author of the Endangered Species Act, who said there was going to be "blood, guts, hair and hide all over the wall."[49] Kenneth Dodd is still employed by the Fish

and Wildlife Service. He presently works as a research scientist at the National Ecology Research Center in Gainesville, Florida.

The retribution attempted against Dodd was atypical, both in its draconian dimensions and as a colossal case of poor judgement, and so succeeded only in embarrassing the perpetrator. But career employees know they can be whisked across the continent to a new duty station on a moment's notice, and there is no encouragement from above to take a strong stand on any sticky issue. This is the mold of timidity that has supremely unfitted the Fish and Wildlife Service to take hold of the endangered species dilemma. Examples are not wanting. It was recently reported that the intended listing of an endangered species—the flattened musk turtle in Alabama—was delayed beyond the deadlines specified in the Endangered Species Act, while the Fish and Wildlife Service reportedly assured the state's congressional delegation that the listing of the turtle would never be the basis for clamping down on water pollution from the coal industry.[50] It was reported that the Fish and Wildlife Service reviewed the plans for Stacy Dam in Texas and judged that it would jeopardize the Concho water snake; it was further reported that when Texas congressmen put pressure on the agency it reversed its opinion and declared the snake would not be endangered after all.[51] A controversial dam project, Two-Forks, in the West, was recently under study by Fish and Wildlife Service biologists to determine if it would jeopardize any endangered species; unseemly behavior was reported from a Fish and Wildlife Service regional director who was inspired to put out the word, prior to the completion of the biological study, that he would insist on a no-jeopardy ruling.[52]

When the Bush administration took office and began filling slots in the federal bureaucracy, environmentalists erupted in protest over a nominee to the U.S. Forest Service who had previously served in the Department of Interior. He was a former Oregon real estate developer who was causing a scandal over the listing of the spotted owl as an endangered species.[53] The spotted owl is at home in old-growth forests in the Northwest. When the Fish and Wildlife Service prepared to list the owl, the timber industry became alarmed, fearing proscriptions on its harvest of the ancient trees. In response to this consternation, the Department of Interior official, who incidentally had no responsibility in the Fish and Wildlife Service, brought pressure against the agency to "sanitize" a report that was being drafted to justify the action. He went so far as to telephone the agency's regional director in Portland, Oregon, Rolf Wallenstrom, to instruct him that the spotted owl would not be listed.[54] When Wallenstrom balked at altering the document, he was fired by Fish and Wildlife Service director Frank Dunkle, a political appointee and former lobbyist for the Montana Mining Association (and former director of the state game agency in Montana). Dunkle also demoted and transferred two assistant regional directors in the Portland office.[55] The Fish and Wildlife Service then obediently revised the report, first in the regional office in Oregon, with additional

changes being added for good measure when it reached Washington, D.C.; conservationists had to bring suit in federal court to reverse the decision—another instance of a citizen's organization having to expend its resources to compel the federal agency to carry out its duty under the Endangered Species Act.

The General Accounting Office investigated the affair. Its summary report begins with the bland statement that ". . . we found several factors that raise questions about FWS thoroughness and objectivity in considering the petition to designate the spotted owl as an endangered species." As to the doctoring of the spotted owl document, the GAO concluded that "the revisions had the effect of changing the report from one that emphasized the dangers facing the owl to one that could more easily support denying the listing petition."[56] The GAO affirmed that "biological criteria are the only basis for listing decisions . . . ," and that, non-biological considerations should not play a part. It went on to say that "factors in addition to the owl's biological conditions were considered in deciding to deny the listing petition. FWS' consideration of such factors is inconsistent with the decision-making process provided for in the Endangered Species Act and its implementing regulations. . . . FWS needs to be able to demonstrate that its review process and ultimate decisions have been as thorough, independent and objective as possible. There is evidence that the spotted owl process did not meet such standards."[57]

So what else is new? It is shown in this book that non-biological decisions are commonplace among the bureaucratic goliaths that are fumbling with the nation's endangered species. These irresponsible exercises are not exclusive to the Fish and Wildlife Service. The management of endangered species in the United States is at the mercy of politics, incompetence, agency paranoia and ideology. Biological objectivity hasn't a chance in this politically-charged bureaucratic environment.

Blowing in the Wind

The General Accounting Office, when called on to do so, visits the Fish and Wildlife Service and catalogs the symptoms of infirmity. Unless an effective cure is found, the symptoms will recur again and again. Nothing will change. A cure will not come without redesigned institutions under able, committed, and politi-cally unshackled, directors. The spotted owl travesty was amenable to correction because it was so blatant—and perhaps because it pitted the welfare of an endangered species against the interests of consumptive users of public land—an issue that made it easy to mobilize environmentalists at the local level. In other kinds of policy conflict, as, say, between the Fish and Wildlife Service and other balky agencies, the absence of black and white symbols can confuse the perception of peril to the species. The spotted owl incident represents only the tip of an iceberg.

And so we can see how the worth of the Endangered Species Act depreciates. Thousands of hours of our congressmen's time went into forming the act. Since the coming of a national awareness about endangered species in the last two decades, the treasury has fed millions to the Fish and Wildlife Service budget, swelling its ranks with biologists to review public works projects that might jeopardize a species, and then a mockery is made of the whole process. This is one more example of how our government squanders millions of dollars on programs that don't work. The malfunctions and wasted tax dollars are often caused by congressmen doing favors for constituents of influence back home. Their proper role is to enact laws and to oversee their fiscal nourishment and execution, not to individually impair the instrument of execution for the statutes they have collectively labored to build.

In making this criticism, I don't overlook the irony of my own attempt to meddle, via my senators, on behalf of the Florida panther, as told in an earlier chapter. My tactic to get measures written into the recovery plan to increase deer numbers on the public lands of southern Florida came to naught because supporters of the National Park Service could be called on to deflect it. We note then that the National Park Service is well buffered from outside interference—unlike the Fish and Wildlife Service. The endangered species mechanism does not have such strength at the grassroots, unless, as in the case of the spotted owl, it can be improvised.

The Fish and Wildlife Service functions are diffuse, and it has also been saddled with the oversight and regulation of other agencies—which are far stronger politically. It has been said that the wildlifers are frequently regarded by the Army Corps of Engineers and other departments (and were by officials in the Reagan administration) as an organizational gnat.[58] One branch of the Service that does evoke citizen patronage is the wildlife refuge system. Here, like the national parks, the agency takes form as a prized plot of ground (or water as the case may be). However, the national wildlife refuges did not begin with an influential band of protective devotees as did the National Parks, and even though the refuges were provided by law with a specific, narrow purpose—the sheltering of wildlife—they came to serve a variety of recreational and commercial purposes, such as hunting, trapping, grazing, mining and boating. Some of these evolved uses have been born of political pressure, and some may be detrimental to wildlife.

For years the National Audubon Society urged its chapters to take a proprietary interest in a local refuge.[59] Environmental groups have recently challenged some unorthodox uses of these sanctuaries. A lake refuge in Nevada allowed water skiing, which was not thought helpful to ducks nesting there. Defenders of Wildlife filed suit to stop the skiing, and won (but Nevada congress-

men introduced legislation to restore the status quo ante).[60] A proposal to hunt deer in the Loxahatchee National Refuge in Florida was defeated by citizens with a proprietary interest in a non-hunted refuge.[61] The point here is to illustrate that when the Fish and Wildlife Service is identified with a protected enclave of cherished ground, citizens may get involved at the local level to fight for it. The endangered species administrative structure within the Fish and Wildlife Service does not emit such earthy charm. Without a strong, attuned constituency, it is wide open to meddling and manipulation by congressmen and anyone else with the right connections.

A complete working system will be needed to identify and recover endangered species. The Endangered Species Act of 1973, upon which environmental organizations have rightly lavished so much protective energy and attention, is only the foundation. The value of a foundation is realized by the structure erected upon it. Without an effective structure, the act is little more than a promise of what could be. If the tool of promise is to be forged, it will require that the environmental organizations invest some of their intellectual and lobbying energies toward institutional reforms, as opposed to a strategy that does not look beyond basic statutory and fiscal tactics. The alternative is to be continually fighting brush fires which the legally mandated, publically funded, fire-fighting institution is too inept to control.

A government agency is composed of people; it is not just an organizational chart. Certain things are essential if any purposeful human aggregate, whether an army, a football team, a business organization, or a government agency is to excel, as opposed to simply achieving and sustaining a corporeal presence. There must be a clear sense of purpose. That purpose must be of worth to the society it serves and there must be capable leaders who approve the mission and strive to fulfill it. Absent a good leader, or absent public support for the agency, and the erosion of morale is predictable. Morale is one of the adrenaline pumps that most humans require to give all they have to an endeavor. What is the effect on morale of Fish and Wildlife Service biologists, who have been conditioned to believe that they may work for weeks or months on a project only to see it swept away by a political decision?

The endangered species branch of the Fish and Wildlife Service is purely an administrative organ. It lacks the vivid identity with a land ideal or with a specialized function of land-management which characterize the other three agencies in the Panther recovery program; it is not guarding any tradition against a "threat," real or imaginary, which might emerge from a recovery strategy; consequently, it has no zealous band of constituents, and thus no political base. It is without power and has only a subsidiary influence on the course of events.

The Fish and Wildlife Service is the sick man of the federal land-management agencies. It has many dedicated employees, but they often labor at tasks that consume their energies for paltry results. This forsaken institution needs only to be consistently led by persons committed to its legally mandated purpose and, in addition, to be buffered by the appropriate institutional arrangements against the eternal bullying and meddling by congressmen and special interests—including other more politically powerful agencies —and to be better supported by the public it is trying to serve. If the necessary reforms aren't brought to bear on its deeply rooted tradition of official timidity, then it will continue to function ineffectively, providing a poor return on withdrawals from the public treasury, and draining the resources of the environmental organizations which are forever having to brace it up and keep it tottering forward.

The Service and the Panther

The agency manages two refuges in southern Florida which are part of the contiguous public lands now constituting a core of secure habitat that might provide the base upon which a viable panther population could be sustained. Loxahatchee National Wildlife Refuge is a 143,000-acre refuge, once a part of the vast Everglades marsh which extended from Lake Okeechobee to Florida Bay. Today it is a diked remnant of that marsh, like those contained within the state Water Conservation Areas. A second refuge is now being acquired—this one specifically to preserve habitat known to be frequented by panthers. The Florida Panther National Wildlife Refuge will encompass the northern portion of the Fakahatchee Strand, but it goes without saying that this sanctuary is far too small by itself to play a meaningful role in recovery. Like every other separately managed segment of southern Florida's sprawling public habitat conglomerate, it cannot hope to be useful unless it becomes part of a coordinated plan for panthers. The obstacles to such a design have been covered in previous chapters, the principal one being that the other agencies will not commit themselves to a unified design.

We have seen evidence, in the original draft of the 1987 recovery plan, that the Fish and Wildlife Service biologists who worked on it knew there was a need for the National Park Service to manipulate deer. We have further seen that the National Park Service was quietly allowed to alter the plan to conform to its biases. We have seen that the Endangered Species Act supersedes any law relating to the management of wildlife in National Parks, but that the Fish and Wildlife Service will not put its foot down. At the FDE panther conference a representative of the Fish and Wildlife Service asserted that "because there is no such thing as a natural ecosystem in south Florida, the issue becomes—to what degree should humans actively manage the system, and what should be the management objectives? . . . and that "all [management actions] must be tried if we're going to give the panther

the best chance for survival."[62] Subsequently we can see the non-influence of these convictions in the administrative documents signed by the Fish and Wildlife Service to guide the recovery program. We have reviewed the minutes of the FPIC's Technical Subcommittee in which, time and again, attempts by Fish and Wildlife Service biologists to build a rational recovery structure were deflected by representatives of the other agencies—without protest. In a later chapter we will see the Fish and Wildlife Service stand passively by while an incompetent state game agency nearly exterminates the world's only known black-footed ferret population.

Chapter 11

THE FLORIDA
DEPARTMENT OF NATURAL RESOURCES

*The objective of natural resource management is to restore
and maintain the resource as a representative sample of an
original Florida ecosystem (original means prior to the
ecological disruptions caused by the arrival of European man
in 1513). With the continuing and accelerating manipulations of ecosystems in Florida, this resource management
philosophy will have increasing scientific, educational,
recreational and aesthetic value for future generations.*

Operations Policy Manual
Florida Park Service
December 1, 1983

The Florida Department of Natural Resources (henceforth referred to as
Florida DNR) is a conglomerate of instrumentalities charged with overseeing the
state's marine and coastal resources and the state park system. It also administers
Florida's program of land acquisition, which is second only to that of the federal
government in the amount of land it annually purchases. The land buying operation
has vital implications for the survival of panthers in Florida. It is the tool of final
configuration for the remains of a native landscape now being rapidly reduced and
sundered by the onrush of asphalt and agriculture. The department's administrative
sub-units are called divisions; the largest is the Division of Recreation and Parks—
more commonly called the Florida Park Service. This is the arm responsible for
managing panthers inhabiting the Fakahatchee Strand State Preserve. The following narrative will largely leave the department behind and focus on the Florida Park
Service. In this affair the division tail has usually wagged the department dog.

The Florida Park Service was a child of the Great Depression, brought
forth less to satisfy a demand for recreation in the great outdoors than to furnish
work-relief to the unemployed. The Civilian Conservation Corps was written into
law to put men to work on government acreage, both on federal and state land. The
economic emergency found Florida with neither state parks nor forests, but they
were hastily designated. State parks were authorized by the 1935 legislature and

placed under a Board of Forestry, which had been created in 1927 to control forest fires and assist private landowners in developing the forest products of their property. Ten parks were in place by 1940.[1] The Civilian Conservation Corps camps were under the supervision of the U.S. Army, and park planning was guided by the National Park Service. Thus, the early sites were chosen for their visual qualities, following the national model.

The 1938-1940 biennial report of the Florida Forest and Park Service complained that disbursements from the Board of Forestry had not been adequate for park needs, prophesying that "the ten park units which now comprise Florida's State Park System represent only a beginning. The ultimate should be a sufficient distribution of state parks to provide wholesome outdoor recreation within traveling distance and pocketbook range of every Floridian. In addition, the historic, scenic or unusual should be preserved."[2] In 1945, perhaps to resolve the unsatisfactory sharing of a budget, the Park Service was given its own executive and granted equal status with the state Florida Forest Service.[3] Four years later a new statute transferred it to the ministrations of its own Board of Parks and Historic Memorials.[4]

World War II terminated the Civilian Conservation Corps. With it went the early professional direction and dynamism that characterized the formative period of Florida's state parks. The agency drifted without firm direction in the post-war period, even while attendance rose steadily in the wake of a general prosperity. Visitation passed the one million mark in 1953.[5] There was no scheme of expansion to meet this rising demand. The system grew, but helter-skelter, primarily though the transfer of surplus military properties and from the occasional donation of estates by the wealthy.[6] In 1963 Congress passed the Outdoor Recreation and Conservation Act, under which a trust fund could be tapped by the states to buy land for outdoor recreation. Officials could now target properties of choice rather than taking what came by chance.

In 1972 attendance climbed to over 10 million. During the 1970s the Florida Park Service entered the modern era. Under Ney Landrum, who became executive director in 1970, institutional reforms were imposed that would slowly improve and refine the quality of operations and move them into a more sophisticated realm. Heretofore the care of parks had been largely measured by the maintenance of buildings and facilities. In the 1970s an academy was founded to give two weeks of basic training to park rangers. Promotion review boards were set up to judge the fitness of those seeking advancement, and training in general was upgraded. At the same time a swelling social awareness, and worry about the environment, brought in a better quality of applicant for career service.

239

During this era the agency also articulated a guiding principle. It postulated the Florida Park Service as the state's principal supplier of outdoor recreation. Properties sought after for parks were those with exceptional natural appeal. The character of these sites suited them to furnish outdoor recreation of a particular kind—that which derived its worth from the special qualities offered only by the natural environment and was therefore termed "resource-based outdoor recreation" to distinguish it from other types, classed as "user-oriented." The latter type included archery, tennis, basketball, swimming pools and the like, activities that could as easily be provided on a city lot or in an urban neighborhood. They were not provided for in state parks, where wildlife and natural scenery offered inimitable surroundings for leisure activities like boating, camping, picnicking, visiting historical and archaeological sites, beach activities, nature study and a pastime clinically termed "natural scenery appreciation."

From this recreational matrix a philosophy of resource management was derived. Its goal was to "restore and maintain the resource as a representative sample of an original Florida ecosystem ("original" meaning prior to the ecological disruptions caused by the arrival of European man in 1513).[7] These tenets drew heavily from those that structured thinking in the National Parks. They elevated management guidance to a loftier plane than before, one consonant with the widespread environmental awakening.

The limitations of reconstituting the rather smallish state parks as "original ecosystems" were obscured by the idealism of making the attempt. A small staff of six biologists was recruited, on a starvation wage, to advise on returning the parks—which had at the time grown to more than 70—to their "original" condition. I was among this group; we set to work with missionary zeal, undaunted by the magnitude of our challenge. We were spread thin and were not greeted with enthusiasm by the old-line regulars who could not understand why anyone would want to start tampering with things. Some of them affirmed that if change came to the park service, it would not happen in their lifetimes. There was no time for research, but much useful work waited; fire had been banned from parks since their beginning (the Florida Park Service was the last agency in the state to rediscover the virtues of managing land with fire); exotic plants infested many parks, particularly in the tropical latitudes, and plans and procedures had to be fashioned for their removal; there were few wildlife or plant inventories, so there beckoned all the basic survey work anyone could wish for.

The expansion of the state park system took a great bound in 1974 when Florida voters approved a $240 million bond issue to purchase environmentally endangered lands. A land acquisition program runs on today supported, in part, by severance taxes on phosphate mining and has added an immense acreage to public

land inventories. The Fakahatchee Strand State Preserve was purchased in 1974. These islands of green have grown and spread, but they will soon be overwhelmed; available lands suitable as parks are diminishing, but there is no foreseeable end to Florida's exploding population. The conflict in outdoor recreation is that at some threshold of saturation, the resource—and thus the quality of the outdoor experience—begins to deteriorate. At the time of this writing there are 145 units in the Florida Park Service. They encompass 340,000 acres of uplands and nearly 82,000 acres of submerged lands. The expansion has placed the agency in control of representative samples of most of the state's biotic communities at a time when its natural land is rapidly being fragmented. The challenge of resource management in the future will be to forestall depletion of the state's biological diversity—in a highly disturbed and modified landscape. Obviously there will have to be some flexibility in the cherished doctrine of simply trying to return every unit of the system to its original appearance. In my agency, in the 1980s, I was moved to introduce this shocking new thought to a protective hierarchy, on the theme of preserving panthers.

Managing for Panthers

Overtures by Game Commission biologists to promote the cause of panthers in the Fakahatchee Strand State Preserve were made to me early in the decade, soon after the advent of radio-telemetry. Suggestions for habitat alterations were informal, and the topic was usually broached in a roundabout manner as if it were an idealized proposal—theoretically useful if not possible. The petitioners knew policy in the state parks did not condone single species management, and I left no doubt in their minds during these exchanges about the correctness of their suspicions. It was within my sphere, not withstanding a modest rank, to reject such a suggestion. I knew the doctrine, and I knew the whole mass of the agency from the base to the summit stood behind me like a mountain.

Radio-telemetry research at first gave a fragmentary picture of the panther population, and there were few data on deer. It was comfortable not to see into the problem of prey scarcity, particularly if approved thinking predisposed against it. My professional orientation had been toward the restoration and care of "natural systems," not single organisms, and in this case one whose requirements far overreached the boundaries of any refuge in Florida. My training had been in a realm that had not primed me to accept the unanticipated challenge now easing its way into my ken. It is not easy to revise the thinking habits of a career (and I have since had to confront the reality that some are incapable of doing so). The aversion to managing deer was easier knowing that the Game Commission was unwilling to restrict hunting.[8] At the bottom of that agency, a few biologists debated the heresy that the harvest of game might be something to worry about; they even probed the chain-of-command to induce the closing of the Fakahatchee Strand—advice not

well-received at the top. They had no data then to justify the prohibition; they were just advocating a common-sense precaution. Field biologists in the Game Commission tend, in some cases, to be less conforming to agency dogma than personnel in other land-management institutions. I suspect this is because they are more often immersed in research—a process that can abrade fixed formulae. As in other agencies this flexibility is less pronounced among administrators, who must treat adventurous schemes that float up from below with great caution.

In September 1983 at the formative meeting of the Panther Advisory Council, Tommy Hines, a Game Commission biologist, was bold enough to advance a proposal for forest clearings in the Fakahatchee State Preserve as a measure for panthers. I countered by advocating controls on hunting. That ended the debate. Either course was unthinkable at the time, and forwarding either of them to Tallahassee would have only elevated blood pressures there. The meeting was a short one. When it ended I found myself elected to the Chair of the Council, and went away feeling an unaccustomed weight starting to bear down on my shoulders. There was a sense of having a large responsibility for a case which might have a low tolerance for error.

As related in a previous chapter, John Eisenberg and Melvin Sunquist, both with a broad knowledge of mammalian predator-prey interactions, were put on the Panther Advisory Council. The recovery program profited from their expertise and from perspectives that were indifferent to the inhibiting constraints that governed strategic thinking in the bureaucracy. Roy McBride was also an influence on my thinking. He carried in his head a store of practical knowledge about predators that would be the envy of any wildlife scientist, and he was not hesitant with opinions. These men sketched the panther situation in southern Florida in broad, simple strokes and offered counsel accordingly: evidence showed an inadequate, perhaps waning, population of panthers; preparations must be made soon for an expanded prey base if the status quo was to be altered to advantage; given the terminal implications of inbreeding, outbreeding might prove unavoidable.

These unaccustomed concepts were unwelcome but inevasible, and I lacked the background to evaluate them properly, having grown comfortable over the years in a professional existence grounded on unchallenged precepts. I was well integrated, attuned to guidance from the top and not alert for troubling new ideas (a common affliction among bureaucrats). To become conversant with the novel responsibilities that had come my way, I drew up a rigorous reading schedule and started burning the midnight oil. It was tempting to believe that the cessation of hunting (legal and illegal) alone would be remedial. I was determined that the burden of management would not fall on state and national parks while the Game Commission refused to confront its responsibility. In June 1984 the Panther

Advisory Council sent recommendations to the Game Commission advising that hunting pressure be eased in the Big Cypress Natural Preserve.

I could not dispel the thought that the Fakahatchee Strand might be a potentially important element in panther survival, and about this time a notion occurred in which the deer management problem might be solved without requiring any unorthodox effort in the Preserve. Golden Gate Estates, the massive land sales project introduced in the first chapter, lies immediately to the west of the Fakahatchee Strand. The 60-square mile portion south of Alligator Alley has long been listed for acquisition as an environmentally endangered land. It is a large, forested area, crisscrossed by a rectangular grid of roads and canals. The aesthetic qualities of this large tract have been so compromised that it lacks any appeal as a park. Deer could, in theory, be multiplied here, next to the State Preserve, without discomfiting any bureaucrat.

I put this idea in a memo and sent it up the ladder with a feeling of self-satisfaction, but then could not rest. It grew on me that each agency was converging on the core issues with constricting preconceptions, embedded in long-standing practice. The National Park Service and the Florida Park Service have vested the original landscape with a near-mystical aura. The Game Commission, committed to the furtherance of sport hunting in a society that had begun to declare its hostility to the practice, was wary of any insinuation that it might have to be curtailed, and its freedom of action was in any case circumscribed by the vigilance of organized hunters.

In the summer of 1984, in the Big Cypress National Preserve, Game Commission biologists began taking deer for analysis and counting tracks for a census. There were not the resources to sample deer all across the Preserve. Efforts narrowed to Raccoon Point and Bear Island. Findings showed that the quality of deer habitat differed markedly between the two collection sites. In Bear Island deer densities were adequate; there, a resident female panther regularly raised young. Raccoon Point was depauperate in deer, a fact already attested to by the few aged, malnourished cats which had been treed there. The remaining sprawling miles of the Big Cypress National Preserve had no panthers. The Stairsteps Unit was a puzzle. Deer harvest records, if compared with those from Raccoon Point, indicated more deer than in the latter unit, but field searches turned up no evidence of panthers in the Stairsteps.[9] In the Fakahatchee Strand it could be reasonably presumed that the emaciated panthers at that site meant few deer. Now came the question of how hunting fitted into the prey supply picture, but it was no longer possible to imagine that conditions for panther survival could be created in southern Florida solely by hunting controls. The habitat would have to supply more deer, and techniques were at hand at least for an experiment, but it was easy to see the granite obstacles waiting in the bureaucracy.

As the 1985 fall meeting of the Panther Advisory Council neared, I began mentally formulating the array of recommendations that would have to be made. Each agency would have to revise traditions which they had relied on for guidance, and collaborate on satisfying the essentials of a panther goal. The problem was on a scale that outstripped precedent, and officials are conditioned to think within definite geographical and administrative bounds. It is usually unrewarding for an agency to stray into the territory of another. A plan would have to be devised (or at least considered) that postulated a minimum number of panthers that could withstand inbreeding, and natural catastrophes as well. A multi-agency refuge would have to uphold a single population. Beyond it to the north, every stone would have to be turned to prevent the loss of habitat on the adjacent private lands.

To assess the form and length that my agency's service to these new principles might take, I looked over maps and aerial photographs of the Fakahatchee Strand. The challenge in this exceptional repository of rare plants, noteworthy for its many epiphytic orchids and bromeliads, was to benefit one endangered species without compromising others. The maps showed a way. Most rare plants are concentrated in a central slough of deeper water that threads the length of the Strand from north to south. Vegetative patterns here were mapped in the 1970s by Daniel Austin, a botanist at Florida Atlantic University.[10] His maps show several forest patches composed of willow and maple trees, scattered through the preserve. In the 1940s and 1950s, after a period of drought which followed logging operations, long fingers of fire burned through the slash, eating downward into the organic soil. These "burnouts" were recolonized first by willows and later joined by maple trees. The replacement vegetation is distinct and still easily recognized. The larger willow-maple associations add up to several thousand acres, and there are other sites near the periphery of the swamp suitable for clearing. The prairies bordering the hardwood swamp were available for forage planting experiments.

As a next step I tried out these volatile ideas on two park managers, to gauge the response of agency professionals who had been indoctrinated in the original Florida school of management. I explained the predicament and the proposed solution first to Robert Dye at Myakka River State Park, and then to Benny Woodham at the Fakahatchee Strand State Preserve, whom I took along on a field trip to investigate the willow-maple growth. Both were shockingly flexible. On federal lands a promising site for deer management was the highly disturbed Hole-in-the-Donut of Everglades National Park. Similar measures would also be needed in the Big Cypress National Preserve.

At this juncture the duty of serving on an independent advisory council was bringing me onto a collision course with an official attitude that stood strongly against manipulative management. I penned a letter to my supervisors explaining

what would have to be done—with emphasis on our duty in the State Preserve, and requested a parley, prior to the upcoming Panther Advisory Council meeting. I was set on seeing the recommendations through the Council regardless, but wanted to alert my bosses to what was coming and to try and sell the idea of the Florida Park Service taking the initiative on deer management. If the state "natural systems" agency would take the lead it could be used as leverage to try and pry the feds into position, and it would not be promising to prod the Game Commission to close the Fakahatchee Strand State Preserve to hunting, unless the Florida Park Service was willing to make reciprocal moves to improve deer numbers.

The meeting in Tallahassee was arranged for September 1985, the day before the Council was to come together. I was extremely tense; this was no casual discussion topic. It had taken me two years to accept that the agency would have to bend if it was to participate in a meaningful recovery program; my superiors had been given two weeks to make the mental adjustment, and was I was not optimistic. On the appointed day I made two proposals. The first was to begin clearings in the willow-maple growth. I had delineated the sites to be cleared on an overlay that covered the checkerboard pattern of public-private ownerships. There were accompanying photographs of the vegetation. The second prescription was for experiments with forage plantings on the bordering prairies. The meeting did not last long; the outcome was part disappointment, part pleasant surprise.

The decision, first, barred the clearing of trees, because the multitude of acre-and-a-quarter lots that had been sold to speculators in the 1960s made ownership uncertain. I argued that since these holdings had never been surveyed none of the owners knew the location of any lot. To survey one would cost thousands, and environmental laws recently enacted eliminated any possibility of building on them. Also, the properties would eventually come to the state, which had been granted the power of eminent domain to purchase the lots but had not yet done so. These arguments had no effect. It was conceded, however, that some selective clearing of tram roads would be acceptable. This was illogical since the tram roads were subject to the same confused ownership; I argued the point without effect. Planting forage plants on the prairies, I was told, was a permissible method and was endorsed without qualification. It was just a matter of working out the operational details. I departed realizing that the options had not been carefully sifted, but with an enormous sense of relief at not encountering the wall of objection I had anticipated. A huge stride forward had been taken in the course of a few minutes. Or so I thought at the time.

The Panther Advisory Council, in September 1985, outlined for the first time a coherent design to advance the cause of panthers in southern Florida. It called for the Florida Park Service and the National Park Service to realize that they had encountered a novel challenge, and pointed out that fresh thinking was in order.

245

It asked the Game Commission to acknowledge that the wildlife management areas having resident panthers were not typical game management units, and that the needs of the cat held preference over recreational hunting. We also put great emphasis on the importance of private lands to the north where panthers were known but not studied. The Game Commission was urged to immediately begin mapping the vegetation and land-use patterns of this region. If sufficient private land was to be held for panthers, mapping was an essential first step.[11]

Following the council meeting I turned my attention to the Fakahatchee Strand and to the task of transforming intentions into a plan. In January 1986 I traveled over the preserve with Jim Schortemeyer, a Game Commission biologist, and Mike Duever, a systems ecologist with the National Audubon Society and an authority on swamp management. We debated alternatives. Clearing forest openings came up again. It is a proven technique for multiplying the browse available to deer. Stepping up the use of fire was also favored, with burning being scheduled for the months of late pregnancy and fawning of deer so as to provide new vegetative growth at the time of greater energy needs by does and fawns. Site-specific research would follow to see how the plan was working.

Then, in April 1986, a Florida Park Service delegation arrived at the Fakahatchee Strand from Tallahassee. It was to investigate the proposals and to approve the specific steps to be taken. The first day was given to a field trip during which I once more tried to promote forest clearings. I showed the party several locations suitable to demonstrate that the measure could be undertaken without threatening any of the rare plants in the Preserve. On the second day we gathered around a table. As the various deer management techniques came up for evaluation, I began to sense that something was wrong. Fault was found with every one that departed from tradition. Forest clearings couldn't be tried. Planting high-protein forage plants on the prairie—which had been agreed to the previous September—was now unacceptable. When I suggested some experiments on a very small scale, that too was rejected. However, it was agreed to step up burning, if possible. That was a long-standing practice.

At this point the discussion began to warm up. I was bitterly disappointed at this turnabout and left no doubts about it. It was a lopsided debate with me on one side of the table and the Tallahassee delegation on the other. "How did I know," it was put to me, that if we began clearing areas in the Preserve that the local County Commission might next want to build an airport there? "How did I know" that our action wouldn't trigger a "downhill slide?" And so it went, with the arguments deteriorating into farce, and me fending off the paranoid absurdities of the central office. Obviously something had happened since our meeting the previous September. The delegation facing me across the table had been sent south on a damage-

control mission. It was unfolding according to a prearranged design of which I had been the only one ignorant.

When things had reached a difficult juncture, I was offered a "deal." I was asked if my "bottom line" was that we increase deer numbers irrespective of method. Curiosity up, I answered that that was essentially it. Very well, two methods were proposed; one was that commercial deer food would be dispensed in feeders; the other was that goats would be set out at scattered spots in the Preserve. I was taken off-guard with these proposals. They were theoretically workable; I doubted that any serious thought had been given to the feasibility, but was not in a position to be choosy so the deal was made. I left the meeting with misgivings about where this turn of events was headed and also about the secretive and defensive cast that was beginning to characterize the attitudes of my superiors. Driving two of the participants back to the airport I was reminded by one of them that a deal was a deal and was cautioned not to "go behind anyone's back." There was little time to ruminate on this development. The following week I conducted Douglas Miller, of the National Wildlife Federation, and Maurice Hornocker, a well-known puma authority from Idaho, on a field trip to southern Florida's panther country. Both men were brought to Florida by Nathaniel Reed for the purpose of making a brief survey of recovery activities and to offer their perspectives at the upcoming panther conference, to be sponsored by Florida Defenders of the Environment. It was scheduled for the week to follow.

Gissendanner's Effort

Early in the next week, on the evening before the conference, I attended a meeting in the office of Elton Gissendanner, the executive director of the Florida DNR. Gissendanner, like others in the ruling circle of the recovery crusade, was scheduled to address the conference, giving his views on his agency's role. The Florida Park Service was well represented at this meeting by its upper echelon. It was unusual for anyone in my lowly position to be asked to attend a high-level pow-wow, but I was on the panther conference agenda as a speaker and as chairman of the Panther Advisory Council, I had taken up the practice of commenting critically on the performance of government agencies—including my own. Gissendanner came straight to the point. He wanted to commit his department to do whatever was necessary so that there would be no further criticism, and he wanted my opinion.

The week following the Fakahatchee field trip, and the disappointing meeting, had been one of great industry in the central office. Some documents of impressive thickness had been drafted. They purported to describe ambitious actions to be taken on behalf of panthers. The finishing touches had been put on the drafts the day of this meeting, and Dr. "G" (as Gissendanner was called) was

now seated at the table making his way through them; I had just been handed a copy and was also reading.

One item was a proposed policy "for the protection and enhancement of Florida panthers in units managed by the Division of Recreation and Parks."[12] The opening paragraph made the usual orthodox statement: "The Division of Recreation and Parks' approach to resource management can be described as natural systems management. This approach is aimed at managing the natural communities of each unit as parts of an interrelated system, rather than managing for the benefit of one or more individual species."[13] However, the second paragraph hinted at a new flexibility: "In most cases, this systems approach will enhance the welfare of all animals and plants within each unit, including endangered species, and no further action, other than protection, is required. However, additional management measures may be used because of unusual circumstances, which is the case with the Florida panther."[14] The policy went on to define, in detail, the various protective, administrative, and other actions to be taken.

In addition to the "new policy," there was a seven-page document entitled "Initial Management Strategy for the Florida Panther in the Fakahatchee Strand State Preserve."[15] It listed in detail the actions about to be launched. These were identified under three objectives, each with a summary, followed by an enumerated list of tasks. The first objective described what would be done to enforce the hunting ban recently declared by the Game Commission. The second was to "Expand Proven Resource Management Activities." In plain words, this meant that we would go forward with methods that would have been used even if panthers had never been heard of. The term "proven activity" meant prescribed burning, which is used in parks throughout the state. The second objective stated, with not a tinge of doubt, that: ". . . The benefit of these measures is that, if fully implemented, they are estimated to provide the largest, most economical, and most long-term enhancement of the panther prey base. Such ecological burning, especially during lightning season, will stimulate new growth of grasses, forbs, and other tender young plant material which provides high protein food supplies for an expanding deer herd. In order to monitor the effectiveness of habitat management, a concurrent research program will be necessary."[16]

It is true that prescribed burning is the most economical, large-scale management tool with which to improve deer habitat, but such improvement is linked to the inherent quality of a given deer range. When the soils and forage are poor, as appears to be the case on much of the public land in southern Florida, the improvement is only in proportion to what is there to be improved upon. The application of fire cannot transform a poor habitat into a good one, and there is no reason to assume that burning alone would give rise to the kind of deer herd that was needed to feed panthers. The deer herd was being expanded prematurely I

thought, but I thoroughly approved of the research. That was the only confident way to get answers to the questions of what would, and would not, produce deer. I was then astonished to see hydrological restoration listed as a "proven resource management activity" to assist in the overall prey-base management effort."[17] Undoing the disruptions of local drainage canals had been an agreed upon need for years, but ballyhooing it as an aid to panthers was pure nonsense.

Objective number three delved into the new flexibility. It was grandly titled: "Expand and Explore Experimental Food Source Enhancement Alternatives." Following a reference to using deer feeders, was a surprising paragraph introducing "active deer enhancement habitat manipulation." It had been made oppressively clear at the Fakahatchee meeting two weeks earlier that measures of this kind of work was not to be considered—even experimentally. "Prey base enhancement," said the report, "may be pursued by establishing food plots or by selectively clearing forested areas, thus stimulating the growth of early successional plant species which are excellent deer browse. However, since these measures would seriously compromise the FSSP resources, other lands west of the preserve will be sought for this purpose. These lands are already seriously impacted, have lower resource values, and are being expressly acquired for panther management purposes."[18] So habitat manipulation was clarified if one read far enough. It was to be practiced on the land next door—which still hasn't been purchased at the time of this writing and may not be for years to come. This was the same magic wand solution I had tinkered with years earlier during a flight of fancy. Nothing has ever come of this daydream.

I didn't say much during the meeting, but there was plenty of anxious chatter from the rest of the park service contingent. Gissendanner was hell-bent on planting forage plants or doing anything else for the panthers. The others viewed the slightest deviation from "natural systems management" as step one on the road to ruin, or the beginning of the "downhill slide" as it had been phrased at the Fakahatchee meeting earlier in the month. The Park Service faithful strove resourcefully to keep Gissendanner on the narrow path that had been mapped out at the meeting two weeks earlier.

I should digress here to explain the clannish nature of the Florida Park Service—which is characteristic of most land management agencies. The agencies are somewhat like large fraternities. The career members spend their professional lives in a common quest to fulfill the institutional credo of public service. The career requires frequent moves that discourage putting down roots in a local community. The agency is the community within which the members interact for decades, a few slowly ascend the hierarchical staircase into the senior management ranks of the central office. Newcomers sometimes make an entry directly into the upper level

via the professional bureaucratic route; for them the process of socialization is rapid—if they want to be accepted into the clan.

The Florida DNR director is a political appointee, and although "the boss," he is usually seen from below as an outsider, unattuned to the values shared by the agency regulars. He is also viewed as a transient. Several DNR directors come and go during the long careers of Park Service professionals. These political chieftains are regarded with varying degrees of wariness, depending on their inclination to tinker with the agency mechanism. I'm sure the same situation prevails with the directors of the National Park Service who are appointed from outside the ranks. The April meeting described here was a classical confrontation between the transient, politically appointed boss and the long-term careerists who were trying to stave off heretical management ideas which had been introduced to him.

All energies were now bent to sell Gissendanner on the arrangement that had been concocted two weeks earlier. "Goats," he shouted. "What do you mean you want to put goats into the Fakahatchee Strand? Goats are ruminants; they will compete with the deer." (Dr. G had been a veterinarian and knew something about animals.) Gissendanner was lavishly assured that pens could be built; all would be taken care of. The palaver went on and on. All the director's concerns were quieted. He tried to draw me out. I went along with the company game, saying that goats and deer feeders would probably work. I had been given assurance that no effort would be spared. I should also point out that I was aware that Governor Graham, who had appointed Gissendanner to his post, was nearing the end of his second term, and it was speculated that the director, who had enemies in the Cabinet, would not be around much longer. It was not a good time for an end run, but I also genuinely wanted to work within the system to get the job done, and believed that the corner had finally been turned. Goats and deer feeders were a bit wacky, but it did seem to indicate a new flexibility and if it proved unworkable, I presumed that common sense would have to break out if these schemes failed to yield results. So ended the meeting.

The FDE panther conference was most encouraging, as related in an early chapter. Officials of the National Park Service sounded flexible and conciliatory, if somewhat contradictory. Dr. Gissendanner radiated a resolve to save the panther. He read the speech which had been prepared for him. It was heavy in emphasizing the Florida Park Service commitment to natural systems management but conceded that "In the case of the Florida panther, however, we cannot assume that this approach will be sufficient to halt the decline of the species. . . ."[19] Gissendanner went through the list of promising actions that had been written for him, and then ad libbed a bit on his own. He promised to evaluate goats (he also added sheep for good measure).[20] "If we have to we'll plant millet. I don't care what we plant in

there; we'll plant whatever they [deer] will eat." Dr. G ended with the, "hope that if we should meet again one year from now, the Fakahatchee Strand State Preserve will no longer be a problem in the saving of the panther."[21] A year later, Gissendanner would be gone and no management measure that deviated from tradition would have been seen.

In the weeks after the conference, I had to dig out from under a backlog of work which had accumulated during April's meetings and field trips. It was June before I could put together thoughts on the practical aspects of goats and deer feeders. I had no experience in this field, but also knew that those who had dreamt up the idea hadn't either, and if I didn't try to think it through it was unlikely that anyone else would. I telephoned Dave Maehr, a Game Commission biologist who was tracking several radio-collared panthers in the vicinity. He promised to help select a location where a goat would more likely to be taken quickly.

I collected odds and ends of information on feeding deer and then called John Lukas at White Oak Plantation. During visits there to observe captive breeding facilities, I had seen deer gathered around feeders. Lukas provided information on kinds of feed, and amounts required, and on the spacing of stations; a feed store quoted costs. The essential point about feeding deer is that high-protein, mineral-rich food can be provided on a continual basis. This is quite a different situation from having food supplied by the natural environment, in which the amount and quality may fluctuate with the season and may vary with climatic shifts from year to year. Feeders can fuel deer abundance until their very density becomes a limiting agent through overcrowding and disease transmission. This is one concern about feeding and something to be avoided. However, individual deer stay within a relatively small area and are not likely to travel any distance to feeders. This meant that many stations might have to be distributed widely. The Fakahatchee Strand is seasonally flooded and is served by a primitive road net. At the time, the staff consisted of a park manager and two rangers. The cost and logistics of this project would quickly get out of hand. Calculating the practice at White Oak Plantation, on the expanded acreage of the Fakahatchee Strand State Preserve, would have required 42,000 lbs of food a week, distributed to 132 feeders. The feed, at an annual cost of $275,000, would have had to be transported many miles to the preserve and then be shuttled to outlying stations. It was an impossible scenario.

I phoned Bill Branan who guessed that panthers might prosper from deer densities well below those maintained at White Oak Plantation. He suggested a pilot project. I wrote a proposal accordingly, scaling it down to something less than ridiculous. These thoughts went to Tallahassee in a memorandum with the warning that once arrangements were in place the work could never flag. It couldn't be suspended if swings in the economy caused budget cuts, and there could be no slacking off during those periods when personnel turnovers caused a temporary

reduction in manpower. The memo ventured that we could probably do the job this way if we wanted to commit all our eggs to such an expensive basket.[22] Such is the thoroughness and professionalism employed in the Florida Park Service to evaluate novel management proposals.

Suppression

During a morning later in the summer of 1986, a phone call came from a boiling Sonny Bass. He had just been told by his supervisors that his service on the Panther Advisory Council constituted a conflict of interest with his duty to the National Park Service, and that he would have to resign. Sonny had derailed this institutional locomotive by demanding a written directive. He was banking (correctly as it developed) that no one in the National Park Service hierarchy would have the gumption to put his signature on such a letter. I tried to convey what moral support I could and urged him to stick.

I was still stirred up about this conversation when less than an hour later a phone call came from one of my superiors. The voice on the phone said that word had been passed to him that he should relay to me that I was to step down from the Chair of the Panther Advisory Council. The source of this instruction, I was told, was unknown. My blood pressure headed for the ceiling. Sonny came instantly to mind. "Can I get this in writing?" I shot back. "Well . . . uh . . . sure, if you want it that way." I am not clear about everything else that was said. I tried not to overdo it, having learned that it's nearly always a mistake to say or write anything in a state of anger. It's nearly always obvious later that more prudent options were available, but not evident at the time. I needed time to think. I suspected that the "unknown source" was purely a fabrication. As in Sonny's case, my agency had begun to feel threatened by pressures originating in the Panther Advisory Council and was moving to suppress that part of it coming from within the ranks. However, I also knew that an administrator from another agency had complained bitterly to Gissendanner about my activities as chairman of the Panther Advisory Council (I was told this by Gissendanner, who said he had responded to these complaints by saying that my activities on the Council were my own affair), and it was impossible not to be struck by the coincidence that Sonny and I had been approached simultaneously, and therefore impossible not to suspect collusion. Unlike Sonny, I had not been told to leave the Council, only to step down from the Chair, but there was no doubt what the next step would be if I complied.

I thought the matter over for several days. There were options, one of which was informing the governor's office. But in the end I took a moderate course and composed a long personal letter explaining why I would not vacate the Chair of the Council. It ended as follows: . . . "Finally I must question the propriety of being instructed to give up the Chair at the behest of some anonymous entity. Is this

political pressure from outside the agency, and if so, how will quietly submitting to it benefit the efforts to prevent the panther's extinction? This is the question that must be asked in every situation. This all seems very irregular and improper to me, and I think it improper that I should simply submit to such pressure without a murmur. Government is not supposed to work this way."[23] Shortly afterward there was another phone call—a short one. "Okay," a voice said, "Forget it."

Both Sonny and I were intimately familiar with the systems we worked in, and with the mental workings of those who peopled them, and we both knew that we were holding the high cards. We couldn't be forced out of positions we held by gubernatorial appointment. These clumsy exercises in intimidation were easily defeated by calling the bluff. But the would-be intimidators knew the game too. They hoped the authoritarian psychology would work—as it usually does in such cases. For them it was a low-risk gamble for what they saw as very high-stakes issue—the protection of the agency missions, which they saw jeopardized by the Panther Advisory Council.

During the course of these difficult years, I often tried to explain to outsiders the intense emotions that coalesce around certain departmental ideals and the encrusting tribal defensiveness that grows up around them. If this proposition is accepted, much seemingly irrational behavior can be understood. But my efforts were often lost on listeners who could not imagine the grip of a land-management ideology. A listener once told me that it wouldn't be logical for an agency to behave in a way inimical to panther recovery, because it would be counter to the agency's own interest to risk having the program fail; further discussion was futile. My observation has been that the emotional nature of beliefs about land, and wildlife, and how it should be managed, can engender the most astonishing capacity for self-delusion. In the bureaucracy, logic is built on a base of values rooted in the institutional calling; it develops to protect orthodox practices from perceived threats; it is not a mode of thinking that will desert its tribal roots and anchor itself on the survival requirements of an endangered species.

Sonny Bass and I were not the only government employees to feel the heat. Our agencies reacted in the manner of all institutions that feel threatened by a dangerous new idea. These responses weren't novel, each one was just another episode in the successive challenges to the ideals of American land-management institutions. A few historical examples will illustrate.

Early in this century, an all-out campaign was mounted to protect forests from arson. In the U.S. Forest Service it became a moral crusade. It wasn't recognized at the time that certain forest types were adapted to a regime of frequent fires, and that fire exclusion would bring unwanted consequences. Pine forests in the Southeast had been subjected to frequent fires for millennia, as a result of

lightning and from burning by Indians. Frontier cattlemen carried on with matches, having superseded the Indians, and learned that if the ground cover in the open pine forests was burned away each year, it produced an annual fresh new growth of succulent forage for cattle. Every year they "burned the woods." The early attempts of the U.S. Forest Service to stop this custom collided with rural folk wisdom. The conflict was a bitter one.

A young biologist named Herbert Stoddard was hired by wealthy sportsmen to find out why quail were vanishing from their hunting preserve in southern Georgia. Stoddard discovered, among other things, that when fire was excluded, suitable food plants for quail began to diminish. Quail, he said, would prosper from frequent burning. Fire properly employed could benefit wildlife. Stoddard's discoveries soon ran afoul of Forest Service dogma, as he recalled in later years:

> The controversy over the use of fire in the pinelands intensified year after year. As the most outspoken advocate of controlled burning in coastal-plain pine forests, I became the focus of that controversy. The battle became even more intense as the course of the new investigations became clear. . . .

> Before publication, manuscripts by employees of the various bureaus had to go "through channels" for approval by the directors of other agencies that might be affected. Since the United States Forest Service was one of the largest and most powerful bureaus in the Department of Agriculture, it exercised enormous influence upon the reports of other agencies. My chapter on fire in *The Bobwhite Quail* immediately ran into trouble when it arrived at the Forest Service, in spite of the fact that I had made my recommendations as mild as my conscience would permit. The critics of the chapter did not question the scientific accuracy of the findings, but they were horrified by the thought of what might happen to their elaborate campaigns against *any* use of fire for *any* land-handling purpose, in the forests of the Southeast or anywhere else. . . . To them, the Florida cattleman who burned off his range had horns and a forked tail. Though they were doubtless aware that there were fire-type coniferous forests elsewhere in the world, they were sure there were none in the United States.

> One of the main arguments against the custom of burning off the longleaf forests was the alleged disastrous effect on game and wildlife in general. In this intensive propaganda the truth mattered little. Motion pictures of deer with hair and hooves

burned off in disastrous crown fires of certain western-mountain forests or in the forests of the Lake States, were regularly shown on southeastern screens without regard to distinctions among the forest types. Dead fish, killed by chemicals washed into streams with the ash from explosive mountain fires, were shown rotting in the sun as examples of what would happen if the Florida Cattlemen did not stop firing the flatwoods.

In illustrated lectures throughout the Southeast pictures of ticks were thrown on the screens to illustrate the iniquity of woods burning—the implication being that burning was responsible for ticks. Malaria was solemnly offered as another result of forest burning. Not only in lectures but also in pamphlets and leaflets handed around by forestry agencies, flat claims were made that the livestock industry was being injured by woods burning—that this old custom of the cattlemen was somehow responsible for the wiry, scrawny condition of flatwoods cattle. It was, in short, the most intensive—and ludicrous—educational campaign that ever insulted the intelligence of American audiences. It was carried on by well-meaning but utterly misinformed persons. . .

It was in this climate that officials in the Forestry Service objected to my first draft of the fire chapter for *The Bobwhite Quail*. I rewrote the chapter several times, trying to make it acceptable without weakening it to a point where it would be entirely counter to the findings. Finally I passed the word that if it was not cleared in its diluted form I would resign and write a book that would really burn them up. Since the funds for the quail investigation were donated by a group of wealthy, and in some cases politically powerful men, my position was a strong one. I felt sure that the subscribers would back me to a man if it came to a showdown. The chapter was finally cleared.

In February, 1929, I was invited to read the chapter at a meeting of the American Forestry Association in Jacksonville, Florida. I have never attended a meeting with a more pervasively hostile atmosphere. . . . At the meeting the chairman, who obviously feared that I might contaminate my hearers, actually cautioned them not to take too seriously what I might say. I fear I took a perverse pleasure in reading the chapter to them, though I had a feeling of futility at the solid wall of opposition with which it was received. (From *Memoirs of a Naturalist*, By Herbert L. Stoddard, Sr. Copyright © 1969 by the University of Oklahoma Press.)[24]

For another example: in the 1930s the land-management agencies were busy exterminating predators, a popular mission nurtured by a cultural attitude inherited from ages past, ordaining that predators, being destructive, must in turn be destroyed. However, a new breed of wildlife scientists were calling the prevailing wisdom into question. Against this background, two wildlife scientists, the brothers Olaus and Adolf Murie, between 1927 and 1939, undertook predator studies for two agencies, the U.S. Biological Survey and the National Park Service, to learn about coyotes and elk. There had been complaints that elk were falling before the ravages · of coyotes. The brother-scientists followed the interactions of both species under wilderness conditions. Olaus worked for the U.S. Biological Survey in Jackson Hole, Wyoming; Adolf was employed in Yellowstone by the National Park Service. Their work showed at both sites that elk herds were in no danger from coyotes, even though individuals could be vulnerable. When the reports came in, both agencies were very unhappy with them. It is reported that the National Park Service wanted to fire Adolf.[25]

Issues and institutional faiths change with time, but the antagonism of comfortable bureaucracies to unsettling initiatives does not. It can be read in the record of intolerance to unwanted news by powers-that-be, as a reflex to eliminate the messenger rather than to confront the disagreeable message. A management problem that seems in any way troublesome to the mission of a land management agency will not be greeted kindly by its officials. The ouster of the Craighead brothers from Yellowstone National Park was just another episode in this long-running bureaucratic theme.

In September 1986 I was notified that goats, as a nutritional supplement for panthers, were being dropped from consideration. In a high-level meeting the specter had been raised that animal rights groups might object. However, I was told that since an operation of this kind was really the sort of thing that ought to be handled by the Game Commission, it would be bounced that way for a decision (and to a predictable greeting). There were also unmistakable signs that the deer feeder plan was losing steam. It had dawned on the decision makers, after receiving my brief on the project, that it would be "too expensive." Thus, now that the FDE panther conference was receding into the past, the innovative resolve displayed by the Florida Park Service was fading fast. Everything would be as before. The assurances that had been given to me had been worthless.

As reported in Chapter 7, six months after the panther conference, Bill Branan of FDE wrote officials who had made presentations, asking for progress on promises made. The return letter from the Florida DNR is too devoid of substance to warrant extensive quoting. There are, however, some interesting passages, like the following about goats: "There is no support from the Game and Fresh Water

Fish Commission for the possibility of using other prey species (goats, sheep, etc.)."[26] Thus, the failure of the phantasmic goats—that creative illusion of the Florida Park Service's imagination—to nourish to the Fakahatchee's emaciated panthers—was deftly laid on the Game Commission; support from that quarter was also commandeered to rationalize the failure to go forward with deer feeders: "It appears that supplemental feeding of deer that we mentioned earlier will have little success and is not recommended by the Game Commission. We do, however, expect to implement a scaled down experiment after the current hunting season."[27] Not the slightest attempt was made to follow through on this promise.

Hope Springs Eternal

About this time I wrote another long, personal letter, mincing no words. I detailed promises that had been made and broken, drawing the unavoidable conclusion that they had been nothing more than expedients of the moment. I commented pointedly on the conduct of those who had made them, and ended by saying that I would not be silent while the rot went on. This brought another telephone call, this time with instructions to go to the Preserve and select promising sites, both for forest clearings and for the planting of forage. A field trip was scheduled by staff from the central office to inspect the sites and approve procedures for them. The sense of relief was beyond description. Time was passing; the months were dragging into years; an enormous amount of work lay ahead if there was to be any reasonable expectation of keeping panthers in southern Florida. The stress of anger and frustration at all this artful avoidance was heavy. My letter, I thought, must have pricked consciences. At last we were on the way—or so I thought at the time.

We toured the Preserve by jeep on a pleasant February day in 1987, in the course of which permission was granted for a "limited treatment" of habit on an experimental basis. A mechanical brush cutter would be used to clear one-half mile of overgrown tram road. Two small areas vegetated by willow, wax myrtle, and small maple trees were selected as experimental sites for clearing. There, hardwood vegetation would be cut low to the ground. The prairies bordering the forested portion of the Fakahatchee Strand State Preserve were crisscrossed with swamp buggy trails. Several of these muddy tracks were selected for the planting of joint vetch (*Aeschynomene americana*), a native legume which in fact grows wild in the Preserve. The plant is rich in protein, and the seeds are sold commercially as a forage crop. The day ended with a renewed sense of relief. These small steps were too restricted for practical value, but they represented the unthinkable. We were over an enormous psychological obstacle. I reasoned that after another year had passed, it would be seen that these tentative steps had not sent the Florida Park Service sliding toward perdition, and work could begin on a meaningful scale.

It was gratifying shortly after the field trip to be instructed to draft a research proposal that would monitor the experiments.[28] I had pushed hard for approval to begin collecting quantitative data. (A research program concurrent with habitat management—to monitor its effectiveness—was yet another promise that Florida DNR had made at the FDE panther conference.) There was an intense dislike in some quarters of the hierarchy to this new direction. The decisions on these measures were being made in verbal free-for-alls, in which well-informed opinions carried no more weight than poor ones, and biases had the run of the field. With idiotic arguments being proffered as confidently as those of substance, the lay administrators who had to make decisions were completely at sea in these debates. For that reason, I was eager to begin assembling data which might form a factual ground for future discussions on how to proceed.

I enlisted the assistance of James Schortemeyer and Walter McCown, two Game Commission biologists. We put considerable time and care into a plan. Several methods are available to assess the capability of forage to support numbers of deer. We selected a nutritional design aimed at sampling the various forage treatments and contrasting the results with adjacent untreated areas. The difference would be measured between the amount, and nutritional content, of forage produced in both the test site and the control site. Crude estimates might then be calculated of the number of deer that could be sustained at a given degree of treatment. The effect of fire on forage was worked into the design; this because much of the opposition to "artificial" habitat management centered on the claim that an intensified burning program alone would suffice to produce an abundance of deer. Forage samples would be collected throughout the year to record seasonal variation in the vegetational response.

We made field trips to the study site. A succession of meetings were held to review sequential drafts of the proposal. The work dragged into the summer when we had to work around vacation schedules, and it was fall before the final product was mailed to Tallahassee for approval.[29] The staff at the Fakahatchee Strand State Preserve had in the meantime been beefed up as part of the Florida Park Service's commitment to panther management. Two rangers had been added and, most gratifyingly, a position had been created for a biologist to do the research. The proposal which was mailed to Tallahassee called for a pilot project the first year to evaluate the design. In the meantime, I recommended that an expanded program of forage treatment be started during the coming year while the monitoring was underway.[30]

In the meantime, small plots of joint vetch had been planted (and were being heavily cropped by deer). A mechanical brushcutter had arrived and cleared

clear small trees and brush from a short segment of tram road. The two one-acre plots in the Strand were not cleared. Dave Maehr who was monitoring radio-signals, advised that movements by a radio-collared female raised the suspicion that she might have young kittens nearby. The work was postponed, and the area was flooded by summer rains before it could be undertaken.

More Obstacles

Another field trip was scheduled by the Tallahassee staff in February 1988. Shortly before the trip I received a rambling memorandum complimenting me on the time and hard work expended on developing the research proposal. "Unfortunately," it said, research would be impossible during the coming year because "neither additional staff nor funding is available for this level of research at this time." However, it implied that something might be possible in the year to follow. The memo then laid out a number of tasks, related to the management of deer, to keep me busy in the months to come. But several of them could only have been completed after seeing results from the research—which couldn't be imple-mented because of "inadequate staff and funding." For example, under a section entitled: "clear cuts," I was instructed to: "a) Develop procedures for clearing that will have minimum impact on the substrate; b) Provide an analysis of the results; c) Cost per acre."[31]

I should comment here that personnel at the Preserve had been increased specifically to aid panther recovery. The park inventory showed the necessary vehicles and equipment, and one objective of the pilot project was simply to judge how the staff would handle the tasks which had been laid out for them so that a reassessment could be made after the first year. The estimated cost was $4300, simply to purchase again the seeds, fertilizer and necessaries for another planting of joint vetch, plus the wire, rebar, clamps and other miscellaneous supplies with which to build exclosures to keep deer out of control sites. The funds could have been easily found, but there was clearly no enthusiasm in the central office for investigations that seemed counter to the approved way of doing things. The memo ended with instructions to forward reports on the various tasks that had been assigned to me. "I look forward to receiving this information and materials," it said.[32] It was not a serious attempt at communication. I never responded, and no inquiry was ever made about it. It went into my file to join the thickening reams of paper, representing an accumulation of man-hours expended in futility.

In February 1988 the visiting delegation from Tallahassee arrived, and the administrative types spent the day riding around the preserve on all-terrain cycles and then boarded their plane for the return flight home. Shortly thereafter, instructions for Fakahatchee's 1988 panther recovery work arrived in the mail. It

was a memorandum of nine lines that, in effect, ordered a repeat of the previous year's piddling work with joint vetch. There was no mention of objectives, methods or anything that could begin to dignify the instructions with the notion that serious research was intended.[33]

There was more at work here than heavy-handed top-down management. The design and implementation of a local research project was being directly supervised from the highest levels of the agency. The utterly nonsensical results of this aberrant procedure left no doubt that the intent was to look busy while insuring against substantive changes in prevailing practice. It had been five years since Tommy Hines, of the Game Commission, first suggested measures to increase deer numbers in the Fakahatchee. It had been three years since I was first promised from above that a new flexibility was indeed in order for special situations, but nothing had changed except appearances. Now another barren year lay ahead while the clock ticked on, counting down on the Florida panther. At this point only a fool would suppose that the future would be any different. Accordingly, I had embarked on a new tactic. I was two months into the writing of a book on the Florida panther recovery program.

Chapter 12

THE BUREAUCRATIC RESPONSE

Hence its activities are reduced to dodging the difficulties of the hour; not solving them, but escaping from them for the time being, employing any method whatsoever, even at the cost of accumulating thereby still greater difficulties for the hour which follows.

José Ortega y Gasset
The Revolt of the Masses
Speaking of government in a mass culture.

"Bureaucratic delay" is an overworked phrase. It is important in analyzing bureaucratic dysfunction to distinguish between the unavoidable delays—wherein actions are held in abeyance by the procedural mandates of administrative routine—and the unnecessary ones. In the conduct of administration, time must be allotted to write research or management proposals, acquire funds, complete purchases, schedule meetings and conduct reviews. Routine matters may move slower or faster depending on the priorities assigned to them. Some agencies are plagued by incompetents sprinkled throughout the hierarchy. These cause inevitable delays and inefficiency. Elsewhere, unhappy working environments in some bureaus contribute to high turnover among personnel, causing procedural sluggishness, since each new employee requires a span of time to learn the job and get up to speed.

But though bureaucracies are sometimes portrayed as unresponsive or torpid, this trait is not invariable—at least not in a land management agency. A challenge can be greeted with lethargy or with zeal, depending on its nature. A key determinant in influencing the tempo and incisiveness of its reply, is a judgement by the agency on whether a task promises to further, or hamper, its own interest. A challenge that promises to bless the mission fires the response with ardor; by contrast, a threatening task usually brings on a paralytic affliction.

But, when a menace looms, the transformation in the operational routine is a marvel to behold. Communications via the leisurely flow of memoranda go by the boards. From central headquarters, telephone messages blitz through the ether to outlying stations. Everyone's schedule is placed at the mercy of the new priority.

Meetings are called on short notice, key decisions are made in minutes. Assignments are quickly delegated to whoever is best qualified to handle them—without regard to rank or station. Adrenaline pumps, and the agency swings into action, transformed into a focused, efficient, swift instrument of self-protection. I offer here a personal example from the Florida Park Service.

Early in 1986, following a routinely scheduled fire at Myakka River State Park, a local paper published a critical article implying that the burn had been conducted irresponsibly, damaging vegetation and so forth. The executive director of the Department of Natural Resources (a political appointee) reacted to the criticism by summarily suspending the use of fire in the park, thereby depriving it of a fundamental resource management tool.

The agency was not passive. Letters quickly accumulated on the department director's desk from research institutions, academics and environmental leaders around the state. Letters from park allies also hit the desk of the newspaper editor. The reporter who wrote the article was invited to a meeting—convened for him at the park. He was given a short but thorough lecture on the principles and practice of fire ecology, by park service personnel and from an array of park allies who had gathered in support. The Florida DNR director was persuaded to visit the park and see for himself that things were not as alleged. The counter-offensive lifted the burning ban. This remarkable thrust of carefully targeted energy came during the time I was arguing in vain for management changes to aid the Florida panther.

The Tosohatchee Conflict

Another example of bureaucratic vigor shows up in one of Florida's great interagency fights, between the Florida Park Service and the state Game Commission. In 1972 the voters of Florida approved a $240,000,000 bond issue to buy environmentally endangered lands. The program was given to the Florida Department of Natural Resources, meaning that most of the purchased lands would be handed to the Florida Park Service. By the late 1970s numerous properties had been bought; several were large tracts which were assigned to the category of state preserves. This classification would emphasize the preservation of natural features, allowing only passive kinds of recreation such as hiking and primitive camping. Voter approval of the bonds had reflected a strong unease in the public mind about Florida's surging populace, which was overpowering the landscape, threatening, among other things, to curtail opportunities for outdoor recreation. Recreational hunting was also being pinched; between 1950 and 1975, hunting license sales soared from 100,000 to 250,000. During the same period the acreage available in wildlife management areas to each license buyer shrank from 40 acres to less than half that amount.[1] The hunting community was not pleased about the exclusion of hunting from the new lands being added to the state's inventory.

In 1977 a tract known as the Tosohatchee Game Preserve (the same mentioned in Chapter 2, relative to the subject of tick eradication) came into state ownership. In the 1920s it had been purchased by a sportsmen's club and added to the state's system of game refuges. By the 1970s the club members were growing older and, having a genuine interest in preserving the land, offered it to the state. Following acquisition, political pressure grew to admit hunters. The Florida Park Service intended no hunting, but the question, now astir and showing signs of a formidable enlargement, was brought before the Governor and Cabinet for a decision. On September 30, 1977, that executive body removed the prohibition against hunting and directed six state agencies to conduct a study of the site to address (among other things) hunting. This faction-ridden investigation must have been contentious judging by the preamble to its findings: ". . . it has been difficult to arrive at anything approaching a consensus on the question of hunting. No two of the six agencies appear to espouse exactly the same position, but four agency viewpoints seem to have emerged: (a) no hunting on any of the tract; (b) hunting on all of the tract; (c) no hunting at this time, but review the situation periodically to determine if hunting should be introduced; and (d) divide the property to prohibit hunting on the most environmentally significant and sensitive part and permit hunting on the rest. The report recommends (d) as the single position having the highest degree of support among the study group."[2]

The divided report went to the Governor and Cabinet in 1978, whereupon the executive body ruled against hunting, but with a qualification (of redundant verbiage and tangled syntax).

> The Game and Fresh Water Fish Commission shall conduct game population studies to monitor the animal population should it become desirable to depopulate, due to overpopulation of deer or other species, damage to Tosohatchee plant life or other adverse effect[sic]. The Game and Fresh Water Fish Commission shall hold public hearings and make a recommendation to DNR [Department of Natural Resources] as to wildlife management within the Tosohatchee area including, if desirable, limited hunting.[3]

What this jumbled pronouncement tries to say is that the Game Commission should monitor the wildlife (meaning deer) at Tosohatchee. If evidence is found that the deer are stressing the resource, the Game Commission can recommend that the herd be reduced—by hunting.

The Game Commission promptly dispatched biologists to the Tosohatchee State Preserve to study the deer herd, which had been protected for many years, subject only to very light hunting. It was in essence a protected herd. The biological investigations revealed what was expected. The physical condition of the animals indicated a herd at carrying capacity. The fitness of adult deer fluctuated seasonally with the availability of forage. The health of the adults was generally very good during the winter and spring with signs of physiological stress during the summer. The physical condition of fawns was generally poor; the fawn survival rate was estimated at 32 percent. Life is difficult for fawns when the habitat is filled to capacity; most of them do not survive. It was a situation in which total numbers might have been expected to vary somewhat from year to year, perhaps dropping during periods of climatic extreme. The pattern is not uncharacteristic of many wildlife populations.

In some parts of the United States, during wide imbalances of deer abundance to habitat, the environment has suffered as deer devoured all the vegetation within reach. In some cases land thus damaged has taken years to recover. However, this misfortune has not been observed in forested habitats in Florida like those at Tosohatchee. The results, stated the Game Commission's biological report, were "typical of what would be expected in a herd not subject to hunter harvest."[4]

The document was forthright. It implied the possibility of future damage from overbrowsing if the deer were to become acutely pressured by environmental stress, but the caveat was buffered by language appropriately cautious. However, the biologists did give an opinion on the ruling by the state's executive body: "The criterion that would permit recreational hunting on Tosohatchee laid down by the Florida Cabinet is biologically untenable." In plain words this meant that no compelling case could be made for hunting deer. A substitute criterion was tendered: "The issue of hunting should be decided on the basis of responsible wildlife management." In plain words this meant that a case could be stated for the harvest of deer at Tosohatchee, the idea being simply to crop enough deer annually to hold the herd "within" carrying capacity.[5] By keeping deer numbers down, the herd would be better nourished, bear more fawns and in theory better withstand any environmental impact it might chance to suffer. The contest over hunting was philosophical, not biological. The question was whether the new lands coming under state stewardship would be used for passive recreation only, or also for hunting. The affair would not be decided by technical reports; it would be fought out in the political arena.

The Florida Park Service and the Game Commission were the contending forces, but convention demands that disaccord on this plane be conducted with

decorum and so it was, at least on the surface, where there was no indication of the passions, elevated adrenalin and intensive lobbying going on behind the scenes. The visible conflict was between opposing leagues of citizens. The Florida Wildlife Federation carried the torch for the Game Commission, while the opposing sentiment, led by the Florida Audubon Society, campaigned for the Park Service position.

On December 2, 1980, the Game Commission presented the findings of its research to the Governor and Cabinet in a packed three-hour meeting and recommended "limited" recreational hunting on the Tosohatchee for 18 consecutive days.[6] The Governor and Cabinet approved hunting, with two dissenting votes cast by Governor Graham and Secretary of State Firestone.[7] The Game Commission planned four hunts, each of three to four days. One hundred fifty permits were authorized for each hunt; applicants were to be selected by a drawing; fourteen thousand applications were made available on December 8; they were exhausted in eleven days; a total of 7,661 applications were returned.[8]

The event was scheduled for January 10. On January 8 the Florida Audubon Society went before the First District Court of Appeals in Tallahassee to stay the hunt. The appeal was not acted upon by the court, but by now the Orange County Board of Commissioners was up in arms and took the case before the circuit court in Orlando, whereupon the local judge granted an injunction on January 9. Word reached the Game Commission headquarters at 5:30 p.m., where an infuriated staff scrambled to notify 150 archers around the state to tell them that the next day's event was not to be. Many didn't get the word until they reached the Tosohatchee gate in the early hours of January 10.[9] Their comments are not on record, but were said to have been colorful. The president of the Florida Wildlife Federation lashed out at the Florida Audubon Society calling it a "fruitcake organization."[10]

A hearing was held in the Orange County Circuit Court on January 13, and the injunction was removed the following day—which was when the second event of four days had been scheduled, but of necessity postponed. The Game Commission staff again went to the telephones to tell the permit holders (muzzle loaders this time) that it would begin a day late, on January 15. On the appointed day the hunt commenced. However the industrious opponents were methodically working the courts and, on the day it began, got another stay at 3:00 p.m., this time from the Fifth District Court of Appeal in Daytona. Once more the Game Commission reluctantly shepherded its angry charges out of Tosohatchee. However, on the next day—January 16—the Game Commission, on its own motion, subsequently lifted that stay and the activities resumed. But on the following day of January 17, the court stayed the Game Commission rules, whereupon the agency

staff once more apprised permit holders that the hunt was off. The outcome of all this hurly burly was a total of two days of hunting at Tosohatchee in 1980 out of the 18 scheduled.[11]

The strife carried over into the following year. The Orange County Commission stood against the hunt and called a public hearing on April 16, 1981. The assembly was a raucous affair, seemingly poised on the brink of riot. The Brevard County Commissioners now weighed into the fight as a counterbalance to Orange County. Brevard was for hunting; the City Councils of Rockledge, Melbourne and Titusville—all in Brevard County—presented resolutions in support.[12] But the battle was over. Hunting was permanently installed at Tosohatchee and was extended to other properties acquired in the Environmentally Endangered Lands Program.

During the conflict the Florida Park Service distributed an information sheet to contest the findings of the deer research and to disparage the notion that culling was necessary. It pointed out that the deer had not been randomly sampled. Eighty-eight percent were taken along a powerline right-of-way (where they were easy to shoot). This was true but probably irrelevant; the physical condition of the deer showed what would be expected in a protected herd; the condition of deer would not likely be different elsewhere in the park. The Park Service information sheet also stated that "a higher level of parasites is to be expected as long as deer must share the same habitat as cattle."[13] This argument was untenable; the parasite loads in the deer were consistent with what was known about a deer herd at carrying capacity whether there were cattle present or not.

The Park Service information sheet also implied that the herd was subject to legal hunting along the preserve boundary and to heavy poaching, and that predators were also taking deer. A deer killed by a bobcat had been found, and the park superintendent estimated that four to five deer per week were taken by poachers. But mortality from poaching is incalculable and at five deer per week, outlaws would have been annually removing one third of the estimated population of 750 deer —aside from predation and boundary hunting. In such a case the deer herd might well have been expected to be below carrying capacity and to have revealed a greater survivorship among fawns.

In connection with the imaginary rate of poaching, Richard Harlow, an authority on the white-tailed deer in Florida was quoted: "even light legal hunting can be very effective in preventing expected herd increases."[14] But Harlow, who was quoted out of context, had been referring to a deer herd at low density in a poor habitat that limited fawn production. The quote had no application to the apparent situation at Tosohatchee. The information sheet finished with several assertions in the following vein: "Homeostasis will occur in a stable environment—parks are

stable environments. There is an automatic self-righting balance between population density and resources." No one would have quarreled with this generalized
proposition. It meant that there was really no biologically compelling reason to hunt
deer—which had been more or less conceded in the written report of the Game
Commission. As for that agency, its propaganda output departed from the standards
of its biological report. A high-ranking administrative biologist in the Tallahassee
office authored a piece in a popular magazine entitled, "Tosohatchee Deer Herd
Ravaged by Overpopulation."[15] State game agencies have more reason than anyone
to deplore the uninformed emotions that influence wildlife policy, but some of them
won't hesitate to play on emotions when an advantage is to be had.

The arguments promoting hunting were as flimsy as those against it; but
as stated before, the rancorous dispute at Tosohatchee was not over biology.
Hunting was opposed by those who valued the opportunity to simply observe deer,
and by those who had principles against shooting animals. It was a no-holds (and
no scruples) barred contest between the two agencies and their respective citizen
backers. As in any emotional contest facts mattered less than results. But the
purpose of revisiting this clash is to illustrate the willful and uncompromising,
single-minded intensity with which the contenders waged it. On one side, an agency
was fighting to prevent an activity which it vehemently believed had no place in
the kind of recreational service it wanted to offer to the public. On the other side,
an agency was alarmed about the diminishing opportunity for the recreational
service it had been founded to supply. A number of Florida's wildlife management
areas are leased from private landowners; the practice began when Florida was a
rural state and land was cheap, and large tracts were available for lease from
cattlemen and from timber companies. But, by the 1970s runaway population
growth was driving up the cost of hunting leases and ultimately threatening the land
itself.

I remember the contest well. At the time it was the only topic of
conversation in the Florida Park Service. For both agencies the struggle had a
priority claim on everyone's time and on all resources. The administrators of the
opposing agencies became studiously involved—more so than in any other event
I can recall. It was a contest between the core values of competing institutions. On
the opening day of the hunt, 14 Game Commission wildlife officers were present,
many of them pulled from duties in other counties. No chances were taken that a
hunter would violate a law. The executive director of the Game Commission arrived
at the site in person to oversee operations. He had written a personal memorandum
to be distributed to every hunter.

MEMORANDUM   December 17, 1980

TO: Tosohatchee Hunters
FROM: Colonel Robert M. Brantly, Executive Director
SUBJECT: Hunting on the Tosohatchee

As you may know, the issue of hunting on Tosohatchee has been extremely controversial. Despite a recent Cabinet decision giving the Commission [Game Commission] clear wildlife management responsibilities on the area, the matter of user policy for Tosohatchee is far from settled. People who oppose hunting charge that hunters are unsafe, leave litter, kill wildlife (including endangered species) indiscriminately, destroy property and commit other abuses on the land. They claim that hunters will spoil the area and its wildlife and they are prepared to go to great lengths to make their case and prove their point.

Fairly or not, you and other hunters with Tosohatchee quota permits will be on trial during the Tosohatchee hunting season. Any garbage left behind, any damaged signs or anything else that is negative will be blamed on hunters and hunting.

This is your chance to show people that hunters are as concerned about wildlife conservation and the environment as anyone — that, in fact, hunters were the original conservationists. Don't let a few people ruin it for everyone. If you see unsportsmanlike behavior, see if you can offer the person some friendly advice and guidance. If that doesn't work, get with a wildlife officer or someone at the check station. If you see trash on the ground, pick it up and carry it out, whether the trash was left by you or not. In short, leave Tosohatchee in better condition than when you found it!

Opponents of hunting on Tosohatchee will be watching closely, looking for proof that hunting should be banned. Deny them the opportunity to find that proof and, instead, go the extra mile to show that they are wrong. Hunters, wildlife, the environment and conservation in general can only benefit. The burden of proof is ours, so let's do what needs to be done. Good hunting![16]

Now, the second—and most important point—to be made of all this ferment is to contrast the energetic, all-out strivings of the two agencies at Tosohatchee against their spiritless, misdirected efforts on behalf of panther recovery. The administrators and senior staffs of both agencies were composed of the same individuals during both episodes. In the Florida panther recovery program, where is the energy? Where is the decisiveness? Where are the bold moves promptly made, the willingness to risk and endure a prolonged controversy—ordinarily an anathema in land-management agencies. And where is the willingness to fight it through to the end, so long as any chance of winning remains. (And for that matter where are the environmentalists?)

The differing behavior of these two camps, when comparing the Tosohatchee controversy to the Florida panther recovery program, is explained by the fact that opposing institutional values were seen to be at stake in the first case, whereas in the second, both parties alike sensed a threat to their ideals. The Game Commission has fretted over hunting being seen as a menace to panthers; it also sees other topics critical to panther survival (such as preserving habitat on private lands) waiting, ripe for eruption. For the Florida Park Service, the thought of compromising to the ideal of treating the resource (the Fakahatchee Strand State Preserve) as a representative sample of an original ecosystem"[17] has caused the greatest consternation—just as it has in the National Park Service.

In one instance both agencies responded with ardor and perseverance, but in the other with lassitude, delay, and obfuscation. The Tosohatchee conflict and the Florida panther recovery program offer a study in contrasts: two bureaucracies in their best fighting form and at their obstructing worst. To observe the workings of a land-management agency when handed a task that seems in some way threatening or disagreeable is to witness ingenuous sloth and misdirection elevated to a departmental art form. Memoranda flow back and forth endlessly; meetings and field trips are scheduled at delayed intervals to discuss and observe the problem, astonishing amounts of time and energy are expended for the thinnest returns; research or management proposals are called for, ignored, and then called for again—and there is never enough money. The otiose bureaucratic merry-go-round rotates slowly, carrying its busy complement on a journey to nowhere. More examples are to come.

The Ethics of the Mission

The mission of a land-management agency is a strong conservative force that imparts a spirited resistance to change—an emotional or principled unwillingness (as opposed to simple inertia) to deviate from ruling ideas and accustomed

269

practices. Like any conservative force it has a value and a liability. Its strength is in aiding internal efficiency; a large organization wants stability and confidence in its direction if it is to be a steady instrument. The mission is the motivating spirit that infuses a cohesive thrust into what would otherwise be little more than an aggregate of individuals. On the negative side conservatism can veil the imperative that comes inevitably to every institution for adjustments to external change.

The agency orders the careerist's life, giving it a path and a plan. It links professional self-expression, through public service, to the greater permanence and purpose of the social order. The agency becomes a dominant presence in life, and more—an extension of the self, craving a favorable perception. This helps to explain, I believe, why agencies react so bitterly to criticism. Within the cloister, the faithful are far more aware of departmental shortcomings than any outsider and are often quite critical of them, but they will respond with anger and dismay to a rebuke from without, which usually sparks a defensive reaction no matter what the circumstances. The recurring censure of an agency can imbue it with a fixed defensive outlook. When Alston Chase brought the bureaucratic shenanigans of the National Park Service to light in an *Outside* magazine article, criticizing the service's grizzly bear policy, the official reaction was choleric. The superintendent of Yellowstone National Park fired off a 27-page broadside at the magazine.[18]

The cover letter for the lengthy Park Service rebuttal began:

Dear Editor:

Yellowstone was waiting for Alston Chase's article "The Grizzly and the Juggernaut." We weren't disappointed. As expected, Mr. Chase is again tilting at windmills with every rhetorical device from innuendo and distortion to misrepresentation and misquo- tation. His regard for accuracy is no better than your choice of an Alaskan bear to symbolize Yellowstone in your January article's featured illustration.

With his sprawling tangle of accusations steeped in a fundamen- tal misunderstanding of park management, he has created an editorial scarecrow calculated more to alarm than to inform.

Mr. Chases's article is a house of cards. The supporting card is his erroneous presumption that the Park Service and the bear's many other defenders are somehow too ignorant to know the difference between science and philosophy. His suggestion that the great assortment of agencies and organizations involved in bear preservation are all blindly following some fashionable

idealistic course is nonsense. The practical character of Park Service management direction is a matter of public record. Anyone who reads these documents and management statements in full (rather than reading Mr. Chase's peculiarly selected excerpts) can see that the Park Service does not now have and never has had a blind commitment to Mr. Chase's absurdly simplified definition of "ecosystems management." For reasons that remain unclear, he has set up this straw man for the convenience of his own journalistic attacks. It is not true, and without it his house of cards collapses. . . . [19]

Angry denial! ". . . a blind commitment to . . . ecosystems management?"—How preposterous! [An] . . ."erroneous presumption that the Park Service and the bear's many other defenders are somehow too ignorant to know the difference between science and philosophy." But, of course, that *is* the problem. Science is an intellectual process that perennially invites challenges to the premises it constructs, whereas we have seen again and again that the National Park Service will brook no challenge to its narrowly interpreted dogma of ecosystems management. It is not Chase who has misjudged. Moreover, it can be seen that the Park Service capers in Wyoming have remarkable parallels in Florida.

The superintendent at Yellowstone tried to set the record straight.

Here is the heart of Mr. Chase's supposed case against the agencies, organizations, and individuals who are attempting to restore a natural grizzly bear population in Yellowstone. He makes his case by setting up a straw man, claiming that the Park Service has an idealistic, impractical goal of primitiveness for Yellowstone. If the agency were as impractical and idealistic as he claims, there would be grounds for criticism. However, the many documents upon which current management is based make it quite clear that there are recognized, practical limits to the degree of primitiveness that can be achieved. Through his practice of selective and out-of-context quotation, Mr. Chase has suggested a course of action that the Park Service simply is not following. Park Service management directions are a matter of public record, and anyone interested in understanding them should refer to the documents rather than to Mr. Chase's highly flavored interpretations of them. . . .

At this point it must be noted that it is Mr. Chase's erroneous assumption that guides and misleads him through the rest of his article. His specific complaint is that a commitment held by the

> Park Service and by a host of other concerned groups, including the Audubon Society, to some unrealistic goal of primitiveness for Yellowstone is keeping all these people from accepting the need to change management. He seems unable to come to terms with the possibility that all these people—who run clear across the political spectrum in private and public life—are convinced that his proposed changes simply aren't necessary. This does not mean that this vast assortment of people (and Mr. Chase's barrage is a broad one) would object to management changes if they do seem necessary. It means only that they do not think they are necessary yet. . . .

> For example, the Park Service has not ruled out the possibility that at some point in the future it may be necessary to supplementally feed grizzly bears. Mr. Chase seems convinced that the Park Service does not consider that option possible, and he is wrong. He builds a case on the supposed intractability of people that he either has not understood or is misrepresenting for some reason.[20]

The Park Service is not resistant to change; it simply isn't convinced that changes are necessary *yet*. Several pages later in this counterattack, the reader is told that "we do not . . . underestimate the importance of keeping the population well above any reasonable estimate of minimum viable population size."[21] Really? Then what are we to make of the National Park Service's words and actions in the Florida panther recovery program—the documented statements of unwavering commitment to ecosystems management, and the flat refusal to consider single-species management? Grizzly bears are numerous enough that the Park Service does have some room to dither and dally (but not forever) in Wyoming, but on the public lands of southern Florida, panthers have dwindled to the most precarious state imaginable. To what low number, one wonders, does a wildlife population have to sink before the National Park Service would no longer object to "management changes"? Just what are these "practical limits of primitiveness" that the superintendent of Yellowstone claims "are recognized"? The replication of resistance in the two situations—grizzly bear and panther— nearly 2,000 miles apart makes clear that the collective state of belief guiding the National Park Service is one which strives to impose an institutional frame of reality on the survival of wildlife. This claim by agency loyalists that they do not act and function apart from the principles of small population biology is transparently incorrect.

As for Chase's charge that the National Park Service had the grizzly downgraded from endangered to threatened status so as not to interfere with

management policy: "Mr. Chase has misunderstood the process by which modern endangered species legislation was developed." Perhaps, but the explanation that followed in the park superintendent's letter did nothing to clear up the misunderstanding. The lesser category of imperilment, termed "threatened," was added to the law to call attention to any species (the term "species" was defined to include any subspecies or any distinct population of a species) likely to become endangered within the foreseeable future.[22] The intent, it seems to me, was to encourage forestalling the endangerment of an organism which appeared to be headed toward difficulty. We are still left to ponder why the small, isolated Yellowstone grizzly population, shrunk by National Park Service policy since it was put on the list for assistance, remains classified as an animal "likely to become endangered in the foreseeable future." It is an odd state of affairs, and will remain vaguely unsatisfying no matter how inventive the arguments put forth to justify it.

The Park Service rebuttal further claimed, in a clever run of words, that the Craighead research in Yellowstone National Park was not terminated. ". . . the objectives of the [Craighead] study were 95% achieved. What was terminated was a proposed extension of the study."[23] The fact that the Craigheads were at the time publicly charging that the Park Service policy had become a hazard to grizzly bears . . . well, that was coincidence.

The response continued:"But behind Mr. Chase's remarkable accusation that all the good guys got together behind the wrong idea is a very troubling thought. How is it that Mr. Chase can be sure that he has this situation figured out better than the host of lifelong professional managers, scientists, and assorted other conservationists who have spent many years sorting out the metaphysical from the facts? . . ."[24] And how is it that in Florida we find assorted conservationists averting their eyes from the unquestionably appalling facts in the panther recovery program? It is a troubling thought indeed!

The reply went on: "Here we find Mr Chase attacking one of the most distinguished of American conservation organizations, the Audubon Society. Audubon, through its officers and magazine, has not been consistently a supporter of the Park Service program but in recent years has indeed backed the program more. [This intriguing statement is not explained.] For Mr. Chase to assume that they are doing so out of some conspiratorial misdirection is outrageous. These people have been conserving and preserving nature for longer than the National Park Service; they may not always be right, but their credentials are infinitely superior to Mr. Chase's."[25] (More will be said later about the National Audubon Society.) The letter goes on and on; one page of apparent outrage follows another; everything is denied; it is all a ghastly misunderstanding on the part of Mr. Chase who "for reasons that remain unclear," is making impossible statements about the

"good guys." [26] This is a normal, shocked reaction from a land-management agency that finds itself skewered by a telling criticism. Having long basked in the glow of public approval, the National Park Service is perhaps more elaborately indignant than an agency grown used to detractors.

The foundation of ethics in the land-management agencies rests on their respective ideals of serving society through the management of land. Careerists see their institution as the instrument of a good cause to be nurtured and guarded against any seeming threat—by whatever means. Any and all actions to guard or further the cause can too often come to be regarded as innately right. For a critic to hold them up to ridicule is unconscionable—the work of a mind unillumined by the vision of ecosystems restored to a state of grace. Most officials who maneuver with such assiduous determination to make a nonsense of recovery programs act from selfless motives. Though the enactments may be aided and abetted here and there by personal ambition, ignorance and incompetence, they are driven in the main by the loftiest (and most uncompromising) ideals. This may help to explain the curious situation in Florida in which four government agencies responsible for planning the panther's survival fashioned a compromise recovery plan without making any rigorous inquiry into its prospects for actually working. The principals were each looking primarily to see that it did not work against their established interests.

Round two of the Alston Chase - National Park Service brawl came in the pages of the *Wall Street Journal* where Chase contributed an editorial in the spring of 1986. The author recapitulated his theme that threats to the National Parks often owed as much to the policies of the Park Service as to the events beyond the park boundaries, but that the policies were immune to criticism from most conservation organizations.[27] Chase's allegations in the *Wall Street Journal* drew a rejoinder from Park Service Director, William Penn Mott, in a letter asserting the flexibility of his agency's management policies. "While we aim for natural perpetuation of ecosystems, policy does provide for human intervention where the effects of human action have been adverse. . . . We have managed population densities of several species where the loss of natural predators and the necessity of fencing and other artificial controls have tended to overpopulate some areas. . . . Our resource management policies are always under review."[28] Mott felt inspired to defend the conservation organizations as critics of his agency: "As to alleged closeness of the Park Service and conservation groups, the frequency of criticisms we receive from such groups appears to indicate they have lost none of their independence. . . ."[29] The letter then proceeded to (what was for me) the culminating irony: "I have suggested to all conservation organizations that we work together toward goals on which we agree, such as protection of the Florida panther. . . ."[30]

The Environmentalists

It might be of interest at this juncture to reopen a discussion of the National Audubon Society by looking into its project to educate the nation about grizzly bears. When, during the course of panther recovery, the FPIC began its image-promotion exercises with the publication of *Coryi,* my curiosity was aroused as to what sort of information the Interagency Grizzly Bear Committee (IGBC) was disseminating. To find out I had my name placed on the mailing list for the IGBC Newsletter. The minutes of an IGBC meeting in November 1987 reveal that a representative of the National Audubon Society had flown from Washington, D.C., to the gathering in Colorado, with a "first cut" of an Audubon film on the grizzly bear. It was due to be aired nationwide on television the following year. The IGBC provided "constructive comments" to the Audubon representative who ". . . agreed to address the IGBC's concerns and provide an opportunity for the committee to review the final before its release."[31] The IGBC complained that "[the] film should not imply that all bears are in the Park" (Curiously, during this critique of the Audubon film, the minutes neglected to identify the speakers). Another anonymous suggestion: "the role of the IGBC should be better displayed, especially its efforts in coordinating research and bear management activities. Overall, the film should depict a more 'optimistic flavor' about whats [sic] happening with the bear."[32]

The IGBC was displaying all the tendencies of its counterpart in Florida. It did not want any unhopeful words going out on the grizzly bear's prospects, and it wanted to insure that its own image was well-burnished. There were all the signs of bureaucrats at work, rather than conscientious wildlife professionals, free of constraint to air the unknowns and to raise hard questions about grizzly survival. The critics were more attuned to easing their passage down an awkward manage-ment path than to fashioning a hard assessment of the erosive potential of time, inbreeding and unpredictable events on a small population of bears, and to exploring all options that might be weighed to reverse them. "Need more upbeat approach at the end," was another anonymous comment.[33] "IGBC consensus was that the film is basically a good effort, but needs fine tuning. The representative from the National Audubon Society promised the ending would be overhauled and changed. He thanked the IGBC for its review."[34] It was with curiosity in the summer of 1988 that I switched on the TV to see the Audubon grizzly bear special.

The viewer was, at the outset, rightly told that there were believed to be only about 45 adult females in the Yellowstone population, and that grizzlies had a very low reproductive rate and that to lose even two bears in any one year would be "alarming." This information was presented while discussing a troublesome female bear that might have to be destroyed. However, these dismal facts, which

275

might have been the start of a meaningful lesson in small population biology, were soon awash in the irrepressible bureaucratic urge to paint over a predicament that offered no easy way out.

The program, narrated by Robert Redford, featured a mix of stunning visuals, interspersed with action scenes. It conveyed the idea that there used to be a conflict between scientists and bureaucrats, but that it had been remedied by the coming of the IGBC. A number of helpful actions had been implemented, and now the future looked promising. The viewer was told that "[radio-collaring] reflects a major change from what management was like back in the 1960s and early 1970s, a time when bear problems were intense, when management was inadequate, when scientists and bureaucrats were bogged down in public quarreling. Bears were dying at a rate so high there were fears the Yellowstone bears were heading for extinction."[35] A remarkable statement. The reader will recall that, according to Alston Chase, it was the Craighead brothers who were sounding the alarm in the early 1970s. The National Park Service, while refusing to modify the new policy that was causing the decline in bear numbers, persisted with the most optimistic interpretation of the data, and the Park Service actions were supported by the National Audubon Society.

The video explained that "the turnaround in the grizzly's recovery began in 1975, with its designation as a threatened species." Another remarkable statement. The viewer was not told that the designation of "threatened" had been a demotion for the grizzly bear from an earlier designation of "endangered." Furthermore, there was no evidence then that a "turnaround" occurred in 1975, nor is there convincing evidence to this day. The term "turnaround," if it is to convey any promise in an affair of this kind, could only be applied to an increase in grizzlies. Park Service policy in the 1970s brought bear numbers spiraling down to a low— where they remain. Verification of this opinion was provided by the minutes of an IGBC meeting in June 1988: "The task force estimates that the Yellowstone population is now increasing at a rate of 0.07 percent to 1.5 percent per year. *This marks the first time the population has shown to be increasing since 1975 when the species was declared threatened in the lower 48 States*[36] (italics added). Unfortunately, the minutes of this meeting, convened shortly after the celebrated Yellowstone wildfires of 1988, expressed worry because of a 15-25 percent destruction of white bark pine trees; the cones of this tree are an important food source for the grizzlies.[37] Clearly, optimism about grizzly survival is fragile at this uncertain juncture when the population is small, and cataclysmic events could easily send it plunging downward again; it is not in line with the principle of erring on the side of caution, which should always reign when managing an endangered species.

The Audubon video, in referring to the "turnaround" year of 1975, stated that "for decades prior to this, individual states like Montana had their own laws to manage the bear. Now the bear was under federal protection which mandated a species recovery plan. The recovery of the grizzly was engineered by a group of people not ordinarily considered to be specialists in coming to the rescue: the managers."[38] So there we have it. When scientists and bureaucrats were bogged down in public quarreling over the recovery of the Yellowstone grizzly, an Endangered Species Act appeared, and a turnaround was engineered by those paragons of common sense, the managers. The reader has by now had enough exposure to the tomfooleries of "managers" not to be encouraged by this revelation. The video explained that "in the late 1970s efforts were begun to straighten out the hodge-podge of bureaucracies and jurisdictions that squabbled over the grizzly's fate. In 1983 a unifying body called the Interagency Grizzly Bear Committee was formed."[39] Ruffles and flourishes. The IGBC was certainly a bureaucratic success, and we have seen that a clone was produced in 1986 to take custody of the Florida panther recovery program. Its performance has been exposed in previous pages.

The production glossed on to an upbeat ending—as stipulated by the IGBC. The TV audience was cheered: "The long decline of the grizzly may have ended for now and managers share a guarded optimism for its future." A Fish and Wildlife Service biologist came on to tell the camera that "we've come a long way I think; the bear is much better off than it was. The important thing we need to do is to keep the momentum up. . . . "[40] And so, two years after William Penn Mott assured readers of the *Wall Street Journal* (in countering criticism of his agency's grizzly bear policy) that the conservation organizations had lost none of their independence as policy critics, we see the National Audubon Society submitting its public explanation of Park Service policies to the IGBC for approval before putting it on the air.

The National Audubon Society also made a television documentary on the Florida panther, which did treat the subject of isolated refuges and small, inbred populations, in fact, many of the themes that are elaborated upon in this book; but the organization seems to treat conservation biology as an abstraction. It has not made a disciplined assessment of how the instrument is being applied in Wyoming or in Florida. The reader might imagine that the National Audubon Society would take unflinching aim at endangered species issues, and in some cases it has—as we will see later with the California condor (Audubon seems to perform best with birds). But with the Yellowstone grizzly and the Florida panther, one of America's most prestigious conservation organizations is doing little more than reinforcing bureaucratic ineptitude.

And the National Audubon Society is not alone. Some environmental organizations that have contributed nothing, or have drifted into a state of lassitude in panther affairs, continue to use the animal for fund-raising and advertising. The Florida Audubon Society featured a large color photograph of a blue-eyed panther kitten on a promotional brochure. The Nature Conservancy put out a fund-raising brochure which announces that anyone who contributes $5,000 will be granted membership in its elite Florida Panther Society.[41] Despite all the fine work The Nature Conservancy has done in Florida (and it is impressive), its acquisitions have not been particularly directed at meeting the habitat needs of panthers. For this The Nature Conservancy can scarcely be blamed; the FPIC has not tried to identify what should be bought, nor has it applied for assistance from organizations like The Nature Conservancy, or the Trust for Public Lands, which might help with a planned strategy of habitat preservation.

In the summer of 1988 I received a request for a donation from Defenders of Wildlife. It announced that "time just ran out for the last dusky . . . as a person who has demonstrated an interest in conservation, and as one who has shown a love for wildlife—I know you are as saddened and angered by this as I am." The reference was to the dusky seaside sparrow. Since a significant portion of the organization's membership resides in Florida, I presume the selection of this recently extinct Florida bird was judged promising in an appeal for contributions.[42] Sadness and anger about the loss of the dusky seaside sparrow should spur a thorough analysis of the failed recovery program to try and ascertain causes. What use is it to watch one species slip into extinction and turn to the next candidate without searching out the lessons of the last disappearance? It should not be presumed that recovery failures were predetermined. It can never be known in the aftermath, whether the program could have won through had it been conducted differently, but it might be possible to spot correctable weaknesses. It is the performance of the rescuers that wants attention.

There is a creeping inclination for prominent environmental organizations to use endangered animals in a careless way to appeal for funds. Following the letter from the Defenders of Wildlife another request for funds came my way from the Sierra Club. Enclosed was a peel-off-the-back sticker with a grizzly bear standing astride the caption: "Sierra Club Legal Defense Fund. . . . If you had the power . . ." queried the letter, "Would you keep oil and gas explorers out of the Deep Creek area of Montana's Lewis and Clark National Forest, home to endangered species like the grizzly bear and the gray wolf?"[43] Perhaps, and while I had such power the Sierra Club would be forbidden to imply that such an action would save the grizzly bear. (The grey wolf has been gone for years.) The letter continued: "But our national parks, forests, wildlife sanctuaries, seashores are under siege today like never before. Small-minded bureaucrats in the Reagan Administration want to develop and commercialize and open to exploitation as many park lands as they can

before they leave office. Their outrageous assaults will leave their mark (their scar) on our parks, forests . . . ."[44] True perhaps, but could the traditional rigidity of the Sierra Club, unwilling to grapple with the unpleasant realities of wildlife preservation in the twenty-first century, leave not a scar but a great emptiness in our national parks from the absence of wildlife species that might have been saved? The Sierra Club in Florida has not been a driving force for the panther.

The National Audubon Society was the third environmental organization to send me an appeal in the summer of 1988 (I have been an Audubon member for 20 years). Audubon bested its competitors by featuring the dusky seaside sparrow, which is extinct, alongside the polar bear, which is in no particular danger,[45] but is presumably rated a good fund-raiser. The question on the envelope queried, in bold, red type: "Will the magnificent polar bear soon suffer the same fate as the dusky seaside sparrow?" The answer is no. The bear situation is in no way analogous to that of the bird, and polar bears are better protected today than in recent decades, according to the *Audubon Wildlife Report 1986*.[46]

The Audubon letter began "Dear Friend of Audubon".

This morning I received a note along with a small donation from someone like you—someone who cares about our nation's wild-life.

The note was short and to the point:

"Why didn't you do something to save the dusky seaside sparrow. It's a darn shame."

I agree. It is a shame. Indeed. it's more than that.

The loss of the dusky is a tragedy—for no one will ever see this little bird again. It now ranks alongside the passenger pigeon and the ivory-billed woodpecker. All are extinct—gone forever.

What could have been done to save this tiny bird?

We could have cared more than we did. And in the 1960s, when we saw that construction and pesticide spraying were destroying its habitat, and reduced its population to 2,000, we could have shouted louder—and longer—and made ourselves heard.

> But we didn't have the time or the money—and believe me, that's
> what it takes to save a species on the brink of oblivion.
>
> For the dusky seaside sparrow, time simply ran out before we
> could make a difference.[47]

Granted, the National Audubon Society has to raise money, and the appeal of endangered animals has obviously become a potent lure, but this cornpone, like the emotional appeals from some other wildlife organizations, is ridiculous. "Shouting" is about the cheapest thing any environmental organization can do, and—allowing for semantics and the license of advertising lingo—shouting is not a common tactic of the staid mainstream environmental organizations. I am convinced of that after observing their tepid performance on behalf of the Florida panther. Environmental organizations have been quick to see endangered animals as a source of funds, but slow to close with the increasingly demanding require-ments of ensuring their survival. There is opportunity aplenty for shouting on behalf of the Florida panther by the National Audubon Society and its kindred organizations, and the results might be salutary, but shouting is not the style favored by many of today's established environmentalists. The National Audubon Society in a recent newsletter on *Problems and Progress in the Everglades* has this to say about the panther.

> Florida panther—This severely endangered cat needs protection
> now. National Audubon supports the Park Service's recommen-
> dations for reduction of hunting deer and other wildlife in the Big
> Cypress Preserve.
>
> National Audubon believes that unless these steps are taken, we
> cannot expect to maintain the Park and its panther population at
> any substantial level. We have the responsibility to protect the
> future of the Park for wildlife and for the appreciation and
> enjoyment of other generations. We must act now to save this
> unique national park and resource.[48]

This position lacks any substance or understanding whatever. There is no grasp of population size, or of the quality of the deer range, or of inbreeding or of any fundamental question. It just parrots the position of the National Park Service. In a later funding appeal in 1991, Audubon told correctly that the Endangered Species Act was under duress by economic interests angered by its strictures. The appeal for money was adorned with photographs of animals that would profit from a contribution to Audubon. Among them was the Florida Panther.[49]

The National Park Trust of the National Parks and Conservation Association submitted its fund-raising entry in the form of a flier. Both flier and postage-free return envelope, display photographs of a Florida panther. The caption informed the prospective donor that "The Florida panther is America's most endangered mammal. There are only 20 to 30 panthers left. You can help purchase critical panther habitat by contributing to the National Parks and Conservation Association."[50] This organization, as we will see in the next chapter, has pointedly rejected anything to do with single-species management on National Park lands. Its funding request will posit in the minds of those who receive it an image of the NPCA taking a special action on behalf of the panther, but as a practical matter it won't amount to a hill of beans. The NPCA has not reckoned with the price of land in southern Florida, nor with the geographic (or other) needs of a panther population.

In 1991 the Environmental Defense Fund headlined the Florida panther in an appeal for money, reacting to a rumor that Manuel Lujan, Secretary of the Interior, wanted to cut cost by ending protection for endangered species. Recipients were asked not to let time run out for the Florida panther. Terminating federal appropriations would certainly do it, but it can be seen as well that to go on spending under the circumstances that now rule, will likely be fatal as well.

There can be no doubt that the mainline environmentalists are in their own way hard at work, doubtless assuming that whatever they choose to do is the best that can be done. But are their unquestionably dedicated energies congruent with the evolving need of the times? This is a fair question, and it should be of vital interest to the mainstreamers, but their course is set and it is hard for them to stop rushing long enough to inquire into it. Knowing their good intentions for wildlife are beyond question, they presume the same of their modus operandi, which increasingly narrows to the path of protective legislation—and litigation to force compliance with the form of the law.

At the top, the organizations are constrained by the decorum of the lobbying culture of Washington, D.C. The imperative to get legislation enacted, seek funding and influence high-altitude policy decisions, can fix perceptions of what is and is not possible and establish a yardstick for success that is part illusion. Their actions on behalf of wildlife are primarily those fixed by tradition: protection, acquisition of habitat, fending off threats to refuges and cajoling money out of the Congress. These have not lost their importance, but they are not enough to rejuvenate an antiquated, foot-dragging bureaucracy.

It is no longer only exploitation and habitat loss that can destroy wildlife. Populations can be eliminated by the very institutions of government charged with saving them. If the agencies are unwilling to follow any advice or words of warning when it points in an unwelcome direction, and if they are unwilling to think through disquieting management proposals that clash with the outlook of a former time, then it is the institutions that can become the agents of ruin. To the long, grim list of threats, a new one can be added: bureaucratic extinction—brought on by departmental ineptitude. Destruction wrought by omission is much harder to fault than vivid calamities like oil spills.

That conservationists should inveigh—impartially—against all agencies not applying the principles of small population biology is not fashionable among the ideas presently guiding them. If the devoted do not recognize the sophisticated new methods essential to overcome novel dangers, they will go on aiding misdirected ventures that are heading nowhere, and it is only the environmental organizations that can alter the balance. Government agencies do not reform themselves, and they will never set the claims of a wildlife species, or any resource, above ingrained notions of self-interest. The favorite formulae being followed by those most responsible for America's declining species are not leading to the needed result. The times call out for innovation, but innovations will not come unless the environmental legions rise against institutional inadequacy.

Chapter 13

ATTITUDES AND AWARENESS

In a democracy it is not sufficient just to have a few trained persons who understand what it's all about; there must also be an alert citizenry to insist that knowledge, research and action are properly integrated.

Eugene P. Odum
Ecology 1963

Land management agencies do not operate in a vacuum. The bureaucratic timidity described in these pages can be accounted for in part by the aversive conditioning of a volatile public arena. The paranoia, the avoidance of a direct and vigorous attack on ills that are clearly the agencies' to treat, the self-delusions and rationalizations that are sometimes employed to prevent them from even defining the problem—owe much to the fear of setting off a grand commotion. Experience has taught officials that debilitating disruptions can spring from anger over issues as disparate as ungulate herd reductions, from groups as diametrically opposed as hunters and animal rights activists, to howls of outrage when an endangered animal dies during a capture, which must inevitably happen on occasion. The only antidote is to educate the citizenry. Citizens care passionately about their wildlife and are determined to have a say in its management, but the profession has not taken great pains in this field—sometimes perhaps because the backward-looking custodians of policy are too poorly informed to instruct laymen.

To illustrate the lack of understanding in these quarters, I offer three examples from my own experience. In writing this book I reviewed the minutes of several Game Commission meetings of the last few years. In 1985 an animal rights advocate spoke at a Commission meeting and "advised that she is against hunting because she believes in the preservation of all species and their habitats. She asked that hunting areas not be expanded because all species have a right to quality life . . . she stated that if there is an overpopulation of deer the Commission should investigate the use of contraceptives for game control." The minutes record that she distributed an article entitled "Family Planning for Deer."[1]

For the second example I offer the president of the National Parks and Conservation Association. I had the opportunity to address the Board of Trustees

of this organization in 1987 and tried to put across to those present that unless measures were taken to increase panthers on the secure public lands in southern Florida, there was little reason to suppose that the animal would survive. I also pointed out that the National Park Service, as the largest single land manager, would be the key to success (or failure), and that it would be essential for the Park Service to arrange for more deer than the agency considered to be "natural." Afterwards I wrote to the president of the NPCA detailing my views in terms I believed any layman could follow. He affirmed in reply that he fully intended to take the necessary actions to save the Florida panther, but stipulated that this would have to be done within the philosophy of ecosystem management rather than single-species management. "Ecosystem management," he said, "was essential to the perpetuation of the national park system. The NPCA . . . will not waiver in its defense of this concept."[2] His solution was to expand the park boundaries and banish hunting from the Big Cypress National Preserve. He had little notion of what he was talking about, in my opinion, but he didn't suspect his knowledge to be in any way lacking. The president of the NPCA is in a position to influence the survival, or loss, of a number of wildlife populations in the United States.

For a third example I turn to the executive director of the state Game Commission. Following a Panther Advisory Council meeting late in 1985, and a review of the bleak data emerging from the field, I sent to this official a dismal assessment of the panther's survival prospects, proposing remedial actions by the appropriate agencies. After four years of radio-telemetry research about 22 panthers could be accounted for—down from about 29 four years earlier. Only about a dozen were known to be using areas with a secure future. Most were on cattle ranches then facing economic pressure that could ruin them as habitat. The relatively few cats that had been examined (Everglades National Park was at this time still disallowing research there) showed a large proportion to be aging. My letter and the recommendations received a wide circulation, stimulating a flow of mail to the Game Commission. In answering, the executive director moved to allay concerns in a reply to Defenders of Wildlife (copied to many others).

> The picture you describe of a panther population comprised of only old age animals that are not reproducing and that are without food is certainly a dismal circumstance, but fortunately that is not the situation with panthers in southern Florida.

> Panthers in and adjacent to the Fakahatchee Strand State Preserve in Collier County, Florida, are represented by individuals of all age classes and both sexes, and reproduction is occurring with an estimated annual recruitment rate of 8 percent.[3]

The director cited, as an example of reproduction, a 34-pound radio-collared kitten which was at that moment following its mother about in the Fakahatchee Strand. The Game Commission got quite a bit of publicity mileage out of this young male. It was the subject of several glowing news releases, and touted as the first panther successfully raised to maturity in the Fakahatchee Strand State Preserve since the advent of radio-telemetry there in 1981. Shortly after becoming independent of its mother in 1987 it was killed by another male. The head of the state's principal wildlife agency presumably possesses a store of cookbook knowledge about game management, but he is as poorly informed about the peril inherent in small populations as the person who would manage game animals by using contraceptives. The land-management agencies, which are presumed to possess the technical competence to care for endangered species, are woefully unprepared. They are bound to tradition, resistant to change—and to learning—and have displayed an aversion to a new discipline which offers the best guidance currently available for designing recovery strategies.

A lack of understanding about wildlife management in general, and endangered species management in particular, pervades our society from the man-in-the-street to the government agencies assigned to save them and to the environmental organizations that we look to for direction against the inadequacies of government. The fascination with animals seems universal. The cultural environment, that sculptor of our feelings about wild creatures, took a radical new form in the United States in the early twentieth century when citizens of the cities and towns came to outnumber those living close to the soil. The dislike of predators and the enjoyment of hunting is a product of the frontier, or rural environment, where we can still observe these feelings in action. The urban experiences of animals is primarily with pets, usually dogs, cats, and, often—in today's affluent environment—with horses, giving rise to feelings of love, affection and paternalism. It is an experience that may lend to a presumption that animals in the wild are simply other versions of the family pet going about their routines in the wilderness.

An odd transformation of the traditional feelings toward large predators can now be observed in which love, affection and paternalism take hold, even where increasing contacts between large predators and humans have once again posed a threat (albeit minuscule) to humans. This can be observed vividly in California. As explained in an earlier chapter, California once undertook an extensive (and unsuccessful) program to exterminate pumas by the payment of bounties. They were granted some protection—as a game animal—in 1969 and were fully protected in 1972.[4] According to statistics, incidents of puma depredation on pets and livestock climbed from less than 10 per year in 1971 to over 70 in 1984. Pumas killed in depredation control incidents also grew from less than 10 per year in 1971

to between 20 and 30 per year in the mid 1980s.[5] There have also been incidents of pumas attacking people. In 1987 the California Game Commission advocated a limited harvest of pumas, thereby agitating opinion in the state. The Mountain Lion Preservation Foundation came into being and blocked the hunt in a California Superior Court.

The Foundation simply took the position that data were inadequate to justify the hunt; it did not specifically oppose hunting. However, the anti-hunting spirit is stronger on the Pacific Coast than anywhere else in the country, and it is the only region in the nation where a majority is opposed to hunting.[6] This undoubtedly influenced the upheaval. But my point is simply to show what powerful feelings can rise to defend a large predator when hunting seems to threaten, and in this instance a controlled hunt could scarcely threaten California's pumas. What a contrast this excited reaction makes when held up to public quiescence about the current bureaucratic danger to large predators like the Yellowstone grizzly and the Florida panther.

Judging American knowledge of, and attitudes toward, wildlife is no longer a matter of guesswork. During the 1970s the Fish and Wildlife Service contracted with Stephen Kellert of Yale University for a series of national surveys on attitudes, knowledge and behaviors toward wildlife. He began his research by categorizing American attitudes towards all animals, wild and domestic, into different types. Kellert devised the following labels to categorize his typology: naturalistic, ecologistic, humanistic, moralistic, scientistic, aesthetic, utilitarian, dominionistic and negativistic. He then canvassed a broad opinion to see how these various attitudes were apportioned. That was followed with a series of questions put to what he termed animal-activity groups. He examined attitudes and knowledge by age, sex, race, education and occupation—and geographically by childhood residence, present residence and by section of the country. Marital status and number of children were also assessed as possible variables. The groups sampled were hunters, backpackers (considered passive recreation viewers of wildlife), bird watchers, pet owners, rodeo enthusiasts, zoo enthusiasts, vegetarians, animal farmers and trappers. A description of the attitude types is as follows:

> *The naturalistic attitude.* Its most outstanding characteristic is a profound attraction to wildlife and to the outdoors in general. The naturalistic oriented have affectionate feelings for pets but tend to regard them as inferior to wild animals. A primary satisfaction is in direct, personal contact with wilderness. . . . Wildlife is valued particularly for the opportunities it provides for activity in the natural environment . . . from experiencing wilderness as an escape from the perceived pressures and deficiencies of modern industrial life.

The ecologistic attitude is also primarily oriented toward wildlife and natural settings, but typically is more intellectual and detached. This attitude views the natural environment predominantly as a system of interdependent parts. Rather than focusing on individual animals, wild or domesticated, the major emphasis and affection is for species of animals in their natural habitats. . . .

The humanistic attitude is distinguished by strong personal affection for individual animals, typically pets rather than wildlife. The pet animal is viewed as a friend, a companion, a member of the family. . . . This concern for animal welfare originates less in any general ethical philosophy or in any particular concern for animal species than in an identification with the experience of individual animals extended from pets to wildlife.

The moralistic attitude. The most striking feature . . . is its great concern for the welfare of animals, both wild and domesticated. Rather than deriving from strong affection for individual animals (the humanistic point of view) or from consideration for animal species (the ecologistic attitude), the moralistic attitude is typically more philosophical. It is based on ethical principles opposing the exploitation and the infliction of any harm, suffering or death on animals.

The scientistic attitude is characterized by an objective, intellectualized, somewhat circumscribed perspective of animals. Animals are regarded more as physical objects for study than as subjects of affection or moral concern. There is typically little personal attraction to pets, wildlife or the natural environment among the scientistically oriented. . . .

The aesthetic attitude also tends to be associated with emotional detachment, but with a central interest in the beauty or symbolic properties of animals. . . . The aesthetically oriented tend to be attracted to animal sporting activities involving considerable artistic display such as animal showmanship, fox hunting and bullfighting. For the most part, they remain aloof from the living animal, enjoying it more as an object of beauty (in paintings, sculpture, movies) or of symbolic significance (in poetry, children's stories, cartoons).

The primary characteristic of *the utilitarian attitude* is the perception of animals in terms of their practical or profitable qualities—largely for their material benefit to humans. While many utilitarian-oriented persons own pets, for example, most believe they should be trained for specific tasks and not kept just as companions or friends.

A sense of superiority and a desire to master animals are defining features of *the dominionistic attitude*. . . skill in competition with animals are typically emphasized . . . as, for example, in rodeos, trophy hunting and obedience training.

A number of quite distinctive attitudes are included within the negativistic category, with the common feature being a desire to avoid all animals. Typical of *the negativistic attitude* are such feelings as indifference, dislike, fear and superstition. . . . For many negativistically oriented persons, an utter gulf of emotion and spirit distinguishes animals from humans.[7]

In dividing attitudes into distinct types, it was understood that some people hold more than one attitude; that not every person would exhibit every characteristic of a particular attitude; that the intensity of commitment varies and so forth, but distinctions had to be made in order to survey differences. My focus is on the management of endangered species, so only some aspects of Kellert's work will be summarized. However, the entire project makes fascinating reading for anyone interested in the subject.

A section of the survey sampled feelings toward several critical wildlife issues, one of which was endangered species, by testing the willingness for economic sacrifice to protect eight different organisms. Seventy-three percent responded favorably to protect the Eastern puma (which has unfortunately been extinct for a century or more, although pumas could in theory be reintroduced). A moderate but significant 56 percent of the national sample supported preserving 5 million acres of national forest land, at the cost of jobs and building materials, in order to protect the grizzly bear. The bald eagle incidentally was favored above all; 89 percent were willing to sacrifice for it.[8] However, all endangered species were not so highly regarded. The American crocodile drew a favorable rating (70 percent), but enthusiasm waned for the eastern indigo snake (43 percent) and for an endangered plant with an uninspiring name—the Furbish lousewort (48 percent). Only 34 percent judged the Kauai wolf spider worthy of an economic sacrifice.[9]

A broad willingness to spend money for wildlife was evident; a significant 57 percent approved of an increased proportion of general tax revenues for wildlife management; a moderate but significant percentage of people were willing to protect habitat despite substantial socioeconomic impacts.[10] Education and sex were the most consistent social differentiators of views towards animals. Those with a graduate education knew more about animals than any other group, were more interested in wildlife and more concerned about the natural environment. Those with less than a sixth grade education were the opposite. They revealed more fear of animals and less affection for them and in fact less interest. Males possess a more generalized interest and understanding of animals, but were more emotionally detached. Females tend to have a more moralistic and protective attitude.[11]

Another interesting difference showed up between urban and rural residents. People in rural areas generally knew more about animals, participated more in wildlife activities, were more supportive of practical uses of animals and were less concerned about animal rights issues than urban residents. Dwellers in cities with populations of more than a million had very low knowledge of animals, were more opposed to hunting and predator control, and more interested in humane or ethical treatment of animals than rural residents.[12] Regions of the country were strongly differentiated in knowledge of animals. Alaskans knew the most, and people from the Rocky Mountain states were next. Those from the Northeast knew the least. Pacific Coast residents gave more importance to ethical treatment of animals and animal rights issues than residents elsewhere.[13] However, shades of knowledge aside, the overall level was extremely low:

The American public as a whole was characterized by extremely limited knowledge of animals. For example, on four questions dealing with endangered species, less than one-third gave the correct answer. Only 26 percent correctly responded to the statement, "The manatee is an insect." and, only 26 percent knew the coyote is not an endangered species. Regarding other knowledge questions, merely 13 percent were aware that raptors were not small rodents, and only one-half correctly answered the question, "spiders have ten legs." A better but still distressingly limited 54 percent knew veal does not come from lamb, and only 57 percent correctly answered the statement, "most insects have backbones.[14]

Kellert's conclusions are noteworthy:

Some general conclusions can be derived from the data presented. Perhaps most important was the majority of Americans appeared to strongly value wildlife and have expressed a willingness to make substantial social and economic sacrifices to protect this resource and associated habitat. Various findings consis-

tently indicated wildlife was not just the concern of an esoteric and elitist minority, but, instead, had broad appeal to many, if not most, Americans. The impression was that an abundant, diverse and healthy wildlife population contributes, in the minds of many, to a high standard and quality of life.

On the other hand, the wildlife views of most Americans appeared to be based on limited factual understanding and awareness. Moreover, interest and concern for animals were largely confined to attractive and emotionally appealing species. While substantial growth in wildlife appreciation is certainly a welcome development, inadequate knowledge and an inordinately narrow perspective must also be recognized and used to form the basis for more innovative public awareness efforts.

The wildlife management field appears to be confronted by a major change in the public it serves, with many new and atypical groups becoming appropriate recipients of professional attention. This expanded constituency must inevitably constitute a threat as much as a challenge to a field that has historically defined itself in far narrower terms. Nevertheless, the challenge represents a rare chance, and it would be a disservice to the profession, let alone to an American public and wildlife resource in need, if the professional reaction was more to avoid an alien reality than a creative and bold response to an evolutionary opportunity.[15]

Coryi

Whose responsibility is it to impart to laymen the arcane technical intricacies about the management and survival of wildlife populations? In the case of the Florida panther the inescapable answer is the component units of the FPIC. It is there supposedly that the expertise resides, and where the cutting edge of research is sifting evidence and building a base of facts with which to press on with the exacting work of recovery. How has this bureaucratic combination performed in transmitting to citizens the information they need to make decisions and act? The centerpiece of the education effort has been a rather elaborate newsletter entitled *Coryi*, a joint product of the FPIC published under the imprimatur of Florida's Game Commission (It has ceased publication since this chapter was written). As an educational project it was without question a complete farce.

The newsletter was paid for out of the private donations of citizens into the Florida panther trust fund;[16] it folded into a 7 1/2 x 11 1/2 paper for mailing.

The address side of the fold informed that "this publication is dedicated to preservation and restoration of the Florida panther, *Felis concolor coryi*. On the reverse side was an eye-stopping pen-and-ink close-up, head-on view of a panther stooping to drink from a pool; the cat had come to water in a narrow clearing in tall reeds; the artist placed it in the left half of the format. The right half of the illustration was balanced with a close-up silhouette of a palm frond. The muscled tension of the drinking animal contrasted with the reflected tranquility of the pool. The cover illustration was the only redeeming feature of *Coryi*; it was appropriately symbolic—an appealing facade for a vacuous publication.

Inside the front cover of the first issue was a section entitled "Perspective." It featured an open letter from the Florida Panther Interagency Committee. It was a heavy dose of agency rah! rah!

"It is with great pleasure that we introduce the Florida Panther newsletter *Coryi*. The intent of this publication is to inform and educate the public about the many actions that are occurring in the state relative to the Florida panther recovery. The panther (*Felis concolor coryi*) is the Florida state animal. The species[sic] is listed as endangered by both the federal government and the State of Florida. Recognizing the animals' critical status, we have launched numerous projects to promote their recovery."[17]

The recovery plan got a pump.

"A technical subcommittee diligently has undertaken the task of revising the Florida Panther Recovery Plan. A draft revision of the recovery plan was released on October 31. The revised plan greatly expands the previous plan and contains detailed information about how the panther can be restored. . . . The recovery plan calls for aggressive actions to protect and enhance the existing populations [sic] of panthers and their habitat, as well as efforts to re-establish additional populations in selected areas of their former range in Florida. Each respective agency is solidly behind this plan and intends to use it as a guide for systematic panther recovery."[18]

Elsewhere the reader was told that "the purpose of a recovery plan is to provide means to combine varied programs of federal[,] state, local and private organizations into effective, efficient, concentrated efforts."[19]

The first issue had an article entitled: "DNR (Florida Department of Natural Resources) Team Hopes to Boost Panthers' Diet and Habitat at

Fakahatchee."[20] As we have seen, the DNR (read Florida Park Service) exertions have been purely cosmetic. An article in the second issue of *Coryi*, contributed by the Fish & Wildlife Service, began with the statement that "perhaps the single most important factor in the long-term survival of the Florida panther is habitat preservation. . . . Land preservation," it said, "is one important link to providing appropriate habitat for the panther. Just as important will be the incorporation of appropriate land management and panther protection measures for these lands."[21] However, despite the reference to appropriate land management measures no specific suggestions were given.

In the third issue was an article by the southeastern regional director of the National Park Service. It was entitled: "Park Officials Manage Ecosystem."

> "The Everglades National Park's healthy, reproducing panther population" [there were then thought to be approximately four adult panthers in the park, one of them a male] "reflects the park's success in 40 years of efforts to protect habitat and preserve the balance and function of the entire ecosystem" [the entire ecosystem reaches north to encompass the chain-of-lakes beyond Lake Kissimmee].

> "The National Park Service policy of ecosystem management is based on the philosophy that the health of the ecosystem should not be compromised to favor a single species that might benefit from selective management. However, that philosophy does not amount to a 'hands off' attitude. . . .

> Everglades National Park's responsibility to maintain natural diversity applies to vegetation as well as wildlife. There is a recognized problem with Schinus (Brazilian pepper) invading native plant communities. Schinus has become established on hundreds of acres in the Hole-in-the-Donut (former agricultural area). The park service is striving to eliminate exotic (non-native) species and restore native plants. The more natural the habitat, the greater the benefit to native wildlife including panthers."[22]

There it is! The length and breadth and depth of the National Park Service's management vision, encapsulated in two easy paragraphs. It's quite simple, you see, "The more natural the habitat, the greater the benefit to native wildlife—including the panthers." One need not trouble the brain beyond this platitude; It holds all the knowledge about conserving wildlife that a National Park

Service authority ever needs to know. In that camp it is the beginning and the end of management wisdom.

Do you suppose that this piece was influenced by the National Park Service's regional scientist who sits at the regional director's elbow to guide him in matters of this kind? Or do you suppose that these opinions are held by the biological staff at Everglades National Park? If so, do you suppose they would have prepared a position paper supported by the appropriate documentation, which places these policy pronouncements on a firm scientific footing and would give the regional director confidence in his statements? If there is a paper, shouldn't it be boldly presented for scrutiny by peers? It would be a prudent move to silence critics like myself, or at least it would establish the basis for an informed debate. It would also, I believe, constitute the level of professionalism we should expect from what is commonly presumed to be the nation's elite land management agency when it is engaged in the task of recovering an endangered species. The reader will recognize that I am being mischievous. There is no such analysis to underpin this blather from the regional director, and nothing in the National Park Service approach that could be dignified with the term "professionalism."

Coryi did contain odd tidbits of interest on research. There were some tantalizing articles that spoke in a broad way to the importance of deer densities to panther health. There were informative pieces about ongoing land purchases and so forth, but the articles did not give a whole picture of the problems or tell what must be done to solve them. If the newsletter were to speak frankly what should it have said? Well, it should present the most important issues first. There might have been a discussion of effective population size. How far short of a viable population does the present estimate fall? Of the lands now known to serve as habitat, what portion is secure for the future and what is still at risk? Are there any ideas for preventing loss of the habitat still in jeopardy? What obstacles lie in the way? What are the arguments, pro and con, of the philosophy and the practicality of managing for more deer? And what about genetics and the various points of view on outbreeding? What are the practical possibilities of recovering the panther in southern Florida, and of reintroduction elsewhere, and what are the respective costs and obstructions? Is saving the panther in Florida realistic? What are the estimated conditions for success? Can they be attained? If they cannot, then should the recovery program be terminated? At what point? These are just some of the issues that would be treated by responsible educators. Compare them to the public relations pablum that has been spooned out.

But of course *Coryi* would never have done those things. Some of the topics mentioned above promise controversy—with its unpredictable fallout. Others threaten favored notions about management, and so of course they would not have been brought up. *Coryi* was a document that allowed each agency to put its best foot

forward. The Florida Park Service could boast about its work to improve habitat in the Fakahatchee Strand State Preserve, whether it was doing anything meaningful or not. The Fish and Wildlife Service timidly offered tantalizing hints of what ought to be done without ever coming out and saying so. The National Park Service ticked off its marginal activities while endlessly reminding readers that the lands it guarded would never be used to benefit a single species. The Game Commission projected an image of great industry with stories headed as: "Commission Plans Panther Poster," "Kitten Studies Gearing Up," "Reintroduction Experiment Challenges GFC's Scientists," "GFC Studies Panther Nutrition." There was nothing inherently wrong with such headings or stories, but the information did not convey to the readership an accurate picture of a dilemma that becomes less amenable to solution with every passing year.

Readers were not told that although Game Commission biologists knew well enough the need for the National Park Service to increase its deer, the Game Commission will not exert any pressure on it to do so. Its leaders see the bright image and popularity of the National Park Service, in contrast to their own, and sense that such tactics could be futile or might even backfire. This is only one item which remained in the closet. Other issues included the pros and cons of outbreeding, the need for security in the form of a captive population, the relentless erosion of panther habitat on private lands in southern Florida and of the need for a statewide interconnected wildlife preserve. The agencies would not raise these vital topics for inspection. *Coryi* never alerted its readers to the plight of panthers in southern Florida or of the need for swift action. That would have raised frightening responsibilities. Not a discouraging word ever appeared in *Coryi*. To use a favored bureaucratic term, the message was "upbeat." *Coryi* sends a out a sense of activity, of great busyness—of doing lots of things. The outsider, reading all the encouraging news, did not know that the goings-on did not conform to a strategic design aimed at grounding a survivable population within the boundaries of a secure refuge.

A genuine tragedy of *Coryi* is that the Florida panther recovery program offers a rich opportunity to a wildlife agency, not only to teach about the specifics of saving a single endangered animal but, by extension and through analogy, about the broad aspects of wildlife ecology and the imperatives of rescuing small populations. This is an important social need, one which the Game Commission in Florida is perfectly positioned to provide. The panther and the ongoing drama of its survival is a subject of great interest to citizens—from which many secondary themes could unfold. It offers openings to elaborate on population dynamics, genetics, the need for refuges of adequate size and the like. The recovery program is, or should be, an educator's dream, producing a cornucopia of lessons.

Educational Resources

The failure of the managing agencies to educate is not because they lack the wherewithal. One of the strong suits of the Fish and Wildlife Service is the quality of its publications. The National Park Service and the Florida Park Service have a superb educational capability through park interpretive programs, and the educational media of the Game Commission are more extensive and sophisticated than all the others. It has an Education and Information Section, a monthly magazine and it has, through its non-game division, recently assembled a talented staff (which includes conservation biologists, by-the-way).

Recently, one of its members, Mark Duda, prepared a thorough treatise on "Floridians and Wildlife." It summarized the findings of opinion surveys, both national and state, and collated them with demographic data to expound on the "Sociological Implications for Wildlife Conservation in Florida."[23] Among Duda's conclusions is that "possibly the most outstanding result of this study is the overwhelming public support for wildlife conservation and environmental protection efforts nationally and in Florida . . . over 60 percent of Floridians believe that spending for the environment should be increased. . . . Concerns over the loss of wildlife and its habitat and other environmental issues are not the concern of an esoteric and elitist minority, but an important concern among the majority. In fact, a disregard for wildlife and other environmental values has certainly become a view of the minority. . . . The new challenge to wildlife professionals is to bring citizens from the 'concern' stage . . . to the action stage. Placing more emphasis on education and research efforts that stress wildlife and environmental action . . . teaching citizens specific actions they can take in order to further environmental protection and wildlife conservation . . . is a relatively new and challenging aspect of information and education efforts."[24] Duda goes on. ". . . if wildlife and environmental professionals are mandated to protect the environment and wildlife resources and are additionally mandated to teach citizens the fundamentals of environmental and wildlife conservation, it is not unreasonable for them also to give citizens the tools with which to constructively act if they choose to do so. . . . Perhaps the most effective wildlife conservation and environmental protection tools the professional can teach citizens are the fundamentals of making government work for the environment. . . ."

I could not agree more. My purpose is to show how the land-management bureaucracy is not working, and if not repaired it can scarcely be expected to teach citizens anything. Duda quotes the National Wildlife Federation:

If you're convinced you can't influence what goes on in Washington, consider this: Millions of acres of pristine Alaskan

wilderness were preserved for future generations because of people like you. The Alaskan Lands Protection Act would never have cleared Congress without the rain of mail that deluged Washington when people from all over the country wrote to their members of Congress. Because of their constant urging, one of the most significant wilderness bills of all time passed Congress and was signed into law by President Carter.

You can influence environmental decisions. Your legislators in Washington will listen to you because your views provide first-hand information on how an issue affects the people 'back home.'

The National Wildlife Federation suggests certain guidelines on how to contact Congress effectively, including writing letters, using the telephone, writing telegrams and personal meetings.[25]

The research concluded that "these actions should be taken at the state and local levels as well. At these, citizen involvement appears to be even more critical. For example, in Tallahassee five personal letters is said to be enough for a legislator to open a file on an issue."[26] (Take note of this you readers who would assist the panther.) The summary runs on and on, through page after page of guidance based on solid data, with key passages and paragraphs underlined. It is a state-of-the-art blueprint for an educational project. But blueprints serve no purpose if they never leave the drawing boards, and talent is useless to a land-management agency that lacks the will and the imagination to use it creatively. The Game Commission, having staffed itself with specialists, who brought forth an excellent design which might have been used "To Save a Great Animal" (the title of a Game Commission brochure on the Florida panther), instead brought forth *Coryi* which did not inform anyone about anything useful. What is the Game Commission's philosophy of education? Are there any guiding principles? During the 1980s it has been budgeting over a million-and-a-half dollars each year for "informational services."[27] What practical return do officials expect from these expenditures? It is clear that money spent to educate the state about the panther has fallen victim to paranoia; elaborate pains were taken to avoid provoking hostile opinion but nothing was done to build a supportive one.

In 1980 Kellert wrote: "it behooves managers to assess existing levels of public understanding and, in circumstances where wildlife knowledge is judged insufficient, to provide information which, hopefully, will render people more capable of forming intelligent perceptions. Of course, a thin and ethically difficult line will often distinguish public awareness and educational efforts from manipulative attempts to influence people toward pre-established viewpoints."[28] Kellert

knew well the self-serving impulses that inevitably push to stage center when a bureaucracy sets out to educate. Who will educate the agencies?

Money, Money, Money

Funding for the Florida panther could be tripled and quadrupled without enhancing its prospects for survival. The problem is not lack of money; it is rather the collective incapacity of tribal institutions to analyze a wildlife management problem and act appropriately. Combining the energies and resources of several land-management agencies in the United States does not necessarily strengthen a program; it can leave it crippled. The agencies struggle to protect their prerogatives, aided or hindered by the political pressure that supportive constituents or adversaries bring to bear. The enterprise bogs down in a slough of conflicting ideologies and fossilized habits. At some point sufficient information comes to hand that would illuminate a strategic direction, but if the strategy menaces tribal notions about correct management, or threatens a controversy, the agencies will evade it—and, as money keeps pouring in, options erode while bureaucrats dither.

During the formation of the FPIC at the meeting described in Chapter 5, a National Park Service representative put on an astonishing performance while parading generous figures for the dollars his agency was readying for the panther. A hundred thousand dollars were set aside for the coming year, he disclosed, with a chance for that much more. In a long, rambling monologue he put on quite a show of not knowing how to best use this gratifying sum. He kept soliciting advice on how it should be spent. This theme was developed to such length that a Fish and Wildlife Service representative was moved to interject helpfully that he might wish to consult his biological staff for ideas. This was ignored and the monologue ran on. The speaker finally tossed out some thoughts of his own, one being that some of the expenditure ought to go for genetic research (I had recently written to him in that regard to urge, again, the importance of getting the radio-telemetry work going in Everglades National Park).

Things then took a stranger turn. The man had a plan. It was, he said, tough to coax the kind of money out of the system that would be needed to save an animal like the Florida panther, but he was bent on getting millions of dollars for research. The word "millions" was subsequently used several times. The plan was to find someone in Florida who owned a captive panther. This person, with panther, would be brought to the Department of Interior building in Washington, D.C. and given an award. The object of this exercise would be to entice bureaucrats from their cubicles, to be enthralled by a large feline parading the halls. The indelible impression made on every functionary could be expected to pay future dividends whenever any of them participated in any discussion, or handled any document,

relating to funding for the panther. The bureaucrats at Interior didn't get excited about much, he said, but a live panther in the building ought to jar them awake.

I thought this devilishly clever and made encouraging sounds; it was right out of Barnum and Bailey. I did however make a mental note never to accept an award from the Department of the Interior (at the time of this writing I am not at risk of being threatened with one). The real meaning of this performance didn't strike me until several hours later. For anyone attuned to the importance to an endangered species program of well-funded research, and accustomed to a dearth of resources, the prospect of millions of dollars can produce instant intoxication. To have a say in how it is spent is an enticement to rapture. I hadn't been immune. It wasn't only the bureaucrats in Washington who were to be baited; it was also those sitting around the conference table that day.

This experience was enlightening, and it produced a lesson, one that should have been arrived at by common sense. It showed that some bureaucrats who have access to money, understand intuitively the researcher's vulnerability to Mephistophlian temptations, and they are willing to use it to purchase the fealty, or at least the neutrality, of potential troublemakers rather than applying it in a disinterested way to research. The lesson is that a recovery program, if it is to have any chance, must be conducted in the open with all the cards up on the table; it must be based on the best scientific foundation available; it must be subjected to open debate, and positions on every important issue should be stated in writing and be available for peer review. In other words, it must be conducted in a professional manner which has not characterized the Florida panther recovery program, or that of Yellowstone grizzly in Wyoming. Recovery programs are not presently being subjected to such standards of professional rigor; they cannot be without an understanding in the bureaucracy of the imperatives of the new science and the inadequacy of venerated doctrines. Without such a shift there will be no improvement in these endeavors, no matter how much money is fed into them or what kind of organizational framework they are fitted into. In the absence of reform, the evasions of land-management officialdom will inevitably make a shambles of any complex enterprise to save an endangered species.

In 1980 the subject of conservation biology was introduced to the world in a book of the same title. The opening chapter announced that "scientific and technological expertise is worthless in the final analysis, if the money and resources required to implement the expertise is absent." An accompanying table showed how much per unit area was provided in budget and personnel to the National Parks of several nations. As might be expected, the relative (and absolute) fiscal allocations to American National Parks exceed those of any other country.[29] But the intent of the authors was to illustrate the insufficient resources at that time for conservation biology.

My experience in Florida has been that the critical blockage is not monetary. Here, though dollars and resources are substantial, and the scientific and technical experts are clamoring to serve, all is wasted because the hands this bounty has fallen into are incapable of making rational use of it. There is an instinctive bureaucratic resistance to spending money in ways that seem to challenge long-standing beliefs, or that bodes a disruption of the orderly flow of operations. The recovery and maintenance of small populations will require a redesigned mental format to restructure operational methods long in place. Bureaucracy has not embraced the new science which pervades the recommendations and commentaries of independent advisors who find themselves in recovery programs; it is within reach, in increasing volume in the libraries, where it should be noticed by the biological staffs of the agencies and transmitted to administrators, but it is neglected. The new ideas portend drastic alterations in the sanctioned way of doing things—an attribute that strengthens resistance to their notice.

This is true not only in the land-management agencies but in their active and vigilant public support groups, which would certainly become aroused by signs that institutional champions were about to drift away from the straight and narrow. A land-management agency usually moves in lockstep with its constituency, much like an elected official; it is not entirely free to amble off on an unfamiliar heading even if it should be inclined. Of course, like an elected official, an agency has the option of trying to educate its constituency when it senses a need for change, but it would be stressful for those in charge and perhaps even risky to arouse the anger of supporters. Many strands of aversion draw together to make avoidance easier. And so those who should be following the signposts of the new science do not—which means the endangered species that fall into their hands have excellent prospects for being lost.

Expenditures

In Florida, as money has flowed to an expanding bureaucratic structure, and while putting the enterprise on a rational course has been avoided, panther recovery has become one of the most expensive wildlife rescue efforts in history. Expenditures to date are I believe in the $30 million to $40 million range. Most have gone to the project in southern Florida.

The Game Commission has spent over $2 million since 1976, most of it on research. A significant portion has been matching funds from the Fish and Wildlife Service. Outlays have climbed steadily and are presently about $400,000 each year.[30] The National Park Service has disposed of $1,236,000 since 1976 and is currently consuming over $400,000 per year. In the current *Florida Panther Recovery Plan*, the tasks identified for the National Park Service called for

expenditures in 1989 of $1,230,000; in 1990 of $1,175,000 and in 1991 of $1,155,000.[31] None of these hoped-for sums are to be used by the National Park Service to increase deer numbers. The Fish and Wildlife Service, in addition to the matching funds it annually gives to the Game Commission ($286,000 in 1988-89), hoped to complete its acquisition of the Florida Panther National Wildlife Refuge in 1988-89, at a cost of just under $20 million. A refuge manager has been supplied; his office will consume approximately $140,000 dollars a year. To handle the ever-increasing flow of paper being generated, a "panther coordinator" position has been funded at a cost of $80,000 a year.[32] The Florida Department of Transportation and the Federal Highway Administration have contributed $13,200,000 to construct 26 wildlife crossings under the Naples-to-Fort Lauderdale leg of Interstate 75, now under construction. Twenty-three of the wildlife crossings will be paid for entirely by the state of Florida, at a cost of $10,750,000—the other three by the federal government.[33] In 1984 the Florida Department of Transportation spent $2,200,000 on modifications to State Road 29, in the hope of engineering a reduction in highway mortalities.[34]

The panther recovery program was set in motion on a paltry budget of approximately $10,000 per year in 1976—a level of spending maintained by the Game Commission through 1980. In these four years, while the recovery team was drafting a recovery plan and the Fish and Wildlife Service was reviewing it, operations were directed largely at survey work through the Game Commission's Florida Panther Clearinghouse. Chris Belden was the principal investigator. The money was budgeted by the Game Commission, aided by private contributions and limited assistance from the Fish and Wildlife Service.[35] The budget constrained the pace in the early years. Research for an animal like the panther is expensive. The National Park Service was also during this period providing nominal amounts for panther research (about $2,000 annually).[36] In fiscal year 1983-1984 expenditures took a huge jump. The Game Commission committed $180,000 in 1983 and $240,000 in 1984.[37] The National Park Service appropriation rose to $70,000 for each of the two years.[38] Most of the money went for research, and the payoff in data was commensurate. As related in a foregoing chapter, by 1985 a general picture of the predicament in southern Florida was visible. Accordingly, it became possible to plot a general course toward recovery. Also, as related earlier, a realistic strategy has been resisted ever since, although expenses have steadily gone up.

Once the agencies are brought nose-to-nose with the things they are not willing to do, they simply go on spending money while avoiding the hard chores staring them in the face. The National Park Service flatly refuses to manage for a single species (at least in the case of the Florida panther); The Florida Department of Natural Resources goes through the motions of managing for more deer in the Fakahatchee Strand State Preserve without actually doing so; and we have seen the inexplicable flip-flop of the Game Commission over captive breeding. The latter

agency also dithers and dithers with the private lands obstacle, and has for years put off sponsoring an interconnected statewide habitat system, which is essential if there are to be panthers (and black bears for that matter) in Florida's future.

The panther recovery program in southern Florida has shunned a strategy. The FPIC refused to identify a number of panthers as an objective (until pressed by external forces—see Chapter 19), and no one has mapped a geographical area that would have to be secured and managed for them. (Mapping would finally get under way in 1992 after a citizen sued the Fish and Wildlife Service.) And so there has been no commonly agreed upon policy, or policies, that might lead the program to the goal. There is no educational design that might awaken citizens to the imaginative tactics that will have to be tried if there is to be any hope of success. The agency administrators who are responsible for this mess have not collectively decided where they want their great campaign to go, and so they have no collective idea of how to get it there. The enterprise is adrift on a sea of bureaucratic expediency. The decision-makers float along, grasping any opportunity that might benefit their agency while veering away from any seeming institutional hazard. The critical questions of what they plan to ultimately obtain by their ceaseless expenditures, and when they hope to arrive, are never asked. The stoutest administrator will quail before a course that may lead to a fundamental reassess-ment of his ingrained operational premises; so the program rolls on, its adminis-trative superstructure growing ever higher; the appropriations that fuel it flow each year; personnel are added; the volume of paper expands, but none of this can remedy a deeply rooted organic incompetence.

Excuses

When confronted with the shortcomings of their performance, land-management agencies often complain that they have not been given enough money. A recent publication from the University of Michigan outlined a history of appropriations for the 1973 Endangered Species Act. The narrative begins with a simple declarative sentence of unimpeachable veracity. "Effective protection for endangered species depends upon adequate financing." So it does. The sentences that follow the lead paragraph, sequentially summarize the purposes to which funds are allocated, one being to "devise and carry out programs to restore the species to viable population levels."[39] And here is where the least obvious obstruction lies—one apparently invisible to scholars and to environmental activists who are trying to push the recovery of endangered species along almost entirely by pounding away at legal and fiscal targets, rarely taking effective aim at the structure of the bureaucracy.

This scholarly review goes on to inform that "the overriding theme of the appropriations history of the Endangered Species Act is that none of these agencies

has been adequately funded to carry out a comprehensive species protection program."[40] The statement is incorrect. The shortcomings in Florida are not linked to money. The California condor program was adequately bankrolled. It broke down for a critical year-and-a-half because of paralysis in a key land-management agency—a paralysis brought on by a controversy that ran to excess, as we shall see later. In the black-footed ferret debacle, considerable private funding had preceded government aid—it could be had on short notice. Consequently, a crack team of private researchers was able to make management recommendations; they were ignored and their talent squandered. The overriding theme now emerging in the implementation of the Endangered Species Act is one of colossal bureaucratic clumsiness, not a shortage of funds.

There is no question that when the 1973 Endangered Species Act arrived, federal dollars and staff were hopelessly inadequate to administer the new statute. It took time to structure a fiscal base, but Congress responded with a steady buildup of appropriations, which grew from less than $5 million in 1974 to over $20 million in 1980.[41] Public apprehension was stirred by the coming of the Reagan administration which was unsympathetic to the idea of spending money for endangered species. Yet the remarkable thing about the Reagan years is that the output from Congress grew steadily to over $31 million[42] despite the undisguised lack of enthusiasm of Reagan's Secretary of the Interior for the assistance. The Reagan administration was completely out of touch with national environmental sentiment—which compelled the increase in spending. The shortcomings of endangered species programs during the Reagan years were in the area of administration and operations, not in funding.

A federal wildlife agency cannot reach its potential if the political appointees who head it combine an anti-federal bias with little interest in endangered species. And a defect of this kind is only partly eased by piling more money on top of it. However, among environmentalists who comment about and scholars who write about the issue, the identification of inadequate funding as the primary deficiency of implementing the Endangered Species Act rarely waivers. Scanning the literature on this matter, raises a suspicion that the dominant view of endangered species issues is being shaped by the lobbying environment of conservation activists in Washington, D.C. There may be a presumption by the literati that the busy toilers in this Olympian milieu are well-informed about recovery shortcomings.

Another focal point for conventional analysis of the Endangered Species Act is the "listing" aspect. Getting a candidate species on the docket is a prolonged procedure. Gains were sluggish at first because of understaffing and controversy (the Tellico snail darter), and listing virtually came to a halt early in the Reagan years because the president's Secretary of the Interior did not want the list enlarged;

some candidates that were enumerated during his tenure made it only under threat of litigation by conservationists.[43] An article on this subject says, that as of May 1988, only approximately 34 percent of likely threatened or endangered species in the United States had been listed.[44] The backlog invites attention because it can be expressed in numbers and percentages—a balance-sheet quantification easily grasped. Its visibility was probably aided by the attention inadvertently brought to it by Secretary Watt's attitude.

Another "numbers issue" is recovery plans. Only 57 percent of listed species in the United States have approved recovery plans.[45] The author of a "listing article" enlightens his readers about the consequences of this backlog: "By the time species 'qualify' for official listing, the ecological situation is frequently critical, and the available options (if known) for successful recovery are quite limited. This often results in high costs for research and management. Thus agencies are constantly faced with balancing high costs and high risk efforts, i. e. those that include data gaps and great uncertainty) against those requiring less resources and having higher chances of success. . . ."[46] The agencies are in a worse predicament than this commentator imagines. There seems to be an assumption on the part of those who write about endangered species problems that the agencies are finely honed instruments, directed to their tasks under the guidance of well-thought-out policies, drafted by industrious state-of-the-science professionals. In fact, some agencies having the most important roles are still mentally in an era that was unconscious of the exacting demands of small population management.

I do not mean to imply that there is no need for large sums. And certainly the administrative foundation of recovery—appropriations, listing, and recovery plans—must be in place before anything else can follow. But these investments have reached a point of diminishing returns. If the funding and listing needs were somehow satisfied overnight, a principal impediment would still be there. This can be seen by peering beneath the surface at the nonsense going on in cases where the species have been listed, recovery plans published and funds provided. The public supporters of the Endangered Species Act are focusing disproportionate attention and energy into pushing more revenue toward the pipeline while there are serious blockages down the way. The output at the other end will be disappointing if the obstruction isn't attended to.

In December 1988 the General Accounting Office criticized the Fish and Wildlife Service (and the National Marine Fisheries Service) in its administration of the Endangered Species Act. Among other things the report announced that "nearly half of the tasks in the 16 approved plans we reviewed in depth have not been undertaken, even though the plans have been approved on average for over four years. Further, the agencies are not systematically tracking undertaken tasks. Officials with both agencies point to a shortage of funds as the primary reason."[47]

I believe it has been shown in this book that the failure to implement some of the most critical tasks in the Florida panther recovery plan (or even to identify them) is in no way related to money. The Fish and Wildlife Service can't tell the GAO that one of its biggest failings is its inability to crack the whip over other agencies for which it has theoretical oversight, so it claims not to have enough money—an excuse that has come to be the prop for all failings.

The GAO report makes several other criticisms and then naively offers a solution: "GAO believes that adherence to guidelines and a priority system will ensure that the recovery plan's value as a recovery tool is maximized and that limited funds are optimally used."[48] The GAO only sees the surface of things, and so proposes an administrative solution. The GAO might, as a mental exercise, ponder a few down-to-earth questions: How can the Fish and Wildlife Service compel the National Park Service to plant forage crops for deer on National Park Service lands in southern Florida? How could the Fish and Wildlife Service have pressured the Wyoming Game Commission to do what independent wildlife scientists in the recovery program were demanding—get some ferrets into captivity while there was time to do so? Remember, a citizen of Wyoming—a champion of Rocky Mountain regionalism—was serving as Secretary of Interior, and a former official of a state game agency had been appointed to oversee the Fish and Wildlife Service. It is no use blandly telling the Fish and Wildlife Service to stick to its guidelines, and it is pointless to criticize when it doesn't. Guidelines will always be abrogated by the prevailing bureaucratic laws of motion. The agencies them-selves need reforming; the crippling flaws are rooted in their fixed beliefs and antiquated structures. And nothing is helped by reducing allocations. The bureau-cracy can squander what it receives, whether it is too little or more than enough. In reviewing the minutes of an FPIC meeting in the summer of 1987, I came to the following statement referencing the captive breeding facility at White Oak Plantation. "In order to proceed with developing [a] larger holding facility at White Oak it was agreed that each agency would seek approximately $15,000 for this project. White Oak Plantation (Lukas) will put together an estimate of what he feels the total needs would be."[49]

I was puzzled as to why each of the four agencies in the FPIC would seek $15,000 to expand captive breeding facilities. It had been my understanding that White Oak Plantation had offered to underwrite the costs. I paused in writing this chapter to call John Lukas and ask. Lukas told me that the incident occurred at the time a facility was being constructed to house "Orphan Annie," the vagabond kitten from Everglades National Park. The suggestion for the agencies to contribute the money had been made by the executive director of the Game Commission; it had not been solicited. "In other words," I asked, "the FPIC spent $60,000 it didn't have to spend?" "That's right," said Lukas.[50] The other agency administrators appar-

ently never questioned this unnecessary expenditure.[51] The money was used for Orphan Annie's facility, but instead of retaining the young female to help establish a captive population, Orphan Annie was soon returned to the wild. Lukas also told me the young female came into estrus while she was being held, but unfortunately there was no proven male breeder available for service.

All the resources of money and manpower, and all the methods of research and all the planning documents cannot compensate for, nor overcome, the frailties of bureaucratic vision and will. The deficiencies can only be supplied by the human factor: the ability and, more importantly, the willingness of decision-makers to think clearly about a problem, no matter how unpleasant the apparent path to a solution, to formulate a plan and then to act decisively. If nothing is done about the present institutional inflexibility, then endangered species programs, particularly those managed by agency coalitions, are unlikely to rise to the standards that citizens should expect of them, except in the unusual situations where the interests of the species in question are not incompatible with the traditional interests and anxieties of the agencies. A growing public desire to prevent the loss of threatened wildlife will continue to find expression in legislation, and in appropriations, but with prospects for success that are being compromised unnecessarily. The bureaucrats will go through the motions without ever getting down to the hard and painful work that must be done; and all the while they will churn out idiotic newsletters proclaiming the fine job they are doing; and when their charges vanish from the earth, there will be no end of excuses, one of which will be that there was not enough money.

PART THREE: OTHER PROBLEMS

Chapter 14

THE CALIFORNIA CONDOR

It is almost a mythical bird that Koford has created. A lot of people are trying to save the mythical bird.Their approach might work for the mythical bird but not for the blood and guts and feathers bird.

John Ogden
"Science" 1980

Things must be done soon and they must be done right. There is no margin of error for the condor.

Constance Holden
"Science" 1980

The California condor recovery program was carefully conceived and well-planned. It was adequately funded and placed in the hands of scientists of proven ability, and it was structurally sound as evidenced by the fact that it withstood a lengthy pounding by an aroused opposition. It was delayed but persevered, emerging fundamentally unaltered only to become mired in another round of conflict between scientific factions within the program. It deserves careful study for the lessons it can offer

California's love affair with its condor has been a long one, closely supported by the National Audubon Society. Actions to save the condor developed early, at a period when carrion-eating birds were not widely esteemed. From a modern perspective it is interesting to note that the condor was a charismatic and protected species for years during which California was striving to eliminate pumas—vainly as it turned out. The aesthetic appeal of many bird species motivated the early strivings to conserve them. The beauty of the condor is in its size and its grace in flight. It does not arouse the aesthetic response at close range. But the condor was seldom seen up close.

History records the condor from Baja California to British Columbia, but by the twentieth century it was no longer found beyond the borders of California. In 1908 a man in that state was fined $50 for shooting a condor (the only conviction of its kind). In 1937 a refuge of 1,198 acres—the Sisquoc Condor Sanctuary—was carved out of a national forest. The National Audubon Society in the 1930s began sponsoring studies of several dwindling bird species. The condor was selected along with other appealing types, including the roseate spoonbill and the ivory-billed woodpecker. In 1939 a three-year fellowship was given to a Berkeley student named Carl Koford.[1] Koford took time off to serve in the navy during World War II and did not finish the field studies until 1946. His report led to the protection of a known nesting area—the 35,000-acre Sespe Wildlife Sanctuary. It was enlarged to 53,000 acres in 1951.

Carl Koford would come to be something of a patron saint of the California condor—an authoritative, protective voice, wielding a heavy influence whenever the schemes of man threatened. As a student Koford's interest was in mammalogy. This he pursued in the circumstances of the time by taking a degree in forestry.[2] He was trained in the exacting methods of Joseph Grinnell, which emphasized detailed field notes based on careful observation. It was a methodology suited to the character of Koford. He was by all accounts a loner, able to endure days of privation sitting motionless for hours with binoculars, filling his field journal with meticulous notations. While a student he sat in a tree for 42 consecutive days studying ground squirrels.[3] These qualities which made him a superb field biologist were marked by his professors and probably influenced their nomination of him for the condor fellowship.

Koford marched off to his assignment with a journal, a pencil, a pair of binoculars, a few things thrown into a rucksack, and with Audubon fellowship money in his pocket to buy groceries. He took a bus to Los Angeles and from there got a lift for himself and a newly purchased stock of food to the study area, where he hiked off into the hills. He found a nest and spent days observing it, filling as many as 20 pages a day in his journal. For up to 40 hours at a stretch he would keep vigil on condors incubating eggs. When Koford's food ran out he would hike 13 miles to a settlement to buy more. Drinking water came from potholes. He eventually succumbed to the temptation for convenience and paid $95 for a model-T Ford.[4] Koford estimated 60 condors remaining, a figure now thought low.[5]

Koford was proud of his skills and endurance and may have cultivated the image of a rugged outdoorsman. He favored plaid shirts (sometimes with holes in them).[6] Jim Layne and John Eisenberg, who have served in Florida on the Panther Advisory Council, worked in the field with Koford. They remember his skills as well as his idiosyncracies. Koford traveled light. John Eisenberg recalls him living on raisins and nuts. Eisenberg and Koford explored the backcountry of Colombia

together. Emerging from several days in the bush, they jumped into a creek to bathe. Eisenberg had hoarded a bar of soap for the occasion, which he offered to share with his companion. However, he learned that Koford disdained the use of soap, believing it contained carcinogens.[7] Jim Layne studied rhesus macaques with Koford in Puerto Rico. Koford would keep his companions going all day in the field, disdaining to pause and eat while they grew weak with hunger. When Layne and Koford went diving for spiny lobsters, Koford insisted on towing a heavy boat from one site to another by swimming with the line clenched in his teeth instead of getting in and using the motor. Layne felt constrained to swim along.[8]

An affair in 1953 displayed the guardian sentiment of California for its great bird, perhaps also predisposing opinion against capture and radio-telemetry—a heated issue years later. The San Diego Zoo, having successfully bred Andean condors, set out to catch the California species for the same experiment. The project aroused strong opposition. It was halted, and the state legislature forbad further captures. The law was unequivocal, mandating it ". . . unlawful to take any condor at any time or in any manner."[9] Carl Koford had been prominent in deflecting the captures. So had the National Audubon Society. It was recently speculated that "with the advantage of hindsight, it seems obvious that the present status of the condor population might be very different if the San Diego Zoo proposal had been allowed to go forward."[10]

In 1963-64, Audubon and the National Geographic Society entrusted another field survey to two ranchers, the McMillan brothers, picked on the recommendation of Koford. The McMillans produced a dire appraisal of 30 percent fewer birds (about 40) than Koford's estimate in the 1940s.[11] Later, scientists in the 1980s who reviewed their work would contend that the McMillan figure was unnecessarily low.[12]

The California condor—along with the Florida panther, the black-footed ferret and the Yellowstone grizzly—was placed on the federal list of endangered species in 1967. The Fish and Wildlife Service assigned a biologist, Fred Sibley, to the diminished and downward-trending bird. His work led to the later naming of another breeding sanctuary in San Louis Obisbo County. During his work Sibley climbed into several condor nests, thereby drawing a storm of protest from protectors of the great bird who believed that such activities were harmful. He had inspected nests in 1966 and 1967, but in 1968 he could only find one nest, sparking a presumption by condor partisans that he had brought on the abandonment of nests.[13] Sibley departed in 1969 and was replaced by Sandford (Sandy) Wilbur. Perhaps alerted to the ruckus raised by Sibley's activities, Wilbur adopted a less adventurous style. His field work was more restrained, though he seems to have been a thorough and methodical worker. Wilbur would be the principal biologist in condor conservation for ten years and apparently did much to bring the program

to the climactic moment of "radical recovery measures." The first California condor entered captivity during this period after biologists spotted two adults not properly caring for a fledgling. The young bird was removed from its nest to the Los Angeles Zoo. It was called Topa Topa, after an Indian name for a mountain near the capture site.

The Recovery Plan

Following the Endangered Species Act of 1973 a newly formed recovery team set to work on a recovery plan. It is not clear precisely when or how the conviction came about among those monitoring the condor that it would be necessary to capture birds for a breeding project. The idea may have incubated for several years, laboring to make the transition to a proposal for action by biologists alarmed by the dwindling flock. They were painfully aware of the anger they would stir by advocating captures. It was not a moment to be seized by the cautious land-management agencies. The captive breeding project might never have seen the light of day if not for the National Audubon Society. John Borneman transmitted the thinking of biologists in the field to Audubon headquarters in New York; assigned by the Society as a condor warden in 1965, he was also responsible for field study and public education. He worked closely with the Fish and Wildlife Service biologists and was on the team that completed the first recovery plan in 1975.

Human exploitation has been the great destroyer of wildlife. Alleviating human-caused deaths early became a keystone of conservation. This tradition had guided the strategy to save condors. Both Carl Koford and the McMillan brothers had emphasized mortality factors.[14] Egg collecting had been a menace early in the century, but the hobby faded by the 1940s. Ian McMillan believed in the 1960s that the main threat to condor survival was "still a man with a gun."[15] A suspected but unproved cause of deaths was the compound 1080, a poison widely used on ground squirrels. Condors had also been observed in fatal collisions with overhead wires.[16]

However, a population severely diminished is in hazard even if protected, and factors other than mortality must be examined. In a decade of study, Sandy Wilbur had increasingly turned to the natality side of the survival problem. Wilbur also estimated more birds than the McMillan brothers, perhaps as many as 60.[17] During Wilbur's tenure an annual census was made by having strategically placed observers count all condors seen in a single weekend and adding up the total. However, there were doubts about the census because no one knew how far or fast a condor could fly, and it was possible that individual birds were being counted more than once. But Wilbur's calculations predicted that even at 60 the condors were headed for extinction.

In the recovery plan, Wilbur presented the dynamics of the population as best as he could discern them.

> With many wildlife species, a large percentage of individuals are capable of reproducing and adding to the size of the population. The reverse is true in the condor population. Because of the long period of sexual immaturity and the low productivity of individual pairs, total annual production was low even when the population was large. Of the estimated 60 condors now in existence, perhaps 40 are of breeding age. Assuming an even sex ratio, no superannuated members in the population and free interchange between all condors in the population, a maximum of 20 breeding pairs can be formed. Because of the probable inequities in sex, age and distribution, a total of approximately 16 pairs seems more likely. With condors nesting regularly every second year, eight pairs would be breeding in an average year. Assuming some nest failure, highest annual production is likely to be somewhat less than eight birds. At this rate, an average annual survival of 90 percent or more is necessary to maintain a static population. The current survival rate appears to be at or above 90 per cent, but cannot be maintained long because of expected old-age losses. Also, production in recent years has not approached the theoretical level of six or eight fledglings annually, so the present imbalance between natality and mortality is even more severe than might be expected.[18]

The recovery plan urged several actions. Some, in keeping with tradition, proposed added strictures on human activity near nesting sites. Supplemental feeding, by encouraging ranchers to leave dead livestock as food for condors, was raised as a possibility. Setting aside more habitat was also put forward. But the recovery plan did not brim with optimism and suggested captive breeding if the bird's status did not improve.[19] In 1977 Wilbur took the next step. He drafted a contingency plan calling for "radical" management techniques, including captive breeding and radio-telemetry, to be activated if the condor's plight worsened.

Enter Audubon

At this juncture the National Audubon Society moved to involve itself directly, in part because it suspected the timid state and federal agencies were not eager to provoke slumbering passions in California.[20] There were other reasons. Activism was in keeping with the Audubon tradition. The Society had funded the first condor research and had maintained a presence in promoting the welfare of

the bird for over 30 years. It also had a capable staff of researchers. Richard Plunkett and Eugene Knoder were the Audubon staff members who stirred the organization to superintend the crisis. Knoder also saw an opportunity for a public education bonanza on endangered species.[21] In addition, Audubon hoped to gain from the publicity. There was however controversy within the staff; some thought the condor doomed, and saw limited resources being siphoned away trying to save it.[22] The first overt step to participation was taken in 1977 when the staff put the issue before its Board. The Directors adopted a resolution approving captive breeding—in principle.[23]

The next step was to put the enterprise on a solid foundation by seeking the best in scientific backing (I cannot resist pointing out that National Audubon's approach to condor recovery stands out in striking contrast to its conduct in the Yellowstone grizzly affair) by soliciting advice from the most appropriate professional society in the country—the American Ornithologists' Union. Nine scientists were named to a panel by the Union in the fall of 1977. The panel submitted its review in May 1978.[24] This report of three parts underpinned the strategy now advocated by Audubon. First, intensified field research using radio-telemetry would expand the skimpy data to more confidently identify the causes of decline. A second objective was to strengthen habitat protection measures. It was hoped that new research would yield more information on where and how protection could best be applied. Obviously the entire 50,000 square-mile region of California used by condors could not be made into a preserve, and trying to protect any part of it would profit if backed by hard data. The third objective called for a captive population from which birds could be reintroduced to the wild. The vulnerabilities to which reproduction and recruitment are subject in a wild population would be guarded against in the security of a captive environment. It was hoped also to return condors to regions where they had been extirpated.

Two parts of this three-part plan would anger condor paladins in California, whose sentiment incorporated several interrelated elements. One element stressed that condor conservation should be exclusively directed at isolating and guarding habitat, and that any other doctrine was illusory. This may have been accompanied in the minds of some by a fear that captive breeding would weaken the thrust toward land preservation. Another element was a bias against technology, or gadgetry (this was directed against radio-telemetry). Another element was the "born free" bias and the feeling that the "wildness" of the condors was sacrosanct and could be irretrievably compromised by captivity. The latter attitude carried over to the notion that if the progeny of captive birds were released, they would be "artifacts" rather than "natural organisms." "Hands-on" was the rubric to which all the abhorrent elements of the proposed recovery program were consigned by the sentiment of condor protection. The opponents wanted the

research strictly limited to the field observation methods of the past—like those used by Carl Koford in the 1940s. For convenience I will henceforth use the terms "hands-on" and "hands-off" to differentiate between these two points of view.

With the report of the American Ornithologists' Union in hand, Eugene Knoder made an appointment with a high-ranking Fish and Wildlife official to propose that the government agency join forces with the private organization to save the condor.[25] Joint action was soon agreed to, and the preparatory events were briskly concluded in 1979. During that year the Fish and Wildlife Service approved the contingency plan drafted by Wilbur. National Audubon petitioned Congress to authorize a 30 to 40-year recovery program for the condor and to grant a special appropriation to it in 1979. Congress did so, committing $750,000 for two years. National Audubon matched this sum with $500,000 over a five-year period.[26] In the final month of the year, the Fish and Wildlife Service presented its ideas for condor research at a public meeting called by the California Game Commission. Shortly thereafter a cooperative agreement was signed by National Audubon and four land-management agencies: the Fish and Wildlife Service, the California Game Commission, the U.S. Forest Service and the Bureau of Land Management. The agreement named the National Audubon Society and the Fish and Wildlife Service to the lead role. Permits, both federal and state, were needed for hands-on research. The federal permit was issued by the Fish and Wildlife Service. The state permit had to be secured from the California Game Commission which was highly sensitive to state opinion.

This novel institutional combination seemed a well-planned design for overcoming public and bureaucratic resistance to a formidable enterprise. A Fish and Wildlife Service biologist, who had spent ten years on the ground and analyzed all available data, had drafted a plan of action. A prestigious body of professional ornithologists had been consulted. A campaign chest had been filled at the outset, and two highly-qualified scientists, one each from the National Audubon Society and the Fish and Wildlife Service, had been assigned to the field. The cautious state and federal land-management agencies had stepped into harness behind a national environmental organization eager to lead the way. The biggest hurdle—the fervid instincts of California's condor fans—had been neutralized. Or so it seemed at the time.

The two scientists who were called to serve were both working in southern Florida. John Ogden, of the National Audubon Society, was in the Florida Keys studying wood storks. Noel Snyder, of the Fish and Wildlife Service, was monitoring snail kites on Lake Okeechobee. Both men had years of hands-on experience with endangered birds. Late in 1979 they packed up and headed for California. In January 1980 they opened the Condor Research Center at Ventura

to serve as the administrative headquarters, and began hiring a staff. The preparations were largely complete by May when they drove to a Game Commission meeting in Santa Barbara for the purpose of requesting research permits.

They found a crowd of over 100 assembled. The meeting dragged; a parade of objectors spoke against the permit. David Brower, president of Friends of the Earth, was present to lend his eloquence to the dissident view. For years to come he would be a leader of the hands-off proponents. As a delaying tactic the opposition had demanded an "environmental impact statement" prior to issuing the permits. The National Environmental Policy Act of 1969 (NEPA) required federal agencies to assess their actions for any possible impact on the environment. To apply the Act to condor recovery was not its intent, but it offered a legal platform to air dissenting arguments. The Fish and Wildlife Service declined to supply the EIS, but did carry out an "environmental assessment"—a more superficial sort of investigation than an impact statement. Of course the agency found no reason not to proceed with a program to which it was now elaborately committed, and the Game Commission released the permits. The resistance had not been a surprise; Ogden had been forewarned by Knoder and Plunkett, but these mentors had guessed that once a few condors had been taken the opposition would fade away. Ogden and Snyder left the meeting with a sense of relief. The extensive groundwork by National Audubon had paid off. A supreme professional challenge lay ahead. The two men headed into the field to get on with the captures, not dreaming of the tribulations to come.

Tragedy

Two active condor nests had been found in the spring of 1980. The scientists wanted to enter them and look at the chicks. Although the opponents of "hands-on" were convinced they knew what should be done to save the bird, the scientists were not certain that the condor's plight had been pinpointed. Sandy Wilbur had suspected trouble with reproduction. To evaluate, Ogden and Snyder wanted to enter nests, not only to examine the nestlings, but to gather bits of eggshell. Weighing and measuring the young at intervals to record growth rates could yield data on their nutritional status and infer the adequacy of food resources; eggshell analysis could spot pesticides and heavy metals, the ingestion of which might affect birth rates.

The first nest entry was easy. It was in a cave high up on a cliff, but could be reached by walking. Nearly an hour was spent with the chick. On June 30 the capture team set out for the second nest, built in a cliff face cave in the San Rafael Wilderness. They ascended an escarpment. The cave was 75 feet below them and could only be reached by rope descent. Unfortunately, neither of the ornithologists were climbers, and the climbers in the party were inexperienced in handling chicks. Nonetheless, the two climbers were sent down to make the diagnosis. Bill Lehman

was to weigh and measure the chick; Jeff Foott was to film the operation. Detailed entries in the recovery journal tell what happened. ". . . 1425 Immediately following the completion of the bill measurements the bird's head is released and Bill notes that it begins to wobble in a few seconds. He releases the bird immediately and calls for advice. Within about 30 seconds of the time he notes the first signs of unsteadiness of the bird's head, the head falls to the ground and the bird appears to have lost consciousness. No signs of pulse or breath are detected from this point onward."[27]

John Ogden avers that the California condor is a physically tough bird, not the least predisposed to drop dead from being handled. In later years six California condor chicks were captured without mishap. In similar work in Florida, Ogden had handled more than a thousand wood stork chicks and more than a hundred young ospreys without ever losing one. When the two scientists later visited South Africa to consult ornithologists who had been working for years with several vulture species, the South Africans were incredulous about a vulture chick dying while being handled. It has been suggested that an experienced ornithologist might have recognized that the chick was stressed and would have backed off. I cannot judge this, but it has been shown that animals when being captured will on occasion die. Endangered species are not excepted. In 1977 when fewer than 75 whooping cranes were left in the wild, a whooper chick died a few hours after being banded. The program went on, however, free of difficulty in 24 subsequent bandings. In the course of recovery programs there are single instances of Florida panthers, whooping cranes, sea otters and California condors perishing during captures. The condor capture team was unlucky.[28]

Public outrage erupted as soon as the news was released. At Ventura, John Ogden fielded more than 40 phone calls from Californians in the first 24 hours after the news broke. The callers were all angry and in a few instances hysterical. Ogden listened patiently to one voice endlessly screaming: ". . . killer! killer! killer! killer! killer! . " The news went nationwide. I read it in the morning paper in Florida, two-and-a-half years before a panther death in the field would bring me back into a recovery program. The California Game Commission folded under the pressure and revoked the permits. The fledgling endeavor was grounded.

The death of the chick confirmed every fear and suspicion of those against hands-on research and fired their resolve to stop it. Bad luck tends to come in swatches and it continued to plague the researchers. While test-firing a cannon net, the detonation ignited a brush fire which burned a hundred acres before it could be extinguished. Under other circumstances it might have gone unnoticed or caused little comment, but not now. Editorial and other writers had a field day promoting the image of ornithological bumblers. One writer conjured up the picture of an unfunny Laurel and Hardy movie.[29] Friends of the Earth rushed into print a 281-

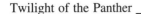

page book disputing hands-on. David Brower began referring to the "Condor disposal program."[30]

The Game Commission reacted by setting up a Citizen's Advisory Council to advise it on condor matters. It is curious that several appointees were known to resent hands-on; others were neutral. In John Ogden's judgement none of them had the expertise to offer counsel. Therefore, the Game Commission, which had initially granted permits and then withdrawn them under pressure, now saddled itself with doubtful advisors who militated against reissuing them. However, the agency biologists, with whom the condor team had early formed a liaison, stood behind the hands-on strategy, but the biologists could not speak out. Thus the agency director, Charles Fullerton, found himself in a box between his professional staff, who urged hands-on, and the commissioners, who were being pommeled by an angry public whose spokesmen they had designated advisors. Faced with a crisis the plodding agency had promptly tied itself into a knot—and the recovery program with it.

It is interesting to note the different response in Florida at a later date when a panther was killed during a capture. In Florida the Game Commission quickly appointed a committee of members known to support radio-telemetry, several of whom were experienced wildlife scientists. In California, the Game Commission may have been flustered by the explosive reaction to the condor chick's death and attempted to placate a citizen uprising by choosing opposition spokesmen as advisors. The authorities could not think beyond an expedient to quell the uproar.[31]

Delay

With meaningful research at an end, Ogden and Snyder began a wearying marathon of appearances at condor meetings, public and private, which would last for more than a year. The assemblies were sometimes noisy and often vehemently against hands-on. John Ogden believes there were over 40 of these events. Many were scheduled by the California Game Commission, but Ogden and Snyder made themselves available to any group that requested their presence. They traveled the length and breadth of the state answering summonses from Friends of the Earth and from Audubon and Sierra Club chapters.

Carl Koford seems to have become something of a cult figure to the opposition. He died in 1980, but his ghost stalked the assemblies as an unmistakable presence. His followers were in evidence, dressed in his likeness (wearing plaid shirts) and carrying copies of his 30-year old condor publication in their hip pockets. The meetings would begin with a statement from the scientists, and it would then be the turn of the audience for an inquisition and for rebuttals. Plaid-shirted Kofordites, who had invested their idol's writings with the sanctity of holy

writ, would read from the scripture to refute statements of the scientists. Rational discussions were often impossible.

For the two scientists it was a time of stress and frustration. It was emotionally draining to be the butt of public wrath, and there was the gnawing awareness that while the recovery program was spinning in a vortex of passion, time was not on the side of the endangered species. The men were strengthened by the conviction that their strategy had been carefully analyzed and the proper course of action chosen. They also had the comfort of knowing that the National Audubon hierarchy stood solidly behind them, and they had the overwhelming support of the scientific community as well. When the controversy brewed up, the American Ornithologists' Union regrouped its condor review panel which lent strong support.

It may be useful at this juncture to examine more closely the arguments of the opposition. The most authoritative source for the hands-off proposition was Carl Koford, as is shown by the arguments of David Brower, its most eloquent spokesman. Brower referenced Koford repeatedly in a long letter to Russell Peterson, the president of the National Audubon Society, in September 1980, where he unfolded his disagreement with the techniques of "intervention." An endangered species, he wrote, should remain "natural, not to become an artifact" or a "managed facsimile of the original." There is a reference to an "obsession with management." The words "wild, wilderness or wildness" make ten appearances in his letter. "Free" is juxtaposed to "captive," and the term "incarceration" is once resorted to. "Excitement, challenge, and romance" are implied as the motivation of researchers (of challenge there is no doubt). In Florida similar thrill-seeking motives were alleged in radio-collaring panthers. A year after the death of the condor chick in California, a critic of the panther radio-telemetry research was quoted in a magazine article. "They want this radio-telemetry to go on because it is fun. You are playing cowboy behind the guy with all his hounds. You have the chase, get the cat up the tree, get him down, put the collar on him, and fly every day in the plane."[32]

Brower suggested that captivity would be deleterious to the condor's genes, yet he showed no awareness of the genetic peril faced by shrunken populations. It is unlikely that the foes of hands-on knew anything about genetics. Few in the wildlife profession were giving much thought to the subject at that time. Friends of the Earth prepared a 26-point alternative to the condor recovery plan. It hammered at guarding habitat and giving added protection. In a larger sense, Brower's arguments make a compelling point. Intervention is the chemotherapy for a planetary cancer; it is not to be compared with preventing the disease, but the cancer is upon us, and any available treatment must be utilized to prevent the malaise from gaining. If faith is placed solely on the timely restoration of diseased

habitats and fragmented ecosystems without considering intervention, then rescue designs for endangered wildlife can be greatly simplified, but if adopted we should anticipate the loss of animals that might otherwise be saved.

Public opinion in California may be an extreme manifestation of attitudes that are widespread (if less explosive) elsewhere and could, perhaps more subtly, skew other programs. John Ogden, who became intimately familiar with the objections, reviewed them in an article in 1983.[33] He dealt first with the class of arguments holding that the effort should not even be made. The foremost of these was the proposition that money was being poured out "to save a species which was almost certainly doomed anyway. . . . , given all that money," the argument goes, "should we invest it in condors or somewhere else?"[34] Ogden pointed out the flaw in that position: much of the money was coming from a special congressional appropriation and from specific donations to the National Audubon Society; terminating the condor program would not transfer earmarked funds to someone else's preferred project.

There were arguments against even trying to save the condor, by some who advocated letting it "die with dignity,"[35] but most just demanded a hands-off strategy, wanting the resources used to save habitat and hold down mortality. Habitat of course was, and still is, a categorical imperative if the future is to see condors wheeling in the sky. But the scientists answered that a lack of suitable habitat had not been demonstrated. There was no evidence of insufficient nesting or roosting sites. There appeared to be adequate places for feeding on private ranches, but the bird's use of these lands was poorly understood. The scientists could not confidently target property for acquisition without better data on feeding behavior.[36] The promise of radio-telemetry was that it might yield the data, and it was certainly the only means that might do so within a period of time appropriate to the crisis. But the opponents of hands-on would not concede the case for radio-transmitters. As for mortality, the scientists argued that there had been no confirmed shooting of a condor since 1976, nor of a probable poisoned bird since 1966. It was not known if these past causes of mortality were still operating or if there might be others that had gone undetected.[37] It kept coming back to the need for intensive research—which the opposition didn't want.

The solitary and wide-ranging habits of condors placed them in 1980 among the poorly understood wildlife populations of the world, despite years of study. The condor picture was a montage, pasted together from the sporadic observations of decades. It did not reveal with any clarity the proper lines for recovery, nor would it have guaranteed that they might be followed expeditiously if they had been obvious. Hence the decision for hands-on research and management: the employment of the promising new technique of radio-telemetry—and the creation of a captive flock, both as security against losing the wild birds and, it was

hoped, to boost the overall rate of productivity as well as to build a stock for reintroduction.

A supporter of captive breeding put it another way: "Since their first contact with the species, humans have saddled the California condor with an unnaturally high rate of mortality. Since it appears unlikely that all forms of people-induced mortality can be entirely eliminated (or even identified) in the near future, the only apparent means of saving the condor is to see that it enjoys an unnaturally high rate of production."[38] Increasing the rate of production, whether in captivity or not, is a sensible measure to provide security to a small, declining wildlife population. It would have been so for the Yellowstone grizzly in the early 1970s (and would be still). It would also be valuable for the Florida panther.

John Ogden did not get into the field during all of 1981. That year the Fish and Wildlife Service tried to get the research moving again with a revised proposal. It was aired in a public hearing on July 28, 1981—13 months after the state permits had been revoked. After a further delay of two and a half months, the Game Commission reissued a three-year permit for limited research. It authorized the trapping of three condors for captive breeding; approval for radio-telemetry studies was postponed.[39]

For trapping vultures, the cannon net had been selected over a variety of methods examined because of its good performance when used by members of the Vulture Study Group in South Africa. It had proved efficient and had a low probability of injuring birds. Four small mortars, or cannons, would be used to fire a large net over condors attracted to a bait—a carcass. One side of the net was staked to the ground in front of the four cannons, which were placed facing the bait in a line parallel to the anchored side of the net. The side of the net to be thrown over the birds was weighted with leads which were then loaded into the cannon muzzles. The trapper would wait inside a blind watching the bait. He held a "trigger" which fired the four cannons simultaneously via an electric impulse sent to detonators in the base of each tube.

A new census technique devised by Noel Snyder and Eric Johnson, another ornithologist, was used for the first time in 1981. It required an accumulation of condor photographs from different locales. Members of the condor team carried cameras with them to bait stations, nest observation sites and any other place where they might be spotting condors. Approximately once a month the team gathered around a table with a map and the photos, and tried to identify individual birds and plot them on a map, matching the date of the photo to the location.

Up to the age of six, when they become mature, the underwing plumage pattern and the skin color of the condor's head and neck gradually changes. During

molt, missing wing feathers were often conspicuous from a distance in photographs. Capitalizing on the possibilities that combinations of observable characters offered for singling out individual birds, the team struggled against the limitations of field photography to sort them out. It was a mind-bending exercise that sometimes went through the night, but it was found that most of the photographed birds could be identified most of the time. Over a period of months confidence grew in the technique, but the conclusions were sobering; by mid-1982 the team believed that approximately 21 condors remained.

Frustration

In January 1982, John Rogers and Noel Snyder of the condor team met with Charles Fullerton in another attempt to loosen the permit restrictions. The team was granted permission to radio-tag condors, but it was contingent upon so many restrictions that they were skeptical about its usefulness.[40] They were allowed to trap up to nine birds (three for captive propagation and six for radio-telemetry). The restrictions are tricky to decipher for any but the cognoscente, but a rendition is as follows: The permissible trapping period would terminate on May 31, because the Game Commission feared trapping condors in hot weather. Adult condors could only be used for radio-telemetry, not for captive breeding. For adult condors the permissible trapping period would terminate on February—only ten days after the issuance of the permit. This restriction was occasioned by the condor courtship period, which peaks in February, March and April; the Game Commission did not want condors trapped while they were courting. The anticipated consequence by the researchers of this ruling was that it would not allow time for captures (this proved correct). For immature birds, or for adults known to be non-breeders (not paired with another adult) that were trapped, the first three—consisting of two females and one male—would be taken for captive breeding. Then, subsequently trapped non-breeders (up to six) could be used for radio-telemetry. Bear in mind that the total number of condors was very small (estimated at about 20), so it would have been reasonable to question whether nine non-breeding birds remained; but now came additional restrictions.

When radio-transmitters had been affixed to the first two condors, no more could be trapped until the procedures were evaluated, and it was determined that the techniques were not inhibiting the birds in any way. The criteria for judging the latter exercise were left undefined.[41] The crowning restriction was that only one bird could be trapped at a time. Taking two birds at once was forbidden. So, if during the period when it was permissible to trap adults, an adult was feeding at a bait and should be joined by another adult eligible to be trapped, the trapper could not fire. The researchers believed it probable that trapping condors would mean long waits in blinds, perhaps weeks, for a bird to be attracted to a bait. The trapper would need

the flexibility to take advantage of any opportunity, otherwise the operation might do little more than waste time.

Although the Game Commission had slightly relented after a year and a half, it was still in a position not unfamiliar to state game agencies—that of political wildlife management. It is not unlike the Florida Game Commission managing the deer herd in the water conservation areas of southern Florida—or managing the Florida panther for that matter. The objective is to minimize controversy and its possible corollary: undesirable political repercussions to the agency. All too often management functions first to protect or benefit the narrow interests of the managing institution. The wildlife resource falls into second place. The California Game Commission was creeping along at a pace it hoped would keep the public volcano from erupting, without weighing the pressure of passing time on the endangered bird.

In January 1982, Ogden and Snyder and their team—filled with foreboding—headed for the field. They set up a trapping site and spent a January week freezing in their blind, staring hopefully at a bait; they never saw a condor. February came, and with it diminished the chances of a capture until the following fall. In early July the condor team asked the Game Commission to extend the permit, complaining that "attracting condors to trap sites has proved to be very difficult. . . . The importance of establishing a captive breeding population has not diminished." To start, the team asked permission to take nestlings or eggs. The application underlined the prospect that "by removing an egg from the condor nest, there is a good chance a second will be laid so that the pair is still productive the following year."[42] Double-clutching is the term used to describe the second laying of eggs when the first have been lost (or removed).

But to the anguish of the condor team, the Game Commission at a meeting in early August clamped on further restrictions. Morale among the researchers hit bottom. Time, energy and money were leaking away with no advantage, and there were no prospects for improvement. John Ogden, in a smoldering memorandum to his superiors, gave his appreciation of the recovery possibilities, along with a clear recommendation for the National Audubon Society.

> In an earlier memo this month, I summarized the features of the permit issued to Patuxent by the California Fish and Game Commission at their 5 August 1982 meeting. . . . In a nutshell, the new permit sharply reduces the number of condors authorized for radio-tagging, and takes us well below the level of telemetry that we consider as absolutely minimal for addressing the key biological questions on condor habitat and limiting factors.

The other revelation from that Commission meeting is that Charlie Fullerton, Director of the California Department of Fish and Game, in spite of his promise of a year ago to support a more liberal and reasonable research program if we would only agree at that time to accept his compromise package following the emotional Commission meeting of July 1981, has decided to continue his independent course of manipulating the condor program in whatever fashion seems to be politically wise at the moment. In spite of promises to the contrary, Fullerton again refused to meet with representatives from Patuxent and Audubon prior to the Commission meeting in order to discuss our positions, and he proceeded to support the recommendations of his at-best unqualified Condor Advisory Committee. Perhaps the most disturbing development was Fullerton's announcement during the Commission meeting that he supports a change in direction for the condor recovery effort, away from trapping and handling of the wild population, and towards habitat preservation as the means for saving condors, coupled with a limited breeding program. . . . The obvious question that no one in the Department of Fish and Game or the Advisory Committee can possibly answer is: What habitat needs saving? Only telemetry may provide truly accurate answers.

I suggest that we either stand up to Charlie Fullerton now, or get out of the research program. . . . Obviously I've approached the point where I'm fed up with this comic-opera (=tragic) approach to wildlife research. If we don't develop a fair amount of backbone over these present issues, then the long-term prognosis for the condor research program cannot be anything less than frustration, unrealized objectives, and a demoralized and burned-out field staff. We have many talented people on our staff who are becoming increasingly despondent over our inability to act on behalf of the condor.[43]

The director of the Fish and Wildlife Service's Patuxent Wildlife Research Center sent a similar memo to his superior in Washington: "Our research has been reduced to gambling . . . our request for taking 3 eggs and 2 chicks has been reduced to one egg and no chicks. . . . The time has come for us to give serious consideration to whether we want to continue to be involved in a research program which cannot be carried out in a rational, integrated manner and on a controllable time schedule." Fuming about the absence of radio-telemetry data, the research director protested that "we are being forced by the State into doing exactly what our detractors have

said—concentrating on a captive breeding program and neglecting the habitat questions.... One of the State's few responsibilities under this agreement [the five-agency cooperative agreement] is to facilitate the permit process. They have not done so."[44]

The popular outcry had paralyzed the Game Commission. Recovery operations had been transformed into a bureaucratic going-through-the-motions, devoid of substance. Land-management agencies are accustomed to such operational nonsense. The agencies take it in stride when compelled to and (as we have seen) will initiate the nonsense when they believe it to be in their interest. But the National Audubon Society had made a large financial commitment and had to keep a sharp eye on the return from its expenditures. And here is a crucial difference between a government agency and a private institution. For the agency, next year's appropriation always comes, whether this year's is spent efficiently or whether it is squandered. Money is not an overarching concern, and marking time in a recovery program carries no threat of a fiscal penalty.

Russell Peterson, Director of the National Audubon Society, acted decisively. Immediately after reading Ogden's memo, he wrote to the director of Fish and Wildlife Service, Robert Jantzen, asking him to petition the state agency with a rational scheme for saving the condor.[45] However, documents of this period leave the impression that the Fish and Wildlife Service had no enthusiasm for confronting the California Game Commission. Apparently considerable pressure had to be brought by the National Audubon Society. First, a meeting was scheduled at the agency's headquarters in Washington on September 7, 1982. Representatives from the state game agency attended. There were several staffers from Audubon. John Ogden flew in from California. His detailed summary of the meeting conveys a glimpse of the various maneuvers that were underway.

> 1. Everyone agreed that the proposed telemetry program is essential, although my comments about the program's urgency (citing our recent population estimate based upon the photography technique of not more than 20 total condors) didn't seem to stir any cries of support from the Fish and Wildlife Service or the State.

> 2. The California Department of Fish and Game recommended against returning to the Commission for a rehearing of the telemetry issue, and Jantzen supports their position. Neither the Department nor Jantzen seemed interested in reconsidering their position, even after hearing from me that we were unable during the Commission meeting on 5 August to present key discussions on the value of telemetry (we were cut off in our testimony before

we could introduce the topic of habitat assessment by telemetry), or on the safety and results of other studies utilizing patagial markers [colored markers attached to the leading edge of the wing - the patagium - to aid in identifying individual condors].
. . .

The Department's position on the question of returning to the Commission is that the Commissioners would not appreciate having to rehear this issue so soon after making their decision, and that elevating the telemetry issue to a full public meeting at this time could result in an entrenchment, rather than a liberalization of the Commission's position on telemetry.

My own view is that the Department is trying to avoid a fair amount of embarrassment over their irrational position on telemetry, which surely would receive wide publicity if this issue were to be reconsidered by the Commission. Several sources in and around Sacramento have reported that the Department has been very much surprised by both the strength and number of statements of dismay and disagreement being made around California regarding their position on telemetry. The press has already picked up on this concern by both scientists and conservationists, and judging from the large number of press calls to our office and the thrust of their printed reports so far, they will provide sympathetic reporting on these issues as we proceed.

3. The Department's counter-offer is that rather than going back to the Commission, that they may be able through administrative procedures to give us what we need in order for Audubon to stay in the program. Specifically, Toffly offered that Director Fullerton could privately poll the Commissioners by telephone, and assuming that he could convince a majority of five Commissioners to change their present position against trapping adult condors, that the Department could issue a written statement in the form of a letter to Jantzen authorizing us to capture adults. That letter is promised to be written on Monday, 13 September.

4. [A long commentary on details of the permit, is omitted.]

5. The response to Audubon's threat to pull out, by both Jantzen and Toffly, was that they would rather have us in the program than out, but if we felt that we must go, then so be it. Toffly stated that the Department would fill our vacancy with a state program,

but I feel certain that they'll never be able to mount any kind of worthwhile research with existing funds and staff. They presently do not have a single biologist who is qualified to do the work, and no money to fund new positions.

6. The overall tactic of the Department was the same as we've seen before, to give up as little as possible, only what it took to keep Audubon in the program. At the same time, they are seeking to make as few changes as possible in the existing permit, which effectively leaves them in control as before, and us at the mercy of their political decisions. . . .

7. So where do we go from here? First, we look at the letter from Fullerton next week, that should contain authorization to capture adult condors (under certain conditions?) and see if it is anything we can live with. If it doesn't allow for capture of adults with or without the presence of immatures, and if we're not able to get rid of the Russian-roulette clause, then I say we close up the research shop. We've cried wolf fairly loudly here, and any backing down at this point will convince Fullerton that he's got this program securely under his control in the future. It is certainly clear now that Fullerton will have no future "problems" from the [Fish and Wildlife] Service, so long as Jantzen is the Director, and if he wins this one with Audubon, well. . . .

A point that Bill Sweeny keeps making is that once we get the first condor radioed, Fullerton knows that it will be much more difficult for us to pull out. Bill is surely correct in his judgement, thus it is most important that we have these issues resolved to our satisfaction before agreeing to fire a net over anything - or announce our withdrawal from research on condors

If next week's letter from Fullerton contains enough to satisfy us, then we should respond in writing as quickly as possible with a detailed statement of what we understand we're authorized to trap, and in what sequence, etc. Copies of our letter should go to the Commission and to the Advisory Committee, to make certain that there is no misunderstanding or differences in interpretation. If we stay in the program, our goal should be to start trapping no later than 1 October. If we pull out, for the sake of our poor, battered psyches, I hope we make that decision just as soon![46]

Some observations might be made here. Note that early in the meeting, Ogden, the scientist, tries to motivate the proceedings by calling up the unencouraging figures of the latest census, a revelation that apparently blew past the assembled bureaucrats; they had not gathered to talk about peripheral issues. The state game agency was in a funk—not surprising for an institution of acute political sensitivity in the midst of a policy uproar, commanded by five political appointees, most of whom hadn't the foggiest notion about the technical aspects of the issue they were supposed to judge. For guidance, they had on one side a howling mob and an advisory council they had appointed in a moment of panic to advise them against hands-on recovery, and on the other side an executive director who had to ponder what advice his five bosses might think acceptable. In predicaments like this, there are powerful pressures on decision makers to abandon biological advice and row off in their lifeboats, leaving the endangered resource to sink.

Nothing could better illustrate the ill-suitedness of the modern game commission to face a complex endangered species challenge. Admittedly, the condor controversy was an atypical monster, as anyone who has ever looked out at an angry crowd of citizens will realize. No game commission had seen anything like it since the days of deer irruptions earlier in this century. The anti-hunting controversies of the 1970s and early 1980s were mild (and brief) by comparison. But game commissions nowadays can be rendered ineffective by any venture that threatens to disrupt the balance of normative relations between the executive director, the appointed commissioners and their assorted volatile constituencies. In a controversy, the commissioners, being laymen, will be unsure of their technical ground, but quite sure that an angry multitude is in need of appeasement.

The tumultuous speaking circuit of Ogden and Snyder, who endlessly repeated the reasons for hands-on research (other scientists in California contributed also in interviews, articles and statements) were shifting the public stance toward hands-on—which redounded to the further discomfort of the hapless Game Commission which didn't know which way to turn. The activities of Ogden and Snyder amounted to a rough-and-ready public education program (a trying one) which was, perhaps, now paying off.

Ogden's summary reveals an apparent maneuver incubating in the central office in Sacramento, whereby the commissioners might be persuaded to give the condor team permission to capture condors without fooling with those infernal permits. An "administrative procedure" it's called. Apparently what happened in the July meeting was that the Game Commission, desirous of getting out of the controversy by any expedient, drifted with the urging of its Advisory Council a few exploratory yards from hands-on, unaware that public opinion had been shifting the other way. But, in September, realizing they were swimming against the

current, officials were trying to turn about. Neither the pleas of the scientists nor the urgings of the advisory council had any controlling importance in this process. They were viewed as the intermediaries of opposing pressure groups. The vital interests of the state agency were not at stake in the condor fracas; it was simply trying to extricate itself.

The Audubon contingent was trying to exert pressure by threatening to pull out (a most distasteful alternative) and leave the agencies to the mob. The agencies were calling what they hoped was a bluff—but as gently as possible. And why did the Fish and Wildlife Service now seem to be in the corner with the California Game Commission? I should point out that the Department of Interior was at this time directed by a political appointee who fervently believed that the federal government should not bully the states. He had appointed a like-minded type as his Undersecretary to oversee the Fish and Wildlife Service. The Undersecretary just happened to have been formerly affiliated with the state game agency in California. And Robert Jantzen, head of the Fish and Wildlife Service, was a former executive director of the state game agency in Arizona.

Ogden, by this time, like every other biologist associated with the program, was in a state of pungent exasperation. Condors were declining; he wanted to get out of politics and get to work, but couldn't move. He sent his superiors a careful appreciation of the condor's prospects and stated his usual clear recommendations as to what should be done. His ire was directed at immediate and visible obstacles: Jantzen and Fullerton, but I believe these were only symptoms of a widespread institutional weakness. The state game agencies have become incapable of functioning effectively outside their customary routine tasks. The social milieu today is not the same that forged them, and the novel exactions of small population biology have pushed the technical and operational requirements of wildlife management into a new dimension, but the game commissions have not been able to follow. Lastly, notice that Ogden's advice to his superiors included an analysis that would rarely be seen in a land-management agency. He attempted to define the conditions for success and recommended terminating the operation if they could not be met. The bureaucratic impulse in such an impasse is to go on doing something, without evaluating its chances.

The Washington meeting ended with no commitment from the California delegation, and of course the agency staffers who had flown there were not empowered to make one. Again, Russell Peterson acted decisively; he called Charles Fullerton and told him Audubon was ready to pull out. The two men arranged to meet quietly for a parley. From New York, Peterson took a plane west, and Fullerton flew east; they met in a conference room at O'Hare airport in Chicago. Unbeknownst to Fullerton, Ogden was also in Chicago having flown in the day before to brief Peterson.

Ogden waited in a hotel room staring at the ceiling. The meeting would shortly determine the direction his life would take. And while the outcome could not guarantee condor survival, it could, he believed, seal the bird's extinction. He had gone to California with high hopes and a strong sense of mission, facing the supreme challenge of a career. He had carried with him a plan for saving one of the nation's most endangered birds, only to encounter public hostility and bureaucratic irresolution as the recovery program became entangled in controversy and red tape. Now he longed for it to be over, and yet he didn't want it to be over. He resented the loss of two years of his professional life and didn't want to waste more time, but he was sure the condor would die out if National Audubon withdrew. The California agency had neither the budget nor the talent to carry on the work. Given time, it might acquire the money and hire the specialists, but here I interject my own view. It is improbable that either the state agency or the Fish and Wildlife Service would resolutely beat into a storm of protest, and they were incapable of fashioning an educational instrument to overcome it. The program would have continued in some form, but it would have been a money-wasting charade.

Advance

When the airport meeting ended, Peterson phoned Ogden to give him the news: Fullerton had made a genuine plea to stay in the program; it was absolutely clear that he did not want Audubon to pull out. Peterson had digested this message, and said that he wanted to finish the job, but that working conditions had become impossible. Fullerton promised to do everything he could to bring the commissioners around to loosening the permit restrictions so the program could get back to speed. Ogden hung up the phone and lay back to stare at the ceiling again. Next morning, he headed back to California.[47]

A pivotal event in the direction of the recovery program took place about this time in Santa Barbara at a meeting called by Charles Fullerton. Noel Snyder believes that Fullerton's objective in calling the meeting was to redirect the program to habitat conservation and have done with the hands-on projects, but it didn't work out that way. For the first time, proponents of all positions came together to interact in a broad review of strategy. The advocates for hands-on, armed with charts and graphs showing the downward slide of survival hopes, won many supporters that day, leading to an important shift in attitudes.[48] At this juncture, the scientists were making a do-or-die drive to salvage the recovery program. While Ogden was lobbying in Washington, Noel Snyder threw caution to the winds and, against specific orders from his superiors, lobbied commissioners of the state game agency directly (subsequently, pressures were brought to have him fired). Governor Brown had recently picked replacements—with non-traditional qualifications—for the Game Commission, who proved to be receptive to the scientists. Snyder's

initiative opened a direct channel to the agency policy makers, eliminating Charles Fullerton as the sole line of information to them.[49]

A few weeks after the Chicago meeting, John Ogden stared out of a blind, seething with frustration. Two condors were feeding on his bait. The permit restrictions still had not been changed. (We may surmise that the Commissioners had quashed the "administrative procedure" proposal—a prudent decision if you think about it.) Ogden couldn't fire. Another embellishment to the program consisted of a game agency employee who was assigned to keep the research scientists under surveillance to insure they complied with the permit. Since the death of the condor chick the researchers were not trusted. On a hill a mile away the agency man was glued to his telescope. Like Ogden, he stared intently at the two feeding condors. Ogden and his team had been waiting in the blind for six numbing weeks. Now, against all odds, two condors had arrived in net range at the same time.

In addition to the permit restrictions, the researchers had been required to draft protocols for various operational procedures. The netting standards for example decreed that the cannons would not be fired when any bird (condor or otherwise) was near to where the weighted edge of the net would land. Also, the cannon would not be fired when a condor was in the head-up position, but only when it was feeding with the head down. Most of the these rules were security precautions, and they were sometimes carried to extremes, but all had been necessary to get the recovery program moving again.

Ogden glared out at the condors. Weeks in a blind, and he couldn't fire because the permit would not allow two condors to be captured simultaneously. He watched the two birds nonchalantly feeding in what might be the twilight of their existence as a species. He thought of the two futile years strung out behind him, going from one emotional public meeting to another, always with the gnawing awareness that time was running out. The two condor heads were bobbing: one up, then the other; then both up; then both down. And then, with the electric trigger clenched tightly in his hands and with the agony of months of frustration welling up against his sense of legal restraint, Ogden did it!

In an exhilarating, ear-splitting roar, sixteen-hundred square-feet of cotton netting blasted out of the cannon barrels and over the feeding condors. A mile away, the newly hired Game Commission employee grimaced in horror through his telescope as the net flashed silently over the bait like a great hand, preceding by a moment the reverberating roar of the detonations reaching his ears from the valley floor. Mouth agape, he saw two endangered condors struggling in the aftermath of a permit violation he was charged with preventing. In a fright he jumped in his vehicle and headed for the nearest telephone at a rural gas station five miles away

to call headquarters in Sacramento. In the instant required in the blind for despair to be transformed into elation, Ogden and his veterinarian were out and running for the net; he had two condors. Hang the consequences!

The sequel was anti-climatic. The state employee was not fired (as he later confessed to Ogden he feared he would be). From the gas station telephone he was put straight through to Fullerton. There was a moment of silence as the drector pondered this disturbing new challenge. He then rendered a Solomonic decision: he instructed his man to go back and tell Ogden to put a radio-transmitter on one condor and release the other one so as to retro-comply with the permit.[50]

In the ponderous manner of game commissions, the California agency began to move. Over the next year it inched forward to loosen restrictions, presumably moving as fast as it dared, keeping a wary eye on mellowing public opinion. Each small step required another public hearing. The recovery program, as it had been originally conceived, was back on track before the end of 1983. The intensive monitoring of condor nests revealed some unexpected causes of mortality. In 1982 two condor parents, during a squabble over who would sit on their egg, knocked it over a cliff ledge. A second egg was then laid, but it was eaten by ravens when left unattended.[51] Also, the scientists began to suspect that the extreme sensitivity of condors to human presence, postulated by Carl Koford, may have owed something to the closeness of his blind to the nest he was watching. Koford's field notes tell that he was 100 to 150 yards from a cave entrance and not well-hidden in the blind. The improved optical equipment of the 1980s enabled blinds to be 800 to 1200 yards distant from the nest.[52]

Critique, Phase One

A review of the condor rescue, beginning in the early 1970s, shows a familiar slow-motion start. Biologists in the field seem to have reasoned by 1975 that so-called radical measures would be needed, but five years passed before operations began. This can be partly attributed to the newness of recovery programs; the administrative and fiscal mechanism was not matured; but it can also be accredited to the reluctance of land-management agencies to tackle a disruptive issue. The actions might have been no swifter even if the Fish and Wildlife Service had been in a more advanced state of readiness. One wonders if the agency would have moved at all if the National Audubon Society had not stepped in. The most vulnerable link in the official chain was the Game Commission, with its acute sensitivity to passions in California. The initial granting of permits in 1980 shows that the agency was not set against hands-on recovery, but it became thoroughly intimidated. In other programs reviewed in this book, the stolid, self-protective conservatism of land-management officialdom has been the primary obstacle to a rational strategy for endangered species. However, in California there was no initial

resistance from the bureaucracy other than simple inertia. No official sensed a direct threat to his tribe from the proposed recovery measures, aside from the expected controversy—against which all hoped to be buffered by the National Audubon Society. There was no fundamental disagreement as to what should be done; all the agencies accepted the remedial package presented to them.

A proprietary and intensely emotional public became the biggest impediment. It must have seemed to the harried researchers that the reactions they encountered were something peculiar to the California mentality, but it is instructive to glance back across the continent where very similar emotions were being expressed (though in less crippling form) in Florida, following the death of a panther during a capture in 1983. The reaction in California may have been an intensive expression of more widespread, and possibly still-evolving, attitudes that could work to the detriment of programs elsewhere. For this reason it is worth trying to identify the elements of the animosity to hands-on. The complex of California attitudes was thoroughly documented, leaving a mine of material for analysis.

As mentioned earlier in the chapter, three principal reasons can account for the intensity and duration of the reaction. First, a long-standing predisposition against capture may have been molded as far back as 1953. Secondly, the opponents of hands-on were no doubt given confidence by prestigious opinion-leaders: a wildlife scientist whose name had become synonymous with condor protection, and a well-known and articulate environmental leader. And there were some other prominent scientists in California who seemed to have lined up with local opinion. Among them were Ray Dasmann[53] and Paul and Ann Erlich.[54] Professional ornithologists in the United States overwhelmingly endorsed the hands-on strategy, but that did not sway local opinion, at least not in the beginning. A third factor that may have been interwoven into the fabric of opinion was the moralistic attitude toward animals which is stronger on the Pacific coast than anywhere else in the country.[55] Moralistic sentiment would have melded with Koford's promotion of the idea that condors were physiologically and psychologically fragile, and with the appeal of the "naturalistic" methods of study characteristic of an earlier era.

It is interesting in this regard to examine the attitude that dictated which procedures were acceptable for condor recovery as against those judged to be wrong. The arguments seem to be keyed to certain buzz words that have come into currency with a popular environmental awareness and perhaps with the emergence of the animal rights movement. The argot of hands-off was keyed to such terms as "wild, wilderness, natural, ecosystem and free." The alternative of hands-on was linked to terms like "captivity, artificial, artifact and incarceration." This complex was interlaced with a streak of romanticism which favored watching, dreamy-eyed and remorseful, while the condors flew off into the sunset. The romantics were bothered

particularly by "science, technology, gadgets," that sort of thing. Radio-telemetry was deemed abhorrent.

Looking further, the condor issue might be usefully set in an even broader historical context. The controversy can be seen as a variation on a theme in the history of American wildlife management—an emotional public response to a new policy believed to be harmful to the wildlife resource being managed. It is like the resistance to earlier changes in deer management policies. Four elements are common to both situations: 1) the need for new so-called "radical" policies as a result of changed environmental circumstances; 2) the attempt by scientists working from a new base of knowledge to implement the unconventional new policies; 3) the resulting conflict with a perception that regarded the proposals as a threat to the animal; 4) the intimidating pressure of the outcry on the bureaucracy. The theme is now being enacted in another setting. Wildlife environments are being altered in a way that threatens the survival of the animals; there is a need for new assessments and "radical" new policies to counter novel threats. But redesigned policies, based on changed conditions and a new scientific discipline, are meeting resistance—not only from the public—but from the bureaucracy as well.

To find a comparable situation to that of the California condor, with features to highlight for analysis, we can return to the "Crime of '43" in Wisconsin, mentioned in Chapter 8. The two controversies differ in that the earlier one centered on a game animal rather than an endangered species. They were similar in that scientists believed an unpopular policy was essential to prevent dire consequences (fatal in the condor case), and that the policy represented a consensus of scientific thinking. It is also similar in that, to the protective layman, it appeared the outcome would be the opposite to that desired. The two predicaments are also alike in that the scientists advocating the policies were subjected to prolonged public anger, but could not alter their stance, being convinced that it was correct. Aldo Leopold was even more isolated in his struggle than Ogden and Snyder, who were aware of the strong institutional and scientific support behind them, albeit at a distance removed from the arena of conflict. Leopold had only the distant moral support of his widely scattered professional colleagues in the field of wildlife management. Also, while Ogden and Snyder were the executors of an unwanted policy, Leopold had the more daunting task of trying to forge a policy in the face of a fierce resistance.

Perhaps some lessons for the future can be drawn from these comparisons. First is the proprietary public feeling about wildlife and its political ramifications; it follows that public education is critical to the rational management of wildlife—no matter what the goal of management. A policy cannot advance until the community is willing to accept it, and policies that affect animals are coming to be among the most emotionally charged in the urbanized nations of the western world. Secondly, the two situations were not aberrant instances of conflict; they were each

related to larger events and widespread attitudes of the time, although they may have derived an intensity or a flavor from the local setting. In Florida there was a similar reaction to the capture death of a panther, but not nearly so strong nor so debilitating as in California. There have since been other emotional eruptions in that state in response to perceived threats to animals. An outcry arose over a proposal in 1987 for a controlled harvest of pumas which had been protected for years and were coming to be a nuisance. An organization sprang up to block the hunt. The puma is in no immediate danger in California.

A third lesson to seek is an understanding of why the policies ultimately prevailed. Again there are parallels. First, the policy positions were solid; there were no serious flaws in them; they carried the weight of the best scientific thinking of the day. In any rational debate they could easily be defended. Second, the agencies responsible for implementing the policies did not have to fight the battles alone. In both the cases considered here, the institutional arrangements featured supporting independent entities: the National Audubon Society in the case of the condor; in Wisconsin it was the Conservation Commission which, of course, was vulnerable, but found a measure of strength in the clear thinking, iron will, energy and communicative skills of Aldo Leopold. Leopold had the character and professional qualifications that, if institutionalized in the appointment of modern game commissioners, might infuse vigor and renewed purpose into the decadent institutions—a subject to be developed in Chapter 18.

In both affrays the managing institutions faltered for a time. The situation in California in the 1980s was retrieved more quickly than in Wisconsin, in the 1940s, where there was no *Deus ex machina* like the National Audubon Society to appear from offstage and move the action forward. Consequently, Wisconsin required years of education before the new policies could be put into practice. And this brings us to a fourth lesson: the ability of the proponents of a well-thought-out policy, backed by sound scientific opinions (and a prestigious scientific body in the condor case), to articulate the policy position and to repeatedly advocate it over an extended period, thereby eventually discrediting the weaker arguments of their opponents. Leopold's writings offer testimony to his gifts as a communicator; Susan Flader, in her book, *Thinking Like a Mountain*, tells of his industry in promoting deer herd reductions in Wisconsin. Leopold understood that educating the public in wildlife ecology must be constantly pursued at every level.

> Although Leopold thought the commission ought not to yield to public opinion on the issue of herd reduction, he was not unconcerned about the problem of gaining favorable public opinion. Indeed, he himself wrote article after article for the *Wisconsin Conservation Bulletin*, national outdoor magazines, and local newspapers; he gave countless talks on the deer

problem to everyone from 4-H clubs and freshman engineers to the Society of American Foresters; he painstakingly explained the facts of deer irruptions to hundreds of bewildered or irate, often abusive, correspondents, granting each the courtesy of a direct, personal reply; and he gratefully acknowledged what few letters he received from supporters.[56]

Ogden and Snyder wrote about condor issues and policy. The articulate, carefully crafted arguments of John Ogden give evidence of his writing skills, and he appears never to have dodged an occasion to present the case for hands-on. Even in the most emotional forums, the hands-on proponents were there to argue their position. Although it may not have been evident at the time, it is likely that this persistence contributed to gaining public acquiescence in the recovery strategy. And this brings us to the fifth lesson: when the data have been analyzed and a solid, defensible base created for a policy, the final and often decisive—but also the most fortuitous—element in any conflict is the will of key proponents and their determination to persevere.

A distillation of reasons for winning through in the condor program can be stated as follows: 1) The best science available at the time was applied to a plan and endorsed by a reputable professional society (it might be worth noting that the planners, in part, were geographically remote from the scene and, thus, unsusceptible to any provincial bias). 2) The basis for the management decisions were clearly stated and available for peer review. 3) A strong supra-agency entity was available to override friction from the agencies. 4) As for the human factor: qualified, determined individuals occupied key positions, and the rough-and-ready public educational program they undertook (of necessity) may have been the decisive factor. Absent any of these strengths, and the obstacles might have been insurmountable. Overall, it was a fine piece of professional work.

Phase Two

In 1983-1984 the condor research design came at last to fruition. Radio-tagging revealed no impairment to free-flying birds (ultimately three of nine with radios died, while 12 of 15 without transmitters would disappear).[57] Closely monitored nests confirmed double-clutching as a behavioral routine, easing the way for authorization to remove eggs. And then the possibilities for replacement clutching became dizzying, when a condor pair laid a third egg after breaking their second one, during a domestic squabble at a nest from which the first had been removed.[58] By the end of 1983 nine birds were in captivity; radio transmitters had been affixed to another seven (nine were carrying transmitters by the end of 1984)[59] and would yield more information on daily activity over the next two years than in the previous 40 the bird had been studied.[60] Radio signals from condors identified

the 13,000-acre Hudson Ranch—slated for housing development—as a feeding site. Lobbying in Washington by the National Audubon Society soon brought forth appropriations for its acquisition.

Anticipating that inflowing data would, over time, illuminate the causes of mortality, and that growth of the captive flock could be speeded, the recovery team plotted a future to accommodate its swelling optimism. In July 1984 a revised recovery plan outlined an early release schedule that would start reintroducing the fledged offspring from each captive family, as soon as five of its members had been secured for a founder stock. The goal was to get 32 breeding adults into zoos; the captive flock would then be used to enlarge the wild population through releases.[61]

But the iron laws that rule small populations take no account of human aspirations. This fleeting illusion of progress was overtaken by catastrophe in the winter of 1984-1985, when six of 15 known birds in the wild vanished. The first inkling of this dramatic loss had come in January 1985, when researchers scouting nesting territories found only single adults in most of them. The death of the wild birds was magnified by its demographic impact; the six deaths reduced five breeding pairs to one.[62] Further losses could not be prudently be tolerated, and in March a suggestion for capturing the remaining wild condors was put forward; it was opposed by some who felt more time was needed to be sure the missing birds were dead. But pressure was now building to bring the free-flying birds in.

The case for total capture gained support in April 1985, when several population geneticists concluded that the limited numbers of captive founders could not guarantee long-term survival of the species. These theoretical postulations were buttressed shortly thereafter by sampling the genetic makeup of most of the remaining condors. Genetic diversity was judged very low in comparison with other bird species that had been studied.[63] At this juncture, in June 1985, there were 16 birds in captivity and 9 in the wild.[64] Sex ratios were unbalanced in both segments: most wild birds were male; most captives female. This asymmetry might have been corrected by capturing some birds while releasing others (it was put forward as an option), but the vulnerability of wild birds had been too grimly demonstrated to win the approval of an early release for the captives.

In the beginning, condor rescue had been stymied by a wave of opinion more passionate than informed. The prompt actions wanted in a crisis had been blocked, leaving prospects for deliverance vulnerable to the remorseless erosion of time. Later, as the optimism of 1984 began unraveling in 1985, the counsel of the technically informed diverged into opposing camps.

The recovery concept featured, simultaneously, intensive research to uncover and correct the causes of decline while withdrawing some birds to captivity as a hedge against disaster. The prescription was imbedded in official thinking and had lost none of its fervor during the months of delay which idled the frustrated researchers. All the principals were not uniformly receptive to the radical turnabout in thinking now gaining adherents, which urged sacrificing the field work to safeguard the entire gene pool. Studying the endangered bird in its threatened habitat promised the best chance for learning the causes of decline and for spotting foraging sites, and for planning reintroduction. Arguments for leaving some birds in the wild thus centered on this pivotal role of research. It was also argued that the absence of birds in the wild would deflate the prospects for land acquisition (the Office of Management and Budget was not enthusiastic about buying the Hudson Ranch).[65]

Noel Snyder was perhaps best-known of the proponents of capturing all condors. His advocacy was not in accord with his agency's position (he would soon be out of the Fish and Wildlife Service), nor with that of the National Audubon Society. The condor committee of the American Ornithologists' Union also apparently took the side of leaving some birds in the wild.[66] The California Game Commission, for its part, voted in June 1985 to terminate the field studies and bring in all condors.

I believe, in the afterlight provided by the near-loss of the black-footed ferrets (Chapter 15) and the loss of the dusky seaside sparrow (Chapter 16), that between these options of desperation, wisdom argued on the side of bringing in all condors. The principle is to err on the side of caution. The field research would have been interrupted, and the already difficult prospects for acquiring more habitat would have worsened, but would not have inevitably been doomed. The captive population could in theory be increased to any size; it could perhaps be made large enough to compensate for the high attrition rate that might be anticipated upon reintroduction—a prospective rate of loss that might have been alleviated by knowledge gained from carrying on with the field research. And with all birds in captivity, the moment of reintroduction would likely be reached sooner, since production rates could be multiplied, and eggs and chicks protected. Whereas if condor numbers dropped below the threshold of terminal inbreeding (there could be no assurance that it had not already), it would all be over. In choosing the course of least risk, the demographic and genetic threats made the most ruthless demands.

In June the Fish and Wildlife Service agreed to capture three free-flying birds. In August the agency agreed to take three more and to capture them all if another wild bird died. However, authorization for the captures was delayed until

October by threatened legal action from the National Audubon Society. In that month a compromise was reached, involving a possible release of three condors in the spring of 1986. In November, an international vulture symposium was held in Sacramento where, it is reported, a resolution was adopted favoring the capture of all wild condors as soon as possible.[67]

However, the release idea was preempted when five eligible condors held by the Los Angles Zoo were turned out of pre-release isolation, thereby fostering an association between food and keepers to whom the birds had been exposed (a situation to be avoided with birds destined for release).[68] Charges of sabotage were leveled at the Los Angles zoo by National Audubon and the Fish and Wildlife Service. The zoo's actions have since been defended by Noel Snyder in an article coauthored with his wife. The Snyders charged that the National Audubon Society and the Fish and Wildlife Service, in proposing to release condors, turned their backs on plans previously agreed to, and "it came as a total surprise to everyone in California (including ourselves). . . . In accordance with planning documents adopted only a few months earlier by the Recovery Team, the USFWS, the GFC and the NAS, these birds clearly did not meet the criteria for release and were to be used instead for captive breeding. Following the unanimous reaffirmation of this policy at the Recovery Team Meeting of April 1985, there was no reason to continue prerelease conditioning."[69]

The administrative grounds of this rationalization are impeccable, but another point of view might be useful to ponder. The recovery plan had been modified several times as perceptions were altered by events. If zoo officials knew that changes (which they found odious) had been set in train (Noel Snyder stoutly asserts they did not and characterizes allegations that they did as slander),[70] they might also have realized they could act in accordance with existing policies to cancel unwanted ones that were impending. Zoo officials undoubtedly acted in a way they believed best for condor recovery, but which, it must be admitted, also happened to coincide with the vested interests of their institution.

Snyder and Snyder, in the introduction to their article, mused that "the condor is not the last endangered species that will be driven to the wall, and a thoughtful review of these matters may help avoid problems for other efforts in the future."[71] One thought (on zoos) is that, while zoological institutions will have an indispensable role to play in the struggle to maintain biological diversity, they have the potential to become one more vested interest, acting independently of the policy-making machinery at the center, adding a centripetal pull to the several that are poised to bring anarchy and paralysis to the administration of recovery programs. A zoo's sense of its own interests may be too binding to permit a detached analysis. (Need I add that the same can be said of the land management agencies?) Indeed, the unrestrained political manipulations of the Greater Los Angeles Zoo Associa-

tion, throughout the condor affair, to install and keep the Los Angeles zoo at center stage were remarkable.

In December 1985 the Fish and Wildlife Service came around to the position that all condors should be in captivity with no releases until numbers were substantially increased. The policy change was in keeping with an apparent trend among scientists, but it has been speculated by one commentator that the policy reversal was imposed by political pressure. "This decision was reached following a great deal of high-level consultation in the Interior Department, possibly involving the President [a Californian] and probably responding to more or less subtle pressures from GLAZA [the Greater Los Angles Zoo Association] but with virtually no consultation outside the department with NAS or with the field staff operating the recovery effort."[72]

The National Audubon Society filed suit to obtain an injunction against capturing the last birds. The Greater Los Angeles Zoo Association and the Zoological Society of San Diego threatened counter litigation, and the condor recovery program was once again transformed into a political circus. Mayor Tom Bradley supported GLAZA, pleading that "the voices of the People of California not be silenced by Washington D.C."[73] The court injunction was overturned later in the year, and the last wild condor was captured on Easter Sunday, 1987.

Critique, Phase Two

We will probably not see a more tempestuous exercise in rescuing an imperiled organism than the one staged in California in the 1980s. If any good can be attributed to the near-ruinous turbulence, it was in bringing out shadowed obstacles that may lie in wait for programs to come—that might have passed unnoticed in a calmer environment. In Florida we have seen the resistance by field researchers to withdrawing any panthers for a captive population (it will be seen again in Chapter 19). A generic lesson is that recovery programs that muddle along unguided by a thoroughgoing doctrine that has been sanctified by scientific consensus are prey to the sometimes disharmonious interests and ideals of institutions and other collectives brought together in the affair. If these entities fall into contention, they will separately strive by any path of influence, political or juridical, to turn the program in a favored direction. In the first phase of condor recovery, the strength of scientific consensus prevailed against a popular opinion that ran strongly in opposition. In the second phase, when scientific consensus dissolved at the center, policies were toppled into in a roiling political arena, there to be fought over.

In such turmoil, with players on both sides intensely committed and propelled by a sense of urgency, any participant with convictions is likely to be

drawn into the infighting. Anyone linked to a political force can be tempted to use it to vanquish (or banish) proponents of another view. An environment is created where officials who air convictions risk getting trampled underfoot (or even hazard their careers). When views on policy cannot prevail in the forum, the courts and the political backstage beckons. Scientists in the condor fracas, whose research skills were cooperatively needed to lead the way to recovery, were pulled to rival sides of the contest, gravitating to any force likely to sympathize with their prescription, there to intrigue against one another. And the unhealthy climate of recovery operations, from the beginning, can be inferred from the evidence of currents flowing below the surface. The maneuvering is poorly documented, but significant; the shenanigans mentioned in this chapter are only the tip of an iceberg. Clearly this is a model to avoid if resources in the future are to be best used in preserving biological diversity. Decisions abandoned to the political arena fall prey to all manner of sectarian interests.

Earlier chapters have lamented the frequent disregard (or disdain) by public and bureaucracy of technical expertise when it was available to serve wildlife management, but laymen cannot be faulted for acting on intuition when scientists cannot agree on policy. A solution will have to come from the scientific community. The scientific consensus that carried the management proposals through the turmoil of the first phase of condor recovery, ended in a confrontation over choosing to capture all birds or leaving some in the wild. In this early recovery experience, the scientists had not thought the matter through to unpalatable contingencies, and there was no coherent management doctrine for managing small populations—no authoritative standard to guide programs and by which to judge them.

A doctrine is needed and will require a broad stamp of scientific approval to muster public support and compel bureaucratic compliance. Desperation tactics should be devised in advance, as is the case in some team sports for the closing moments of a game when a team is behind. The tactics are founded on the statistical probabilities of risk in various tactical options, and the participants are schooled in the need to employ them if the game is going badly in the late moments. The discipline of small population biology now offers a theoretical basis for devising criteria that can weigh at any juncture, the need for further research against the probabilities of extinction through declining numbers. A prepared doctrine, bearing the prestige of approval by professional scientific associations, should be presented to the Fish and Wildlife Service with a recommendation that it be used to guide programs. As an administrative tool, it could be mandated for inclusion in recovery plans. This subject will be elucidated in Chapter 18.

The California condor is not safe yet. The expertise and the money are there, and a staff is at work. The remaining condors are in captivity, protected from the indifferent vicissitudes that can ravage large populations and exterminate small

ones. Eventually they will be released into the wild for one more try at survival. Two overwhelming questions remain. The first is: will there be an adequate habitat? Land use policies in California will decide. It can only be hoped that some of the energy of citizen groups that was poured into the struggle against a hands-on recovery program will be directed at working to ensure that the condor will have a habitat when it returns. The second question regards the effect that years of reduced numbers in the condor population have had on its genes; it has been suggested that the bird may already be doomed.[74] The question can only be answered by time, and perhaps not with certainty for a very long time. But if the suggestion proves out, the condor could have been biologically extinct as Ian McMillan pondered the causes of its decline, or as young Carl Koford tramped the backcountry with his rucksack and binoculars nearly a half-century ago. The insidious effects of inbreeding would not have been observed, nor suspected.

Chapter 15

THE BLACK-FOOTED FERRET

If such a mess can be made of efforts to save a creature as attractive as the black-footed ferret in a country as well organized and prosperous as the United States, prospects for conservation in other parts of the world are indeed bleak.

Robert May
Nature, 1986

A bureaucratic misadventure featuring the black-footed ferret illustrates anew the folly that ensues when a conservative institution finds itself in uncharted waters. The performance of the Wyoming Game Commission was no worse than those of other agencies set forth in this book, but the outcome was dramatic. Most of the agencies thus disoriented have avoided muddling away the resource—at least so far (the Fish and Wildlife Service excepted: it lost the dusky seaside sparrow). However, the Wyoming Game Commission came close. It held every advantage in the way of expert advice, excellent field research teams and captive breeding facilities at its disposal, but the agency could not see past its traditional blinders.

The now familiar black mask across the ferret's face has endowed the small mammal with a special charm. The only ferret native to North America is a nocturnal predator, dependent on prairie dogs for food; it also shelters in their burrows and there raises its young. It will take other prey, opportunities arising, but it is best suited to catching prairie dogs, most of which are probably killed underground. Although ferrets were once common and widespread, their nocturnal and subterranean habits concealed them. By the time our culture matured to an interest in preserving ferrets, and mastered the techniques to understand them, we had nearly ended their existence.

The credit for discovering the animal for science goes to two famous naturalists: John Audubon and John Bachman. They described it as a species from a skin given to them by a trapper in Fort Laramie in 1851.[1] The domain of the black-footed ferret once stretched from Alberta and Saskatchewan to Texas. A half-million of them may have lived on the western prairies in 1920.[2] In 1931 statutory

authority for the federal government to "eradicate, suppress or bring under control animals thought to be harmful to agricultural crops and livestock"[3] was granted by the Animal Control Act—a law that sealed the ferret's decline. Prairie dogs fell into the category for treatment; cattlemen thought they competed with cattle for forage. As prairie dog colonies were poisoned away, the ferrets ebbed with them. Canine distemper, to which ferrets are vulnerable, was an added threat. The disease may have arrived on the continent with European man and his domestic animals and could have contributed to the decline.[4]

The first official list of endangered species in 1967 included the black-footed ferret. The only population known at the time was a small colony in South Dakota which had been discovered in 1964. The Fish and Wildlife Service monitored this colony in the field for ten years. A few were taken to the Patuxent Wildlife Research Center in Maryland for a captive breeding experiment. In 1974 the ferrets in South Dakota vanished. The captives died one by one, afflicted with diabetes mellitus, monorchidism, breeding disorders and malignant tumors, due perhaps to genetic causes, or perhaps in part to the advanced age reached in captivity.[5] And so it seemed that the final page had been turned in the story of the masked predator of the prairies.

But there was to be another chance. In 1981 a Wyoming rancher brought a dead animal he could not identify to the local taxidermist in the small community of Meeteetse; it had been killed by the rancher's dog. The taxidermist recognized the species and immediately called the Fish and Wildlife Service. Two biologists, Steve Martin and Dennie Hammer, came to investigate near the ranch and soon caught a ferret. They fitted it with a radio-collar and began checking signals at five-minute intervals; they went on for 16 grueling days. The radio eventually went dead, but not before the peregrinations of the animal wearing it led the researchers to nine others of its kind.[6] Against all odds the black-footed ferret still lived.

The Wyoming ranchers on whose property the rediscovered creature went about its nocturnal affairs had worked their land for decades unaware of ferrets. It is a testament to the elusive nature of the species that it had been found fortuitously despite intensive searches that had been underway since the loss of the South Dakota colony in 1974. One of the searchers was Tim Clark, an adjunct professor of biology at Idaho State University, who had taken up the investigation a year before the South Dakota extirpation. When a conference on the endangered mammal had been held in that state, the Wyoming game agency apparently had no interest in participating. Clark, an expert on prairie dogs, was chosen to attend by default.[7] When the South Dakota ferrets died, Clark sought grants to make a systematic search for surviving colonies. His quest was made under the auspices of his wildlife firm: BIOTA Research and Consulting, Inc.

344

The BIOTA project had been funded from several sources. A slide series and a ferret movie were used in talks to service clubs, conservation groups and others. Clark had stumped Wyoming to lecture on ferrets and to pass out "Wanted" posters that described the species and promised a $250 reward for information leading to its rediscovery.[8] He had made an intense 25-month survey in Wyoming in 1973-1975, in which 9,000 self-addressed ferret post cards were distributed, and numerous news releases and longer articles were published in media having a combined circulation of 100,000. The publicity brought many reports but none of them led to ferrets.[9] But in 1981 ferrets were found. Tim Clark soon arrived at Meeteetse. On short notice he garnered research funds from private sources.[10] His team of researchers soon joined those of the Fish and Wildlife Service. Like the California condor recovery program, the ferret endeavor attracted an independent contingent, backed by private capital, to participate in research and to advise on management.

In February 1982 the Fish and Wildlife Service designated the Wyoming Game Commission (officially the Wyoming Department of Fish and Game) as the lead agency. The Game Commission found itself in an interesting position; it had been given responsibility for a recovery program in which it did not control the research. In addition to the team fielded by the Fish and Wildlife Service, there was an independent, highly regarded group, supported by prestigious environmental institutions, helping to assemble the data needed for conservation. To the outside observer it might seem that the Game Commission would be delighted at its good fortune; the use of time can be crucial to the rescue of a species (although land-management agencies have thus far proven to be notoriously impervious to this fact), and state game agencies are not usually fitted by their administrative or fiscal procedures (nor by temperament) to accommodate to the requirements of an unanticipated assignment. However, anyone acquainted with the psychology of state game agencies will sense that the arrangement portends trouble. An independent research team can focus exclusively on its subject, move at an expeditious tempo and make its opinions known without the slightest inhibition. This approach is precisely what a recovery program demands, but it is anathema to a land-management agency.

The Wyoming Game Commission soon mustered an ad hoc advisory body called the Black-footed Ferret Advisory Team (henceforth referred to as BFAT). Central to ferret recovery was the fact that most of the known habitat was on private ranch lands, with the bulk of it within the confines of a single ranch. BFAT was needed, because the goodwill of the landowner(appointed to BFAT) was essential. The landowner, Jack Turnell of the Pitchfork Ranch, seems to have easily made a commitment to act in the interest of the ferret—even to deferring the production of oil on his property.[11] BFAT was formed ostensibly to advise the Game

Commission. In practice it appears to have been primarily a discussion group through which the Game Commission—clearly the dominant agency—coordinated (and sought to control) all activities relating to the ferrets. BFAT included one member from an environmental organization: the National Wildlife Federation. The agencies were represented by the Fish and Wildlife Service, the Bureau of Land Management, the U.S. Forest Service and the State Land Board. There was also a representative from the University of Wyoming.

The field research initially had two broad thrusts: to census the population and define its geographical boundaries. Two methods were used: reading sign and spotlight counts. Reading sign is simply an intense search for tracks, scats or any distinctive markings made by the species of interest. It is a preliminary method that identifies zones of activity and gives an idea of the creature's abundance and movements. Prairie dogs plug their burrows to hibernate. The black-footed ferret digs into the burrows and then backs out to deposit the excavated soil in a distinctive shape that leaves unmistakable evidence of its passing. The removed soil becomes an elongated mound that can extend as much as eight feet from the burrow depending on the industry of the ferret. As the digging progresses, a trough is usually formed down the length of the mound as the ferret repeatedly moves backward, pulling more soil with its front legs. Digging increases in the winter when prairie dogs hibernate. Evidence of the excavation remains visible up to two months.[12] Snow-tracking also proved useful. The above-ground wanderings of the ferrets could be read clearly in the new-fallen snow, and each snowfall cleaned the slate, so to speak, for another revelation. Spotlight counts were made by moving about at night, probing for the reflected shine of ferret eyes with the beam of a powerful light. Within the eyes of some nocturnal mammals is a layer of crystalline cells that reflects light back to the retina, thereby enhancing vision in the dark. The spotlighted eyes of a black-footed ferret return a bright emerald green glow which can be seen at a distance of nearly 200 yards. The researchers found ferrets to be most active just after dusk and during the two hours before dawn.

Field work was daunting in the Wyoming winter. The researchers lived in the open much of the time, searching the ground intensively during the day, working their lights at night, crawling into sleeping bags on the bare ground when fatigue overcame them. By April 1982 they had plotted 275 ferret digs and had frequently sighted the animal. The zone of activity proved extensive. Surveys would eventually map 37 white-tailed prairie dog colonies spread over nearly 7,400 acres, dotted with about 125,000 burrows.[13] A census was hindered by the widely dispersed burrows, but by the spring of 1982 Tim Clark estimated the population at no fewer than 22 animals, based on track counts. The Fish and Wildlife Service stated a more conservative minimum of nine, apparently staying within the bounds of individual sightings.[14]

The research biologists looked forward to the first summer when young ferrets venture up for a look at the world above ground. The eyeshine of the young is set apart by an icy blue-green color.[15] They are easily found at this season, and the counting of the young discloses much about the health and fortunes of the population. A census in early August yielded a figure for adults and young combined. The August tally, repeated annually, would become the index for reading population size and trends. During 1982 the census work was still being sorted out; nevertheless, based on an incomplete survey the estimate of total numbers was put at 61.[16]

From the beginning the Wyoming Game Commission embraced caution, as state game agencies with their acute sensitivity to local opinion are wont to do. The Fish and Wildlife Service men, Martin and Hammer, who had radio-collared ferrets, were criticized for moving in haste.[17] Martin and Hammer believed data should be gathered expeditiously, an opinion shared by the BIOTA research team, but not by the Game Commission as its director of biological services made clear early in 1982. "We don't know what could happen. We do know the last ferret population that was studied doesn't exist. Nobody can tell us why it disappeared, but it did. We have to be very cautious."[18] The approach of choice by state game agencies is to move by the smallest increments (the creep approach), preferably over a period of years, when dealing with any volatile issue. But the measured tempo heretofore taught to the agencies by experience would prove no buffer against controversy and criticism in treating with the endangered ferret.

The state game agencies formed a national association in 1902.[19] The department heads annually convene to attend the matters common to their profession. It seems unlikely that the upper echelons of the Wyoming Game Commission would have been unaware of the upheaval and operational disruptions that followed the capture death of a California condor in 1980—and of a similar case with a Florida panther which would occur later, in 1983. At a black-footed ferret workshop in 1984 a Game Commission spokesman commented that "visions of past endangered species problems loomed uncomfortably over BFAT's shoulders [meaning over the Game Commission's shoulders]."[20] The agency's ingrained wariness would not have been lessened by a knowledge of angry eruptions over the death of endangered species in other states. Anyone attuned to this undercurrent could have predicted that the operational pace of the bureaucracy would not conform to advice given by independent advisors. The researchers were state-of-the-science biologists, focusing quite correctly on the biological aspects of conserving a small population. The cumbersome state agency, with a mentality shaped by the lessons of an earlier era, saw a different picture. All the bureaucratic instincts prompted caution.

By the end of 1982 the research teams had hit their stride. The Fish and Wildlife Service supplied the costly apparatus of radio-telemetry. Radio-collars were affixed to several ferrets, and the higher hills around Meeteetse sprouted antennas, mounted on trailers—hauled to Wyoming from the Denver Wildlife Research Center.[21]

As with the condor, the black-footed ferret venture would show the strengths and limitations of a private entity working in tandem with a government agency. The strengths were comparable in both situations. They consisted of adequately funded, competent professionals, with years of experience, who were specialized for the biological problem at hand; they were unfettered by the rigid structure of a bureaucratic hierarchy with its administrative and "political" constraints; they could set their own priorities and work at their own vigorous pace. The Wyoming Game Commission was not capable of financing or staffing an unexpected operation on short notice. It diverted some personnel from other duties and then set about the search for funds through legislative appropriations and by soliciting contributions from the Fish and Wildlife Service and the Bureau of Land Management. The California condor program had surged ahead (at first) when a strong private organization united with a politically weak federal agency. In Wyoming the private segment of the recovery program contributed funding and expertise, but the political backing was diffused among several organizations which were not integrated into the program as the National Audubon Society had been with the condor. The Wyoming Game Commission was politically very strong vis-a-vis the private segment.

The research attracted volunteers, most of them college students, drawn by the appeal of knowing with their hands, and eyes and hearts, what they were working to assimilate from textbooks and in classrooms. Much of the labor was routine walking and sweat, and typical pen and notebook tedium, but there were also the elevating moments of discovery and transcendence. There was the first truck ride of anticipation through the dark, stopping to follow the traversing searchlight beam across the sagebrush-dotted flats, and driving slowly on to stop again and sweep the light across the prairie and to sweep it back. And then the ferrets, known until now only as a sensory promise, imagined from the printed page and nurtured in the recurring dreams of day, became bright, living emeralds dancing at the end of a long lance of light, under the star-studded chill of a Wyoming night. And a threshold was crossed in the observer's life. The creatures became the perpetual captives of experience, and for those who watched the hyperactive emeralds dance closer and closer to become the small, masked mammalian forms once thought to have vanished from the earth, there could be no return to a time before ferrets.

A summer volunteer left us her impressions.

I am at the center of the light beam, the radius reaching 150 meters out into the night. The moving light is like a movie screen on which the cast of characters keeps changing: pronghorn antelope, cottontails, jackrabbits, mule deer, badgers, coyotes, deer mice, long-tailed weasels, and other night-prowling prairie inhabitants, including, at times, the black-footed ferret. . . . I may never see another ferret after this summer, or spend whole wakeful nights out on the Wyoming prairie, but I will like just knowing that they are here, and knowing that the world of darkness is at least alive and active as the world of light. . . .[22]

The volunteers entered a nonpareil wildlife class, engaged in a study of the only known remnant of a little-known species, facing a dubious future which might hinge on timely, well-directed research. Steve Forest, Louise Richardson and Tom Campbell executed much of the field work for the BIOTA team, while Tim Clark worked to keep funds flowing in. However, Clark himself had entered a class which would serve up some hard and bitter lessons—but few answers. His intimation of trouble was soon alluded to in the first of several articles he would write on dysfunction in a recovery program. It was entitled *Biological, Sociological and Organizational Challenges to Endangered Species Conservation: The Black-footed Ferret Case*. After outlining the biological and sociological themes, he touched on the countervailing pressures boiling up in Wyoming.

Many interests are focused on the Wyoming ferrets—private, national and international conservation groups, universities, and state and federal agencies. All parties in the ferret program want a model conservation and recovery effort. But there are great differences among the key actors, from ranchers to bureaucrats, and from professionals to careerists to politicians (Wilson, 1980), all with a varying organizational model of operation and greatly varying power bases. The question then becomes: how best do we organize these varying interests to meet the biological and sociological challenge? The organizational structure implemented by the state in the ongoing ferret program is diagramed by Clark (In press) and shows the formal relationships between the principal state, federal, and private interests.[23]

1983 was a hopeful year for the researchers. They were well organized now and accumulating a variety of data. The census of 1983 showed what was beginning to look like an annual yo-yo effect in numbers: a high in summer followed by a sharp

drop the next spring. The spring count of 1983 had dipped well below that of the previous August. However, the 1983 August census turned up 88 ferrets—more than the 61 estimated in the incomplete August survey of 1982. So although the figures each year bounced from a spring low to a summer high and down again, the trend was upward. It was surmised that the annual loss was partly due to the dispersal of young as they matured and began to leave their natal area. Deaths among the young were believed extremely high—as much as 85 percent. Probably none of the young ferrets that departed the study area survived, since there were no other prairie dog colonies near Meeteetse. However, dispersal aside, annual losses among small mammal populations are typically very high, but are compensated for by a high rate of replacement. Even among adults the annual mortality was estimated at 50 percent. Although the ferrets were predators, they were themselves preyed upon by owls, hawks, eagles, coyotes, foxes and badgers.[24]

The biologists were mindful that they might be analyzing the world's only remaining ferret colony. The yearly loss implied that a percentage of each summer's increment could be considered "surplus"—in the sense that their presence was not essential to the well-being of the population. Therefore, those that might be expected to perish could be taken into custody as a hedge against calamity in the wild. The captive animals could then serve as stock for reintroductions. In 1983 BIOTA brought forth a paper exploring recovery options and strongly recommending captive breeding.[25] It was based on work done by Louise Richardson, the principal author.[26] The recommendation was rejected by the Wyoming Game Commission.[27]

Tim Clark would not rest with this decision and took his case to the conservation organizations that were underwriting his research. At one of the organization's request, a meeting was called by the Wyoming Game Commission in Cheyenne in the spring of 1984 to discuss captive breeding. The assembly represented the extended network of federal and state agencies and private organizations engaged in ferret recovery.[28] On the appointed day the participants came directly to the subject. Tim Clark and his colleagues presented enough demographic data to suggest that the Meeteetse ferret colony was stable or even growing.[29]

Wildlife Conservation International, one of the private organizations, was represented by Archie "Chuck" Carr III, who had flown west with James Doherty of the Bronx Zoo. The two visitors offered, on behalf of the American Association of Zoological Parks and Aquariums (AAZPA), to arrange zoo accommodations. They hit a brick wall. The reaction of the bureaucracy was unexpected and bordered on the hostile. Carr and Doherty heard themselves categorized as "Easterners." An official barked: "I'll be damned if I'll ever see a ferret leave the state of Wyoming."[30] Wyoming wanted to build its own captive breeding facility.

Regional tensions have grown in the United States over the use of resources on federal lands—most of which are in the West, but are greatly in demand by the more populous East.[31] Pride, resentment and a majority of registered Republicans, it has been remarked, characterize the eight states of the "Mountain West" (Montana, Idaho, Wyoming, Colorado, Utah, Nevada, New Mexico and Arizona). "The people of the Mountain West are inclined to think, as Southerners once did, that they have a unique 'way of life' that sets them apart from and a bit above other regions."[32] This provincialism is no doubt well-ripened in a state land-management agency that is highly sensitive to local opinion, in a state where half the land is controlled by the feds. Of the various biologically irrelevant factors recounted in this book that have marred decisions on endangered species management, this regional hubris is one of the most outlandish. Chuck Carr was taken aback; he saw himself coming to offer assistance. State officials apparently saw covetous Easterners who wanted to pinch Wyoming's ferrets.

Some of the best zoological facilities in the world were put at the disposal of Wyoming, but its delegates were vehement that under no circumstances would they allow ferrets leave the state—and certainly not to be placed in the care of any "Easterners." So there it was. The captive breeding project would be governed under the terms dictated by a state agency. Chuck Carr's after-the-event recollection of the meeting indicates that everyone present knew the hazards in delay.[33] But if the state wildlife agency recognized the importance of time, they were unwilling to take a stitch by utilizing the zoological facilities offered them. Carr wrote: "Simultaneously they declared that their own Sybille Canyon Wildlife Research Unit [where it was intended to house the ferrets] was unsatisfactory as a captive breeding facility, an ironic viewpoint as things turned out, and they concluded that federal and/or private agencies should pay the cost of building and staffing a proper facility in Wyoming."[34]

The ironies accumulate. The stubborn states-righters in Wyoming, who found themselves with the responsibility of managing an endangered national resource, could not conceive of allowing ferrets to be housed beyond the borders of their state which itself had not mustered the necessary capital to provide for captives. The provincial attitude insisted that the money would have to come from those who did not live in Wyoming. And of course it was provided, but not in time. And once again we see the Fish and Wildlife Service—the federal agency ostensibly in charge of the nation's endangered species programs—functioning as a passive observer and a funnel for appropriations with little real say over how they will be spent.

National attention had descended on Wyoming. In addition to the provincial myopia that afflicted strategic thinking, institutional pride may have been smarting. The Game Commission heard a summons to direct a high drama,

but events were moving at a profoundly disturbing pace for the pedestrian agency. It had little control over the researchers who were causing all manner of awkwardness. Their opinions were made known without clearance from headquarters, and they were pounding the table at meetings demanding greater speed, and now departmental pride was threatened by having captive breeding removed to some faraway place. "We'd have no control over them," lamented an official."[35] The agency saw itself threatened with relegation to a subsidiary role in a prominent event and resented it. The April meeting ended with the captive breeding project in the unyielding grip of the Game Commission—which had neither the facilities nor the expertise to conduct it. The Easterners went back East, and the researchers returned to Meeteetse.

The ferrets soared to an all-time high that summer. The August census stood at 129. Prospects looked very good, but it was to prove a season of illusory optimism. The first sign of trouble had come two months before the census, not among the ferrets, but in a threat to their food supply. Sonya Ubico, a graduate student at Colorado State University, began a study of diseases in the Meeteetse prairie dog towns. She sent samples of fleas to the Center for Disease Control at Fort Collins, Colorado. When the samples returned, five of eight locations sampled tested positive for sylvatic plague.[36] An epidemic disease had hit the prairie dogs. A month later a BIOTA researcher, Steve Forrest, drove to Meeteetse. As he was standing in front of a burrow a prairie dog crawled out, went into spasms and died at his feet. Forrest walked around the prairie dog complex for three nights and did not see a single ferret.[37]

Warning lights went on in the offices of the state game agency, as seen by its reactions. A project of unprecedented scale was launched to treat prairie dog towns by dusting them with flea powder (5 percent carbaryl). A contingency plan was drawn up to capture and remove black-footed ferrets to the inadequate facilities at Sybille. Three years after this event, in 1988, a Wyoming Game Commission official would write that "arrangements were made to move, after a preliminary quarantine period, ferrets in excess of 12 to the Smithsonian Institution's Wildlife Conservation and Research Center, Front Royal, Virginia, and the Fish and Wildlife Service's Denver Wildlife Research Center."[38] This later account gives the impression that the arrangements were a fact, but the minutes of a BFAT meeting of August, 1985, leave a different impression: "a proposal . . . to send an additional group of ferrets to another facility [is] . . . under consideration—it depended on the population estimate of the Meeteetse ferrets."[39] Since the Wyoming officials had a propensity to estimate ferret numbers optimistically, it seems unlikely that these "arrangements" later remembered in 1988 progressed beyond the agency's dreamworld assessments prior to 1985. In any case the 1988 account informed that "because ferrets were not shown to be adversely affected by plague, these contingency plans were not implemented."[40]

In the summer of 1985 only 58 ferrets could be accounted for during a census by BIOTA and the Fish and Wildlife Service. The evidence strongly suggested fewer ferrets than the previous summer when 129 had been tallied, and it would have been reasonable to anticipate a decline. If the ferret prey base was afflicted with an epidemic disease, the predators would not be expected to escape the impact. During the 1985 census, many of the ferrets had been seen only once, unlike in past years when once located they could be found night after night.[41] In August, BIOTA, in yet another report, argued in the strongest terms for withdrawing ferrets from the wild. The need for urgency rings through its strident sentences.

> Captive breeding ferrets is the single best recovery option. In 1983, towards such an objective we prepared . . . *some options.* . . . In 1984, we stated at the April Cheyenne meeting that 10-12 ferrets should be taken into captivity that fall. Again, this recommendation was repeated at the Laramie Ferret Workshop: "Ferrets should be transplanted via a captive breeding program immediately. . ." and "The single ferret population is currently highly vulnerable to extinction. This fact alone has significant implications for species recovery including the timely implementation of captive breeding/translocation efforts which we recommend should begin this fall. . . ." Dr. Mike Bogan, USFWS, at the same conference said. . . "We should begin now to remove a few 'test' animals to captive situations." To date these recommendations have been rejected. In 1985, again we recommend ferrets (6 or more) be taken for captive rearing (and not just holding).[42]

BIOTA's 1985 census had been completed on August 6. However, others went on searching for several weeks, sighting more ferrets. About these latter findings: in a BFAT meeting on August 29, a spokesman for the Wyoming Game Commission is credited with saying that "the survey performed after BIOTA's effort resulted in raising the population estimate by 30 percent, which suggests that the initial effort lacked thoroughness." A BIOTA representative, Tom Campbell, countered. "The [BIOTA 1985] effort was greater [in locations] where ferrets were found in 1984. He argued that their [BIOTA] data showed [a] substantial decline in ferret numbers."[43] However, the officials insisted on an optimistic interpretation of the data. If the situation was as serious as BIOTA claimed, it would follow that some drastic actions were in order. Nothing is more abhorrent to a state game agency than the prospect of taking drastic actions.

Despite an outward aplomb, the Game Commission began inching its way in the direction of common sense. In September it pulled two ferrets out of Meeteetse, promising that four more would be taken shortly.[44] In the 1988 accounting of this episode by the Wyoming official, he states that this decision had

been taken at a meeting in Denver in May 1985. "The ferrets to be captured in the fall of 1985 were to serve as a hedge against a catastrophe befalling the single known colony of ferrets and also to serve as founder animals for a captive breeding effort."[45] However this may be, the creeping precautions being taken at last in the fall of 1985 were too late; a calamity, unseen (except indirectly via the census), was well-advanced. During the months while meetings were held and census data debated, and letters and documents were passing to and fro, ferrets were dying beneath the ground at Meeteetse.

Six ferrets were finally withdrawn to the state facility at Sybille Canyon, and in the central office it may be surmised that sighs of relief were heard. The agency had insulated itself with what it thought was insurance against disaster. Six is the rule-of-thumb minimum used by animal breeders for a founder stock. Long before an understanding of genetics, animal breeders had learned empirically that a minimum of three males and three females usually gave a reasonable insurance against inbreeding defects when starting a new herd or flock of domestic animals.[46] But the premise is that the stock from which the breeders are drawn is genetically sound. This was not a well-founded assumption with the Meeteetse ferrets; they may have been isolated for decades. Six animals is otherwise theoretical, because it assumes that the three animals of one sex will freely breed with the other three. But in some wildlife species, individuals are finicky about mates. The black-footed ferret is such a species. Females choose from among several suitors and will not necessarily accept any male that human breeders pair her with. When the Fish and Wildlife Service had tried in the 1970s to breed ferrets from South Dakota, while holding only two females and three males, one female had refused all advances from the males.[47]

Meanwhile, as these inadequate precautions were being arranged, biologists from BIOTA and the Fish and Wildlife Service went again to Meeteetse for another census, this time using a mark-and-recapture method to strengthen confidence in the finding. A limitation in the visual count is that with many species only a few individuals can be seen at any one time, so that some animals will go uncounted; others may be counted more than once. This imprecision now allowed the skeptics of urgency to interpret the data in favor of their biases. The mark-and-recapture technique makes a statistical assessment from a sample of the population that can be positively identified. Several are caught and marked in some way (in this case by small ear tags) and then freed. Subsequent random captures are made, and the population size is estimated from the ratio of marked to unmarked animals.

On September 10 the project was completed. The computations showed 31±8 ferrets. At this stage it would seem to have required an act of will for anyone watching the falling numbers to remain optimistic about the future of the Meeteetse ferrets. Further trapping on October 9 produced an estimate of 16± ferrets.[48] With

census figures plummeting downward, fast closing on zero, Wyoming officials were at last animated. They scheduled a gathering of BFAT in Cheyenne to talk over the problem—in two weeks, on October 22. An article in *Natural History* magazine tells that "for the next two weeks, all the players in what had quietly become a black-footed ferret crisis argued fiercely over the meaning of the new numbers."[49] The author says that the state officials seized on one last detail which permitted them to adopt the most sanguine view: none of the large prairie dog towns had been entirely wiped out by the plague, therefore the ferrets must still have food. The apparent drop in ferrets, they persuaded themselves, was due to the annual dispersal of young from their parent's territories. The BIOTA researchers countered with data from three previous years of study, showing that the current drop had started before the expected months of dispersal. The *Natural History* article reported that the state agency simply dismissed the dispersal data.[50] On October 11 the sixth ferret had been withdrawn to the facility at Sybille. Perhaps officials felt that security measures were now in place even if the worst happened at Meeteetse. A Wyoming Game Commission spokesman about this time is credited with the statement: "what we have here is a damned bunch of fools running around saying the sky is falling."[51] The author of the *Natural History* article lamented that four days later, at the meeting in Cheyenne, the sky landed.

It is written that early in the October 22 meeting, agency staffers were still doubting that ferrets had declined.[52] At midday, the Game Commission veterinarian arrived from the facility at Sybille to tell those assembled that one of the captives had just died of canine distemper, a second was ill, and the ferrets had not been in captivity long enough to have contracted it at Sybille. It was probable that the wild population at Meeteetse was afflicted, and since all the captives had been housed in one room, all were likely infected with the epidemic disease.[53]

And so it came about that opportunities to safeguard the world's only known black-footed ferrets were allowed to slip away, and the widely-known enterprise found itself in the most awesome crises. On this point there at last seemed to be a consensus—at least in the meeting room in Cheyenne. A generous period for rational analysis and planning had fallen victim to the self-interested delusions of bureaucrats. Salvation now was left to one last throw of the dice.

There is probably no instance of a land-management agency ever having been brought face-to-face with the consequences of its miscalculations so abruptly. But even in this extremity the cumbersome state game agency—under the direction of appointed lay commissioners who were remote from any understanding of the biological problem—could not free itself from its inhibitions and act decisively. The best hope at this juncture was an immediate move to trap any survivors. If any had avoided exposure to the disease they could be vaccinated, and it was vital to preserve whatever genetic variation remained in the surviving individuals. But

when researchers returned to Meeteetse for a final trapping expedition, they were incredulous to find that certain areas had been placed off-limits to trapping.

A review of the minutes of the eventful BFAT meeting of October 22 illuminates the incapacity of an agency coalition to act in a crises. Ulysses Seal appears in the pages of these minutes. He had been asked to Wyoming to advise the Game Commission on managing the black-footed ferret. Seal was mentioned briefly in Chapter 7. During the 1980s, Seal and a team of specialists who represent the cutting edge of the discipline of conservation biology, came to function as an endangered species fire brigade which careens from crises to crises with state-of-the-science advice on the emergency moves best calculated to avert calamity. Seal's prescriptions are usually preceded by a standard crash course on small population biology which is directed at "naive professionals," as he tactfully puts it. His compressed course of instruction is a masterful didactic exercise, but his students are at times too biologically retarded to get the hang of things, or else they are the delegates of decision-makers who are (retarded), and who fear to attend class and risk exposure to frightening new ideas. Seal's exertions are not always fruitful.

The minutes tell that, after learning of the canine distemper, Seal leaves no doubt as to the proper course.

> Seal said data suggests the entire area is exposed to the disease, and it was his conclusion that we need to consider all of the animals are at risk for exposure to the disease and from that point of view we have a 'new ball game.' Seal suggested that we bring in any surviving animals that can be captured. . . . Seal said by leaving animals in the wild and doing nothing at this point, the disease may cause total mortality of the wild population. Seal pointed out the ferret complex on a map, and suggested trying to get every ferret that can be found starting tomorrow (October 23, 1985).[54]

However, none of the agency delegates were empowered to act. The Fish and Wildlife Service representative said his agency's decision would have to be made by its (regional) director, Galen Buterbaugh. The Game Commission man says that of his agency will have to come from "Director Bill Morris and the Wyoming Game and Fish Commission." Presumably Morris will have to track down the commissioners—who are as close to (what they believe to be) the provincial opinion of Wyoming as they are distant from the assessment of Ulysses Seal—and get a reading from each of them. As the meeting adjourned, a Game Commission representative warns those from BIOTA research, not to contact the press until someone from the Wyoming Game Commission sends out a [news] release.[55]

We should assume that upon adjournment, telephones were frantically busy, although who said what to whom will probably never be known, but the outcome of the high-level pow-wow was that the desperation proposal to capture all the ferrets was denied. It can be deciphered from the oblique wording of an announcement made by the Game Commission Director, Bill Morris. At a press conference in Cheyenne on October 24, 1985, he outlined the course adopted by the Game Commission (with the concurrence of the Fish and Wildlife Service, of course).[56] Point one of Morris' announcement was that "as many ferrets as possible will be captured and removed from the area where the risk of mortality is the highest, recognizing from the start it will be impossible to capture them all. . . ." Point two was that "in two outlying areas, where ferrets may not have been exposed to the disease, all human access and activity, except normal ranching operations, will be curtailed immediately so as not to stress the ferrets or increase transmission of the disease."[57] It is hard to grasp how the latter part of the remedy relates to the malady, but Morris went on to assure all listeners that "as always, this agency's primary concern is the welfare of the wild ferret population and we are doing everything possible to protect the remaining ferrets in outlying prairie dog colonies." In plain words, the Game Commission rejected the recommendation to round up all the surviving ferrets. But alert to the potential of the crisis to generate money, the director's message ended with an appeal to citizens to "send their donation to the [Wyoming] Ferret Fund."[58]

A magazine article reported that the Wyoming Game officials insisted that a few outlying prairie dog towns be left untouched "so that the public could be assured that there were some ferrets living in the wild."[59] The researchers were given leave to catch six ferrets, again the minimum of convention for a founder stock of domestic animals. Any others would be left to cope with canine distemper—in addition to the usual causes of mortality. This decision (I can only suppose) was made to satisfy the Wyoming Game Commission's sense of what would be most likely to pacify the general mood in Wyoming. It is one more example of many related in this book, of a vital move by a government agency which lacks any biological merit whatever. It was made against the best state-of-the-science advice that could be had, but the performance is not atypical. It is a sad commentary on the state of wildlife professionalism in American land-management agencies.

In March 1986, five months after the second crisis trapping of six ferrets, BFAT convened once more. The minutes offer a glance into a bureaucratic fantasy world. First there was a dismal accounting of recent searches for evidence of ferrets. Sign had been found on three occasions in November, none at all in December, once in January and once in February. Ulysses Seal had sent to Wyoming his prescription for the crisis. This report is taken up by the participants.

Harry Harju [of the Game Commission] reviewed the rationale leading to the invitation of CBSG [Ulysses Seal and his Captive Breeding Specialists Group] to advise on the captive breeding effort. He reviewed their report of January 19, 1986, and the 14 recommendations. Basically, the recommendations are appropriate except those relating to the management of the Meeteetse wild population. The recommendation to add an adult male ferret to the captive group was not implemented because of winter weather which was either too severe (sub-zero temperatures make trapping risky) or because the lack of snow cover did not indicate the location of remaining ferrets. We are presently past the deadline for implementing the action and the addition of ferrets to the Sybille group will be postponed until August.... The recommendation concerning removal of additional ferrets from the wild lapses into management [an interesting expression] and requires more consideration. Harry said that the decision to exterminate the wild population [a Freudian slip?] will be made by the Director of the Wyoming Game and Fish Department and the USFWS Regional Director after the July/August litter survey is complete and BFAT has the opportunity to make such a recommendation. The decision will be based on scenarios for ferret numbers and distribution described in the contingency plan which is being developed. . . . Harry mentioned some of the reasoning behind resistance to put all ferret recovery options into captive breeding. He admitted that distemper affected ferret numbers but the fact that 10 of the 12 captive ferrets were not diseased when captured suggested that the disease outbreak may have been over-emphasized, in any case. Harry predicted that the pressure to capture all the wild ferrets will be extreme if the summer survey results in very low numbers. Jack Turnell [owner of the Pitchfork Ranch] described his impression of Meeteetse public opinion. He believes most Meeteetse residents would prefer that we not remove all the ferrets even if BFAT concurs with the recommendations. Harry said that the reasoning for maintaining wild ferrets may be only political and that CBSG understood that aspect of the decision. . . . Further discussion of the option to capture all the wild ferrets followed. Lyman McDonald [of the University of Wyoming] asked if the sentiment to maintain wild ferrets was very strong. Harry answered that proponents of removing all the wild ferrets were more vocal but the public reaction to removal would be difficult to predict. . . .[60]

The Game Commission is paralyzed; it is tinkering with another contingency plan; it can't move to bring in the remaining ferrets, because it doesn't know how the public might react and fears to find out. This is the message emanating from the rambling monologue of an official who in one sentence concedes that the decision is political and elsewhere makes excuses why it can't be done, or seems to be trying to convince himself that maybe it isn't necessary . . . Maybe canine distemper was "over-emphasized". . . Maybe there only seems to be a crisis. The minutes raise a suspicion that some agency biologists must realize (or at least suspect) that it would be sensible to capture the last ferrets, but the decision will not be theirs. It resides in a hierarchical realm above their heads, and it has been reached in discussions for which there are no records, but it seems plain enough that it was caused by worries about the slumbering giant of public opinion. Calculations about the survival of the endangered species were off on the side somewhere.

In a published article two months later, Tim Clark gave readers an update. State officials were belatedly entertaining expert guidance on the operation of the facility at Sybille Canyon, but they were still not accepting advice to capture more ferrets.

In short, ferret recovery, which was well along in 1984, is now highly problematic.

The Captive Breeding Specialists Group (CBSG) of IUCN [International Union for the Conservation of Nature] is now advising the WGC [Game Commission] and USFWS [Fish and Wildlife Service] on the 6 captive ferrets. Chaired by Ulysses Seal, the CBSG consists of Jim Doherty of the New York Zoological Society, Chris Wemmer of the National Zoological Park and Mike DonCarlos of the Minnesota Zoological Garden. CBSG has met three times since early December, 1985. They have significantly contributed to captive breeding efforts by reviewing WGF facilities, resources, personnel, support, and plans. They have concluded that it would be genetically desirable to have at least 20 breeders as founders of the captive population for maximum retention of genetic diversity. On this basis, and because the 2 male ferrets in captivity were immature and unlikely to breed in 1986, CBSG said "It is of highest priority that every effort be made to secure 2 adult male or young males from the wild population." This recommendation was not taken by WGF and USFWS. The CBSG estimated that the 2 immature males stood only a 10% chance of breeding success in 1986. The

results are in now and the 6 captive ferrets produced no young this year. . . .[61]

The second trapping of six ferrets had been carried out in haste, which did not permit selections based on age and sex criteria; the subsequent failure of the captive animals to produce young is believed due to the absence of sexually experienced adult males in the second group of captives.[62] It is thought that over the summer of 1986, two more juveniles and one (unconfirmed) adult ferret vanished from Meeteetse. Finally, in late 1986, a year after the population crash, the cautious agency brought in the last ferrets. There were eleven. The last was trapped in March 1987, bringing the total to 18[63]—two short of the 20 stipulated by Ulysses Seal as a desirable minimum.

Like its counterpart in the Florida panther recovery program, the Wyoming Game Commission was much concerned about its image during all this hullabaloo. The minutes of the BFAT meeting of March 21, 1986 record that a report under the heading of "media review" was given. An article critical of the Game Commission had appeared in *Natural History* magazine. A speaker (from the Game Commission) makes the cryptic statement "that the recent article. . . did stir some people in Washington, D.C. but did not stimulate overwhelming public reaction." He went on to say that the Game Commission "had received only a half dozen letters in reference to the article." Then he raised another worrisome issue. In the past the agency had gnashed its teeth over information given to the media by BIOTA, which was not what the agency wanted the media to hear, and now another independent group led by Ulysses Seal was coming to Wyoming. "He expressed concern over how CBSG will handle news releases describing their involvement." One must always be thinking ahead to the vital issues in a recovery program; it is very important that the public be given the right sort of information. The speaker then "reported progress towards objectives of the Game & Fish Department's 'Media Plan'."[64] Whatever might happen to the ferret, appropriate attention would be given to making the agency look good.

Public opinion lives and breaths in the minutes of this meeting through the words of a rancher who conveys his reading of community feeling: it does not want Meeteetse denuded of ferrets, and his words will ring hard in the ears of Wyoming officials. However, the citizens, according to the material I have read, seemed interested in the welfare of the ferrets. If they had been made aware of the importance of saving whatever remained of the invisible gene pool, they might have agreed to an all-out capture, but the community did not know because no one had told them. That was the responsibility of the Wyoming Game Commission; it had an educational arm (which, as we have seen, is hard at work on a media plan) whose function should be to educate citizens with the facts they will need to make responsible decisions about their wildlife. But now the question arises as to whether

the Game Commission staff was informed. An answer is suggested in the minutes of a BFAT meeting held eight months later on November 10, 1987. By this time Ulysess Seal and his team had been working hard to enlighten the staff. The minutes show that Seal was meeting with staffers, two to three times a year, to review the captive breeding project.[65] But the wording hints that the CBSG may have run into trouble. The strategic goal was to get enough ferrets from Meeteetse (events, as already related, would show that none remained at large) to raise the founder stock at Sybille to 20 animals. The minutes then record that the Wyoming official who was the recovery program coordinator stated that "he still did not understand the term founder and wanted to know what 20 founders meant."[66] And so we can see at least one fundamental reason why the agency was incapable of acting rationally: key members of the biological staff did not understand the principles of small population biology, and so of course it would be impossible for the agency to educate anyone.

The information was within reach, but there was apparently little motivation to dig it out of the literature, even under the stimulus of a crisis. This may be explained I believe, in part, because the staffs of state game agencies, particularly in the upper levels of the bureaucracy, live in and breath the atmosphere of political expediency; this they rightly sense is the crucial determinate of policy. The grasp of, and emersion in, this bureaucratic reality is essential if one is to function successfully. No awards are given in the land-management agencies for dragging in the novel, unsettling ideas emerging from academia. There is no incentive to rethink the way things are done. Even if the agency administrator should grasp the need for change, the cumbersome, outdated political structure of his department would not permit him to wheel it up an unfamiliar street as if it were an automobile. The politically appointed commissioners are not simply passengers; they dictate the course—without the advantage of an up-to-date road map. And the inertia of their collective opinion can usually be predicted by the executive director—a fact that can influence the choice of route he will suggest to them. The built-in rigidity of this policy-making system imposes its weight on the thinking of all upper level staff. Thus, the modern game commission, designed to meet a turn-of-the-century need for wildlife protection, has become a hopelessly inept instrument for recovering endangered organisms.

At this point I would like to leave the Wyoming scene for a moment and bring the reader forward to January 1989, to an assembly in a beachfront hotel in Naples, Florida. Here Ulysses Seal and his industrious team of specialists was conducting a two-day workshop on the Florida panther, for representatives of the participating agencies, to spell out the options for Florida's diminished panthers. Much of the first day was given to trying to instruct the assembled officials from the Florida Game Commission and the National Park Service in how the persistence of small populations is influenced by genetics and various environmental and

catastrophic events—the ABC's of conservation biology. Seal then probed officials on their thoughts about possible lines of action, the idea being to pit institutional valuations against expert assessments of the consequences in an open debate.

When a hypothetical question arose about removing a single, possibly isolated, panther from a remote part of the Big Cypress National Preserve (it was referred to as the "last" panther) for captive breeding, a National Park Service official objected, saying, "the public needs to know that there is a panther there." I asked what would be the point of leaving it there if it was the last one? The firm and confident rejoinder came that "the public needed to know it was there." I then suggested that if the public knew what a predicament its panthers were in, it might vote for captive breeding.[67] Citizens in Florida don't know the panther's predicament, or the options that might alleviate it, because no one has told them. And no one tried to explain in Wyoming the various measures—some of them "extreme"— that might foil extinction.

Now back to the ferrets. By the summer of 1988 the captives had increased to 58.[68] They survived the genetic bottleneck, and, it is hoped, fatal impairment. The black-footed ferret may yet return to the North American prairies. Luck is still with this amazing mammal; but endangered species programs should not be run on luck in a wealthy nation that pioneered wildlife management, is now pioneering conservation biology, and is awash in scientific talent and material resources. Wars and revolutions have done for military and political institutions what endangered species programs now promise to do for those we have entrusted with the nation's imperiled organisms: the programs offer the institutions splendid opportunities to collide with their delusions. Some military and political institutions have not survived their misjudgments. Nothing so drastic will befall American land-management agencies, but it can overtake the creatures they are supposed to be saving. It is therefore important that the correct lessons be drawn from the early experiences in this new field. That requires, among other things, an examination and assessment of the errors that have been made.

Wyoming bureaucrats in the aftermath of the disaster, to judge from available sources, were resistant to admitting error. One spokesman called criticisms of its performance "Monday morning quarterbacking."[69] But the phrase implies that what should have been done can only clearly be seen post-facto. This defense is not credible. Officials were repeatedly urged to take reasonable precautions, and prestigious facilities were put at their disposal. Another Wyoming official offered this defense: "I don't think we've lost the ferrets, even if we lose Meeteetse. . . . I'm convinced there are more ferrets here in Wyoming."[70] His prediction was parroted by a regional director of the Fish and Wildlife Service— who apparently took his cues from the state agency.[71] Management of the only

known population of a species should not be planned on the chance that if it is lost others will turn up. They may not.

Early in 1988 an article appeared in the *Journal of Conservation Biology* treating the subject of "Disease and Endangered Species," using the black-footed ferret. The senior author is a Wyoming Game official, and the article appears to function partly as an apologia. One section gives a history of the recovery program. The reader learns early that the Fish and Wildlife Service "shared the responsibility for making decisions necessary for preserving the species with the Wyoming Game Commission," an implication that decisions were only partly made by the state entity. We can see that although the Fish and Wildlife Service had no power to influence ferret management, it is enlisted to share the blame when things go wrong. The history is a curious one in that BIOTA research, one element of the program's field research arm, is never mentioned. The reader is left with a mental picture of the Wyoming Game Commission and the Fish and Wildlife Service working in company only with a citizen's advisory team (BFAT). The rather emphatic (and ignored) advice of BIOTA, Wildlife Conservation International and others does not intrude into this vignette. A historian has recently written of partisan histories that "loyalty and discretion may result in the suppression of discreditable evidence especially if all ultimately turns out well."[72] The aphorism certainly fits here.

The history may have more serious defects. It comments that "in retrospect it is unfortunate that ferrets were not captured for captive breeding in 1984, when the population reached its peak size." It mentions that the measure had been recommended (without saying who recommended it), but goes on to allege that ". . . in 1984 there was neither promise nor even a suggestion of short-and-long-term funding for a captive propagation effort from either federal, state, or private agencies and organizations, "nor," it states unequivocally, "had any offers been made by institutions outside of Wyoming to take ferrets and participate in captive breeding."[73] However, as related earlier in the chapter, in April 1984, Chuck Carr, of Wildlife Conservation International, and James Doherty, of the Bronx Zoo, went to Wyoming on a futile mission to offer their services in arranging zoological accommodations.[74] So we can see in the writings of an agency loyalist that overtures to accommodate ferrets by several zoos beyond the borders of Wyoming are not remembered, and the state agency's troublesome, independent research arm, BIOTA, (whose members published more than 50 scientific papers on their ferret investigations and experiences) is excluded from a "historical" account of the recovery program. This phenomenon is worth a brief digression.

Alston Chase, in his book, *Playing God in Yellowstone*, describes the treatment of former independent researchers by the National Park Service following the disturbance over grizzly bear policy in the early 1970s.

> Pengelly and other University biologists who had worked in Yellowstone during the Garrison [a former park superintendent] administration, were no longer required by the Park Service, however. In the spirit of the Leopold Report calling for all science to be under government control and to be "mission oriented," no university or independent researchers were invited to take part in testing the new natural-regulation hypothesis. Those who had participated in the days of Garrison and were now associated with the discarded policies no longer found themselves recipients of Park Service research funds or participants in discussions on management. Their works, expunged from official bibliographies of wildlife studies published by the research office, were no longer assigned reading for park naturalists. From the Park Service point of view, they had simply disappeared.[75]

The institutional tendency to rewrite history so that it always portrays present policy-makers in the most favorable light is well known in our time, because attention has been called to extremes of the practice in totalitarian nations whose discredit we have found rewarding. A psychologist has written that "the ego is characterized by biases that are strikingly analogous to totalitarian information-control strategies. Like totalitarian regimes, the ego organizes knowledge in a way that exalts itself, distorts new information, and revises past experiences to justify its own premises."[76] And thus we see how the institutional mind—that abstract, inspiriting mirror of its devotees—is inclined to tidy up the past. History can offer perspectives that we would not otherwise have, and case histories of endangered species programs have the potential to serve as a corrective for past mistakes. This tool is diminished if accounts are not chronicled accurately.

"Concern about the effects of the disease," the reader is told, was best demonstrated in the spring of 1985 by the response to the discovery of sylvatic plague in the prairie dog population which, as the author says, "may have been the most extensive non-public health, non-urban sylvatic plague control effort" ever enacted. A campaign was set in motion to dust tens of thousands of prairie dog burrows with flea powder. The scale of these exertions is suggested by the BFAT minutes of August 7, 1985. The Game Commission got permission from the ranchers to treat the prairie dog burrows; then the Fish and Wildlife Service ordered the largest supply of flea powder ever accumulated, from a supplier in Nebraska; then, the manufacturer of the applicators in Pennsylvania was asked to ship his

entire stock to Wyoming. Treatment started on July 5, two days after the arrival of the chemicals and supplies. By the time of the August 29, BFAT meeting, approximately 1600-man days had been expended in dusting burrows. Volunteers were mustered from the National Park Service, BIOTA, the U.S. Forest Service, the University of Wyoming, the Bureau of Land Management, and the Colorado Division of Wildlife. A representative of the Fish and Wildlife Service said "he thought the arrangement was beneficial to the ferret program."[77] This seems doubtful. The project was likely defeated by its geographical dimensions. Repeatedly, agency officials refused, except for the most minimal steps, to heed the common-sense advice that was pressed on them; dusting prairie dog burrows however did not threaten institutional interests—or risk adverse public reaction. This massive and costly orchestration was an easy route.

Brian Miller, a graduate student at the University of Wyoming capitalized on his participation in the ferret program with a doctoral thesis. Among its conclusions are that "the recent history of the black-footed ferret demonstrates an excellent reason to have a captive propagation plan for threatened and endangered species in the initial recovery plan. It illustrates the vulnerability of small, isolated populations to random events regardless of the intensity of field conservation efforts."[78]

The Wyoming Game Commission did not approach its task from the principle of managing for the minimal risk to the species. The intuitive bureaucratic axiom that ruled operations was intended to minimize the risk of disruption and embarrassment to the agency. The conventional wisdom of Game Commissions, when compelled to act in any potential controversy (providing that it appears to offer no clear departmental gain), dictates the minimum measures, by the smallest increments, at the slowest pace, over the longest time—a pace inappropriate to the imperatives of conservation biology. The old shuffle is not adequate to the new challenge, but this elemental premise is what our unaroused bureaucracy cannot come to terms with. This can plainly be seen in the actions of Florida's Game Commission in the panther recovery program. In Wyoming the gamble failed.

Chapter 16

THE DUSKY SEASIDE SPARROW

What have we learned from
the extinction of the dusky
seaside sparrow?

Herbert W. Kale II

A continental fringe of coastal marsh, stretching hundreds of miles from Massachusetts to the Rio Grande, is the abode of seaside sparrows. This strand of sea-edge grass anchors in a dark and soppy soil that is daily nourished by the saline push and ebb of the tides. It is an eye-pleasing vista of waist-high grasses and rushes whose mesmerizing "Length and breadth and sweep" captivated the muse of Sidney Lanier in the late nineteenth century, leaving to posterity an evocative word picture of one man's pensive contemplation of a maritime fen. Several feathered vertebrates have habituated to this graminoid littoral, among them the clapper rail, the black rail, the marsh wren and the seaside sparrow.

Here the seaside sparrow, like the clapper rail, finds year-round sustenance, although some populations of both species migrate southward in winter. The small bird's plumage varies somewhat over the length of its range. The practice of describing subspecies, as explained with the puma in an earlier chapter, was applied also to the seaside sparrow with the result that several subspecific forms were distinguished. However, when the sparrow in the marshes of central Florida's east coast was discovered, it was declared a separate species, being distinctly darker than others of its kind and isolated from other populations. It was first called the "black-and-white-shore finch" by the ornithologist, Charles Maynard, who found it in 1872.[1] He visited Florida in the winter and saw only one of the small, dark birds. They are not readily observed except during the breeding season when males claim a territory in which each announces its occupancy by singing from a perch high on a grass or rush stem. It was only during the singing period, from March to early July, that the sparrows could be censused. Females were not commonly visible, so when census takers eventually arrived on the scene, some of them multiplied by two on the presumption that each singing male had a mate.

The seaside sparrows of Florida were eventually split into six taxa: one specific form, compromising four subspecies, plus two more species. The dusky, along with the Cape Sable sparrow at the southern tip of the peninsula, was declared a specific form.[2] When the biologists of a later era came to study the dusky, they found the bird's tolerance of habitat conditions to be narrow and exacting even within the confines of its marshy home. Nest locations plotted on a topographical map fell into a zone between the 10 and 15-foot contours. Below the 10-foot line, the upper reach of the tide prevented nesting, since most nests were within two feet of the ground. At the other extreme, above the 15-foot contour, the ground was dry enough to favor the growth of occasional cabbage palms, and the dusky, it was learned, was partial to a view of the unbroken horizon when selecting a nesting site.[3] The birds stayed well away from trees because, according to speculation, trees serve as perches for predatory birds that might eat sparrows or their nestlings. Also, the land above the 15-foot contour was drier and therefore susceptible to more frequent fires of greater intensity than could be tolerated by the sparrows with their peculiar preference for vegetative arrangements.[4]

The birds preferred a mixture of short and tall grasses (from a height of two to four-and-a-half feet) at a density of 1700 stems per square yard. The soil moisture gradient of the preferred habitat was such that periodic fires burned only part of the grass, leaving patches suitable to the needs of sparrows. After a fire, fewer of them used the spottily burned habitat than before, but since the regrowth of grass was rapid they returned in force within a year or two.[5] The range of the species was one of the most restricted in North America, being limited to the north portion of Brevard County in east-central Florida, a span of probably not more than 25 miles.[6] And it can be seen that its existence hung on the shifting variables of a delicately balanced environment that could withstand only limited human disturbance.

Historical Background

For a century after becoming a part of the United States, the lower Florida peninsula was lightly settled, being used primarily for cattle grazing. The first improvements in pasturage began on a modest scale in the 1920s. Cattlemen, intent on drainage, pushed a few dikes and ditches into the marshes of the St. Johns River. It is not known how these limited works might have changed the sparrow's habitat, but certainly the impact was not severe. In the 1940s further alterations of the river marsh arrived with nascent ambitions for truck farming.[7] This disturbance also is believed not to have been great enough to have threatened the sparrow. It is the degree and the cumulative effect over time that can make such disturbance extirpative. In the 1950s duskies were still abundant on Merritt Island where it was estimated that 2,000 pairs were present. But it was also in the 1950s that the dusky

seaside sparrow began its precipitous decline to extinction, following habitat disarrangement on a massive scale. Post-war affluence and mobility, and the combined forces of the American space program and Mickey Mouse, would bring down the dusky seaside sparrow. Mickey Mouse would strive for redemption in the end; Disney World would put up the capital and provide the facilities for a last ditch attempt at rescue by captive breeding.

In the decade of 1950 to 1960, Brevard County experienced an explosive population growth of 370 percent, which by 1966 had doubled again—fueled by the expanding launch facilities at Cape Canaveral. Florida's coastal marshes, during the warm months, produce salt marsh mosquitoes (*Aedes taenoirhynchus* and *Aedes solicitans*) in uncountable billions. *Aedes* is not a hovering, singing type of mosquito; it is a tiny, blood-seeking organic missile whose numbers exceed available targets by a vast and ravenous margin. The pre-war inhabitants had learned to cope by means of oil of citronella and cheesecloth netting, and by positioning themselves downwind in the smoke of slow-burning smudges. The modern post-war community had the technology, and an expanded tax-base, from which to wage war on the mosquito. Soon after World War II the Brevard County Mosquito Control District was formed. At first DDT was used, but the mosquitoes soon became resistant. Aircraft were used from 1947 to 1962 to spray the marshes with insecticides.[8] This practice cannot have been beneficial to the sparrows. Although they eat some seeds, the bulk of the diet is made up of spiders, grasshoppers and crickets with lesser quantities of beetles and snails.[9]

Another method of control was the impoundment. Dredges and draglines moved into the marshes, digging trenches and piling the excavated material (the spoil) to form a series of enclosing dikes. Salt marsh mosquitoes lay their eggs in the "high marsh," just above the normal range of daily tides. The eggs hatch when a surging tide, pushed by wind or drawn by the moon or raised by heavy rain, or by some accrual of these forces, flows into the upper ground of the high marsh. Permanent flooding will deny the mosquitoes a place for egglaying. It also destroys vegetation not adapted to standing water. Mosquito impoundments in the sparrow habitat rendered it unusable by them. Other encroachments would add to the destruction as we shall see, but impoundments displaced the sparrows *en masse*.

A further threat arose from a regional water control strategy. Visionaries of the era when a utilitarian philosophy governed attitudes toward the use of land, dreamed of draining Florida's swamps and marshes to make the submerged lands "usable." The dream attained its culminating institutional expression in 1947 (the same year that the Brevard County Mosquito Control District was formed). Disastrous flooding from a hurricane in that year spurred the formation of the Central and Southern Florida Flood Control District. With the help of the U.S. Army Corps of Engineers, the district began work on a water control plan that

promised the sky; it would furnish flood protection, supply water to cities of the lower east coast, prevent saltwater intrusion, enhance fish and wildlife, store surplus water and improve navigation.[10] The mechanism for this expected beneficence was a gigantic system of dikes, pumps, canals and water control structures. The project partly delivered what was promised to various interests—with the exception of enhancing fish and wildlife. However, such "benefits" as were gained came at an exorbitant environmental cost for which corrective measures are today being attempted at astronomical public expense. The engineered wetlands with their erratic fluctuations of surface water were calamitous for certain wildlife species of the region.

As the hosts of wildlife destruction gathered momentum, the instruments of wildlife rescue, following the usual pattern, were created to follow in their trail. In 1967 the dusky seaside sparrow drew attention from the federal government. In 1968 an ornithologist named Brian Sharp, a graduate student from the University of Wisconsin, came to make the first comprehensive survey of the species. He found two remaining populations. Only about 30 birds were left on Merritt Island—a dangerously insecure few. An estimated 1800 birds were in the marshes along the St. Johns River.

In his report Sharp cast a wary eye on the impending dikes and spillways of South Florida Water Control Project for the upper St. Johns River, then still in the planning stage. He speculated on the changes that might be anticipated from a manipulated hydrology. Alterations in moisture gradients and salinity balances could be expected, which in turn would cause shifts in vegetative composition. There might be an enhanced potential for cattle grazing and real estate development—activities not thought to be compatible with sparrows. Sharp's assessment was not optimistic. His commentary of the late 1960s is of interest because his thinking seemed ahead of the times:

> In any event management for the Dusky, if it involves habitat preservation, as it will obviously have to do, should be of sufficient magnitude to allow the species the opportunity of further evolution. Only in this way can it remain viable. By 'magnitude' we mean not only a physical area adequate to preserve a minimal population of birds as an "outdoor museum exhibit" but an area containing a non-homogeneous gradient of habitat choices, each slightly different, so that the species can demonstrate the versatility of habitat preferences it seems to have.[11]

In 1969 another insult was added to previous habitat injuries when the county commissioners of Brevard decided to extend a road into the sparrow's

369

domain in the St. Johns River marshes. I am informed on reliable authority that the commissioners had been taken by the notion that a reform school for girls would be suitable there.[12] Nothing came of this inspiration of course—except the road; it is still there, known officially as the Hacienda Road and unofficially as "the road to nowhere." Meanwhile, with the coming of Disney World the Orlando metropolitan area mushroomed all over the central Florida landscape, and the transportation artery connecting Orlando to the Atlantic beaches became packed with crawling vehicles. To ease traffic congestion another highway, the Beeline Expressway, was laid across the wetlands—right through the dusky's habitat—leaving a roadside canal which contributed to drying out the marshes. As the environment deteriorated, sparrow numbers came down, down, down. In 1970 the Fish and Wildlife Service began acquiring 4,000 acres of the St. Johns River marsh for a refuge. In 1972 an agency biologist, Jim Baker, was assigned to the dusky seaside sparrow case. In his first census he found 110 singing males in the 4,000-acre site.

The early 1970s were years of drought in Florida. Across the state hundreds of thousands of acres burned, and for weeks the smell of smoke permeated the air. The impact of these fires on the ditched and desiccated wetlands was intensified by all the drainage. Whereas the dusky seaside sparrow habitat on Merritt Island was ruined by too much water through impounding, that in the St. Johns River marshes now suffered from too little. In 1972 two severe wildfires flamed across the parched riverine grasslands. When Jim Baker returned for the spring census in 1973, he concluded that the population in the refuge had been halved from the previous year—to 54 countable birds.[13]

Crisis

At this point the survival of the dusky had clearly come to crisis. The rate of decline was precipitous and had drawn numbers down to a precarious low. The predicament of the endangered sparrow at this stage, illustrates the hazard posed to a withered population by catastrophic events that would have only made marginal inroads on a large one. With the loss of the protective buffer afforded by a mass of individuals, the fate of the last few hangs by a vulnerable thread, and the reduction enlarges the proportions of a new threat—from inbreeding.

At this critical juncture the dusky seaside sparrow was affected by an oblivious taxonomic revision. The American Ornithologists' Union (A.O.U.), among its other functions, passes judgement on the classification of birds in North America, making revisions as research reveals new information. The judgements are made known in the A.O.U. checklist—a list of standardized common and scientific names for the North American birds. In 1973 the A.O.U. published a revised checklist that "downgraded" the dusky seaside sparrow from a species to

a subspecies. Thus, during an ongoing program to prevent its demise, the creature of concern, while it did not cease to be endangered, did cease to be a species.

Herb Kale, an ornithologist, who for 21 years was deeply involved in the struggle to save the bird (he organized the first dusky seaside sparrow conference in 1969), believed that the dusky lost political support from its "birdwatcher constituency" after being demoted.[14] Many practitioners of birding, or birdwatching, keep a tally of the species they have seen. To some devotees, "listing" can take on an obsessive character, which has been derided as "bird bingo" by those who suspect that the interest in birds by some aficionados does not extend beyond the creature's value in enlarging the birder's list. However this may be, Kale believes the dusky's birdwatching supporters abandoned it to fate after the taxonomic revision. Enthusiasm in the bureaucracy also subsided—as we shall see.

By 1973 the acres for a refuge were accumulating, but land-buying by the government is a slow business under the best of conditions. By the end of that year only about half the 4,000 acres had been acquired.[15] Some owners would not sell their plots of riverfront marsh, sending the transactions to court for condemnation of the land—with the inevitable delays that accompany such proceedings.[16]

A recovery team was formed in 1974 in accordance with provisions of the preceding year's revised Endangered Species Act. The team was composed of Jim Baker of the Fish and Wildlife Service, Herb Kale, the ornithologist, and Lovett Williams, a wildlife biologist in the Florida Game Commission. The recovery team urged, in the emergency, getting a swamp buggy that could clear fire lanes around the critical zones in the marsh. According to Herb Kale, the request sat on a desk in the Fish and Wildlife Service regional office in Atlanta for two years while the sparrow's environment burned in Florida. The swamp buggy would finally arrive Christmas Eve, 1976, too late to prevent the burning of 5,000 acres of marsh in 1975, by fires that seared 75 percent of the remaining dusky domain along the St. Johns River. The last females probably vanished at this time. Earlier in the year of 1975, Jim Baker had sighted five females with fledglings. They were the last females ever seen.[17]

By 1978 no more sparrows could be found on Merritt Island, and only 24 males were counted that year in the new refuge. By now the Fish and Wildlife Service had spent $2.6 million for the 6,000-acre refuge and $500,000 repairing it.[18] But work to restore the badly disturbed marshes had come too late. Although some ditches were plugged, and fences taken down, and fire lanes cleared, a population made up of solely males had little time remaining to it.

Desperation

Still hoping to find females in 1979, biologists searched hard but only found 13 males along the St. Johns River. No birds were sighted on Merritt Island. The only option for recovery left was outbreeding—mating the remaining males with females of another subspecies. By such an expedient the offspring from these unions could then be backcrossed with the dusky males to accrue dusky genes in the progeny. But this portal of hope led to a collision with Fish and Wildlife Service policy.

Late in 1979 biologists captured three dusky males and transported them to the Game Commission's wildlife research laboratory in Gainesville. In 1980 one of the captive birds died (in March). The following year three of the remaining four wild males were brought in (one evaded capture). On June 19 and 20 of the latter year a special meeting was scheduled to ponder outbreeding. Fish and Wildlife Service officials came to Merritt Island from Washington, D.C., and although nothing was officially decided, Herb Kale came away feeling there was a tentative agreement to try outbreeding.[19] He had given the opinion that six generations of outcrossing would produce a sparrow with 98.4 percent of the dusky's genes.[20] Two possible sites for the captive breeding facility—both in Gainesville—were identified: the Florida State Museum at the University of Florida, or the Santa Fe Community College which operated a teaching zoo. The meeting adjourned and the solemn participants went their respective ways. The case was desperate, but there was still a chance of keeping outcrossed sparrows in being. Then, three weeks later, the biologists in Florida were stunned to hear from Washington that there could be no outbreeding project. They were sent an agency solicitor's opinion written in 1977 which asserted that the Endangered Species Act was not meant to protect "hybrids."[21]

Meanwhile in Gainesville, William Post, an ornithologist under contract to the Game Commission, had already begun breeding sparrows on his own without approval from the Fish and Wildlife Service.[22] One male dusky was mated to a Scott's seaside sparrow—a subspecies found on Florida's west coast. Of the offspring two were female and one male. They were dubbed 50 percenters because they were 50 percent "dusky." However, the Fish and Wildlife Service was adamant against further outbreeding, anchoring its position on a legal opinion (albeit an in-house one). The Agency answered with a final "no" on outbreeding in July 1980. Federal funds were allocated only for "captive maintenance" of the last five males, in case mates for them should be discovered unexpectedly. The sparrows were moved across town from the Game Commission's Wildlife Laboratory to the Santa Fe Community College Teaching Zoo.[23]

In 1980 a Fish and Wildlife Service official justified the denial of outbreeding: "Emotions tell you one thing. Economic necessity, logic and hard decisions are something else. Legally, a 98.4 dusky isn't a dusky (and not protected under the Endangered Species Act). That's the key point: The bird we would be getting would not be the bird we are losing. It would not be the endangered species [sic]. . . ."[24] It can be seen that this opinion rests in part, on a judgement of the imperatives of "economic necessity"—something to be kept in mind when we return to this issue later in the chapter.

The government contract with Santa Fe Community College was due to expire in October 1983 and the duskies had nowhere to go. At the request of Florida Audubon Society officials Disney World agreed to take them in. With Disney agreeing to foot the bill, Peter Mott, President of the Florida Audubon Society, approached the Fish and Wildlife Service for permission to cross-breed. Mott got a "yes" from the Fish and Wildlife Service in less than a week.[25] Subsequently, in the summer of 1983, the backcrossed sparrows hatched a 75 percent female which closely resembled a dusky. Soon after, the birds went to the zoological facility at Disney World, and over the next two years begat a 75 percent dusky male and three 87.5 percent offspring (two males and a female).[26] The last 100 percent dusky died on June 16, 1987. He had been mated to a 75 percenter. There had been four offspring—87.5 percenters—only one of which survived.[27] And so the drama concluded, with the last dusky departed and all the actors stilled. Their labors could not prevail against the press of time and shrinking numbers which had relentlessly multiplied the odds against them.

Hybrids

In assessing the dusky seaside sparrow case it appears that furnishing fire-fighting equipment at a critical moment in the mid-1970s may have been avoidably sluggish. The marsh fires of that decade pushed the sparrows beyond recovery. Herb Kale has been critical of the federal agency for its lack of resolve in removing roads and plugging drainage ditches, and for its lackadaisical methods in general at the refuge.[28] And in the end the agency stood against cross-breeding. However, from the beginning the dusky appears to have been a star-crossed bird. The momentum of forces hindering survival gathered early and was so great that only extremes of vigor and imagination might have prevailed against it, and the bureaucracy did not measure up. The transformation of mosquito breeding sites ("source-reduction," in the idiom of mosquito control professionals) on Merritt Island virtually eliminated duskies there. Those in the St. Johns River marshes were thereafter subjected to the violent impact of multiple habitat disturbances.

Unfortunately, no sparrows had been taken captive for security. The cost would have been small for this tiny bird. It is interesting to speculate about what might have been achieved in 1979 by outbreeding. The opinion of the Fish and Wildlife Service that "hybrids" are not covered under the Endangered Species Act has been a controversial one, and it has loitered backstage in the Florida panther recovery program as explained in Chapter 7. The Fish and Wildlife Service policies based on this opinion have ramifications for other species, now—and in the future, and so warrant a digression here.

When personnel of the Fish and Wildlife Service expound on the issue of outbreeding listed species, they refer to the solicitors: the solicitor's office, the solicitor's opinion, etc.[29] A belief has gained currency that the agency's intransigent legal arm could not reconcile biological subtleties to the law. However, a review of the internal memoranda relating to the origins of the opinion dispels this fiction. The solicitors were simply supplying legal interpretations that were requested of them.

The history is as follows. On April 27, 1977, the chief of the Division of Law Enforcement of the Fish and Wildlife Service sent a memo to the assistant solicitor seeking an opinion on whether a hybrid of an endangered or threatened species was covered by the Endangered Species Act. The law enforcement officials were disquieted by reports that endangered crocodiles in Southeast Asia were being crossbred to a non-endangered species, with the intent to market the offspring. The officials worried that success in this business would lead to increased captures of the endangered crocodile for breeding stock, thereby further diminishing the wild populations.[30]

The solicitor complied with the request of the Division of Law Enforcement in a memo of May 18, 1977: "Language of the statute, its legislative history, and one of the law's purposes indicate that hybrids of endangered or threatened species are covered by the Act." It went on to explain, "Because it defines `fish or wildlife' to include any offspring without limitation, the Act's plain meaning dictates coverage of hybrids of listed animal species. The legislative history buttresses this conclusion for animals and also makes clear its applicability to plants." The author of the memo made his point once more: "Thus, the statute's language and its legislative history show clearly that the Endangered Species Act of 1973 is intended to cover hybrids of endangered or threatened species. Moreover, such coverage is required if the Act's policy of reducing commercialization of listed species is to be given effect."[31]

This unequivocal opinion was not to stand for long. When the brief reached other departments within the agency alarms went off. On July 7, 1977, a

memo, with "ASAP" scrawled across the top, was sent from the deputy associate director of federal assistance, to the solicitor's office. It was headed: "Reconsideration of Solicitor's Opinion with Regard to Hybrids." The opening sentence came directly to the point: "We would like to request your reconsideration of this solicitor's opinion as quickly as possible," it said, "since it is having profound effects on our treatment of endangered and threatened species matters. . .we find it difficult to believe that the original intent of Congress was other than to have the offspring of endangered species classed as endangered only when both parents [sic] are endangered."[32]

This sharp reaction was driven by concern about another problem called genetic swamping, a consequence of the union of two species capable of interbreeding. If one population is small (as with the red wolf) and the larger (as with the coyote), the phenotype of the small population might be absorbed into the larger one over several generations. At best the outcome might be an intermediate form. Mixing of this kind has occurred in nature, but the term "genetic swamping" commonly connotes human agency—an induced and unnecessary mixing of life forms with a potential outcome thought best to avoid.

The specific concern referenced in the memo of July 7, 1977, was the endangered red wolf, a remnant species thought to be interbreeding with coyotes. The agency biologists believed that sound management (and the Endangered Species Act) required preserving the red wolf as an existing phenotype. As the memo phrased it, the agency could be placed in a "biologically unsound position" if the offspring of coyote-red wolf crosses were protected under the Endangered Species Act. A real Pandora's box there; remember, at this time one branch of the Fish and Wildlife Service was in the business of poisoning coyotes. The solicitor's opinion on crocodiles threatened, by trying to solve one problem, to create others.

In any case the solicitor's opinion of May was reversed in August, in a memo explaining that ". . . we have received additional biological information from your office and other sources in the Service indicating that coverage of hybrids would hinder the conservation of endangered or threatened species and possibly jeopardize their continued existence. It was pointed out that hybrids of some species might well interbreed with the few remaining purebreds so as to dilute or eliminate the original gene pool. In addition, hybrids are frequently larger, more vigorous, and more adaptive than either of their purebred parents. . . ."[33] The solicitor's office had revisited the statute forthwith, reversing its opinion. It was this memo of August 2, 1977 that became the justification in July, 1980, for the Fish and Wildlife Service decision to prohibit outbreeding.

So it can be seen how the policy of excluding the offspring of any outcrossed taxon from coverage by the Endangered Species Act evolved. First, the

law enforcement arm of the agency sought an opinion to block the threat posed to an endangered species of crocodile by the commercial utilization of its offspring. But that strategy could have undermined the defense against genetic swamping—specifically in the red wolf. The counter-remedy then came to hand as a policy against outcrossing, not only between species, but by extension, between the ephemeral, and sometimes uncertain, taxon of the subspecies. The policy was a makeshift, born of the conflicting exigencies of a moment. Two diametrically opposed legal opinions were, within a brief span of time, promulgated from the same office, both justified by quoting different portions of the same statute and its legislative history. One conclusion to draw is that the statute is not a suitable instrument to resolve such an abstruse issue. The congressmen who produced the Endangered Species Act were simply creating a mechanism to prevent the loss of life forms their society deemed worthy of saving, neither they nor their technical advisors anticipated the outcrossing complication. Incidentally, the threat to crocodiles was taken care of by a similarity of appearance ruling.

When the Fish and Wildlife Service ruled in 1980 on the dusky seaside sparrow, it raised the ire of several scientists, some of whom published criticisms.[34,35] An agency spokesman responding to the critics, revealed through a choice of words, that the concept as it is posited in the collective mind of the agency was not exactly (for lack of a better term) "scientific." Some quotations to illustrate this point are as follows: "once the dusky has been contaminated with whatever genes, the biological entity that was there is no more. . . so, what other than an artifact—a new caged bird—are we producing here. . . . We interpret 'which interbreeds when mature' to imply a natural situation. The Scott's-dusky hybrid is a human manipulation of naturally separate gene pools and so doesn't qualify."[36]

The phrasing conveys a notion that the deliberate mixing of genes, since it would not have happened in nature (at least under the circumstances attending this case), is unsavory. The population being afflicted by this mixing would become "contaminated." It would then be an "artifact." Some of the terms bring to mind the attitudes in California of those opposed to a captive breeding program for condors. Unfortunately for our generation, much of the natural world, in a strict sense, is gone. It endures only in fragments encompassed in refuges, and in portions of the earth unsuited, or poorly to human habitation. To save many life forms human manipulation will be essential. It only remains to define the degree.

In giving thought to outbreeding, the population selected as the genetic donor might differ only slightly in genetic composition from the recipient population. In a small, endangered population, a previous human-caused genetic alteration may have been inflicted via the reduction in numbers and consequent loss of genetic variation. If that were so, then introducing genetic material from elsewhere would not be the first human alteration of the gene pool, but the second

—made with the aim of intentionally improving survival odds compromised by artifice. Neither of these hypothetical alternatives is "natural." The question is which is more desirable? The present policy elevates the existing genetic composition of an endangered organism to the position of controlling value in deciding whether to save it or allow it to vanish. It prizes the static biological isolate, even when the genotype has been altered unnaturally. The policy does not weigh the case for keeping the organism as a functioning part of an interacting system of organisms—an ecosystem, if you will. No guidance is given to assay existing genetic species against the worth of the evolving species.

The Endangered Species Act addresses ecosystems (for whatever it might be worth). "The purposes of this Act are to provide a means whereby the ecosystems upon which endangered and threatened species depend may be conserved. . . ."[37] The act contains two pages of definitions, which immediately follow its statement of purpose. However "ecosystems" is not among them. This is just as well I think. The lawmakers who framed the act in 1973 knew that ecosystems were good things to conserve, however they might be defined; the awful things beings done to them were being talked about by all the best environmentalists. And an ecosystem, legally, is like a hybrid in that it could be defined by policy to deal with whatever practical problem was at hand. We (all of us who want to save whatever we can of organisms—and ecosystems) still have to wrestle with the question of exactly what we want to save and why.

The most recent episode in the dusky seaside sparrow saga emerged in February 1989. Two researchers at the University of Georgia compared a random sample of genetic material from the extinct dusky seaside sparrow to genetic material from several other subspecies, both from Atlantic and Gulf Coast populations. The amount sampled from each bird was extremely small; that from the dusky showed no difference from the other Atlantic Coast populations. However, there was some "genetic distance" between the Atlantic Coast seaside sparrows and those of the Gulf Coast.[38] One conclusion of the authors was that "in this study we provided evidence that a taxonomy for the seaside sparrow, which was initiated in the last century and upon which management decisions continue to be based, does not properly summarize the evolutionary genetic relationships of the populations involved."[39] A good point, but until such relationships for organisms are summarized by some voice that will be regarded as authoritative—and the new way of thinking about them becomes accepted in the circles that count—endangered species decision-makers will still have to work with antiquated biological classifications. The out-of-date taxonomies have a strong grip on thinking because they are there, and the programs are off and running. The overloaded bureaucrats at the Fish and Wildlife Service, looking for practical ways to deal with a gargantuan problem new to history, and unprecedented in its complexity, don't have the time or the inclination to rethink the issue. If guidance for alternative

policies is to be established, it will have to originate outside the agency by some authoritative consensus.

The techniques of genetic investigation used in the recent seaside sparrow study were not available in 1980. The researchers suggested that if they had been, the "exceptional preservation efforts mandated by the Endangered Species Act would not have applied to the Brevard County population." They observed that "this is not the first instance in which a faulty taxonomy has resulted in well-intentioned but misdirected efforts in endangered species management. A widened concern with the phylogenetic bases for taxonomic decisions should contribute to the recognition and conservation of biotic diversity."[40,41]

An increased awareness of genetics has, at least in scientific circles, drawn the focus of conservation values to, maintaining the world's existing genetic diversity. This is a genetic refinement of the utilitarian philosophy of natural resource management, which is still, after a century, the most broadly compelling argument for conservation. The gene complexes contained within the earth's remaining organisms might be utilized for many purposes, from treating cancer to creating disease-resistant food plants. There can be no doubt that an incalculable number of uses are undiscovered and, as the organisms are lost, as many of them are going to be, the potential benefits will go with them. So considering the dusky problem within this scheme of values, it would be important to save the two genetic complexes represented by the two measurably distinct seaside sparrow popula-tions—the one of the Atlantic Coast, and that of the Gulf Coast. Since the dusky seaside sparrow population was an isolated segment of one of these genetic complexes, the argument goes, it would not have justified the effort.

However some questions may still remain. Writings in conservation biology have stressed the importance of maintaining not just existing biological diversity but the conditions for its continuing creation—populations that can continue to evolve (truly we have come to play God). Although the dusky was genetically similar to other Atlantic Coast sparrows, it was an isolate with a quite distinctive appearance, an indication that there were genetic differences, even if too slight to measure in the recent investigation. Given time, the genetic distance between what might be an evolving new lineage and the populations to the north, could have been widened. The dusky population could have been genetic diversity aborning, an incipient species—a potentially different gene complex which was snuffed out in the evolutionary womb. Arguing against trying to rescue the discrete dusky population on the grounds of its genetic similarity to other populations seems to presume a static view of evolutionary processes.

Should a consideration of this kind be given weight in making recovery decisions? It might be argued that such an elaborate defense of a small, fragile

sparrow population is frivolous in view of the extinction apocalypse galloping down on us, but the question is inseparable from a larger one, which lacks a completely satisfactory answer. What precisely among the multifarious living forms do we want to save, where and why? The question should not be dismissed simply because it was raised within the limited scope of the dusky affair. Other situations taxonomically similar could have much broader implications.

Budget Constraints

Economics has been bandied about as a sifter for choosing which taxa to save. This is the issue of allocating scarce, or at least limited, resources. It was mentioned earlier in the chapter as a justification used by representatives of the Fish and Wildlife Service to deny support for outcrossing the dusky. However, a review of the memoranda underpinning the present policy does not confirm that the economic argument contributed to it, thereby lending to the suspicion that economics became an add-on justification, employed in a supporting role after the 1977 memo came to occupy the position of a policy against outbreeding. That of course is irrelevant to the issue of allocating scarce resources.

An economic decision in the dusky situation requires asking how much additional money outcrossing would have taken, relative to the amount already expended? By 1980 the recovery program had consumed over three million dollars. Research had assembled a data base for managing a wild population and the refuge had been bought. It had staff and equipment. The only thing lacking was sparrows. The increment of funds would not have been great. The Fish and Wildlife Service has a captive breeding facility at Patuxent, Maryland, for chores of this kind. And we have seen with the dusky seaside sparrow (and the Florida panther as well) that captive breeding is one aspect of recovery programs for which private capital is sometimes available (although admittedly that was not evident in 1980). The economic argument against outcrossing the sparrow lacks strength.

However, before making a judgment on the economic argument. two other factors that may have been in the minds of decision-makers should be examined. One is the weight of precedent. Would approving the outcrossing of the dusky then overwhelm the recovery mechanism through more requests for like projects, at the expense of more productive management alternatives? There is sometimes a tendency for agency decision-makers to become afflicted with a secondary-concern syndrome, which postulates an improbable chain of consequences for a proposed decision, that it is feared, will dissipate the agency mission, perhaps to ruin. Fears about flawed precedents are not irrelevant, but the scenarios are not always rigorously examined and can become props for a flawed policy. If the fear of a precedent weighed in the economic arguments against outbreeding, I suspect it rested on insubstantial calculations.

The second factor to consider is the funding context of the decision. How much money was available at the time, compared to the amount judged essential for supporting other endangered species programs? In 1980, appropriations for the Fish and Wildlife Service had risen from $4.7 million in 1974 to slightly over $20 million. (it would rise to $32 million by 1988.)[42] These funds were judged at the time to be inadequate to the total demand (see Chapter 13), but the history of endangered species funding has been one of steady increase. There have been no reductions or cut-backs (although as pointed out in previous chapters, the political weakness of the Fish and Wildlife Service can work against the efficient expenditure of funds). Again, the economic argument used against outbreeding the dusky seaside sparrow does not seem to be sound.

Beyond the question of saving organisms for their utility lie the metaphysical questions for which no quantifiable criteria can be devised. An animal in the wild offers encounters that enrich the experience of living. What are such moments worth? What will they be worth in the future? In the spring of 1979 I waded into the waist-high grasses along the St. Johns River and headed north from the road. The sky was cobalt blue, and the day was warm, and as the highway receded in the distance behind me, the world became a sea of grass with a horizon punctuated by distant palm trees. Eventually the faint call of the sparrows came across the still air of early day, and soon the small dark forms took shape. I had come this weekend morning for a farewell look at a passing bird. I tried to fix in memory the yellow lores, and fuscous wings and back, and streaked underparts. Long and long I looked at the small feathered forms swaying on supple perches, calling lustily to a marshy world, for mates that did not come. No one will ever do that again.

PART FOUR: THE SOLUTION

Chapter 17

A FUTURE REFUGE?

*The forests that now wave with such maj-
esty around, will be levelled to the earth,
and every vestige of those beauties which
at present are able to attract the notice of
even the most illiterate and unfeeling,
vanish before the destructive influences
of human cupidity.*

Captain John E. LeConte,
U.S. Army Geological Survey,
Some Observations on the Soil and Climate of East Florida, 1822.

If there are panthers in Florida's future where will they live? They must
have great, wide and wooded spaces where the human presence is light; that space
must be demarcated if they are to remain with us. The cats have persevered through
500 years of post-Columbian travail, but they will not withstand the massive
disturbance now rolling over the land unless a secure portion of it is set aside for
them. In Florida the future is cascading in. The time left in which to pick lands that
might serve as a refuge and to set the rescue measures in motion is wasting. The
"natural" landscape, whatever remains of it, is disappearing under asphalt and
concrete, or being cleared for agriculture—often a transitional phase soon supplanted by urban development.

Florida's natural landscape, a once unbroken habitat, is fracturing into an
archipelago. The larger islands will themselves be disjoined and broken again, and
again. The panther will perhaps be the first animal to be lost if steps are not soon
taken to prevent it. The Black Bear will not be far behind. Bears also have a patchy
distribution in the state, with densities similar to those of panthers; only a large
region can sustain a population. The bigger animals will go first, but many
sanctuaries when isolated will be too small even for bobcats and white-tailed deer.
The few that survive on the island sanctuaries will decline and vanish.

This foreseeable calamity could be ameliorated somewhat. The broad
citizen concern is there, and that is the essential ingredient; it is the foundation upon
which to build, both with programs that have been proven and with innovative new

designs wanting a test. The environmental organizations will have to move these designs to the public arena and promote them. By obligation, this task should have been undertaken by the FPIC with the Game Commission leading the way. It would not have been easy, but this promising new departmental combination might have made impressive gains, had it been willing to test the enormous potential of the popular cause it represents.

Fragmenting habitat is recognized now as a world-wide threat to the earth's biological diversity. Media coverage is highlighting the vanishing rain forests (where most terrestrial life forms are to be found) and the constricting pressures on Africa's spectacular wildlife parks. It is less widely known that an acute case of this malady stalks the North American continent—in Florida. Here the hinterland is being degraded, not by campesinos with machetes or herds of Masai cattle, but by an affluent avalanche of retirement villages, golf courses, and $100,000 to $300,000 homes and high-rise condominiums. Florida's population growth rate, at four percent per year, is one of the fastest on earth.[1] The growing conurbations spawned from this austral mass-migration of an affluent populace require a continuous spread of arterial asphalt to link them together. The new highways sometimes seek a path of least resistance in the uncrowded countryside; they have been growing at three miles per day for 50 years, and are making an impact on wildlife through the cleavage of habitats and by direct mortality.[2]

Florida is prominent among the states having endangered life forms,[3,4] but is probably without competitors in the vulnerability of its species—by reason of a rapidly eroding habitat. The state's coastal lowlands long discouraged intensive settlement; the poor soils offered an unpromising subsistence to the agrarian immigrants of the past. But in today's nation of affluent urbanites, a sub-tropical climate lures refugees from northern winters. The unencouraging sands that once dissuaded immigration—thereby granting a measure of protection to animals that were exterminated elsewhere in eastern North America—are a barrier no longer. The most visible and immediately threatened symbol of this novel menace is the Florida panther. If the panther symbolizes the impending wildlife debacle, the responses of our inept land-management agencies embody the principal impediment to a rescue. For resolving the most challenging biological task imaginable, we are saddled with the worst institutional arrangements possible.

If there is to be a future refuge for the panther in Florida it must be created deliberately. It will not just happen. Someone must do the hard thinking, try to sketch the options and put them out for debate. There should be three phases, starting with a single plan for the great expanse of public land in southern Florida— the logical foundation for a sanctuary. Panthers are there, and it is the largest, single, contiguous tract of preserved wildlife habitat in the eastern United States. The second phase should be to build protective corridors northward from the

present refuge; this is the "private lands issue." The eastern portion of Collier County, and much of rural Hendry County and points north, is wholesome country for panthers. The third phase should be to link existing refuges into an unbroken, or nearly unbroken, sanctuary throughout Florida and on to the north.

The Public Lands

The public land at the southern tip of the peninsula is divided into several administrative units which are managed by five different state and federal agencies. The National Park Service oversees Everglades National Park and the Big Cypress National Preserve. The Fish and Wildlife Service is responsible for Loxahatchee National Wildlife Refuge and the Florida Panther National Wildlife Refuge. The Florida Department of Natural Resources operates the Fakahatchee Strand State Preserve, and the South Florida Water Management District controls the water conservation areas. The Game and Fresh Water Fish Commission administers several wildlife management areas including J.W. Corbett, Holey Land, Rotenberger, White Belt Ranch, and is authorized to manage wildlife in the Big Cypress National Preserve and in the Water Conservation Areas. The core of this conglomerate— Everglades National Park and the Big Cypress National Preserve—is the domain of the National Park Service.

Everglades National Park

The present park boundaries encompass about 1,400,000 acres. However, if the submerged lands offshore and those dominated by mangrove swamp and tidal marsh are excluded, the space usable by panthers is probably reduced by a third. The Park Establishment Act of 1934 excluded an interior tract of about 7,000 acres of agricultural land from the park. The enclosed fields became known as the Hole-in-the-Donut,[5] a site introduced in an earlier chapter. Environmental sentiment during the 1970s spurred the political pressure to buy these private inholdings. The use of fertilizer and pesticides in the interior of a national park had been a particular cause for alarm. Farmers objected strenuously to federal acquisition, but the inholding was purchased and agricultural operations terminated in 1975. A federal research report on Hole-in-the-Donut stated in 1981 that "Wildlife populations in the Donut area increased dramatically within the years following abandonment of the fields. Bobcats and predatory birds became abundant, and there were numerous sightings of the endangered Florida panther. The National Park Service explored various means of restoring some semblance of the original vegetation, but with little success since the substrate had been so drastically altered."[6]

"Objectives were quickly shifted," added the report, "from restoration of original ecosystems to maintenance of biotic diversity and minimizing the impact

of exotic species on adjacent native vegetation." The investigations reported here were begun in late 1977 with the aim of "gaining an understanding of old-field succession on these lands."[7] The report summarized four studies which, in effect, did little more than monitor the transformation of abandoned farmlands into a gigantic patch of exotic weeds. As the controversial opposition of farmers died away, institutional somnambulism overtook the promising energies that had been committed to restore Hole-in-the-Donut to a natural state.

The de facto policy of neglect was reassessed in the 1980s, when suggestions to manipulate the weed patch to aid panthers raised the specter of single-species management. The National Park Service's idea for another try at restoring the Hole-in-the-Donut was supplied by the regional office in Atlanta. "With reference to Hole-in-the-Donut, we are beginning to develop a rehabilitation plan for this area. Prior to any implementation of a rehabilitation plan, research must be conducted to determine the best techniques and alternatives. Everglades National Park is in the preliminary stages of developing a proposal to conduct an experimental project to test methods for rehabilitation. The estimated cost for conducting such research is $100,000."[8]

The Big Cypress National Preserve

Legislation creating the Big Cypress National Preserve, carried forward on a broad wave of environmental feeling, was enacted by Congress in 1974. The big swamp was imperiled by an impending jetport to be positioned midway between Naples and Miami. Massive development would have followed, creating an urbanized strip across the southern peninsula. Hydrological concerns were paramount in the acquisition. The Big Cypress Swamp is the drainage basin for the western portion of Everglades National Park, including the estuary of the Ten Thousand Islands.

Several organizations labored to create the Preserve. One of the most vigorous leaders was "Johnny" Jones of The Florida Wildlife Federation. Jones was a model of energy; his conservation organization encompassed most of the state's organized hunters. The Big Cypress Swamp was a favorite hunting ground in southern Florida, and Jones took a hand in drafting the Big Cypress National Preserve Act. The enabling legislation makes interesting reading and hints at a jockeying for position between the interests of "preservation" and "utilization." Oil was known to lie beneath the miles of cypress and prairie, and many private owners who sold land to the government kept the mineral rights. "No . . . oil and gas rights," reads the statute, "shall be acquired without the consent of the owner unless the Secretary [of the Interior] in his judgement, determines that such property is subject to, or threatened with, uses which are, or would be, detrimental to the purposes of the preserve."[9] It might be possible to "determine" that oil exploration would be

detrimental, but the cost of purchasing mineral rights would be exorbitant. Several oil companies have conducted seismic explorations in the Big Cypress National Preserve; no doubt others will follow. These explorations sometimes require the clearing of a right-of-way so that equipment can move through cypress strands. This is a most undesirable activity in any public park, although probably not a direct threat to panthers.

I attended a presentation by Shell Oil Company in 1987, given to describe the techniques that would be used in an upcoming search for oil. Shell was only the latest of several companies to explore the region. During the meeting I questioned why the companies didn't collaborate on a single search and pool the data, thereby dispensing with the cumulative impact of repeated explorations. The answer was that each company's method of exploration was a carefully guarded secret and would never be revealed for fear of yielding an advantage to a competitor. Unfortunately, this competitive aspect of free enterprise does not yield any advantage to the public resource being explored for oil. I have often wondered if a legislative cure would be worthwhile.

The Big Cypress Act further authorizes ". . . the Secretary [to] permit hunting, fishing, and trapping . . ."—but makes a qualification—". . . except that he may designate zones where and periods when no hunting, fishing trapping or entry may be permitted for reasons of public safety, administration, floral and faunal protection and management, or public use and enjoyment."[10] The law also stipulates that the lands shall be administered ". . . in a manner which will assure their natural and ecological integrity in perpetuity. . . ."[11] The possible interpretations of these countervailing mandates guarantee a perpetual wrangle between the utilizers and the preservers of the Big Cypress. Whoever has the greatest political leverage at any given time calls the shots. Approximately 146,000 acres of land to the northeast will eventually be added to 570,000 acres already under administration. The provision for additional acreage came about through congressional action in April 1988.[12]

The Fakahatchee Strand

The Fakahatchee Strand lies immediately to the west of the Big Cypress National Preserve. State Road 29 reaches south, from Immokalee to Everglades City, threading its way between the Fakahatchee Strand and the Big Cypress National Preserve. The extraordinary aesthetic and botanical treasures of the Fakahatchee Strand have been recognized since early in this century. One account credits Henry Ford with buying the land and offering it to the state as a gift in 1922. His offer was refused.[13] The towering cypress trees were felled by a timber company beginning in 1944. Dan Beard, the first superintendent of Everglades National Park, inspected the land in the late 1940s, when it had been partially cleared by the

lumbermen. He recommended acquisition by the federal government, but the times were not propitious. In the 1960s a new highway, dubbed Alligator Alley, sliced through the Fakahatchee Strand to link Naples to Fort Lauderdale. North of Alligator Alley the Fakahatchee Strand was in the hands of a private hunting club. The southern part of the swamp was purchased by the Gulf-American Land Company, a land-sales enterprise.

In the 1960s a Miami attorney named Melvin Finn made the goal of public ownership of the Fakahatchee a personal cause and worked for ten years to that end. In the 1970s difficulties overtook the Gulf-American Land Company because of its illegal dredge-and-fill activities along the Florida coast. In retrenching, the company divested itself of holdings in the Fakahatchee Strand by selling them to the state. Thus, the southern part of the swamp became a state preserve in 1974. However, some 6,000 private owners still hold title to lots there. The Gulf-American Land Company peddled these holdings, in acre-and-a-quarter lots, to speculators. Although the property was submerged during much of the year and could never have been developed, the lots sold like hotcakes.

The Fakahatchee Strand has drawn attention because of its consistent use by panthers—this despite a dearth of prey south of Alligator Alley, a fact reflected in the poor physical condition and poor reproduction of panthers that have been studied there. The Fakahatchee Strand has been a dependable locale for capturing panthers, although the dense vegetation can make the work arduous. The Preserve boundaries enclose approximately 60,000 acres between Alligator Alley and the Tamiami Trail (U.S. 41). This portion of the Preserve is potentially available for panther management (the tidal marsh and mangrove acreage south of the Tamiami Trail is excluded from consideration). The objective here should be to increase deer numbers. There would necessarily be constraints on the kind and extent of measures used, since botanical and scenic values could not be disregarded. However, there is much that could be done without degrading other resources. The portion of the Fakahatchee Strand north of Alligator Alley abuts private lands, where large prey animals (deer and hogs) are more abundant—as seen in the health and reproduction of panthers north of that highway. The northern portion of the Fakahatchee Strand has been purchased by the Fish and Wildlife Service and dubbed the Florida National Wildlife Panther Refuge; it comprises some 30,000 acres. Yet an area of this size will be of little use unless all the contiguous public land—and suitable private lands as well—are managed together for the common goal.

The Water Conservation Areas

Immediately to the east of the Big Cypress National Preserve, and to the north of Everglades National Park, are the diked impoundments called Water

Conservation Areas. They, along with a portion of Everglades National Park, are the remnant of the original Everglades —the "River of Grass" which flowed south from Lake Okeechobee to Florida Bay. The altered segment, the 550,000-acre Everglades Agricultural Area, is being used to grow sugar cane. This is a short-term agricultural activity and a short-sighted use of land, since the farming is slowly oxidizing the organic soil. The days of agriculture are numbered and will be terminated when bedrock is reached. While it lasts, agriculture is a hazard to Lake Okeechobee and to the remaining undrained portions of the original Everglades marsh—the National Park and the Water Conservation Areas—because of nutrient-laden waters pumped into them from the Everglades Agricultural Area and from regional dairy farms. The big lake was declared eutrophic in 1976.[14]

Draining the Everglades to farm the rich organic soil was a dream that wouldn't die. An attempt was made in the 1880s and failed. An Everglades Drainage District was formed in 1905 and made modest progress in peripheral areas. A few shallow canals were dug and low muck dikes were raised. These tentative projects were soon undone by hurricanes which drove the waters of Lake Okeechobee southward, sweeping the human settlements and all the flimsy works of man before them. The waters of a 1928 hurricane receded leaving 2,000 dead. Following a hurricane in 1947, the Central and Southern Flood Control District was formed to tame the Everglades once and for all. By that time technology and an improved tax base had made the dream possible. The Flood Control District was charged with preventing floods and attending to the needs of agricultural interests. The District, working with the Army Corps of Engineers, set about converting the rivers, lakes and marshes of southern Florida into a gigantic water-storage system. The work enlarged and increased the inadequate canals of the earlier drainage enterprise. Three large impoundments, the Water Conservation Areas, were built to store great volumes of water during dry periods that would recharge the subsurface aquifer of porous limestone, from which the urban belt along the southeast coast drew its supply.

Such vast manipulations subjected the remaining natural portions of this water-driven ecosystem to enormous stress. The backpumping of nutrient-laden waters into Lake Okeechobee stimulated the growth of algae in the lake's shallow waters. The Water Conservation Areas, designated one, two and three, also received a surfeit of nutrients. Number one, the most northerly, became the Loxahatchee National Wildlife Refuge; it is 145,000 acres in size. Number two, just to the south, encloses 135,000 acres. The southernmost impoundment abuts Everglades National Park and the Big Cypress National Preserve; at 480,000 acres it is the largest of the three. The Water Conservation Areas were made by raising dikes to enclose natural segments of the Everglades marsh; but within the impoundments seasonal water levels were not the same as before. The diked areas, although quite large, enclosed portions of the marsh much smaller than the

original. The undiked half-million acres of sugar cane fields were kept drained by canals, with the "excess" water being pumped into the impoundments. Unfortunately, the pumped water, laden with nutrients, is affecting the vegetative character of the marsh, transforming its botanical variety into a dense monoculture of cattails.[15] These changes appeared initially in the vicinity of the water discharge points, later spreading downstream in the marsh.[16]

This capacious plumbing system was designed for the averages of climate. However, rainfall occasionally exceeds the average 55 to 65 inches—going up to 120 inches in very wet years.[17] When heavy rains sent extreme volumes of water sluicing through the canals to the limited storage areas, it accumulated more rapidly than in pre-drainage times, severely stressing the marshes—both within the diked Water Conservation Areas and downstream in Everglades National Park. Water levels rose rapidly, often staying up longer. The damage was measured most dramatically in wildlife mortalities, particularly of deer. The snail kite, a snail-eating hawk of the Everglades marsh, also suffered from the disarranged movement of water. Historically, wildlife populations had always suffered from flood and drouth, but the engineered alterations of the region's hydrology exacerbated the impact of natural events.

In the late 1950s a study of the deer herd in the Water Conservation Areas—what has come to be known as the Everglades deer herd—was undertaken by a Game Commission biologist, Charles M. Loveless. It showed that the physical condition of deer varied with seasonal water level fluctuations. The depth of water in the Everglades is very shallow, enabling deer to feed on aquatic plants. Depths vary with the season, and the marsh is often dry for a part of each year. Loveless found that when the depth exceeded two feet, deer crowded onto tree islands that dotted the marsh, during which time body weight and health declined. As the waters receded in winter and spring, the deer again dispersed in the marsh to feed. Most fawns were born in the dry period when the herd was in better health. If high water persisted through the winter, the deer became desperate. Unable to reach palatable plants in the marsh, and having consumed the usable forage on the islands, they went on eating the nutritionally inadequate upland plants, stripping away the foliage as they died of malnutrition. The younger ones succumbed first, then the does; the bucks being stronger held out longest.[18]

Deer die-offs recurred, and in 1970 a team of five independent wildlife scientists undertook a review. Their report emphasized the futility of treating symptoms and pressed for far-reaching hydrological restoration measures. They did point out however that ameliorating effects for deer might be provided by building artificial islands and by placing layers of organic muck atop the rocky spoil banks of the impounding dikes. The hope was that native vegetation would grow and provide additional resting and foraging sites for deer.[19]

390

An interagency "Everglades Recreational Planning Board" assembled in 1973 and drew up a five-year plan for the recreational development of the Water Conservation Areas. It recommended that "during the five-year period ending December 1978, a total of 350 wildlife islands should be constructed," predicting that this measure "together with other habitat management practices will help maintain the Everglades deer herd at a reasonable population." Another proposal was to place a muck layer six to twelve inches thick atop the spoil banks of the Miami Canal—a dike that stretches diagonally across Water Conservation Area number three.[20]

In June 1980, James Schortemeyer, a Game Commission biologist, evaluated wildlife conditions in Conservation Area Three with regard to water management practices. He wrote that "... in mid-1979, for the second time in recent years, documented panther sign was discovered in this area indicating at least two different animals to be present."[21] The report described the damage done to deer habitat by periods of excessive water. It also noted the loss of organic soil from fire, as a result of periods of extreme drought.[22] He drew up a second lengthy appreciation later in the same year. It examined "Potential Habitat Management Programs on the Everglades Wildlife Management Area," and repeated many of the same recommendations of previous reports, including the construction and enhancement of artificial wildlife islands and adding muck to spoil banks upon which forage plants for deer could be planted.[23] Subsequently, it is reported that over 300 deer islands were constructed in Conservation Area Three, but they were inadequately vegetated with forage plants.[24] Only a fraction of the upland habitats in the Water Conservation Areas have ever received the attention that would be needed to manage deer as a food source for panthers. In fact, there has never been a sustained effort to manage habitat for deer in the Water Conservation Areas. Following the 1982 "mercy hunt" fiasco described in previous chapters, Game Commission enthusiasm for any kind of deer management waned perceptibly—and with good reason.

In the 1990s the welfare of the Florida panther raises new questions about the Everglades deer herd. Is it amenable to a management scheme that might aid the endangered cat? The question could only be answered by implementing the appropriate measures and observing the result. The miles of dikes within and around the Water Conservation Areas could, in theory, function as travelways for panthers, as do the tramways in the Fakahatchee Strand. If the dikes were mucked and vegetated with plants, suitable for cover and forage for deer, panthers could, in theory, benefit, marginally perhaps, in such a severe habitat, but if any serious effort is to be made on behalf of panthers in southern Florida (none has been), all possibilities should be appraised. Deer management in the Water Conservation Areas should be evaluated as part of a unified strategy of seeing the contiguous

public and private lands of southern Florida function as a single unit for panthers. Deer would have to be multiplied, and during times of prolonged flooding many would have to be shot to prevent the degradation of the upland habitats; and here is another point of friction. The frenzied reactions of animal rights organizations could be expected to derail such measures—unless the public could be prepared to accept it in advance. These troublesome ideas are unlikely to be greeted with enthusiasm by the appropriate agencies.

Private Lands

This issue has been touched upon throughout the text. It will be isolated here and traced chronologically. The term "private lands" refers to properties extending northward from the edge of the Big Cypress National Preserve and the Fakahatchee Strand, which are presently known to be used by panthers. In theory the private and public lands of southern Florida might be orchestrated to serve the needs of panthers. This region is presently hospitable to the cats, but not for long, given trends in land alteration.

During the mid-1800s cattlemen drove their herds southward into this wilderness, then peopled only by fugitive Indians who had evaded deportation to the West during three wars inflicted on them by the American government. Captain F.A. Hendry was one of the first recorded cattlemen to cross the Caloosahatchee River.[25] The rural county now bearing his name is still largely given to ranching. Some ranches are quite large; they support several panthers. Today the most immediate threat to these lands as panther habitat is through conversion from cattle ranching to the production of crops, primarily citrus. In the early 1980s unusually cold winters devastated the state's citrus groves in central Florida, prompting a shift to the south. Lands traditionally used to raise cattle now promise a greater monetary return from groves. The transition of natural land to crop production in southern Florida is often an interim use, sometimes a brief one, soon followed by urban development. Agriculture is exempted from many of the regulations that govern development. Therefore a brief phase of agricultural use, that is often little more than a subterfuge to prepare the land for building, often precedes urbanization. It is an abuse of the legitimate function of agriculture—which is to provide society with food and fiber.

In the late 1800s, Barron G. Collier, a Tennessean, amassed a fortune through a nationwide business in street car advertising. Looking for new worlds to conquer after the turn of the century, Collier began quietly buying up land in southwestern Florida, eventually garnering over a million acres. The county that bears his name became a political entity in 1923. (Thirteen of Florida's counties appeared on the map between 1921 and 1925.)[26] What remains of the original Collier holdings is owned by two descendant branches of the family. The acreage

is tallied in the tens of thousands, much of it inhabited by panthers. I do not mean to create the impression that these are the only large, single ownerships of important panther lands—they are not—or even that they are the key to maintaining a functional refuge for panthers, although they are important—but from here one might speculate on how to extend the refuge northward. The allure of this point of departure is that one branch of the Collier family, Collier Enterprises, has declared that any of its lands are for sale. The one and only guaranteed method of preserving upland wildlife habitat at present is by fee-simple acquisition. There are both government programs and private organizations in Florida devoted to acquiring lands for preservation.

In November 1984 the Panther Advisory Council was called to Tallahassee by Governor Graham to recommend a boundary configuration for lands in the northern Fakahatchee Strand, which were then being proposed for acquisition by the Fish and Wildlife Service. There was a dispute with a landowner who wished to keep a portion of the property wanted for the refuge. It was at this meeting that a representative of Collier Enterprises announced that it was a willing seller— given the right price, of course. This matter is also of interest because planning is presently underway to transform thousands of acres of these holdings to citrus groves.[27]

As told earlier, a general picture of the panther situation began to emerge in 1985 and was summarized in the recommendations of the Panther Advisory Council late in that year, with emphasis on private lands: ". . . unfortunately, these private lands to the north are beginning to be converted to intensive agriculture and may, someday, be unavailable as habitat. Ten thousand acres of Collier County agricultural land presently being used to grow citrus, is expected to jump to 40,000 acres in the next five years. If a means cannot be devised to preserve this vital habitat on private lands then the survivability of the *F. c. coryi* population in southern Florida may ultimately depend entirely on the habitat encompassed by the boundaries of contiguous public lands that are primarily in the Fakahatchee Strand, the Big Cypress Swamp and the Everglades—a very grim prospect."[28]

Economic pressures are rapidly clearing the hammocks and pine forests from this vulnerable domain of the panther, supplanting them with citrus groves, pastures and scattered houses. Any preservation strategy would have to begin with a map that identified habitat types and contrasted present land uses against those projected for the future. Among other recommendations from the Panther Advisory Council to the Game Commission in 1985, one emphatically encouraged a "hasty mapping project" of this region, because "it is urgent that we improve our understanding of the situation on these private lands."[29]

In May of 1986, at the formative meeting of the FPIC, the need for a management plan for private lands was deliberated—whereupon the Game Commission representative voiced a reluctance to wave a "red flag" at private landowners. However, the issue remained under discussion during the year-long preparation of the revised recovery plan. It survived a year of review and was written into the plan as a recovery objective.[30] But at the end of 1991 there was still not anything resembling a management plan for private lands, nor was there a map, which is essential to planning. Also in May 1986, at a Panther Advisory Council meeting, a Fish and Wildlife Service man announced that "anticipated applications for drainage permits may soon affect up to 70,000 acres of single-owner land within the known range of the Florida panther." "In view of this discouraging news," ran our subsequent correspondence to the Game Commission, "it would seem that the Council's estimates of the previous October about the amount of land in panther habitat to be converted to citrus in the next five years had been greatly underestimated, and that panther habitat on private lands could soon be lost if something is not done to arrest these trends. Some interagency mechanism would be useful to coordinate the modification of private lands in a way that doesn't obliterate panther habitat. The Council would encourage the Commission to exert its influence to this end."[31]

In June of 1986 a memorandum from the newly formed FPIC disclosed that an "information strategy"—ostensibly to inform the public about the problems of, and plans for, panther survival—was in the offing.[32] On behalf of the Panther Advisory Council I sent suggestions to the Game Commission on what the public should be told, urging that the strategy pay particular attention to the private lands problem.[33] As often happened with written replies to our letters, the answer implied that the agency had already drawn the same conclusions and was at work on the matter: "We concur with the Council's beliefs regarding the foundation of a public information policy. We will continue to pursue a truthful, if not quite as pessimistic as you suggest, disclosure of the plight of the Florida panther. We share your concerns regarding the four 'crucial issues' that you identify. Nevertheless, we draw optimism from recent documentation of Florida panther reproduction, and continue to insist that Council conclusions regarding the adequacy of their prey base extend well beyond the limits of the Commission-generated data that form their basis. . . ."[34] However, in all the pages and pages of *Coryi*, the information organ of the FPIC, there was never an explanation of the role of these lands in panther conservation.

By October 1986, at the fall meeting of the Panther Advisory Council, the Game Commission had made no move to begin mapping the private lands as recommended a year before. However, as briefly mentioned in Chapter 5, a promising initiative came from Larry Harris, a professor of wildlife ecology at the

University of Florida having expertise in habitat analysis and access to cartographic tools. His offer to do the mapping was well received at a Council meeting, where the Fish and Wildlife Service delegate suggested that he go to the next FPIC meeting scheduled for January 1987, and make his pitch to the administrators. Harris agreed. Following the meeting, the Panther Advisory Council sent a letter to the Game Commission pounding away at this key problem. Soon afterward, Harris was asked by the head of the Game Commission's research lab in Gainesville to send a proposal. He was elated, and arranged for a graduate student to work on the project, but his hope for bringing it before the FPIC for sanction came to nothing; the reason is not clear. He was called by a Fish and Wildlife Service official and told that his appearance at the January meeting would not be particularly useful.[35] This is odd, because at a meeting of the FPIC's Technical Subcommittee on January 13 a Game Commission spokesman outlined several projects being contemplated by his agency, one of which was to work with Larry Harris on developing a land use map for Southwest Florida.[36]

Meanwhile, Harris forwarded his proposal to the Game Commission. It was bounced back and forth for revisions as the summer slipped away. When weeks passed with nothing settled, he repeatedly called the agency's research laboratory in Gainesville. Each time he was assured that approval was expected soon. In August, Harris, in exasperation, called directly to Game Commission headquarters in Tallahassee to get an answer. There an official informed him that he, the official, had "only now seen this proposal for the first time. There is no money available; this project is not fundable."[37] And so it goes in the administrative chaos of panther recovery. It was another bitter disappointment for the Panther Advisory Council. When I probed some individuals in the Game Commission, they shrugged and said in resignation that it was "the bureaucracy." But how could officials in the central office be so out of touch as not to know that the mapping plans had been broached to the FPIC's Technical Subcommittee the previous January by their own delegates?

Linkage

The habitat linkage idea first came to me in a letter from John Eisenberg in December 1984.[38] He cautioned that keeping panthers in Florida was unrealistic unless habitat could be guaranteed on an appropriate scale—an uncertainty, given the state's rampant urbanization. Eisenberg enclosed a paper on the subject, written by Larry Harris and one of his students, Reed Noss, which outlined thoughts on regional habitat linkage. The paper highlighted two global trends: the rapid reduction in total forest acreage, and the fragmentation of the remainder; both are fatal to organisms that cannot be sustained within the decrement of space left to them. The authors advocated the comprehensive planning of landscapes to insure interconnected natural environments. The agricultural and the built environment

would have to develop in concert with the conservation of the natural environment. "If we can establish a system of intensive conservation preserves," they speculated, "integrated with extensive conservation easements and management programs that will work for these flagship species (e.g. large mammal, bird and reptile carnivores, and elephants), we believe it will very nearly suffice for all other species as well."[39]

It made sense; it ought to be done, and if there were to be panthers (and black bears) in Florida's future, it would have to be done. The challenge was to transform the idea into a program. It seemed that the popular goal of preserving panthers could be the perfect vehicle to set up the working arrangements. In February 1985 the Panther Advisory Council sent the idea off in a letter to the Game Commission as "a matter for attention."[40] The outcome of this episode was given in detail in Chapter 4. To summarize: prior to a Panther Advisory Council meeting meeting in May 1985, the Game Commission expressed an interest in the idea and wanted it discussed at the upcoming meeting. It was, but the agency officials then declined to organize a workshop aimed at sponsoring legislation. So following the meeting I phoned Bill Partington who agreed to organize the workshop. It was scheduled for December 1985. To stimulate interest, Partington asked Harris to write an article on the concept aimed at a general audience. The product, entitled Conservation Corridors: A Highway System for Wildlife, was published by Partington's Florida Conservation Foundation as an *ENFO* report.[41]

The workshop was a huge success with over 200 in attendance. There were representatives of local governments, agricultural interests, legislators, many planning and environmental officials, environmental leaders, a representative from the governor's office and a gubernatorial candidate. Here was a fertile ground in which to plant, and a high promise of what might come with a little nurturing. After the workshop Bill Partington immediately sent out a synopsis of the issues asking for comments:

> . . .We must maintain existing habitats. The system must be comprehensive, from state on down through to regional and local governments. We have sufficient baseline data now to design an effective corridor system. . . . The rate of habitat loss has never been greater and will only increase . . . much can be started now at state and local level, which should encourage legislative action. . . . We can start with our excellent assortment of publicly owned or controlled lands . . . and private preserves. . . . A cooperative, understanding attitude is needed in dealing with private landowners and in helping them meet their needs while creating a quality system. Varied strategies, some new and unproven must be tried. . . . A steering committee of dedicated and

knowledgeable persons needs to be established, to develop a plan of action dealing with all these issues. Overall state guidance is necessary but much can be accomplished on regional and local levels. . . .[42]

In June of 1986 a bill was introduced into the state legislature that would have had the Game Commission undertake a feasibility study and submit a written report by 1988.[43] It was heavily attacked in the Senate by lobbyists representing large landowners and failed early in the session.[44] At the Panther Advisory Council meeting later that year the assembled group was told by Tommy Hines of the Game Commission that his superiors had not been enthusiastic about the bill.

Late in 1986 Bill Partington made ready for another try at legislation. He met with an ad hoc "wildlife habitat group," which concluded that unless the Game Commission was willing to throw its weight behind the legislation, the project would be futile. But no one knew where the agency stood. To find out, Partington recessed the meeting and phoned Alan Egbert, the agency's assistant director. Egbert said there were "problem areas." He identified three: some vocal dissenting biologists, worried landowners and government agencies. However, Egbert said he would call back with an answer after checking with the director, which he did soon after.[45] He would not endorse the idea of legislation in 1987, but neither did he indicate that his agency would oppose it. Armed with a definite maybe from the Game Commission, Partington decided to forge ahead. To insure that there would be no misunderstanding of his conversation with Egbert, he followed the telephone conversation with a letter outlining his thoughts on how to proceed; the bill to be introduced in 1987, wrote Partington, should stipulate a joint study by the Game Commission and Florida DNR to survey existing refuges, enumerate research needs, identify funding sources and so on. The bill would seek appropriations to get the staff work underway and provide an advisory committee made up of agency representatives, landowners and non-government scientists. From this modest beginning a more ambitious design would be charted for legislative action in 1988 or 1989.[46]

Egbert, to insure that there would be no misunderstanding on where the Game Commission stood, sent an answer.

> . . . The need for such a project is clear. . . . Before we can recommend definite actions to the Legislature . . . we need to have a better idea of our protection priorities and needs. The Commission has already taken the first step in the development of a wildlife habitat plan, obtaining 1986 Legislative approval of a project to study the efficacy of using LANDSAT to inventory and

monitor plant communities and wildlife habitats. The next logical step is to identify what species should be incorporated into a habitat protection plan, determine what lands are important to these species and decide what degree of protection may be necessary. Combining this information with LANDSAT results (assuming the feasibility study shows positive results) should provide quantitative recommendations of statewide application. . . . Contrary to what I earlier stated, I envision this phase taking two full years. . . . During this phase, I am against involving formal advisory committees; this phase is biological in nature and an advisory committee would not enhance progress. . . .

The second major phase . . . would be the actual development of legislation. . . . It is in this phase . . . that we can consider some type of advisory committee . . . (An advisory committee can be appointed by the Commission and need not be created through legislation.) Obviously, our thinking on this matter has evolved somewhat, and this approach may cause problems for you. For one thing, it would not come as quickly as even I envisioned and further it does not presume that connecting corridors is the single best approach. I most certainly do not wish to delay or create hurdles for a fast-train corridors approach, but only to point out that our participation will be devoted to a broader perspective.

I am sure that a number of people in the environmental community feel we have all of the information necessary to go straight to the legislation phase. However, I think the more orderly progression is advisable. Failure to adequately lay a biological framework for political action will only lead to additional divisiveness among environmentalists, researchers, and resource managers that will kill, in my opinion, any proposed legislation. I think we have seen too much of that phenomenon in the past. With the exception of the longer time frame, our proposal is similar to yours.

Finally, I must tell you that the question of institutionalization of a wildlife habitat system is very clear in our minds. Apparently, there is a view that this should be split up or maybe even that a new institution be established. We believe this agency, as the State's constitutionally authorized wildlife agency, is the place for any new program, freely admitting that we have a parochial attitude. But this attitude is vested in the sincere belief that we are

the responsible body and the one best equipped philosophically
and organizationally to handle it. . . .[47]

There it is. The point is clearly made that independent advisory bodies are
not wanted, and the Game Commission intends to take its customary creep
approach (if it acts at all) to a crises that will not wait forever. The agency claims
it wants to carefully prepare a biological framework before seeking any supporting
legislation. The idea might be commendable if not for the fact that more than
325,000 people a year are pouring into the state. The prospects for a "statewide
habitat protection plan" will crumble under an oncoming migration that is rapidly
foreclosing all options. It would be prudent to seek the enabling legislation (which
might take several years of lobbying), to hire a staff and get them settled into
quarters. This would not interfere with ongoing biological planning. And the letter
seems to hedge on the follow up for the LANDSAT project ("assuming the
feasibility study shows positive results"). The cautious types at the Game Commission always insure that any commitment has an escape hatch. But the letter leaves
no doubt that, if and when such a program emerges, the Game Commission wants
dominion over it—and (it hopes) without any legislatively imposed advisors. What
a struggle it has been to get the prospects for linking habitat statewide disinterred
from that graveyard of innovative ideas known as the Florida Game and Fresh
Water Fish Commission.

Meanwhile, during the period described here in which the corridor, or
linkage, idea was emerging, and environmental groups were futilely struggling to
create a legal framework to underpin the concept as a public policy, a political storm
brewed up in central Florida over an actual corridor issue. The state of Florida is
administratively divided into five Water Management Districts. Each with a
professional staff, guided by a director, who serves a board of five members chosen
by the governor. It is another of those public institutions directed by political
appointees who are not required to have professional qualifications commensurate
with their responsibilities—a damaging institutional flaw today when water must
treated as a depleting resource. But as Florida careens into an uncertain future, the
leadership quality of water management boards is subject to the same hit-or-miss
process of political appointments that afflicts other environmental and conservation agencies.

In September 1985, a citizen organization, Friends of the Wekiva River,
asked the St. Johns River Water Management District to restrict development near
the Wekiva River, being alarmed about the ever-expanding Orlando metropolis
which was encroaching on their river basin. The Wekiva is one of Florida's famous
clear-water streams that boil up out of crevices in the state's limestone substrate.
The fears of environmentalists stemmed from previous damage done by develop-

ment to the Little Wekiva River, a tributary of the Wekiva. There, trees had been stripped from the river's edge and houses built in the floodplain, and riverbanks had eroded to be carried downstream, thereby changing the configuration of the river and threatening riverside residences. Homeowners had then demanded that local governments come to the rescue of their threatened property.[48]

The Water Management District staff went to work on the request made by Friends of the Wekiva and in January 1986, announced plans for a protective buffer along the river that would exclude development. A howl of opposition immediately went up from homebuilders' associations and from a wealthy developer who charged that buffer regulations were an unconstitutional land grab which constituted the taking of property without due process of law. The opponents threatened a legal challenge.[49] It afflicted the governing board of the Water Management District with cold feet. The board was unsure of its legal position and lacked a "damn the torpedoes" attitude that would put it to the test. At a meeting in December 1986 it delayed voting on a buffer—at the request of a developer.[50] But the issue would not be stilled. The environmentalists had a sympathetic press and wide support. The Water Management District Board responded to the ruckus, in the words of an editorial in the *Orlando Sentinel*, ". . . as if a water moccasin just dropped into its canoe."[51] The Board met again in July 1987 to consider the matter and, following the well-trodden path of irresolute decision makers, it ordered a study.

By this time reverberations from the fracas were rattling windows in the state capitol. A month after the Water Management District contracted with the University of Florida's Center for Wetlands for a study, the Governor and Cabinet endorsed the idea of a no-development buffer for the river. In November 1987 Mark T. Brown, a co-author of the study, reported to the Board that a substantial buffer should be maintained between the river's wetland borders and any new development.[52] However, to the dismay of environmentalists, the Board decided to wash its hands of the troublesome affair, declaring that it didn't have the authority to impose the ban. One might pause here to wonder why, if the Board didn't believe it had such authority, it paid $8,000 for a study.

The turbulence did not subside, and the environmentalists regrouped for the next moves. The Florida Audubon Society and Friends of the Wekiva River formally petitioned the Water Management District to create the protective buffer.[53] Also, the East Central Florida Regional Planning Council stepped in. The Regional Planning Councils were created by Florida's Growth Management Act of 1972. The intent of the act was to impose a degree of order on runaway urban sprawl. The statute mandates counties to produce management plans that conform to statewide criteria for orderly growth. The planning councils have to consider protective measures for rivers and endangered species. On January 1988 the Regional

Planning Council unanimously endorsed a buffer policy.[54] The same month, Florida's Governor Martinez urged local governments to establish the buffers. He also took steps to expedite the purchase of four parcels of land along the river, totaling 24,600 acres, which were on a long list of candidate properties for acquisition by the state. The governor also assigned a task force of state, regional and local officials to propose measures that would protect the river.

The Water Management District's governing board had been left behind by the surge of popular sentiment and now, marooned in the mire of its irresolution, found itself starring in the role of lonely bureaucratic wimp. The *Orlando Sentinel* heaped editorial abuse on the faltering decision makers.[55] The board was thereby prompted to reevaluate its stance, and in April 1988 it enacted a new rule that would ban development along the Wekiva River. The District's executive director said that creating a buffer would step into a legal gray area, but he recommended that the board take the risk. He compared the buffer endeavor to a football game and urged the board members to run for a touchdown. "If developers and home builders want to quibble with the buffer, let a judge referee."[56] The developers and home builders, as it turned out, eyed the rising wrath of citizens and elected to remain quiet. The environmentalists, still riding a popular wave, lobbied successfully in the 1988 legislature to produce The Wekiva River Protection Act. The law virtually ordered the St. Johns River Water Management District to adopt a rule establishing protective buffers adjacent to the river. It also mandated a welter of other restrictions on the density of urban development in the river basin.[57] The Wekiva battle reveals the latent citizen support for environmental protection, which can be mobilized when a threat becomes evident, and brought to bear when the threat is clarified and a reasonable solution is offered. The *Orlando Sentinel*, and other media as well, did an excellent job of educating the public and promoting protective policies. When the 1988 legislature convened in the spring, protecting the Wekiva River had become an unstoppable political bandwagon.

The strong environmental safeguards in the Wekiva River Protection Act could be applied elsewhere in the state, as pointed out by Charles Lee of the Florida Audubon Society:

> The Wekiva River Protection Act should be looked upon as a model comprehensive approach to protecting sensitive ecosystems. If replicated elsewhere in Florida by the legislature, it could bring true protection to such treasures as the Suwannee River, which currently lies completely vulnerable to development in an area of the state where local governments have no inclination of their own to develop protective plans and ordinances. . . . Imagine this envelope of protection surrounding the Myakka, the Mana-

tee, Little Manatee, and remaining natural portions of the Peace and St. Johns rivers.[58]

Threats to wildlife were raised as an issue in protection of the river.[59] The forested land around the Wekiva is Florida black bear country, and its dismemberment a threat to the subspecies. The Game Commission was scarcely visible during this controversy, although an unparalleled opportunity was offered which could have been used to raise public awareness about the importance of linking habitat and to build support statewide for the idea. But in a time when Florida's wildlife faces its greatest threat, the Game Commission's outlook is narrow and primarily defensive. Opportunities come and go that an alert agency could use to make great strides in protecting the state's wildlife against the onrushing destruction. It could also use such opportunities to present itself as a crusading defender of the state's threatened wildlife—an image-building exercise based on substance. But there is no imagination and no will—and no substance. Meanwhile, regional planning councils, county planning departments and land planning initiatives in general have started to incorporate the concept of wildlife corridors into their projects, but without guidance from the state agency that should be leading the way.

One of the most sensitive indices of environmental quality in a region is the composition of native wildlife species. It follows that if the line is to be held on environmental quality in Florida, we must limit the space allotted to the built environment and the space given over to agriculture. And we must ultimately limit the intensity of human uses in the natural environment. Providing for such species as the manatee, the black bear and the panther will preserve them so that they might save for us a Florida worth living in. That will demand a large habitat, and to save it will require land-management institutions with qualities of foresight and fortitude that are not presently evident.

For all its imposing achievements, Florida's drive to acquire land is falling behind in the race to preserve a sufficiency of the natural amenities that make the state a desirable place to live. The revenues for buying land come primarily from documentary stamps and from severance taxes on minerals (mainly phosphate). The percentage allotted to the purchase of land is currently about 77 million dollars a year, while the funding needs for properties presently awaiting purchase is between 2.4 and 2.8 billion dollars.[60] The cost of land escalates, and developers, of course, will not wait for the overburdened acquisition machinery to catch up. A prize parcel in the Wekiva River corridor was recently sold to an eager developer.[61]

A one-cent increase in the sales tax would raise a billion to 1.5 billion dollars a year.[62] Tax increases are not popular with citizens—or legislators—but opinion polls have indicated a willingness of the majority of citizens to contribute

additional revenue to save land and wildlife. In 1988 citizens of Marion County voted an increase in their property taxes—which will remain in effect for 30 years—for purchasing environmentally sensitive lands in the County to, "preserve as wildlife habitat, parks or other recreation and conservation uses."[63] If it was made clear that the tax would be earmarked solely for the preservation of the woods, waters and wildlife of the deteriorating Florida peninsula, citizens might agree to a "green penny tax." No finer opportunity would ever be offered to a generation to buy a future for the next.

Chapter 18

REFORM AND EDUCATION

In any great endeavor there comes a moment
when the will to press ahead falters in the face
of the enormity of what has to be done.

The Economist, October 1, 1988
Speaking of Mikhail Gorbachev's frustrated attempts
to reform the world's most intractable bureaucracies.

The administration of endangered species programs in the United States is inexcusably defective. It cannot improve until the appropriate institutions are prepared to dispense with all concerns except biological reality in drafting designs for secure, self-sustaining populations. Until then the disappointing stories told in this book will go on repeating. We cannot advance unless the land-management agencies learn to perform objective analyses and spell out the conditions for success; they must then go forward where they can, while articulating the way, and the obstacles to, the final goal. It has been shown that public acquiescence is essential, and its active support will often be the lever that moves obstructions aside. It follows that in all cases the issues must be clearly and frankly laid out. A solution to this epidemic dysfunction of bureaucracy falls into two broad categories: institutional reform and education.

The cases dissected in these pages have been habitually troubled by upper-level fears having nothing to do with biology. Politically-appointed agency administrators are usually laymen who have learned to keep a weather eye on the horizon. Too often they steer policy wide of troubled waters with too little regard for destination and schedule. They are rarely picked for qualities that might promise the keenest service: personal strength combined with professional acclaim, or at least a demonstrated competence, in their field of appointed service, as is the case with chairmen of the Federal Reserve Board, for instance, or a director of the National Health Service (we have had the good sense to put the central banks and the nation's health service beyond the reach of amateurs). Too often the appointee qualifies solely by a philosophical outlook similar to his political patron's—which may have no relevance to the professional demands of the service he or she is to provide—or by nothing more than pliancy. Even in an agency headed by an innovative and talented appointee, constraints can be imposed by careerists in the

404

ranks devoted to safeguarding tradition—institutional scientists and biologists not excluded. There is no scarcity of biased expertise in the land-management profession.

The Game Commissions

Reform should be directed at freeing agencies from politics, convention and orthodoxy. It might be undertaken by several methods. First among these would be the installment of professionally qualified bodies to oversee agency policy. Secondly, specialists should advise and interact with the agency staff on technically demanding tasks. Another measure, the periodic independent review, will be brought up in conjunction with the federal agencies. There is a precedent for independent professional oversight in this field—one that worked. It can be seen in the early quasi-independent state game commissions, an institutional design that was fostered by an alliance of conservationists to overcome the debilitations of political patronage. They saw that new laws, refuges and departments did little good when the requisite human qualities were not installed to make them go.

The commission system proved sound until the march of time brought transformations of the natural and social environment which have reduced it to a feeble and aversive state. A recent article in *Audubon* magazine chronicles yet another case of dysfunction-through-controversy avoidance, this time bringing disaster to a resource. For two decades the California fish and game agency would not heed warnings about the impending decline of winter-run king salmon in the upper Sacramento River. In 1989 only 500 fish made the spawning run (down from 117,000 in 1969), this after the agency director assured interested parties the year before that the salmon run had been stabilized. The political forces that would have been discomfited by the appropriate regulatory correctives were agricultural and development interests. When the threat ripened to crisis, the California Game Commission too late granted the fish endangered status, opening a way for action that might have earlier prevented endangerment.[1] This is a second-hand account of the affair, but it is in accord with the laws of bureaucratic motion demonstrated in previous chapters.

Even when game commissions recognize a need to act, they typically will go forward only by fractional increments. The gopher tortoise in Florida furnishes yet another example of this creep approach. For ten years this beguiling reptile suffered the distinction of having been declared an imperiled species—which could be legally harvested. Under the persistent lobbying of conservationists, the Game Commission finally ended the paradox, but it yielded at the pace of a bureaucratic tortoise. The *Bulletin of the Gopher Tortoise Council* sketched a history of this labor of a decade for its readers. "Possession limits were established at 10 (per person) and subsequently reduced to five and then two; at the same time, open

season was reduced by 3-month increments from year-round to permanent closure. . . . March 4, 1988 was a day in history that Gopher Tortoise Council members should long remember. By a unanimous vote, the five members of the Florida Game and Fresh Water Fish Commission formally approved the end of gopher tortoise harvesting. . . . The vote marked the culmination of ten years of effort by many GTC members to bring Florida's regulations into line with the status and biology of the declining species."[2]

There is a theoretically simple solution to this weakness. There are in the universities and research institutions of Florida, wildlife and fish scientists eminently qualified to serve on the commission. They have an understanding of research and management and of how the one relates to the other, and their profession is centered on the study of wildlife (and fish). They are generally more receptive to new ideas, and sooner abreast of advances in new fields, than their counterparts in the bureaucracy. They cultivate a wide range of professional contacts upon which to draw for information. Perhaps most important, they understand that under appropriate circumstances wildlife can be managed for harvest, so their appointments should not threaten hunters (or organized fishermen) who comprise the shrinking base of political power for the commissions. A further advantage is that, in the inevitable controversies that are coming to attend the management of wildlife, they would have a competence to defend policies that cannot be supplied today by lay commissioners. Instituting the professionally qualified commission would simply be updating George Bird Grinnell's nineteenth-century formula to accommodate the more complex demands of the present.

No institution attains perfection, and the professional commission would surely reveal its own peculiar flaws; but there are degrees of unserviceability, and the system now in place desperately wants improving. A commission of professionals might be no more immune to riotous constituency pressures than any other assemblage of mortals, but its technical strength would stand as a barrier against policy by capitulation—an advantage denied the unschooled. I believe such a body of professionals would have moved quickly to restrict hunting in the Big Cypress National Preserve when data indicated the precarious status of the panther there, and I do not think an informed commission would have sat inert in 1987, permitting the National Park Service to have its way with the Florida panther recovery plan. I believe that under a body of wildlife professionals the whole apparatus of recovery would boast a record of greater directness and clarity of purpose. Such a body might also see the link between education and the future of wildlife in our urban society, and start up the steep hill of enlightening citizens on all wildlife issues. The challenges that will stand before state game agencies in the next century are written large today in Florida, with its dismal catalogue of endangered organisms, where habitat is vanishing with alarming rapidity. Florida urgently needs a strong, knowledgeable Game Commission, imbued with an innovative self-confidence.

Wildlife in the Sunshine State can no longer be adequately attended to by an institution designed for a bygone era, which works at the sleepytime tempo of the 1940s.

Quasi-independent, professional commissions need not be limited to the oversight of wildlife resources. The public interest would prosper by applying the concept to other environmental agencies. In the 1980s the Florida Legislature moved to protect the state's marine fisheries by creating a commission to formulate rules for harvesting. The legislators neglected to specify scientific credentials for the positions, but it happened that capable scientists were named to them anyway. This body operates administratively within the Department of Natural Resources, but is still answerable to the Governor and Cabinet. It is independent of the agency, but not of the executive branch of government. The system has worked well; of 70 recommendations to the Governor and Cabinet over the years, only two were rejected.[3] As pressures weigh ever more heavily on the earth, all aspects of environmental administration are becoming as technically demanding as they are vital to the public welfare. The current wildlife situation in Florida is easily comparable to the severities looming at the end of the last century. It is not prudent to guard the depleting natural resources of this state (or of the nation) through an antiquated practice of political patronage that cannot consistently place the best-qualified persons in the most important slots.

Only by installing procedures for excellence at the top can the growing bureaucratic apparatus of environmental stewardship be made consistently sound. The runaway growth now threatening this flat and vulnerable peninsula cries out for regulation through a system of rock-ribbed professionalism. Persons placed on oversight commissions should have a technical grasp of environmental issues and a demonstrated competence in their respective fields. Such appointed bodies should have the authority to install at the heads of departments under their jurisdictions talented administrators who not only possess a zeal for safeguarding the environment, but who have been properly trained for the work.

The lack of keenness that can afflict politically appointed environmental administrators is indicated by a recent newsletter of Manasota 88, an environmental organization in southwestern Florida:

SECRETARY HAS TO GO___Manasota-88's June-July newsletter noted, "If as he purports, Governor Martinez is committed to the protection of Florida's environment, he will take immediate steps to replace Secretary of the Department of Environmental Regulation Dale Twachtmann."

One year later our position regarding Mr. Twachtmann has not changed. Manasota-88 has filed suit against EPA [Environmental Protection Agency] to force Florida to comply with the provisions of the Clean Water Act. The Department has permitted conservation easements to be accepted as wetlands mitigation. The Department has delayed the clean-up of Lake Okeechobee. The Department is promulgating rules for effluent reuse that fail to adequately protect the public health. The Department has developed rules for incinerator ash that will permit increased groundwater pollution. The Department has weakened the wetlands mitigation rule to such a point that Manasota-88 has had to develop its own wetlands compliance study.

If, as the Governor's Chief of Operations Brian Ballard stated, Twachtmann is just carrying out the Governor's wishes, the state environment will be further degraded. Instead, Manasota-88 hopes the Governor will refute Ballard's statement by replacing Twachtmann. We need a person who understands that Florida's future is tied to good policies and restoration projects that undo the harm we have done to our environment.[4]

The reader should note that Manasota-88 is one environmental organization that thinks clearly, acts decisively and isn't afraid to "shout." Although it is a small, local organization it is one of the most effective in Florida.

A scheme to rectify the ailing administration of Florida's environment emerged from an Environmental Efficiency Study Commission appointed by the Governor in 1986. It suggested to the state legislature changes for bringing order to the welter of laws and institutional jurisdictions that have evolved for environmental protection. One was aimed at rectifying the flaws of political patronage. "Appointments to all collegial bodies acting as heads of environmental agencies, except the Governor and Cabinet, will be made by the governor from three possible choices forwarded to him by a new Environmental Appointments Board. The members of the EAB will be appointed by the Governor, Senate President and Speaker of the House for designated terms. Appointees to agency boards will be selected based on qualifications established in the organic acts relating to each agency. The governor's appointee must be confirmed by the Senate."[5]

This idea falls short of a mandated professional commission, but would be a large improvement over the present appointments roulette. Unfortunately, it was the recommendation of a minority (composed of environmentalists) of the

Environmental Efficiency Study Commission—which was weighted in favor of developers whose interest in efficiency settled on smoothing the route to permits for their activities.[6] The minority report would also have bridled the Game Commission by making it a department answerable to the Governor and Cabinet (presumably doing away with commissioners). This action would be vexed by the difficult and uncertain recourse to a constitutional amendment, and it is worth reflecting that political commentators since Edmund Burke have cautioned against reforming institutions by demolition. Rather than wrenching the agency out of its historical foundations, it would seem more promising to update a mechanism that once worked well, simply by updating the qualifications for commissioners. The early success of this design strongly recommends it as a dependable model for rehabilitation. The need for amending the constitution could be by-passed by having the Senate formally define the professional qualifications of a commissioner. That body must approve the governor's nominees, although this check has typically been a perfunctory exercise.

Scholarship

Scholars have looked for a cure for the bureaucratic antics now parading as recovery programs in the United States. Three wildlife professionals in the West recently mined the literature of political science. Tim Clark, Ron Crete and John Cada, in an incisive paper, began by looking at studies on the dysfunctional behavior of organizations; they then reviewed methods that have improved the performance of business and industry.[7] They advocate setting up parallel organizations alongside the balky bureaucracy. The authors outlined two classes of parallel organizations: task forces and project teams. "Task forces are temporary teams focused on short-term problems, whereas project teams are more permanent. . . ."[8] The authors moreover favored bringing the special skills of trained coordinators into the melee. The coordinator's role would be to mediate between the various factions and to insure the flow of essential information to all appropriate parties, most importantly, at the lofty plane where ruling decisions are made. The authors noted the observation of a political scientist, T. M. Douglas, that "in bureaucracies, the site of decisionmaking is high up the hierarchical ladder, and it is carried out by people who are often physically removed from much of the task environment and who are least in contact with its essential details."[9]

The work of Clark, *et al.* is a commendable stab at shoring up an inept structure, but the question is how to make the bureaucrats take the medicine? The authors weren't naive; they cautioned that ". . . even if parallel organizations are set up, agency administrators must insure that they are not taken over by bureaucratic values and procedures."[10] But unfortunately that is what will happen—as predictably as the sun sets in the west. Parallel organizations in the land-management agencies are either co-opted (or more accurately established as fronts)

as with the IGBC, the FPIC and BFAT, or ignored if possible, as happened with the Panther Advisory Council and with BIOTA research in the black-footed ferret debacle. The Fish and Wildlife Service ought, in theory, to be an imposing parallel organization. But the agency is so weak it can only fill the incongruously merged roles of sugar-daddy and hand-maiden. In January 1989 the Florida panther recovery program was blessed by the advent of a parallel organization (an imposing one)—the Captive Breeding Specialists Group of the International Union for the Conservation of Nature. It was brought in by the Fish and Wildlife Service. At the time of this writing it has helped some, but the bureaucratic resistance has been formidable as we will see in the final chapter.

Parallel organizations and coordinators could usefully serve a multi-institutional recovery program, but they are secondary measures. Fundamental reform—in the nature of oversight by professionals—will have to be instituted before the agencies will embrace (or even tolerate) such refinements. Parallel organizations and coordinators may have worked as institutional adjuncts in business and industry; when marketing products in a competitive environment, efficiency cannot long be ignored. But land-management agencies are not subject to the ruthless imperative of efficiency; they are driven by ideology and conflict aversion, and are quite willing to squander money and other assets to protect their tribal prerogatives and ideals.

The U.S. Fish and Wildlife Service

The appalling afflictions illustrated in this book could be improved by strengthening the federal agency that administers the Endangered Species Act. The setting today is not unlike the one faced by George Bird Grinnell a century ago when the government was incompetently working to save wildlife. Grinnell, as a crusading magazine editor, had spurred on the sportsmen's clubs, and in 1886 organized an affiliation of local Audubon Societies. A year later he and Theodore Roosevelt founded the Boone and Crockett Club ". . . to do for the larger mammals what the Audubon Society . . . was doing for birds."[11] Laws were enacted and departments set up to enforce them. Then it was seen that laws are only print on the page of a book, and no more, without a sound instrument to send to the field. Today history comes around in a fresh cycle. No improvement is possible unless the endangered species administration of the Fish and Wildlife Service is put out of reach of local nabobs, meddling congressmen and the political hacks who are sent to reign at the Department of Interior. It would be in the interest of the various environmental organizations to collectively direct the kind of energy and persistence to departmental failure that was applied by George Bird Grinnell a century ago. The rewards would be commensurate. Nowadays environmentalists ceaselessly expend their meager assets in trying to push agencies along paths where they ought to be making their own vigorous and creative way.

The federal endangered species mechanism will have to be freed from its political hobbles if it is to contribute anything to difficult recovery programs. It might be of use to examine Grinnell's corrective to see if it might be applied to the apparatus of the Endangered Species Act. He faced a similar obstacle in the state of New York in 1888 when he began editorializing for a reform of the New York Fisheries, Game and Forest Commission. As a scientist and businessman he took his administrative ideology from those realms. He repeatedly drove home the simple and utterly sensible idea that all renewable resources benefited from efficient administration.[12] Grinnell campaigned in Forest and Stream to separate oversight of the state's natural resources from politics and put it in the hands of impartial experts.[13]

When Grinnell set out on his long march, conservation sentiment appropriate to his purpose was poorly formed. Supportive opinion had to be laboriously shaped and strengthened over a period of years. He hammered at his theme and, aided by William T. Hornaday and others, finally forged a responsive instrument. In 1912 the power to regulate hunting seasons was assigned by legislative act to the New York state Conservation Commission, prompting a grateful Hornaday to declare, ". . . it is a privilege and a pleasure to be a citizen of a state which has thoroughly cleaned house. . . ."[14] Today, considerable resistance would greet any move to install a professional body over the endangered species arm of the Fish and Wildlife Service, but there will be no serious advance without putting some backbone into this great federal wimp. An unfettered team of experts with a proven competence in the new discipline of small population management, their credentials fixed by statute, should be formulating policy and checking the operations of the nation's endangered species programs.

The National Park Service

The ancient Greeks metaphorically embodied labor at strenuous tasks in figures who worked in fanciful surroundings. The story was told of Sisyphus, King of Corinth, who angered Zeus for reasons now obscure. He was therefore punished when he reached the underworld by being assigned the chore of pushing a large stone up a hill. The job defied solution, because each time he neared the top the stone rolled down again. Anyone who tries to bring sanity to an endangered species program will soon come to feel like Sisyphus trying to get his burden to a hilltop in Hades.

Hercules, being a paragon of physical strength, accomplished seemingly impossible tasks more readily. He once made a deal with the King of Elis, named Augius, to clean his sprawling stables in exchange for a tenth of the King's herds—provided only that the work be completed in a single day. There were 300 cattle,

411

and the stables had been neglected for 30 years. Augius agreed to the bargain; he knew a deal when he saw one. Hercules, in addition to his great strength, seems to have been an unconventional thinker, brimming with fresh ideas. He set to work and diverted two nearby rivers, flushing out the stables before sundown. Augius, furious at this unexpected feat, sent Hercules packing—without the promised cattle. Even Hercules met with frustration when dealing with government officials. Moving a mountain of dung was simple by comparison.

The labors of Sisyphus and cleansing the Augean stables are germane metaphors for reforming the National Park Service. Nonetheless, there have been recent rumblings about doing just that. A year after the publication of *Playing God in Yellowstone*, the author, Alston Chase, contributed an article to the *Atlantic Monthly*. It offered 12 specific recommendations for Park Service reform.[15] The first, and perhaps strongest, rested on the principle of periodic evaluation by an independent review panel. It called for a Presidential Commission to review the purposes, policies and performance of the National Park Service. Chase suggested that it be aided by the National Science Foundation, and that it include prominent scholars who have not been associated with the Park Service in the past. Agencies on occasion are inspired to set up their own review or advisory panels, but usually on occasions of duress, when wishing to be braced against criticism. The tendency is to ask those judged likely to say what the agencies want to hear. Such groups may in fact render a valuable service as the Leopold Committee did in 1962, but the choosing of inquisitors by those to be examined favors opinions more supportive, or protective, than objective or critical.

Chase also recommended that the National Park Service be pulled out of the Department of Interior, presumably because of the parent department's recent neglect in cases of external threats to national parks. But a need at least as great is for this famous agency to be unshackled from its own ideology. The key lies in institutional safeguards that will buffer against pressure coming through the political back door, but also against parochial ingrowth and a blind defense of the status quo. The "autonomy" needed by all agencies charged with managing of natural resources in the broad public interest is oversight by scientists of proven ability. The trouble with autonomous agencies that lag behind is getting them to mend their ways; autonomy can add to the difficulty. The National Park Service has gained a measure of *de facto* autonomy by virtue of the esteem in which it is held by the country. Its broad base of citizen approval enables it to fend off many threats (real as well as imaginary) of the kind that could not be deflected by a weak agency like the Fish and Wildlife Service. The fact of near-autonomy is evidenced by the confidence that has recently animated the National Park and Conservation Association to seek autonomy *de jure* for the agency.[16] Chase further proposed subjecting candidates for director of the Park Service to Senate confirmation. This

might at least keep the job from being handed out as a political plum by presidential administrations. It is a safeguard that could also be productively applied to the Fish and Wildlife Service.

Another Chase recommendation, in line with the principle of outside involvement in research, was that one-fourth of all researchers should be recruited from academia, thereby opening the door to views unconstrained by official dogma. A companion measure was aimed at minimizing the co-option of outsiders who work in national parks—a recognition of the narrow line they may have to walk if their findings bump against the prevailing management gospel. In such cases it is not prudent to challenge orthodoxy if funding is to follow on. The expulsion of the Craighead brothers from Yellowstone stands as an enduring admonition. Chase's model would follow the National Endowment for the Humanities and the National Science Foundation. He advocated the allocation of money to academic research through peer-review panels composed of non-government scientists. Other of his proposals addressed the Service's laggard research capability—a recognition that resource management will be no better than the research base it rests upon, and that it should have more latitude to follow the findings of research rather than being cramped by a philosophical formula.

Chase called for wresting the research arm of the Park Service away from the dominant operations branch which cannot use it properly. This was well illustrated by the prolonged resistance of the superintendent of Everglades National Park to research on deer and panthers—against the pleas of his own staff. In the design put forth by Chase, researchers would get their own line of authority to a coordinating office in Washington. Chase thought the operations branch, for its part, should be upgraded by making graduate training in a resource management discipline a requisite for career advancement. At present, most national park superintendents are laymen who ascend the promotional ladder from a ranger profession zealously bent toward park protection, but poorly schooled in the natural sciences. This measure would, in the long-term, promote a consonance of views between operations, research and resource management, tilting it more toward a scientific orientation.

Almost a year after the *Atlantic Monthly* article, the National Parks and Conservation Association unveiled its comprehensive plan for the National Park Service. The NPCA commentary was quite frank in admitting inadequacy in research—and a poor performance in resource management as well. Whereas 8.7 percent of the Fish and Wildlife Service budget and 5.6 percent of the U.S. Forest Service budget goes for research, the National Park Service spends 2.4 percent. The U.S. Forest Service employs 767 scientists and the Fish and Wildlife Service, 509; the National Park Service has 285 researchers, including those for cultural

resources and in the social sciences. Some National Park Service researchers have been diverted to other tasks, and have done little or no research work in their field for years, are not given adequate opportunities to attend scientific meetings and suffer from a lack of policy guidance from the Washington Office.[17] Aside from highlighting the lack of money and manpower, the report tells the tale of a scientific staff dominated by laymen having little understanding of, or regard for, the research arm—which is neglected accordingly. And if the ruling mind does not understand or value research, simply pumping in money and adding positions will not produce the right return on the investment.

The NPCA plan makes 14 recommendations for improving research. Several of them are very close to those made by Chase, such as enlarging allocations from the annual budget to ten percent, separating the research arm from the operational line of authority and phasing out park superintendents untrained in disciplines applicable to resource management. The plan also endorses the promising prescription for an independent Science Advisory Board of "demonstrably qualified experts," to be established by Congress, and calls for a nationally recognized scientist to head a science policy, planning and coordinating center which would direct the research arm. Additional science advisory boards are called for at the regional and park level. Presumably membership on these regional and local boards would be at the invitation of the National Park Service.[18]

These ideas might help counter the agency's ideological introversion. The NPCA plan incorporates the principle of the independent advisory group, though apparently limiting it to the central office. This would be a valuable but not complete reform measure. The blueprint does not appear to encourage research by outsiders, a measure that could inject doctrine-free ideas at the park level. It identifies a need for an "independent" research arm, but the term as used by the NPCA means only that research will be independent of the dominant operations faction.

A glitch lurking here is the question about the NPCA's willingness to entertain challenges to management dogma. While favoring some outside advice, and calling for the biological education of park superintendents, it seems chary of non-agency researchers. As for the principle of periodic outside review, the NPCA considers itself sufficiently free of bias to discharge that duty. In introducing the plan to its membership, *National Parks* magazine is assertive on the point. "Because of our mandate to protect the parks, our strong citizen base, and our knowledge of the National Park Service, NPCA was able to maintain an independent point of view while analyzing the needs and flaws in the park system."[19] The clause of the preceding sentence is a *non sequitur*—a fact probably obvious to anyone not on the NPCA staff. At any rate the NPCA chose itself to investigate the park system. It also named a commission, whose findings will be presented later, to review resource management and research policy.

To find a model for a truly independent review panel, it is useful to see how a study team was picked to look at wildlife management in South Florida's Water Conservation Areas in 1970. The managing agency, then called the Central and Southern Florida Flood Control District, asked that a slate of five qualified scientists be submitted by the Florida Chapter of the Wildlife Society—an association of wildlife professionals with diverse backgrounds and institutional affiliations. The agency then submitted the slate of candidates to another body— the state wildlife agency—for its approval. Thus, the agency that requested its policies be reviewed initiated the review process, but distanced itself from the appointments, giving the task to wildlife professionals chosen by their peers.[20] Yet, in fairness, while the NPCA is scarcely a paragon of detachment, it must be given credit for acting rather than just reacting defensively to criticism—as the National Park Service did.

There can be little doubt that the current spasm of reform owes much to the criticism Alston Chase poured on the Yellowstone grizzly foolishness (it is unlikely that the NPCA would ever admit to this or even admit the existence of Chase). However, I doubt the NPCA is ready to sponsor an objective program of scientific research in the National Park Service. A ruling flaw in this agency's stewardship is its rigid adhesion to "ecosystems management" which is unyielding in situations seeming to have any implications, however slight, for modifying the landscape. The extraordinary bureaucratic intrigue described in *Playing God in Yellowstone*, and in the pages of this book, testify to the strictness of the orthodoxy. The NPCA is as fixed in its stance on this issue as the institution it claims to be able to evaluate with an independent point of view.

In reacting to criticism of the bureaucratic exercises in Yellowstone, the NPCA would improve the biological education of park superintendents, expand the scientific staff and solicit advice from independent advisors. Presumably the NPCA faith in its interpretation of ecosystems management is such that it feels the philosophy would not be questioned by an expanded staff of scientists. That presumption is unlikely to stand up as the squeeze tightens on the nation's biological resources. A few institutional scientists will always have an incorrigible habit of being guided by their data even when it brings them afoul of a ruling dogma. A few may not be submissive if they are told to be quiet. The inadequacy of isolated refuges is being belabored in scientific journals. The subject is also showing up in popular magazines (though usually without indicating a need for flexibility by government agencies). Thus, the NPCA has set itself on a track that could ultimately lead to modes it does not presently accept. It has not thought its dilemma through and is incapable of providing fresh thinking about dead-end problems like the grizzly bear and the panther. The NPCA documents leave the impression that it can conceive of no remedy for the small population tangle other than the dubious

ones of expanding park boundaries or persuading neighbors to treat their land as if it were part of the park. A reinforced scientific staff might begin pushing for the same sort of distasteful tactics that have been put forth for panthers in southern Florida and grizzly bears in Wyoming. What then? Such counsel would still confront an ideology which has as yet shown no sign of bending despite all the talk about reform.

The NPCA plan has not been the only initiative pointed at Park Service policies. In 1986 William Penn Mott convened a task force to define the role of the agency in protecting biological diversity. Scientists from across the nation gathered in company with National Park Service partisans. I was told by some who attended that considerable heat radiated from the deliberations—perhaps not unexpectedly. Mott wanted the conclusions refined into a biological diversity plan for the National Park Service. The product of this conference has yet to see the light of day. Mott is gone, and draft copies have been meandering around inside the agency ever since. In fact, there is not one draft but two, which have been christened, sensibly enough, *Option One* and *Option Two*—a biformity seeming to suggest a divergence among the drafters. Neither meets the "refinement" criterion laid down by William Penn Mott; both are sketchy.

Option One is little more than an outline, and does not reflect a tolerance of innovations. It says things like "emphasis should be on fine tuning ongoing programs to ensure that the Servicewide priority of preserving biological diversity is given appropriate emphasis. . . . The NPS is already conducting a large number of projects which concern biological diversity. The present program is weak in some areas however,"[21] and, "existing statutes and policies generally identify the Service's role in conserving biological resources."[22] *Option Two* makes a more promising start, proclaiming itself to be organized around six major goals, one of which is to "clearly establish the NPS role in conserving biological diversity."[23] But the pages that follow do not promise any real changes. It is a compendium of broadly worded goals, such as: "assess native species populations in the NPS, identify those that are rare and/or endangered, and determine which populations may require mitigating actions [the term intervention is avoided]. . . . Develop Action Plans to mitigate the threats and sustain the populations in question."[24]

One searches the pages in vain for wording that would counter the repeated assertions by National Park Service spokesmen that they will never manage for more than a "natural" number of deer and panthers in southern Florida; but only the cautionary and prohibitive sentences glow from a web of imprecision and vagueness; otherwise the documents simply display that bureaucratic fraudulence of idiom which endeavors to write obscurely so as to avoid any unpleasant consequences that might result if readers understand what is being said. The agency

scribes can, however, communicate with precision and relevant detail when needing to convey word of a genuine threat to a national park.

One promising ovule is trying to germinate on the hard ground of National Park Service ideology. It also is a draft document presently circulating within the agency, one that would set new guidelines for natural resource management. One section, on endangered, threatened and rare species management, actually comes straight to the issue in a lucid exposition beginning with the first sentence: "Endangered and threatened species present unique management situations for the National Park Service. They require special management with single species priority within an ecosystem concept."[25]

It goes on to say:

> The goal of endangered and threatened species recovery efforts is generally to increase populations and secure sufficient suitable habitat to "recover" the species to acceptable levels (pre-decline or some designated level). Endangered species, therefore, cannot simply be preserved; they must be actively managed for recovery. If we only continue to preserve, those species will simply continue to decline because their habitats may no longer be suitable for survival, reproduction and recruitment. . . .

> Once a park or Region enters into a recovery program for a threatened or endangered species, a judgement concerning that species has already been made—that the species' recovery is of great enough value to warrant exceptional actions in the management of that species. . . . If such actions are necessary for the success of recovery programs, they must be regarded as acceptable management alternatives. . . . they should take priority over other species management and park operations. Significant modification of habitats and landforms is discouraged *unless* [italics added] necessary to prevent extirpation or extinction of the species.[26]

Another paragraph begins by making the important but rarely considered point that management for an endangered species should not be mandatory: "In considering manipulative activities, the park manager must consider potential impacts on other native species and park operations."[27] This is reasonable; if there are sound reasons to suppose that assisting one species would threaten another, or cause clearly identifiable harm to other park values, or unjustifiably hamper park operations, then it would be right not to launch the recovery, and the reason for not doing so should be stated forthrightly. The thing to avoid is a prolonged, costly,

going-through-the-motions, in an ill-planned venture that has no plausible basis for success. That has been the form with the Florida panther.

The above quotes are taken from proposed management guidelines drafted by a few scientists in the National Park Service. Whether this prospectus will ever be seen in official print is an interesting question. It is clearly not in tune with sanctioned views as they have been displayed to date. The draft guidelines state that "management will be in accordance with approved recovery plans."[28] But in the Florida panther recovery program it has been the other way around. The recovery plan was brought in line with ideological censures imposed by the National Park Service.

The NPCA Study Commission Report, 1989

In April 1988 the NPCA set up a 17-member Commission on Research and Resource Management Policy in the National Park System. The body spent a year meeting and touring national parks. It summed up its conclusions in a symposium billed as "National Park Research and Resource Management Policy into the Next Century: A Successor to the Leopold Report." However, the final product, released in March 1989, makes no pretense of the directness of the Leopold report, which was a clear exposition of shortcomings followed by a slate of rectifying goals, policies and methods, which were reinforced by plentiful allusions to specific parks. The 1989 report speaks in generalities. Unlike the Leopold report few illustrations are given. The looseness may be partly the function of a ponderous committee—17 members (modestly alluded to by the NPCA as 17 of the nation's best minds)[29] from an array of disciplines—in contrast to the five-member Leopold committee (all wildlife experts).

The 1989 committee's aspirations for the National Park Service unfold along four main lines: conduct resource management based on an ecosystem perspective; a greatly strengthened research program; a need for professionalism; and a significant expansion of the agency's educational mission. The need for research and professionalism were previously raised by Alston Chase and by the NPCA itself. The emphasis on education is new; but it is the treatment of ecosystems management that warrants the closest scrutiny, it being the controversial and sensitive stimulus of the reform initiatives. The report fights shy of using actual debates to justify its conclusions—despite the flagrant availability of the Yellowstone grizzlies, and despite the golden moment presented by having 17 of the best minds in the nation assembled to ponder the devilish contradictions. A comparable omission by the Leopold report would have been to neglect any mention of elk. In the end the reader is left uninformed about how the National Park Service will respond to the pressing planetary crisis of preserving biological diversity in the scattered shards of landscape we call National Parks.

There are in fact tantalizing passages in the 1989 report that seem to recognize the limitations of the Leopold formula, such as the following:

> The Leopold Report provided the National Park Service with a critical push toward ecological management. Examples across the system include efforts to remove feral animals and develop combined natural fire/prescribed fire regimes in many National Park System units. Nonetheless, the resource management tradition of the national parks is rooted in scenery management—preserving or recreating various types of "facades"—and the park service has yet to fully transcend that emphasis to provide stewardship for the elemental components and processes that in many cases stand behind and compose the shifting face of the facade.[30]

and:

> Ecosystem management, then, should focus on site-specific efforts to retain key resources directly serving park goals; creative solutions may not fit conventional wisdom about either nature or its manipulation.[31]

Elsewhere, however, are contradicting passages like the following: "The National Park System was founded on the belief that selected landscapes and artifacts of our nation have intrinsic worth and that people benefit from their contemplation and enjoyment. All future benefits of the National Park System depend upon the integrity of this resource base...."[32] These quotations encapsulate conflicting views of resource management which the report does not try to resolve. Their interpretation is left to an agency with a record of treating imperiled wildlife as a threat to orthodoxy, not as a problem having its own imperatives. The failure to confront these elemental differences leaves them to suppurate.

The 1989 report is grandly titled *National Parks: From Vignettes to a Global View*. But the National Park Service is far from a global view in these troubled days. The world's most reactionary land-management institution, which is tenaciously devoted to policy-as-it-is, has no innovative ideas to offer on the global preservation of biological diversity—which it is preeminently positioned to provide. Despite all the comings and goings of panels, symposia and the enlightened wording of some draft documents, nothing has really changed in the National Park Service. All this energy and motion amounts to no more than the writhings and gyrations of an institution that seems to sense the need to stride boldly in a new direction, but can't come to terms with its inhibitions and actually take the step.

The recovery plan for the Florida panther is still rigged to shield the National Park Service against modifying its narrow interpretation of ecosystems management. And the Draft General Management Plan for the Big Cypress National Preserve, which finally emerged for review in the late summer of 1989, gave no sign that a new day is about to dawn on the Park Service's care of the Florida panther.[33] Its verbiage bespeaks the unvarying pattern in a land-management agency that refuses again, and again and again, to mentally accommodate an unwelcome new reality. It is vainly articulating panther recovery with the terminology of park protection and ecosystems management, just as the Game Commission habitually labors at the task with a blueprint designed to parry its impact on recreational hunting and to avoid controversy. The cerebral tools of the agencies were not designed to cope with modern emergencies. The fundamentals of small population biology are easily grasped by anyone with an uncluttered mind, but those conditioned by dogma are less supple. A management doctrine is a fact-proof screen. Once a guiding idea gets into the collective head of a bureaucracy it is incredibly difficult to redirect it.

There is a way, in theory, to by-pass the National Park Service and manage for a greater number of deer. Sizeable tracts of land within the boundaries of the Big Cypress National Preserve belong to Dade County and to the state of Florida. Dade County owns an entire township (36,000 acres). The state of Florida owns 12,500 acres in school sections—tracts of land, each a square mile in size, scattered through the Preserve at a ratio of one per township. Also, Florida will soon come into temporary ownership of 25,000 acres of land in the Preserve, prior to conveying title to the federal government—as a result of state assistance in acquiring the right-of-way along Interstate-75. But the state agencies also have demonstrated no zeal for experiments to boost deer numbers. The Panther Advisory Council once recommended to the Game Commission that it start some experimental work, but there was no reply.[34] The Florida Park Service's deer management caper was detailed in Chapter 11.

The Draft General Management Plan, although it makes a number of grim statements about the status of the panther, also includes the obligatory optimism about panther survival—and doffs its hat to the FPIC.

> There are, however, reasons for guarded optimism about the ultimate survival of the Florida panther. Cooperation for panther management among the Florida Game and Fresh Water Fish Commission, the Florida Department of Natural Resources, the National Park Service, the U.S. Fish and Wildlife Service, and other resource agencies has been improving. The Florida Panther Interagency Committee, formed in 1986, and the revised Recov-

420

ery Plan in 1987 will better coordinate panther protection programs. Federal legislation has been passed, and efforts are underway at the state and federal levels to increase public ownership of panther habitat by almost 200,000 acres, including the 146,000-acre expansion of Big Cypress National Preserve. Equally important, the Game and Fresh Water Fish Commission is involved in the captive breeding of panthers to sustain the gene pool and to eventually return offspring to the wild.[35]

This resembles the upbeat ending the IGBC had inserted into the National Audubon Society's video on grizzly bears, does it not?

The New Dialectic

An endangered species crisis is like a medical emergency or perhaps like a battlefield problem, in that it will invariably deteriorate to a final, undesirable end in the absence of prompt, well-grounded actions to mend it. The time needed for retrieval may be measured in months or several years rather than in the seconds or minutes of the emergency room, or the hours or days of the battlefield, but in this new field of endeavor the time is precious in proportion. Complex recovery programs today are at the mercy of the dice. There is a need for a few directing principles, if order is to supersede muddle. A theoretical knowledge of the hazards intrinsic to small populations is now available, but there is no set of generally agreed-upon standards to guide the institutions (which respond intuitively), and to measure their performance. Records on current and past programs must be assembled to formulate a grammar of conservation management which might be inculcated as a doctrine (a body of accepted ideas to guide procedures) in the land-management agencies. Such an approach has long been in effect for medical emergencies, and in the profession of arms, to train practitioners to think and move in crisis situations that tend toward chaos and calamity. Like patients arriving at a hospital emergency room, each case will be different, but they are generic enough to devise a teachable framework for action. The great trouble will come in persuading officials that the method must be risk-minimal to the endangered species, not to the bureaucratic tribe. Inroads might be made by scientific consensus—if scientists were willing to speak out on the issue, a theme we shall return to momentarily.

Successful conservation management will mandate the organization of time and space (the ground where organisms must live) and fuse them with the available and potential assets of money, manpower and supportive public opinion. This new venture will join the discipline of conservation biology, and the research and management techniques of wildlife biology, to a reconnaissance of the setting where the recovered population (or populations) will be expected to persevere. The

novelty here is that the ground may stretch beyond the traditional purview of a single agency and so introduce a challenge to minds accustomed to administrative and geographically circumscribed calculations. The environment to be evaluated must include the social and political forces where operations are to be carried out. The conditions for success must be defined; the obstructions must be clearly pointed out. Citizens must be kept fully informed of the complexities and details during all phases of the work. In the long term it is not advantageous to keep the direction of affairs veiled against a wide understanding. How is the sometimes unpredictable lay public ever to become acquainted with the essentials of saving endangered wildlife—a goal the majority clearly desires? There will always be a raucous few with fixed opinions, sometimes with the clout to stall the program—all the more reason to try and educate the majority. If the majority is deemed intractable what is the use? The turmoil is not something agencies should fear to meet, but to be anticipated and planned for. Building acceptance may be long and trying, but this formidable undertaking goes with the hard profession of service in the public land-management arena, where many of the greatest attainments cannot succeed without struggle and stress.

The country as a whole has signaled a desire to save endangered species, but component parts of this opinion can threaten, retard or derail recovery programs. Some believe the cure begins and ends with saving habitat and ending exploitation of the animals, or in setting aside protected preserves. To others the path to salvation is a rigidly interpreted philosophy of restoring ecosystems. Still others believe that if the animals are left alone and not frightened or harassed (as with radio-collars), things will work out—somehow. Some lean to magic wand solutions like pushing the national park boundaries outward or persuading (or perhaps compelling) the park's neighbors to treat their plot of ground as an extension of the park. Opposing factions are selectively hostile to some land-management agencies while upholding others. Environmental leaders may be no more inclined to confront the forces of tradition than agency administrators. They soldier on, not pausing to ponder a redirection of methods, and are generally unattuned to the pivotal role they might play in overhauling institutions. They, like agency administrators, are leery of wading into the murky waters of controversy and conflict with their peers and constituents. *Perestroika* is not an easy or a secure track for anyone.

The Educational Imperative

An educational thrust to unite this refracted energy will have to instill a foundation of the biological principles and practices of conservation management and explore how they might fit at a given site. The responsibility for this tutelage rests mainly on the participating agencies. They have the staff and resources to do the job. A sound educational instrument, or the lack thereof, may well be the most

telling criterion by which the professionalism of an agency can be gauged. And by sound education, I mean not just the skill with which information is transmitted and images projected but the degree to which the message portrays the realities of a task. Without public acquiescence, and sometimes active support, the technical skills of managers cannot be used to advantage. And if bureaucrats cannot present a clear picture to the community they are unlikely to have defined the problem to themselves.

Land management history offers examples of new policies that had to overcome resistance. The most vivid are from the field of deer policy where strife has reigned for years, but there the need for recasting policies rested on a factual basis and the dilemma would not go away, and here and there progress has been made. Facts often move slowly against passions in the early stages of a teaching venture, but may win out if presented with sufficient clarity—and promoted with tenacity. The tenacious dimension of an educational endeavor was illustrated in the California condor controversy by the extemporaneous performance of scientists who had to assume the burden of promoting hands-on recovery in the face of heated resistance.

With the panther the pedagogical actions of the agencies have been vigorous only when defending conventional practice. Too often in this program information has been juggled to allow each party the widest latitude to pursue whatever course seems to best guard its interest. Political scientists have observed that "the control of information is of course a major source of power for a bureaucracy, and if it can convince those outside the organization that it is one of the few possessors of a certain body of information then it has an advantage vis-a-vis those that do not have it."[36] In the absence of basic reforms is there any way to correct the dispensing of self-serving blather in lieu of facts needed by citizens to support endangered species programs?

History offers a possible solution. During the Wisconsin deer controversy in the 1940s, Aldo Leopold criticized the placid irrelevance of the state game agency's *Conservation Bulletin*. Subsequently, an editorial board was formed for the *Bulletin*, apparently sharpening its output.[37] A similar remedy might help in Florida. An editorial board could be legislated for *Coryi*. The appointive require-ments should join editorial experience to wildlife expertise. Of course the board would be resented by some agency administrators who desire to keep the image of their agency bright, their thoughts shrouded, their options open and all decisions firmly in hand, but at the present I see no other hope for a meaningful educational endeavor. The only chance for *glasnost* in the Florida panther recovery program is through an independent editorial board that would infuse more matter and less art into the flummery from the FPIC. *Glasnost* is a difficult virtue for an agency to cultivate, but it is healthier in the long term than the self-serving treatment of

information. If this hard lesson is now being learned by the world's totalitarian governments, it ought to be learnable by bureaucracies in a free society.

Another technique for getting critical information to the marketplace of ideas is by formally encouraging the exposition, challenge and debate of the central issues of an endeavor in appropriate forums where all important parties are brought together to make recorded presentations. Walter A. Rosenbaum, who authored *Environmental Politics and Policy*, offered opinions on the potential benefits of such a practice:

". . . agencies, no less than individuals, are guilty of using scientific data selectively, sometimes with gross negligence. . . . All agencies at some time practice a garden variety of data manipulation. One of the virtues in wide public exposure of regulatory proceedings is that opportunities will exist for experts to expose and challenge such manipulation."

The great potential in policy conflict for disrupting sound scientific inquiry and distorting data emphasizes the importance of permitting an open, prolonged, and comprehensive scientific review of major environmental policy decisions. Such a process does not ensure that any scientific consensus will emerge upon strategic issues. But it does permit the widest latitude for scientific debate—for the uncovering and publicizing of information as well as for challenging and refining interpretations of data. It encourages among policy makers greater clarity about the full range and limits of the technical information confronting them. It invites a public airing of issues that experts otherwise might keep to themselves or confine to a small cadre of governmental and scientific insiders who become by virtue of their privileged information a powerful technocratic elite. It helps to discriminate between plausible and unrealistic policy options. If the politicizing of science in environmental issues is inevitable it should at least be exploited to advantage when possible.[38]

The Professional Societies

The professional societies: the mammalogists, ornithologists—those associated with the classes of vertebrate animals and, of course, the Society of Conservation Biologists, might play a role in institutional reform. These associations do not always have a sense of their potential prying power in institutional policy and are not always inclined to plunge into this exasperating arena, where so much energy can be expended for so little gain. But scientists can sometimes be influential if they are willing to speak out, preferably with a collective voice. There

have been occasions when professional societies have thrown their weight into policy conflicts—sometimes with good effect. The American Ornithologists' Union, in its formative years, was an authoritative voice in the campaign to prevent the extinction of plume birds. The A.O.U. also lent its support to overcoming militant opposition to radio-collaring California condors. In the early part of this century, the American Society of Mammalogists was divided against itself over predator control—an internecine conflict that spilled into the open. This professional society also once helped campaign against killing bears in Alaska. At the present difficult juncture in the struggle of conservation biology to find effective vehicles, the societies might assist. Carefully worded resolutions, for instance, might, over time, bring a measure of forward motion from many small pushes. The prestige of the professional societies can be used to advantage, as the case of the California condor showed.

A Society for Conservation Biology has formed and has tried to animate the cause of preserving biological diversity by introducing the discipline to the land-management agencies. It has worked with the Society of American Foresters.[39] It also conducted a Workshop on Biological Diversity for the National Park Service, after which a Society member beamed that "the Society is pleased that it was able to assume a leading role in this revolutionary policy shift."[40] Unfortunately, dispite this well-meaning attempt, no such shift has come to my attention (except on paper), though I am well-positioned to notice one should it occur. The Society is working also for a statutory solution, advocating federal legislation to underpin a national policy.[41] But as these pages argue, appropriate statutes, funding and research are already far in advance of the bureaucratic capability to use them. Passing another law and spending more for research, without an effective instrument, will bring only a marginal return. it is no use hitching bigger and newer wagons to the same broken-down horse. The most promising target for legislation would be the structure of the hide-bound land-management bureaucracy.

Unfortunately, it must be remarked here that in 1988 the Society for Conservation Biology gave the Interagency Grizzly Bear Committee an award for its "exemplary leadership in coordinating the efforts of government and private organizations to promote the recovery of grizzly bear populations in the western United States." The committee . . . ," reported the Society's journal, "overcame many obstacles in developing a unified plan."[42] The IGBC is as shady a candidate for a conservation biology award as is ever likely to come down the pike. The cause will not be advanced by rewarding bureaucratic legerdemain.

Case Histories

Case histories can serve as an instructive record of cumulative experience. Several have been attempted in this volume. Others will be needed. We have to learn

fast. We do not have decades to absorb and apply the lessons now being proffered. Most wildlife professionals in the United States will never have the opportunity in a career to work in more than one complex endangered species program (for this they may wish to be thankful). An exception may be in geographical regions like Florida where endangered species abound and the environment is in decline. There is room in case histories for the social sciences; it is abundantly clear that much more is involved than the mere application of a scientific discipline to a biological problem. This turmoil of factional counter-productivity offers a fertile ground for work by sociologists, social psychologists and political scientists. Some useful analytical work employing the findings of the social sciences has come from Tim Clark of the black-footed ferret disaster, who has drawn on studies of organizational behavior by political scientists and coauthored papers with workers in several disciplines.[43-48]

The Florida Panther

How could the principles of conservation management be applied to the Florida panther predicament? The first objective is to agree on is a population number. Current theory in conservation biology postulates 300-500 breeding adults to insure against inbreeding. Such a figure is probably impossible in Florida today, meaning that neighboring states would have to participate in long-range planning. The second objective is to identify all potential remaining habitat on public and private lands. Schemes would have to be explored to link the preserved lands in an unbroken refuge. Private lands must be purchased outright or guaranteed by conservation easements that would suit them to panthers—in perpetuity. Government land must be managed for more panthers. A third objective is to open the outbreeding question to debate. If outbreeding were permitted, some mountainous difficulties could be swept away. Lingering questions about genetic fitness could be made to disappear, and the expense of maintaining a captive population would be greatly reduced. These are the essentials of a recovery strategy, greatly simplified here. Each element would have to be broken into components for detailed treatment. But these foundational components have for years been side-stepped by the responsible authorities as if they were dynamite sticks that could explode, sending everything into ruin. If the bureaucracy will not confront the fundamentals, it is idle to plan further.

The agencies, working through a series of ad hoc task force committees, could hammer out a rough strategy in less than three months if the administrators were motivated. And if the institutions could become as inspired about saving panthers as they are about protecting tribal prerogatives—as demonstrated in the Tosohatchee battle, or in the prolonged antagonism to the supplemental feeding of grizzly bears—you can believe that a hard-nosed strategic design would be ready in short order, and officials would be promoting it with all the energy they could

426

muster. The design would have to be laid out for inspection, and of course it would be ferociously attacked by fearful interests, and by ideologues of diverse persuasion who would see it placing some favored concern in jeopardy. But there is no rational—or honest—way of trying to come to terms with this complicated dilemma other than to openly delineate all its disturbing and troublesome dimensions and wade into battle with it. There would be no guarantee of victory, but defeat is certain if a champion won't take to the field.

But this fantasy cannot safely be anticipated; the battle cannot be fought; the state of generalship is deplorable. The senior staffs of the agencies are not practiced in large operations (having repeatedly avoided opportunities to learn the skills) and are anyway incompetent to plan moves other than those in their own narrow interests. The few who do see the larger needs (those in the Fish and Wildlife Service) are too prudent (or intimidated) to call attention to the failings all around them. There is a wealth of non-government expertise to draw on, but as we have seen, the agencies do not seek expertise and are wary when it appears. No state of affairs could better summarize our plight. The environment that sustains us grows worse; enormous tasks lie ahead in managing a dwindling supply of biological resources for a human population making ever greater demands upon them—tasks much more demanding than the ones for which our bureaucracy is presently inadequate. There is a great need to take the formulation of policy from political hacks and to put it in the hands of apolitical professionals with specialized training in the appropriate fields.

And finally, beyond the need for a doctrine built on principles, and beyond the structural dimensions of reform and the need to apply the best available science to management of small populations, it is essential to recognize the evanescent, innermost reaches of recalcitrance: the last unrepentant, ingrained resistance residing in the mystical pull of institutional ideals—those abstract conduits for the instincts that direct the upright social animal, *Homo sapiens*, in the imperative of service to his kind. The mechanics of reform and the findings of science can only facilitate the expression of ideals; they cannot redirect them, nor entirely overcome their friction. Without an acceptance of alternative ideals, the institutional spirit will inexorably work its will to evade and hamstring the intent of statute, organization and policy. A new ideal stands ready to serve, if only it would be accepted: a commitment to the preservation of the earth's biological diversity. Here is the waiting spark to ignite new ways of thought and movement. But the unwillingness glares forth from the unmistakable adhesion to ingrained ideologies, held with the blind strength of limpets clinging to a rock. In the end the character of institutional operations will always reflect the ideological bent of the executors.

Chapter 19

FINALE: THE INTERNATIONAL UNION
FOR THE CONSERVATION OF NATURE

*The present population appears to be declining
and no proposed interventions solely directed at
the wild population are likely to ensure survival of
the Florida panther. . . .The potential for a catastrophic loss of the population, as was experienced
with the black-footed ferret, was not strongly
emphasized in our final summary. I wish to point
out that this small population is highly vulnerable
to such an event at any time. This only emphasizes
the need for timely action if the Florida panther is
to [be] preserved.*

Ulysses S. Seal
March 3, 1989

Shortly after the publication of the revised *Florida Panther Recovery Plan*
in June 1987, an interesting item arrived by mail in the form of PANTHER INFO-
58, recounting the appearance of specialists from the IUCN. Founded by Sir Julian
Huxley in 1948, the IUCN (International Union for Conservation of Nature and
Natural Resources) is headquartered in Gland, Switzerland. It is a network of
government and conservation organizations and experts in 114 countries. The
IUCN monitors ecosystems and species worldwide and provides assistance for
conservation planning and action.[1]

PANTHER INFO-58 disclosed that the FPIC (and its Technical Subcommittee) had convened in the unlikely locale of a Key Largo resort to ponder the path
ahead now that the recovery plan exercise had been put out of the way. The minutes
of this meeting of July 19-20 reveal that "Dr. U.S. Seal and Dr. T. Foose made a
presentation on genetic management strategies for small populations. They are
involved with the Captive Breeding Specialist Group of the IUCN and have assisted
in projects involving the red wolf, California condor, and black-footed ferret, as
well as many other critically endangered species worldwide. Through organized
workshops involving all personnel knowledgeable on a particular species (biology,

ecological relationships, habitat, limiting factors, genetics, population composition, recovery objectives, etc.), they develop a conservation strategy, a Species Survival Plan."[2] It seemed that another sub-plot in the Florida panther recovery epic was beginning to unfold. The lads from the Fish and Wildlife Service were up to something. Having seen their efforts of the past year culminate in a sterile recovery plan, they were taking a different tack, with a proposal to bring Ulysses Seal into the fray. Seal, and his work on behalf of endangered species, was first alluded to in Chapter 7. His services during the black-footed ferret misadventure were recounted in Chapter 15. There was a potential for this team to function as the sort of instrument that the FPIC had rejected at its formative meeting—an independent advisory group of technical experts, a Technical Subcommittee in fact if not in name.

If Seal and his team showed up to analyze panther problems there would be no nonsense. They would not be influenced by factional interests or provincial views. And there could be no doubt that these experts would sound the call for drastic measures of some kind if the slide towards extirpation were to be reversed. They would be sure to give the sort of advice that key decision makers in the FPIC had thus far demonstrated a marked unwillingness to entertain. However, the likelihood of disturbing recommendations from these specialists might not be immediately apparent to the lay administrators to whom the proposal was being made. The IUCN team is called the Captive Breeding Specialist's Group (CBSG), implying a rather narrow specialization with captive wildlife.

The FPIC took the bait and posted a list of suggested workshop participants to Seal. In September he mailed back a proposal for conducting a "population viability analysis workshop." His letter remarked that "the suggested participants do not include any of the citizens groups or several other scientists who have been involved with the Florida panther. This partly reflects an effort to control numbers and partly the need to focus on this exercise as a technical event. However, I have no problems with inclusion of any other people that you see as necessary or desirable as long as we can establish ground rules."[3] The proposed workshop was showing signs of not being designed to include a very broad representation of interested parties.

1988 had been another bad year for panthers. An alarming rate of loss had been recorded. Seal's proposal of September, distributed in PANTHER INFO-60, expressed a need for urgency. "Because of recent events (starting with the death of #15 at ENP [Everglades National Park] and ending with the death of #25 in N. Fakahatchee Strand), which have resulted in a significant decline in the number of radio-instrumented panthers in the wild (down from 17 to 11), it is felt that such a workshop is certainly appropriate, and that we should immediately move forward with plans for conducting it. . . . The FWS will cover the CBSG costs ($4,900) for

conducting the workshop. We are of the opinion that it should be held prior to the end of the year."[4]

The CBSG Workshop

The workshop was scheduled for January 4-6 of the following year (1989). Seal had recommended that the "workshop might best be conducted in Florida at a site that would minimize distractions . . . and minimize travel costs for a majority of participants."[5] Instead, the site selected was a beachfront resort hotel in Naples, Florida at the height of the tourist season. I was not invited but went anyway. In addition to having a professional interest, the manuscript for this book was reaching an advanced stage, and the events then unfolding would comprise an important chapter. The workshop was an impressive exercise. It was a tightly structured, no-nonsense affair. Ulysses Seal projects energy and remains firmly in control, but exudes a geniality that is valuable in deflecting the tensions of a group exercise which brings out intensely held, divergent opinions. The first morning session was given to lectures on the fundamentals of small population biology. Seal character-ized the Florida panther situation as a "population in a crisis circumstance."[6] True, of course, but no official to date in the Florida panther recovery program had ever conceded that by word or act.

The afternoon session featured the assembling of data on everything presently known about the life history of the Florida panther and its current status in the wild. The source of these data was the field research biologists of the Game Commission and the National Park Service—the persons who had been gathering it in since the research began. Everyone was encouraged to speak, to get opinions out into the open and to challenge anything that was being said. While Seal chaired the discussions, his associates sat in the back of the room clickety-clicking away at the keyboards of their portable computers, recording the exchange and entering data that would be fed into population models.

Among the interesting debates were those arising from an intense and determined resistance by some field biologists to the suggestion that any panthers be removed from the wild. Arguments for this position centered on the theme that the information being gained by the research was too valuable to interrupt and that there was no urgent need to act. If anything should go wrong, went this line of reasoning, and panther numbers began to decline, there would be plenty of time to bring the survivors in (this opinion was precariously in league with one holding that a rather impressive number of uncollared panthers were still at large). Early in the workshop Ulysses Seal had commented that "a common experience in these workshops is to have individuals view captive breeding as a threat and to be resistant."[7] I was well acquainted with the obstruction in the panther recovery program. Seal, from previous experience, was anticipating it.

The meeting consumed a long afternoon, after which the CBSG members worked at their computers until late in the evening, entering the population data into a series of models. The following day the computer runs were presented and survival strategies aired for debate. Seal solicited reactions from the assembly to assess the "reality" of a range of remedial scenarios and to various strategies. A month later he forwarded his report. A cover letter gave an assessment of the status of the population and its prospects for survival. It should be explained that while inbreeding is known to cause extinction, the existing state of knowledge did not allow confident predictions of when. Chapter 6 told of populations that long persisted with low genetic diversity (though it cannot be known how many others so affected might have expired). In evaluating the preliminary genetic investigations of the panther, Seal found diversity low but within the range of many species of mammals. He could see no direct evidence of inbreeding, but cautioned that effects of that kind are not easily proved since they can be manifested indirectly in unpredictable ways. Sperm abnormalities and cryptorchidism could easily be symptomatic of such infirmities. The impairments of inbreeding might not be detectable, but neither could they be ruled out; and the uncertainties about fitness in this case had to be evaluated in an environmental and demographic context that portended catastrophe: "The present population appears to be declining and no proposed interventions solely directed at the wild population are likely to ensure survival of the Florida panther . . . . The potential for a catastrophic loss of the population, as was experienced with the black-footed ferret, was not strongly emphasized in our final summary. I wish to point out that this small population is highly vulnerable to such an event at any time. This only emphasizes the need for timely action if the Florida panther is to [be] preserved."

The population viability analysis drew the grim conclusion that the Florida panther was a ". . . declining population with an 85% probability of extinction in 25 years and a mean time to extinction of 20 years. . . . A reduction in fitness may already have occurred as reflected in the high incidence of cryptorchidism and sperm abnormalities."[9] If the Florida panther population was to survive in the wild, the CBSG report warned, it would require "the establishment of a captive and multiple wild populations. The surplus from the captive population would provide the animals to establish 3 to 10 new geographically separate wild populations of at least 30-50 adults each. These populations will require monitoring, periodic exchange of animals (about one every five years), and replacement in the event of local extinction."[10] The executive summary affirmed that "the establishment of a captive population is the only management intervention that can assure survival of the Florida panther for 100 years."[11] The basic strategy was to build a captive population at the earliest moment and rapidly expand it to 250-300 animals;[12] a rapid propagation of cats would be necessary to prevent any further loss of genetic diversity; contracts with a number of zoos would be needed, and animals

would have to be periodically moved among the zoological parks to insure the mixing of genes. Obviously huge sums of money would have to be found, even to begin this vast project for safeguarding a constituency of genes that might already be dangerously compromised.

At this point the reader should be aware that the CBSG operated under a constraint. The analysis was conducted "on the basis that the gene pool of the present population of Florida panthers is to be preserved with no additions or replacements with animals from other geographically distant populations."[13] In plain words the concept of outbreeding was not to be aired in the workshop. But outbreeding should not have been barred from debate; it had the potential to moderate projections about where and how to house this great host of captives, and it could substantially lower the cost of holding so many cats. All discussions of mean time to extinction could be made irrelevant; plaguing genetic uncertainties could be wiped away. By the infusion of new genes, a panther could be created which would be little different in appearance (or none at all. Remember that the population was exhibiting two phenotypes: the one in Everglades National Park, and the other one), but with improved chances for long-term survival. There should still be a captive population for security purposes, but it would not have to be on the scale of the one contemplated. Also, it is most important to bear in mind that the strategic cornerstone of outlining where all these animals were to live in the wild still remained to be laid.

Seal emphasized the importance of losing no more time in beginning the captive arrangements. He urged taking at least six panthers less than 18 months old to form a captive population before the end of 1989.[14] The next step was for the FPIC's Technical Subcommittee to meet and enact the fiction of evaluating the proposal for the FPIC. When the months passed without a meeting it was evident that the CBSG warning had failed to implant a sense of gravity in the hierarchial stratum that mattered. At last a Technical Subcommittee gathering was scheduled for the final two days in May. On May 30, 1989, I attended my first meeting of this body, enormously interested in seeing how the bureaucracy would react to the call to action by the Captive Breeding Specialist Group.

The Technical Subcommittee Meeting

In addition to the captive breeding proposals, the agenda announced a review of the status of each task of the 1987 Recovery Plan. The reader will recall that the recovery plans (in theory) identify the tasks that are judged necessary to prevent the extinction of the target organism. The enumerated tasks are then placed on an implementation schedule which assigns each one to an agency, or a combination of agencies, and specifies a date for its completion. The reader may also recall from a previous chapter that in December 1988, the General Accounting

Office sent a report to Congress critical of the Fish and Wildlife Service's execution of the Endangered Species Act, among other reasons because ". . . nearly half of the tasks in the 16 approved plans we reviewed in depth have not been undertaken, even though the plans have been approved on average for over 4 years. Further, the agencies are not systematically tracking undertaken tasks. Officials point to a shortage of funds as the primary reason for existing shortcomings."[15]

The Technical Subcommittee meetings are always chaired by a representative of the Fish and Wildlife Service, since that agency theoretically directs the recovery program. The chairman announced that the review of the implementation schedule would be the first since the recovery plan was approved two years earlier. He then went down the list of tasks. Some, such as those identified for the Florida Panther National Wildlife Refuge, had not been implemented because the refuge was not yet acquired. Others were bypassed because they involved ongoing research and monitoring activities that would be presented by agency biologists on the following day. However, it was plain to see that some tasks hadn't been done, and there seemed to be little interest by the Technical Subcommittee in inquiring into the causes. The impression was of a reluctance to create embarrassment by dwelling on tasks for which no action had been taken.

Task number 1215 of the implementation schedule, to "modify hazardous roadways," was an exception. Under this obligation the Florida Department of Transportation (DOT) was to "physically alter segments of roadways determined to be hazardous to panthers."[16] A DOT delegate announced that planning was underway and that repairs to State Road 29, between Alligator Alley and the Tamiami Trail, would have protective measures for the panther incorporated into the design. As reported previously in this book, there are plans to spend millions of dollars on modifying highways—which will be useless to panther recovery if other more fundamental measures are avoided.

Another interesting task was number 126: "Florida Department of Natural Resources (DNR), FGC [Game Commission], FWS [Fish and Wildlife Service], and NPS [National Park Service] will develop or revise existing comprehensive land-management plans that address the needs of the panther on their respective lands within the current known range of the panther. . . ."[17] The reader will remember that in the preparation of the revised recovery plan of 1987, the agencies would not jointly subscribe to a unified management strategy. Instead, each agency insisted on developing its own plan.

Now each agency reported its progress. Florida DNR had a plan for the Fakahatchee Strand State Preserve "under department review." The Fish and Wildlife Service promised to have a plan six months after acquiring the Florida Panther National Wildlife Refuge (which was then impending). The Game

433

Commission had nothing to report although it manages thousands of acres of deer habitat in the Water Conservation Areas (remember the deer hunting controversy) and in several other wildlife management areas (and, in theory, in the Big Cypress National Preserve).

The plan that the National Park Service was developing to "address the needs of the panther" seemed, from the presentation, somewhat complex and, for me, hard to follow. As I understood it the management plan for Everglades National Park was still more than a year away. As for the Big Cypress National Preserve, a General Management Plan was in preparation (it was mentioned in the previous chapter). In addition to this general plan, several topical plans for resource management activities were being readied for such things as prescribed burning, the eradication of exotic plants, and so forth—all the standard thrusts of recreating vignettes of primitive America. These were presented by the National Park Service as the fulfillment of its responsibilities to panther management.

Task 1317 states that: FGC [Game Commission] will offer to work with MSIT [Miccosukee and Seminole Indian tribes] to evaluate the deer status on Indian lands and cooperatively initiate and evaluate a variety of management techniques and strategies to enhance deer populations."[18] The Game Commission representative reported "no action." And there were no questions. The discussion moved perfunctorily to the next item.

Task 127 requires the Game Commission to "initiate a system for marking and maintaining records on captive cougars in the state." The narrative explains that:"It has been estimated that there are over 1,000 captive cougars in Florida (Capt. Barry Cook, pers. comm., 1986). These animals pose a potential problem to the recovery of the Florida panther due to the confusion over the true status and distribution of the native population as a result of escapes and intentional releases. Some system of marking (such as tatooing) and careful record-keeping is needed to keep track of these captive animals and to make the owners responsible for the continued upkeep of them in captivity (Belden 1982)."[19] The Game Commission representative reported "no action." And there were no questions. The discussion moved on.

Task 1312 requires all agencies to "evaluate habitat protection and management actions on their respective lands and initiate actions to enhance panther conditions as appropriate." This is the task which contains the escape clause for the National Park Service: "To perpetuate the natural distribution and abundance of the Florida panther and its primary prey, it will be necessary, [etc.]. . . ."[20] The National Park Service representative announced that his agency was working to control exotic plants, using prescribed fire, and investigating oil pad restoration—all matters that would be slated for attention if there were no panther.

Nothing had changed in the National Park Service. The accomplishments of the Florida Park Service were presented: Three deer feeders had finally been approved for installation, and a biologist had been thorough in monitoring the strips of joint vetch that had been replanted in 1989, but his work had not been guided by a research design of any thoroughness; from the central office, no expression of enthusiasm for management measures that diverged from tradition had ever made itself felt at the Fakahatchee Strand State Preserve. The Game Commission representative had nothing to report, and the discussion moved on.

Task 1318 had assigned the "Florida DNR and the Game Commission to test the effectiveness of supplementing the prey base in the Fakahatchee Strand State Preserve."[21] The representative of the Game Commission stated "that it had been resolved not to proceed with that program"[22]—an assertion that was incorrect. What actually happened was that the Game Commission had refused to cooperate in the experiment which was supposed to monitor the release of radio-collared deer. Both the executive director of the Florida DNR,[23] and later the executive director of the Florida Park Service, had asked for the deer releases. Both requests had been refused.[24,25] The discussion moved on.

Task 191-A, tagged as a "management priority one," was to prepare a "contingency plan for removal of panthers." All four agencies had been assigned responsibility but nothing had been done. The reader may remember that the contingency plan concept had started out as a recommendation of the Panther Advisory Council in May 1985, when a meeting was held with the Game Commission staff to discuss captive breeding—which was being pushed in that year by the Game Commission as a matter of the gravest urgency. At the time, the Game Commission did not act on the recommendation, but the contingency plan concept had subsequently been shuffled into the revised recovery plan in 1987, as a joint responsibility of all four agencies of the FPIC. Now midway through 1989 not a finger had been lifted to prepare a contingency plan. If an emergency came, in which it was judged prudent to bring in the remaining panthers, the work might be chaotic. All the arrangements for transporting and housing animals in an unprecedented wildlife rescue would have to be improvised on the spur of the moment. There is certainly no reason to treat seriously assertions by the Game Commission in 1986 that ". . . if such a need should arise, the level of investigation that is currently being devoted to the panther should reveal the need in ample time"[26]—if the agency would not bestir itself to plan for such an emergency.

The Fish and Wildlife Service representative tried vainly to draw the other three agencies into a commitment on the contingency plan, but there was no enthusiasm. The Game Commission representative commented helpfully that since the CBSG workshop had raised the prospects of creating a captive population, maybe a contingency plan wouldn't be needed. (These same evaporative prospects

435

had served as an excuse for inaction for years.) The Fish and Wildlife Service representative wouldn't give up and tried to force the issue by suggesting that the group identify a date for completion of the task, whereupon the Game Commission representative quickly asked if the Fish and Wildlife Service was willing to take the lead (this task promises a good deal of work)—to which the answer was yes! And so the review of this item ended on a positive note; what was to have been jointly prepared by four agencies was loaded onto a representative of one—who was willing to press the issue and do the work. A draft contingency plan was scheduled for completion on October 1, 1989.

Task 191-B.6 referred to the need to acquire jetport property in the Big Cypress National Preserve. It was explained in the last chapter that the Dade County Port Authority owns an entire township—36,000 acres—within the boundaries of the Big Cypress National Preserve. The land is the site of a proposed jetport in the 1970s, the threat of which helped stir the movement to acquire the Big Cypress Swamp as a public preserve. One intriguing possibility for this land is that it might be used for experimental measures to swell deer numbers, since it is not under the control of the National Park Service (yet). However, no action had been taken; no ideas for action were exchanged, and the jetport task was left in limbo—as were several others. The contention by the Fish and Wildlife Service that more money would enable it to complete scheduled tasks in its recovery plans is patently ridiculous.

On day two of the meeting the assembly turned to the report of the CBSG. Ulysses Seal had argued forcefully for taking steps in 1989 to forestall any further genetic loss. The months had slipped by with no sign that high-level decision makers had been any more impressed with Seal's call for urgency than with ones made repeatedly in previous years by the Panther Advisory Council. Now, six months into the year, a Technical Subcommittee had convened to confer on the report.

The chairman stepped to a blackboard and chalked a list of questions.

(1) Is it appropriate to bring animals into captivity at this time?
(2) Do we accept the CBSG recommendations?
(3) If we don't, do we develop our own?
(4) Do we develop a SSP (species survival plan)?
(5) Do we map out how we will comply with regulatory requirements?
(6) Which zoos will be designated to maintain the animals?
(7) How will all this be funded?
(8) What will we recommend to the FPIC?

When the general discussion opened, the first move was an attack by the partisans of field research on the findings of Seal and his associates; it was claimed that his premises had been flawed and his statistics inaccurate, causing the dire prognostications for Florida panthers to be invalid. But of course the arguments against a captive population were not a spontaneous reaction to supposed flaws in the calculations. Opposition to removing cats from the wild was entrenched long before there was any thought of soliciting guidance from the CBSG. These reactions only point up the value of bringing in the analytical skills of technically expert outsiders (the task force discussed in the previous chapter). A balkanized multi-agency recovery program will invariably stifle objective thinking, and in the Florida panther recovery program the private agendas of extra-agency factions have further diffracted the coalition energies.

The CBSG had wanted to retain two young female panthers from Everglades National Park, taken out of the wild for rehabilitation, as founders for a captive population. The question of using these cats had been put directly to Park Service representatives at the workshop in Naples where the response had been non-committal; but now the National Park service representative informed the group that his agency had done "some internal soul-searching." He implied a reluctance by the National Park Service to surrender its cats (one—Orphan Annie—had been returned to the park by this time; the other, recuperating from broken legs, would ultimately remain in captivity).

The Game Commission spokesman said that captive breeding would be essential at some point for reintroduction, to which he said his agency was committed. However, it became clear that the creep approach—now familiar to the reader—would rule the pace. "We don't have enough information to make a decision at this time," he said. "There's a whole lot more meat that needs to be hung on this rack first." Seal and his group would have to furnish more particulars. And what sort of additional information was wanted? "What is the time frame?" was one question; another was: "what are the exact steps that will have to be taken and in what sequence?" And: "what impact will taking panthers from the wild have on those that remain?"

As for the effects on the wild population caused by withdrawing animals, the Panther Advisory Council had been over that ground in 1983-1984. The Council's initial caution about reducing the wild population was soon over-whelmed by what appeared to be a dangerously high mortality rate, one that continues to seem so and which in effect consigns the elimination of cats from the wild to chance, forfeiting the discrimination that would mark a deliberate effort to selectively remove them to captive security. It will be remembered that Jim Layne suggested as far back as 1981 that effects on the wild population could be minimized

by taking kittens. The suggestion was made again by Robert Baudy in 1983 and more recently by the Panther Advisory Council in 1985; and Seal had addressed the question in the PVA report. "... the survivorship pattern, which exhibited high juvenile mortality for ferrets, as it does also for cougars, suggested that young animals destined to die in the wild anyway might be removed with little or no impact."[27]

Delay

Two weeks after the Technical Subcommittee meeting, Dennis Jordan, the Fish and Wildlife Service's Florida Panther Coordinator, informed Ulysses Seal that the scheme to accelerate captive propagation had been suspended until the PVA workshop report could receive further review. Jordan then solicited written appreciations from all agencies. By early August he had one each from the National Park Service and the Game Commission, and two from specialists in the Fish and Wildlife Service. The Fish and Wildlife Service reviewers had several nits to pick with the hastily gathered and processed data, but agreed in essence with the conclusions of the report. The supervisor of the Cooperative Research Units Center commented:

> ... the net result of all these quibbles is that they don't matter. If the data on reproduction and mortality and population size are reasonably representative, then this subspecies' population is of extremely limited size, probably declining and certainly extremely vulnerable, even in the short term (next 5 years). ... There are striking similarities between this situation and both the condor and the black-footed ferret. In both of those preceding situations the decision to begin captive breeding was delayed so long that eventually all known individuals in the wild had to be brought into captivity. There is a chance to avoid repeating these hard lessons with the panther, but doing so will require moving with some dispatch.[28]

The National Park Service review picked at details and worried about disruptions to the wild population that might be caused by captures, but it was unequivocal in supporting the findings:". . . The plain conclusion from the simulation models is that, on its own, the present wild population of Florida panthers cannot survive through the next century. One can nitpick forever, but we feel certain the population parameters used will prove over the decades to be too optimistic, rather than the reverse. The vigorously ongoing loss of habitat on private lands will take care of that."[29] The written response of the Game Commission gave tentative support for the withdrawal of some panthers, but once again stressed the need for more information before making a decision.[30]

After receiving replies from three agencies, Jordan, on August 4, forwarded them to his regional office in Atlanta urging that "it is essential that we proceed as quickly as possible, as we are already running a month behind the schedule we established at the TS [Technical Subcommittee] meeting."[31] The regional office posted a letter to Ulysses Seal the same day suggesting "that the Technical Subcommittee meet with you as soon as possible to revisit any pertinent points of the PVA [population viability analysis] that may need addressing, and discuss details of proceeding with the preparation of a Species Survival Plan."[32] And so Seal prepared to confront the system and plough through the arguments once more.

At this juncture the Fish and Wildlife Service stalwarts laboring to animate a somnambulant bureaucracy received an unexpected boost, in an unlikely guise, when Hurricane Hugo roared onto the South Carolina coast in September. Passing over Puerto Rico the hurricane had cut by half the forty-odd population of Puerto Rican parrots on the island. The parrots, an endangered species, had been slowly increasing during the past decade. In South Carolina Hugo wreaked havoc among the old-growth pine trees used by red-cockaded woodpeckers (another imperiled species) for nest cavities. And among the poorly reported anxieties of Hugo's passage were those of several wildlife specialists monitoring red wolves that had been experimentally released on a coastal island which was battered by the tempest. Even though the wolves miraculously survived a 17-foot tidal surge, the Fish and Wildlife Service was able to use the publicized rack and ruin of the storm to impress on procrastinators the exterminating potential of cataclysmic events on small populations.

The CBSG Workshop Repeated

On the last day of October the Technical Subcommittee gathered for another marathon session with Ulysses Seal and the CBSG. The announced purpose of the conclave (moved to Atlanta, Georgia) was to draft a species survival plan (in effect, the essence of an unofficial recovery plan). An undeclared purpose was to overcome the bureaucratic resistance to the new project. The meeting went on for three days. Early on, Seal emphasized that the report of the CBSG had understated the problems rather than overstating them.[33] In a review of the population modeling he, and others, spoke at length on the nature and limitations of the models that were used. Some points of interest in this expostulation were that more animals were entered (45) than were known (less than 30), on the chance they might exist; the effects of past inbreeding could not be quantified for use in the models; the potential impact of a catastrophe on the remaining panthers was not modeled—and so on.[34] Seal again asserted that, for security against a catastrophe and to halt the erosion of genetic diversity, 20 founder animals—a number believed

to contain about 97.5 percent of the remaining genetic diversity[35]—were immediately needed to start a sheltered population. The founders would have to be rapidly multiplied to prevent attrition of the captive genes. Five hundred captive and wild panthers combined, it was estimated, would be needed to guard against short term extinction (if the non-breeding age classes of this population were included it would, of course, yield a higher total).

The distributive proposal for this numerical goal, featured three wild populations, each with a minimum of 50 breeding cats, within the designated historic range of *Felis concolor coryi*. The population maintained in custody would have to be sufficiently large to safeguard the surviving complex of genes over the time the captives would serve the conservation exigency. Genetic exchange would be effected through periodic transfer of cats among the four populations. The fiscal requirements of this elaborate operation would be enormous. The primary costs would have to be born by the participating zoos. The zoo contribution could approach $1,000,000 in capital outlays for facilities and over $500,000 each year in operating costs. However, several zoos were willing to participate; representatives of five zoological institutions attended the Atlanta meeting; they were collectively prepared to receive about 40 panthers.[36] The participating agencies for their part would immediately need $50,000 above existing expenditures and much more in the future.[37]

Unfortunately, when the assembly began assessing everything known about panther lineages, only 19 could be identified for a founder stock. The analysis dictated that the entire population would have to be captured to approach a secure number. However, the decision made by the Technical Subcommittee fell short of this most rigorous of the options put forth by the CBSG; it was to capture only half the recommended founders during the first year: "The captive breeding program will take from the wild 4 adults and 6 kittens in 1990 and 1 pair of adults and 6 kittens per year through 1993."[38] The procedure chosen would attempt to assemble the necessary founder stock over a period of years by taking a few adults and a trickle of their offspring. Two baleful difficulties glare from this compromise. First, in the mathematics of genetic management it takes five offspring per founder to get 97 percent of the founder's genes; and second, given the rate at which panthers are known to perish in the wild, choosing to prolong actions intended to salvage the remaining genes courted disaster. Crucial decisions in a recovery program were again being made with the dice.

The following commentary on this decision appears in the executive summary of the species survival plan, dated November 17, 1989.

> If all the Florida panthers were removed from the wild immediately then there would be less of a loss of genetic diversity because

most of the remaining founders would be protected. Our proposed strategy would capture animals at a slower rate over a 3-6 year period and it is likely that mortality of some founders would occur during this time. This loss would be minimal but clearly represents a loss of genetic diversity that could be preserved if all animals were taken immediately. However, the consensus of the SSP working group members and the Technical Subcommittee was that maintenance of the wild population had greater priority than an incremental loss of genetic diversity.[39]

A warning attended the commentary on prolonging the withdrawal of founders: "It should be clearly understood that this plan represents a biological compromise necessary to maintain the existing wild population while developing a captive population to ensure long term survival of the taxon. There is a clear biological tradeoff involved." And: "It would not be recommended if this population were the last remnant of a full species (such as the California condor, black-footed ferret, red wolf) rather than a subspecies."[40]

This last monition was not explained. Did it imply that if disaster strikes, levies of *Felis concolor* from elsewhere could be drafted to reinforce the decimated ranks in Florida (or to replace the population if extirpated)? The outbreeding option had never been sanctioned, and if it was to be an option, why wait for a calamity to even begin thinking about it? Or did the monition mean that since *Felis concolor* as a species was in no danger, the subspecies in Florida was tacitly presumed expendable. If so, it is startling to think that more money has perhaps been committed to its recovery than to any other creature in history. Here we see a pattern of behavior remarkably like that in the Wyoming ferret case—where decision-makers were confronted with far more compelling evidence of an impending disaster. Having apparently ruled out any consideration of outbreeding—which could banish worries about genetics, and at a fraction of the cost of the course they had chosen—the bureaucrats would not act decisively to safeguard whatever genetic strength remained.

The prudent strategy would be to secure an adequate number of founders and then increase them as rapidly as circumstances allowed (ideally in one generation), followed by reintroductions at the earliest possible moment. The advantage in taking all founders in at once is that the security and nutrition provided to captives could greatly reduce mortality and increase fecundity—and guarantee a high rate of survival in the offspring. The disadvantage of dragging out the project over several generations is that genetic combinations not suited to withstand the ravages of nature could pervade the stock of cats destined for release.

The role of captives should be to provide security to the wild population (or populations)—only for the briefest time. The CBSG had emphasized that principle at the workshop: "Genetically, the faster you can build up the numbers and the sooner you can release [reintroduce captives to the wild] the better."[41] This of course meant that places for reintroduction must be identified, and the means investigated to secure them; the dismal record of aversion in this field can be found in Chapter 17. The species survival plan was ominously vague on where future populations of panthers would reside. One of its recommendations was to "establish reintroduction sites which, in combination with the extant populations[sic], are capable of supporting 300 breeding adults by the year 2010. At least one of the sites would be within the state of Florida." It offered no details. The schedule approved by the FPIC in January 1990 allowed 20 years to assemble the 500 panthers needed to provide security against short-term extinction. The goal was to have 130 breeding animals combined in wild and captive populations by the year 2000. The final goal was to be attained by 2010.

The National Park Service was not a driving force in the expedient provision of founders. There was a continuing reluctance to allow captive breeding to threaten the presence of panthers on National Park lands. Yet panthers in Everglades National Park late in 1989 had been reduced to a state of apparent hopelessness. The only female (one of two in the park) to produce a litter during this year did so by breeding with the only available male—who was her son. After breeding with his mother the young male then left the park by moving west across Shark River Slough. The female that gave birth was identified as a possible founder for the captive population. Not only was the Park Service unwilling to let her leave, the agency wanted a male from elsewhere in the wild to be captured and transferred to the park. Accordingly, at the October meeting, five males were evaluated as candidates for stud service to the two females in Everglades National Park; after much discussion one was chosen (known as 33), because he was the only one of the five who was not cryptorchid. So number 33 (also tagged as a possible founder) was slated to be sent to the park, even though there was no certainty he would remain there. Seal voiced a reluctance to see this male used in such a high-risk enterprise.[42] But Seal has no authority, he can only advise. Vested interests continued to deflect hard-headed analyses and expedient decisions in an endangered species crises.

In the Big Cypress National Preserve, the CBSG judged the "subpopulation" of panthers to be "functionally extinct" (like the one in Everglades National Park). However, the Park Service response was to promote the delivery of replacements—to be brought in from other locations, justified as follows: "1) Translocated wild cougars have a better likelihood of surviving in the wild than captive-bred stock. 2) It is projected that it would take a minimum of 5 years before

captive-raised panthers would be ready for reintroduction into the wild. Since suitable habitat exists, the use of this habitat by panthers should not be delayed."[43]

As has been much written about, the finger of suspicion about the panther's hardship in this region points vividly at the dearth of deer—the result of a nutrition-poor environment (a situation not improved by deer hunting). Nonetheless, the above quoted passage also stated that "since 1980, documentation of panthers in the Big Cypress National Preserve south of Alligator Alley has decreased from a reproducing population to possibly only a few males. Causes of this gradual decline are unknown but it is believed that both the habitat and prey base can support panthers."[44] In the official executive summary of the species survival plan of December 15, 1989, the recommendation for importing panthers to Raccoon Point was condensed to the following statement: "During the next annual review and revision to the SSP, a plan should be developed to define the recovery steps to repopulate the Raccoon Point area of the Big Cypress National Preserve."[45] It is interesting to reflect that in northern Wyoming the National Park Service, and its supporters among the environmental organizations, are pushing hard for the reintroduction of a predator, the Rocky Mountain wolf—while in southern Florida the same agency maneuvers assiduously to avoid sensible measures that might prevent the extinction of another hard-pressed predator, the Florida panther. Both projects are driven by a quest for the mythical grail of ecosystems management.

Controversy

Early in 1990, news releases, and the *Federal Register*, conveyed word to the public about the captive breeding scheme, and there was soon an outcry against it. Letters of opposition poured in. "Many reflected the belief or opinion that adequate habitat preservation, accompanied with actions to eliminate or reduce existing human related threats would in itself lead to recovery. In summary, many comments reflected a feeling that programs to secure, restore, and improve the quantity and quality of panther habitat should be expanded."[46] The opposed reasons were similar to those advanced to buttress a hands-off approach to saving condors in California, and there were discomfiting signs that a replay of the condor fracas might be unfolding in Florida. The voices of Earth First and the Humane Society of the United States were among those raised.[47] The Fish and Wildlife Service had planned to issue permits in late March, but backed down, fearing litigation.[48]

An environmental assessment was written; public meetings were scheduled in Gainesville, Tampa and Miami; and the Fish and Wildlife Service, in an unusual display of energy, made plans to meet national conservation leaders in Washington, D.C. to gain their support. The recovery program was again trundling in a circle with few prospects for seeing panthers in captivity in 1990. The FPIC,

having failed to educate the public on the need for a sound recovery strategy (because it had never fashioned one), now paid the price with further delays from an aroused and uncomprehending sentiment. The educational gimmick wheeled out for the emergency, only attempted to persuade opponents of the necessity of implementing a poorly conceived captive breeding project; there was still no recovery strategy. The long-overdue necessity of identifying a habitat to sustain the three wild populations, as called for in the species survival plan, was again pushed forward into the mists of the future. The Fish and Wildlife Service rationalized this neglect in the *Federal Register*:

> The Fish and Wildlife Service recognizes that an increased panther population could eventually lead to reintroduction of the species in carefully selected habitats within its original range. However, this aspect of the recovery would be speculative since the ability of a captive breeding program to produce a sufficient number of animals for a reintroduction program is unknown at this time. Such a program if warranted, would be a separate action and the Fish and Wildlife Service will address them in accordance with the National Environmental Policy Act when, and if such a program becomes viable.[49]

This dissembling is unconscionable. There was no reason to assume that a captive population of panthers would not produce sufficient offspring for reintroduction—despite the poor breeding performance of Big Guy. The species, *Felis concolor*, has bred readily in captivity for many years. But there was a reluctance to raise "red flags" by identifying reintroduction sites. Nonetheless, the pronouncements of officials resolutely implied that reintroduction was just around the corner. The *Fish and Wildlife Service News* informed its readers that "the [species survival] plan calls for the immediate establishment of a captive breeding program for the panther, expansion of efforts in managing and monitoring the wild population, reintroduction of the species into former habitats and habitat conservation. . . ."[50] The *Miami Herald* quoted agency spokesmen as saying that ". . . captive breeding will be paired with a habitat conservation and wild panther management [plan] to strengthen both the animals and the land they live on.[51]

And The Band Played On

In the summer of 1990 the Society For Conservation Biology held its annual meeting at the University of Florida, in Gainesville. Biologists from the state's land-management agencies were prominent among the speakers. A Florida Park Service representative gave a talk on an agency operational practice known as resource managements audits, whereby a team of three biologists periodically visits a park to assess whether its resource management is complying with agency

objectives—which in the case of the Florida Park Service, was to "manage these lands as natural systems providing representative samples of the biological communities and landscapes of Florida prior to alteration by European man."[52] The audit team is a good idea, but it did not sway the course of management to benefit the Florida panther. In November 1986, three field biologists (including me) had visited the Fakahatchee Strand State Preserve and recommended, among other things, special measures to increase deer numbers.[53] The agency's failure to manage for deer has been explained. Unfortunately there is no mechanism in the institution to examine whether resource management policy is keeping up with current thinking on preserving biological diversity.

Another paper from the Florida Park Service was entitled "the Management of Florida's State Lands Must be Guided by Scientific Research if Biological Diversity is to be maintained."[54] The speaker informed the gathered scientists that "through restoration of ecosystems, biodiversity will be enhanced." However, we have seen that in the Florida Park Service, as in other land-management agencies, research has been the servant of management dogma, not the director of management.

A high-ranking game commission staff biologist delivered a lecture entitled: "Conservation Biology, Rainmakers, and Casey at the Bat; A State Wildlife Agency Perspective."[55] The term "rainmakers" seemed to be an unsubtle jab at the theoretical aspects of conservation biology. The word "theoretical" was wielded elaborately during the lecture. The speaker contrasted the theoretical nature of conservation biology with his agency's practical way of doing things. He proclaimed that "Conservation biology lives in the programs of the Game and Fresh Water Fish Commission" (however, to give the speaker credit for being frank, he admitted never having heard of conservation biology until 1988). He asserted that his agency "was not just another hook and bullet outfit, not just theoreticians, but doers of deeds [the doers of deeds phrase was repeated twice more]. . . . We cannot be timid in the application of science," he said, "the game we play is too important to future generations."

He then hurried through a list of "recent accomplishments" by the Game Commission. His agency was at work on a GIS (Geographic Information System) that would be "the basis for designing a plan for guiding land acquisition, which would become a focus for preserving biodiversity." He alerted the audience to his agency's recent collaboration with Ulysses Seal in formulating a population viability analysis for the Florida panther. The Game Commission, he said, had also helped to develop a species survival plan for the endangered animal. He praised his agency's role in designing a captive breeding project. (He did add that captive breeding was "on hold pending questions on the issuance of the permit by the Fish and Wildlife Service.") And so we see the land-management bureaucracy rolling

ponderously on, easily appropriating the trappings of conservation biology, claiming to be in the front rank of the new movement, indeed claiming (and no doubt believing it) to have been there all along.

Tomorrow?

Looking forward from this grim chronicle of wasted years and dollars, and dissipated energies, what are the prospects for the Florida panther? We have seen time after time in the workings of the FPIC, and its Technical Subcommittee, behavior that contravenes the spirit of the Endangered Species Act, and subverts the recovery process in tacit mutual agreements that do little more than protect the respective interests of the dominant players. The program seems at last to be lurching toward the margin of security that a captive population offers, but by the most high-risk, expensive and dilatory method that could ever be devised, and without evaluating the outbreeding option. The sluggish tempo has largely been a product of the combined frictions of departmental dogma, bureaucratic aversion to precipitate actions, and the protective instincts of field researchers toward their subjects.

What of saving the habitat on private lands presently known to support panthers? The new species survival plan, produced under the stimulus of Ulysses Seal and his team, contains a promising recommendation: "Immediately establish and pursue a goal of no net loss of habitat value for the existing populations of Florida panthers in south Florida and potential reintroduction sites in north Florida and southern Georgia."[56] But sadly, the hour for effective action has grown late. The futile energies expended in that direction by the Panther Advisory Council in years past have been described. And how can the FPIC "immediately establish and pursue" such a goal if the species survival plan remains mute about the steps to be followed? It offers not a hint of a thought for getting there. Is there a reason to believe that the FPIC will suddenly depart from its record of avoiding the chore and dash forward in a burst of committed determination? Is there a reason to believe the National Park Service will alter its oft-stated refusal to manage its extensive holdings for more panthers than the "natural system" will support? The subject is not mentioned in the species survival plan, and it can be seen in the final pages of this chapter that decision-makers in the National Park Service continue to wander in a cloud-cuckoo land of wildlife management fantasies.

We should strive to save the large carnivores, and to reintroduce them whenever we can. By preserving the vast natural spaces needed to sustain them, we could insure space for a multitude of less-demanding creatures that will surely in their turn be brought to the same desperate pass in years not far ahead. The panther, prowling in modest numbers from the mangrove coast to the Tallahassee hills,

could be a great agent to help preserve a Florida where we humans might escape the overcrowded future that is coming down on us like an avalanche.

When I opened an envelope from the governor's office nine years ago, a glowing prospect of holding onto a fading natural heritage unfolded in the letter of appointment to advise on panther recovery. It was a grant to serve a vast and vital project to benefit not just panthers, but the land community in Florida and the people who are nourished by it. John Eisenberg's vision, expounded in the private deliberations of our past council meetings, has been an even broader one: since the widespread deer herds that fed the eastern puma before declining a century ago are now restored, the sparsely peopled Appalachians, from Georgia northward through the Adirondacks, are biologically ripe for the return of *Felis concolor*. And given the growing strength of opinion favorable to wildlife and for holding on to what remains of our natural environment, the dream might unfold in a decade or two— or three—with the proper orchestration. But those of us who have fed the hard years with ceaseless labor at this herculean chore in Florida have seen our energies drained off in the sand. Every vibrant initiative is swallowed up by a leviathan of interlocked bureaucracies standing astride the path of change. Nothing can move if it is not in an officially sanctioned channel.

Why should anyone think the elaborate exercise that has passed itself off as a recovery program will be miraculously transformed into a credible instrument for saving the Florida panther? In 1989 the Fish and Wildlife Service was able to capture the initiative in the bureaucratic maneuvering by enlisting Ulysses Seal and his team, but even with this imposing and energetic band of experts only the slowest and most dubious headway is being made. All the agencies should be clamoring for the technical advice of the CBSG. Instead, the Fish and Wildlife Service must resort to using it as an institutional goad to try and lever other reluctant, defensive participants onto a course that might be meaningful. Without the CBSG there would be no movement at all. And there are all the dismal signs that the captive breeding project will end as another in a succession of moves, begun without enthusiasm and prosecuted without vigor, that cannot lead anywhere. The Florida panther may have survived a half-millennia of carnage inflicted upon it and its habitat, but it will need a miracle to survive the ministrations of the institutions we are employing at such great expense to save it.

Without meaningful reforms in the structures of the controlling government agencies they will remain permanently locked in their own introversions. If sufficiently embarrassed the reluctant bureaucrats might be jolted forward a few steps more, but they would undertake the distasteful tasks forced on them with all the enthusiasm of taking poison. They might prance industriously about for a bit, but only so long as the spotlight was on them. They would soon be back to their bad old ways.

When the situation was manageable it was neglected, and now that it is thoroughly out of hand, we apply too late the remedies which then might have effected a cure. There is nothing new in the story. It is as old as the Sibylline books. It falls into that long dismal catalogue of the fruitlessness of experience and the confirmed unteachability of mankind. Want of foresight, unwillingness to act when action would be simple and effective, lack of clear thinking, confusion of counsel until the emergency comes, until self-preservation strikes its jarring gong—these are the features which constitute the endless repetition of history.

- Winston Churchill, 1935

EPILOGUE

Events have not been still between the closing sentence of my manuscript and the publication of *Twilight of the Panther*. A summary of happenings through 1991 will be of interest.

Everglades National Park has experienced modest success with its project to control alien growth in the Hole-in-the-Donut. Sixty acres have been cleared of exotic vegetation by the radical expedient of removing all plants, and several inches of topsoil, so that the plot of ground will be flooded for a longer period, thereby preventing the reentry of Brazilian pepper. The cost of treating this fractional acreage of former farm fields is reported at $665,000. That sum would have purchased a huge amount of research, and probably tangible results, on managing Hole-in-the-Donut to supplement the prey base for panthers.

In late 1990 the Game Commission concocted a plan to divest itself of the Panther Advisory Council. This was to be accomplished by lobbying the governor to abstain from filling a vacancy that had opened when a member stepped down. Evidently the plotters were confident of holding the political cards for an achievement of this kind. An agency official was brazen (or imprudent) enough to inform the Council of its imminent demise. Word of this scheme by bureaucrats to erase a creation of the state legislature soon got in the air (see the appendix), to the anxious discomfort of the perpetrators. Perhaps in consequence, the agency has since displayed a remarkably congenial regard for the opinions of its advisors, even taking up some past recommendations that had languished for years. Life was breathed anew into the statewide habitat linkage project about this time (the one recommended at the dawn of 1985); the mapping it is said will be finished sometime in 1992. Unfortunately, during the seven wasted years since the urging of the work, immigration to the sunshine state has expanded the census by ten percent. Agricultural transformations, too, of natural lands that might have served an expanded refuge have ceaselessly subtracted from the available assets. These years of crowding and depletion have not been kind to the prospects of 1985.

Early in 1991 the recovery mechanism was jolted forward a few more steps by a Gainesville citizen, Holly Jensen, who sued the Fish and Wildlife Service over the issue of captive breeding. The federal agency settled out of court, acceding to the plaintif's demand that, in conjunction with taking cats from the wild, it must evaluate the outbreeding option and present a concrete scheme and schedule for the return of panthers to the wild. It was agreed that kittens could be taken in 1991, but no adults—not until the Fish and Wildlife Service could demonstrate credible intent to strive for a non-captive future for the Florida panther. Thus it cost the Fish

and Wildlife Service $8,000 in legal fees to agree to an action that competence and common sense should have moved it to initiate years earlier.[1]

Some aspects of Jensen's action might be criticized, like the insistence on leaving all adults in the wild, when Seal's analysis highlighted the importance of getting sufficient founders into captivity to preserve the dwindling gene pool. But remember, the FPIC avoided the same advice, and it entirely shunned the outbreeding option which should have weighed in such a momentous decision. Holly Jensen, backed by the Fund For Animals, did what other sleepwalking conservation organizations should have done long ago. After suspecting a problem, she investigated, drew some sound conclusions and then jumped on the problem with both feet. She spoke out and took to the courts to try and bludgeon sanity into panther policy.

Soon after the settlement was reached, Ulysses Seal and his CBSG were called again to service, this time to draft a federal policy on "Subspecies, Populations, Hybridization and Conservation of Threatened Species." At last an expert opinion was to be formed on the outbreeding question. In a 22-page report, Seal evaluated all recovery options, expressing hope (but not certainty) that the existing genetic composition might still be salvageable (if the existing variation can be captured, and if the founder base can be expanded rapidly—the same conditions he had emphasized early in 1989). He also urged that outbreeding experiments begin immediately just in case inbreeding has taken the panther past the point of no return. Seal picked the trans-pecos subspecies, *Felis concolor stanleyana*, as the closest extant geographic population to the Florida panther, noting that the surrogates from Texas apparently adapted well during the reintroduction trials in northern Florida. He also resurrected questions about the long-ignored Piper cats, pointing out that "this captive stock has some Florida panther ancestry, and may even contain Florida panther genes no longer present in the wild."[2]

His passages on the darkening evidence of consanguinity in the Florida panther make somber reading. The signs of inbreeding, which should have caused alarm among officials years ago, have steadily advanced. "There are a number of indicators that inbreeding and losses of genetic diversity are having damaging effects on the population. . . . As of 1991, 90% of male Florida panthers are cryptorchid(M. Roelke, FL GFWFC).Vaginal fibropapillomas were observed on two female panthers. These papillomas are thought perhaps to impede penetration during copulation and affect sperm motilization. The two females did not breed during 6.5 years of observation even though they were in regular contact with breeding males (1990 FP Report, FL GFWFC)."[3]

450

Meanwhile, as these lamentable signs of lost opportunity have, year by year, festered and spread—and while the administering circle of the panther bureaucracy has spent great sums and avoided a serious inquiry into captive breeding—Robert Baudy, working alone, has raised and sold at a profit, more than 100 offspring from the Piper stock he transported to his compound in 1981.

APPENDIX

August 1, 1990

Jack Pons, Chairman,
Florida Panther Technical Advisory Council

Dear Jack:

Herein, as you requested, is my estimation of the worth of the Florida Panther Technical Advisory Council (FPTAC) to the Florida Panther Recovery Program, and the Council's posture versus the agency it was created to advise: the Florida Game and Fresh Water Fish Commission.

As I understand it, an official of the Florida Game and Fresh Water Fish Commission, at the July meeting of the FPTAC, explained that the Governor had not appointed a replacement for John Eisenberg, who is stepping down, because of the Game Commission's desire (intent?) to "sunset" the FPTAC. The agency reasoning, as given at the meeting, is that events have taken the program beyond the limited capacities of the FPTAC.

This appraisal portrayed things in reverse. I believe the Game Commission has failed to keep pace with doable actions urged upon it by the FPTAC, that are essential if there is to be a panther in Florida's future. For example, the agency has never identified the boundaries of a refuge in southern Florida that will be needed to sustain a panther population (FPTAC recommendations, Nov.'86). It apparently has not even prepared a map of the private lands upon which to plan the refuge (FPTAC recommendations, Oct.'85). While on the subject, it is interesting to note that the Recovery Plan (June '87) also calls for the U.S. Fish and Wildlife Service and the Game Commission to "...develop a Comprehensive Habitat Management Plan for the panther on private lands in cooperation with the landowners within the known distribution of the panther (page 38)." However I am not aware that such planning is underway, and it is hard to see how it could begin without first identifying the boundaries of the project.

The captive breeding project (of present controversy) was first proposed by the Game Commission in early 1985, after facilities were made available—gratis—at White Oak Plantation. The FPTAC supported the initiative, advising minimal disturbance to the wild population by selecting kittens for the project.

However, despite repeated urging from the FPTAC (especially after the crash of the black-footed ferrets in Wyoming), a captive population never materialized. So, five years later, instead of having a back-up population for security, we now have a controversy. This affray might have been avoided (or certainly contained) if the Game Commission had taken the trouble to develop a sound public education program that clearly presented the panther's dilemma and explained the difficult options available for recovery. But the Commission, having failed to educate the state on the demands of a sound recovery strategy (because it has never fashioned one), now pays the price with further delays from an aroused and uncomprehending sentiment. Citizens have a passionate, proprietary interest in their wildlife resources, and rational management of these resources can sometimes prove impossible when the managing agencies do not make a forthright effort to put the citizenry in the picture. A state game agency ought to know this better than anyone.

The FPTAC tried to get the Game Commission to broadcast the necessary message (see the appended letter of July '86), but instead of being informed about the crises, people have been fed a lot of public relations baloney from *CORYI*.

In 1985, we urged the Game Commission to begin work on a plan to link habitat statewide (FPTAC recommendations, Feb.'85). The agency at first seemed interested. At an FPTAC meeting in May '85, I tried to get the commission staff to organize a workshop that would get the project going. When no one on the staff would respond, I called Bill Partington and he—with the assistance of Larry Harris and myself—did the job. There was a large turnout, and the endeavor was praised by the press. But although Partington held several more well-attended workshops, there was never any further support from the Game Commission. Today, water-management districts, regional planning councils and even some counties are taking up the "corridor" idea, but the Game Commission has steadfastly refused to play a leadership role, although few projects could be more vital to the future of wildlife in this state.

I could go on, but this should be adequate for your purposes, You can see that it is not the FPTAC that has fallen behind the Game Commission. While the FPTAC has been urging a strategy for saving panthers in Florida, the Game Commission has been fretting about taking actions that might cause a controversy (rather ironic considering the way things turned out).

I also understand, that it is the opinion of the Game Commission, that when the Florida Panther Interagency Committee (FPIC) formed its own Technical Subcommittee—of agency representatives—the FPTAC (a statutory body appointed by the Governor) became superfluous. This is odd, because the Recovery

Plan (June '87), in discussing the establishment of the Technical Subcommittee, states that: "Expertise and input from other appropriate sources will be utilized by the subcommittee in accomplishing its objectives (page 33). Surely the FPTAC, created by the state legislature (which specified that appointees have appropriate research and management experience) to advise on panther recovery—qualifies as appropriate source of expertise.

Setting aside the questionable legality of tampering with a statutory advisory body, any suggestion by the Game Commission that the FPIC's Technical Subcommittee can usefully replace independent advisors, some of whom have a wealth of professional experience not available in the agencies, is absurd.

The representatives of some government agencies cannot operate outside their agency's biases. That's why the FPTAC was created—to give biological advice that would be uncensored by political or narrow institutional constraints. The role is invaluable. In my experience, biological considerations, which should be paramount in managing endangered species, can be crushed underfoot when they collide with bureaucratic fears and conventions.

I understand that a further justification for wanting (trying?) to terminate the Governor's advisory council is because Ulysses S. Seal and his group of captive breeding experts from the IUCN have been brought to the program, thereby rendering the FPTAC unnecessary.

Seal's arrival is a promising development. His arguments to act expediently, through captive breeding to preserve further erosion of genetic diversity, are in my view, unanswerable. However, anyone watching closely will have seen that his disturbing advice has been greeted with less than frantic enthusiasm in some quarters of the bureaucracy. His urgent calls for action (since Jan. 1989) still await implementation, and the tempo exhibited thus far by the bureaucracy does not match the one he recommended. As a consequence, the remaining genetic diversity in the panther population will be subjected to greater risk than Seal has indicated is desirable. And the issue of outbreeding—which could reduce risk and cost, and perhaps shorten the time to reintroduction—is apparently barred from debate.

Seal has managed to pump some air into the deflated captive breeding project, but I suspect his role in strategic recovery planning will be limited from here on. The bureaucratic tolerance for enthusiasts with innovative ideas is as short as its resistance to them is long. I have appended a paper that will give you some insights into the bureaucratic rigidities that are impairing endangered species programs. It will show that the Game Commission, in trying to deep-six its legislatively imposed advisors, is simply following a bureaucratic instinct to mould

the environment to parochial advantage, a trait well understood by political scientists and other investigators of organizational behavior. The paper was coauthored by Tim Clark, who experienced departmental intransigence at first hand in the near-disastrous black-footed ferret recovery program.

I heard rumors that the Game Commission staff had tried this caper (unsuccessfully) the last time vacancies occurred on the FPTAC. I can't imagine that the Governor would be drawn into such unsavory maneuvers. I hope these brief comments are of some use.

Sincerely,

Ken Alvarez, former Chairman
Florida Panther Technical Advisory Council

cc: Council Members

NOTES

Abbreviations Used in the Notes

BFAT   Black-footed Ferret Advisory Team
DNR   Florida Department of Natural Resources
ENFO   A publication of the ENVIRONMENTAL INFORMATION CENTER of the Florida Conservation Foundation, Inc., 1191 Orange Ave., Winter Park, Florida 32789
FDE   Florida Defenders of the Environment
FPIC   Florida Panther Interagency Council
FPRT   Florida Panther Recovery Team
FPTAC Florida Panther Technical Advisory Council
FWS   U. S. Fish and Wildlife Service
GFC   Florida Game and Fresh Water Fish Commission
NAS   National Audubon Society
NPS   National Park Service
TS   Technical Subcommittee (of the FPIC)

Chapter 1: *FELIS CONCOLOR*: THE GREAT AMERICAN UNSPOTTED CAT

1.   Stanley P. Young and Edward A. Goldman, *The Puma: Mysterious American Cat* (Washington, D.C.: The American Wildlife Institute, 1946) 9.
2.   Ibid., 1-2.
3.   Allen E. Anderson, *A Critical Review of Literature on Puma(FELIS CONCOLOR), Special Report Number 54* (Colorado Division of Wildlife, February 1983) 1.
4.   Peter C. H. Pritchard, "Endangered Species: Florida Panther," *The Florida Naturalist*, vol. 49, no. 4, (August 1976) 15.
5.   Anderson, *Critical Review*, 1.
6.   Young and Goldman, *The Puma*, 2.
7.   Ibid., 3.
8.   Ibid., 4.
9.   Ibid. [The same page as in the preceding note.]
10.   David L. Lendt, *Ding: The Life of Jay Norwood Darling* (Des Moines, Jay N. "Ding" Darling Conservation Foundation, Inc., 1984) 7.
11.   Ed. Bradford Torrey and Francis H. Allen, *The Journal of Henry David Thoreau*. In 14 Volumes bound as two, Vols. VII-XIV, November, 1855-1861 (New York: Dover Publications, 1962) 985.
12.   Kenneth R. Dixon, "Mountain Lion," *Wild Mammals of North America* (Baltimore: The John Hopkins University Press, 1982) 712.
13.   John C. Seidensticker IV, et al., "Mountain Lion Social Organization in the Idaho Primitive Area," *Wildlife Monographs, no. 35* (Washington, D.C.: A publication of the Wildlife Society, December 1973) 45.
14.   Harley G. Shaw, *Mountain Lion Field Guide, Special Report No. 9* (Phoenix: Arizona Game and Fish Department, November, 1983) 12.
15.   Roy T. McBride, "Population Status of the Florida Panther in Everglades National Park and the Big Cypress National Preserve" (Homestead: Everglades National Park, 1985). McBride mentions

finding one mound during his years of field work in Florida. David Maehr (personal communication) of the Game Commission has found two.

16.   Personal Communication, David S. Maehr.

17.   D. S. Maehr, J. C. Roof, E. D. Land and J. W. McCown, "First Reproduction of a panther (Felis concolor coryi) in southwestern Florida, USA," *Mammalia*, t. 53, no. 1, 1989. 130.

18.   Bruce Akerman, "Cougar Predation and Energetics in Southern Utah," Master's Thesis (Logan: Utah State University, Fisheries and Wildlife, 1982) 67.

19.   George B. Schaller, *The Deer and the Tiger: A Study of Wildlife in India* (Chicago: The University of Chicago Press, 1967) 289.

20.   Maurice G. Hornocker, "Analysis of Mountain Lion Predation Upon Mule Deer and Elk in the Idaho Primitive Area," *Wildlife Monographs, no. 21* (Washington, D.C., a publication of the Wildlife Society, March 1970) 18.

21.   John Eisenberg (personal communication) suggests that cases of infanticide may not involve the young of the killer but could involve an alien male, assuming that a resident male can recognize his own young.

22.   Allen E. Anderson, *A Critical Review of Literature on Puma (FELIS CONCOLOR), Special Report No, 54* (Colorado Division of Wildlife, February 1983) 50

23.   David S. Maehr, "Panther Food Habits and Energetics," (Tallahassee: Florida Game and Fresh Water Fish Commission,1987-88) 2.

24.   Melody Roelke, et al., "Medical Management and Biomedical Findings on the Florida panther, Felis concolor coryi, July 1, 1983 to June 30, 1985,"(Tallahassee: Florida Game and Freshwater Fish Commission, September 24, 1983-85) 65-66.

25.   Hornocker, "Analysis of Mountain Lion Predation."

26   Donald L. Neal, "The Effect of Mountain Lion Predation on the North Kings Deer Herd in California," ed., Jay Roberson and Frederick Lindsey, *Proceedings of the Second Mountain Lion Workshop* (Salt Lake City: Utah Division of Wildlife Resources, 27-29 November 1984) 139.

27.   R. P. Hanson and Lars Karstad, "Feral Swine in the Southeastern United States," *Journal of Wildlife Management*, Vol. 23, No. 1 (January 1959) 64.

28.   Ibid., 66.

29.   William B. Frankenberger and Robert C. Belden, "Distribution, Relative Abundance and Management Needs of Feral Hogs in Florida." Reprinted from the *Southeastern Association of Game and Fish Commissioners 30th Annual Conference 1976*, 641.

30.   Mark Shaffer, "Minimum Population Sizes for Species Conservation," *Bioscience*, Vol. 31, 131-134.

31.   Michael E. Soule, "Conservation Biology and the `Real World" in ed. Michael E. Soule, *Conservation Biology: The Science of Scarcity and Diversity* (Sunderland: Sinauer Associates, Inc., 1986) 1-34.

32.   Ian Robert Franklin, "Evolutionary Change in Small Populations" in ed. Michael E. Soule and Bruce A. Wilcox, *Conservation Biology: An Evolutionary-Ecological Perspective* (Sunderland: Sinauer Associates, Inc., 1980) 135-149.

33.   Brian James Miller, "Conservation and Behavior of the Endangered Black-footed Ferret (Mustela nigripes) With a Comparative Analysis of Reproductive Behavior Between the Black-footed Ferret and the Congeneric Domestic Ferret (Mustela putorius furo)," Ph.D. Dissertation (Laramie: University of Wyoming Department of Zoology and Physiology, December 1988) 21.

34.   Franklin, "Evolutionary Change," 141.

35.   Ulysses S. Seal, "The Realities of Preserving Species in Captivity" in ed. R. J. Hoage, *Animal Extinctions* (Washington, D.C.: Smithsonian Institution Press, 1985) 72.

36.   Seal, "The Realities."

Chapter 2. *FELIS CONCONCOLOR CORYI*: THE FLORIDA PANTHER

1.   Frank Hamilton Cushing, "Exploration of Ancient Key Dwellers' Remains on the Gulf Coast of Florida," *Proceedings of the American Philosophical Society*, 35:153 (December, 1896) 387.

2.   Cris Cristoffer and John F. Eisenberg, "Report No. 2 on the Captive Breeding and Reintroduction

of the Florida Panther into Suitable Habitats" (Task I report prepared for the Florida Game and Fresh Water Fish Commission, Florida State Museum, University of Florida, Gainesville, 15 January 1985) 5.

3.   John Grier Varner and Jeanette Johnson Varner, eds. and trans., *The Florida of the Inca* (Austin: University of Texas Press, 1951) 65-66.

4.   Ibid., 66.

5.   Charles E. Bennett, trans., *Three Voyages*, Rene Laudonniere (Gainesville: The University Presses of Florida, 1975) 9.

6.   Mark Van Doren, ed., *Travels of William Bartram* (New York: Dover Publications, Inc., 1955) 63.

7.   Charles W. Arnade, "Cattle Raising in Spanish Florida, 1513-1763," reprinted from *Agricultural History*, Vol. 35, No. 3 (St. Augustine: Publication No. 21, St. Augustine Historical Society, 1965) 5.

8.   Jim Bob Tinsley, *The Florida Panther* (St. Petersburg: Great Outdoors Publishing Co., 1970) 13.

9.   Tinsley, *Florida Panther*, 50-60.

10.   Outram Bangs, "The Florida Puma," *Proceedings of the Biological Society of Washington*, Vol. 13 (31 January 1899) 15-17. Bangs does not explain why another name would have to be found. I presume there was a conflict with the rules of taxonomical nomenclature of the period.

11.   Ibid.

12.   Ibid.

13.   Young and Goldman, *The Puma*, 11-43.

14.   Van Doren, ed., *Travels*, 63

15.   John K. Mahon, *History of the Second Seminole War*, 1835-1842 (Gainesville, University of Florida Press, 1967) 281.

16.   Tinsley, *Florida Panther*, 43.

17.   C. J. Maynard, "The Mammals of Florida," *The Quarterly Journal of the Boston Zoological Society*, Vol. II, No. 1, January 1883, 2.

18.   Tinsley, *Florida Panther*, 21.

19.   Gloria Jahoda, *River of the Golden Ibis* (New York: Holt, Rinehart and Winston, 1973) 164. Unfortunately the author does not document this report.

20.   James Layne and Mindy N. McCauley, "Biological Overview of the Florida Panther," in Peter C. H. Pritchard, *Proceedings of the Florida Panther Conference, March 17-18, 1976* (Florida Audubon Society, published in cooperation with the Florida Game and Fresh Water Fish Commission) 25. Layne and McCauley state that "Persecution by man appears to have been the primary cause of the decline of the Florida panther, and illegal killing and highway mortality probably continue to be the major forces depressing the population below carrying capacity."

21.   Jay Robertson and Frederick Lindsey, *Proceedings of the Second Mountain Lion Workshop* (Salt Lake City: Utah Division of Wildlife Resources, 27-29 November 1984) 13.

22.   Ibid., 14.

23.   Ibid. [The same page as in the preceding note.]

24.   Carl B. Koford, "The Welfare of the Puma in California, 1976" (Wildlife-Fisheries, Dept. of Forestry and Conservation, and Museum of Vertebrate Zoology, University of California, Berkeley) 1-2.

25.   Kenneth R. Dixon, "Evaluation of the Effects of Mountain Lion Predation, 1966-67" (Colorado Game, Fish and Parks Department) 145-149.

26.   Robertson and Lindsey, *Proceedings*, 64. The figures given in the text were summarized from a table.

27.   Rainer H. Brocke, "Reintroduction of the Cougar Felis concolor in Adirondack Park: A problem Analysis and Recommendations," New York State Department of Environmental Conservation (1981) 13.

28.   Richard E. McCabe and Thomas R. McCabe, "Of Slings and Arrows: An Historical Retrospection" in ed. Lowell K. Halls, *White-tailed Deer: Ecology and Management*, A Wildlife Management Institute Book (Harrisburg: Stackpole Books, 1984) 19-72.

29.   Melinda Nunn McCauley, "Current Population and Distribution Status of the Panther, *Felis concolor*, in Florida" (Master's Thesis, Tampa: University of South Florida, December, 1977) 58pp.

30. Ibid., 33-34.

31. Joe A. Akerman, Jr., *Florida Cowman: A History of Florida Cattle Raising* (Kissimmee: Florida Cattleman's Association, 1976) 138.

32. Ibid., 139-140.

33. James N. Layne, "The Land Mammals of South Florida" in ed. P. J. Gleason, *Environments of South Florida: Present and Past*. Memoir 2 (Miami, Miami Geological Society, 1974) 399.

34. David Newell, "Panther," *The Saturday Evening Post*, 13 July 1935, 10.

35. Ibid. [The same page as in the preceding note.]

36. Ibid., 11.

37. McCauley, "Status of the Panther," 22.

38. Ibid., 35.

39. Jim Vanas, "The Florida Panther in the Big Cypress Swamp and the Role of Everglades Wonder Gardens in Past and Future Captive Breeding Programs" in ed. Pritchard, *Proceedings, 1976*, 110.

40. Peter C. H. Pritchard, Series ed., *Rare and Endangered Biota of Florida*, 6 volumes (Gainesville: University Presses of Florida). Earl Frye was executive director of the Game Commission as the Endangered Biota series emerged in the 1970s. He wrote a foreword which was inserted into each volume. It contains the following phrase indicating that there was resistance to protecting the panther: ". . . when David C. Jones of Naples in 1958 fought an uphill battle in influencing other members of the Game and Fresh Water Fish Commission to protect the Florida panther, which like all predators was traditionally considered the archenemy of man. . . ."

41. O. Earle Frye with Bill and Les Piper, "The Disappearing Panther," *Florida Wildlife*, October 1950, 8-9, 31-32.

42. Interview: Melody Roelke, 11 April 1989.

43. McCauley, "Status of the Panther," 34.

44. Van Doren, *Travels*, 182-184.

45. Richard F. Harlow and F. K. Jones, *The White-tailed Deer in Florida, Technical Bulletin No. 9* (Tallahassee: Florida Game and Fresh Water Fish Commission, 1965) 9-11.

46. J. B. Royall, Commissioner, *Report, Department of Game and Fresh Water Fish Commission, for Biennium Ending June 30, 1928* (Tallahassee: Florida State Library) 39.

47. F. Trench Townshend, *Wild Life in Florida: With A Visit to Cuba* (London: Hurst and Blackett, Publishers, 1875).

48. Ibid., 44-48.

49. Ibid., 105.

50. Ibid., 264-268.

51. Ibid., 44 and 268.

52. Harry A. Kersey, Jr., *Pelts, Plumes and Hides: White Traders among the Seminole Indians 1870-1930* (Gainesville: The University Presses of Florida, 1975) 19.

53. Ibid., 30.

54. Ibid., 47.

55. Clay MacCauley, "The Seminole Indians of Florida," *Fifth Annual Report of the Bureau of Ethnology to the Secretary of the Smithsonian Institution 1883-84* (Washington, D.C. Government Printing Office, 1887) 513.

56. Kersey, *Pelts, Plumes and Hides*, 131-132.

57. James A. Henshall, *Camping and Cruising in Florida* (Cincinnati: Robert Clarke & Co., 1884) 62-75.

58. Ibid., 159.

59. Ibid., 132-133.

60. Ibid., 88.

61. Ibid., 201-209.

62. Charlton W. Tebeau, *The Story of the Chokoloskee Bay Country* (Miami: University of Miami Press, 1955) 62-63.

63. Henshall, *Camping and Cruising*, 226

64. Maynard, *The Mammals of Florida*, 3.

65. *Biennial Report, Florida Game and Fresh Water Fish Commission, 1947-48*, (Tallahassee: Florida State Library) 36.

66. T. Gilbert Pearson, *Adventures in Bird Protection: An Autobiography* (New York: Appleton-Century, Inc., 1937).

67. E. Z. Jones, Commissioner, *First Annual Report of Department of Game and Fish, Tallahassee, Florida, 1914*. (Tallahassee: Florida State Library) 8.

68. Ibid., 20.

69. E. Z. Jones, Commissioner, *Second Annual Report, State of Florida. Department of Game and Fish, Tallahassee, Florida, 1915* (Tallahassee: Florida State Library) 26.

70. Ibid., 35.

71. *Florida Commission of Game and Fresh Water Fish, Biennial Report for period ending December 31, 1938* (Tallahassee: Florida State Library) 11.

72. Kersey, *Pelts, Plumes and Hides*, 46.

73. Charlton W. Tebeau, *Florida's Last Frontier: The History of Collier County* (Miami: University of Miami Press, 1966) 202-203.

74. Ibid., 179-182.

75. The estimated capacity of Florida's deer range is well under one million. Cristoffer and Eisenberg (see note no. 2) estimated an original carrying capacity of 400,000. The figure might be higher with modern land-management practices.

76. *Biennial Report, Commission of Game and Fresh Water Fish of the State of Florida, Biennium Ending December 31, 1940*, 14.

77. Harlow and Jones, *The White-tailed Deer in Florida*, 125.

78. *Biennial Report, Game and Fresh Water Fish commission of the State of Florida, Biennium Ending December 31, 1944* (Tallahassee: Florida State Library) 18.

79. McCauley, "Status of the Panther," 35.

80. J. E. Williams, "The Why and Wherefore of Florida's Deer Killing Program," *Florida Cattleman* (Kissimmee November 1939). This document and several others which summarize events leading up to the 1939 deer killing episode in Collier County can be found in the Florida State Archives. The documents are in the files of the State Livestock Sanitary Board of Florida.

81. The figures given for the size of this refuge vary somewhat with the source, and with the date. It is possible that the size varied over time.

82. *Miami Herald*, 16 October 1939.

83. *Miami Herald*, 1 November 1939.

84. *Orlando Sentinel*, The clipping is in a scrapbook which was maintained by the Livestock Sanitary Board of Florida. It is now in the state archives. My notes do not record a date, but it would have probably been in the late months of 1939.

85. T. H. Watkins, "The Terrible-Tempered Mr. Ickes," *Audubon*, Vol. 84, No. 2 (March 1984) 93-111.

86. Interview, Roy Komarek, November 1988.

87. W. J. Hamilton, Jr., "Notes on Some Mammals of Lee County, Florida," *The American Midland Naturalist*, Vol. 25, 1941, 689.

88. Letter: Page to Edminister, 26 December 1939, (Aldo Leopold Papers, "Florida Deer Tick Controversy," Division of Archives, University of Wisconsin, Madison).

89. Letter: Edminister to Halt, 3 January 1940 (Aldo Leopold Papers).

90. Letter: Leopold to Baker, et al., 11 January 1940 (Aldo Leopold Papers).

91. Watkins, "The Terrible-Tempered Mr. Ickes," 107-109.

92. Curt Meine, *Aldo Leopold, His Life and* Work (Madison: University of Wisconsin Press, 1988) 403.

93. Letter: Leopold to Ickes, 6 March 1940, (Aldo Leopold Papers).

94. Letter, Roy Komarek to John Baker, 15 September 1944. Komarek informed Baker that "Deer killing by BAI [Bureau of Animal Industry] was terminated August 14 last, and all of the Hendry County and part of Collier County are expected to be released from quarantine December 1 of this year."

95. John H. Davis, Jr., *The Natural Features of Southern Florida: Especially the Vegetation, and*

the Everglades (Tallahassee: State of Florida, Department of Conservation, Florida Geological Survey, Geological Bulletin No. 25, 20 October 1943) 238-239.

96.   *Biennial Report, State of Florida Game and Fresh Water Fish Commission, For period Ending December 31, 1946*, 18.

97.   *Biennial Report, 1944*, 37.

98.   *Orlando Sentinel*, 27 February 1941.

99.   *Biennial Report, Florida Game and Fresh Water Fish Commission, 1949-50*, 20.

100.   *Royall, Report: Biennium 1928*, 51-58.

101.   Young and Goldman, *The Puma*, 22-23.

102.   George H. Lowery Jr., "A Preliminary Report on the Distribution of the Mammals of Louisiana," *The Louisiana Academy of Sciences*, March, 1936, 23.

103.   Ibid., 19.

104.   Royall, *Report: Biennium 1928*, 51-58. There is a discrepancy in the report. The figures for animals killed are displayed in a table showing returns for each species, by county. The figures in the deer column add up to 577 and so is indicated in the table. However, the narrative summary of the table states that 1,111 deer were taken. Either way, it is obvious that there were few deer in Florida. The discrepancy may have been the result of faulty clerical work; another is shown for squirrels: the figures in the table show a total of 128,610; the narrative summary omitted the first digit, with the result that 28,610 squirrels are reported as the harvest total.

105.   Frankenberger and Belden, "Feral Hogs in Florida," 641.

106.   *World Almanac, 1927*, 374.

107.   Agricultural Statistician, Hogs: Inventory, Numbers, Pig Crops and Disposition, Florida 1924-63 (Orlando: U.S.D.A Statistical Reporting Service) 24.

108.   Frankenberger and Belden, "Feral Hogs in Florida," 641.

109.   Compiled under the direction of the County Commission, Glades County, Florida History (Moore Haven: Rainbow Books, 1985) 135.

110.   John S. Otto, "Open-Range Cattle-Ranching in South Florida," *Tampa Bay History*, Vol. 8, No. 2, 32.

111.   Ibid., 32-33.

112.   *Biennial Report, Florida Game and Fresh Water Fish Commission, 1949-50*, 20.

113.   Harlow and Jones, *The White-tailed Deer in Florida*, 125.

114.   McCauley, Status of the Panther, 35.

115.   Ross Allen and Wildfred T. Neil, "The Florida Panther," *Florida Wildlife*, Vol. 7, No. 6, November, 1953, 33.

116.   Koford, "The Welfare of the Puma in California, 1976," 3.

117.   Hornocker, "Analysis of Mountain Lion Predation," 18.

118.   Melody E. Roelke, "Florida Panther Biomedical Investigation, 1987-88," (Tallahassee: Florida Game and Fresh Water Fish Commission, 1988) 21-24.

119.   Ibid., 24.

120.   Melody E. Roelke, Elliot R. Jacobson, George V. Kollias and Donald J. Forrester, "Medical Management and Biomedical Findings on the Florida Panther, Felis concolor coryi, 1985-86" (Tallahassee: Florida Game and Fresh Water Fish Commission, 1986) 21.

121.   Roelke, "Florida Panther Biomedical Investigation 1987-88, 122.

122.   The New York Times, 29 August 1989.

Chapter 3: IN THE BEGINNING

1.   Personal communication, Robert C. Belden. After cursory examinations of these remains by several persons, doubts were expressed as to whether they were those of *Felis concolor*. The identity of the species cannot be stated with certainty.

2.   Personal communication, Robert C. Belden. The hide of this animal hangs on the wall of an office of the Florida Game and Fresh Water Fish Commission in Ocala.

3.   Robert C. Belden and Lovett E. Williams, Jr., "Survival Status of the Florida Panther" in ed. Pritchard, *Proceedings, 1976*, 86. The records are listed under category one, records of the Florida

Game and Fresh Water Fish Commission. In the winter of 1974 the U. S. Fish and Wildlife Service seized a hide which had been sent from Immokalee, Florida to be tanned in Wyoming. This record was not listed in the report mentioned above.

4.   Vernon G. Henry, "The Recovery Team Concept of the Fish and Wildlife Service as it relates to the Florida Panther" in ed. Pritchard, *Proceedings, 1976*, 59-77. A recent historical perspective on endangered species legislation is offered by Dennis Drabelle, "The Endangered Species Program," in ed. Roger L. DiSilvestro, *Audubon Wildlife Report 1985* (New York: The National Audubon Society, 1985) 61.

5.   Ibid., 63.

6.   Pritchard, *Rare and Endangered Biota*.

7.   Robert C. Belden, "Florida Panther Investigation—A 1978 Progress Report" (Tallahassee: Florida Game and Fresh Water Fish Commission, 1978) 6.

8.   GFC memo, Belden to Williams, 18 April 1978.

9.   Kent A. Reeves, "Preliminary Investigation of the Florida Panther in Big Cypress Swamp" (Homestead: South Florida Research Center, Everglades National Park, August 1978) 5.

10.   Hornocker, "Analysis of Mountain Lion Predation."

11.   Seidensticker, et al., "Mountain Lion Social Organization."

12.   Robert C. Belden, "The Capture and Handling of Panthers: Literature Review and Plan for Use in Florida" (Tallahassee: Florida Game and Fresh Water Fish Commission, 15 January 1981).

13.   Robert E. Baudy, "Transcript of a speech given at a meeting of the Florida Panther Recovery Team meeting, 27 September 1978, at Bushnell, Florida."

14.   Corey O'Gorman, "The Florida Panther: Teetering on the Brink," *The Florida Naturalist* (March 1983) 7.

15.   "Resolution: Florida Panther Tracking Program," Board of Directors, Florida Audubon Society, 22 January 1983.

16.   Chris Belden, "It was the Hunt of a Lifetime," *Florida Wildlife* (May-June, 1981) 22-24. Belden provided a narrative of his first panther capture. It imparts the detailed freshness that characterizes first experiences and was the basis for the account given here.

17.   FPRT Minutes, 16 June 1981.

18.   FPRT Minutes, January 1982.

19.   Belden, "Florida Panther Recovery Plan Implementation," 14.

20.   GFC Letter, Brantly to Landrum, 17 January 1983.

21.   Belden, "Recovery Plan Implementation, 1982 Progress Report," 10-11.

22.   "Resolution: Florida Panther Radio Tracking Program," Board of Directors, Florida Audubon Society, 22 January 1983.

23.   Letter, Setterblade to Graham, 24 January 1984.

24.   Letter, Taylor to Editor, *The Miami Herald*, 6 February 1984.

25.   Editorial, *The Miami Herald*, 19 January 1984.

26.   *Fort Myers News-Press*, 3 December 1986.

27.   GFC Letter, Brantly to Humphrey, 22 March 1983.

28.   Memo, Humphrey to Panther Advisory Committee, 19 July 1983.

29.   "Florida Panther Recovery: A Status Report to the Governor and Cabinet, July 7, 1983" (Tallahassee: Florida Game and Fresh Water Fish Commission) 2.

30.   Ibid., 3.

31.   FPTAC Minutes, 9 September 1983.

32.   FPTAC Minutes, 3 November 1983. A history of off-road vehicle use in the Big Cypress National Preserve, through the year 1978, had been documented by the National Audubon Society's Ecosystems Research Unit at Corkscrew Swamp Sanstuary. The research had been contracted by the National Park Service. Fred Fagergren, the Preserve Superintendent, brought the Panther Advisory Council up to date on ORV activities since the Audubon Society's report. The subject occasioned long discussion.

33.   This statement first appeared in a report by Colonel Robert Brantly to the Governor and Cabinet on the status of Florida panther recovery, 7 July 1983. It appears again in the FPTAC minutes of 3 November 1983. In a letter to Mrs. Bette Kissick on 20 March 1984, Colonel Brantly informed that

"Normal sport hunting activities pose little threat to the panthers, as evidenced by their movements during hunting season, and the absence of any documented deaths of panthers caused by hunters." The last statement is incorrect. A hunter killed a panther on 3 March 1978.

34.   Peter B. Gallagher, "Panthers Caught in the Middle," *The Orlando Sentinel*, Sunday, 26 May 1985.

35.   Robert E., Baudy, Comments on "Recommendations of the Florida Panther Technical Advisory Council to the Game and Fresh Water Fish Commission, November 14, 1983." Baudy's comments were appended to the recommendations when they were forwarded to Game Commission Headquarters on December 9, 1983, in a letter, Alvarez to Brantly.

36.   Peter B. Gallagher, "A Panther Treed is Not a Panther Collared," *St. Petersburg Times*, 22 May 1984. The account of this incident is based on the story by Gallagher, supplemented by my conversations with members of the capture team.

37.   Melody E. Roelke, et al, "Medical Management and Biomedical Findings on the Florida Panther, 1983-1985 (Tallahassee: Florida Game and Fresh Water Fish Commission).

38.   FPTAC Recommendations, 12 June 1984, in letter, Alvarez to Brantly.

39.   Gerald Grow, "New Threats to the Florida Panther," *ENFO* (Winter Park: Florida Conservation Foundation, 1984) 11-12.

40.   This account of Big Guy's rescue and medical treatment was reconstructed from several newspaper articles (*Naples Daily News*, 4,5,15 November 1984; Miami Herald, 3, 4, 6 November and 11 December 1984, and from an interview with Walt McCown, Game Commission biologist.

41.   GFC Minutes, Tallahassee, Florida, 7 March 1985.

42.   FPTAC Recommendations, 14 November 1983.

43.   FPTAC Recommendations, 28 May 1985.

44.   GFC letter, Brantly to Morehead, 18 July 1985.

45.   NPS letter, Morehead to Brantly, 2 August 1985.

46.   Ibid.

47.   Letter, Alvarez to Mott, 17 September 1985.

48.   NPS Letter, Mott to Alvarez, 18 November 1985.

49.   Letter, Alvarez to Brantly, 1 February 1985.

50.   Roy McBride, "Population Status of the Florida Panther in Everglades National Park and Big Cypress National Preserve" (Homestead: Everglades National Park, 1985) 3.

51.   Ibid.

52.   McBride, "Population Status," 46.

53.   Ibid. [The same page as in the preceding note.]

54.   Ibid., 57.

55.   Ibid.

56.   W. B. Robertson, Jr. O. E. Bass, Jr. and R. McBride, "Review of Existing Information on the Population of the Florida Panther in EVER, DICY and environs with Suggestions for Needed Research, 23 April 1985" (Homestead: Everglades National Park) 1.

57.   Ibid.

58.   Roelke, et al., "Medical Management, 1984-1985, 90-91.

59.   Ibid., 65.

Chapter 4: THE FLORIDA PANTHER INTERAGENCY COMMITTEE

1.   Alston Chase, "The Grizzly and the Juggernaut," *Outside*, January, 1986, 30.

2.   Ibid. [The same page as in the preceding note.]

3.   Chase, "The Grizzly and the Juggernaut," 33.

4.   Ibid., [The same page as in the preceding note.]

5.   Ibid., 34.

6.   National Academy of Sciences, "Report of Committee on the Yellowstone Grizzlies" (Washington, D.C.: National Academy Press, July 1974). My reading of the report leaves an impression that it was somewhat less emphatically supportive of the Craigheads than impled by Chase in the magazine

article. The Committee did not feel that the garbage dumps had increased grizzly bear numbers and implied that the killing of bears was simply an occurrence in the readjustment of the bears to a period of "exclusively wild feeding." The Committee stated that there was "no evidence as to the role and importance of garbage food sources in the fecundity or mortality rates of grizzly bears.... There is no convincing evidence that the grizzly bears in the Yellowstone ecosystem are in *immediate* [italics added] danger of extinction. It recommended "against supplemental feeding as being unnecessary to maintain the Yellowstone grizzly population." The Committee acknowledged a substantial reduction in bear numbers between 1968 and 1973, but it *believed* [italics added] that compensatory mechanisms would lead to a replacement of bears that had been killed. However, it suggested that the bear population could not survive mortality rates as high as those it was subjected to in the years 1970-72, while also stating that "mortalities and control actions declined in 1972 and 1973."

However, the Committee admitted that it couldn't determine the trend in population numbers because of inadequate data and stated that "at best, grizzly populations are vulnerable when high rates of mortality are imposed." It also recommended that man-caused mortalities be held to "about" 10 [per year] until research could clarify the picture. The Committee was critical of the National Park Service research program calling it "inadequate to provide the data essential for devising sound management policies of the grizzly bears...." The Committee was also critical of the bureaucratic mechanism the National Park Service had erected to oversee the program (the Interagency Grizzly Bear Study Team and its Steering Committee): "its close ties to management supervision and management authority impose severe constraints on its effectiveness." The Committee recommended a non-governmental mechanism as a remedy, but this went against self-protective bureaucratic impulses and was never implemented.

The Committee also seemed to implicitly criticize the Park Service for expelling the Craigheads. "We recommend that the National Park Service and the U. S. Forest Service pursue a policy of supporting and encouraging independent research on Yellowstone grizzlies. The freedom of scientists to conduct research throughout the Yellowstone ecosystem is imperative if the data essential to successful management of Yellowstone grizzlies are to be obtained; the presence of independent investigators will enhance and invigorate study programs undertaken by land-management agencies."

7.   Chase, "The Grizzly and the Juggernaut," 34.
8.   Dennis Drabelle, "The Endangered Species Program," in ed. Roger L. DiSilvestro, *Audubon Wildlife Report 1985* (New York: The National Audubon Society, 1985) 75.
9.   Chase, "The Grizzly and the Juggernaut," 57.
10.   NPS Letter, Mott to Alvarez, 18 November 1985.
11.   Chase, "The Grizzly and the Juggernaut," 57.
12.   "Panther Recommendations, Everglades Coalition, 18 January 1986," in Letter to Governor Graham, 20 January 1986 (signed by representatives of the Florida Audubon Society, National Audubon Society, Defenders of Wildlife, Conservation Foundation, Friends of the Everglades, Florida Chapter of the Sierra Club, Wilderness Society, and National Parks and Conservation Association.
13.   Robert L. Downing, et. al., "Deer Management Review Panel Final Report," submitted to Big Cypress National Preserve, National Park Service, Ochopee, Florida, 13 March 1986.
14.   References to the deer panel report reappeared in 1989 in the draft General Management Plan for the Big Cypress National Preserve—in the course of commentary provided by Game Commission biologists.
15.   Ed. Wm. V. Branan, Proceedings, "Survival of the Florida Panther: A Discussion of Issues and Accomplishments, 24-25 April 1986" (Tallahassee: Florida Defenders of the Environment).
16.   Ibid., 43-45.
17.   Ibid., 43.
18.   Ibid., 45.
19.   Mancur Olsen, "The Yellowstone Primer," *The New York Times*, 13 May 1990, 12.
20.   Branan, Proceedings, "Survival of the Florida Panther," 45

Chapter 5: THE FPIC IN ACTION

1.   FPIC Agenda, 27-28 May 1987.

2.   TS Minutes, 18 June 1986 (PANTHER INFO-4).
3.   Draft, Florida Panther Recovery Plan, 16 May 1986, 19a.
4.   TS Minutes, June 1986 (PANTHER INFO-4).
5.   Ibid.
6.   Letter, Branan to Christian, 31 July 1986.
7.   TS Minutes, 30 June and 1 July 1986 (PANTHER INFO-11).
8.   Draft, Florida Panther Recovery Plan, 16 May 1986, 38.
9.   Draft Revision, Florida Panther Recovery Plan, 5 June 1986, 38.
10.   TS Minutes, 15 January 1987 (PANTHER INFO-21).
11.   Ibid.
12.   Ibid.
13.   Ibid.
14.   Ibid.
15.   Ibid.
16.   PANTHER INFO-22.
17.   Ibid.
18.   Letter, Alvarez to Pulliam, 26 April 1987.
19.   FWS Letter, Pulliam to Alvarez, 26 May 1987.
20.   Letter Alvarez to Pulliam, 20 June 1987.
21.   FPIC news release, 26 June 1987 (PANTHER INFO-33).
22.   FDE Letter, Branan to Baker, 27 April 1987.
23.   NPS Letter, Baker to Branan, 29 May 1987.
24.   Richard Hamann and John Tucker, "Legal Responsibilities of the National Park Service in Preserving the Florida Panther" (Gainesville: Center for Governmental Responsibility, University of Florida College of Law) 26 October 1987.
25.   FDE Letter, Branan to Baker, 9 November 1987.
26.   *National Parks*, November/December 1986, 7.
27.   GFC News Release, 30 July 1986.

Chapter 6: INBREEDING, OUTBREEDING AND THE SUBSPECIES QUESTION

1.   Donald Culross Peattie, *Green Laurels: The Lives and Achievements of the Great Naturalists* (New York: Simon and Schuster, 1936) 111.
2.   Charles Darwin, *The Voyage of the Beagle* (Danbury: The Harvard Classics, Grolier Enterprises, originally published in 1845) 383-384. Stephen Jay Gould in an essay entitled "Darwin at Sea and the Virtues of Port" explains that Darwin's observations during the voyage raised suspicions about evolution, but did not dispel his creationist views until his collection of specimens was examined by experts back in England. Darwin, the amateur, had not the detailed knowledge to thoroughly interpret what he saw. It is interesting though, that after his collections were studied, Darwin drew the proper conclusions about evolution, while some of the experts who examined the collections remained confirmed creationists. Gould, who in this essay, cites the work of Frank Sulloway, a historian of science, writes that the Galapagos finches played no part in Darwin's incipient ideas about evolution during the voyage. I learned all this while reading for pleasure Gould's book, *The Flamingo Smile*.
3.   George Gaylord Simpson, *Principles of Animal Taxonomy* (New York: Columbia University Press, 1961) 148.
4.   Ibid., 171.
5.   Young and Goldman, *The Puma,* 181.
6.   Ibid. [The same page as in the preceding note.]
7.   Ibid. [The same page as in the preceding note.]
8.   Ibid., 188.
9.   Simpson, *Principles of Animal Taxonomy*, 179.
10.   Ernst Mayr, "Of What Use are Subspecies?", *The Auk.*, Vol. 99, 595.
11.   "Notes and News," *Oryx*, Vol. XVI, No. 4, June, 1982, 298-299.
12.   Stephen J. O'Brien, David E. Wildt and Mitchell Bush, "The Cheetah in Genetic Peril,"

Scientific American., Vol. 254, No.5, 84.

13.   Ibid., 88.

14.   Ibid., 87.

15.   Melody E. Roelke, "Florida Panther Biomedical Investigation, 1986-87" (Tallahassee: Florida Game and Fresh Water Fish Commission) 31-34.

16.   FWS Memo, 2 August 1977.

17.   Tom J. Cade, "Hybridization and Gene Exchange among Birds in Relation to Conservation," in ed. Christine M. Schonewald-Cox, et al., *Genetics and Conservation: A Reference for Managing wild Animal and Plant Populations* (Menlo Park: The Benjamin/Cummings Publishing Co., Inc., 1983) 306.

18.   J. Comrie Greig, "Principles of Genetic Conservation in Relation to Wildlife Management in Southern Africa," *South African Journal of Wildlife Research*, Vol.9 (1979) 57-78.

19.   Dennis Drabelle, "The Endangered Species Program," in ed. Roger L. DiSilvestro, *Audubon Wildlife Report 1985* (New York: The National Audubon Society, 1985) 78.

20.   FWS Memo, Schreiner to Region 4 Director, 14 October 1976.

21.   Laurie Wilkins and Robert C. Belden, "Distinguishing Features of the Florida Panther" (Tallahassee: Florida Game and Fresh Water Fish Commission, 23 August 1982) [Second Draft]

22.   Robert C. Belden, "Florida Panther Recovery Plan Implementation — A 1982 Progress Report" (Tallahassee: Florida Game and Fresh Water Fish Commission, 29 September 1982) 20.

23.   Robert C. Belden, "The Florida Panther," in *Audubon Wildlife Report, 1988-89* (New York: National Audubon Society,1988) 524. This document of 1988 is the earliest in which I could find a reference to 1,000 captive pumas. However, the figure was bruited about during recovery team deliberations in the late 1970s.

24.   John F. Eisenberg, "The Density and Biomass of Tropical Mammals," in Soule and Wilcox ed., *Conservation Biology: An Evolutionary-Ecological Perspective* (Sunderland, Mass: Sinauer Associates Inc., 1980) 35-55.

25.   Tinsley, *The Florida Panther*, 23.

26.   Branan, Proceedings: "Survival of the Florida Panther," 17.

27.   Ibid. 15.

28.   U.S. Endangered Species Act, 1973.

29.   Branan, Proceedings, "Survival of the Florida Panther," 15.

30.   Ibid. 64.

31.   Ibid. 63.

32.   Ibid.

33.   Ibid., 64.

34.   FWS Letter, Christian to Branan, 18 November 1986.

35.   Interview, Melody Roelke.

36.   Oron L. Bass, Jr. and William B. Robertson, Jr., "Preliminary Report on Florida Panther Research in Everglades National Park, November 1986-April 1987" (PANTHER INFO-25, 12 May 1987).

37.   PANTHER INFO-65, Minutes of 30 May-1 June, 1989, Technical Subcommittee Meeting. The minutes state that "[panther] #'s 16 & 27 successfully crossed Shark River Slough during the dry season. This represents the first documented crossing of what was generally considered a physical barrier preventing east/west movement of panthers in that area.

38.   Video Tapes: James Billie trial, courtesy Peter B. Gallagher.

39.   Ibid.

40.   FWS Memo, Wesley to Regional Office, December 1986.

41.   FWS Memo, Jordan to T. S., FPIC (PANTHER INFO-25, 12 May 1987).

42.   FPIC Issue Paper (PANTHER INFO-50, 28 March 1988).

43.   FPIC Memo, Jordan to Technical Subcommittee (PANTHER INFO-50, 28 March 1988).

44.   *Tallahassee Democrat* (9 March 1988) ". . . A big cat killed Wednesday night in Jefferson County—which appears not to be an endangered Florida panther—has state Game and Fresh Water Fish officials puzzled, a game official said Friday. . . . "I don't think we're ever going to know for sure," said Tom Logan, head of wildlife research for the commission. . . . Logan said a necropsy had been

performed on the animal, which was hit by an unknown driver near Capps. The cougar didn't have "any of the characteristics that the game commission normally finds in Florida panthers," he said. The 74-pound cat did not have fused vertebrate in its tail, white spots on its back or a characteristic cowlick on its shoulders. . . . "More lab work will be done to try to determine what kind of cougar the cat was," Logan said. . . .

    Tallahassee Democrat (9 April 1988) ". . . Before the source of the cat was discovered, wildlife biologists had been called in to figure out its identity. . . ."The confusion was that this cat did not have the characteristics of the Florida panther," Cabbage said, describing it as "typically having a crooked tail, white flecks on the back, and a cowlick on the shoulders."

45.   GFC Letter, Logan to Wesley, 19 July 1988.

Chapter 7: CAPTIVE BREEDING AND REINTRODUCTION

1.   Robert E. Baudy, "Breeding Techniques for Felines Destined for Release in the Wild" in Pritchard, *Proceedings, 1976*, 99.

2.   Jim Vanas, "The Florida Panther in the Big Cypress Swamp and the Role of Everglades Wonder Gardens in Past and Future Captive Breeding Programs," in ed. Pritchard, *Proceedings*, 1976, 110-111.

3.   Biennial Animal Census Report for Everglades National Park, January 20, 1958 (Homestead: Everglades National Park files). Dr. William B. Robertson Jr., a research scientist at Everglades National Park (personal communication) talked to Bill Piper during the course of the 1957 release. Robertson's recollection is that Piper said the two introduced cats were about two years old and had been captured in the Big Cypress Swamp as kittens. Robertson's account does not seem to agree with the information provided by Jim Vanas.

4.   Superintendent's Monthly Narrative Report for Everglades National Park, September 1965 (Homestead: Everglades National Park files) 5.

5.   NPS Letter, Allin to Pipers, 25 March 1968 (Homestead: Everglades National Park files).

6.   Baudy, Statement (1 June 1978)

7.   Letter, Baudy to Belden, 9 June 1978.

8.   Robert E. Baudy, "Observation of the First Complete Mating of Florida Panthers at the Rare Feline Breeding Compound" (23 September 1978).

9.   FPRT Minutes, 27 September 1978.

10.   Ibid., "Speech given by Robert E. Baudy, Member of the Florida Panther Recovery Team, September 27, 1978—Bushnell, Florida, Hosted by the Rare Feline Breeding Compound."

11.   FPRT Minutes, 16 January 1979.

12.   FPRT memo, Belden to Team Members.

13.   Letter, Baudy to Belden, 27 March 1980.

14.   FPRT Minutes, 4 June 1980.

15.   FPRT Letter, Belden to Baudy, 19 August 1980.

16.   FPRT Minutes, 16 June 1981.

17.   FPRT Minutes, January 1982.

18.   GFC Letter, Logan to Gerde, 29 November 1988.

19.   FPTAC Minutes, 9 September 1983.

20.   Letter, Baudy to Alvarez, 28 November 1983.

21.   "Proposal to Conduct Research Relevant to the Breeding and Reintroduction of the Florida Panther in Suitable Habitats," letter, Eisenberg to Logan, 9 December 1983.

22.   Cris Cristoffer and John F. Eisenberg, "Report No. 3 on the Captive Breeding and Reintroduction of the Florida Panther in Suitable Habitats (Tallahassee: Report Prepared for the Florida Game and Fresh Water Fish Commission, 2 August 1985).

23.   FPTAC Recommendations, 12 June 1984.

24.   GFC Letter, Egbert to Fagergren, 14 March 1985.

25.   Attachments, FWS License/Permit Application, GFC to FWS, 15 April 1985.

26.   Ibid.

27.   Ibid.

28. Letter, Alvarez to Logan, 1 April 1985.
29. GFC Letter, Egbert to Alvarez, 19 April 1985.
30. Ibid.
31. FPTAC Recommendations, 28 May 1985.
32. Ibid.
33. Ibid.
34. FPTAC Recommendations, May 1986.
35. GFC Letter, Brantly to Alvarez, 4 November 1986.
36. Letter, Alvarez to Brantly, 19 November 1986.
37. Ibid.
38. FPTAC Recommendations, 9 November 1986.
39. Ibid.
40. TS Minutes, 29-30 April 1987 (PANTHER INFO-29).
41. Letter, Alvarez to Brantly, 17 January 1987.
42. FPIC Minutes, 15 January 1987 (PANTHER INFO-26).
43. GFC Letter, Brantly to Alvarez, 13 February 1987.
44. Letter, Alvarez to Brantly, 14 April 1987.
45. PANTHER INFO-26, 13 May 1987, 26.
46. Ibid.
47. TS Minutes, 22-23 June 1987 (PANTHER INFO-32).
48. GFC Letter, Egbert to Alvarez, 19 April 1985.
49. Attachments, FWS License/Permit Application, GFC to FWS, 15 April 1985.
50. TS Minutes, 29-30 April 1987 (PANTHER INFO-29).
51. TS Minutes, 22-23 June 1987 (PANTHER INFO-32).
52. Ibid.
53. Ibid.
54. Ibid.
55. TS Minutes, 3-4 December 1987 (PANTHER INFO-46).
56. TS Minutes, 22-23 September 1987 (PANTHER INFO-42).
57. *Florida Panther Recovery Plan* (Washington, D.C.: U.S. Fish and Wildlife Service, 17 December 1981) 8-9.
58. *Florida Panther Recovery Plan, June 1987* (Washington, D.C.: U.S. Fish and Wildlife Service) 14.
59. Tommy C. Hines, Robert C. Belden and Melody E. Roelke, D.V.M., "An Overview of Panther Research and Management in Florida," in ed. Ron R. Odom, Kenneth A. Riddleberger and James C. Ozier, *Proceedings of the Third Southeastern Nongame and Endangered Wildlife Symposium,* Athens, Georgia, 8-10 August 1987 (Georgia Department of Natural Resources, Game and Fish Division) 142.
60. Ibid. [The same page as in the preceding note.]
61. Ibid. [The same page as in the preceding note.]
62. Robert C. Belden and William B. Frankenberger, "Potential Panther Reintroduction Site Evaluation," appendix to "Florida Panther Reestablishment," (Tallahassee: Florida Game and Fresh Water Fish Commission, 1985-86) 3-4.
63. William B. Robertson Jr. and Oron P. Bass, "Preliminary Report on Florida Panther Research in Everglades National Park, November-December, 1986."
64. Cristoffer and Eisenberg, "Report No. 3."
65. *Palm Beach Post*/University of Florida Poll.
66. Branan, Proceedings "Survival of the Florida Panther," 37.
67. Letter, James B. Estes, County Extension Director, to Brantly. The letter was worded as follows: "The Franklin County Board of County Commissioners have instructed me to write to you in regard to the Florida Game and Fresh Water Fish Commission's Panther Relocation Program.

We were informed approximately a year ago that the Commission, in cooperation with some wildlife specialists from the University of Florida, were considering relocating some panthers in Franklin County that your department raised in captivity. I was asked to assist with this program by providing

information in regard to whether or not owners of livestock would object to the program.

We made a survey and found that there was no objections[sic] as far as the owners of cattle and other livestock were concerned.

Since that time, we have been informed that other counties where the panthers were relocated had severe restrictions placed on them by your department in regard to the use of 4-wheel drive vehicles, 3-wheel recreational vehicles, dog hunting, and fishing in the areas where panthers were released.

The Franklin County Board of County Commissioners would like to go on record as opposing the Panther Relocation Program in Franklin County because of the above listed restrictions being imposed on the hunters and fishermen of the county.

68. Belden and Frankenberger, "Reintroduction, 1985-86," 5-6.
69. Ibid., 6.
70. Robert C. Belden and William C. Frankenberger, "Candidate Panther Reintroduction Sites," appendix to "Florida Panther Captive Breeding/Reintroduction Feasibility," (Tallahassee: Florida Game and Fresh Water Fish Commission 1986-87) 3.
71. Cristoffer and Eisenberg, "Report No. 3."
72. Robert C. Belden and William C. Frankenberger, "Florida Panther Captive Breeding/Reintroduction Feasibility," (Tallahassee: Florida Game and Fresh Water Fish Commission (1987-88) 2-3.
73. Ibid., 5-6.
74. Ibid., 6.
75. Ibid., 6-7.
76. Ibid., 10.
77. Associated Press news item, reported in the *Sarasota Herald-Tribune*, 21 April 1989.
78. FPIC Memo, Pulliam to Baker, Brantly and Gardner, 1 May 1989.
79. Ibid.

Chapter 8: THE FLORIDA GAME AND FRESH WATER FISH COMMISSION

1. William T. Hornaday, *Our Vanishing Wildlife: Its Extermination and Preservation* (New York: New York Zoological Society, 1913) 277.
2. James B. Trefethen, *An American Crusade for Wildlife* (New York: Winchester Press, 1975) 177.
3. T. Gilbert Pearson, "Florida Bird-Life," in Jones, *Second Annual Report, 1915*, 60-61.
4. Hornaday, *Our Vanishing Wildlife*, 278.
5. Royall, *Report, 1928*, 39.
6. Jones, *First Annual Report, 1914*, 10.
7. Ibid., 17.
8. Ibld., 23-24.
9. Ibid., 9.
10. Ibid., 8.
11. Ibid. [The same page as in the preceding note.]
12. Ibid., 60.
13. T. Gilbert Pearson, "Wildlife Protection in the United States," *Proceedings: International Association of Fish and Wildlife Agencies, 1938* (Washington, D.C.: International Association of Fish and Agencies) 61.
14. Jones, *Second Annual Report, 1915*, 10.
15. Ibid., [The same page as in the preceding note.]
16. Ibid., 42.
17. Ibid., 19-20.
18. Dian Olson Belanger, *Managing American Wildlife: A History of the International Association of Fish and Wildlife Agencies* (Amherst: University of Massachusetts Press, 1988) 25.
19. Ibid., 26.
20. Lovett E. Williams Jr. and Larry L. Martin, "Nesting Populations of Brown Pelicans in Florida," *Proceedings, 24th Annual Conference of the Southeastern Association of Game and Fish Commis-*

sioners, 1970 (Tallahassee: Reprinted by the Florida Game and Fresh Water Fish Commission) 168. The authors state that "Another question which remains unanswered is whether the adult population has ever been any higher in Florida than during the period of this census. In spite of frequent allegations to that effect (by laymen, primarily) we find no evidence that current populations of about 13,000 nesting, adult pelicans are 'low'."

21.   Pearson, "Wildlife Protection," 59.

22.   William T. Hornaday, *Wildlife Conservation in Theory and Practice; Lectures Delivered Before the Forest School of Yale University* (New Haven: Yale University Press, 1914) 167-168.

23.   A Tribute by the Board of Directors, "T. Gilbert Pearson, 1873-1943, In Memoriam" *Audubon*, Vol. 45 (1943) 371.

24.   Pearson, "Wildlife Protection," 61.

25.   John F. Reiger, *American Sportsmen and the Origins of Conservation* (New York: Winchester Press, 1975) 53. Reiger has provided a valuable perspective on the development of the movement to protect and conserve fish and wildlife resources prior to 1900.

26.   Belanger, *Managing American Wildlife*, 170.

27.   Trefethen, *An American Crusade*, 112.

28.   Reiger, *American Sportsmen*, 53.

29.   Ibid., 39.

30.   Trefethen, *An American Crusade*, 110.

31.   Ibid., [The same page as in the preceding note.]

32.   Ibid., 109.

33.   Reiger, *American Sportsmen*, 142.

34.   Ibid., 144.

35.   Hornaday, *Our Vanishing Wildlife*, 80.

36.   Katherine Barton and Whit Fosburgh, "The U.S. Forest Service," in ed. Rodger L. deSilvestro, *Audubon Wildlife Report* (New York: National Audubon Society, 1986) 6-7.

37.   Trefethen, *An American Crusade*, 113.

38.   Pearson, "Wildlife Protection," 60.

39.   *Royall, Report, 1928*, 39.

40.   Ibid., 59.

41.   *Biennial Report, Florida Commission of Game and Fresh Water Fish, Biennium Ending December 31, 1936* (Tallahassee: Florida State Library) 29.

42.   C. C. Woodward, State Game Commissioner, *Fourth Biennial Report of the Department of Game and Fresh Water Fish, Florida, 1932* (Tallahassee: Florida State Library) 6.

43.   Trefethen, *An American Crusade*, 217.

44.   Meine, *Aldo Leopold*, 348.

45.   Chapter 170.16. Laws of the State of Florida.

46.   Section 30 added to Article IV, 1885 Constitution by Committee Substitute for Senate Joint Resolution 28, 1941.

47.   *Biennial Report, 1944*, 10.

48.   *Biennial Report, Commission of Game and Fresh Water Fish of the State of Florida, Biennium Ending December 31, 1942* (Tallahassee: Florida State Library) 10.

49.   J. J. Murray, "T. Gilbert Pearson, An Appreciation," *Audubon*, Vol. 45 (1943) 28.

50.   Jones, *First Annual Report, 1914*, 51.

51.   Belanger, *Managing American Wildlife*, 22.

52.   *Biennial Report, Florida Commission of Game and Fresh Water Fish, Biennium Ending December 31, 1940* (Tallahassee: Florida State Library) 47.

53.   E. L. Cheatum, "The Outlook," in ed. Halls, *White-tailed Deer*, 791-792. Cheatum writes: "All too often there is a wide gap between what is theoretically possible and what is actually achievable. In a society where management objectives and regulatory authority are subject to the sway of public opinion, the agency charged with wildlife management may find its authority limited or constrained, whether by law or by self-imposition as the result of political pressure. The lack of inflexibility of authority is cited by several authors in this book as inhibiting sound deer management. It is a legitimate complaint, but I see little hope of it changing soon unless much greater confidence in management expertise and

responsiveness can be engendered in the minds of the citizens the agencies serve. This will require demonstrated results and greater persistence as well as continuing education and debate...."

54.   Susan Flader, *Thinking Like a Mountain, Aldo Leopold and the Evolution of an Ecological Attitude Toward Deer, Wolves and Forests* (Columbia: Univesity of Missouri Press, 1974) 222.

55.   *Biennial Report, 1947-48*, 7.

56.   Edward E. Langenau, Jr., Stephen R. Kellert and James E. Applegate, "Values in Management," in ed. Halls, *White-tailed Deer*, 712-13.

57.   *Everglades Wildlife Management Committee: Final Report to Governor Graham, August 1983* (Tallahassee: Office of the Governor) 3.

58.   Ibid. [The same page as in the preceding reference.]

59.   Estus Whitfield, "Restoring the Everglades," in ed., William J. Chandler, *Audubon Wildlife Report 1988-1989* (San Diego: Academic Press, Inc, 1988) 474.

60.   "Everglades Wildlife Management Committee."

61.   Larry D. Harris and O. Earle Frye Jr., "Florida's Wildlife and Hunting Resource," in ed. A. S. Jensen, *Mutual Opportunities for Forest, Range and Wildlife Management, Resource Report No. 4* (Gainesville: School of Forest Resources and Conservation, University of Florida) 17.

62.   *Florida Game and Fresh Water Fish Commission, 1986-87 Annual Report*.

63.   GFC Memo, 27 April 1978.

64.   GFC Letter, Brantly to Graham, 21 October 1982.

65.   Big Cypress Area Management Task Force, "A Report to the Governor and Members of the Cabinet: Sensitive Natural Resources of the Big Cypress Area of Critical State Concern" (Tallahassee: Florida Game and Fresh Water Fish Commission, 21 February 1984).

66.   Florida Panther Management Policy Statement: Game and Fresh Water Fish Commission (undated, probably late 1982 or early 1983).

67.   FDE Letter. The letter was signed by the following: John H. Kaufman, Ph.D., Chairman, FDE Panther Policy Committee; F. Wayne King, Ph.D., James N. Layne, Ph.D., Kathleen S. Abrams, Ph.D., Stephen DeMontmollin, Esquire, In Cooperation With: Archie Carr, Ph.D., Graduate Research Professor, University of Florida; John Eisenberg, Ph.D., Ordway Professor and Curator of Ecosystem Conservation, University of Florida, Florida State Museum; David Smith, Ph.D., Nepal Tiger Tracking Project, University of Minnesota; Larry Harris, Ph.D., School of Forest Resources and Conservation, University of Florida.

68.   "Florida Panther Recovery: A Status Report to the Governor and Cabinet, July 7, 1983" (Tallahassee: Florida Game and Fresh Water Fish Commission)

69.   Ibid.

Chapter 9: THE NATIONAL PARK SERVICE

1.   William C. Everhart, *The National Park Service* (New York: Praeger Publishers, 1972) 199.

2.   Alfred Runte, *National Parks: The American Experience* (Lincoln: University of Nebraska Press, 1987) 335pp.

3.   Ibid., 22.

4.   Ibid., 6.

5.   Ibid.

6.   Ibid.

7.   Ibid., 48.

8.   Ibid., 61-62.

9.   Runte, *National Parks*., 69.

10.   Ibid., 131.

11.   Lee Clark Mitchell, *Witnesses to a Vanishing America: The Nineteenth-Century Response* (Princeton: Princeton University Press, 1981) 31-32.

12.   "Report of the Advisory Board on Wildlife Management" (The Leopold Report), *National Park Magazine*, April 1963, pp I-VI.

13.   Curt Meine, Teaching Conservation: The Leopold Legacy," *Environmental Education in Wisconsin*, Vol. 3, No. 3 (February 1987) 1.

14.   Flader, *Thinking Like A Mountain*, 183.
15.   "Leopold Report," p. III.
16.   Susan P. Bratton, "National Park Service Management and Values," *Environmental Ethics*, Vol. 7 (Summer 1985) 123.
17.   Curt Meine, *Aldo Leopold: His Life and Work* (Madison: University of Wisconsin Press, 1988) 18-21. Meine in his biography of Leopold, discusses the restraints Leopold's father practiced in taking game — also a credo preached in the early sportsmen's magazines. There is no mention that his father preached atavistic values. In A Sand County Almanac, written near the end of his life, Leopold discussed the 'split-rail value' of any experience that reminds us of our distinctive national origins and evolutions. He used the analogy of the boy "who goes Daniel Booneing in the willow thicket below the tracks."
18.   Aldo Leopold, *A Sand County Almanac* (New York: Oxford University Press, 1949) 177-178.
19.   Stewart L. Udall, *The Quiet Crisis* (New York: Discus Books, 1963) 118.
20.   Belanger, *Managing American Wildlife*, 14.
21.   Flader, *Thinking Like A Mountain*, 10-11.
22.   Ibid., 153.
23.   Ibid., 155-156.
24.   Robert H. MacArthur and Edward O. Wilson, *The Theory of Island Biogeography* (Princeton: Princeton University Press, 1967) 203.
25.   J. Grinnell and H. S. Swarth, "An Account of the Birds and Mammals of the San Jacinto Area of Southern California," in William E. Ritter and Charles A. Koford, eds., *Zoology*, Vol. 10, No. 10 (Berkeley: University of California Press, 1912-13) 385-386.
26.   Paul Jaccard, "The Distribution of the Flora in the Alpine Zone," *The New Phytologist*, Vol. XI, No. 2 (February 1912) 37-50.
27.   Stanley A. Cain, "The Species-Area Curve," *The American Midland Naturalist*, Vol. 19 (1938) 573.
28.   Olof Arrhenius, "Species and Area," *Journal of Ecology*, Vol. 9 (1921) 95.
29.   J. Braun-Blanquet, *Plant Sociology* (New York: McGraw-Hill, 1932) Trans. by G. D. Fuller and H. S. Conard.
30.   Aldo Leopold, *Game Management* (New York: Charles Scribner's Sons, 1933) 85-86.
31.   Motoo Kimura and James F. Crow, "The Measurement of Effective Population Number," *Evolution*, Vol. 17, No. 3 (September 1963) 279.
32.   Phillip J. Darlington, Jr., *Zoogeography: The Geographical Distribution of Animals* (New York: John Wiley and Sons, Inc., 1957) 482.
33.   MacArthur and Wilson, *Island Biogeography*, 4.
34.   Michael Soule and Bruce A. Wilcox, eds., *Conservation Biology: An Evolutionary-Ecological Perspective* (Sunderland, Mass: Sinaur Associates, Inc., 1980).
35.   Alston Chase, *Playing God in Yellowstone: The Destruction of America's First National Park* (Boston: The Atlantic Monthly Press, 1986).
36.   Ibid., 400.
37.   Ibid., 144.
38.   DNR Letter, Gardner to Parker (copy to Chiles), 1 December 1987.
39.   GFC Letter, Logan to Parker (copy to Chiles), 20 November 1987.
40.   FPIC Letter, Pulliam to Gerde, 2 July 1987.
41.   NPS Letter, Baker to Graham, 14 September 1987.
42.   Letter, Graham to Gerde, 16 March 1988.
43.   "A Policy Position regarding Deer and Panther Habitat Management in the Big Cypress National Preserve (BCNP)" Executive Committee of Florida Wildlife Federation, (27 May 1987).
44.   "Resolution," Florida Defenders of the Environment, Passed 30 May 1987, Spring Trustees Meeting, Cedar Key, Florida.
45.   "Deer and Panther Habitat Management in the Big Cypress National Preserve: Proposed Resolution No. 20," Submitted by: Florida Wildlife Federation, 1988.

Chapter 10: THE U. S. FISH AND WILDLIFE SERVICE

1.   Jeanne Nienaber Clarke and Daniel McCool, *Staking Out the Terrain: Power Differentials among Natural Resource Management Agencies* (Albany: State University of New York Press, 1985) 80.

2.   Ibid., 77-91. Also see: Steven Lewis Yaffee, *Prohibitive Policy: Implementing the Federal Endangered Species Act* (Cambridge: MIT Press, 1982).

3.   Thomas R. Dunlop, *Saving America's Wildlife* (Princeton: Princeton University Press, 1988) 35-36.

4.   Ruth Norris, "The Federal Animal Damage Control Program," in ed. Roger L. DiSivestro, *Audubon Wildlife Report 1987* (Orlando: Academic Press, Inc., 1987) 224.

5.   William J. Chandler, "The U. S. Fish and Wildlife Service," in ed. Roger L. DiSilvestro, *Audubon Wildlife Report 1985* (New York: The National Audubon Society, 1985) 7.

6.   Lendt, *Ding*. [See the first page of "An Album," following page 55.]

7.   Ibid., 69.

8.   Meine, *Aldo Leopold*, 317-318.

9.   Ibid., 318.

10.   Ibid., 319.

11.   Lendt, *Ding*, 69-70. Lendt states that "many years later Darling still harbored the suspicion that Roosevelt had appointed him less for what he could do for wildlife conservation than for what silencing Ding could do for the New Deal.

12.   Ibid., 74-75.

13.   Ibid., 79.

14.   Ibid., 83.

15.   Douglas H. Strong, *Dreamers and Defenders: American Conservationists* (Lincoln: University of Nebraska Press, 1988) 152.

16.   Ibid., 59.

17.   Thomas B. Allen, *Guardian of the Wild: The Story of the National Wildlife Federation 1936-1986* (Bloomington and Indianapolis, Indiana University Press, 1987) 29.

18.   Lendt, *Ding*, 85-86.

19.   Ed. Richard H. Straud, *National Leaders of American Conservation* (Washington, D.C.: Smithsonian Institution Press, 1985) 162-163.

20.   Frank Graham Jr. and Richard Frant, "Durward Allen: A Clear-eyed View of the Natural World," *Audubon*, Vol. 87, No. 2 (1985).

21.   Drabelle, "The Endangered Species Program," 74.

22.   William C. Reffalt, "United States Listing for Endangered Species: Chronicles of Extinction," *Endangered Species Update*, Vol. 5, No. 10 (Ann Arbor, University of Michigan School of Natural Resources, August 1988) 10.

23.   Ibid. [The same page as in the preceding note.] It is not clear from my references who published the Redbook in 1966. Reffalt states that it was published by the IUCN. Dennis Drabelle in *Audubon Wildlife Report 1985* states that it was published by the Interior Department [page 75].

24.   Kathryn Kohm, "Letter from the Editor," *Endangered Species Update*, Vol. 5, No. 10 (Ann Arbor, University of Michigan School of Natural Resources, August 1988) 2.

25.   Nathaniel P. Reed and Dennis Drabelle. *The United States Fish and Wildlife Service* (Boulder: Westview Inc., 1984) 87.

26.   Clarke and McCool, *Staking Out the Terrain*, 85-89.

27.   Lynn A. Greenwalt, "Reflections on the Power and Potential of the Endangered Species Act," *Endangered Species Update*, Vol. 5, No. 10 (Ann Arbor, University of Michigan School of Natural Resources, August 1988) 7-9.

28.   Archie Carr III, "The Black-footed Ferret," *Great Basin Naturalist Memoirs, No. 8* (Provo, Brigham Young University, 1966) 4.

29.   Clarke and McCool, *Staking Out the Terrain*, 86.

30.   Ibid., 55-56.

31.   Reed and Drabelle, *The United States Fish and Wildlife Service*, 96.

32.   Ibid., 97.
33.   Ibid., 146.
34.   Rose Marie Audette, "The Bush Men," *Environmental Action* (March/April, 1989) 13.
35.   Douglas Jehl, *Los Angeles Times*, reported in the *Sarasota Herald Tribune*, 23 March 1989.
36.   "Wildlife Advocates," *St. Petersburg Times*, Saturday, 12 May 1990.
37.   John Kenney, *National Parks*, September/October 1989, 14.
38.   "Turner named Fish and Wildlife Service Director," *Fish and Wildlife News* (June-July, 1989) Fish and Wildlife Service, 1.
39.   *The Tampa Tribune*, 21 July 1989.
40.   Nannette Holland, *The Tampa Tribune*, 26 July 1989.
41.   FWS Letter, Dodd to Dominque's, 12 September 1979.
42.   Letter, D'Ermo to Dodd, 23 September 1979.
43.   Interview, C. Kenneth Dodd, Jr., August 1989.
44.   FWS Letter, Greenwalt to Dodd, 10 October 1979.
45.   Ibid.
46.   Bill Gold, "The District Line," *The Washington Post*, 15 October 1979.
47.   *The Washington Post*, 12 October 1979.
48.   Ibid.
49.   *The Washington Post*, 18 October 1979.
50.   Michael S. Bean, "The 1973 Endangered Species Act: Looking Back Over the First 15 Years," *Endangered Species Update*, Vol. 5, No. 10 (Ann Arbor, University of Michigan School of Natural Resources, August 1988) 6.
51.   Ibid. [The same page as in the preceding note.]
52.   Ibid.
53.   Jean Heller, "Lumber Was Favored Over Rare Spotted Owl," *St. Petersburg Times*, 6 April 1989.
54.   Ibid.
55.   Charles Callison, "The Owl Caper," *The Amicus Journal*, Fall, 1989, 43-44.
56.   *U.S. General Accounting Office Report, Endangered Species: Spotted Owl Petition Evaluation Beset by Problems* (Gaithersburg, Maryland: U.S. General Accounting Office, February 1989) 1.
57.   Ibid., 3.
58.   Ibid., 145.
59.   Interview, John Ogden, 23 February 1989.
60.   Reed and Drabelle, *The United States Fish and Wildlife Service*, 60.
61.   Chandler, "U.S. Fish and Wildlife Service," 170.
62.   Branan, Proceedings, "Survival of the Florida Panther," 43-44.

Chapter 11: THE FLORIDA DEPARTMENT OF NATURAL RESOURCES

1.   *Sixth Biennial Report of the Florida Forest and Park Service, July 1, 1938-June 30, 1940*," Tallahassee, Florida, 34.
2.   Ibid.
3.   "History," 1 September 1985. Operations Policy Manual: Policies and Procedures for Managing Areas of the Florida Park Service, (Tallahassee: Florida, Department of Natural Resources, Division of Recreation and Parks, Bureau of Park Operations, 1 September 1985).
4.   Chapters 375, 258 and 418, Florida Statutes.
5.   "History," Operations Policy Manual.
6.   Notes, Lecture given by Ney Landrum, Florida Park Service Superintendent's Workshop, Wekiwa Springs State Park, 2 October 1977.
7.   "Resource Management," Operations Policy Manual, Table 3 - Table 4.
8.   "Florida Panther Recovery: A Status Report to the Governor and Cabinet, July 7, 1983," (Tallahassee: Florida Game and Fresh Water Fish Commission).
9.   McBride, "Population Status of the Florida Panther."

10.   Daniel F. Austin, Bradly C. Bennett and Julie Jones "Vegetation Maps and Plants of Fakahatchee Strand State Preserve," Department of Biological Sciences, Florida Atlantic University, Boca Raton, Florida.

11.   FPTAC Recommendations, 24-25, September 1985, in letter, Alvarez to Brantly, 4 October 1985.

12.   Anonymous, "Policy for the Protection and Enhancement of Florida Panthers in Units Managed by the Division of Recreation and Parks," in, Initial Management Strategy for the Florida Panther in Fakahatchee Strand State Preserve (Draft) 23 April 1986. (Tallahassee: Florida Department of Natural Resources)

13.   Ibid.

14.   Ibid.

15.   Ibid.

16.   Ibid.

17.   Ibid.

18.   Ibid.

19.   Ed., Branan, Proceedings, "Survival of the Florida Panther," 38.

20.   Ibid., 40.

21.   Ibid. [The same page as in the preceding note.]

22.   DNR Memo, Alvarez to Conklin, 26 June 1986.

23.   This was a hand-written, personal letter.

24.   Herbert L. Stoddard, Sr., *Memoirs of a Naturalist* (Norman: University of Oklahoma Press) 243-247.

25.   Dunlap, *Saving America's Wildlife*, 74-75.

26.   DNR Letter, Gissendanner to Branan, 1 December 1986.

27.   Ibid.

28.   DNR Memo.

29.   DNR Memo, Alvarez to Stevenson, 29 October 1987.

30.   Ibid.

31.   DNR Memo, Stevenson to Alvarez, 4 February 1988.

32.   Ibid.

33.   DNR Memo, Hardee to Stevenson, 15 March 1988.

Chapter 12: THE BUREAUCRATIC RESPONSE

1.   Larry Harris and Carroll Glynn, Growth Implications," Florida Wildlife (July 1976) 13.

2.   DNR Mcmo, Shields to Governor and Cabinet, 5 April 1978.

3.   L. C. Chappell and C. R. MacCracken, "White-tailed Deer Investigations, Tosohatchee State Proserve, September 1978 through August 1980," 108.

4.   Ibid., 109.

5.   Ibid. [The same page as in the preceding note.]

6.   "Proposal and Recommendations for Tosohatchee State Reserve Hunting," Presented to the Florida Governor and Cabinet 2 December 1980 (Tallahassee: Florida Game and Fresh Water Fish Commission).

7.   "Tosohatchee Should Not be Opened to Hunters," *The Times*, 17 December 1980.

8.   "Supplemental Report," Division of Wildlife (Tallahassee: Florida Game and Fresh Water Fish Commission, 25 February 1981) 122.

9.   Ibid. [The same page as in the preceding note.]

10.   *Orlando Sentinel Star*, 10 January 1981.

11.   "Supplemental Report," 123.

12.   "Summary of Hearing, Public Hearing, TOSOHATCHEE INTERAGENCY TASK FORCE, April 16, 1981 - 7:00 P.M., Orange County Courthouse, Orlando Florida."

13.   Florida Division of Recreation and Parks information sheet, 1980.

14.   Harlow and Jones, *The White-tailed Deer in Florida*, 117.

15.   Frank H. Smith, Jr., "Tosohatchee Deer Herd Ravaged by Overpopulation," *Florida Out of*

Doors, 8.
16. GFC Memo, Brantly to Hunters, 17 December 1980.
17. "Resource Management," Operations Policy Manual.
18. "A Detailed Response from the National Park Service to The Grizzly and the Juggernaut by Alston Chase," *Outside*, January, 1986, 4.
19. NPS Letter, Barbee to Editor, *Outside*, 31 December 1985.
20. Ibid., 5.
21. Ibid., 26.
22. Endangered Species Act, 1973.
23. "A Detailed Response," 12.
24. Ibid., 19.
25. Ibid., 20.
26. NPS Letter, Barbee to Editor, *Outside*, 31 December 1985.
27. Alston Chase, "Sometimes What Threatens Our Parks is the Park Service," *The Wall Street Journal,* 8 April 1986.
28. William Penn Mott Jr., "National Park's Priorities," *The Wall Street Journal*," 7 May 1986.
29. Ibid.
30. Ibid.
31. IGBC Minutes, 19 February 1988, 7.
32. Ibid.
33. Ibid.
34. Ibid.
35. "Grizzly and Man: An Uneasy Truce," Video Series, National Audubon Society Specials, 4.
36. IGBC Minutes, 30 June 1988, 4.
37. IGBC Minutes, 29-30 November 1988, 2.
38. "Grizzly and Man," video.
39. Ibid.
40. Ibid.
41. The Nature Conservancy, a request for funds.
42. Defenders of Wildlife to "Friend," a request for funds, Summer 1988.
43. Sierra Club Legal Defense Fund, a request for funds, Summer 1988.
44. Ibid.
45. Steven C. Amstrup, "Polar Bear," in ed. Roger L. DiSilvestro, *Audubon Wildlife Report 1986* (New York: National Audubon Society, 1986) 791-804.
46. Ibid.
47. National Audubon Society Letter, Berle to Dear Friend of Audubon, a request for funds (undated).
48. "Everglades Update," Vol. 4, No. 1 (April 1988) National Audubon Society.
49. NAS Letter, Berle to members, 1991.
50. National Parks and Conservation Association, a request for funds.

Chapter 13: ATTITUDES AND AWARENESS

1. GFC Minutes, Tampa, Florida, 11 January 1985.
2. Letter, Prichard to Alvarez, 6 June 1987.
3. GFC Letter, Brantly to Fitzgerald, 27 January 1989.
4. Robertson and Lindsey, *Proceedings*, 23.
5. Ibid., 25.
6. Stephen R. Kellert and Joyce K. Berry, "Knowledge, Affection and Basic Attitudes Toward Animals in American Society, Phase Three results of a U. S. Fish and wildlife Service funded study of ``American Attitudes, Knowledge and Behaviors Toward Wildlife and Natural Habitats,'" 92.
7. Stephen R. Kellert, "Perceptions of Animals in American Society," *Proceedings: Forty-First North American Wildlife Conference, 1976*, 534-537.

8.   Stephen R. Kellert, "Americans' Attitudes and Knowledge of Animals" *Proceedings: Forty-Fifth North American Wildlife Conference, 1980,* 112.
9.   Ibid. [The same page as in the preceding note.]
10.   Ibid.
11.   Kellert, "Perceptions of Animals," 539.
12.   Ibid., 541.
13.   Ibid. [The same page as in the preceding note.]
14.   Kellert, "Americans' Attitudes," 115.
15.   Ibid., 123.
16.   *Coryi,* Vol. 1, No. 3.
17.   *Coryi,* Vol. 1, No. 1.
18.   Ibid.
19.   Ibid.
20.   Ibid.
21.   *Coryi,* Vol. 1, No. 2.
22.   *Coryi,* Vol. 1, No. 3.
23.   Mark Damaian Duda, *Floridians and wildlife: Sociological Implications for Wildlife Conservation in Florida, Technical Report No. 2* (Tallahassee: Florida Game and Fresh Water Fish Commission, April 1987).
24.   Ibid., 100-101.
25.   Ibid., 102.
26.   Ibid., [The same page as in the preceding note.]
27.   *Florida Game and Fresh Water Fish Commission 1985-86 Annual Report.* In the 1985-86 fiscal year, the agency reported that $1,648,834 were spent on informational services. The 1986-87 Annual Report indicated an expenditure of $1,673,373, and an additional $158,458 spent for the same purpose from the Nongame Wildlife Trust Fund.
28.   Kellert and Berry, "Knowledge," 7.
29.   Michael E. Soule and Bruce A. Wilcox, "Conservation Biology: Its Scope and its Challenge," *Conservation Biology: An Evolutionary-Ecological Perspective* (Sunderland: Sinauer Associates, Inc., 1980) 3-4.
30.   GFC Letter, Logan to Gerde, 29 November 1988.
31.   NPS Letter, Baker to Gerde, 13 June 1988.
32.   FWS Document, Fish and Wildlife Service, Southeast Region, Initiatives, Florida Panther Recovery, Section 6 (Funding Allocations and Requests, 1986-1991).
33.   Estus Whitfield, "Restoring the Everglades," in ed. William J. Chandler, *Audubon Wildlife Report 1988/1989* (New York: Academic Press, Inc., 1988) 483.
34.   *Daily Naples News,* 27 January 1984.
35.   GFC Memo, Belden to FPRT, 13 September 1977. Belden stated that the Florida Panther investigation was funded by Shikar-Safari, Inc. and the National Wildlife Federation.
36.   NPS Letter, Baker to Gerde, 13 June 1988.
37.   GFC Letter, Logan to Gerde, 29 November 1988.
38.   NPS Letter, Baker to Gerde, 13 June 1988.
39.   Faith Campbell, "The Appropriations History of the Endangered Species Act," *Endangered Species Update,* Vol. 5, No. 10 (Ann Arbor: The University of Michigan School of Natural Resources, August 1988) 20.
40.   Ibid., 14.
41.   Ibid. [The same page as in the preceding note.]
42.   Ibid.
43.   Reed and Drabelle, *The United States Fish and Wildlife Service,* 99.
44.   William C. Reffalt, "United States Listing for Endangered Species: Chronicles of Extinction?" *Endangered Species Update,* Vol. 5, No. 10 (Ann Arbor: The University of Michigan School of Natural Resources, August 1988) 11.
45.   Ibid. [The same page as in the preceding note.]
46.   Ibid., 12-13.

47.   *U.S. General Accounting Office Report, Endangered Species: Management Improvements Could Enhance Recovery Program* (Gaithersburg, Maryland: U.S. General Accounting Office, December 1988) 3.
48.   Ibid., 5.
49.   FPIC Minutes, 22-23 June 1987 (PANTHER INFO-32, 17 July 1987).
50.   Interview, John Lukas, 16 May 1989.
51.   Interview, Jack Pons, 7 May 1991. Pons, an official of the Florida Department of Natural Resources, represented the agency at this meeting. He would not commit DNR, saying he questioned the propriety of conveying the money to a private zoological institution. However, his demurral was not recorded in the minutes of the meeting, and his reluctance on behalf of DNR was later overruled.

Chapter 14: THE CALIFORNIA CONDOR

1.   David Darlington, *In Condor Country* (Boston: Houghton Mifflin Co, 1987, 78.
2.   David Phillips and Hugh Nash, *The Condor Question*: Captive or Forever Free (San Francisco: Friends of the Earth, 1981), 86.
3.   Darlington, *Condor Country*, 79.
4.   Phillips and Nash, *Condor Question*, 87.
5.   Noel F. R. Snyder and Helen A. Snyder, "Condor Biology and Conservation," *Current Ornithology*, Vol. 6, 1989. The authors state that ". . . many questions simply were beyond the capacities of a solitary worker to resolve, especially with the tools then available for research. . . . Where he drifted into difficulty was in estimating numbers of condors in the population (an essentially impossible task at the time, given the sorts of data he had available). . . . In our judgement, Koford very likely had been dealing with a population somewhere in the vicinity of 120 to 180 individuals. . . .", 182-184.
6.   Phillips and Nash, *Condor Question*, 29.
7.   John Eisenberg, Interview 28 November 1988. David Darlington, in *Condor Country*, records Ian McMillan's reminiscence of Koford's idiosyncracies. The reported staples of Koford's expedition diets show some variation. McMillan stated that he went off for days with his pockets filled with prunes and cheese, 85.
8.   Letter, Layne to Alvarez, 19 July 1989.
9.   "Chronology of Significant Events in California History," *California Outdoors* (September-October, 1983), 42. (Years 1602 through 1975 are from Appendix IV of Sanford R. Wilbur's monograph on the California condor, 1978).
10.   Lloyd Kiff, "An Historical Perspective on the Condor," Outdoor California (September-October, 1983) 35.
11.   John Ogden, "The California Condor," *The Audubon Wildlife Report 1985*, 392.
12.   Snyder and Snyder. In the opinion of the authors: "The population estimate of 40 individuals was based largely on comparisons of sizes of the largest flocks these researchers could document with the largest flocks documented by Koford; thus the accuracy of their estimate depended crucially on the accuracy of Koford's estimate . . . we would estimate that the actual condor population during the Miller et al, study [Alden Miller at Berkeley provided academic oversight of the McMillan's work; he was a coauthor] was somewhere between 80 and 120 condors, 185-186.
13.   Phillips and Nash, *Condor Question*, 69-70.
14.   Noel F. R. Snyder, "California Condor Reproduction, Past and Present," in ed. Stanley A. Temple, *Bird Conservation*, Vol. 1 (Madison: University of Wisconsin Press, 1983) 68.
15.   Ian McMillan, *Man and the California Condor* (New York: E. P. Dutton & Co., 1968) 14.
16.   Snyder, *Bird Conservation*, 68.
17.   Snyder and Snyder, "Condor Biology." The authors state that ". . . we believe his estimate of 50-60 birds in 1968 and 25-35 birds in 1978 (Wilbur, 1980) were excellent, although recent evidence shows that some of his assumptions were not entirely justified," 191.
18.   Sanford R. Wilbur, et al., *California Condor Recovery Plan* (Portland, 1974) 3.
19.   Ibid., 11.
20.   Interview: Eugene Knoder, 22 December 1988. Knoder, met with a high-ranking Fish and

STRATFORD LIBRARY ASSOCIATION
06 JAN 97 11:28am
Celebrating the library's 100th birthday

Renewal - Change Due Date

Patron Name: KALAPOS, JACLYN

The death of common sense : how
34003057252045   Due: 27 JAN 97 *

Noah's choice : the future of endan
34003057279378   Due: 27 JAN 97 *

Twilight of the panther : biology,
34003057169132   Due: 27 JAN 97 *

Wildlife Service official to propose joint action by that agency with the National Audubon Society. The official was chary of getting entangled with the U.S. Forest Service, the California Game Commission or with an emotional public in California. He also told Knoder that so far as the Fish and Wildlife Service was concerned the species was doomed and had been written off. Knoder assured him that Audubon could take the heat, would work to coax funds from congress and would contribute money and personnel of its own.

21. Ibid.
22. Interview: Jerry Cutlip, 8 November 1988. Cutlip was manager of National Audubon's Corkscrew Swamp Sanctuary during the 1970s. He attended a staff meeting at Greenwich, Connecticut when the staff was informed of National Audubon's impending involvement in the condor recovery program. Cutlip said a small number of the staff were strongly opposed, believing that the condor was doomed, and National Audubon would be expending a large portion of its limited resources in a lost cause. The opposing argument was that the National Audubon Society had a moral obligation to try and save the condor, and also that the organization hoped to benefit materially from the publicity attending the recovery of a popular species. Cutlip stressed that the opposition came from refuge managers who were trying to cope with budget cuts and were appalled at the enormous sum of money about to be committed to an enterprise with dubious prospects of success.
23. Phillips, *Condor Question*, 271.
24. Ibid. [The same page as in the preceding note.]
25. Interview: Eugene Knoder, 22 December 1988.
26. Constance Holden, "Condor Flap in California," *Science*, Vol. 209 (8 August 1980) 670.
27. Phillips and Nash, *Condor Question*, 192-96.
28. Snyder and Snyder, "Condor Biology," 235. The authors, nine years after the death of the chick, with more experience to draw on, maintain that "sadly, although the loss was completely unexpected, it was a preventable loss had better precautions been taken. The fact that handling of late-stage condor chicks (both Andean and California Condor) involves considerable risks of overstressing individuals—risks that do not exist with many other species or other-aged condors—was not known at the time, although it has become clear since.
29. Phillips and Nash, *Condor Question*, 271.
30. Ibid., 257.
31. Interview, Noel Snyder, 21 July 1990. Snyder, in a review of the chapter, found this assessment of the commissioners harsh. He felt the commissioners at this juncture were not making good decisions because they were not being given sound information. Both he and Ogden had been cautioned by superiors not to communicate directly with commissioners. Later in the program, when Snyder (against orders) initiated a liaison with the commissioners, he found them willing to make hard decisions to move the program forward.

However, this raises the question of why the commissioners, whose responsibility it was to make policy, did not themselves, create a forum to learn the thinking of the scientists at first hand, in what surely was one of the most contentious and important issues they had been called upon to judge. Snyder's later attainments in working directly with the commissioners may have been aided by changed circumstances, not the least of which was that Governor Brown appointed to the commission, persons of above-average ability and independent thought (according to Snyder) who were not inclined to passively follow the executive director of the agency. There may have been other factors: new data showed convincingly the precarious low number to which condors had fallen, and perhaps the public mood had shifted toward hands-on. I was not persuaded to revise my opinion, stated repeatedly in this book, that the game commissions have become inadequate instruments for the demanding task of endangered species management. The most promising solution would be to stipulate qualifications for the appointive positions that would assure they be occupied by persons whose credentials are commensurate with their responsibilities.
32. Peter B. Gallagher, "Among the Panther Men," *Defenders*, June 1981, 28.
33. John Ogden, "The California Condor Recovery Program," in ed. Stanley A. Temple, *Bird Conservation*, Vol. 1 (Madison: University of Wisconsin Press, 1983) 91-4.
34. Frank A. Pitelka, "The Condor Case: An Uphill Struggle in a Downhill Crush," *Point Reyes Bird Observatory Newsletter 53* (Spring 1981) 4-5.

35.   Rich Stallcup, "Farewell Skymaster," *Point Reyes Bird Observatory Newsletter 53* (Spring 1981) 10.

36.   Ogden, *Bird Conservation*, 93-94.

37.   Ibid, 93.

38.   Kiff, *Outdoor California*, 37.

39.   *California Outdoors*, 42.

40.   Interview, Noel Snyder, 21 July 1990.

41.   Minutes, Monthly Condor Meeting, 25 January 1982.

42.   William D. Sweeney, FWS California Condor Trapping Permit Extension Application, 7 July 1982.

43.   NAS Memo, Ogden to Paulson and Sprunt, 28 August 1982.

44.   FWS Memo, Rogers to Associate Director, Research, Washington, D.C., 9 August 1982.

45.   NAS Letter, Peterson to Jantzen, 27 August 1982.

46.   NAS Memo, Ogden to Paulson and Sprunt, 9 September 1982.

47.   Interview: John Ogden, 28 November 1988.

48.   Interview, Noel Snyder, 21 July 1990.

49.   Ibid.

50.   Interview, John Ogden, 28 November 1988.

51.   Jennifer Meyer, "Field Work Seeks Cause of Decline," *Outdoor California* (September-October, 1983) 30.

52.   Ogden, "The California Condor Recovery Program," 100.

53.   Interview: John Ogden, 28 November 1988. Ray Dasmann, an accomplished wildlife ecologist, served on the California Game Commission. Ogden and Snyder believed that if they could "turn anybody around" who was opposed to hands-on recovery, it would be Dasmann. Accordingly, they paid him a visit early in the recovery program. They found him unwilling to yield his opposition.

54.   Phillips and Nash, *Condor Question*, 11-13. The Ehrlichs authored the foreword to the book. They expressed an opinion that [California condor] "numbers . . . quite clearly are too low to ensure long-term survival." They went on to state:

    The most experienced students of the condor quickly learned that the birds are excruciatingly sensitive to human interference. The mere appearance of a person within several hundred yards of a nesting site may cause interruption of feeding or incubating behavior long enough to result in loss of the chick, for instance.

    More recently, well-meaning biologists relatively inexperienced with condors and heedless of the warnings issued years before by others more knowledgeable, have sought to photograph and film the birds' behavior, not hesitating to invade nests in the process. Further, they have attempted to weigh and measure the chicks and even plan to operate on adults to determine their sex and to attach radio transmitters to them in order to monitor their far-flung foraging flights.

    Most outrageous of all, a formal "Recovery Plan" of the U.S. Fish and Wildlife Service aims to capture a substantial portion of the remaining condor population for breeding in captivity, returning the progeny to the wild at some unspecified but far-off future date. One wonders whether a better plan could be devised to hasten the extinction of the California condor! Indeed, the death of a chick at the very start of the program from pure fright at being manhandled by investigators came as no surprise to those familiar with this giant vulture. But the event demonstrated to a startled world the incompatibility of condors with this space-age technology intended to "save" them.

    . . . This book is a plea to save the condor in a sane, sensible, and reasonable fashion—not through inappropriate technological gimmickry and harassment. There is a way to do it right that is both less costly and will protect other species as well: leave the condor alone and protect its habitat. It remains to be seen whether Homo sapiens can summon that much wisdom, however. We hope that this book will mark a turning point in treatment of the condor. The one thing we hope it will not be is an epitaph.

55.   Kellert and Berry, "Knowledge," 89-102.

56.   Flader, *Thinking Like a Mountain*, 219-220.

57.   Snyder and Snyder," Condor Biology," 204.

58.   James A. Tober, *Wildlife and the Public Interest: Nonprofit Organizations and Federal*

Wildlife Policy (New York, Prager Publishers, 1989) 69.

59.   Interview, Noel Snyder, 21 July 1990.

60.   John Ogden, *Audubon Wildlife Report, 1985*, 395.

61.   Tober, *Wildlife and the Public Interest*, 70.

62,   Ibid. [The same page as in the preceding note.]

63.   Ibid., 239.

64.   Interview, Noel Snyder, 21 July 1990.

65.   Tober, *Wildlife and the Public Interest*, 71

66.   Snyder and Snyder, "Condor Biology," 240.

67.   Ibid., 241.

68.   Ibid., 240.

69.   Ibid., [The same page as in the preceding note.]

70.   Interview, Noel Snyder, 21 July 1990.

71.   Snyder and Snyder, "Condor Biology," 177.

72.   Tober, *Wildlife and the Public Interest*, 73.

73.   Ibid., 74.

74.   John F. Lehmkuhl, "Determining Size and Dispersion of Minimum Viable Populations for Land Management Planning and Species Conservation," *Environmental Management*, Vol. 8, No. 2 (New York: Springer-Verlag, Inc., 1984) 167-176.

Chapter 15: THE BLACK-FOOTED FERRET

1.   Joan Nice, "Endangered Species: A Wyoming Town Becomes Ferret Capital," *Audubon* (July, 1982) 106.

2.   Tim W. Clark, "Black-Footed Ferret Recovery: A Progress Report," *Conservation Biology*, Vol. 1, No. 1 (May 1987) 8.

3.   Roger L. DiSilvestro, "The Federal Animal Damage Control Program," in ed., Roger L. DiSilvestro *Audubon Wildlife Report* (New York: The National Audubon Society, 1985) 131-132.

4.   Max Schroeder, "The Black-footed Ferret," in ed., Roger L. DiSilvestro, *Audubon Wildlife Report 1987* (Orlando: Academic Press, 1987) 450.

5.   Ibid., 449.

6.   Nice, "Endangered Species," 108.

7.   Helen Ballew, "Stalking the Prairie Bandit," *Orion Nature Quarterly*, Vol. 4 (1985) 50.

8.   Dick Randall, "Survival Crisis at Meeteetse," *Defenders* (January-February, 1986) 5.

9.   Tim W. Clark, "Current Status of the Black-footed Ferret in Wyoming," *Journal of Wildlife Management.*, Vol. 42, No. 1 (1978) 128-134.

10.   Tim W. Clark, "Black-footed Ferret Recovery," 10. Funding came from the New York Zoological Society's Wildlife Conservation International, Wildlife Preservation and Trust International, World Wildlife Fund—U.S. National Geographic Society, Charles A. Lindbergh Fund and other conservation organizations.

11.   Jack Turnell, "A Private Landowner Perspective" in ed. Stanley H. Anderson and Douglas B. Inkley, *Black-footed Ferret Workshop Proceedings* (Laramie: Wyoming Game and Fish Department, March, 1985) 6.3,.

12.   Tim W. Clark, et al., "Handbook of Methods for Locating Black-footed Ferrets," *Wyoming BLM Wildlife Technical Bulletin No. 1* (Cheyenne: U. . Bureau of Land Management, November, 1983) 5-6.

13.   Tim W. Clark, "Black-footed Ferret Recovery: Just a Matter of Time?" *Endangered Species Technical Bulletin Reprint Vol. 2, No. 8* (Ann Arbor: School of Natural Resources, The University of Michigan, June, 1985).

14.   Nice, "Endangered Species," 107.

15.   Ballew, "Stalking the Prairie Bandit," 47.

16.   Archie Carr III, "The Black-footed Ferret," *Great Basin Naturalist Memoirs, No. 8* (Provo: Brigham Young University, 1986) 5.

17.   Nice, "Endangered Species," 109.

18.   Ibid. [The same page as in the preceding note.]

19. Belanger, *Managing American Wildlife*, 10.
20. H. J. Harju, "Black-footed Ferret Advisory Team Efforts" in ed. Stanley H. Anderson and Douglas B. Inkley, *Black-footed Ferret Workshop Proceedings*, 4.3.
21. Ballew, "Stalking the Prairie Bandit," 54.
22. Ibid., 55.
23. Tim W. Clark, "Biological, Sociological, and Organizational Challenges to Endangered Species Conservation: The Black-footed Ferret Case," *Human Dimensions in Wildlife Newsletter*, 3:1-15 (1984) 12.
24. Tim W. Clark, "Black-footed Ferrets on the Edge," *Endangered Species Technical Bulletin Reprint.* Vol. 3, No. 7 (Ann Arbor: School of Natural Resources, The University of Michigan, May, 1986) 3.
25. Ibid. [The same page as in the preceding note.]
26. Louise Richardson, et al., "Black-footed Ferret Recovery: A Discussion of Some Options and Considerations," *Great Basin Naturalist Memoirs, No. 8* (Provo: Brigham Young University, 1986) 169-184.
27. Tim W. Clark, Louise Richardson Forrest, Steven C. Forrest, "Some Recommendations Concerning the Current Plague Outbreak at Meeteetse" (Pocatello: Idaho State University, 6 August 1985) 4.
28. Carr, "The Black-footed Ferret," 5.
29. Ibid., 6.
30. Interview: Archie Carr III, 18 November 1988.
31. Tom Arrandale, *The Battle for Natural Resources* (Washington, D.C.: Congressional Quarterly, Inc., 1983) 185-216.
32. George F. Will, *New Season: A Spectator's Guide to the 1988 Election* (New York: Simon and Schuster, 1988) 48.
33. Carr, "The Black-footed Ferret," 6.
34. Ibid. [The same page as in the preceding note.]
35. David Weinberg, "Decline and Fall of the Black-footed Ferret," *Natural History* (February 1986) 65.
36. Ibid., 66.
37. Ibid., 66-67.
38. E. Tom Thorne and Elizabeth Williams, "Disease and Endangered Species: The Black-footed Ferret as a Recent Example," *Conservation Biology*, Vol. 2, No. 1 (March 1988) 68.
39. BFAT Meeting Minutes, 29 August 1985, 10.
40. Thorne and Williams, "Disease," 68.
41. Clark, "Black-footed Ferrets on the Edge," 3.
42. Tim W. Clark, Louise Richardson Forrest, Stephen C. Forrest, Thomas M. Campbell III, "Some Recommendations Concerning the Current Plague Outbreak at Meeteetse," A report to the Wyoming Game and Fish Department, U. S. Fish and Wildlife Service, et al, 6 August 1985 (Jackson, Wyoming, Biota Research and Consulting, Inc.) 4.
43. BFAT Meeting Minutes, 29 August 1985, 1.
44. Weinberg, "Decline and Fall," 67.
45. Thorne and Williams, "Disease," 68.
46. Ulysses S. Seal, "The Realities of Preserving Species in Captivity," in ed. R. J. Hoage, *Animal Extinctions: What Everyone Should Know* (Washington, D.C.: Smithsonian Institution Press, 1985) 76.
47. Randall, "Survival Crisis," 8.
48. Clark, "Black-footed Ferrets on the Edge," 3.
49. Weinberg, "Decline and Fall," 67.
50. Ibid., 63.
51. Ibid. [The same page as in the preceding note.]
52. Randall, "Survival Crisis," 7.
53. BFAT Meeting Minutes, 22 October 1985.
54. Ibid.

55. Ibid.
56. Remarks presented by Bill Morris, Director, Wyoming Game and Fish Department, October 24, 1985, Cheyenne News Conference (Laramie: Wyoming Game and Fish Department).
57. Ibid.
58. Ibid.
59. Weinberg, "Decline and Fall," 63.
60. BFAT Meeting Minutes, 21 March 1986.
61. Clark, "Black-footed Ferrets on the Edge," 3.
62. Brian James Miller, "Conservation and Behavior of the Endangered Black-footed Ferret (*Mustela nigripes*) with a Comparative Analysis of Reproductive Behavior between the black-footed ferret and the Congeneric Domestic Ferret (*Mustela putorius furo*), (PhD dissertation, University of Wyoming, 1988) 23.
63. Ibid., 25.
64. BFAT Meeting Minutes, 21 March 1986, 7.
65. BFAT Meeting Minutes, 10 November 1987, 1.
66. Ibid., 3.
67. "Draft minutes, Florida Panther viability workshop, 17 January 1989."
68. *Endangered Species Technical Bulletin*, Vol. XIII, Nos. 6-7, Department of Interior, U.S. Fish and Wildlife Service, Washington, D.C. (1988) 1.
69. Randall, "Survival Crisis," 10.
70. Weinberg, "Decline and Fall," 69.
71. Randall, "Survival Crisis," 8.
72. Michael Howard, *The Causes of Wars: and other essays* (London: Unwin Paperbacks, 1984) 212.
73. Thorne and Williams, "Disease," 70.
74. Interview: Archie Carr III, 23 February 1988.
75. Chase, *Playing God in Yellowstone*, 60.
76. A. G. Greenwald, "The Totalitarian Ego: Fabrication and Revision of Personal History," *American Psychologist*, Vol. 35 (1980) 603-618.
77. BFAT Meeting Minutes, 29 August 1985.
78. Miller, "Conservation and Behavior of the Endangered Black-footed Ferret," 21.

Chapter 16: THE DUSKY SEASIDE SPARROW

1. *Dusky Seaside Sparrow Recovery Plan* (Washington, D.C.: U.S. Fish and Wildlife Service, December, 1978) 1.
2. Alexander Sprunt, Jr., *Florida Bird Life* (New York: Coward-McCann, Inc., 1954) 475.
3. James L. Baker, "Dusky Seaside Sparrow" in ed. Herbert W. Kale II, Vol. 2, Birds, series ed Pritchard, *Rare and Endangered Biota*, 17.
4. Brian Sharp, "Let's Save the Dusky Seaside Sparrow" in vol. 42, no. 2, *The Florida Naturalist* (April, 1969) 69.
5. Ibid. [The same page as in the preceding note.]
6. Sprunt, *Florida Bird Life*, 478.
7. James L. Baker, "Preliminary Studies of the Dusky Seaside Sparrow on the St. Johns National Wildlife Refuge," in ed. Arnold L. Mitchell, *Proceedings of the 27th Annual Conference, Southeastern Association of Game and Fish Commissioners*, Hot Springs, Arkansas, October 14-17, 1973, 208.
8. Peter B. Gallagher, "The Edge of Extinction," *St. Petersburg Times*, Monday Floridian.
9. Baker, "Dusky Seaside Sparrow," 17.
10. Whitfield, "Restoring the Everglades," 472.
11. Sharp, "Let's Save the Dusky Seaside Sparrow," 70.
12. Interview, Herb Kale, 25 February 1989.
13. Baker, "Preliminary Studies," 207.
14. Interview, Herb Kale, 25 February 1989.
15. Baker, "Preliminary Studies," 208.

16.   Gallagher, "The Edge of Extinction."
17.   Ibid.
18.   Ibid.
19.   Interview, Herb Kale, March 1989.
20.   Dusky Seaside Sparrow Recovery Team Minutes, 24 June 1980.
21.   Ibid.
22.   Ibid.
23.   Gallagher, "The Edge of Extinction."
24.   Ibid.
25.   Ibid.
26.   Personal Communication, Herbert W. Kale II.
27.   Herbert W. Kale II, "The Dusky Seaside Sparrow: Have We Learned Anything?", *The Florida Naturalist*. (Fall 1987) 2.
28.   Herbert W. Kale, II, "A Status Report on the Dusky Seaside Sparrow," *Bird Conservation News and Updates*, 131.
29.   David Wesley, in Branan, Proceedings: "Survival of the Florida Panther,"63.
30.   FWS, memo, 18 May 1977.
31.   Ibid.
32.   FWS, memo, 7 July 1977.
33.   FWS, memo, 2 August 1977.
34.   Tom J. Cade, "Hybridization and Gene Exchange among Birds in Relation to Conservation," in. ed. Schonewald-Cox, *Genetics and Conservation*, 288-309.
35.   Frances C. James, "Miscegenation in the Dusky Seaside Sparrow?", *Bioscience*, Vol. 30, No. 12 (December 1988) 800-801.
36.   Peter Steinhart, "Synthetic Species," *Audubon*, 8-10.
37.   Endangered Species Act of 1973.
38.   John C. Avise and William S. Nelson, "Molecular Genetic Relationships of the Extinct Dusky Seaside Sparrow," *Science*, Vol. 243 (3 February 1989) 648.
39.   Ibid., [The same page as in the preceding note.]
40.   Ibid.,
41.   Herb Kale (personal communication) uses the same faulty taxonomy argument against claims of taxonomical separation based solely on the extranuclear mitochondrial DNA of an organism. He concedes that nuclear inheritance materials play a large role in inheritance and taxonomy, but believes that any one aspect of inheritance is a tenuous basis for classification. Kale invokes the proverb of the blind men describing an elephant. He points out that Avise and Nelson avoided phenotypic distinctions between the disjunct dusky seaside sparrow and other East Coast populations.
42.   Faith Campbell, "The Appropriations History of the Endangered Species Act," *Endangered Species Update*, Vol. 5, No. 10 (Ann Arbor: The University of Michigan School of Natural Resources, August 1988) 20.

Chapter 17: A FUTURE REFUGE?

1.   Larry Harris and John Eisenberg, "Enhanced Linkages: Necessary Steps for Success in Conservation of Faunal Diversity," in ed. David Western and Mary Pearl, *Conservation for the Twenty-first Century* (New York: Oxford University Press, 1989) 176.
2.   Ibid. [The same page as in the preceding note.]
3.   *Endangered Species Technical Bulletin*, Vol. XIV, No. 8 (Washington, D.C., Department of the Interior, U.S. Fish and Wildlife Service, August 1989). The number of listed species in the United States is given by state and territory. California leads with 86 species, followed by Florida with 69. The remaining states in the top ten are, in descending order: Texas, 61; Hawaii, 58; Alabama, 55; Tennessee, 46; North Carolina and Arizona, 41; Virginia, 39; Georgia, 36; New Mexico and Puerto Rico, 32.
4.   "Diversity/Wealth Table: July, 1989" (Arlington, VA: The Nature Conservancy). The table gives the number of endangered "elements" in each state. An element is defined as any exemplary or

rare component of the natural environment. The designation encompasses more than individual species and includes such things as plant communities, bird rookeries, springs, sinkholes or other ecological features. California has the greatest number (581), followed by Hawaii (441), Texas (235) and then Florida (216).

5.	Lloyd L. Loope and Vicki L. Dunevitz, *Investigations of Early Plant Succession on Abandoned Farmland in Everglades National Park, Report T-644* (Homestead: Everglades National Park, October 1981) 1.

6.	Ibid. [The same page as in the preceding note.]

7.	Ibid.

8.	Letter, Baker to Gerde, 13 June 1988.

9.	Public Law 93-440, 93rd Congress, H.R. 10088, 11 October 1974, An Act to Establish the Big Cypress National Preserve in the State of Florida and for Other Purposes, 232.

10.	Ibid., 234.

11.	Ibid.

12.	Public Law 100-301, The Big Cypress National Preserve Addition Act, 29 April 1988.

13.	Charlton W. Tebeau, *Florida's Last Frontier: The History of Collier County* (Miami: University of Miami Press, 1966) 94. Tebeau's account states that "four men who comprised the [Lee Tidewater Cypress] Company . . . gave an option to an agent of Henry Ford who was to buy the Big Cypress Swamp for $2,250,000. Ford intended to give it to the state of Florida for a park, but the state was in no position in the depression years to build the necessary roads and the matter was dropped." The company named here owned the Fakahatchee Strand. I do not know the geographical extent of the proposed land deal.

14.	Whitfield, "Restoring the Everglades," 479.

15.	"Lake Okeechobee Technical Advisory Council (LOTAC II), Interim Report to the Florida Legislature" (Tallahassee, 29 February 1988) 23.

16.	Ibid., 4.

17.	Ney C. Landrum, et al., "Recreational Development of the Florida Everglades Water Conservation Areas: Five-year Plan 1973-1978, Submitted to the Florida Game and Fresh Water Fish Commission by the Everglades Recreational Planning Board," (1 January 1974) 20.

18.	Charles M. Loveless, *The Everglades Deer Herd Life History and Management, Technical Bulletin No. 6* (Tallahassee: Florida Game and Fresh Water Fish Commission, 1959) 41-43.

19.	Charles M. Loveless, et. al., "Report of the Special Study Team on the Florida Everglades" (West Palm Beach: South Florida Water Management District, 1970) 27.

20.	Landrum, et al., "Recreational Development," 170-171.

21.	James L. Schortemeyer, An Evaluation of Water Management Practices for Optimum Wildlife Benefits in Conservation Area 3A (Tallahassee: Florida Game and Fresh Water Fish Commission, June 1980) 26.

22.	Ibid., 11.

23.	James L. Schortemeyer, "Potential Habitat Management Programs on the Everglades Wildlife Management Area," (Tallahassee: Florida Game and Fresh Water Fish Commission, December 1980) 15-17.

24.	Ibid., 8-9.

25.	James W. Covington, *The Story of Southwestern Florida* (New York: Lewis Historical Publishing Co., 1957) 161.

26.	Tebeau, *Florida's Last Frontier*, 83-95.

27.	"Citrus in Southwest Florida" (West Palm Beach: Information Services, South Florida Water Management District, 4 September 1986) 2.

28.	FPTAC Letter, Alvarez to Brantly, 4 October 1985.

29.	FPTAC Recommendations in Letter, Alvarez to Brantly, 4 October 1985, 6-7.

30.	*Florida Panther Recovery Plan*, June 1987, 38-39.

31.	FPTAC Recommendations, 6 June 1986 (Tallahassee: Florida Game and Fresh Water Fish Commission).

32.	FWS Memo, 11 June 1986, 21 July 1986 Minutes, TS, FPIC Meeting, 30-31 July and August, 1986 (PANTHER INFO-4).

33. Letter, Alvarez to Brantly, 21 July 1986.

34. GFC Letter, Brantly to Alvarez, 17 October 1986. In addition to stating the issue of "the precarious status of habitat on private lands," my letter of 21 July recommended that the FPIC should clearly explain three others: (1) extremely low numbers (2) an inadequate prey base on public lands and (3) the inbreeding problem.

35. Personal communication, Larry Harris, July 1989.

36. Minutes, TS, FPIC Meeting, 13-14 January 1987 (Panther Info 25) 5.

37. Interview, Larry Harris, July 1989.

38. Letter, Eisenberg to Alvarez, 4 December 1984.

39. Larry D. Harris and Reed F. Noss, "Problems in Categorizing the Status of Species: Endangerment with the Best of Intentions," in *Proceedings, 16th Session of the General Assembly of IUCN and 16th IUCN Technical Meeting, Madrid, Spain, 5-15 November 1984.*

40. Alvarez to Brantly, 1 February 1985.

41. Larry D. Harris, "Conservation Corridors: A Highway System for wildlife," *ENFO* (Winter Park, Florida: A publication of the Florida Conservation Foundation, November 1985).

42. Memo, Partington to Wildlife Habitat Group [Persons interested in following up on the December 14, 1986 habitat meeting] (23 December 1986).

43. CS for SB 1073.

44. Interview, David Gluckman, 7 September 1989. Gluckman lobbies for environmental causes in the state legislature.

45. Memo, Partington to Wildlife Habitat Group.

46. Letter, Partington to Egbert, 25 November 1986.

47. GFC Letter, Egbert to Partington, 13 January 1987.

48. Lisanne Renner, "Wekiva's Fate on the Line," *Orlando Sentinel*, 7 December 1987.

49. Ibid.

50. Lisanne Renner, "Water Board Reconsiders Wekiva Buffers," *Orlando Sentinel*, 14 April 1988.

51. Editorial, *Orlando Sentinel*, 8 December 1988.

52. Mark T. Brown and Joe Schaefer, et al., *Buffer Zones for Water, Wetlands and Wildlife: A Final Report on the Evaluation of the Applicability of Upland Buffers for the Wetlands of the Wekiva Basin* (Gainesville: Center for Wetlands, University of Florida, October, 1987).

53. Renner, "Water Board."

54. Lisanne Renner, "Buffer Zone for Wekiva gets Support," *Orlando Sentinel*, 16 January 1988.

55. Editorial, *Orlando Sentinel,* 8 February 1988.

56. Renner, "Water Board."

57. Charles Lee, "The Wekiva Protection Act: A Model for Saving Florida's Rivers," *Florida Naturalist*, Fall, 1988, 10.

58. Ibid., 10.

59. Editorial, *Orlando Sentinel*, 8 February 1988.

60. Report, Florida House of Representatives, Natural Resources Committee, September 12, 1989, "The Need for Increased Funding for State and Local Land Acquisition" (Winter Park: The Nature Conservancy, Florida Chapter).

61. Kevin Spear, "Paradise Lost," *Florida Magazine*, November 5, 1989.

62. Report, Florida House, Natural Resources Committee.

63. *The Tampa Tribune*, Friday, 8 December 1989.

Chapter 18: REFORM AND EDUCATION

1. Frank Graham, "Talk of the Trail," *Audubon*, November 1989, 8.

2. Ed. Ellen Nicole, "Gopher Tortoise Protected in Florida," *The Tortoise Burrow: Bulletin of the Gopher Tortoise Council*, Vol. 8, No. 26 (March 1988) 1.

3. Jon Wilson, "Florida Marine Fisheries leader is taking on a new challenge," *St. Petersburg Times*, Sunday, 10 December 1989.

4. Newsletter, Manasota 88, June-July 1989.

5. David Gluckman, Marilyn Crotty and Carol Rist, "Environmental Efficiency Study Commission:

Report of the Minority" (Tallahassee: Office of the Senate Natural Resource Committee, February 11, 1988) 6.

6. Donna Blanton, *The Orlando Sentinel*, 3 November 1987.

7. Tim W. Clark, Ron Crete and John Cada, "Designing and Managing Successful Endangered Species Recovery Programs," *Environmental Management*, Vol. 13, No. 2 (1989) 161.

8. Ibid., 165. The quote is from M. T. Douglas, *How Institutions Think* (Syracuse, Syracuse University Press, 1986).

9. Ibid., 164.

10. Ibid. [The same page as in the preceding note.]

11. John Franklin Reiger, "George Bird Grinnell and the Development of American Conservation, 1870-1901," PhD. Dissertation, Northwestern University (Evanston, Illinois, June 1970) 173.

12. Ibid., 179.

13. Ibid., 226.

14. Hornaday, *Our Vanishing Wildlife*, 290.

15. Alston Chase, "How to Save Our National Park," *The Atlantic*, Vol. 260, No. 1 (July, 1987) 35-44.

16. William J. Lockhart, "External Park Threats and Interior's Limits: The Need for an Independent National Park Service," in ed. David J. Simon, *Our Common Lands: Defending the National Parks* (Washington, D.C.: Island Press, 1988) 1-72.

17. *Investing in Park Futures, The National Park System Plan: A Blueprint for Tomorrow*, Executive Summary (National Parks and Conservation Association, 1988) 7-9, 18. These numbers alone are not necessarily an indicator of the respective research capabilities of the agencies named. To make that assessment, one would have to know how each agency defines a scientist, how many slots filled by biologists are specifically for research and so on.

19. Ibid. [The same page as in the preceding note.]

20. Charles M. Loveless, et al., "Report of the Special Study Team on the Florida Everglades, August, 1970 (West Palm Beach: South Florida Water Management District) 42 pp.

21. Prepared by the National Park Service Steering Committee for Biological Diversity, "Draft Biological Diversity Plan for the National Park Service (Option One)" (Washington, D.C.: National Park Service, October 1988) 2.

22. Ibid., 6.

23. Ibid (Option Two) 1.

24. Ibid., 18.

25. Draft, Natural Resource Management Guideline, Chapter 2 (Washington D.C.: National Park Service), 145.

26. Ibid., 146-147.

27. Ibid., 147

28. Ibid.

29. Paul C. Prichard, "To the Reader," in *National Parks: From Vignettes to a Global View*, A Report from the Commission on Research and Resource Management Policy in the National Park System, 1989.

30. Ibid. 5.

31. Ibid. [The same page as in the preceding note.]

32. Ibid. 4.

33. *Draft General Management Plan and Draft Environmental Impact Statement, Big Cypress National Preserve* (Atlanta: Southeast Regional Office, 75 Spring St., SW, U.S. National Park Service, 1989) 36.

34. FPTAC Recommendations, 6 June 1986.

35. Draft General Management Plan., 6.

36. Clarke and McCool, *Staking Out the Terrain*, 220-221.

38. Walter A. Rosenbaum, *Environmental Politics and Policy* (Washington, D.C.: CQ Press, A Division of Congressional Quarterly, Inc., 1985) 97.

39. "News of the Society," *Conservation Biology*, Vol. 3, No. 2. 113.

40. "News of the Society," *Conservation Biology*, Vol. 2, No. 3. 235.

41. Ibid., 236.
42. "News of the Society," *Conservation Biology*, Vol. 2, No. 4, 305.
43. Tim W. Clark, "Biological, Sociological, and Organizational Challenges to Endangered Species Conservation: The Black-footed Ferret Case," *Human Dimensions in Wildlife Management Newsletter*, 3:1-15 (1984) 10-15.
44. Tim W. Clark, "Professional Excellence in Wildlife and Natural Resource Organizations," *Renewable Resources Journal*, Vol. 4, No. 1 (Winter 1986).
45. Tim Clark and Ron Westrum, "Paradigms and Ferrets," *Social Studies of Science*, Vol. 17, No. 1, (February 1987) 3-33.
46. Tim W. Clark, "The Identity and Images of Wildlife Professionals," *Renewable Resources Journal* (Summer 1988).
47. Tim W. Clark and John R. Cragun, "Organization and Management of Endangered Species Programs" (unpublished manuscript).
48. Tim W. Clark and Ron Westrum, "High Performance Teams in Wildlife Conservation: A Species Reintroduction and Recovery example," (unpublished manuscript).

Chapter 19: FINALE: THE INTERNATIONAL UNION FOR THE CONSERVATION OF NATURE

1. H.R.H. Prince Philip, Duke of Edinburgh, *Down to Earth: Speeches and Writings of His Royal Highness, Prince Philip, Duke of Edinburgh, on the relationship of man with his environment.* (Lexington, Massachusetts: The Stephen Green Press, 1988) 37.
2. TS Minutes, 19-20 July 1988 (PANTHER INFO-58).
3. Letter, Seal to Christian, 5 September 1988 (PANTHER INFO-60).
4. PANTHER INFO-60, 16 September 1988.
5. "Florida Panther Population Viability Analysis Workshop Proposal, September 5, 1988," Captive Breeding Specialist Group, Species Survival Commission, International Union for the Conservation of Nature and Natural Resources, U. S. Seal, CBSG Chairman.
6. Ibid.
7. "Draft Minutes, Florida Panther Population Viability Workshop, 17 January 1989." 2.
8. Letter, Seal to Christian, 3 March 1989, in "Florida Panther Population Viability Analysis, February 23, 1989," Captive Breeding Specialist Group.
9. J.D. Ballou, et. al., Florida Panther, *Felis concolor coryi, Population Viability Analysis and Recommendations, Captive Breeding Specialist Group, Species Survival Commission IUCN* (23 February 1989) 34.
10. J.D. Ballou, et al, *Florida Panther*, 3.
11. Ibid. [The same page as in the preceding note].
12. Ibid., 2.
13. Ibid., 1.
14. Ibid. [The same page as in the preceding note].
15. *U.S. General Accounting Office Report, Endangered Species, Management Improvements Could Enhance Recovery Program, December,1988.*
16. *Florida Panther Recovery Plan*, June,1987, 15.
17. Ibid., 16.
18. Ibid., 17.
19. Ibid., 26.
20. Ibid., 27.
21. Ibid., 30. Task 1318 reads as follows: FGC [Florida Game & Fresh Water Fish Commission] and DNR will continue to test and evaluate on an interim basis the effectiveness of supplementing the prey base for panthers is the FSSP [Fakahatchee Strand State Preserve]. In March 1986, 12 radio-collared, sterilized hogs were released in FSSP and the southern Golden Gate Estates to examine the feasibility of supplementing the diets of two adult female panthers. One hog was killed by an adult male panther on July 14, 1986. Other predators including black bears, and an alligator killed four others. Three were taken by humans and four were lost due to radio failures or unknown causes. All hog

collars failed or were collected by January 1, 1987 (David Maehr, pers. comm. 1987). Additional experimental releases should be attempted using deer to temporarily supplement the prey base for selected individuals that are in poor physical condition.

22. The comments of speakers are taken from my notes, made on May 30-31, which were used to write this section of the chapter on June 3-4, 1989.

23. DNR Letter, Gissendanner to Brantly, 16 December 1986 (This letter was written as the plan was being revised).

24. GFC Letter, Brantly to Gissendanner, 16 April 1987.

25. GFC Letter, Montalbano to Landrum, 26 April 1988.

26. GFC Letter, Brantly to Alvarez, 4 November 1986.

27. J. D. Ballou, et al., "Florida Panther," 13.

28. FWS Memo, Supervisor Cooperative Research Units Center, 7 June 1989.

29. NPS Memo, Deputy Associate Regional Director, Science and Natural Resources, SERO to Jordan, 30 June 1989. 4-5.

30. GFC Letter, Logan to Jordan, 1 August 1989.

31. FWS Memo, Florida Panther Coordinator to Christian.

32. FWS Letter, Christian to Seal, 4 August 1989.

33. "Florida Panther SSP Masterplan Workshop Minutes, U.S. Fish and Wildlife Service, October 31, 1989."

34. Ibid.

35. John Christian, "Florida Panther Species Survival Plan, Executive Summary (Version 2), November 1989."

36. "Florida Panther SSP Masterplan Workshop Minutes."

37. "Florida Panther Species Survival Plan, Executive Summary 17 November 1989."

38. Ibid.

39. Ibid.

40. Ibid.

41. "Florida Panther SSP Masterplan Workshop Minutes, 8.

42. "Florida Panther Species Survival Plan, Executive Summary (Version 2) 2 November 1989."

43. "Florida Panther Species Survival Plan Draft, 21 November 1989, 10."

44. Ibid.

45. "Florida Panther Species Survival Plan, Executive Summary, 17 November 1989."

46. Dennis Jordan,"Draft Environmental Assessment: A Proposal to Issue Endangered Species Permits to Capture and Hold Florida Panthers (Felis concolor coryi) for the Establishment of a Captive Population," (U.S. Fish and Wildlife Service).

47. Michael Griffen, "Activists rip breeding plan for panthers," *Orlando Sentinel*, Saturday, 10 March 1990.

48. FWS Memo, Jordan to Florida Panther Interagency Committee and Technical Subcommittee Members, 18 May 1990.

49. *Federal Register*, Vol. 55, No. 32, Thursday, February, March, 1990.

50. Viki Boatwright, Public Affairs Officer, Atlanta, "Captive breeding initiatives underway for red wolf, Florida panther," *Fish and Wildlife News*, January, February, March, 1990, 15-16.

51. Ellen McGarrahan,"Panthers to be bred in zoos," *The Miami Herald*, 10 January 1990.

52. Patricia A. Maclaren, Office of Land Use Planning and Biological Services, Florida Department of Natural Resources, Tallahassee, Florida 32399, "Bridging the Gap Between Biologists and Managers: Resource Management Audits," *Program and Abstracts, 4th Annual Meeting, Society for Conservation Biology, 17-20 June 1990*, Gainesville, Florida, USA. 30.

53. Rozi Mulholland, Ken Alvarez, Dick Roberts, "Resource Management Evaluation, Fakahatchee Strand State Preserve, District VI, 25 & 26 November 1986 (Tallahassee: Florida Department of Natural Resources, 1986) 4-5.

54. James A. Stevenson, Florida Department of Natural Resources, Tallahassee, Florida, 32304, "The Management of Florida's State Lands Must be Guided by Scientific Research if Biological Diversity is to be Maintained," *Program and Abstracts*, 32.

55. Frank Montalbano III, Florida Game and Fresh Water Fish Commission, 620 S. Meridian St.,

Tallahassee, Florida 32399-1600, "Conservation Biology, Rainmakers, and Casey at the Bat; A state Wildlife Agency Perspective," *Program and Abstracts*, 31.
56.   "Florida Panther Viability Analysis and Survival Plan, Summary and Recommendations, 15 December 1989."

EPILOGUE

1.   Settlement Agreement, Civ. No. 91-076 (TPJ), U.S.Fish and Wildlife Service, February 1991.
2.   Captive Breeding Specialist Group IUCN - The World Conservation Union, "Subspecies, Populations, Hybridization And Conservation of Threatened Species," CBSG Working Group Draft Policy, Washington, D.C., 29-30 May 1991. 17.
3.   Ibid. 14.

Index

A

Academy of Natural Sciences in
  Philadelphia 42
Acadia National Park 204
Adirondack Mountains 61
Aedes solicitans 368
Aedes taenoirhynchus 368
Aeschynomene americana 257
Africa 134
African lion 127
Alabama 38, 182, 232
Alachua County 36, 48
Alaska 205, 212
Alberta 343
Albright, Horace 203–204
Allen, Durward 223
Alligator Alley 21, 29, 30, 60, 71, 88, 91,
  122, 162, 167, 169, 196, 243
American Association of Zoological Parks and
  Aquariums 149, 350
American Ornithologists'
  Union 54, 314, 315, 319, 338, 370, 425
American Society of Mammalogists 425
Andean condor 311
Andrus, Cecil 225, 230
Animal Control Act 344
Animal Damage Control Program 220
Apalachicola National Forest 174
Aquinus, Thomas 130
Archbold Biological Station 61, 63, 141
Arizona 25, 39, 42, 46, 135, 209, 228, 329
Arkansas 24
Army Corps of Engineers 234, 368, 389
Arrhenius, Olaf 211
Atchafalaya River 56
Atlantic ridley turtle 106
Audubon, John James 36, 343, 405
Audubon Wildlife Report 1986 279
Augean stables 412
Augius 411–412
Austin, Daniel 244
Australia 210

B

Bachman, John 343
Baja California 310
Baker, Bob 104, 116, 121, 122-123, 171,
  292
Baker, Jim 370, 371
Baker, John 52, 54
Bangs, Outram 37, 131, 137, 144
Bartram, William 36, 38, 44
Bass, Sonny 74, 89, 252–253
Baudy, Robert 63, 65, 67, 70, 76, 136,
  147, 148–150, 155, 158, 438, 451
Bauhin, Caspar 127
Bear Island 21, 80, 88, 103, 162, 164,
  171, 243
Beard, Dan 387
Beck, Tom 221
Beeline Expressway 370
Belden, Chris 22, 63, 64, 67, 69 - 70, 76,
  77, 137, 143, 144, 150 - 151, 160, 173 -
  174, 176, 300, 434
Berkeley 209
Big Bend Gambusia 106
Big Bend National Park 106
Big Cypress 74, 79, 82
Big Cypress National Preserve 65, 70, 73,
  75, 76, 80, 85, 88, 91, 99, 386 - 387
Big Gasparilla Island 48
Big Guy 84, 87, 154, 157, 160, 161, 169
Billie, James 143–144, 145
Biological Conservation 230
Biological, Sociological and Organizational
  Challenges to Endangered Species
  Conservation: The Black-footed Ferret
  Case 349
BIOTA Research and Consulting, Inc. 344,
  363, 365, 410
Black River 56
Black-footed ferret 35, 159, 160, 163, 168, 172,
  237, 302, 311, 338, 343-365, 410, 426,
  428, 431, 438
Black-footed Ferret Advisory Team
  (BFAT) 345
Bogan, Mike 353
Bonita Springs 53, 67, 147, 149
Boone and Crockett Club 208, 410
Borneman, John 312
Bowles, Samuel 201
Bradley, Mayor Tom 340
Branan, Bill 100, 101, 103, 116, 122,
  125, 139, 141, 142, 251, 256
Brantly, Colonel Robert 73, 82 - 83, 85, 171,
  198, 268
Brazilian pepper 124, 214, 217, 292, 449
Brevard County 37, 41, 266, 367, 368
Brevard County Mosquito Control District 368

N

Order Form

Ken Alvarez's
Twilight of the Panther:
Biology, Bureaucracy and Failure
in an Endangered Species Program

To order by credit card call:
1-800-444-2524 ext. 300 (toll free)
1-813-758-8094 (international orders)
1-800-777-2525 (fax orders)

Or send a check or money order to:
Book World
1933 Whitfield Loop, Suite 300
Sarasota, Florida 34243

Yes, I want __ copies of *Twilight of the Panther* at $19.95 each, plus $3.75 shipping for first book, and $1.50 for each additional book. (Florida residents please add 6% sales tax. Canadian requests must be made by a postal order in U.S. funds and add $5.00 for first book, and $2.50 for each additional book.)

Name _____

Address _____   _____

City, State, Zip _____

Country _____

_____ Check or money order enclosed

Charge my __VISA ___ Master Card

Expires _____ Signature _____

Card # _____